REFERENCE GUIDE TO UNITED STATES MILITARY HISTORY 1865–1919

REFERENCE GUIDE TO UNITED STATES MILITARY HISTORY 1865–1919

CHARLES REGINALD SHRADER
General Editor

Facts On File

REFERENCE GUIDE TO UNITED STATES MILITARY HISTORY 1865–1919

Facts On File, Inc.
460 Park Avenue South
New York NY 10016
USA

Library of Congress Cataloging-in-Publication Data
(Revised for volume 3)
Reference guide to United States military history.

Includes bibliographical references (v. 1, p. 265-268) and index.
Contents: v. [1]. 1607–1815—v. [2]. 1815–1865.—v. [3]. 1865–1919.
1. United States—History. Military—To 1900.
I. Shrader, Charles R.
E181.R34 1991 973 90-25673
ISBN 0-8160-1836-7 (v. 1)
ISBN 0-8160-1837-5 (v. 2)
ISBN 0-8160-1838-3 (v. 3)

A British CIP catalogue record for this book is available from the British Library.

Composition and Manufacturing by the Maple-Vail Book Manufacturing Group
Printed in the United States of America

10 9 8 7 6 5 4 3 2 1

This book is printed on acid-free paper.

Contents

List of Contributors

Ted Alexander
Antietam National Battlefield

Martin W. Andresen
Lieutenant Colonel, U.S. Army
U.S. Army Military History Institute

Louise A. Arnold-Friend
U.S. Army Military History Institute

Daniel T. Bailey
University of Wisconsin—Madison

Fred Arthur Bailey
Abilene Christian University

M. Guy Bishop, Ph.D.
Seaver Center for Western History Research
Natural History Museum of Los Angeles County

James C. Bradford, Ph.D.
Texas A&M University

Jerry Cooper, Ph.D.
University of Missouri—St. Louis

Leo J. Daugherty III
Ohio State University

James Sanders Day
Captain, U.S. Army
U.S. Military Academy

George B. Eaton
Captain, U.S. Army
U.S. Military Academy

Uzal W. Ent
Brigadier General (Ret.),
Pennsylvania National Guard

Peter R. Faber
Major, U.S. Air Force
Yale University

David Friend

Lloyd J. Graybar, Ph.D.
Eastern Kentucky University

Russell A. Hart
Ohio State University

John A. Hixson
Lieutenant Colonel (Ret), U.S. Army

Jonathan M. House
Major, U.S. Army

Richard F. Kehrberg
University of Wisconsin—Madison

Roger D. Launius, Ph.D.
Chief Historian
National Aeronautics and Space Administration

Stephen J. Lofgren, Ph.D.
U.S. Army Center of Military History

Richard B. Meixsel
Ohio State University

Deborah L. Mesplay
Southern Illinois University

Ralph P. Millsap, Jr.
Captain, U.S. Air Force
U.S. Air Force Academy

Rod Paschall
Colonel (Ret.), U.S. Army

Mark Pitcavage
Ohio State University

Robert D. Ramsey III
Lieutenant Colonel, U.S. Army
U.S. Army Command and General Staff College

Carol Reardon, Ph.D.
Penn State University

Charles R. Shrader
Lieutenant Colonel (Ret.), U.S. Army

Carol E. Stokes
Command Historian
U.S. Army Signal Center

Thomas W. Sweeney
Colonel, U.S. Army
Director, U.S. Army Military History Institute

Anne Cipriano Venzon, Ph.D.

Steve R. Waddell
Texas A&M University

R. John Warsinske
2d Lieutenant, U.S. Army Reserve

Karen S. Wilhelm
Captain, U.S. Air Force
U.S. Air Force Academy

Vernon Williams, Ph.D.
Abilene Christian University

Robert A. Wooster, Ph.D.
Texas A&M University

John F. Wukovits
Woodhaven, Michigan

Donald A. Yerxa, Ph.D.
Eastern Nazarene College

Photographic services by Jim Enos, Carlisle, Pennsylvania

Introduction

The period from 1865 to 1919 was an era both of continued growth and of dramatic change for the United States. The country completed its westward expansion, and internal development, particularly industrialization and urbanization, reached a high level by the end of the 19th century, just in time for the nation to be thrust on the international scene by the war with Spain and the subsequent requirement to govern overseas territories and defend American interests in a world increasingly rent by national competition and conflict. The half century after the Civil War also saw the maturation of the U.S. Armed Forces and their emergence to world responsibilities and prominence. In military terms, the era can be divided into three distinct periods: an era of relative neglect and introspection (1865–97); the Spanish-American War of 1898 and a consequent period of reform and broadened responsibilities (1898–1916); and, finally, the major challenge of World War I (1917–19). The military threats, organizational structures, doctrines, technological developments, and other issues dominant in each of these periods shaped the armed forces and elicited responses that led to further growth and change.

Having defeated the rebellious Confederacy and lacking any considerable external threat, the armed forces of the United States returned to their traditional small size and preoccupation with internal development and security in the years following the Civil War. The army, scattered in small groups around an enormous country, focused on the employment of small units to maintain law and order in the conquered South, on the advancing western frontier, and in various labor disturbances. By 1890, the major challenge posed by the resistance of the Indian tribes of the Plains and the Southwest to white expansion had been met successfully. The period was one of relative isolation and chronically inadequate funding for the army, but it was also a period of introspective professional study and internal reforms that would prepare the army for the challenging role that it would be called upon to play in the early 20th century. The U.S. Navy and Marine Corps, similarly neglected in the immediate post-Civil War period, also strove to achieve internal reforms. The navy in particular became preoccupied with the process of adopting and adapting new technology and new concepts of tactics and strategy. The rapid evolution of steel ships, armor plating, naval weaponry, and auxiliary matériel prompted determined efforts by U.S. naval officers to keep pace with developments abroad, and the navy soon broke out of the doldrums and drove ahead to create a truly competitive "modern" navy.

The short, successful war with Spain in 1898 thrust the United States onto the world stage and imposed new and far more difficult missions upon both the army and the navy. The requirement for the services to work in concert to support operations far from the American homeland and to protect and administer the newly won overseas territories demanded not only large military and naval forces but also emphasized the inadequacies of organization and coordination in the existing structure. The period from 1898 to 1916 was thus one in which both the army and the navy underwent fundamental internal reorganization and improvement in order to meet the challenges of new, worldwide responsibilities. At the same time, the pace of technological change continued to accelerate, and the armed services worked to evaluate and integrate the new engines of war and the new organizations, strategies, and tactics they required.

The degree to which the army and navy met the challenges of new technology and new ideas in military and naval organization and doctrine in the first two decades of the 20th century was tested by the belated U.S. entry into World War I. From April 1917 to November 1918, the reformed structures, the newly incorporated weapons and concepts, and the improved coordination of the U.S. Armed Forces were put to a severe test by the raising, equipping, training, moving, and fighting of an army of some 2,000,000 men in France. The management of a mass army equipped with modern weapons and the requirement to act in concert with allies revealed the existence of serious faults remaining to be corrected, but on the whole, the services successfully met the challenge and made a major contribution to the defeat of the Central Powers. This contribution assured the United States of a prominent place at the peace conference that followed, as well as a leading role in world affairs that would be retained for the remainder of the century.

In large part, the history of the United States is a history of its military establishment—the story of its military leaders and the forces they have commanded in peace and in war. The *Reference Guide to United States Military History* provides a fresh perspective on this important story. As with each of the other four chronologically organized volumes of the *Reference Guide,* this volume comprises a thorough examination of the role of the military and its leaders in American life during a given period. Introduced by a short description of the organization, equipment, and doctrine of U.S. military forces, the narrative portion of the volume includes an extended discussion of the course of events and the development of U.S. military institutions from 1865 to 1919. The seven narrative chapters of this volume are supplemented by biographical profiles of the military and naval leaders of the period, detailed descriptions of the principal battles and events, and discussions of special topics. The text of the volume is further enhanced by maps and illustrations depicting the nation's military leaders, military life, battles, and other events. This survey of U.S. history as viewed through the perspective of military activities thus provides a unique reference work for school and library use and should appeal to a variety of readers interested in this crucial aspect of the national experience.

Obviously, every detail of the military history of the United States cannot be addressed even in a five-volume series. The editors of the *Reference Guide to United States Military History* have thus selected for emphasis only those aspects that seem to be most important for understanding the course of U.S. military history and the role of the military in American society. Any selection process is sure to omit personalities and events that many readers may consider very significant. To guide the selection of persons and events for inclusion in the *Reference Guide,* a number of prominent themes and key topics in American military history are stressed repeatedly in all five volumes of the series. These themes and topics represent those that the editors believe to be most important to the development of U.S. military forces and of attitudes toward the military in the United States from the colonial period to the present. Special attention is given to such key questions as what should be the role of armed forces in a democratic society and what should be the size, nature, and functions of such armed forces. Similarly, the themes of citizen (militia) forces versus professional (standing) forces, competition among the various elements of the U.S. military establishment for resources and prestige, and ways in which American attitudes toward such matters have differed in times of peace and in times of crisis are also emphasized. The unique American solutions devised to coordinate military strategy and the organization of forces to meet perceived threats are investigated in some depth. The adaptation of technology to military ends occupies an especially important place in U.S. military history in view of the nation's consistent preference for substituting technology for manpower and thus receives special attention. Another prominent theme that is stressed is the perpetual and characteristic failure of the United States to prepare adequately for war in time of peace. The attitudes toward soldiers, sailors, and their leaders displayed by political leaders and ordinary citizens is another important aspect on which the *Reference Guide* focuses. Throughout the five volumes, special care has been taken to highlight the independent nature of the U.S. soldier and sailor and the conditions under which he or she was required to operate. By repeatedly returning to these themes and topics, the editors hope to give focus to the series as well as to explain better the course and importance of military affairs in U.S. history.

The contributors to this as well as to the other volumes of the *Reference Guide to United States Military History* are among the best of the younger generation of scholars working on the problems of U.S. military, naval, and airpower history. Some are serving military officers; others are civilian historians in government service, professors in colleges and universities, or independent scholars from across the nation. Each contributor was chosen for his or her expertise on a particular topic as well as the ability to explain complex ideas and events clearly and concisely. Chapter authors are identified in the table of contents, and all contributors are recognized in the list of contributors.

The editors have worked diligently to make this volume of the *Reference Guide to United States Military History* as complete, accurate, and readable as possible. It is to be hoped that we have succeeded and that the readers of this and all other volumes of the *Reference Guide* will find the work useful for their purpose regardless of their individual interests and levels of expertise. Errors of fact and interpretation are inevitable in any work of this magnitude. Readers are therefore encouraged to bring any errors to the attention of the editors for correction in subsequent editions.

Charles R. Shrader, Ph.D.
General Editor
Reference Guide to United States Military History

PART I

The Organization of American Armed Forces and Their History

1

The Organization of Military Forces: 1865–1919

The 50 years after the Civil War constituted a period of dramatic change in American life in which the United States completed its westward migration, accelerated internal development, and emerged as a major player in world affairs. The pace of both scientific discovery and industrialization quickened in the late 19th century, and the application of science and industry to military ends thoroughly transformed the art of war. After the Spanish-American War of 1898, the new requirement to administer overseas territories and to support forces deployed outside the United States made the continued isolation of the nation from world political, economic, and technological change impossible. New missions, weapons, organization, and doctrines forced the rapid modernization and professionalization of the army and navy after 1880. American participation in World War I further expanded the process of doctrinal, organizational, and technological change and determined the essential character of the U.S. Armed Forces for the remainder of the 20th century.

DEFENSE POLICY

The United States faced few serious threats to its sovereignty and continued national existence from 1865 to 1919. Canada remained friendly, and Mexico posed only a minor threat to U.S. persons and property. The European powers had little interest and even less capability of invading the United States, although after 1898, Japan, and to a lesser extent Britain, did threaten U.S. territorial and commercial interests abroad. Even the Spanish in 1898 posed no real threat to the United States. However, in the second decade of the 20th century, imperial Germany presented a new type of threat, that of an aggressive expansionist nationalistic philosophy that was incompatible with American ideals and was threatening to friends of the United States if not to the nation directly.

Internal threats were a more significant problem. Following the Civil War, the southern states that had been in rebellion were perceived by many in the North to harbor desires for continued resistance that had to be quashed. The perceived threat of class insurrection in the form of labor disputes also caused concern, however ill-merited. The armed resistance of native Americans to the steady deterioration of their way of life caused by the westward expansion of white Americans was a more substantial problem. The Indians of the Plains and Southwest were formidable opponents but lacked the inclination to coordinate their opposition. The overwhelming tide of U.S. migration and an increasingly effective army had decisively suppressed these Indians by 1890. After 1898, native insurrection in the newly acquired Philippine Islands, while practically unnoticed at home, required another long counterguerrilla campaign.

Strategies

Between the Civil War and World War I, the focal point of U.S. national security strategy was the coastal defense of the continental United States; Indian opposition, civil unrest, and minor Mexican border incursions required only

Ely Samuel Parker, an engineer of Seneca Indian ancestry, served as military secretary (1864–69) to Gen. Ulysses S. Grant and as Commissioner of Indian Affairs (1869–71) during Grant's presidency. (U.S. Army Military History Institute)

the use of small numbers of troops using long-established tactics. However, the war with Spain and the consequent overseas expansion demanded a well-defined strategy to protect U.S. economic interests and territories abroad, the more so since the rise of the United States as a world power coincided with an intensification of international rivalries. The American strategy devised early in the 20th century retained as its cornerstone the defense of the continental mainland. Other key elements included enforcement of the Monroe Doctrine and the active defense of new U.S. possessions and interests in the Caribbean and the Pacific. To achieve its strategic objectives, the nation committed itself to the concept of a balance of power, while continuing to avoid "entangling alliances" to the maximum extent possible.

Public Attitudes

Public attitudes toward the army and navy followed the traditional pattern after 1865. Soldiers and sailors remained widely despised or simply ignored, and many an officer was patronized by civilian acquaintances with seeming sympathy for his underpaid, hazardous, and isolated existence. When threats arose, however, the soldier and sailor became members of a popular and even honored class. Indian uprisings, labor unrest, the war with Spain, and World War I all precipitated periods in which the army and navy were viewed by the public as indispensable guardians of the public welfare. But every conflict also involved significant antimilitary sentiment. The vocal opposition of antiimperialist factions to U.S. occupation of the Philippines and of pacifist, pro-German, and isolationist factions to American participation in World War I reflected traditional American attitudes. On balance, however, the public attitude toward professional military and naval forces took on a more positive cast as the half century after 1865 progressed, in large part because the professional military class was augmented in times of crisis by increasingly large numbers of citizens temporarily inducted for the duration.

Budget Levels

Throughout the period, the concerns of Congress and the public regarding military issues were made manifest in the debates over appropriations for various new weapons systems, over approval of organizational changes, and over the permissible size of the army and navy. Although, of necessity, the army received a high proportion of annual defense appropriations, the need for modern naval forces and their value to the preservation of U.S. interests and prestige were increasingly recognized after 1880.

Between 1866 and 1919, War Department expenditures amounted to about $19.3 billion. Army expenditures, 1866–97, amounted to about $1.85 billion and averaged about $58 million per year, although Reconstruction-related costs in the 1860s skewed the average, which from 1870 to 1897 was more nearly on the order of $45 million per year. The cost of maintaining the army slowly increased after 1898. From 1898 through 1916, the total approached $3.15 billion and averaged about $166 million per year.

Annual expenditures of the Navy Department from 1866 to 1919 totaled just over $6.3 billion. Expenditures averaged about $30 million per year from 1866 to 1869 and about $21 million from 1870 to 1897. The total for that period was somewhere in excess of $714 million. Between 1898 and 1916, the total expenditures of the navy were

Expenditures of the U.S. War and Navy Departments, 1865–1919

Year	*War Department*	*Navy Department*
1865	$1,031,323,000	$122,613,000
1870	57,656,000	21,780,000
1875	41,121,000	21,498,000
1880	38,177,000	13,537,000
1885	42,671,000	16,021,000
1890	44,583,000	22,006,000
1895	51,805,000	28,798,000
1900	134,775,000	55,953,000
1905	126,094,000	117,550,000
1910	189,823,000	123,174,000
1915	202,060,000	141,836,000
1919	9,009,076,000	2,002,311,000

Source: *Historical Statistics of the United States—Colonial Times to 1970, Part 2* (U.S. Dept. of Commerce, Bureau of the Census, 1975).

just over $2 billion, an average of about $105 million per year.

The total expenditures of the federal government, as might be expected, increased significantly between 1917 and 1919. War Department expenditures in those years approached $14.3 billion, an average of nearly $5 billion per year. The peak came in 1919, when War Department expenditures exceeded $9 billion. Navy expenditures, 1917–19, totaled more than $3.5 billion, an average of nearly $1.2 billion per year. The direct World War I-related outlays of the U.S. government were approximately $23.5 billion, plus loans of some $9 billion to allies. This amounted to about $1 million per hour for two years and equaled the total expenditures of the U.S. government for the entire period 1791–1914.

THE ARMY: 1865–1919

After 1865, the principal mission of the U.S. Army remained the defense of the continental United States against external attack, but other more pressing tasks took priority. Following the Civil War, a major portion of the army occupied and maintained order in the states of the Confederacy. In addition, the Bureau of Refugees, Freedmen and Abandoned Lands, headed by Maj. Gen. Oliver O. Howard, played a major role in dealing with the large number of displaced and disoriented former slaves. The formal end of Reconstruction in April 1877 did not, however, free the army from duties more appropriate to a policeman than to a soldier. In the summer of 1877, Pres. Rutherford B. Hayes used the army to control the first great national labor dispute, the railroad strikes. Subsequently, the suppression of labor troubles as well as the enforcement of law and order and the collection of revenues were to be important army missions. The army also governed (1867–77) the new territory of Alaska. Army officers explored and mapped new territory, recorded weather observations, and conducted scientific experiments. Providing assistance in natural disasters such as floods and earthquakes also came to be a common army function, and the Corps of Engineers contributed to the development of the nation's water resources and the construction of public buildings. Such civil works were capped with the construction of the Panama Canal, completed under the direction of Maj. Gen. George W. Goethals in 1914.

All such missions were secondary; for 25 years after the Civil War, the main task of the army was to protect the growing settlements and migration routes west of the Mississippi River. Between 1865 and 1891, the army fought 10 campaigns and 1,067 separate engagements against hostile Indians. Few of these campaigns involved as many as 4,000 men, but the task occupied the bulk of the army's resources and stood foremost in the public eye until the war with Spain (1898) brought the army new and greatly expanded responsibilities. After 1898, the army was required to pacify and administer the newly acquired territories in the Caribbean and the Philippine Islands. The U.S. occupation of Cuba ended in 1902, but the United States felt compelled to intervene repeatedly in Caribbean affairs until the Good Neighbor Policy, announced in 1934, ended such interventions. In the Pacific, the China Relief Expedition in 1900 required army participation, and the suppression of the Philippine Insurrection and its Moro offshoot lasted until 1913.

The task of guarding the volatile border with Mexico was among the more important army missions throughout the period. The intensification of unrest and revolution in Mexico after 1900 drew a major portion of the army's strength to the border from 1913 to 1917. Two direct interventions on Mexican territory also occurred: the expedition to Veracruz in 1914 and the pursuit of Pancho Villa in 1916.

With U.S. entry into World War I in 1917, the missions of the army changed substantially. No longer was the task simply to maintain order and to protect the continental United States and its territories and possessions. Henceforth, the army would also be required to conduct operations designed to protect very abstract U.S. interests and even such philosophical concepts as democracy and freedom. Comprehending that mission and organizing and deploying forces to accomplish it would be major tasks for the army for the remainder of the 20th century.

Size of the Army

The enormous Union army of the Civil War was quickly disbanded after May 1865. In July 1866, Congress authorized an establishment of 54,302 officers and men in 45 infantry, 10 cavalry, and 4 field artillery regiments, but in March 1869, the authorized number of officers and men was cut to 45,000 and the number of regiments was cut to 25 infantry, 10 cavalry, and 5 field artillery. In addition, some 1,000 Indian scouts were authorized. Further cuts were imposed in 1876. The number of authorized regiments remained the same but the authorized strength of the army was reduced to 27,442 officers and men, where it remained until the Spanish-American War (1898). The reduction was accomplished by leaving 2 companies of each 10-company regiment unmanned.

On Mar. 8, 1898, 2 new field artillery regiments, the 6th and 7th, were added, and the other 5 were reorganized, bringing the authorized strength of the regular army to 28,747. Thus, in April, the regular army consisted of 2,143 officers and 26,040 men in 25 infantry, 10 cavalry, and 7 field artillery regiments (plus the staff bureaus, Corps of Engineers, and Coast Artillery Corps). The day after the declaration of war with Spain, Congress doubled the au-

The End of Reconstruction

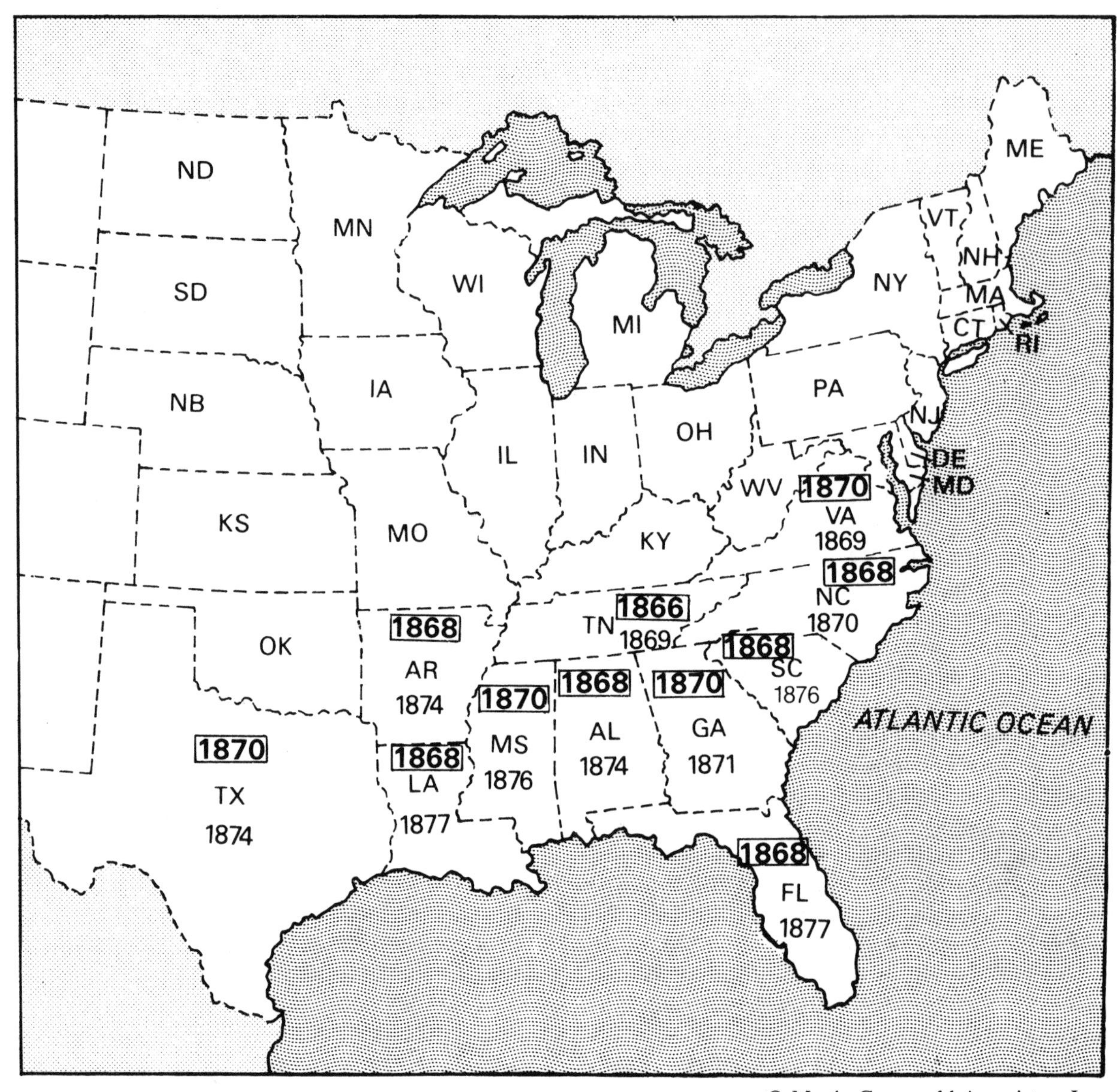

Dates in bold—Readmission to the Union
Dates in light—End of Carpetbagger Government

© Martin Greenwald Associates, Inc.

thorized size of the regular army, and a battalion organization was adopted, each regiment to have 2 battalions of 4 companies each plus 2 skeleton, unmanned companies. The president was later authorized to add a third battalion of 2 full companies and 2 skeleton companies to each regular regiment. Congress, on May 11, also authorized 3 regiments of volunteer cavalry, a 3,500-man volunteer engineer brigade, and 10 regiments (6 white and 4 black, totaling 10,000 men) of volunteer infantry, composed of men supposedly immune from tropical diseases.

On April 23, Pres. William McKinley also called for 125,000 state volunteers; in May, he called for 75,000 more. The call for volunteers produced 5 regiments and 17 troops of cavalry, 16 batteries of light artillery, 1 regiment and 7 batteries of heavy artillery, and 119 regiments and 10 battalions of infantry. Barred from overseas service, many National Guard (militia) units converted to volunteer organizations in order to serve in Cuba, Puerto Rico, and the Philippines. By the end of the war in August 1898, the army consisted of a total of 11,108 officers and 263,609 enlisted men of whom about 59,000 were regulars and about 216,000 were volunteers.

At the conclusion of the hostilities with Spain, most of the volunteer forces were mustered out. However, the new worldwide responsibilities assumed by the army precluded the usual return of the army to its prewar size. A new series of volunteer regiments was created in 1899 to replace state units whose enlistments had expired, and on Feb. 2, 1901, Congress increased the size of the regular army to 30 infantry regiments (the 26th–30th being added), 15 cavalry regiments (the 11th–15th being added), and an artillery corps of 30 batteries of field artillery and 126 companies of coast artillery, plus 3 battalions of engineers. The new authorized strength of 3,820 officers and 84,799 enlisted men was augmented by a regiment of Philippine Scouts and the Puerto Rican regiment. Each infantry regiment was authorized a band and 3 battalions of 4 full companies each. The equivalent units in cavalry regiments were designated squadrons and troops. Infantry companies consisted of 65–146 men and cavalry troops of 100–164.

The expansion of the army for World War I was even more spectacular. On Apr. 1, 1917, the organized strength of the army included 127,588 regular army officers and enlisted men and 80,446 officers and enlisted men in the National Guard. By the end of the war on Nov. 11, 1918, the total strength of the army was 3,685,458, of which 2,057,675 were serving with the American Expeditionary Force (A.E.F.) in France. In all, more than 4,500,000 American men served in World War I, and their demobilization was equally spectacular. In the nine months after the armistice, 3,250,000 men were returned to civilian life, and by the beginning of 1920, the army had been reduced to about 19,000 officers and 205,000 enlisted men.

U.S. Secretaries of War, 1862–1921

Name	*Term*
Edwin M. Stanton	Jan. 20,1862–May 28, 1868
John M. Schofield	June 1, 1868–Mar. 13, 1869
John A. Rawlins	Mar. 13, 1869–Sept. 6, 1869
William W. Belknap	Oct. 25, 1869–Mar. 2, 1876
Alphonso Taft	Mar. 8, 1876–May 22, 1876
James D. Cameron	May 22, 1876–Mar. 3, 1877
George W. McCrary	Mar. 12, 1877–Dec. 10, 1879
Alexander Ramsey	Dec. 10, 1879–Mar. 5, 1881
Robert T. Lincoln	Mar. 5, 1881–Mar. 5, 1885
William C. Endicott	Mar. 5, 1885–Mar. 5, 1889
Redfield Proctor	Mar. 5, 1889–Nov. 5, 1891
Stephen B. Elkins	Dec. 17, 1891–Mar. 5, 1893
Daniel S. Lamont	Mar. 5, 1893–Mar. 5, 1897
Russell A. Alger	Mar. 5, 1897–Aug. 1, 1899
Elihu Root	Aug. 1, 1899–Jan. 31, 1904
William H. Taft	Feb. 1, 1904–June 30, 1908
Luke E. Wright	July 1, 1908–Mar. 11, 1909
Jacob M. Dickinson	Mar. 12, 1909–May 21, 1911
Henry L. Stimson	May 22, 1911–Mar. 4, 1913
Lindley M. Garrison	Mar. 5, 1913–Feb. 10, 1916
Newton D. Baker	Mar. 9, 1916–Mar. 4, 1921

Command and Staff

Between 1865 and 1919, the administrative and logistical support of the army continued to be provided by the staff departments, or bureaus, headquartered in Washington. In 1898, there were 10 such bureaus: Adjutant General's Department, Inspector General's Department, Judge Advocate General's Department, Medical Department, Ordnance Department, Paymaster General's Department, Signal Corps, Subsistence Department, Quartermaster's Department, and Corps of Engineers. Each was supreme in its area of expertise, and all were led by chiefs who were very powerful due to their longevity in Washington and their close relationships with the secretary of war and the Congress. The staff departments were generally very competent in performing their assigned tasks. The real problem lay in the army's inability to coordinate properly their actions and to plan for future operations.

New worldwide responsibilities after 1898 brought significant expansion and reorganization of the staff departments. A military intelligence capability was established in 1885. By August 1918, it was incorporated in the Military Intelligence Division (G-2) of the War Department General Staff. The Army Medical Department, with the establishment of the Army Hospital Corps in 1887, was the first staff bureau to obtain a real corps of enlisted specialists. An Army Nurse Corps and a Dental Corps were added in 1901 and an Army Veterinary Corps in 1916. Perhaps the most significant change was the consolidation in 1912 of the Subsistence, Quartermaster, and Paymaster General departments to form a single Quartermaster Department. At the same time, a Quartermaster Corps was created that provided for a limited number of enlisted men to perform logistical tasks. Fiscal responsibilities were withdrawn from the Quartermaster General with the reestablishment of a separate Finance Corps in 1918. Several other new staff agencies were also created during World War I. In 1917, the Office of Provost Marshal General was reestablished to administer and enforce the Selective Service Act. In 1918, a Military Police Corps was activated in the A.E.F. in France, and a Motor Transport Corps, an Embarkation Service, and other agencies were created only to be dissolved after the war. However, the Chemical Warfare Service, established on June 28, 1918, survived after 1919 as the Army Chemical Corps.

The short, successful war with Spain in 1898 highlighted a number of deficiencies in the organization and planning ability of the army. Accordingly, Sec. of War Elihu Root, who took office in 1899, initiated a series of reforms in which new techniques derived from the business world were applied to correct the shortfalls in army organization and planning. The three most pressing areas requiring adjustment were the conflict between the line units and the staff of the army; the uncertain division of authority among the Commanding General of the Army, the secretary of war, and staff bureau chiefs; and the lack of a planning and coordination agency.

The conflict between line and staff was of long standing. In part a matter of envy by line officers of the perquisites and power enjoyed by staff officers assigned to comfortable posts in Washington, the conflict also arose from the frustration of line officers over their inability to control all aspects of the management of their forces in the field. Line officers believed that the staff did not understand the problems of field service, and the chiefs of the staff bureaus were convinced that line officers did not understand the complexities and difficulties of supplying and administering the army. In theory, the sole purpose of the staff was to support the army in the field, but in reality, the power of the bureaus, gained by long service and close relationships with the secretary of war and with Congress, allowed the bureau chiefs to act as they pleased. Several measures were taken before the Spanish-American War to reduce the power and privilege of the staff departments. For example, regulations in 1894 required that all appointments to positions in the staff departments come from the line. A regular interchange of officers between line and staff positions was also a feature of the Root reform program.

The conflict between line and staff was encapsulated in the authority dispute among the Commanding General of the Army, the secretary of war, and bureau chiefs. This problem arose from the lack of statutory definition of the functions of the commanding general. The army in the field was under his direction with regard to discipline and military operations, but the army's fiscal affairs were conducted by the secretary of war through the staff departments, and the commanding general did not command the bureau chiefs who reported directly to the secretary of war. The commanding general's inability to control the logistical and administrative support of the army limited his ability to direct troops in the field. Gen. Ulysses S. Grant and William T. Sherman had failed to correct the problem after the Civil War, but Secretary Root proposed to reduce the power of the bureau chiefs and to clarify the relationship between the commanding general and the secretary of war. In 1903, he achieved his goal with legislation that replaced the Commanding General of the Army with a chief of staff who stood in line directly under the president and secretary of war as their principal adviser and executive agent with control over the staff departments as well as the line of the army.

The Spanish-American War revealed that the army largely had lost its capacity for planning and conducting large-scale operations. There was no advanced planning and little coordination among the staff bureaus. Commanders lacked experience in managing large-scale, complex military operations. The creation of an army general staff to plan and coordinate operations had long been advocated by military reformers such as Emory Upton, and Congress had investigated the concept of a general staff for several decades but failed to act, primarily because of unwarranted fears of a "Prussian General Staff." In 1901, Secretary Root established an ad hoc War College Board whose chief function was advanced planning and, incidentally, the training of officers for the management of large, complex operations. Finally, legislation passed by Congress on Feb. 14, 1903, established a General Staff Corps (as of Aug. 15, 1903) to consist of the new chief of staff, two other general officers, and 42 junior officers. The primary function of the General Staff was to plan and coordinate military activities.

The fledgling War Department General Staff suffered considerable growing pains, mainly through confusion over its proper role and function. It was also strongly opposed by some members of Congress and some of the staff department chiefs. Military secretary (Adj. Gen.) Fred C. Ainsworth led opposition to the General Staff. His defeat by Chief of Staff Leonard Wood and Sec. of War Henry L. Stimson in 1911 significantly reduced opposition to the General Staff, although Congress continued to limit its operations. The so-called Manchu Law of August 1912, for example, required officers detailed to the General Staff to have served at least two of the immediately preceding six years with their regiment. The idea was to prevent development of a "permanent" general staff. The National Defense Act of May 1916 also hampered the General Staff by limiting the number of officers who could serve at the same time in or near Washington. The attempts of the General Staff and the staff departments to plan ahead for inevitable entry of the United States into World War I were also limited by Pres. Woodrow Wilson's personal opposition to planning for war. Thus, in April 1917, the War Department General Staff consisted of only 41 officers (compared to 232 for the British and 650 for the Germans), and of these only 19 served in Washington.

Gen. Peyton C. March became chief of staff in early 1918 and undertook a thorough reorganization of the General Staff as well as a further definition of the primacy of the chief of staff over both the line and staff officers. The General Staff was reorganized into four main divisions: Operations; Military Intelligence; War Plans; and Purchase, Storage and Traffic. The 55-man statutory limit on the number of General Staff officers was repealed, and the General Staff was increased to 1,072 officers. It also began to assume operational direction as well as planning and coordination tasks, particularly with regard to logistical matters. Armed with the authority of the Overman Act of May 1918, General March completed the subordination of the bureau chiefs by requiring them to report to the secretary of war only through the chief of staff and by replacing many of the old, experienced bureau chiefs. By a law of May 12, 1917, the chief of staff was to take rank and precedence over all officers of the army. However, Gen. John J. Pershing, commander of the A.E.F., considered himself senior to Chief of Staff March, and the two men found themselves in a serious conflict that was not fully resolved until Pershing became chief of staff in 1921.

Administrative Organization

From 1865 to 1877, about one-third of the army was stationed in the southern states, but most served at one of the more than 250 small posts scattered about the country, mostly in the West. The large number of small remote posts contributed to the army's isolation and lack of expertise in large unit operations but was continued for some time by congressional pressure. The pattern began to break in the late 1880s when the desire to make army troops readily available to suppress labor troubles made their assemblies near railroad junctions a necessity. By 1896, there were only 77 posts, and the new, worldwide requirements for army forces after 1898 changed forever the old stationing pattern. In the years after the Spanish-American War, about one-third of the army served overseas, mostly in the Philippines, but also in Alaska, Hawaii, Cuba, Puerto Rico, China, Panama, and elsewhere. More than 2,000,000 men also served in England, France, Belgium, Italy, and Germany between 1917 and 1920.

The territorial organization of the army adopted before the Civil War was continued after 1865. The number and names of geographic divisions, departments, and districts changed frequently. In 1879, the existing 8 departments and 11 districts were distributed among 3 major territorial divisions: Atlantic, Pacific, and Missouri. By 1897, the system had been reorganized into 8 geographical departments: East, Missouri, Platte, Colorado, Dakota, Texas, California, and Columbia. Each department was commanded by a general officer who reported to the Commanding General of the Army in Washington and who was assisted by a staff of officers detailed from the various bureaus in Washington or drawn, in the case of "operations" assistants or "aides-de-camp," from the line units under control of the departmental commander. By Apr. 6, 1917, the number of territorial departments had been reduced to 4 (Eastern, Central, Southern, and Western) plus Alaska, Hawaii, the Philippine Islands, Puerto Rico, and the Panama Canal Zone. On May 1, 1917, 2 additional departments were established (Northeastern and Southeastern). The 6 departments continued to exist until after World War I, when the continental United States was redivided for administrative purposes into 8 army corps areas.

Tactical Organization

The Civil War brigades, divisions, army corps, and field armies were disassembled in 1865, and until 1898, the infantry regiment was the largest authorized formation. However, few soldiers saw a full regiment assembled between 1869 and 1898; most operations were conducted by company-size units or even smaller patrols and detachments. It was not until the 12th Infantry was massed for field exercises in 1887 that commanders were again able to practice the tactical employment of even regimental-size units.

The mobilization of significant forces for the war with Spain saw the return of larger units. On Apr. 22, 1898, Congress authorized the organization of the regular and volunteer forces mobilized for the war into brigades of three regiments, divisions of three brigades, and army corps of three divisions. Army General Order No. 36 of May 7, 1898, created seven army corps, all of which were in fact activated for the duration of the war. The brigade, division, and corps structure was discontinued by 1902, and until the entry of the United States into World War I in April 1917, the largest tactical unit of the army was once again the regiment.

The 1905 Field Service Regulations provided for the organization of divisions in time of war, and in 1910, the new General Staff prepared a plan for three permanent peacetime infantry divisions composed of designated regular army and National Guard regiments. Troubles on the Mexican border in 1911 prevented execution of the plan. A temporary maneuver division of 13,000 officers and men was formed at San Antonio, Texas, in August 1911, and another maneuver division was assembled in Texas in 1913, but the army was unable to achieve a permanent division structure until World War I. Thus, in May 1917, there were no divisions or larger units, and the necessary superstructure had to be reformed quickly.

The U.S. "square" division of World War I consisted of about 28,000 officers and men divided into 2 infantry brigades (each with 2 infantry regiments of 3 battalions and a machine-gun company); a field artillery brigade (of 1 heavy and 2 light field artillery regiments); a regiment of engineers; a division machine-gun battalion; a signal battalion; and divisional supply, engineer, sanitary, and ammunition trains. In all, the division, commanded by a major general, incorporated 72 field artillery pieces, 260 machine guns, and 17,666 rifles. The World War I square division was larger than most Civil War army corps and was approximately twice the size of the divisions of the other Allies or the Germans. It was, therefore, somewhat clumsy and difficult to maneuver but did have tremendous striking and staying power. Moreover, it minimized the impact of the army's lack of trained staff officers. The division was a self-contained combat force and could be shifted from the control of one corps headquarters to another. Divisions were normally supported by a variety of attached units such as engineer gas companies, additional medical units, telegraph battalions, balloon companies, and aero squadrons. In all, the United States organized 62 such divisions, of which 42 saw service overseas.

Units of division size or smaller were fixed in size. The infantry platoon consisted of 58 men led by a lieutenant.

Future U.S. president Theodore Roosevelt (left) *was among the officers deployed to San Antonio, Texas, in 1911 to police the U.S.-Mexican border.* (U.S. Signal Corps)

The infantry company, commanded by a captain, consisted of 6 officers and 250 men. Four companies constituted a battalion led by a major, and three battalions plus a machine-gun company and assorted supporting troops constituted a regiment containing 112 officers and 3,720 men commanded by a colonel. The infantry brigade, commanded by a brigadier general, consisted of about 8,500 officers and men in two regiments and a machine-gun battalion. Units above division level were flexible in size. A corps commanded by a major general might control from two to six divisions. An army commanded by a lieutenant general could control three to five corps, and an army group commanded by a full general might control two or more armies.

Reserve Forces

The voluntary militia survived the Civil War intact despite its obvious faults and the opposition of many regular army officers. Still operating under the antiquated law of 1792, almost all militia units were poorly equipped and ill-trained. Although of little value, the militia was very strong politically, and its advocates, who resisted amalgamation with or control by the regular army, generally prevailed. Civil disturbances in the 1870s led some state legislatures to improve their organized militia units. A National Guard Association was formed at Richmond, Virginia, in 1877, and between 1881 and 1892, every state revised its military code. Most called the resulting reorganized militia units the National Guard. In 1887, the National Guard Association secured a doubling of the $200,000 annual federal grant for weapons, but in general, federal legislation to correct the problems of the National Guard were stymied by antimilitary sentiment, apathy, and a residual insistence on states' rights.

Many military reformers wanted to replace the ineffective militia system with a strong regular army backed by a mass conscription system on the European model. Key aspects of this reform program included universal military service, some form of reserve officer training corps, and the unification of state militias with the federal armed forces and/or the replacement of the militia by a genuine federal reserve force. Some U.S. military reformers fell under the spell of the Prussian system, which provided a large pool of trained men organized to move rapidly to mobilization points where they could be armed and equipped from stockpiles and then moved rapidly to combat positions. However, the Prussian system was extremely expensive, and the maintenance of the necessary mobilization machinery was a great burden even for the most advanced industrial nations. In any event, a large standing army, even in the form of ready reserve, was contrary to the U.S. tradition of a small regular force supplemented in time of need by citizen volunteers and was extremely distasteful to the politically powerful advocates of the National Guard.

The Spanish-American War drove home the need for reform of the U.S. militia system. Despite a paper strength of 9,376 officers and 106,251 men in 1898, the National Guard was of little practical value, since under existing laws it could not be deployed outside the United States. Additionally, most National Guard units were unfit for active service without an extended period of training and reequipment. Once again, the United States had to rely on the small regular army and a volunteer army raised especially for the occasion. However, a few of the better-prepared National Guard units enlisted en masse in the volunteer forces and to all intents and purposes served as National Guard units in federal service.

After the Spanish-American War, Secretary of War Root obtained legislation that corrected the most glaring deficiencies of the militia system. The Militia Act of Jan. 21, 1903, commonly known as the Dick Act after its sponsor, Congr. Charles W. Dick of Ohio, thoroughly revised the obsolete 1792 Militia Act. The militia was divided into two classes: a reserve militia to be called out only in case of dire necessity, such as the invasion of the United States, and an organized militia (or National Guard) that would be organized, trained, and equipped to federal standards with federal funds.

Although the Dick Act was a significant step toward creating an effective National Guard, the process was completed only with passage of the National Defense Act of 1916. In a study entitled "The Organization of the Land Forces of the United States," Maj. John McAuley Palmer argued for abandonment of the old expansible army idea in favor of a ready-to-fight regular army with brigades and divisions and the mobilization of a citizen army in time of crisis. Many of Palmer's ideas were incorporated in another study issued in September 1915 by Sec. of War Lindley M. Garrison, entitled "A Proper Military Policy for the United States." This study called for an effective citizen army, the doubling of the regular army, increased spending on the National Guard, and the creation of a new 400,000-man continental army (reserve) whose training would be under federal control.

The continental army concept was vehemently opposed by National Guard advocates in the House of Representatives, notably Representative Hay of Virginia, but the Mexican Punitive Expedition of 1916 precipitated agreement on the central idea of a citizen army as the foundation of the U.S. military establishment, but with the National Guard rather than a new continental army as its core. The National Defense Act passed on June 3, 1916, was the most comprehensive military legislation enacted up to that time. The act reasserted the obligation of all men between the ages of 18 and 45 to military service and established the three principle components of the army: regular army, National Guard, and organized reserve. The authorized peacetime strength of both the regular army and the National Guard was increased, and federal support and control of the National Guard were improved. The act also provided for a system of summer training camps to furnish additional officers for an expanding army and established both an officer and an enlisted reserve corps to supplement the regular army in time of crisis.

There was also provision in the National Defense Act of 1916 for a volunteer army to be raised only in time of war, but when war came in 1917, the only true volunteer force to serve was the Slavic Legion authorized by an act of July 9, 1918. More than two-thirds of U.S. land forces in World War I were provided by operation of the Selective Service Act of May 18, 1917. The act relied on district and local civilian boards to register all males between the ages of 21 and 30 (later extended to 45). In less than 18 months, the Selective Service System registered more than 24,000,000 men and delivered 2,810,296 men for service, 180,000 in the first three months of the system's operation. Draftees formed the bulk of the million-man national army. The remainder was provided by 285,000 men of the regular army, doctors and other specialists from the organized reserve, and 475,000 National Guardsmen, who formed 40 percent of the divisions in the A.E.F. in France and gave a good account of themselves on the battlefield.

Officer Personnel

Between 1865 and 1919, the U.S. Military Academy at West Point continued to be the principal source of commissioned officers for the regular army, but the increased demand for officers after 1898 focused attention on alter-

Senior Officers[a] of the U.S. Army, 1864–1921

Name	*Term*
Lt. Gen. Ulyssess S. Grant[b]	Mar. 9, 1864–Mar. 4, 1869
Gen. William T. Sherman	Mar. 8, 1869–Nov. 1, 1883
Gen. Philip H. Sheridan	Nov. 1, 1883–Aug. 5, 1888
Lt. Gen. John M. Schofield	Aug. 14, 1888–Sept. 29, 1895
Lt. Gen. Nelson A. Miles	Oct. 5, 1895–Aug. 8, 1903
Lt. Gen. Samuel B. M. Young	Aug. 15, 1903–Jan. 8, 1904
Lt. Gen. Adna R. Chaffee	Jan. 9, 1904–Jan. 14, 1906
Maj. Gen. John C. Bates	Jan. 15, 1906–Apr. 13, 1906
Maj. Gen. James F. Bell	Apr. 14, 1906–Apr. 21, 1910
Maj. Gen. Leonard Wood	Apr. 22, 1910–Apr. 20, 1914
Maj. Gen. William W. Wotherspoon	Apr. 21, 1914–Nov. 15, 1914
Maj. Gen. Hugh L. Scott	Nov. 16, 1914–Sept. 21, 1917
Maj. Gen. Tasker H. Bliss	Sept. 22, 1917–May 18, 1918
Gen. Peyton C. March	May 19, 1918–June 30, 1921

[a]General in Chief, 1866–1903; Chief of Staff, from 1903

[b]General from July 25, 1866

native commissioning methods. In general, the War Department failed to exploit the program of military training in land-grant colleges established by the Morrill Act of 1862, but the National Defense Act of 1916 and the efforts of Chief of Staff Wood embodied in the Plattsburgh concept of summer training camps for college men were of some help. Nevertheless, in 1917, only 9,000 officers were available to meet a requirement for 200,000. The needs of the large national army and expanded regular army and National Guard were met by commissioning regular army enlisted men and graduates of the Reserve Office Training Corps, the Student Army Training Corps, and 16 officer training camps established in division cantonments (and later consolidated into 8 officer training schools), which produced some 96,000 "90-day wonders," or about one-half the total World War I officer requirement. Many specialists, particularly doctors, received direct commissions.

Until well after the turn of the century, the senior officers of the army were Civil War veterans. Most of these men were technically competent but generally set in their ways. As a group, they were also remarkably long-lived and thus blocked advancement of their juniors. Consequently, officers who entered service after the Civil War had very limited prospects. Pay was low, promotions were slow, and for many, the duty was both dangerous and monotonous. But by the turn of the century, the army's junior officers, exercised in basic soldiering and toughened by service on the Great Plains, were better educated and more introspective. Interested in their profession and the army as an institution, this corps of junior officers promoted professional development and a number of reforms that transformed the army after 1898.

The consolidation of the army on larger posts was an important factor in facilitating professional development, but the major impetus was an effective, progressive system of officer education. The key institution was the School of Application for Cavalry and Infantry established on the order of General Sherman at Fort Leavenworth, Kansas, on May 7, 1881. The "Leavenworth Schools" flourished after the turn of the century under the guidance of a small group of army educators, and in 1903, the Army War College was established to stand at the pinnacle of professional officer education. Initially an adjunct of the new General Staff, the War College provided a training ground for the study of strategy and the raising and management of the large, mass armies that would dominate 20th-century warfare. The effect of these postgraduate army schools, as well as the revitalized branch schools, was to disseminate basic professional knowledge and establish standards of competence necessary for a modern professional army.

The growing sense of professionalism was accompanied by a number of positive administrative changes. By 1870, voluntary retirement, at the president's discretion, after 30 years service was possible, and in 1882, compulsory retirement at age 64 was instituted with good effect. In 1890, a system of promotion by seniority in arm, corps, or bureau replaced the old regimental seniority system, and examinations for promotion for all officers below the grade of major were instituted to insure a minimum level of professional competence. In the mid-1890s, a system of character and efficiency reports for all officers was adopted, and physical standards were enforced by periodic physical examinations and practical tests such as the annual officer riding test. These measures did much to increase the vigor and professional competence of the officer corps of the army.

Enlisted Personnel

Under the direction of hard-bitten noncommissioned officers, many of whom were Civil War veterans, the soldiers of the late-19th-century army became tough, experienced campaigners with all the vices of the "old trooper": drunkenness, gambling, and a propensity for contracting venereal disease. Between 1865 and 1898, many of the men who enlisted in the regular army were immigrants unable to find jobs in the East. Others served for a variety of reasons, not excluding the avoidance of civil justice. The conditions of service were harsh and often dangerous, and pay was low, only $15 per month as late as May 1917. The term of enlistment was five years until 1894 and thereafter was three years. Desertion was a significant problem. The harsh conditions and better opportunities in an expanding West precipitated a steady stream of deserters. In 1871, some 8,800 men, nearly one-third of the entire enlisted complement, deserted. The number of desertions fell in the 1870s but rose again to 3,721 men in 1882. Thereafter, there was a steady decrease in the number of desertions as the conditions of service were improved.

The consolidation of army units on larger installations definitely improved conditions for enlisted personnel. Opportunities for education were provided, the temperance movement had some effect, and army leaders strove to provide alternative recreation in the form of organized sports and more effective marksmanship programs with financial incentives for superior performance. Rations and uniforms were also substantially improved. The physical and moral quality as well as the educational level of the enlisted corps were also significantly enhanced by the broader spectrum of men, many with advanced education, inducted for the war with Spain and World War I. Many of these men stayed on to contribute to the peacetime regular army and raised the professional standards of noncommissioned officers and troops beyond anything experienced before 1898.

Army camp life in Arizona in 1871, although harsh and primitive, allowed periods of relaxation for the soldiers stationed there. (Library of Congress)

Tactical Doctrine

The subjugation of the Plains Indians and the other missions assigned to the army in the late 19th century required little in the way of formal tactical doctrine beyond an emphasis on scouting, rapid movement, and the application of maximum firepower in attack and defense. The Spanish-American War brought a return to more formal tactical precepts, but the codification of late-Civil War practice presented by Colonel Upton in the 1880s seemed to suffice, particularly when active operations against the Spaniards were quickly over. The subsequent suppression of insurrection in the Philippines no more required a formal tactical doctrine than had the campaigns against the Indians, and after 1901, most army field operations took the form of counterguerrilla campaigns.

While U.S. troops practiced Civil War–era Uptonian tactical evolutions on the parade ground and Indian war tactics in the jungles of Luzon, the rapid advance of military technology transformed the tactics of land warfare. The changes were first evident in European armies and were the subject of much academic study by U.S. soldiers. Although machine guns and improved indirect fire artillery bolstered the defense, most tacticians gave the advantage to the attacker and the principles of mass and momentum came to be seen as the foundation of successful tactics. New weapons made the use of cover and concealment essential to survival on the battlefield, but linear tactics were still dictated both by tradition and by practical control considerations. Improved strategic transport and better staff techniques meant that leaders could mass enormous numbers of troops with highly lethal weapons on the battlefield and could in fact sustain them there, but the means for command and control of such forces on the battlefield continued to lag. Direct visual contact remained essential for the artillery as well as the infantry and cavalry commander. The situation changed only after the adoption of certain technical breakthroughs in communications such as the field telephone, radio, and airplane.

World War I began with armies on both sides emphasizing mobility and the offensive. The real impact of the new weapons and of mass warfare became apparent only gradually, and the war then stabilized into a war of position with extended field fortifications in depth. These fixed trench lines continued for some time to be assaulted by linear formations with supports in a secondary line, usually with only limited success. The extent of the fortified line almost demanded a frontal assault. Divisions normally attacked with brigades abreast and regiments on line with battalions deployed in depth. Preplanned artillery barrages were employed to fix and destroy the defender and his fortifications, particularly his barbed wire emplacements and communications lines. The rolling barrage was developed to maximize the protection of advancing infantry but frequently caused as much damage to friendly forces as to enemy forces. For the defender in well-prepared positions, protective artillery barrages coupled with heavy infantry rifle and machine-gun fire against attackers who had been channeled into designated killing areas by obstacles were usually sufficient to halt such frontal attacks. Gradually, the opposing forces learned to dispense with the linear frontal attack in favor of small assault groups maneuvering independently in their assigned zones, sometimes even without preplanned artillery support. Such tactics promised

The new weapons of World War I included the tank; the British Mark IV tank is shown here, behind U.S. troops of the 107th Infantry, 27th Division, in France's Somme region in September 1918. (U.S. Army Signal Corps)

to restore the power of the offensive by making penetrations possible and decisive. Special new weapons such as the airplane, the tank, the flamethrower, and poison gas played mostly secondary roles, although the use of tanks en masse in support of advancing infantry did influence defenders to maintain an area defense with strong reserves placed in supporting lines at the expense of the first line.

When the U.S. Army entered the fray in 1917, the tactical practices of the Allies were adopted, but with one important exception. General Pershing and his subordinates, brought up in a tactical environment that demanded good individual soldier skills, initiative, and rapid movement, continued to believe in the primacy of the offensive and relied on superior U.S. riflery and élan to overcome the strengths of the prepared German defenses by breakthrough and exploitation. In point of fact, the Americans came in at a time and with an effect that finally forced the more mobile offensive war that they favored. Although U.S. tactical doctrine focused on the offensive and the trained rifleman, there was also a growing tendency to emphasize technology over manpower as the prime arbiter of the battlefield, and this tendency would continue for the remainder of the century.

THE NAVY: 1865–1919

After 1865, the principal missions of the U.S. Navy remained U.S. coastal defense and the protection of American seaborne commerce. The strategic ideas of Alfred Thayer Mahan, focusing on the defeat of the enemy main battle fleet in time of war, gradually took hold, but the traditional commerce raiding mission of the wartime navy lingered. After 1898, the navy was used increasingly to support U.S. foreign policy and to protect new overseas possessions. The enforcement of the Monroe Doctrine in the Caribbean and the Open Door policy in China were almost entirely the task of the navy and elicited the term "gunboat diplomacy." The involvement of the United States in World War I brought new responsibilities for protecting the steady stream of merchant vessels in the "bridge of ships to France," a mission for which the navy had to develop new tactics and new types of vessels. Exploration and scientific work had been important secondary missions of the navy during the period 1842–61. Such activity was resumed after the Civil War, and the contributions of the navy in hydrography and arctic exploration were quite important.

Size of the Navy

In 1865, the actual strength of the navy was 6,759 officers and 51,537 enlisted men, but the Civil War navy demobilized rapidly. In 1867, Congress fixed the number of enlisted men at a maximum of 8,500, and for three decades, the actual number on duty was usually substantially less. Despite a progressive rebuilding program after 1880, the authorized number of seamen was actually reduced to 8,250 between 1881 and 1893. In 1893, the authorization rose to 9,000 men, and in June 1896, the number was increased to 10,000. An additional 1,750 men were added in 1897. The Spanish-American War required a significant increase in size, and in 1898, the actual strength of the navy reached 1,432 officers and 21,060 enlisted men. Despite increased responsibilities after 1898, the size of the navy shrank slightly, but by 1910, it had again increased to 2,699 officers and 45,834 enlisted men. The navy underwent a tremendous expansion to meet the demands of U.S. participation in World War I. In 1918, the navy had 23,631 officers and 424,975 sailors on duty.

In 1865, the navy had some 700 ships, many of which were of relatively modern design, but the U.S. lead in naval technology was soon lost through scant appropriations and a preference on the part of influential senior naval officers for a return to wooden sailing ships for reasons of economy and tradition. Between 1864 and 1881, Congress authorized construction of only 2 experimental torpedo boats and 8 small steam war vessels. Existing vessels were repaired repeatedly under a political spoils system that did little to improve the number of available seaworthy vessels. The usual number of ships in commission was only about 50. In January 1881, the navy had only 139 ships, all outdated types, but the neglect of the 1870s was a blessing in disguise. Naval technology had advanced rapidly since 1865, and new ships built during that period would have already been obsolete by the early 1880s when the American public and Congress recognized that an efficient, "modern" navy was needed to protect U.S. seaborne commerce and other interests abroad.

Prompted by Sec. of the Navy William E. Chandler, in March 1883, Congress appropriated $1,300,000 for the construction of 4 modern steel ships. The light steel cruisers *Atlanta, Boston, Chicago,* and *Dolphin* were only a beginning. Development accelerated under Sec. of the Navy Benjamin F. Tracy in the early 1890s. Tracy sought a two-ocean navy of 100 ships: 20 battleships, 20 coast defense vessels, and 60 cruisers. In 1889, the U.S. Navy was just 12th in strength in the world with only 39 modern ships, but by March 1897, the "new navy" had 78 new ships completed, under construction, or authorized, and on the eve of war with Spain, the U.S. Navy had risen to 6th in the world.

The increased responsibilities that followed the Spanish-American War prompted demands for a navy "second to none but that of Britain." The navy added some 131 ships during the war, and for a decade after 1903, naval expenditures were substantial. Two capital ships were laid down each year, and by 1910, the navy had a total of 371 ships, 58 of which were armored. Of the total, 308 were fit for service, 31 were under construction, 20 were authorized but not yet begun, and 12 were unfit for sea service. By 1917, the U.S. Navy was third largest in the world, exceeded only by those of Britain and Germany. In February 1917, President Wilson called for the "greatest navy in the world," and Congress responded in a most positive manner. In 1918, U.S. naval strength in European waters alone included 5 battleships, 95 destroyers, and many other vessels. Most of the ships authorized in 1917–18 were not completed until after World War I, but in 1919, the U.S. Navy was indeed the largest in the world, with more than 2,000 ships of all types.

U.S. Secretaries of the Navy, 1861–1921

Name	*Term*
Gideon Welles	Mar. 7, 1861–Mar. 3, 1869
Adolph E. Borie	Mar. 9, 1869–June 25, 1869
George M. Robeson	June 26, 1869–Mar. 12, 1877
Richard W. Thompson	Mar. 13, 1877–Dec. 20, 1880
Nathan Goff, Jr.	Jan. 7, 1881–Mar. 6, 1881
William H. Hunt	Mar. 7, 1881–Apr. 16, 1882
William E. Chandler	Apr. 17, 1882–Mar. 6, 1885
William C. Whitney	Mar. 7, 1885–Mar. 5, 1889
Benjamin F. Tracy	Mar. 6, 1889–Mar. 6, 1893
Hilary A. Herbert	Mar. 7, 1893–Mar. 5, 1897
John D. Long	Mar. 6, 1897–Apr. 30, 1902
William H. Moody	May 1, 1902–June 30, 1904
Paul Morton	July 1, 1904–June 30, 1905
Charles J. Bonaparte	July 1, 1905–Dec. 16, 1906
Victor H. Metcalf	Dec. 17, 1906–Nov. 30, 1908
Truman H. Newberry	Dec. 1, 1908–Mar. 5, 1909
George von L. Meyer	Mar. 6, 1909–Mar. 4, 1913
Josephus Daniels	Mar. 5, 1913–Mar. 4, 1921

Command and Staff

Following the Civil War, the affairs of the navy were regulated in the traditional manner by the secretary of the navy and by the heads of the staff bureaus. The senior naval officers on duty, Adm. David Farragut and Vice Adm. David Dixon Porter, exercised a great deal of influence, but the real day-to-day management of the navy remained in the hands of the all-powerful bureau chiefs. The chief of the Bureau of Navigation gradually assumed the unofficial senior position, particularly because he controlled assignments of naval officers.

The inadequacies of the staff bureaus led to agitation for their reform through consolidation, realignment of responsibilities, and the establishment of a board to coordinate their work. President Grant's reform proposal failed in the House of Representatives in 1869, but some progress was made in the late 19th century. The position of assistant secretary of the navy was reestablished in 1882. In 1892, Secretary of the Navy Tracy reorganized the Bureau of Provisions and Clothing into the Bureau of Supplies and Accounts, the navy's finance office. In June 1889, the Office of Detail in the Bureau of Navigation was stripped out to form a Bureau of Personnel, and the former Bureau of Equipment and Recruiting became simply the Bureau of Equipment. Meanwhile, the four "manufacturing bureaus" (Construction and Repair, Steam Engineering, Ordnance, and Equipment) were greatly increased in size and importance and became more specialized. By 1898, there were eight realigned and partially reformed bureaus: Navigation, Equipment, Ordnance, Yards and Docks, Construction and Repair, Steam Engineering, Supplies and Accounts, and Medicine and Surgery.

Calls for a naval general staff to plan and coordinate properly the navy's various activities were generally ignored until the Spanish-American War demonstrated the need for immediate reform. A temporary organization, the Naval War Board, was created during the war to advise the secretary of the navy on naval strategy and to assist him in coordinating intelligence and strategic planning as well as in the conduct of naval operations. After a long period of gestation, a permanent General Board of the Navy was finally established on Mar. 13, 1900. Consisting of nine officers—including the chief of the Bureau of Navigation, the chief intelligence officer, the president of the Naval War College, and the Admiral of the Navy as board president—the General Board was charged with making plans for the effective preparation of the fleet for war and with advising the navy secretary on the proper number and type of ships, the number and ranks of officers and enlisted men of the navy, and plans of naval operations. The board was also charged with coordinating the activities of the Naval War College, the Office of Naval Intelligence, and other activities. Although granted some authority to coordinate the activities of the bureaus, the General Board was not given the power to direct their operations, and the bureaus continued to be powerful, independent, and often conflicting centers of authority. In 1915, Rear Adm. Bradley A. Fiske, against the wishes of Sec. of the Navy Josephus Daniels, succeeded in forcing the creation of the position of chief of naval operations (CNO) as the ranking officer of the navy, a position analogous to the new chief of staff of the army. An act of Aug. 29, 1916, gave the new CNO a staff of 15 assistants to prepare war plans and coordinate activities. However, the act failed to provide the CNO with adequate power to control the bureaus, a situation that would not be corrected until World War II.

Organization

In 1865, the navy reorganized the foreign squadrons established before 1861. The Mediterranean and African squadrons were merged to form the European Squadron, the Brazilian Squadron became the South Atlantic Squadron, and the former Pacific Squadron was divided to form a new Pacific Squadron and an Asiatic Squadron. The former Home Squadron was replaced by a North Atlantic Squadron and a Gulf Squadron. In 1873, there were 10 ships assigned to the North Atlantic Squadron, 5 to the European, 9 to the Asiatic, 3 to the South Atlantic, and 7 to the Pacific. By 1882, there were also nine navy yards (at Portsmouth, New London, New York, League Island, Boston, Washington, Norfolk, Pensacola, and Mare Island) and six naval stations (at Newport, Annapolis, Port Royal, Key West, New Orleans, and Sacket's Harbor). In 1883, Secretary of the Navy Chandler closed the yards at Pensacola, League Island, and New London, but in 1891, a new naval station was established on Puget Sound. Until after the Spanish-American War, U.S. naval facilities overseas were limited mainly to a few coaling stations (Samoa from 1879 and Hawaii from 1893, for example) and a naval hospital established in 1872 at Yokohama, Japan.

From time to time, the navy also assembled fleets for special purposes, such as the so-called Squadron of Evolution (1889–91), created to test new strategic and tactical principles devised by the Naval War College. The Squadron of Evolution toured to impress foreigners and the domestic public, as did the famous "Great White Fleet," which made an around-the-world cruise (1907–09) on the orders of Pres. Theodore Roosevelt to advertise America's new status as a first-class naval power.

During the Spanish-American War, the navy was forced to operate in two theaters. The fleet oriented toward the Caribbean and Spanish homeland consisted of three squadrons (Blockading, Flying, and Northern Patrol) under Rear Adm. William T. Sampson. The fleet oriented toward the Spanish possessions in the Philippines consisted of one squadron under Rear Adm. George Dewey. At the time of his great victory in Manila Bay on May 1, 1898, Dewey's squadron was composed of seven combat vessels: four cruisers, two gunboats, and one revenue cutter.

The quick victory over Spain in 1898 brought the navy increased responsibilities, particularly in the Caribbean and in the western Pacific. New bases were established at Guantanamo Bay in Cuba, in Puerto Rico, on Guam, and in the Philippines. The navy's wider operational deployments, plus the threat of Japan in the western Pacific, led to increased strength to protect the Pacific lines of communication and an increased interest in a canal across the Isthmus of Panama to provide the ability to transfer ships rapidly from the Atlantic Ocean to the Pacific. In 1904–05, the European and South Atlantic squadrons were consolidated with the North Atlantic Squadron, and in 1907, the Pacific and Asiatic squadrons were amalgamated. The reorganized Pacific Fleet consisted of three squadrons and the 1st and 4th Torpedo Flotillas, a total of 35 vessels. The Asiatic Squadron was reestablished in 1910. From 1913 to

1915, the bulk of the U.S. fleet was concentrated in Mexican waters, but the entry of the United States into World War I in April 1917 caused a redeployment of most naval strength to the North Atlantic to protect the convoy routes to Europe. Adm. William S. Sims, the U.S. naval commander in Europe, eventually commanded some 375 ships, 5,000 officers, 70,000 enlisted men, and 45 bases.

Reserve Forces

The principal augmentation for the navy in time of war was provided by the Coast Guard, which was formally established on Jan. 28, 1915, by joining the Revenue Cutter Service and the Life Saving Service. Some 856 coastguardsmen served with the navy in the Spanish-American War. In World War I, the Coast Guard augmented the navy with 15 cutters and more than 200 officers and 5,000 men. Coast Guard vessels and crews hunted submarines and surface raiders and guarded the troop transport convoys en route to France.

There was no federal naval reserve in the 19th century, but an effort by the states to establish naval militia units began with a bill in Congress on Feb. 17, 1887. A naval militia was established in Massachusetts in 1890, and other states soon followed. In March 1891, Congress appropriated $25,000 for arms and equipment of the naval militia, and by 1896, 14 states and some 3,339 men were involved. More than 3,800 naval militiamen served in the war with Spain. Several attempts were made to create a permanent national naval reserve in the years after 1898 but met with little success until the 1920s.

Officer Personnel

The first two decades after the Civil War were not a happy time for the officers of the navy. Pay was low, and promotions were slowed by the "hump" created by the accession of Civil War volunteers, 150 of whom were retained after 1866. The old internal conflicts over retirement plans, the relative pay and status of line and staff officers, and commissioning practices also continued to preoccupy many naval officers. In addition, the small and aging fleet offered little opportunity for command at sea. Conditions began to improve after 1885 with the advent of the "new navy" building program and accelerating professionalism among naval officers. The increased number of new ships meant more opportunities for command, and improved professional education was provided after 1885 by the Naval War College. The founding of the U.S. Naval Institute in 1873 provided an additional outlet for the new sense of professionalism. The real turning point came with the Spanish-American War and the increased responsibilities that followed. On Mar. 3, 1899, the longstanding dispute between engineers and line officers was resolved by the amalgamation of the two categories and by regulation of both the number of officers and the flow of promotion. The Naval Personnel Bill of 1899 also increased pay and allowances and abolished the rank of commodore. By World War I, most of the serious impediments to professionalism in the naval service had been eliminated, and the expansion occasioned by World War I, as well as the increased opportunity for command and other important assignments, further increased the satisfaction of the naval officer corps, which continued to be recruited largely from graduates of the Naval Academy.

Enlisted Personnel

Improvements in the conditions of service for enlisted men of the navy paralleled those of the officer corps. Following the Civil War, seamen of American birth and nationality were difficult to attract because of commercial civilian opportunities, and the enlisted personnel of the navy continued to be drawn largely from the foreign-born. In 1889, the enlisted strength of the navy counted 4,278 foreign-born seamen and only 3,668 native-born. The foreign-born included natives of some 57 countries, and a full 11 percent were from Ireland. In 1897, about 25 percent of the enlisted men of the navy were foreigners, but by 1904, conditions had improved to the degree that only 9 percent were foreigners, 11 percent were naturalized citizens, and 80 percent were native-born. Throughout the period, the navy faced difficulties in obtaining the required number of seamen of any nationality to man the steadily increasing number of ships, and vessels often operated with only 50–75 percent of their authorized complement. The lack of seamen and the increased demand for mechanically inclined sailors for the new, more technologically sophisticated ships of the "new navy" led to attempts to improve pay and conditions and to train young men for naval service. A new apprentice system was initiated in October 1875, and training for seamen steadily improved.

Tactical Doctrine

The essence of naval warfare in the late 19th century was to find, close with, and destroy the enemy's men-of-war or merchant ships by rapid, accurate naval gunfire. However, technological advances changed naval tactical doctrine in many ways. The capital ship remained the basic tactical instrument, but the perfection of the torpedo led to increased emphasis on small, fast torpedo boats. More lightly armed vessels, such as the armored cruiser, were developed for long-range scouting, warding off torpedo attacks on the main battle line, and commerce raiding. By 1910, the use of destroyers mounting rapid-fire guns to screen the capital ships was accepted doctrine in all world navies. The construction of effective submarines led to their integration in fleet protection and inshore defense operations, but their value as commerce raiders was not realized until 1914, when the threat posed by German submarines to Allied transatlantic merchant shipping assumed major proportions. The submarine threat thus provoked interest in the development of effective antisubmarine warfare techniques, including convoys and the use of smaller rapid vessels such as the destroyer to find and kill submarines with depth charges. World War I also increased reliance on mining as part of conducting naval operations. The operation of fleets far from home after 1898 also required the seizure and protection of naval bases overseas. Accordingly, the U.S. Navy and Marine Corps developed effective techniques and tactics for amphibious operations.

THE MARINE CORPS: 1865–1919

Following the Civil War, the U.S. Marine Corps provided guards aboard naval vessels and at shore installations, manned naval guns, acted as expeditionary infantry in support of naval operations, and occasionally was called upon to enforce civil laws. The advent of the "new navy" in the 1880s signaled some changes in Marine Corps missions. The traditional ship guard function was challenged by the advocates of the "new navy," but the commandants of the Marine Corps were ultimately successful in keeping marines abroad ships. The strategic emphasis of the "new navy" and the overseas expansion after the Spanish-American War brought other opportunities for the marines. After 1885, the prospect of major expeditionary duties was used to argue for manpower increases in the Marine Corps, and the marines were used increasingly for diplomatic show-of-force and protection tasks such as the defense of the international compound in Peking in 1900. After 1898, the Marine Corps was also involved in the administration of overseas territories and in a number of "diplomatic" interventions in the Caribbean. In Cuba, Nicaragua, Haiti, the Dominican Republic, and Mexico, marines "pacified" unrest and often contributed significantly to internal development.

A major marine landing was made at Guantanamo Bay, Cuba, on June 14, 1898, and amphibious operations subsequently became a Marine Corps hallmark. Created in 1900, the General Board of the Navy focused on amphibious operations to seize advance bases, and in March 1902, a marine battalion was organized especially for the mission of capturing and defending advance bases for the navy. Between 1910 and 1914, the Advance Base Force idea evolved from concept to reality. The marines also engaged in other sustained operations ashore in the early 20th century. A marine regiment was organized for service in the Philippine Insurrection and later expanded to form the 1st Marine Brigade. The 1st Marine Brigade was disbanded in 1914, but World War I once again involved a large force of marines in major sustained ground operations as the 4th Marine Brigade, consisting of the 5th and 6th marine regiments, fought as part of the army's 2d Division of France.

Commandants of the U.S. Marine Corps, 1864–1920

Name	*Term*
Brig. Gen. Jacob Zeilin	June 10, 1864–Oct. 31, 1876
Col. Charles G. McCawley	Nov. 1, 1876–Jan. 29, 1891
Maj. Gen. Charles Heywood	Jan. 30, 1891–Oct. 2, 1903
Maj. Gen. George F. Elliott	Oct. 3, 1903–Nov. 30, 1910
Maj. Gen. William P. Biddle	Feb. 2, 1911–Feb. 24, 1914
Maj. Gen. George Barnett	Feb. 25, 1914–June 30, 1920

The actual strength of the Marine Corps at the end of the Civil War in 1865 was 78 officers and 3,177 men. In 1874, the Marine Corps was reduced to 1,500 privates, and between 1878 and 1889, Congress annually funded only 75–85 officers and about 2,000 enlisted men. During the war with Spain, the actual strength rose to 116 officers and 4,700 men, and by 1908, the authorized strength had risen to 332 officers and 9,521 enlisted men. In 1916, on the eve of U.S. entry to World War I, the actual strength of the Marine Corps was 341 officers and 10,056 enlisted men. By the end of the war in November 1918, Marine Corps strength had reached 2,462 officers and 72,639 enlisted personnel, including 305 women of the Marine Reserve (female).

During this period, the Marine Corps, like the army and the navy, developed an increased professionalism with better preparation of officers and better training for enlisted men. A major step forward came with appointment of marine officers from the Naval Academy. Between 1882 and 1898, all new marine lieutenants were Naval Academy graduates. Schools and examinations for serving officers were also introduced. The training of enlisted men was also much improved. The Washington Marine Barracks served as a school of application for the Marine Corps after 1891, and various commandants stressed marksmanship and other individual skills. Although the Marine Corps, like the army, suffered a high desertion rate in the years after the Civil War—ranging from one-third to one-fourth of its strength annually—improved training, better facilities, and, above all, improved morale and esprit de corps did much to alleviate the problem. The public image of the Marine Corps was also much improved by the efforts of the Marine Corps Band under the direction of John Philip Sousa after 1880.

In terms of organization, the marines continued to follow the army pattern, with companies, battalions, and later brigades. Independent marine divisions were not formed until after World War I. Marine Corps tactical doctrine for land operations generally followed that of the army, but of course the marines themselves took the lead in developing doctrine for amphibious operations.

AIR FORCES: 1865–1919

Air power began to emerge as an important component of military power at the end of the 19th century. Prof. E. A. Lowe's tethered balloons had been used by the Union army for observation and primitive artillery fire direction early in the Civil War, but the experiment was soon abandoned. Although interest in military ballooning was revived in the 1890s, the future of military aviation lay with powered heavier-than-air craft. Wilbur and Orville Wright's attempts to achieve manned, powered flight succeeded at Kitty Hawk, North Carolina, on Dec. 17, 1903, and the airplane soon attracted notice in the army. An Aeronautical Division, under the chief signal officer, was established on Aug. 1, 1907, and in February 1908, the Wright brothers signed a contract with the War Department for delivery of a military airplane to cost $25,000. The Wright airplane was accepted by the army in August 1909, but not before the army suffered its first military aviation casualty, Lt. E. E. Selfridge, who was killed in the crash of the Wright Flyer on Sept. 17, 1908.

However tragic, Selfridge's death did not derail interest in military aviation, and in 1909, Congress appropriated $30,000 for army aviation. In September 1909, the first military airfield was established at College Park, Maryland, the site also of the first military aviation school in 1911. The army's first aviation unit, the 1st Aero Squadron (provisional), was activated at San Diego, California, on Mar. 5, 1913, and was quickly deployed to Texas City, Texas, as part of the force then being assembled on the Mexican border. On July 18, 1914, a full-fledged Aviation Section was established in the Signal Corps with a complement of 60 officers and 260 enlisted men, and in 1916, Congress authorized the creation of eight aero squadrons in the Officer and Enlisted Reserve Corps. Meanwhile, the 1st Aero Squadron, commanded by Maj. Benjamin D. Foulois, joined Brigadier General Pershing's Punitive Expedition into Mexico. The unit of 11 officers, 82 enlisted men, and a civilian mechanic struggled to keep the eight original aircraft in the air but proved the worth of the airplane as a military reconnaissance and liaison tool.

World War I Expansion

Due to low funding and strong resistance in the military bureaucracy, the United States entered World War I well behind in military aviation. On Apr. 6, 1917, the Aviation Section of the Signal Corps consisted of 131 officers (of whom 26 were qualified pilots), 1,087 enlisted men, 55 trainers and observation aircraft, and 224 other airplanes, none of which were combat models and all of which were obsolete when compared to those in war service in Europe. Seven tactical squadrons were in existence or were being organized. Both the army and the Congress moved quickly to repair the defect. On July 24, Congress appropriated $640,000,000 for development of military aviation, the largest sum ever appropriated for a single purpose up to that time. Overall, the World War I expenditure for aeronautical purposes was $868,100,671.

A semi-independent Air Service, U.S. Army, was created in May 1918, and by the end of the war, there were 45 U.S. squadrons in France: 20 fighter, 6 day bombardment, 1 night bombardment, and 18 observation. In addition, 35 balloon companies were formed, and 23 saw active front-line service. Of some 2,900 airplanes used, only 696 were of U.S. manufacture, the remainder being French or British models. Air Service personnel in France on Nov. 11, 1918, included 767 pilots, 481 observers, and 23 aerial gunners. In 1918, the size of the Air Service reached 20,708 officers (including 11,425 flying officers) and 174,315

Wilbur and Orville Wright's first powered flight at Kitty Hawk, North Carolina, on Dec. 17, 1903, paved the way for the establishment of an Aeronautical Division of the U.S. Army in 1907. (Library of Congress)

enlisted men, most of whom were in training in the United States. In March 1919, the Air Service became a recognized branch separate from its parent Signal Corps, and the strength of the Air Service subsequently fell to 25,603 officers and men, or about 3 percent of the total army.

The achievements of the Air Service in France were remarkable for a force so raw. Some 781 enemy planes and 73 balloons were shot down, in contrast to an Air Service loss of 289 planes and 49 balloons. American pilots performed all of the recognized aviation tasks: reconnaissance, liaison, observation and direction of artillery fire, ground attack, air-to-air combat, and bombardment by both day and night. They dropped some 275,000 pounds of bombs in more than 150 bombing raids.

Naval and Marine Corps aviation also began in the years immediately preceding World War I and proved its value in that conflict. Naval aviation began in November 1910 with the launching of a Curtis biplane from the deck of the USS *Birmingham* in Hampton Roads, Virginia. Naval airpower expanded in World War I from 39 pilots to 1,600 and from 54 to 2,000 airplanes. Marine Corps aviation began with the qualification of Lt. Alfred A. Cunningham on May 22, 1912. In 1917, 6 Marine officers were designated as naval aviators and were supported by 1 warrant officer and 45 enlisted men. Marine Corps aviation developed at a rapid pace in World War I, and four squadrons of marine bombers served in France. In all, 282 officers and 2,180 enlisted men served in marine aviation in World War I.

TECHNOLOGICAL DEVELOPMENTS

The half century after the Civil War was a period of tremendous scientific and technological change throughout the world. Theoretical breakthroughs in the basic sciences were rapidly translated into practical tools. Although U.S. scientists and inventors played a prominent role in scientific discovery, the U.S. Armed Forces lagged behind their European counterparts in adopting the new technology to military ends. The lack of available funds, coupled with traditional military conservatism and the difficulties of resolving the problem of when to "buy into" the rapidly developing technology, served to retard modernization of the U.S. Armed Forces. But once it came, the U.S. response was rapid and thorough, particularly because between 1865 and 1917, American industry became dominant in almost every technological field.

Infantry Weapons

In 1872, an army ordnance board met to examine and test new infantry weapons. The result was the 1873 Springfield breechloading rifle in center-fire .45–.70 caliber. The 1873 Springfield had greater muzzle velocity and greater penetrating power than its predecessors, but it was a single-shot weapon, used black-powder cartridges, and was heavy, as was its ammunition. A modification, the 1889 Springfield, was the principal weapon of the National Guard as late as 1898.

By 1890, the trend was toward repeating arms using smokeless powder cartridges, which permitted higher velocity and flatter trajectory with smaller caliber. In 1892, the army adopted the Danish .30-caliber bolt-action Krag-Jörgensen rifle with a box magazine containing five cartridges, but Congress delayed production for two years in order to permit further tests of U.S. rifles. The Krag's high muzzle velocity and flat trajectory meant great range and greater accuracy with stopping power equivalent to the older 1873 Springfield. The soldier's burden was reduced by the Krag's lighter weight, and the lighter weight of its ammunition meant the soldier could carry more cartridges.

By the start of the Spanish-American War, only the regular army was armed with the Krag, and volunteers continued to use the old Springfield against Spaniards armed with the modern Mauser. The real constraint was not so much rifle production as the production of smokeless powder with which to fill the cartridges. In 1898, only one factory in the United States was producing such smokeless powder. The Krag-Jörgensen continued as the standard U.S. infantry weapon until 1904, when production was halted with the introduction of the new 1903 Springfield, considered by many to be the best infantry rifle ever made. The .30-caliber bolt-action Springfield, with its clip-fed five-round magazine and improved range and accuracy, remained the standard U.S. infantry weapon until World War II and continued in use long after as a special-purpose weapon.

Two other new weapons introduced in the early 20th century had an equally long service life. The Colt .45-caliber automatic pistol, introduced in 1911, was developed for use against the Moros in the Philippines. It remained the standard U.S. sidearm for almost 70 years. The .30-caliber Browning automatic rifle was introduced about the same time, and it remained the standard automatic weapon of the infantry squad until the early 1960s.

Developed during the Civil War, the multibarreled Gatling gun was finally adopted as a standard army weapon in 1866. The Gatling was seen as an auxiliary to artillery and was thought to be most useful for the defense of fixed installations such as bridges. In 1885, Hiram Maxim introduced a true recoil-operated machine gun, which was adopted by the British army in 1889. A gas-operated model was invented by John M. Browning in 1895. Maxim and an American, Isaac N. Lewis, took the lead in further development of the machine gun, but it was little appreciated in the United States before World War I. From 1898 to 1916, Congress could be persuaded to appropriate only an average of $150,000 annually for machine-gun procurement. A

The Gatling gun, used throughout the Civil War but not adopted officially by the army until 1866, is demonstrated by cadets at West Point, about 1905. (Library of Congress)

$12,000,000 machine-gun procurement was approved in 1916 but was delayed until 1917 so that an optimum choice could be made. The result of such foot-dragging was that the army entered World War I with only four machine guns per regular army infantry regiment and even fewer for National Guard units.

The machine gun proved to be the dominant infantry weapon in World War I, but many other innovations were also introduced in that conflict. Among them were massive barbed fortifications, improved hand grenades, and the flamethrower. Perhaps equal with the machine gun in its portent for the future was the tank, a tracked armored vehicle mounting machine guns and cannon and used to support infantry attacks. A Briton, Col. Ernest Swinton, is usually credited with being the driving force behind development of the tank, which was first used by the British at Cambrai, France, on Nov. 20, 1917. The U.S. army in France used various models of British and French tanks including the heavy Mark VII, a 30-ton model with 16 millimeters of armor and a 6-pounder gun, and the light "Whippet," a 14-ton tank with 4 millimeters of armor and a .303-caliber machine gun. The development of both tank tactics and tank technology moved forward rapidly, but when World War I ended, the tank was still viewed primarily as an infantry-support weapon. A concept of independent tank operations emphasizing mobility and shock action would have to wait until the 1920s and 1930s.

Artillery Weapons

Three important improvements in artillery weapons were breechloading, advances in interior ballistics, and the development of an effective recoil mechanism. All were products of the late 19th century, as was the development of true indirect fire techniques. Between the Civil War and World War I, the Army Ordnance Department developed breechloading field and coast artillery as well as improved projectiles, propellants, and explosives. Rifled pieces replaced smoothbores, and steel replaced iron; steel carriages, pneumatic and hydraulic brakes, and improved mechanisms for elevating, traversing, and sighting artillery pieces were all introduced. Nevertheless, the United States lagged behind European armies in the development of accurate rapid-firing field artillery weapons. The principal shortfall was in the production of the new smokeless powder. Only after 1903 did U.S. production of smokeless powder suffice to support army needs.

Representative of the advantage held by European armies was the French 75-millimeter field gun introduced in 1897. A rifled breechloader with a superior on-carriage recoil system and using smokeless powder, the "French 75" was light, highly mobile, and could shoot farther, faster, more accurately, and with greater terminal effect than most contemporary field artillery pieces. The 3-inch field gun with advanced recoil mechanism adopted by the U.S. Army in 1902 was every bit as good as the French 75. It might have achieved equal recognition had it been available in sufficient quantities for U.S. forces in World War I. As it happened, U.S. artillery units in France were equipped primarily with the French 75; of 2,250 field guns used by Americans in France, only 100 were of American manufacture.

In World War I, the machine gun played a major role in stifling offensives, but artillery was the big killer. In one year of World War I, the U.S. artillery alone fired 8,000,000 rounds, and Allied forces fired some 160,615,000 rounds in all. World War I artillery ranged from small 37-millimeter infantry assault guns to the enormous German "Big Bertha," a 420-millimeter monster howitzer, and the "Paris Gun," which fired a 250-pound shell 75 miles. New weapons such as the 3-inch Stokes trench mortar and various antiaircraft guns were also introduced, and high-explosive shells, shrapnel, and time fuzes contributed to the deadly effectiveness of artillery.

Chemical Weapons

Poison gas was another World War I development. Dispersed from ground-mounted cylinders or by exploding artillery shells, chemical agents added another dimension of terror and suffering to the battlefield. Gas was first used by the Germans at Ypres, Belgium, on Apr. 22, 1915, and it soon was added to the arsenals of all the belligerents. Classified as blistering agents, choking agents, and blood agents, World War I gases caused enormous numbers of casualties, most of whom were incapacitated rather than killed. About 25 percent of all American casualties in World War I were from gas. Of these, 2 percent died (compared to 25 percent fatalities from casualties by other weapons). About 75 percent of American gas casualties were from mustard gas, an extremely painful and debilitating blistering agent that was seldom fatal unless inhaled.

Naval Weapons

The last half of the 19th century witnessed a revolution in naval technology. The transition from sail to steam and from wooden to steel ships was completed, and improved guns and ammunition, better armor, oil-burning boilers, better ship ventilation, and new electrical and hydraulic gear all served to modernize the navies of the world. These trends were merged in 1906 in the British *Dreadnought,* a large, fast, expensive vessel with heavy armor and 10 12-inch guns and an antitorpedo battery of 12-pounders.

The 15 years after the Civil War saw a transformation of naval ordnance as rifles replaced smoothbores, breechloaders replaced muzzleloaders, and wrought iron replaced cast iron in the manufacture of guns. After 1881, all new naval guns were made of built-up steel. Shell replaced shot in naval projectiles after 1870, and after 1873, naval guns were increasingly mounted in revolving turrets and equipped with effective recoil mechanisms. The range of the new guns increased from 6,000 yards in 1898 to 20,000 yards in 1914, and the time required to fire went from 5 minutes to about 40 seconds. Accuracy increased as well. By 1910, the standard naval gun was a 12-inch cannon some 46 feet long and weighing 62.5 tons (108 tons mounted). A built-up steel gun, it fired an 870-pound projectile with a maximum charge of 400 pounds of smokeless powder at a muzzle velocity of 2,800 feet per second to a maximum range of 12 miles. At a fighting range of 5,000–6,000 yards, it could penetrate 14 inches of steel armor.

The development of new, more powerful and more accurate naval guns prompted related improvements in ship armor. Between 1860 and 1880, the average thickness of armor at the water line increased from 4.5 inches to 24 inches. Wrought-iron armor was replaced by composite steel. The so-called new-process armor developed by the German firm Krupp was 20–30 percent more resistive and was thus adopted by most navies by 1898. The first U.S. armored vessels, the battleships *Maine* and *Texas,* were not launched until 1886, but by 1917, the U.S. Navy was fast catching up with the British and Germans.

The United States led rather than followed in the adoption of new electrical and hydraulic devices to facilitate the working of ships and guns. Rear Admiral Fiske invented numerous devices, including new sights, turrets, ammunition handling equipment, and the engine order telegraph. The new dreadnaughts mounted all big guns of the same caliber, thereby making fire control somewhat easier, but for some time, the ordnance technology outran the means to direct naval gunfire accurately at long range. However, by 1914, the continuous aiming battery firing system developed by Fiske and electrical engineer Elmer A. Sperry was in general use. Coupled with improved ship construction, engines, and armor, the developments in naval guns, projectiles, and fire control all but ended close-range naval actions by the turn of the century. In World War I, naval actions could be conducted with the opponents all but out of sight of each other.

The second half of the 19th century also saw rapid development of other naval weapons, such as the mine, the torpedo, and the submarine. The self-propelled mine, or torpedo, was invented by a Scot, Robert Whitehead, and was generally adopted by 1873 with many improvements being made thereafter. The torpedo led to an emphasis on fast-moving torpedo boats, and they in turn sparked the development of the destroyer with quick-firing guns. The submarine was introduced during the Civil War, as was the periscope invented by Thomas H. Doughty, but the first really practical submarine was produced by the Frenchmen Bourgeous and Brun in 1863. In 1884, the Britons Campbell and Ash perfected an all-electric submarine with an effective range of 80 miles, and by 1899, submarines with a range of about 150 miles were in service in several world navies. John P. Holland's *Plunger* was the first true submarine contracted by the U.S. Navy. Completed in 1900, it utilized steam power for surface cruising and storage batteries for submerged operations.

The Germans are rightly noted in connection with submarines. The first satisfactory diesel-powered U-boat was launched in 1913. On Aug. 8, 1914, the *U-15* fired a torpedo at the British battleship *Monarch* without success in the first use of a torpedo fired from a submarine against an enemy vessel. Subsequently, the Germans achieved considerable success in the use of submarines and torpedoes against Allied shipping. That success provoked a counter-reaction, and various means were developed to deal with the submarine menace. The hydrophone was first used successfully by the British to locate a submerged submarine in April 1916, and destroyers, depth charges, and the convoy system were also used to counter the submarine threat, which would prove an even more significant factor in World War II.

Aviation

The development of the airplane in the early 20th century transformed the nature of modern war. At the beginning of World War I, military aircraft were still few and primitive, but they evolved quickly under the stimulus of war. Initially used for reconnaissance and artillery fire control, bomber variants were soon developed, including long-range aircraft with four engines. The invention of a method to synchronize the firing of a machine gun between the blades of the propeller by Dutchman Anthony H. G. Fokker led to air-to-air engagements as well as the strafing of ground troops and the destruction of observation balloons. Among the many other aviation-related developments during World War I were improvements in engines and airframes leading to bigger, faster, and more survivable aircraft; cotton airplane and balloon fabrics; the use of helium gas for balloons; oxygen masks with telephone connections and electrically heated clothing for operation at higher altitudes; the adaptation of radios for air-to-ground and air-to-air communication; and aerial photography. Although still in its infancy in 1918, the airplane promised to become a major factor in warfare, and its subsequent development was to be rapid and far-reaching.

Communications

In 1867, responsibility for electrical field telegraphy was restored to the Army Signal Corps, which proceeded to construct telegraph lines on the East Coast and in the Southwest and Northwest to link army posts. By 1881, nearly 5,000 miles of telegraph lines had been erected. The flying, or field, telegraph train using battery-powered sounders and insulated wire was also improved and provided the beginnings of tactical communications in the field. In the late 1870s, the army experimented with the use of Alexander Graham Bell's telephone to link Fort Whipple and offices in Washington, and by 1892, 59 of the army's 99 garrisons had telephone service. A field telephone kit consisting of a Bell telephone, a Morse key, and a battery was developed in 1889 but proved too expensive for issue at the time. Older methods of field communications were also employed. The heliograph saw extensive use in the sunny Southwest, and after 1878, there were experiments with the use of homing pigeons to carry messages.

The real breakthrough in field communications came with the invention of the radio by Guglielmo Marconi. In 1897, Marconi transmitted a message 9 miles, and by 1901, his device could span 3,000 miles. The U.S. Navy was quick to sense the importance of Marconi's invention and entered negotiations with him in 1899 leading to the use of radio equipment aboard most major naval vessels early in the 20th century. The U.S. Army also saw the usefulness of radio and adopted radio equipment early in the century as well. Although radio communications were still primitive, they were used extensively on land and sea and even in the air in World War I and transformed tactical as well as strategic communications, giving the commander in the field a far greater ability to command and control large forces spread over a battlefield that was rapidly expanding in size to accommodate the new weapons and tactics.

Mobility

Railroads and steamships remained key factors in strategic mobility throughout the 19th century. Indeed, the movement of military forces and equipment by railroad and steamship was still at the center of strategic plans and operations in World War I. By skillful use of the railroads, European armies mobilized and moved their mass armies to battle; and by steamship, the United States moved a decisive 2,000,000 men and 8,000,000 tons of supplies to France.

For most of the period, tactical mobility remained the same as in the Civil War, limited to the pace of man and animal, but the invention of the internal combustion engine in the late 19th century was a key technological breakthrough that brought about a revolution in military transportation. Germans took the lead in the development of the internal combustion engine. Dr. Nikolaus A. Otto developed the first successful gasoline engine in 1874, Gottlieb Daimler produced the first lightweight model in 1882, and Rudolf Diesel introduced his engine in 1895. The production of a satisfactory fuel for such engines was a major problem. Commercial oil production began in Rumania in 1857 and in the United States in 1859. Soon, methods of refining were developed to produce a satisfactory fuel. Rubber was also essential to motor transport. Charles Goodyear invented the vulcanization process in 1839, and various rubber products were in use during the Civil War. In 1906, George Oenslager of Akron, Ohio, discovered how to produce uniform rubber products and how to speed the process of vulcanization. In doing so, he made possible the production of tires, hoses, belts, and other rubber items essential to the mass production of automotive matériel.

The eventual perfection and application of the gasoline engine to the truck, airplane, and tank was to have a most profound effect on civilian life as well as on military strategy, tactics, logistics, and organization, but for the most part, that impact would not be felt until after 1918. Although the gasoline-powered truck was beginning to be an important factor in tactical mobility, by the end of

By 1869, railroads spanned the continental United States when a gold spike completed the tracks at Promontory, Utah, where the Union Pacific and Central Pacific railroads met. Railroads were depended upon for many years to move troops and equipment to battle sites. (Union Pacific Railroad)

World War I, armies everywhere still depended upon animal-drawn transport for supply and movement of artillery and other equipment in the field. Indeed, many "modern" armies would continue to depend upon the older methods through World War II.

Medical Developments

Enormous progress was made in every aspect of medical treatment and preventive medicine between 1865 and 1919. Louis Pasteur contributed the germ theory, Jacob Lister the concept of antisepsis, and Wilhelm C. Roentgen the x-ray process. Surgical techniques were greatly advanced, and the use of improved anesthetics became general, as did the use of more potent painkillers such as morphine. Inoculation against infectious diseases, particularly those such as typhoid that were particularly threatening to massed military forces operating under poor sanitary conditions, also became common.

U.S. military physicians were major contributors to the advance of medical science. George M. Sternberg, who became army surgeon general in 1893, was a recognized pioneer in the field of bacteriology. The famous discovery of the mosquito as the vector for yellow fever by Maj. Walter Reed at the turn of the century led to the reduction of one of mankind's more serious ills, and the subsequent efforts of Col. William C. Gorgas to control malaria and yellow fever made possible the construction of the Panama Canal.

The effect of such medical advances on the treatment and survival rates of sick and wounded soldiers was profound. In the Civil War, the rate of death from disease was 71.4 per 1,000. In the Spanish-American War, it fell to 34.0 per 1,000, and in World War I, it was 16.5 per 1,000. The rate of death from wounds also fell. The rate was 14.1 per 100 in the Civil War but only 6.7 per 100 in the Spanish-American War. The rate rose slightly to 8.1 per 100 in World War I (exclusive of gas casualties) due to the greater destructiveness of modern weapons, but the downward trend was only beginning. In World War II, the rate of death from disease would be further reduced to 0.6 per 1,000 and the rate of death from wounds would drop to 4.5 per 100.

CONCLUSION

Between the parade of the Grand Army of the Republic in Washington in 1865 and the Victory Parade in 1919, the armed forces of the United States came of age. Awakened to new global responsibilities and aware of the crucial importance of new technology and the new organization and doctrine it required, the army, navy, Marine Corps, and fledgling Air Service proved their mettle in numerous small engagements and in the major crisis of a world war. Although these forces would again regress in size and funding in the 1920s and 1930s, they would emerge by 1945 as the key components of the dominant military power of the world.

2

Reconstruction and the Indian Wars: 1865–1891

The nation's traditional fears of a large military establishment remained evident after 1865. Both the army and the navy thus suffered major reductions. During the Civil War, the navy had assembled a mighty armada of 671 warships, but by 1867, only 103 ships remained in active commission. Numbering more than 1,000,000 men at the close of the Civil War, the army was cut to just over 54,000 in July 1866. Further congressional measures in 1869, 1870, and 1874 reduced that figure by another 50 percent.

In 1877, House Democrats renewed their attacks on the regular army. Opposed to the military's role in Reconstruction and buoyed by recent political gains, Democrats demanded that the army be reduced to 17,000 and be withdrawn from areas where Republicans still controlled state government in the South. When the Senate refused to go along with such draconian measures, the resulting impasse left the army without appropriations and the soldiers without pay for several months.

MILITARY ORGANIZATION

As sectional rivalries diminished, Congress moved on to other matters and left the size of the army intact. Organized into 10 cavalry, 5 artillery, and 25 infantry regiments, the army garrisoned 200–300 military posts. Although official doctrine used the regiment as the basic tactical formation, the multiple demands on the small regular establishment made the concentration of an entire regiment impossible. As such, the company served as the basic building block for army action.

Officially, a captain and two lieutenants led each company. Rarely, however, were all officers present for duty, as recruiting details, personal leaves, courts-martial, and service on official boards stripped the companies of commissioned personnel. Inadequate recruiting budgets, sickness, and extra duty left companies chronically short of enlisted men, a weakness exacerbated by annual desertion rates of 30–40 percent.

The reorganized army included four regiments of black enlisted personnel: the 9th and 10th cavalries and the 24th and 25th infantry regiments. Led by white officers, these regiments built impressive combat records. They also proved immensely loyal to the army itself, reenlisting at high rates and deserting much less frequently than their white counterparts. Indian scouts and auxiliaries added to the mix, providing invaluable service in the field and in combat. Experiments during the 1880s and 1890s went so far as to add a company of Indians to the regular regiments.

The Multipurpose Army

The nation assigned the army a wide range of functions. Defending the nation's seaboards retained high priority, although little systematic study was given the question until 1885, when Congress authorized the appointment of an army-civilian board headed by Sec. of War William Endicott to study the crumbling coastal defenses. This group recommended a $127,000,000 program of torpedo boats, mines, rapid-firing artillery, and searchlights the following year. Although funding fell short of what was needed to fully implement the Endicott recommendations, the huge

Members of the Wheeler geographical expedition (1871–74) make camp on the banks of the Colorado River near Painted Canyon. (Library of Congress)

appropriations incumbent with such projects remained an attractive political plum.

The army also took an active role in scientific affairs. George M. Sternberg, surgeon general 1893–1902, was a pioneer among American bacteriologists. A branch of its Signal Corps was expanded to form the U.S. Weather Bureau. In addition to providing escort and support services for scientists such as Francis Hayden and Clarence King, from 1871 to 1878, Lt. George M. Wheeler and a team of army engineers headed the U.S. Geographical Surveys west of the 100th meridian.

In contrast to the years before 1861, the army's explorations in the contiguous United States focused less upon "pure" discovery and more upon filling in the gaps left by previous explorations. In Alaska and the far north, however, exciting new discoveries were still forthcoming. Expeditions led by Capt. Charles Raymond (1868–69) and Lts. P. Henry Ray (1881–83), Frederick Schwatka (1883), and Henry T. Allen (1885) did much to open Alaska to U.S. settlement and provided scientists with a wealth of new information. And although much of his command died, Lt. Adolphus Greely's epic studies along Lady Franklin Bay (1881–84) propelled that officer to a successful term as chief signal officer.

The army also assisted the western railroads. Supportive of the nation's efforts to achieve what they believed to be its manifest destiny, regular officers enjoyed good relations with railroad managers and engineers, many of whom they had served with during the Civil War. As such, the army protected railroad surveying and work parties on a regular basis. In 1871, 1872, and 1873, for example, large military expeditions accompanied railroad parties on the Northern Plains as they pushed into Sioux country.

The army also continued to sponsor a range of domestic improvements. Headed by its Corps of Engineers, military projects included work on a number of rivers and harbors as well as capital improvements. Particularly symbolic was the army's supervision of work on public buildings, such as the Washington Monument and the State, War, and Navy buildings in Washington.

The preservation of domestic order remained another important function of the Gilded Age military. The army distributed food, clothing, and blankets to settlers made destitute by natural disaster. In 1877, 4,000 troops assisted management and the government in asserting their authority against railroad workers protesting recent wage cuts. Regulars also intervened in several strike-torn mining and urban areas. More soldiers were used in 1894, when nearly 750,000 workers went on strike. More often than not, officers closely allied themselves with management during such duties.

These quasi-military responsibilities consumed significant time and manpower, but assisting westward expansion remained the army's primary task. The indigenous peoples of the West, rationalized most Americans, were savages whose cultures, lifestyles, and intellectual development left them far below the more "civilized" whites. Although few military officials advocated the physical extermination of the tribes, they did agree that the Indians must accept the ways of the white man. In order that non-Indian migration might continue, the natives should be concentrated on reservations and transformed into Christian farmers.

The consensus on goals rarely translated into an agreement on means. Army officers complained that the transfer of the Bureau of Indian Affairs to the Department of the Interior had divided the government's authority. Ideally, bureau agents staffed the reservations, distributed government annuities, headed educational efforts, and conducted diplomacy with the tribes. The army patrolled the reservation boundaries, keeping white trespassers out and Indian renegades in. But the division of authority often produced grievous misunderstandings among agents, the army, and Indians. Repeated army calls for the transfer of the Indian office back to the War Department threatened many in the Department of the Interior; corruption within the latter agency led some military men to blame all Indian outbreaks on dishonest agents.

The army made little effort to formulate strategic plans in a systematic fashion. On occasion, commanding generals William T. Sherman and Philip H. Sheridan made vague references to the use of total warfare against their new foes. Their influence over the faction-riddled postbellum army, however, is easily overstated. Most campaigns were undertaken with little advance planning and depended for their success on the experience and ambition of officers in the field rather than strategic direction from above.

Administration and Weapons

Administratively, the post-Civil War army retained most of the features of its antebellum predecessor. The Division of the Missouri generally included the Departments of Texas, the Missouri, the Platte, and Dakota. Those of Arizona, California, and the Columbia composed the Division of the Pacific. Rounding out the divisional structure was that of the Atlantic, which was divided into the Department of the East and the Department of the South upon the completion of Reconstruction in 1877.

Drawn for convenience rather than according to any overall strategic guidelines, the number of divisions usually correlated with the number of major generals on active duty. A brigadier general could expect to command a department. As the number of high-ranking Civil War veterans diminished over time, Congress reduced the number of separate administrative units correspondingly.

Plagued by congressional parsimony and technical conservatism, the postbellum army was indifferently armed. The single-shot, breechloading Springfield .45-caliber rifle, adopted in 1873, packed a powerful punch and a long range. Cavalrymen carried a smaller carbine version, as well as a six-shot Colt 1873 revolver. Small Hotchkiss mountain howitzers and Gatling guns added additional firepower, but many officers deemed such field pieces too cumbersome for warfare against the Indians. Line officers complained that their Indian foes, who sported a variety of weapons including the deadly lever-action magazine-fed Winchester rifle, sometimes outgunned their men.

POSTWAR CHALLENGES

Major tasks confronted the army upon the collapse of the Confederacy. Restoring federal authority over the secessionist states seemed difficult enough, as the social, economic, and political collapse of the South would take wisdom, patience, and extraordinary amounts of sensitivity. But the West also demanded close attention. During the Civil War, volunteers had supplemented and often replaced regular units on the frontiers, where violence between Indian and non-Indian had increased in frequency and intensity. Finally, some 35,000 French troops had propped up the tenuous reign of Archduke Ferdinand Maximilian as emperor of Mexico and seemed a major threat to U.S. hegemony in Central and North America.

On the latter issue, Sec. of State William Seward quickly made his displeasure known to Napoleon III of France. In July 1865, the United States began assembling a 50,000-man army along the Rio Grande. To reinforce the point, Gen. John M. Schofield was dispatched on a special diplomatic mission to Paris to demand a French withdrawal. Shorn of French protection, Maximilian quickly fell from power.

Reconstruction

The federal reorganization of the postwar South—labeled "Reconstruction"—proved complex. Neither precedent nor statute law offered much guidance to federal military forces. To assist former slaves, the Bureau for the Relief of Freedmen and Refugees had been established under the command of Gen. Oliver O. Howard. Congress eventually broke with Pres. Andrew Johnson over the scope and intent of Reconstruction; through the spring and summer of 1866, individual officers sought to reconcile the wishes of Congress with the often contradictory proclamations of the president. Racial incidents mounted, especially when the garrisons included black regiments.

Elections that fall returned an overwhelming Republican majority to Congress. With a veto-proof legislature, Congress divided the South into five military districts and directed the army to supervise civil officials, voter registration, and constitutional conventions. But President Johnson fought back, reassigning Sheridan, whose Republican sympathies concerned conservatives, from his Reconstruction duties in Texas and Louisiana to command of the Department of the Missouri. Transfers were also issued to Daniel E. Sickles and John Pope. An angry House of Representatives impeached the president when he attempted to force Sec. of War Edwin Stanton's resignation. Barely escaping Senate conviction, a cowed Johnson allowed congressional Reconstruction to proceed.

INDIAN WARS

By the time the Civil War ended in 1865, the promise made by President Andrew Jackson in the 1830s of a "permanent Indian frontier" had been all but forgotten by a war-weary American public, who, at war's end, was soon captivated by the entrepreneurial enthusiasm of westward expansionists. Charged with the protection of U.S. interests in the West, the U.S. Army for 25 years (1866–91) engaged in countless operations against virtually every Indian tribe and faction that resisted U.S. territorial advancement.

Initial Army Actions

As the army implanted Congress's wishes, controversies concerning government policy toward the Indians left military and political leaders at frequent loggerheads. The fiercely independent Plains tribes were in a restless mood, for societal traditions of raiding and unimpeded bison

Civil War veteran George Crook spent most of his military career on the western frontier; he was relentless and ruthless in his pursuit of the Indians but treated them fairly and with respect in captivity. (U.S. Army Military History Institute)

hunting would not be ended by the uncertain treaty promises made by a few chiefs.

Military leaders were unsure as to how to deal with the situation. Most felt more comfortable fighting Confederates than the mounted Plains warriors, whose unconventional styles bewildered their opponents. But the army supported western expansion, so regulars occupied scores of military posts throughout the Midwest and along the Santa Fe, Oregon, and Bozeman trails.

Oregon demanded the army's immediate attention. Here, volunteer units vainly sought out the Paiute Indians in 1865 and 1866; only when Lt. Col. George Crook and the regulars swung into action did the military compel a peace. One of few army men who attempted to study Indian life in anything resembling a systematic fashion, Crook mounted an unending series of expeditions that featured large numbers of allied Shoshone scouts and pack mules. After some 40 engagements, the Paiute accepted the U.S. terms in the summer of 1868.

Sherman, head of the sprawling Division of the Missouri, believed the Indians had no right to block the progress of his civilization. The Indians, however, saw the situation from a different perspective. Recent paper treaties notwithstanding, their lands were being invaded and their traditional ways threatened. The Teton Sioux and Northern Cheyenne seemed especially determined in their efforts to block the Bozeman Trail. Isolated skirmishes culminated on Dec. 21, 1866, with the annihilation of Capt. William Fetterman's party just outside Fort Phil Kearny, Wyoming.

Peace Commissions

Heavy snows prevented immediate retaliation against the Sioux. Before the army could launch a spring offensive, Congress, influenced by the Indian Bureau and a recent reassessment of the Sand Creek Massacre, appointed a peace commission to investigate the Northern Plains. Until the commissioners reached a verdict, the troopers satisfied themselves with establishing a perimeter of forts around the Sioux. Even attacks against detachments from Forts C. F. Smith (the Hayfield Fight) and Phil Kearny (the Wagon Box Fight) in early August 1867 drew no immediate counterstrokes.

No such interference precluded Winfield S. Hancock from taking action in his Department of the Missouri. Convinced that a show of force was necessary, Hancock took the field with nearly 1,400 troops in the spring of 1867. But Hancock's expedition started rather than averted an Indian war. As the soldiers returned to their forts after an unsuccessful effort to overawe the tribes, Sioux and Cheyenne warriors roamed the southern overland trails. Local authorities screamed for protection even as another civilian-dominated peace commission concluded treaties with the Southern Plains tribes along Medicine Lodge Creek, Kansas, in October 1867. The northern tribes drove a harder bargain, and pacts concluded at Fort Laramie, Wyoming, called upon the army to abandon its Bozeman Trail posts.

Continuing Tangles

In May 1868, the Republican party nominated Gen. Ulysses S. Grant as its next presidential candidate. Congress readmitted Alabama, Arkansas, Florida, Louisiana, and the Carolinas to the Union the following month. Upon Grant's victory that November, Sherman took command of the army. But even a soldier in the White House could not untangle the army from the twin webs of Reconstruction and Indian policy. As attacks against blacks and the federal government continued in the South, regular soldiers remained even in those states already readmitted into the Union.

These political controversies helped to explain the army's actions on the Southern Plains. Upon assuming command of the Department of the Missouri in March 1868, Sheridan found but an uneasy peace. Preoccupied with its struggle with President Johnson, Congress had delayed action on the Medicine Lodge treaties and Indian appropriations. Such delays encouraged the war factions among the Cheyenne, Sioux, and Arapaho, who struck several Kansas

Indian Battles and Skirmishes in Wyoming, 1854–76

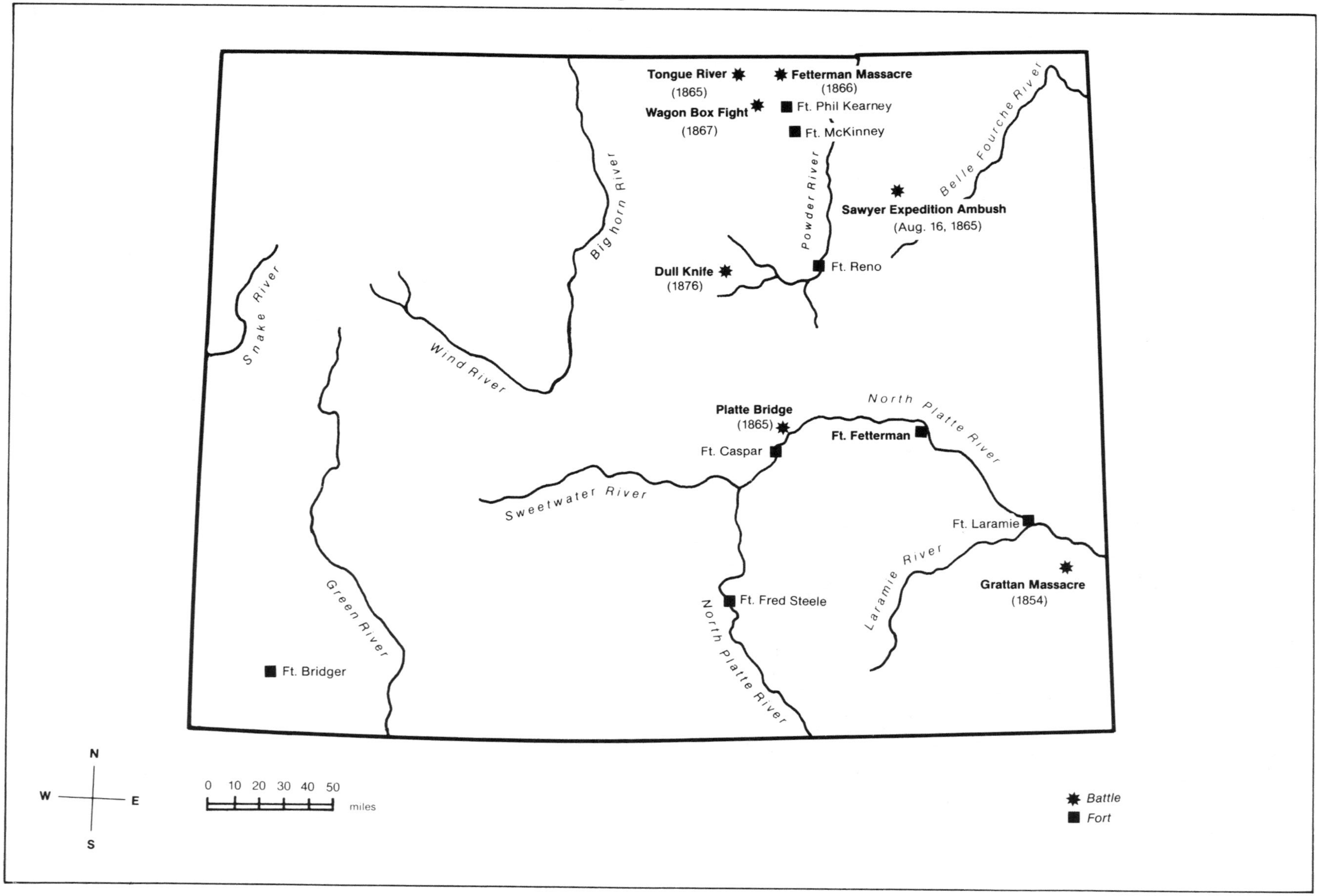

Belle Fourche River
Sawyer Expedition Ambush (Aug. 16, 1865)
Fetterman Massacre (1866)
Ft. Phil Kearney
Ft. McKinney
Tongue River (1865)
Wagon Box Fight (1867)
Powder River
Ft. Reno
Dull Knife (1876)
Big horn River
Wind River
Snake River
Green River
Ft. Bridger
North Platte River
Ft. Fetterman
Platte Bridge (1865)
Ft. Caspar
Sweetwater River
Ft. Laramie
Grattan Massacre (1854)
Laramie River
Ft. Fred Steele
North Platte River

Battle
Fort

0 10 20 30 40 50 miles

N E S W

James Butler Hickok, nicknamed "Wild Bill" for his exploits in the West, aided the U.S. Army during the Indian wars. He later served as a U.S. marshal in Kansas at Fort Riley, Hays City, and Abilene. (U.S. Signal Corps)

settlements. In September, Maj. George A. Forsyth and a company of scouts fought off a week-long siege at Beecher's Island.

Southern Plains

The peace commission provided official sanction for military reprisals in early October 1868. With Gen. Christopher C. Augur having replaced a senior civilian, the army opted to force the Southern Plains tribes onto Indian Territory reservations. Those Indians who desired peace were ordered to gather under the command of Col. William B. Hazen; all others were declared hostile.

Theorizing that the lack of forage would limit the Indians' mobility, Sheridan timed the new campaign to coincide with the onset of winter. From New Mexico, Maj. Andrew W. Evans would push eastward down the South Canadian River. Maj. Eugene A. Carr was to lead another column out of Fort Lyon, Colorado. The main force, including Sheridan himself and featuring Lt. Col. George A. Custer's 7th Cavalry Regiment, set out from Fort Dodge, Kansas.

As the infantry from Fort Dodge established a field depot, Custer's troopers plowed through deep snows into present-day Oklahoma. On the night of Nov. 26, 1868, scouts located Black Kettle's Cheyenne village along the Washita River. The chief had recently returned from tentative peace talks with Colonel Hazen. Custer, however, did not know of Black Kettle's entreaties. Fearing that the Indians might escape, Custer divided his men into four detachments and stormed headlong into the village at dawn on November 27. Achieving surprise, the cavalrymen cut down the Indian pony herd and destroyed the lodges. Only the loss of Maj. Joel Elliott and 19 men to a larger force from nearby Kiowa, Arapaho, and Cheyenne villages marred Custer's victory.

Reinforced by the 19th Kansas Volunteer Cavalry, Sheridan and Custer determined to finish up the Indians. News of the attack on Black Kettle's band had alarmed nearby Indian camps. No longer could they assume that the onset of winter would drive the soldiers back to their forts. Evans destroyed a Comanche camp at Soldier Spring in December. Just east of the Wichita Mountains, Col. Benjamin Grierson began erecting strategic Fort Sill. After refitting their forces, Custer, Evans, and Carr again combed the region through the early spring as growing numbers of Indians surrendered. Carr delivered a final blow on July 11, 1869, destroying a Cheyenne "Dog Soldier" camp at Summit Springs, Colorado.

The Southern Plains offensives of 1868–69 left a strong imprint upon the Indians and the soldiers alike. By striking at the homes and families of their foes, the army had forced the Indians to fight on less-than-favorable terms. But the campaigns also pointed up several weaknesses in the U.S. Army. Supply shortages had been chronic and leadership less than impressive. Finally, efforts to distinguish friend from foe had been less than successful, with Sheridan convinced that Hazen had offered safe haven to too many Indians.

Piegan Controversy

Events in Montana dealt the army a major political blow in the wake of the recent offensives. On Jan. 23, 1870, Maj. Eugene M. Baker, encouraged by Sheridan, struck a Piegan encampment along the Marias River. Official reports allowed that the soldiers had killed 173 Indians, including 53 women and children. The army left another 300 Piegan to face the brunt of the Montana winter without their lodges or winter stores, destroyed during the attack.

This type of warfare found few supporters, especially when it became clear that the Piegan struck by Baker had not been associated with hostile bands. Reinforced in its distrust of the military, Congress reasoned that Indian affairs must remain under the aegis of the Interior Department and that church-sponsored agents rather than army officers should fill the Indian Bureau's field posts.

Resentful of the intrusion of whites into their territory, the Modoc fought back, waging an excellent defense with armed fighters, such as the one shown above, against a much larger army force. (U.S. Army Military History Institute)

Apache Wars

With access to the reservations controlled by the Interior Department and its numbers stretched thin by the continuing demands of Reconstruction, the army assumed a defensive posture on the Plains. But angry Arizonans believed more decisive action was necessary, and on Apr. 30, 1871, a mob slaughtered 86 Apache at Camp Grant. But Indian raids in Arizona—by army count, 54 during the previous 12 months—continued to plague the region. Transferred from the Pacific Northwest to command the Department of Arizona in the wake of the Camp Grant affair, Lieutenant Colonel Crook swung into action. Using unconventional tactics, Crook forced most of the Indians back to their reservations by the close of 1873. For his efforts, President Grant promoted Crook to brigadier general.

Modoc War

Long-simmering tensions between the Modoc Indians and white settlers in Oregon also boiled over. In 1872, the army determined that Captain Jack (Kintpuash), 60–70 warriors, and their families must be removed from their homes along the Lost River. Initial efforts to drive the Modoc from these lava beds proved futile despite the army's four-to-one numerical advantage. When renewed peace talks stalled, Brig. Gen. Edward R. S. Canby, commanding the Department of the Columbia, was given control of negotiations. But in a desperate attempt to force government concessions and regain control of militants within his own camp, Captain Jack murdered Canby at the peace table on April 11.

Canby thus became the only regular general of the U.S. Army ever killed by Indians in the field. Still, the Modoc held out, their superb defensive positions and marksmanship combining with poor army leadership to blunt several assaults. Finally, Col. Jefferson C. Davis took command and tightened the siege. Resistance collapsed in June, and Captain Jack and three other leaders were hanged.

Texas

Violence also shattered the Texas frontiers. As the campaigns of 1868–69 faded from memory, depredations attributed to the Indians increased. According to Texan accounts, nomadic tribes were armed by illegal Comanchero traders and used the international boundary to the south and the reservations to the north as safe havens. The danger was emphasized when a Kiowa war party just missed General Sherman while he was on an inspection tour near Fort Richardson in May 1871.

Declining interest in Reconstruction allowed the army to redeploy more troops to the frontiers. Spearheading the campaign across the Llano Estecado was Col. Ranald Mackenzie, a hard-bitten Civil War veteran. On Sept. 29, 1872, Mackenzie's 4th Cavalry surprised a large Comanche

William Frederick Cody, known as "Buffalo Bill," served as a valuable scout for Gen. Philip H. Sheridan during the Indian wars; he also supplied buffalo meat for railroad construction crews during the 1860s and 1870s. (Library of Congress)

encampment in the Texas Panhandle near McClellan Creek, killing scores of Indians, taking 124 captives, and burning the village. The loss of the captured pony herd to an Indian counterstroke, however, prevented Mackenzie from claiming total victory.

Sheridan assigned the young colonel to an even more dangerous task in 1873. In a secret meeting with Mackenzie at Fort Clark, Sheridan assured his subordinate that the high brass would support efforts to end Kickapoo raids across the Rio Grande into Texas. Taking his cue from Sheridan, Mackenzie led two dozen Seminole-black scouts and 400 cavalrymen into Mexico on May 17. During the 60-hour foray that followed, the troops burned three Indian villages near Remolino and took 40 captives before riding back into the United States. True to his word, Sheridan defended this breach of international law. Sherman, although bitter about not having been apprised of the project, also stepped in to shield Mackenzie from retribution.

Red River War

To the north, the release of several captured chiefs from a Texas penitentiary seemed only to encourage more Kiowa, Cheyenne, and Comanche raids during the spring and summer of 1874. An unsuccessful assault against two dozen bison hunters at Adobe Walls, Texas, that June renewed the Indians' determination to blunt the U.S. intrusions. A squad of Texas Rangers was ambushed the following month at Lost Valley. In mid-July, the Interior Department finally gave the army permission to pursue Indian raiders onto the reservations.

Sheridan called upon departmental commanders Augur (Texas) and Pope (Missouri) to draw up plans for an offensive. Other than demanding that the campaign begin as soon as possible and instructing all concerned to ignore departmental boundaries in their pursuit, he left the details up to his subordinates. Augur recalled Mackenzie and the 4th Cavalry from South Texas to lead a heavy column north from Fort Concho. Lt. Col. George P. Buell was to drive north from Fort Griffin. To fulfill the Interior Department's demand that peaceful tribes be spared from retribution, Lt. Cols. John W. Davidson and Thomas H. Neill would operate near the Kiowa-Comanche and Cheyenne-Arapaho agencies.

Initially, Pope had sought to convince Sheridan to delay the campaign until winter. Failing in this, he called upon Col. Nelson A. Miles to move south from Fort Dodge and operate west of the Wichita Mountains. Major William R. Price was to drive up the Canadian River from Fort Bascom, New Mexico. The six army columns had twice the number of fighters as their enemy, estimated at some 1,200 warriors.

Fighting commenced in August when Davidson failed to disarm the Kiowa and Comanche near Fort Sill. On July 30, Miles encountered a sizeable Cheyenne band near the Salt Fork of the Red River. Supply shortages, however, forced the colonel to call off the pursuit after a running skirmish. Threats against his communications then paralyzed Miles's column for nearly a month, but Mackenzie surprised several Cheyenne, Kiowa, and Comanche camps in Palo Duro Canyon on September 28. Most of the inhabitants fled to safety, but only after Mackenzie's troopers had destroyed most of their possessions and their ponies. Buell hit two more villages in mid-October; leading a detachment from the Miles column, Lt. Frank Baldwin defeated another Cheyenne party near McClelland Creek on November 8.

Heavy December snows led Davidson, Buell, and Mackenzie to break up their commands. Miles, anxious to prove himself after nearly nine years away from a combat command, led a final sweep in January 1875. Like the offensives of 1868–69, the grueling campaigns had achieved no decisive battlefield victories but had rendered the Indians destitute and demoralized. The once-proud warriors of the Southern Plains straggled into their reservations throughout the winter and spring.

Great Sioux War

To the north, the Fort Laramie treaties had delayed open conflict between the Plains tribes and the government. However, the approach of the Northern Pacific Railroad to the Black Hills and the Yellowstone River valley met stiff resistance. In 1873, 1,500 soldiers unsuccessfully tried to overawe the tribes. Rumors of rich mineral deposits and the desire to build a new military post led the army to mount another column, led by the flamboyant Custer, the following year.

In November 1875, Sheridan and Crook met with President Grant and Interior Department officials. Since the army could not check trespassers excited by the rumors, stemming from the Custer expedition, of gold deposits, the Indians would have to cede additional land. Sec. of the Interior Zachariah Chandler authorized the military to force the Sioux and Northern Cheyenne to accept the new order on Feb. 1, 1876.

Sheridan hoped that a winter strike might again prove decisive. From the Department of Dakota, Gen. Alfred H. Terry readied to push west out of Fort Abraham Lincoln. Recently transferred to the Department of the Platte, Crook accompanied Col. Joseph J. Reynolds and 900 men out of Fort Fetterman, Wyoming, on March 1. Reynolds and Crook spent a shivering month in desultory campaigning before retiring; heavy snows held Terry's force at Fort Lincoln.

Renewed efforts followed. On March 30, Col. John Gibbon began marching toward the Yellowstone Valley from Fort Ellis, Montana. Crook pushed out from Fort Fetterman in late May. With Custer's 7th Cavalry in the vanguard, Terry left Fort Lincoln that same month to

George Custer, shown here with fellow hunters and their quarry, spent most of his military career in the West. (National Archives)

complete the converging movement. From division headquarters, Sheridan assured his field commanders that large numbers of hostile Indians would remain together for no longer than a week.

While previous experience supported this conclusion, this summer was different. Ably led by Crazy Horse, Sitting Bull, Lame Deer, and Hump, five Sioux tribal circles (Sans Arc, Miniconjou, Hunkpapa, Blackfoot, and Oglala) had joined with the Northern Cheyenne and a smattering of Arapaho to form an immense encampment of as many as 15,000 people. On June 17, they met Crook at the Battle of the Rosebud. The general claimed victory but pulled back to await reinforcements. Lacking communications with Crook, Terry and Gibbon hoped to trap what they believed to be a large enemy camp. Custer's 7th Cavalry rode ahead to form the southern pincer, while Terry and Gibbon labored to bottle up the Indians in the north.

Custer learned that a large Indian camp lay along the Little Bighorn River on June 25. Fearful that the enemy would detect his presence, he divided his command to converge upon the village. But this would be no repeat of the Battle of the Washita. Maj. Marcus A. Reno and Capt. Frederick Benteen were checked in their flanking movement and driven back with heavy losses. Still unsure of the enemy's dispositions or numbers, Custer and five troops rode directly toward the villages. Emboldened by their recent success at the Rosebud, Indian warriors swarmed over Custer's command, killing the five companies of bluecoats to a man.

Stunned by Custer's fate, Terry and Gibbon withdrew to the mouth of the Rosebud. Reinforcements brought Terry's command up to 1,700; Crook, now searching for the Indians with 2,000 men, blundered into Terry on August 10. Their combined forces lumbered eastward toward the Powder River. They separated again in late August, with Crook engaging elements of the enemy force at Slim Buttes, South Dakota, on September 9. He then limped back to Fort Fetterman. Terry had in the meantime detached Miles to establish a position on the Yellowstone River before breaking up his command.

Having failed to defeat Indian forces in battle, the army moved to prevent any more reservation peoples from joining the fighting. Inhabitants of the Red Cloud, Standing Rock, and Cheyenne River agencies were disarmed and dismounted. Crook, having received more reinforcements, including Colonel Mackenzie and the 4th Cavalry, led another 2,200-man column into central Wyoming that November. Mackenzie and the cavalry struck Dull Knife's Cheyenne village on November 25. Sparked by their Indian auxiliaries, the soldiers burned the lodges and captured several hundred ponies after a fierce fight. Miles had also been patrolling the Yellowstone. Undeterred by heavy Montana snows, his hardy infantrymen drove off a series of Sioux and Cheyenne attacks at the Battle of Wolf Mountain on Jan. 7–8, 1877.

Thousands of demoralized Sioux and Cheyenne turned themselves in through the spring and early summer. Miles continued to harass the more recalcitrant tribes, routing Lame Deer's band at the Battle of Little Muddy Creek on May 7. Sitting Bull and a few hundred followers fled to Canada; although shameless in his own self-promotion, Miles doggedly patrolled the Canadian boundary until Sitting Bull also surrendered in 1881.

Pacific Northwest

Even as the wars against the Sioux continued, another major war erupted in the far Northwest. Here, officials decided that the nontreaty Nez Percé must be removed from the Wallowa Valley. Rather than accepting government terms, Chief Joseph and his followers opted to flee east across the Rocky Mountains. The Nez Percé repulsed attacks by Capt. David Perry and a mixed force of regulars and volunteers at White Bird Canyon, Idaho, on June 17. The Indians in turn defeated General Howard on July 11 at the Battle of Clearwater River.

A discouraged Howard rejoined the pursuit only after a three-week delay. As Chief Joseph fled east, Gibbon moved out from Missoula to offer battle. Leading 161 regulars and 45 volunteers, the colonel surprised the Nez Percé near the mouth of the Big Hole River on August 9. Initially shaken, the Nez Percé warriors managed to pin down their antagonists as their families escaped. Heavy losses, including fully a third of Gibbon's command and upwards of 100 Nez Percé—including many women and children slain in the opening melee—marked the bitter engagement.

Howard and Gibbon combined their commands while Col. Samuel Sturgis attempted to block Joseph's escape

Indian Battles in South Dakota, 1876–91

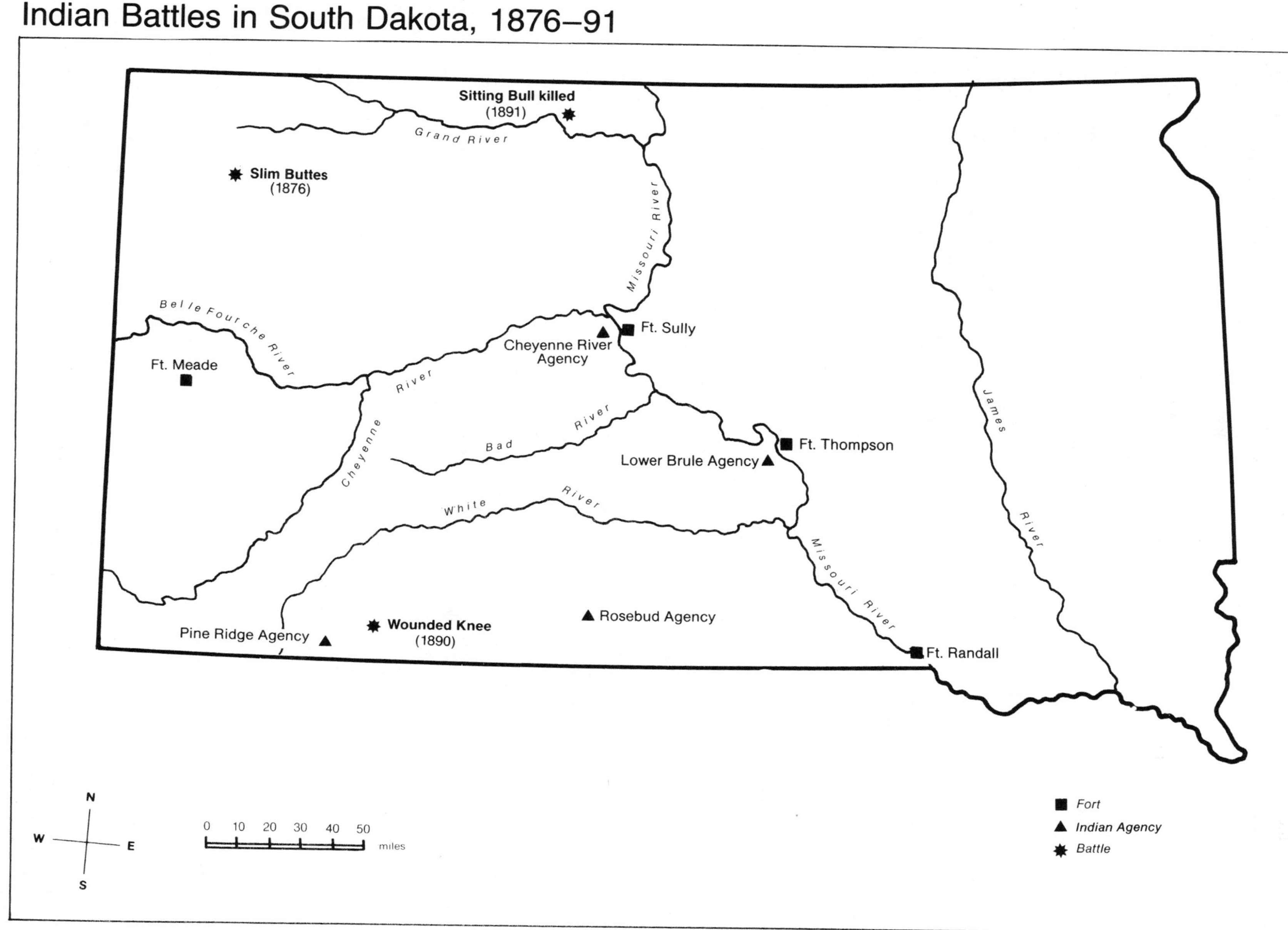

through the Yellowstone Valley passes. Sturgis, too, met defeat at the Battle of Canyon Creek (September 13), but the Nez Percé slowed enough to allow the indefatigable Miles to catch them as they approached the Canadian border. Stiff resistance at Bear Paw Mountain forced Miles to lay siege to the Indian camp on September 30. Howard rode in four days later with a small escort. Chief Joseph surrendered with some 400 men, women, and children on October 5.

The army did better in subsequent campaigns. In 1878, General Howard organized three columns to converge upon a coalition of Bannock and Paiute Indians enraged by encroachments onto the Camas Prairie. Displaying keen tactical skills, Capt. Reuben F. Bernard defeated some 400 warriors at Silver Creek and again at Pilot Butte, Oregon. Ute rebellions against government assimilation programs at the White River Agency, Colorado, necessitated military intervention in 1879. The insurgents blocked the first column and killed its commander, Maj. Thomas T. Thornburgh. Only the decisive intervention by Sec. of the Interior Carl Schurz prevented even more violence.

Geronimo, a Chiricahua Apache, was known for his resistance to the federal government's removal policy that confined Indians to reservations; he eluded capture several times before settling with his family at Fort Sill, Oklahoma, in 1894. (Library of Congress)

Southwestern Borderlands

Texas and the Southwest remained of special concern. Mackenzie's 1873 raid had temporarily slowed illegal borderlands trafficking, but an upsurge in such crossings led Brig. Gen. E. O. C. Ord, commanding the Department of Texas, to encourage a series of military expeditions into Mexico. State Department prodding even led Mexico to agree to reciprocal crossings in hot pursuit (the "Ord Order") from 1877 to 1880. War fever rose on both sides of the border until the excitable Ord was forced to resign in late 1880.

To the west, Arizona's complex political and administrative situation had baffled Crook's successors. Led by Victorio, about 150 Warm Springs, Mescalero, and Chiricahua Apache had bolted the agencies in 1879. Only in Texas, where Grierson garrisoned water holes throughout the arid trans-Pecos, was Victorio checked. Stung by skirmishes at Tinaja de las Palmas (July 30, 1880) and Rattlesnake Springs (Aug. 6, 1880), he fell back across the Rio Grande, where Mexican troops killed the dynamic Indian leader.

Geronimo

Others also chafed under the government's tenuous authority and ran circles around the regulars. As the army commanders came to recognize the region's economic potential, Crook was transferred back to Arizona in 1882. Replacing civilian agents with army officers and enlisting Apache scouts to fight for the government, Crook waged fierce campaigns against small bands of tribesmen. After a grueling chase deep into the Sierra Madre, many of the Indians returned to the San Carlos Reservation in June 1883.

Two years later, however, Geronimo and 42 warriors again fled the reservation. Nearly 3,000 men guarded the Southern Pacific Railroad and key water holes while columns composed of white officers and Apache auxiliaries again trudged into Mexico. Leading one such force, Capt. Emmet Crawford was killed by Mexican militia. Crook kept up the pressure but was replaced by Miles upon word that Geronimo had again bolted in March 1886.

Sheridan, who had three years earlier replaced Sherman as the army's commanding general, demanded that regulars now assume the brunt of the campaigning. As the summer wore on and his bluecoats seemed nowhere near success, Miles quietly returned to Crook's methods. Lt. Charles B. Gatewood made the first significant contact with Geronimo in August. Miles had, however, added one new twist, ordering the removal of all Chiricahua and Warm Springs Apache—even those who had already surrendered—to Florida. Demoralized by news of this action, Geronimo and the other leading warriors surrendered in September 1886.

Wounded Knee

Scattered incidents kept soldiers in the Southwest on the alert for years to come even as Miles introduced annual field maneuvers to his department. Ironically, Miles was promoted to command the Division of the Missouri just in time to confront another major Indian outbreak in late 1890. Many Sioux had sought comfort in the Ghost Dance, a religious movement that was sweeping across the North-

Indian Reservations, 1883

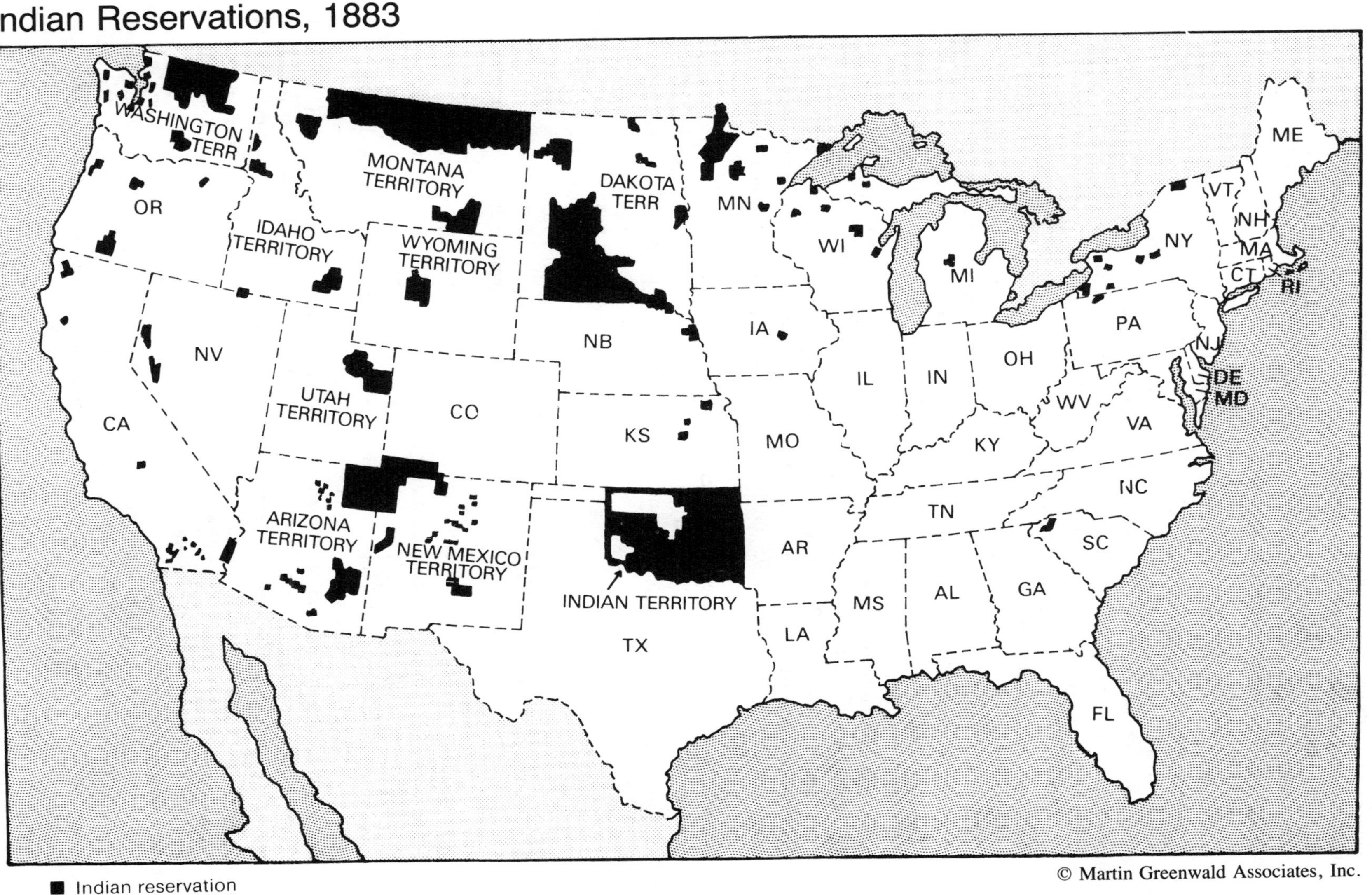

■ Indian reservation

ern Plains. Panicky civilian agents in South Dakota and Nebraska called for army assistance. Miles hoped to stifle any trouble by seizing potential leaders and stationing large garrisons on the reservations. But such plans went awry when Indian police killed Sitting Bull during an attempted arrest in December 1890.

As thousands of Indians stampeded from the agencies, Miles poured in reinforcements. One column caught up with one group of Miniconjou and Hunkpapa Sioux, led by the respected Big Foot, on December 28. That night, Colonel Forsyth arrived at the camp along Wounded Knee Creek with orders to disarm the entire Indian contingent. Forsyth botched the effort the next morning. Although his 500 soldiers and four Hotchkiss cannon outnumbered the 120 Indian warriors, the colonel allotted too few troopers to the job of collecting weapons. A scuffle over a rifle led to general firing. Men, women, and children scampered for cover as the Hotchkiss guns pounded the village and the covering forces swung into rifle range. When the firing ended, 25 soldiers and 150 Indians littered the field.

With 3,500 soldiers at his disposal, Miles prevented a more general conflict. By February 1891, the Sioux had been forced back to their reservations for years to come, especially during the eight-year tenure (1895–1903) of Miles as the army's commanding general. This continued attention to Indian affairs seemed only natural for a general of the officers raised on the Indian wars. Only later would Wounded Knee be known as the last of the major army-Indian confrontations in the American West.

BUREAUCRACY AND COMMAND

Men like Miles, Crook, and Mackenzie had proved their military abilities against traditional armies during the Civil War. Their experiences against the Indians broadened their horizons as combat leaders. However, skirmishes against the Indians, argued army intellectuals, did not amount to "real" warfare. Thus, the more cerebral officers studied and at times sought to copy their European counterparts.

Limited efforts to improve army education were made during the late 19th century. Sherman, who envisioned a series of postgraduate and branch schools that might benefit junior officers, led the charge. Housed at Fort Leavenworth, the School of Application for Infantry and Cavalry emphasized tactical training. To stimulate further interest in military affairs, the Military Service Institution was formed in 1879. Its bimonthly *Journal,* along with the rival *United Service* magazine, published a wide range of articles. The *Cavalry Journal* was founded in 1885, with the *Journal of the U.S. Artillery Corps* established seven years later. Following the lead of the navy, the army created a Division of Military Intelligence in 1889.

Intraservice rivalries, however, impeded reform. Civil War veterans often scorned their younger comrades and skirmished among themselves over their own wartime exploits. Slow promotion lay at the heart of such squabbling. Proud soldiers accustomed to the meteoric promotions of the Civil War resented their loss of status. Major generals of volunteers who had once commanded entire corps now became regular colonels who rarely saw more than four or five companies at any one time; lieutenants who had once led regiments of fine veterans could expect to wait 10–15 years before achieving even a company command.

Rivalries between staff and line also split the officer corps. Many regimental officers yearned for a station near an eastern city, where it would be easier to send their children to a good school and where their wives might enjoy more refined comforts. It was unfair, argued line officers, that their rivals in staff positions dominated the choice postings and curried undue influence with key congressional leaders.

Army

The regular army itself had a legion of critics. Several leading industrialists embraced a pacifistic stance that reinforced traditional fears of a standing army. Labor leaders, noting the army's less than neutral role in the labor unrest of 1877 and 1894, also criticized the regulars. Several congressmen, led by ex-general John A. Logan, an Illinois Republican, criticized West Point and claimed that the volunteer effort during the Civil War had confirmed the nation's reliance on nonprofessionals. State militias, contended Logan and his supporters, should dominate national defense. By the mid-1890s, these units were four times as large as the regular establishment.

Countering these internal and external challenges was a daunting task, particularly when one of the army's champions, Lieutenant General Sherman, sought to disengage himself from politics. Appointed commanding general in 1869, Sherman had little stomach for the unseemly deals of the Gilded Age. Less vocal about their disdain for politics, Sherman's successors as commanding general, Sheridan (1883–88) and Schofield (1888–95), nonetheless failed to match the political efforts put forth by the navy. Miles took a more active interest in currying congressional favor, but the latter's overweening ambition and astonishingly poor interpersonal skills did the army's cause more harm than good.

Feuds among Sherman, Sheridan, and Secs. of War William W. Belknap and Robert T. Lincoln did nothing to improve the army's public image. To retain control over the army, the president acted through his civilian cabinet advisers. But if the secretary of war controlled the army, what did the commanding general command? Did the secretary of war need to go through the commanding general's office on all army matters? If so, did this not

Gen. Philip Sheridan succeeded William Tecumseh Sherman as commander in chief of the army in 1883, a position he held until his death in 1888. (U.S. Military Academy Archives)

place the civilian secretary at the mercy of the general? Recently revised regulations specified that while the commanding general controlled the military establishment, the staff departments were responsible only to the secretary of war. In practice, this created a giant loophole, for the financial and logistical support needed to mount a field campaign might be withheld from the commanding general's authority.

Sherman fled Secretary Belknap's meddling in 1874 for the freedom of St. Louis. The move satisfied Sherman's pride but left the army without its chief spokesman during a critical period in the wars against the Indians. Only when Belknap later resigned to escape impeachment for having sold post sutlerships did Sherman return to the capital. Subsequent secretaries refused to press the limits of their authority against Sherman, who also adopted a more conciliatory stance. Upon assuming command in 1882, Sheridan determined to force the issue. Secretary of War Lincoln parried Sheridan's thrusts, but the question of authority was not resolved until the next century.

When considering such difficulties, it seems no irony that the army's leading theorist, the principled, pessimistic Col. Emory Upton, would commit suicide before completing his most influential work. A West Point graduate of 1861, Upton had risen to the rank of brevet major general of regulars during the Civil War. Disinterested in Indian warfare, Upton hoped to reshape the army on a German model. Lambasting the performance of volunteers and militia, he demanded that civilians enlarge and reorganize the standing army to allow for wartime expansion.

Wracked by a painful brain tumor, Upton committed suicide in 1881 before completing his magnum opus, *The Military Policy of the United States*. The manuscript was circulated in unfinished form among interested officers, and Peter Smith Michie's *Life and Letters of General Emory Upton* (1885) publicized its basic theories. But the sense of impending doom that embodied Upton's life also permeated his *Military Policy*. Doubtful that the nation would adopt his reforms, his contempt for civilian leadership and unwillingness to consider political realities limited his manuscript's influence with more general readers.

Navy

The U.S. Navy endured a period of uncertainty similar to that of the army after the Civil War. Controversies between

Col. Emory Upton modeled the reorganization of the army on Germany's army in his work The Military Policy of the United States, *but, plagued by illness, he committed suicide before the manuscript was completed.* (U.S. Army Military History Institute)

line and staff officers rivaled those on land, as did the discouragingly slow pace of promotion. Plagued by budgetary problems, ship commanders were implored to use their coal-fired engines only during emergencies. Such limits demoralized a generation of officers accustomed to the excitement found during the Civil War.

Citing these concerns, the postbellum years have often been described as the dark ages of the American navy. Yet the reductions of the late 1860s and 1870s were consistent with the national mood. Americans resented and feared a large military establishment, for Europe seemed a very distant threat at most. The availability of a few larger vessels, however, was deemed an acceptable necessity, to show the flag at exotic ports and to protect U.S. commerce. But defense of the nation's coastlines, not control of the seas, remained of prime importance.

Intermittent war scares—with Britain over the *Alabama* claims and with Spain concerning the seizure and execution of the crew of the *Virginius,* a gunrunner used to supply Cuban insurgents—briefly sparked calls for a larger navy. But Congress remained satisfied with its force of something over 100 aging vessels, for the existing fleet seemed perfectly capable of protecting ports and assisting economic ventures. Uninhabited Midway Island was made a coaling station in 1867. Naval and marine landing parties secured concessions in Japan, Fiji, Formosa, Korea, China, and Panama. Robert W. Shufeldt took the USS *Ticonderoga* on a two-year world cruise in 1879 on an avowedly commercialist mission. Small-scale gunboat diplomacy thus flourished as naval officers cooperated with State Department consular officials on a regular basis.

Even continentalists conceded that advances in naval architecture and technology necessitated some modernization. In 1882, Sec. of the Navy William H. Hunt secured support from Pres. Chester A. Arthur for new construction. The four transitional "ABCD" craft (cruisers *Atlanta, Boston,* and *Chicago,* plus the dispatch boat *Dolphin*) that resulted boasted steel hulls, compartmentalization, steam engines, and electric power plants, but also carried full sail rigging and breechloading rifles with slow-burning powder.

The navy also escalated its professional education and lobbying efforts. The Naval War College was established at Newport, Rhode Island, in 1884. Its first president, Rear Adm. Stephen B. Luce, had been instrumental in creating the U.S. Naval Institute 11 years earlier. A cadre of junior officers, frustrated by slow promotion and by opposition among older officers to new technology, enlisted the support of business and industry for an expanded fleet. New naval construction, they pointed out, would increase employment and stimulate industrial growth; a larger navy would encourage new international markets. Congress agreed, authorizing eight new protected cruisers, three armored cruisers, three unprotected cruisers, and six steel gunboats between 1884 and 1889.

Pres. Benjamin Harrison, called the "soldiers' friend," was instrumental in the passage of the Dependent Pension Act (1890), which provided pensions for all disabled Civil War veterans, and supported expansion of the navy and merchant marine during his term (1889–93). (Library of Congress)

The navy received a tremendous boost from these lobbyists, but without a policy to capture the public's imagination, it would remain a third-rate fleet. Capt. Alfred Thayer Mahan provided the necessary antidote. Asked by Luce to join the Naval War College staff in 1885, Mahan delivered cogent lectures that drew wide acclaim. His first book, *The Influence of Sea Power upon History, 1660–1783,* was published in 1890. Mahan's thesis—that sea power held the key to national greatness—captivated military and political leaders alike. By controlling the seas and dominating maritime commerce, concluded Mahan, Britain had seized world power. The United States might secure a similar place by removing its continentalist blinders, building a strong merchant marine and a powerful big-ship fleet, and acquiring new colonies.

Sec. of the Navy Benjamin Tracy set out to capitalize on the naval renaissance. In 1889, he combined the ABC cruisers and a steel gunboat into a "squadron of evolution" that served as a precursor of a peacetime battle fleet. The acrimonious congressional debate that followed authorized construction of three battleships of limited ranges. The latter provision, rationalized continentalists, would ensure that the big new ships would remain defensive in function. Subsequent battleships authorized during the mid-1890s, however, carried no such legal restrictions.

Marine Corps

Like the navy, the U.S. Marine Corps underwent significant changes during the late 19th century. Commandant Jacob Zeilin helped block congressional efforts to abolish the corps in 1866 and 1867. Although technological change had nearly eliminated their usefulness in ship-to-ship combat, marines took an active role in the gunboat diplomacy of the late 19th century. Two marine companies seized the forts guarding Korea's Han River in 1871. Another marine landing party accompanied the British force that occupied Alexandria, Egypt, in 1882. Three years later, marine detachments landed at Panama to protect U.S. economic interests on the revolution-torn isthmus.

Charles G. McCawley succeeded Zeilin as commandant of the Marine Corps. McCawley methodically reformed standards of enlistment and training and in 1882 began feeding Naval Academy graduates into the marines. Despite the efforts of Zeilin, McCawley, and McCawley's successor, Charles Heywood, slow promotion and internal rivalries continued to plague modernization efforts.

Conclusion

Although the navy seemed ready for the new century, past glories, internal jealousies, and financial shortages had retarded technological and intellectual development in all branches after 1865. Its own halting steps toward professionalization notwithstanding, the army seemed particularly beset by such difficulties. The military was by no means isolated from public life and society, but it had not yet been able to forget its recent Civil War past. In the coming years, substantial reform would therefore be necessary as the nation assumed additional imperial responsibilities.

3

The Spanish-American War: 1898

The Spanish-American War marked both an end and a beginning in American military history. War in 1898 tested a system that had evolved over the preceding century and, despite its many flaws, had met the challenges of war in 1812, 1846, and 1861. The major land and naval commanders in the Spanish-American War were products of that system. They shared common experiences, the most important of which had been extensive service as young officers during the Civil War. For those who remained in the services after 1865 there was as well the shared background of peacetime garrison duty and Indian campaigns, or overseas squadron service. In many respects, mobilization in 1898 resembled the call to arms in April–May 1861, with heightened public enthusiasm and improvisation the dominating themes. Public opinion and political impatience once again pushed the army into combat before it was fully organized. The later war, however, did not follow the same pattern as conflict in 1861. The nation's soldiers and sailors overcame a flawed system in 1898 to produce a quick victory in what Sec. of State John Hay called the "splendid little war."

Victory in 1898 was the last to be achieved under the decentralized U.S. military system. The defeat of Spain took the United States beyond the North American landmass and ended a century-long policy of continental defense. Overseas acquisitions had to be governed, defended, and even pacified. Equally important, the need to reform the administrative institutions responsible for the glaring defects revealed during the war fostered what can truly be called a military-naval-diplomatic revolution. In the aftermath of 1898, the army, the navy, the State Department, and the nation's approach to world affairs would undergo dramatic change to deal with the nation's newfound place in the world.

BACKGROUND TO WAR

The reemergence of a drive by Cubans to win independence from Spain in February 1895 led eventually to U.S. intervention. Having failed in an earlier revolt (1868–78), Cuban insurgents now adopted a guerrilla campaign aimed at destroying the Cuban sugar crop, disrupting internal transportation, and wearing out Spanish troops. The insurgency, led by José Martí and Gen. Máximo Gómez, severely tested an economically weak and politically unstable Spain. When early efforts to suppress the insurrection failed, the Conservative Spanish government sent Gen. Valeriano Weyler y Nicolau to take command. Weyler adopted a strategy that divided Cuba into three areas of operations. Within these areas, separated by two fortified trenches running north to south across the island, Weyler established so-called reconcentration camps to centralize the rural population. Despite the influx of Spanish regulars, which approached 100,000 in early 1898, and the organization of 80,000 loyalist Cuban volunteers, Weyler failed to crush the insurgency.

Guerrilla war and Weyler's harsh reconcentration policy devastated the Cuban economy and created much human suffering. At least 100,000 Cubans, called reconcentrados, died in the camps and a like number of Spanish soldiers perished in combat or succumbed to disease. While General Gómez's irregulars rarely exceeded 30,000, Spanish forces could not suppress them. The never-ending conflict caught

William Randolph Hearst used his newspaper, the New York Journal, *to champion the Cuban revolt of 1895 and to report the brutality of the Spanish in Cuba in a sensational, often exaggerated, style known as "yellow journalism."* (Library of Congress)

the attention of the American press. While in exile in New York, Martí had cultivated the city's press as well as some congressmen in Washington. From the outbreak of the insurrection in 1895, the Cuban junta in New York exploited these connections to lobby Pres. Grover Cleveland for recognition of the Cuban Republic, which Martí formed when he returned to Cuba. Martí died a hero's death in March 1895, but the junta succeeded in its effort to publicize the cause. New York papers, especially William Randolph Hearst's *New York Journal* and Joseph Pulitzer's *New York World,* competed in flamboyant accounts of Cuban heroism and suffering. Weyler's reconcentration program, the cause of such misery, became the focal point of journalistic hyperbole, labeled "yellow journalism" at the time.

The Cuban insurgency continually intruded in U.S. politics. Americans had an historical interest in the Caribbean, as seen in pre–Civil War filibusters to Cuba and several Central American countries, and even in U.S. proposals to annex the island. Investors from the United States played a substantial role in the Cuban economy, with holdings near $50,000,000 that the insurgency threatened. Ironically, an 1894 U.S. tariff law levied a heavy duty on Cuban sugar, which depressed the island's economy and partly fostered the insurrection. Discussions among naval officers and civilians interested in building a larger navy focused attention on the need for an isthmian canal. They argued that political stability in the region, which the insurgency threatened, was essential to the defense of a canal. Some contended that as the United States approached the 20th century, a new meaning should be attached to the Monroe Doctrine by eliminating all European powers from the Caribbean basin. The Cuban insurgency reinforced these impulses and led navalists to urge intervention.

President Cleveland approached the Cuban affair cautiously, despite the varied interests calling for action. His policy was to pressure Spain to lessen its harsh rule in Cuba and offer Cubans home rule, but Cleveland had no intention of threatening Spain with armed force. Furthermore, his administration vigorously suppressed filibustering expeditions and arms shipments to Cuba from the United States. The inauguration of William McKinley in March 1897 brought an eventual policy change. While not announced publicly, McKinley pursued the diplomatic goal of convincing Spain to grant Cuban independence. Steady American pressure throughout 1897, in addition to the advent of the Liberal government of Práxedes Mateo Sagasta, brought some results. In January 1898, Sagasta announced a new policy of autonomy, or home rule, for Cuba. He had no intention of granting independence but hoped that delay, gradual change, and ultimate victory against the insurgency would keep the McKinley administration from intervening.

Sagasta's autonomy policy failed. The insurgents rejected it outright in their drive for independence. Spanish colonial officials, army officers at home, and Cubans loyal to Spain spurned it as well. In the United States, the press and pro-insurgent congressmen denounced autonomy as a half measure. Announcement of home rule brought riots in Havana in mid-January 1898 by Spaniards and Cubans opposed to it. In response, President McKinley sent the USS *Maine* to Havana on January 25 to protect U.S. citizens and indicate his concern with Spanish recalcitrance. February brought two events that made war virtually unavoidable. On February 9, the *New York World* published a letter that Spanish ambassador Enrique Dupuy de Lome had written to a friend, depicting McKinley as weak-willed, indecisive, and a prisoner of public opinion. The yellow press treated de Lome's letter as a national insult. Far more ominously, on February 16, the *Maine* exploded in Havana harbor, killing 260 sailors.

McKinley had followed two policies since his inauguration: pressure Spain to free Cuba and avoid war. With the sinking of the *Maine,* the latter goal became virtually unachievable. McKinley was careful in public comments not to blame Spain for the *Maine* disaster, although con-

The United States in the Caribbean, 1898–1916

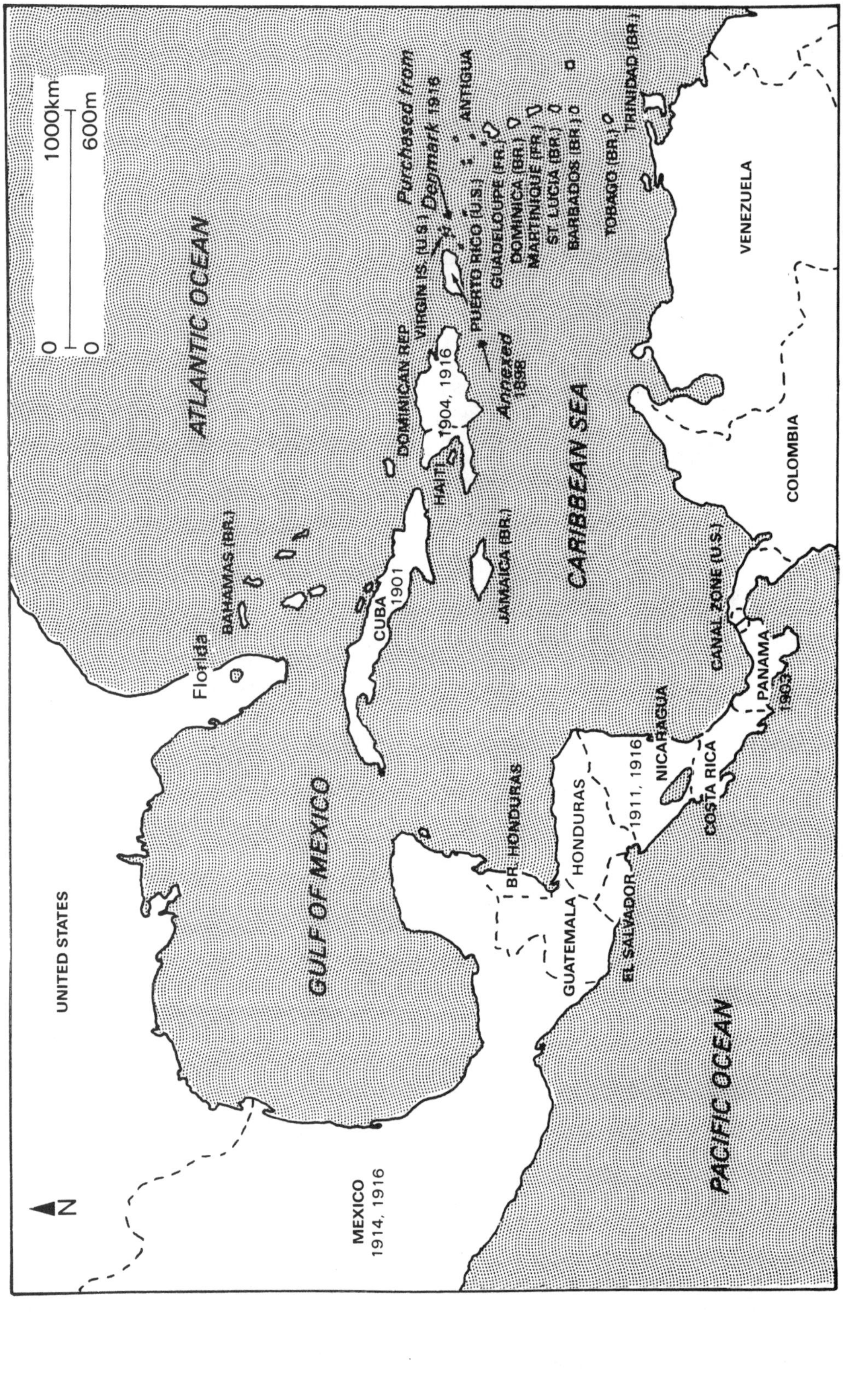

Dates Indicate Years of United States Involvement

gressmen and the press were not so restrained. In the United States, "Remember the *Maine!*" became a media-expounded rallying cry against the Spanish, even though the cause of the catastrophe was clearly undetermined. (A credible study published by Adm. Hyman G. Rickover in 1976 concluded that the explosion occurred internally, probably as the result of internal combustion in its coal bunkers.) Aware he could not control public pressure for war very long, the president intensified his efforts through March and April to convince Spain to let Cuba go. At the same time, McKinley quietly directed the armed services to prepare for war. The Sagasta government procrastinated but had no intention of accepting McKinley's demand. To do so would mean rebellion in Spain. On March 26, McKinley directed his ambassador to Madrid to demand of Sagasta a plan to free Cuba, to be offered by March 31. Sagasta rejected the U.S. proposal. Negotiations continued into April, but the demand for war in the United States was irresistible. On April 11, McKinley asked Congress for authority to intervene, which it granted eight days later. When Spain learned of the action, it broke relations with the United States, then declared war on April 24. Congress did likewise the next day, noting that a state of war had existed since April 21.

The die had been cast earlier, however, when the *Maine* went to the bottom of Havana harbor. Neither McKinley nor Sagasta wanted war in 1898, but neither would alter policies that were likely to bring conflict. While lacking the economic and political capacity to maintain its empire, Spain nonetheless stubbornly clung to its overseas possessions. For the United States, a combination of humanitarian solicitude for the Cuban people, concern for private economic interests on the island, a growing sense of power and nationalism, and a desire to assert authority in the Caribbean led the nation to war in an atmosphere of heady enthusiasm. McKinley in part acted in response to public pressure, but he never abandoned his goal of Cuban independence. Lost in the gloom at Madrid and the elation in Washington was the initial cause of conflict, the Cuban insurgency. Had there been no uprising or had Spain quickly quelled the insurrection, it is far less likely war would have come. Significantly, despite pressure from Congress and the press, when McKinley asked for war, he refused to recognize the Cuban Republic or grant the insurgents belligerency status. This would be a war between nation-states.

STRATEGY AND WAR PLANS

Strategy, the application of power to achieve policy objectives, is determined first and foremost by those objectives, for if they are limited in nature, so too will be the military means used to obtain them. If war aims are total, then much greater military force will have to be applied. Strategy is further shaped by the resources available to both belligerents and by the political support given to the governments waging war. Ideally, a nation goes to war with clearly defined policy objectives, institutional arrangements to determine the military means necessary to win, and a political leadership capable of explaining its war objectives and military methods to the public. In the Spanish-American War, neither the United States nor Spain approached this ideal.

Reluctant to go to war, President McKinley determined from the outset to wage a quick, limited conflict. The United States would fight Spain on its periphery and not attack the homeland. As the Cuban insurgency was the immediate cause for war, a key American objective was to end Spanish sovereignty there. McKinley, however, said little about the fate of the Cuban republic. As the war progressed, American objectives changed, partly as the result of battle, partly as the McKinley administration grasped opportunities it had not originally anticipated. The new objective came to be the acquisition of part of Spain's overseas empire, particularly the Philippine Islands and Puerto Rico. Territorial annexation had not been a stated objective when war began, but despite the addition of new war aims, U.S. strategy remained the same.

Naval War Plans

McKinley found it easy to adopt a clear strategic approach because the navy had developed contingency war plans that suited his goals. The president and his advisers sought to wage a largely naval war, an approach based on Spain's geographic separation from its overseas possessions and on the greater naval power of the United States. War planners hoped that ground operations could be confined largely to occupation duty and indirect aid to Cuban insurgents.

The Naval War College and the Office of Naval Intelligence (ONI), established in the mid-1880s, began serious planning for a war with Spain when the Cuban insurgency broke out in 1895. Plans underwent several modifications, but from mid-1897, ONI assumed that the objective of such a war would be Cuban independence and did not anticipate annexation. Of particular import to the actual campaign, the final plan called for the U.S. Asiatic Squadron to assault the Spanish fleet at Manila. Other provisions included blockading Cuba, formation of a major fighting force in the Caribbean to meet any naval challenge from Spain, and a possible attack on Puerto Rico. Successful implementation of the navy plan would isolate Spanish forces in Cuba and the Philippines and would hold islands under U.S. control as hostages to peace negotiations. General in outline, subject to Spanish behavior, and less than orderly when put into action, the navy's war plan nonetheless governed conduct of the war.

The navy was able to implement its plan because it possessed the essential ships to carry it out, a relatively modern fleet augmented by additional purchases in March and April. The U.S. Navy began serious modernization in the early 1890s and by 1898 had 4 first-class, well-armored battleships with moderate sailing range, carrying main batteries of four 13-inch guns. An older battleship, the USS *Texas,* sister to the *Maine,* and 12 modern cruisers, some armored, completed the fighting fleet. The navy lacked balance, falling short of colliers, fast scout vessels, and torpedo-boat destroyers. As Spanish-American relations deteriorated, Congress approved a $50,000,000 appropriation on March 9 to bolster the army and navy, the latter receiving $29,000,000 of the fund. The Navy Department purchased a variety of ships to fill out the fleet, especially auxiliaries to conduct blockade duty. Naval personnel strength more than doubled during the war, from 12,982 officers and men to just over 26,200.

Despite the addition of 131 new vessels and thousands of new officers and men, the navy's peacetime ships, officers, and crews formed the fighting fleet. The navy entered the war not only with a contingency war plan but with a fighting doctrine as well, which its thoroughly professional officer corps was determined to follow. As defined by Capt. Alfred Thayer Mahan, navy doctrine stressed concentrating combat ships in squadrons whose main objectives were to seek out the enemy fleet, fight it, and sink it. Destruction of enemy forces would allow the navy to blockade ports and support land operations. The McKinley administration deviated from Mahan's doctrine early in the war, much to the chagrin of high-ranking naval officers, but the Spanish ultimately obliged U.S. commanders eager for fleet combat. Spain's naval force in Manila Bay simply awaited the arrival of Commodore George Dewey's Asiatic Squadron, and in the Caribbean, Adm. Pascual Cervera y Topete brought his ships from Spain direct to the area of operations where the most powerful U.S. ships lay in wait.

The Navy maintained a relatively effective command system throughout the war. Relying in part on the planning experience at the Naval War College and ONI, Sec. of the Navy John D. Long drew on informal meetings of senior officers who often met under the chairmanship of Asst. Sec. of the Navy Theodore Roosevelt as war beckoned. Long formally convened a Naval War Board in March, recalling Captain Mahan from England to serve on it. A Massachusetts Republican, Long ably presented the Board's views at McKinley's war council meetings and vigorously directed navy operations. On March 7, for example, he ordered the USS *Oregon,* a first-class battleship, to steam to the Caribbean from its port at Bremerton, Washington. The *Oregon* immediately began a dramatic two-month voyage, avidly covered by the press, which brought the ship off the Cuban coast just in time to take part in the largest naval fight of the war.

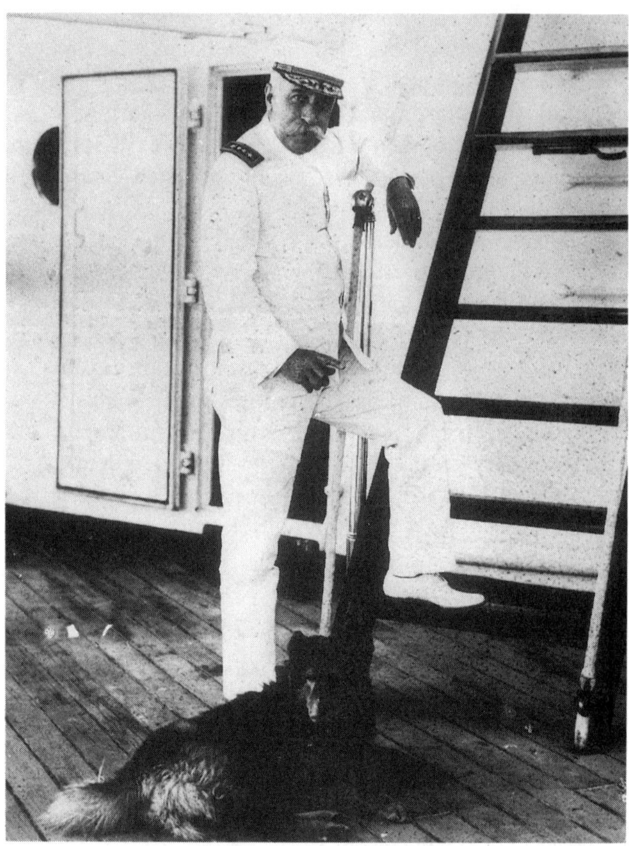

In January 1898, Adm. George Dewey (shown aboard the Olympia*) was given command of the Asiatic Squadron, which consisted of nine ships, and was ordered to sail to Hong Kong in February; orders to attack the Spanish at Manila Bay came in April.* (U.S. Navy)

Long had the active navy on a war footing by the end of March, with the Naval War Board functioning, auxiliary ship purchases well under way, and detailed plans to blockade Cuba in place. The secretary even had a primitive intelligence network active, with agents in Havana and other Caribbean ports. Long created five operational squadrons, one being Dewey's Asiatic Squadron, reinforced during March and temporarily anchored at Hong Kong. On the Atlantic coast, the secretary established the Flying Squadron, under Commodore Winfield S. Schley, operating from Hampton Roads, Virginia, and the North Atlantic Squadron, commanded by Rear Adm. William T. Sampson, serving out of Key West, Florida. Two other lesser squadrons patrolled Atlantic coast areas north of Hampton Roads. Naval officers opposed creation of the Flying Squadron, whose role was coastal defense, as the action reduced the North Atlantic Squadron's strength, dispersing the fleet in violation of Mahanian doctrine.

Army War Plans

The U.S. Army proved less effective in preparing for war. The army's institutional problems and its secondary role in prewar planning hampered the service's efforts to ready itself for combat. The army's greatest problem was its inability to expand from a peacetime footing to a wartime force, as it could do nothing without congressional approval. Unlike the navy, the army could not fight a war with its peacetime combat units. Additional men and units would have to be organized. The War Department wasted much time by sending a bill to Congress early in March 1898 to expand the regular army from its peacetime strength of roughly 25,000 enlisted men to 100,000 and to add a third battalion to its active regiments. The bill fared badly as it stimulated old fears of a large professional army and angered National Guard officers who fully expected to serve in wartime state volunteer regiments. Consequently, Congress did not approve a manpower bill until April 22, which allowed President McKinley to call for state volunteers and gave National Guard units first preference.

Uncertainty over the army's role in the war also hampered planning. Unsure precisely how the naval war would develop and hesitant to introduce large numbers of troops immediately into Cuba, the McKinley administration wavered in its plans for ground operations. The army received only $19,000,000 from the $50,000,000 prewar appropriation, and Sec. of War Russell A. Alger allotted $15,000,000 of the sum to improve coastal fortifications. In retrospect, it became clear that the money, however inadequate, should have been spent on preparing training camps and stockpiling arms and equipment for an expanded wartime army. Alger, however, received no clear direction from McKinley as to what the army might do or even how large it might be. Furthermore, as creation of the Flying Squadron suggested, the administration believed it had to respond to public fears, however exaggerated, that Spanish ships might descend on Atlantic port cities.

Careful planning from the army was not likely to be forthcoming in any event, as it continued to suffer from its decades-long administrative confusion. The commanding general, Maj. Gen. Nelson A. Miles, held little authority over the supply bureaus and could only recommend to Secretary Alger on the disposition of the combat regiments, normally scattered across the country in battalion-sized garrisons. Lacking agencies similar to the Naval War College and ONI, the army had limited means to prepare contingency plans. Alger, a Civil War cavalry regimental commander, wealthy Michigan lumberman, and major contributor to the Republican party, was an honest, earnest administrator but lacked imagination. He administered the War Department by established routines but failed to anticipate the problems and possibilities of war. His uniformed counterpart, General Miles, proved an irascible and unpredictable colleague. Another Civil War veteran, Miles had earned a brigadier generalcy of volunteers at age 25, just before entering the regular army in 1865. He gained a national reputation as an Indian fighter and an equal notoriety for self-promotion and egoism. Promoted to commanding general in 1895, Miles provoked clashes with the bureau chiefs, and from the time Alger took office in 1897, he squabbled with the secretary of war. Miles sometimes offered sound advice during the war, but his contrary personality and frequently eccentric views led McKinley and Alger to ignore him. The army would suffer during the war both from its institutional failings and the inability, often willful refusal, of Alger and Miles to work together.

McKinley as Commander in Chief

In 1898, the United States lacked an effective command and control system to wage war. While the navy possessed an informal command system, led by a vigorous secretary, it had no uniformed chief similar to the army's commanding general. Miles, on the other hand, bore the title but could not command and had no rudimentary staff system to coordinate army planning and operations. President McKinley learned quickly that he would have to serve as an active commander in chief, coordinating foreign policy with military action, imposing order within the fractious War Department, and compelling army-navy cooperation in joint operations.

McKinley asserted control before war was declared and closely supervised affairs in all major operations after April 25. He directed the creation of a "war room" in the White House, with large maps pinned to the walls. Fed from the room were 20 telegraph lines and 15 telephone lines, the former to major military concentrations, such as Tampa, Florida, and eventually Cuba, and the latter to cabinet offices in Washington. Thus, McKinley made the key decisions that led to victory.

The president early on displayed skepticism on the value of the War Department advice and in April asked retired lieutenant general John M. Schofield (former Commanding General of the Army) to advise him. Schofield's addition to the war council understandably offended General Miles, so much so that thereafter Miles found fault with nearly all the war council's decisions. Distrustful as well of Secretary Alger, McKinley came to rely on the army's adjutant general, Brig. Gen. Henry C. Corbin, yet another Civil War veteran and long a member of the adjutant general's corps. For all intents and purposes, Corbin became de facto chief of staff of the army, the man to whom McKinley turned for military advice and for the coordination of the War Department's mobilization effort.

The McKinley war council, including Secretaries Long and Alger, Generals Schofield and Miles, and one or more members of the Naval War Board, began meeting regularly

Lt. Gen. (ret.) John McAllister Schofield, former Commanding General of the U.S. Army (1888–95), advised Pres. William McKinley during the Spanish-American War. (U.S. Army Military History Institute, M. F. Steele Collection)

from mid-April. Despite the overall navy plan to attack the Spanish fleet and seize Spanish islands, much indecision marked early strategic discussions. The navy objected to the division of the North Atlantic Squadron and disliked blockade duty off Cuba, for it too dispersed the fleet. However, until a Spanish naval force appeared in the theater, there was little else for the sailors to do.

At an April 20 meeting, the council accepted a plan proposed by Miles. He recommended that the navy blockade Cuba and await the Spanish fleet. At the same time, navy ships should support small army landings in Cuba's southeast provinces. The soldiers would reconnoiter Spanish troop dispositions and give arms to Cuban insurgents. Meanwhile, the War Department would organize, train, and equip volunteers and await the passing of the Cuban fever season. Once the Spanish fleet was destroyed and summer had passed, the army would invade Cuba. Over Secretary Long's objection, the council approved the proposal. Cuba quickly came under blockade, and the army began to organize its first Cuban raid at the end of April.

In the next few days, two widely dispersed events at sea altered these plans; thereafter, the dictates of war, not prewar plans, determined U.S. military action. McKinley cancelled the Cuban raid when he learned on April 30 that Admiral Cervera's force of four armored cruisers and three destroyers had left the Cape Verde Islands sailing westward.

On May 3, the United States was thrilled to learn that Commodore Dewey's Asiatic Squadron, sailing out of Hong Kong, had destroyed Spanish naval forces in Manila Bay two days earlier. The war to free Cuba had seen its first casualties 10,000 miles from the insurgency. A sortie on Manila had been part of the navy's plans since 1896. McKinley had personally signed the order on April 20, directing Dewey to attack. However, the public knew nothing of the plan and was astounded by Dewey's easy success. The weakest of the three fighting squadrons, Dewey's force included four modern cruisers: *Olympia, Raleigh, Boston,* and *Concord.* Its Spanish opponents manned decrepit old ships, none of which had armor-plated decks and the largest of which was made of wood. Two-thirds of the Spanish guns were muzzleloaders. In seven hours of sporadic combat, Dewey's men sank three enemy ships and burned six more. Some 161 Spaniards died, and another 210 were wounded. The Americans suffered 9 wounded sailors. The overwhelming U.S. victory at Manila Bay on May 1, 1898, altered the conduct of the war and fundamentally changed McKinley's war objectives.

MOBILIZATION

While the nation absorbed the import of Manila and made Dewey an instant hero, the McKinley administration labored to mobilize an army. Mobilization came late, virtually on the eve of war's declaration. Congress approved a manpower bill on April 22, 1898, and on April 23d, McKinley surprised the War Department by issuing a call for 125,000 volunteers, on the advice of General Schofield, twice the number the army recommended. Young men everywhere scrambled to find a place in the National Guard regiments, which generally had first choice to fill state quotas assigned by the War Department.

Recruiting men proved easy, but as the War Department had feared when it proposed to meet war needs by expanding existing regular regiments, the understrength, poorly equipped, ill-trained guard regiments were filled to war strength with men who had no training. The recently revived state soldiery proved able to mobilize and concentrate nearly 120,000 men far more rapidly than had been the case in April–May 1861. The very rapidity of mobilization, however, overwhelmed both state military systems and War Department supply bureaus.

National Guardsmen were not the only soldiers straining the mobilization. As a token to the army, Congress agreed to expand the service to 61,000 enlisted men late in May, requiring more than 35,000 new recruits. It further authorized recruitment of 3,000 U.S. Volunteers, commanded by officers commissioned by the president. From this authority came the 1st, 2d, and 3d volunteer cavalry regiments, the 1st soon known familiarly as the Rough Riders. Further legislation provided for 3,500 volunteer engineers and 10,000 volunteer infantry, 10 full regiments. The latter were to be filled with men purportedly immune to tropical diseases, hence their popular designation as "the Immunes," which proved a misnomer. Four of the volunteer infantry regiments were black troops (the 7th through the 10th), although all their officers except the lieutenants were white. Finally, on May 25, President McKinley issued a second call for 75,000 volunteers, in part to bring National Guard units to full war strength but also to provide troops for the Philippines. All told, at the end of August, the army totaled 11,108 officers and 263,609 enlisted men. In just over four months, the army had grown from 27,000 to nearly 300,000.

The army's greatest challenge in the Spanish-American War was to overcome logistical difficulties in order to make this force an effective military organization. It never quite met the challenge. Congressional tight-fistedness before the war prevented the service from stockpiling arms, clothing, and equipment. Little federal aid went to the National Guard, and few states spent enough money to keep the Guard equipped. Thousands of volunteers brought nothing to the war but their enthusiasm. Indeed, the shortage of arms and equipment was such that it is not clear how the War Department had intended to equip enlistees.

Every necessity to equip and train the volunteers had to be acquired just as war began. The army did not maintain training camps in peacetime and lacked posts sufficiently large to hold the wartime regiments. While the volunteers mobilized at National Guard camps or temporary state facilities, the War Department designated Chickamauga Park, Georgia, named Camp Thomas, and Camp Alger in Falls Church, Virginia, as the main volunteer mobilization camps. The army did not maintain peacetime organizations above the regiment level. With the administration eager to begin military action, the War Department ordered state regiments to move to the camps on May 15 so they could be organized into brigades, divisions, and corps. The army ultimately formed eight corps, with both divisions and corps commanded by regular army officers. Unfortunately, many regiments were not yet sworn in and neither Camp Thomas nor Camp Alger had yet completed providing water, sanitation, or cooking facilities when the order went out.

Volunteer regiments began to arrive by May 20, commanded by colonels unfamiliar with feeding and caring for 1,000 soldiers on extended field duty. Few of the regulars commanding the divisions and corps had experience with the logistical needs of thousands of men, and many failed to manage the proper feeding, supply, and health of the raw volunteers. Corps and division commanders quickly fell prey to supply bureau peacetime procedures, with all requisitions having to be properly filled out and forwarded up the chain of command. For weeks, commanders were denied permission to purchase on the open market the most desperately needed supplies. Washington bureau chiefs worked diligently to meet the demands but were temporarily overwhelmed. In the Quartermaster Department, for example, just 57 officers and 80 quartermaster sergeants were on duty as war broke out. The Subsistence Department reflected similar manpower levels.

The shortage of modern shoulder weapons was particularly acute. Although the army had adopted a new breechloading rifle firing smokeless powder in 1892, the .30-caliber five-shot Krag-Jörgensen, it barely had enough to equip regulars. Guardsmen carried the 1873 Springfield .45, a single-shot breechloader firing black gunpowder cartridges. U.S. troops would go into battle with two different rifles, complicating supply during combat. The problems represented by weapons appeared with all essential equipment needs.

By the end of July, through tremendous work and significant personnel expansion, the logistics bureaus overcame most shortages. Alger did his best work in solving the supply problem, assisted by Corbin. Some corps commanders displayed energy and foresight. Maj. Gen. Wesley Merritt, commanding VIII Corps at San Francisco, proved best at caring for his volunteers, moving them quickly into a vigorous training program and taking care of their health. Some volunteer units, notably the Rough Riders, with Leonard Wood as colonel and Theodore Roosevelt as lieutenant colonel, benefited from political connections. The Rough Riders received the Krag-Jörgensen, light canvas uniforms, and a healthy camp (personally chosen by Wood) near San Antonio, Texas. Such was not the case for most volunteers, who initially experienced chaos, confusion, bad food, and little to wear. Ultimately, they would face tropical disease, an enemy more implacable and deadly than the Spanish.

The logistical difficulties plaguing mobilization affected combat operations as well, especially in Cuba. An acute shortage of wagon transportation hampered mobilization at Tampa and Maj. Gen. William R. Shafter's V Corps campaign against Santiago, Cuba, as well as complicated supply efforts in the mobilization camps. The War Department's belated realization that it needed ships to transport troops overseas was indicative of the army's failure to plan and marked the single greatest strategic shortcoming of the McKinley administration's conduct of the war. How the nation might carry on land operations against Spanish-held

Despite the U.S. Army's logistical difficulties in the late 1890s, Maj. Gen. Wesley Merritt's troops underwent vigorous training and were fit for battle when orders came to depart for the Philippines in 1898. (U.S. Army Military History Institute)

islands without the means to transport troops did not arise until early May. McKinley's war council, between May 1 and May 4, decided to launch an invasion of Cuba and send 5,000 troops to the Philippines. Responsibility for transporting them fell to the Quartermaster Department, not to the navy. With little experience or forethought, the Quartermaster Department rapidly purchased a variety of cattle boats, coastal freighters, and other merchant ships ill-fitted to carry human beings. It then hastily converted them to troop transports. While ships going to the Philippines from San Francisco were somewhat better than those operating in the Caribbean, many of the most vivid and hateful memories for Spanish-American War veterans came from time spent on quartermaster transport vessels.

Contemporary observers and historians castigated the War Department's logistical bureaus for their dismal performance in 1898. Secretary of War Alger, in particular, became a target for sharp criticism, based largely on the sentiment that Alger and his bureau chiefs had enough information at their disposal to have anticipated wartime needs and to have made reasonable preparations on how to address such needs but failed to do so. In fact, when the war began, the bureaus had made little provision to abandon peacetime supply requisition procedures. The army, concurrently, lacked authority to purchase so much as an extra rifle without congressional authorization, did not know how large the wartime army would be until McKinley issued his 125,000-man call on April 23, and had no centralized coordinating agency to direct a united logistical effort.

Had McKinley heeded Miles's early advice to take in some 60,000–80,000 volunteers slowly, to train and organize them through the summer, and then to launch a Cuban invasion in September, many of the worst aspects of mobilization and supply shortages could have been avoided. War, however, inevitably develops an impetus of its own that often outruns the careful plans of professional soldiers. Not unlike the advice of Cmd. Gen. Winfield Scott in April 1861, to prepare carefully and go slow, Miles's recommendations lost out to public demands for action and McKinley's desire to end the war quickly. McKinley bears much of the responsibility here, for he made the crucial decisions and pushed his generals to act, particularly Shafter. Eager to capitalize on Dewey's remarkable victory in Manila, McKinley altered the basic war plan and the nation's objectives when he approved the movement of troops to the Philippine Islands.

COMBAT OPERATIONS

Although intent on keeping the war brief, McKinley and his war council proved unable through the end of May to devise an operational plan for the Caribbean area. The exact location and ultimate destination of Admiral Cervera's squadron remained a mystery from April 29 through May 20, and until the U.S. Navy solved that puzzle, plans for land operations continually collapsed. The initial intent to send part of Shafter's V Corps as an armed reconnaissance to southeast Cuba was cancelled upon receipt of word that Cervera had left the Cape Verde Islands. Remarkably, on May 2, the war council then decided to attack Havana with up to 50,000 men as soon as possible. Anxious to be relieved of blockade duty off Havana, the navy pushed for a land attack against the port city. An overly optimistic Shafter asserted that his V Corps could leave Tampa by May 16. Reports of Cervera's arrival at Martinique, however, led the council to delay the Havana operation.

In any event, V Corps was in no condition to begin combat operations. Some 12,000 regular troops had just arrived in Tampa, and volunteer regiments likely to be assigned to Shafter were just then filtering into Camp Thomas at Chickamauga Park. Miles went directly to McKinley and told him bluntly that the army was not ready to fight. Having performed this sound service, Miles then offered his own plan, urging an invasion of Puerto Rico while making only raids into Cuba. With Cervera on the loose, an attack on Puerto Rico was no safer than one on Cuba. Miles reiterated one version or another of this scheme for the rest of the war, including a proposal late in May to place a full cavalry corps ashore in northeast Cuba for an overland attack on Havana from the east. Increasingly, McKinley and the war council ignored the commanding general, whose every idea ran counter to the council's consensus.

Search for Cervera

Land operations would not begin in Cuba or Puerto Rico until the navy located Admiral Cervera. Secretary Long had ordered blockades of Havana and other Cuban ports on April 23 and simultaneously established patrols throughout the Caribbean to scout for Spanish ships. Scouting and blockading severely tested Sampson's North Atlantic Squadron, reduced in numbers by creation of the Flying Squadron. The Caribbean area of naval operations was large, the distance from Havana to San Juan, Puerto Rico, for example, being just over 1,100 miles. U.S. Navy ships, many recently acquired auxiliary cruisers, scouted passages from south of Puerto Rico to the Venezuelan coast, and north from Puerto Rico to the Bahamas. In the age before radio telegraphy, coordinating these efforts was challenging. Only with some difficulty could Sampson or Long communicate with ships at sea. Long sent cables to various Caribbean ports from which dispatch boats sought out U.S. ships to deliver messages. Sampson also relied on speedy small ships to communicate with his command when they were not near cable stations.

The navy experienced great difficulty in finding Cervera's squadron. Having learned that Cervera had left the Cape Verdes, Sampson could only guess at his destination. Havana or San Juan seemed the most likely places. Sampson assumed the latter and on May 4 pulled several vessels, including the battleships *Iowa* and *Indiana,* away from the Havana blockade and made for San Juan. Eight days later, he arrived off the city but found no Spanish squadron. He bombarded the town for two hours, to no real purpose, then departed. Only on May 16, off the north coast of Haiti, did Sampson learn that Cervera had briefly put in first at Martinique, then Curacao, and was once again on the high seas. Out of touch with the navy for two weeks, Sampson received a sharp order from Long to return to Key West immediately.

Eager to bring Cervera to bay, the navy directed Commodore Schley to take his Flying Squadron to Key West on May 18 and unite with Sampson. The navy had learned from its agent in Havana that Cervera had sailed into Santiago Bay, on Cuba's southeast coast, on May 19. Although the report proved to be correct, neither Sampson nor Schley, nor the Navy Department, accepted it. Long directed Sampson to screen Havana while Schley took his squadron to watch Cienfuegos, on Cuba's south-central coast. Schley unaccountably took three days to move from Key West to Cienfuegos, arriving there on May 24. Even more puzzling, he took another two days to obey Sampson's order to go to Santiago.

Schley made a brief appearance before Santiago on May 26 and conferred briefly with auxiliary cruisers there. He then inexplicably turned around to sail for Key West to recoal without ascertaining whether Cervera was in the harbor. Under orders from Long and Sampson, Schley at last took station off Santiago on May 28 and confirmed the next day that at least some of Cervera's ships were in the bay. Nearly 10 days had passed since word of Cervera's arrival had been learned, and 5 days since Schley had been ordered from Cienfuegos to Santiago. At any time during that period, Cervera could have escaped. He did not. When Sampson's North Atlantic Squadron joined Schley on June 1, the elusive Spaniard was at last trapped. In the final act of the navy's curiously inefficient search, Sampson did not determine that all Cervera's ships were present until June 11, when he sent ashore a lieutenant who, with the aid of Cuban insurgents, counted and identified the entire enemy fleet.

Once Sampson established his blockade in front of Santiago, he requested use of the only organized Marines Corps battalion, then sitting idle at Key West. Marines normally served aboard ship as guards and acted as gunners on rapid-fire secondary batteries aboard cruisers and battleships. However, Long had approved formation of a six-company infantry battalion of 24 officers and 633 enlisted men. Sampson wanted the unit, commanded by Civil War veteran Lt. Col. Robert W. Huntington, to seize a position on Guantanamo Bay, east of Santiago, for use as a coaling station. Huntington's force went ashore on June 10, under the guns of the recently arrived USS *Oregon,* and, aided by Cuban insurgents, wrested control of the bay following four days of sharp Spanish resistance. The marines gained a coaling station for the navy, a direct cable line to the United States, and nationwide press attention from the first U.S. ground combat against the Spanish enemy.

Capture of Santiago

Locating and blockading Cervera's squadron in Santiago harbor broke the war council's indecision on land operations in the Caribbean. Even before Schley moved to Santiago, McKinley and his advisers dropped the Havana attack plan, and on May 26 decided to land Shafter's V Corps near the harbor city. In a reversal of prewar planning, the army went to aid the navy. Unlike Manila harbor, the entrance to Santiago was narrow, covered by highlands to the east and west. The Spanish had mounted guns in well-fortified positions on the heights. Even if Sampson forced a passage through this channel, he faced a constricted outer harbor and a second narrow passage, easily mined, into the larger inner harbor. Secretary Long and the Naval War Board wanted the army to seize the fortified batteries on the seacoast, attack Santiago, and force Cervera to leave

Spanish-American War, 1898—Caribbean Campaign

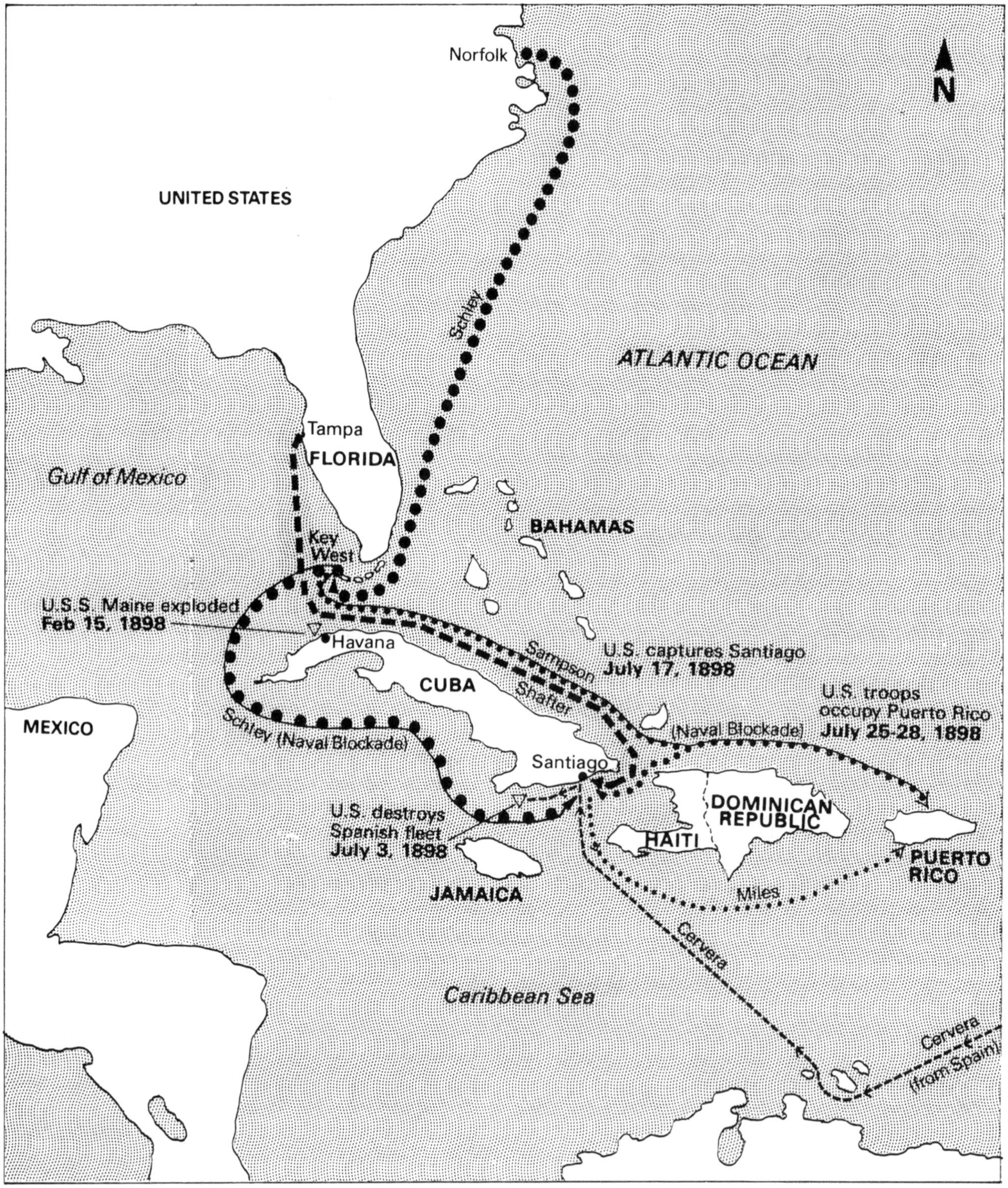

Norfolk
N
UNITED STATES
Schley
ATLANTIC OCEAN
Tampa
FLORIDA
Gulf of Mexico
BAHAMAS
Key West
U.S.S. Maine exploded
Feb 15, 1898
Havana
Sampson
U.S. captures Santiago
July 17, 1898
CUBA
Shafter
U.S. troops occupy Puerto Rico
July 25-28, 1898
MEXICO
Schley (Naval Blockade)
(Naval Blockade)
Santiago
DOMINICAN REPUBLIC
U.S. destroys Spanish fleet
July 3, 1898
HAITI
PUERTO RICO
JAMAICA
Miles
Cervera
Caribbean Sea
Cervera (from Spain)

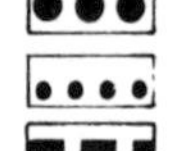

Com. Winfield S. Schley
Adm. William T. Sampson
Gen. William Shafter

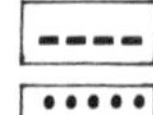

Adm. Pascual Cervera
Gen. Nelson Miles

port or surrender. Shafter was urged to take his V Corps to Cuba as quickly as possible.

Embarkation at Tampa

The organization, embarkation, and deployment of Shafter's command to Santiago highlighted the failings of the mobilization. Selected because it was the U.S. port closest to Havana, Tampa proved to be woefully inadequate as a major troop concentration point and port of embarkation. First in importance, the town lacked sufficient rail lines to accommodate the influx of more than 25,000 soldiers and the near 1,000 freight cars that funneled into Tampa. Two single-track lines served the city, but only one went directly to the docks. The army's shortage of wagons left it with only 17 vehicles to carry freight forward to the docks. While on average 50 cars arrived daily, V Corps quartermasters could unload only 3 a day. Rail congestion created a monumental traffic jam in mid-May, with freight cars backed up more than 100 miles to the north. The absence of a single agency to coordinate the flow of supplies to Tampa compounded the logistical bottleneck. The arrival of freight was disorganized, without advance notice or bills of lading.

The V Corps command organization proved unable to correct supply problems. In peace, the supply bureaus handled logistics routinely, but now their overcentralization left field commanders such as General Shafter with no experienced quartermaster or commissary officers. He assigned line officers from the regiments to the jobs, a common peacetime practice, but inexperience led to many errors. Shafter worked diligently to create order, but conditions in Tampa and his own inexperience produced only limited success. A Civil War veteran with long service commanding black troops in Texas, "Pecos Bill" Shafter did not earn a generalcy until 1897 and had never commanded above the regimental level in combat. At age 63, weighing more than 300 pounds and often garbed in a long white coat, he became an easy target for the yellow journalists who derisively dubbed him "the floating tent." Most of the problems at Tampa were not Shafter's fault, but the blunt old regular often gave the appearance of inefficiency.

Shafter had little control over use of his command. Informed on May 26 to take the V Corps to Santiago, he received increasingly strident orders to get under way. McKinley, always with an eye to end the war quickly, was eager to dispose of Cervera. Unaware of the chaotic conditions at Tampa, the president and Secretary Alger bombarded Shafter with orders to embark. The V Corps officers, directed by Shafter's efficient adjutant general, Lt. Col. Edward J. McClernand, strove to load ships with enough equipment and supplies to sustain the corps for a short campaign but discovered the transports were too small to carry the entire force and its full combat load.

Directly ordered to set sail without further delay on June 7, Shafter lost control of the final loading. Regiments scrambled to board any available ship, and supplies were loaded without thought. Shipping shortages forced Shafter to leave some 8,000 of his men behind, largely National Guard volunteers, and most of his horses and wagons. The V Corps departed with two infantry divisions, each with nine regiments organized into three brigades, and a dismounted cavalry division of two brigades with three regiments each. A small independent infantry brigade, six batteries of artillery, and three volunteer regiments—the 71st New York Infantry, the 2d Massachusetts Infantry, and the 1st U.S. Volunteer Cavalry (Rough Riders)—filled out the corps, some 17,000 officers and men. Eighteen regular infantry and five cavalry regiments formed the heart of the force. Prominent among the regulars were all four of the army's black regiments—the 9th and 10th cavalries and the 24th and 25th infantries. An additional 300 civilian teamsters, 89 journalists, and 15 foreign military observers accompanied Shafter. The V Corps rendezvoused in Tampa Bay on June 8, only to sit under the sweltering sun for six days while the navy vainly searched for a phantom Spanish raiding force rumored to be in the Caribbean. At last, the rumor punctured, the corps left on June 14 under naval escort and joined Admiral Sampson off Santiago on June 20.

Cuban Land Campaign

General Shafter was ordered to Santiago to "capture or destroy the Spanish fleet" with the aid of the navy. War Department instructions did not detail how this was to be done. Shafter arrived off Santiago with no campaign plan or much intention of cooperating with the navy. Maj. Gen. Arsenio Linares y Pombo commanded Santiago Province, with some 28,000 men under him. Only 13,000 defended Santiago City, other forces being dispersed throughout the province to watch insurgents. With Cervera blockaded in the harbor and Cuban rebels controlling the high ground to the city's north and west, Linares had to fight with the forces at hand. While extensively fortified, the city suffered food shortages and rampant disease. Linares stoically awaited Shafter's arrival, intent on conducting a static defense.

General Shafter ignored Admiral Sampson and, after conferring with insurgent Gen. Calixto García Íñiquez, decided to land at Siboney and Daiquiri, small towns lying 11 and 17 miles east of the city, respectively. Sampson had wanted landings west of the harbor entrance. From there, the army could take the fortified highlands and allow naval forces to enter the outer harbor. Shafter rejected the idea, fearing it would be too costly. With García's insurgents disposed largely to the west of Santiago, Shafter thought Spanish resistance would be less in the east.

Under the guns of the disgruntled Sampson's fleet, and with García's men controlling the beaches, the V Corps

Cuban insurgents, here deployed in trenches, controlled most of the high ground surrounding Santiago. (U.S. Military Academy Archives)

carried out a disorderly landing, first at Daiquiri, then Siboney, between June 22 and June 25. Once again, logistical deficits plagued the corps, yet another indication of its hasty departure. The U.S. convoy lacked landing craft other than the transports' small boats and a few steam launches. Without small craft, and with a lack of docks, landing troops and supplies became slow and difficult. Soldiers had no choice but to push horses and mules over the side to swim ashore. Many swam out to sea and drowned. The shortage of landing craft seriously delayed unloading the ships, which had been hastily and improperly loaded in the first place. When coupled with the fact that Shafter had been forced to leave behind many of his supplies, logistics support for the corps appeared grim. In particular, it was desperately short of tents, medical supplies, fresh food, and wheeled transportation. Because soldiers never got the tropical uniforms that had been sent to Tampa, they fought the campaign in blue woolen uniforms.

Shafter recognized his severe logistical problems. He intended to expand his beachhead before starting his campaign and urgently requested the War Department to forward supplies left at Tampa. Instead, he received orders to begin action immediately. The Spanish made no effort to resist the American landings but placed a force of 2,000 at Las Guásimas, a village four miles inland from Siboney. Shafter issued vague orders for an armed reconaissance toward the village, but Maj. Gen. Joseph Wheeler, commanding the dismounted 1st Cavalry Division, brashly attacked the position on June 24. Wheeler, ex-Confederate cavalry commander and the only West Pointer among V Corps generals, pushed his outnumbered men, fewer than 1,000 troopers including the Rough Riders, directly into the Spanish lines. The cavalrymen drove off the Spanish after a sharp firefight. Sixteen Americans and 10 Spaniards died in this unnecessary skirmish.

The V Corps was not properly ashore and organized for combat on June 24, and in the ensuing days, it continued to unload as Shafter and his staff struggled to organize the beachhead and create an effective supply line to the interior. Unable to put off Washington's demands that he start fighting, Shafter prepared plans for a July 1 attack. With intelligence from insurgents, he positioned his forces late on June 30 to assault the twin ridges of San Juan and Kettle hills, which screened the more heavily fortified lines protecting Santiago's eastern flank. Shafter ordered the 1st Infantry Division, commanded by Brig. Gen. Jacob F. Kent, and Wheeler's cavalry division to take the hills. Brig. Gen. Henry W. Lawton's 2d Infantry Division was to take the fortified village of El Caney, lying on the U.S. right flank, then join the San Juan Heights assault.

The July 1 combat marked the only land fighting in Cuba. It did not go smoothly. Despite Lawton's promise to take El Caney in two hours, his 6,600-man command fought from 6:00 A.M. to 4:00 P.M. before taking the 500-man garrison. Meanwhile, the advance on the heights began

Maj. Gen. Joseph Wheeler (foreground), *a West Point graduate and a Confederate Civil War veteran, came out of retirement to lead a volunteer cavalry unit during the Spanish-American War.* (U.S. Army Military History Institute)

Troops of Brig. Gen. Henry W. Lawton's 2d Infantry rest in the trenches before their 10-hour fight to gain El Caney, a battle that should have taken no more than two hours. (U.S. Signal Corps)

at 8:00 A.M. and lasted until 1:30 P.M. before the 500 defenders there gave way to the nearly 8,000 attacking Americans. At the end of the day, Shafter's men fired from San Juan Heights into Santiago's inner defenses. The V Corps extended its lines to the north and west on July 2, joining Cuban insurgents on the west. Santiago was effectively surrounded on land and sea.

During the two days of combat, 220 Americans died and another 1,300 suffered wounds. It was not an impressive performance, as just over 1,000 Spaniards had held off nearly 15,000 Americans. Many individuals displayed uncommon courage on July 1, Theodore Roosevelt hardly being the only one, although he reaped the greatest publicity from the action. Difficult terrain, lack of command and control, and the absence of combat experience at all levels marred the American performance.

The terrain near San Juan Heights forced Shafter's men to move forward along muddy trails paralleling the Aguadores River. High ground and thick jungles channeled soldiers to the more open ground in front of the hills. As they passed from the Aguadores trails, troops had to wade the San Juan River and only then deploy in a firing line. Throughout the advance along the Aguadores and during the deployment, Spanish artillery and rifle fire harassed the Americans, who were unable to return fire. The presence of a Signal Corps observation balloon provided the enemy an excellent firing point. Under the constant Spanish sniping, the 71st New York Volunteers lost cohesion and moved into thick jungle to sit out the battle.

Shafter played no part in the battle. Sick and exhausted, he remained in the rear and took battle reports over a telephone. His adjutant general, McClernand, positioned on a hill called El Pozo, gave what cohesion there was to the U.S. attack. The fight at El Caney went wrong because Lawton failed to concentrate his artillery fire and initially misaligned his attacking brigades. When ordered by Shafter to break off the fight early in the afternoon and join the San Juan Heights assault, Lawton continued his attack on El Caney. Along the slowly forming assault line at the base of the heights, brigade and division commanders displayed personal courage by exhorting their men forward, but none directed the action. The American assault succeeded as units at last deployed across the San Juan River and enveloped the enemy flanks. When Lt. John H. Parker's four-gun Gatling battery raked the Spanish trenches at about 1:00 P.M., U.S. soldiers simply surged up the hills and drove the Spanish off. Numbers and bravery overcame the lack of combat experience in the V Corps.

The Rough Riders, shown entrenched at Santiago, Cuba, was a volunteer cavalry group for which Theodore Roosevelt resigned his post as undersecretary of the navy; their horses were left behind in Florida. (U.S. Army Military History Institute)

Death of Cervera's Squadron

However haphazardly organized and led in combat, Shafter's V Corps achieved its strategic purpose. Two days after the San Juan Heights battle, and against his own wishes, Admiral Cervera reluctantly led his ships out of Santiago and into the guns of Admiral Sampson's fleet. At 9:30 A.M., July 3, 1898, Cervera's ships, forced to steam in line out of the narrow harbor entrance, entered the sea one by one. Heavily outgunned by the U.S. battleships *Indiana, Oregon, Iowa,* and *Texas,* as well as by the U.S. armored cruisers, the Spanish ships were doomed. By 11:00 A.M., three of Cervera's four armored cruisers and both his destroyers were sunk or beached. The last Spanish ship, the *Cristobol Colon,* was driven aground by the *Oregon* at 1:15 P.M. Cervera not only lost his ships but saw 323 of his men killed and 151 wounded. More than 1,700 Spanish sailors were captured. Minimal U.S. losses (one man killed, one wounded) and minor damage to the *Texas,* the *Iowa,* and the cruiser *Brooklyn* made the victory even more dramatic.

Despite the overwhelming success, Sampson did not become an instant naval hero. By coincidence, he was not present when the fight began. He had gone to Siboney to confer with Shafter on the next phase of the campaign. As a consequence, Commodore Schley directed the tactical battle. Sampson reached the scene aboard the cruiser *New York* in its final stage. His cable report to Secretary Long, however, neglected to mention Schley, a fact quickly noted by the press, which extolled Schley and criticized Sampson. A Sampson-Schley controversy divided the navy into the 20th century, a counterproductive squabble for glory.

Surrender of Santiago

Victory on July 1 surprisingly left Shafter and many of his officers pessimistic, a mood not lightened by Cervera's defeat. U.S. naval triumph assured the Spanish defeat ultimately, but it did not eliminate the possible necessity to attack Santiago. Army officers had been shaken by the chaos of the July 1 battle and by the relatively high casualties and Spanish tenacity. Shafter even briefly considered withdrawing from the heights on July 2 to reorganize. More and more, logistical problems hindered the V Corps, subject to oppressive heat, rain, a growing sick list, and woefully insufficient food and medical supplies. The lack of wagons and the primitive roads from Siboney to the San Juan Heights made daily supply an onerous task.

Shafter stayed put on orders from Washington, and from July 3 through July 17, he and Santiago's new commander, Gen. José Toral, negotiated the city's fate. Almost daily, Shafter and Sampson bickered over which service should attack Santiago, a debate that extended to the war council, where Secretaries Long and Alger took up the argument. Shafter wanted the navy to force its way through the harbor entrance to bombard the city. Sampson wanted the army to take the harbor entrance forts first. Neither commander would give way. The Spanish garrison increasingly fell subject to sickness and lack of food, which broke Toral's resistance. From July 10 onward, reinforcements came to the V Corps, including General Miles. Miles and Shafter met with Toral on July 13 and threatened a combined naval and land attack on the city. Toral gave in, and surrender ceremonies took place on July 17. In a final blow to army-navy relations, Shafter neglected to include Sampson in the affair. He also omitted General García. The latter, his honor deeply offended because insurgent forces had assisted the V Corps throughout the campaign, resigned in indignation.

Return of V Corps to the United States

Shafter eagerly sought Toral's surrender in large part to save his command, whose health was rapidly deteriorating. Capture of Santiago allowed the Americans to use the harbor for supply, but it was too late, as yellow fever, typhoid, dysentery, and, above all, malaria, swept through the corps. At the end of July, nearly 20 percent of Shafter's men lay in hospitals. The War Department believed it best, at first, to leave the force in Cuba to wait out the epidemics, but an August 3 report from Shafter reported that 75 percent of his men suffered from malaria, and he urged an immediate return to the United States. The general had asked for his division and brigade commanders' views. All reported serious sickness and recommended returning home. Later dubbed the "round robin," these reports were leaked to the press, as was a similar letter of Roosevelt's to Sen. Henry Cabot Lodge.

The "round robin" leaks created a sensation and embarrassed the McKinley administration. They simultaneously made the administration appear callous and inept. Furthermore, McKinley was in the midst of negotiating an armistice with Spain. If the V Corps was incapacitated, it gave Spain greater bargaining power. Secretary of War Alger had already designated Montauk Point, on Long Island, as a recuperation camp for the corps a week before the "round robin" appeared. Press attention, however, made it seem as though the administration was relieving the troops only because its own generals pleaded for help. The War Department speeded up the V Corps' voyage home, the last units leaving on August 25, accompanied by General Shafter. It left behind more than 500 of its men dead of disease. Yet again, however, events backfired on the War Department. Many of the transports taking men home were unfit. Worse yet, Montauk Point was not ready to take in the stricken V Corps, and early arrivals found no bedding, little food, and a disorganized medical system. Further press attacks lambasted the War Department in the harshest

Epidemics of yellow fever, typhoid, dysentery, and malaria left large numbers of troops sick and in need of medical attention; some of the sick in Puerto Rico were transported to military hospitals by wagon. (National Archives)

terms yet seen during the war. The return home was a sorry end to the problem-plagued V Corps.

Puerto Rican Campaign

As the V Corps awaited its fate, Commanding General Miles at last gained his chance to make a mark. Since mid-April, Miles had urged an attack on Puerto Rico. The original Santiago plan called for Shafter to take Santiago quickly, then reembark and go to Puerto Rico. By the time the V Corps left for Cuba, the war council decided instead to give Miles the assignment. In early June, McKinley decided to seek permanent annexation of Puerto Rico, and it was necessary to place a U.S. force there to insure the demand. Miles and part of his force first went to Cuba to aid Shafter but never disembarked and left for the mission after Toral surrendered. Controversy attended Miles wherever he went. He carried on an acrimonious wrangle with Admiral Sampson over the size of a naval escort, an argument finally settled by McKinley.

Miles left Cuba on July 21 with some 3,400 troops. He was to be joined off Puerto Rico by troop transports sailing direct from the United States. As originally planned, Miles was to go ashore at Cape Fajardo, at the island's eastern end, then advance on San Juan. Once at sea, the unpredictable general altered the plan. Placing a cruiser at the cape to direct transports from the United States to follow him, Miles conducted a bloodless landing at Guánica on the southern coast on July 25. Three days later, Maj. Gen. James H. Wilson, an ex-Union cavalry commander, took Ponce, to the east of Guánica, again without casualties. Other forces arrived through August 5. Miles then commanded more than 16,000 men to deal with the 7,000 Spanish troops on Puerto Rico. Eleven of the 13 infantry regiments in the force were National Guard volunteers.

The force Miles led was far better organized and equipped than the V Corps, and its disembarkation went smoothly. Miles, however, had placed his command about as far from his objective, San Juan, as was geographically possible on the island. Outnumbering the Spanish by two to one, he nonetheless divided his command into four columns, some separated up to 20 miles. Beginning on August 9, the columns moved northward toward San Juan. Miles's disposition left his columns open to defeat in detail, but Spanish resistance was minimal. The sharper conflict came between Miles and Sampson. Left with little to do, the navy offered to bombard San Juan into submission and incidentally deny the army credit for capturing the city. McKinley again had to intervene to restore interservice peace by rejecting Sampson's proposal. Spain and the United States agreed to an armistice on August 12. With the loss of 4 men killed and 40 wounded, Miles on that date controlled two-thirds of the island, but the closest U.S. force still lay some 25 miles south of San Juan.

Manila Campaign

Following Dewey's May 1 victory at Manila Bay, the nation's attention shifted to the search for Cervera and the fighting in Cuba. Throughout May, June, and July, however, the McKinley administration refined its war objectives, largely with an eye to the Pacific. The war council decided to send 20,000 troops to the Philippines at the end of May. By that time, McKinley had determined to demand that Spain cede at least a portion of the archipelago. Troops were needed in the islands, not only to force the Spanish garrison's surrender but to watch over Filipino insurgents who surely would resent U.S. annexation. Insurgent leader Emilio Aguinaldo, brought to the Philippines with U.S. assistance after Dewey's victory, reinvigorated the insurrection and declared Philippine independence on June 12. An insurgent army then besieged Manila. Dewey and other U.S. officials had at first treated Aguinaldo as a virtual ally, but by early June, the administration ordered them to make no promises nor treat the Filipino as a national leader.

In the meantime, the War Department belatedly created the VIII Corps, on May 12, and assigned Major General Merritt to its command. A West Point Graduate, Civil War hero, and Indian War cavalry officer, Merritt brought impressive credentials to the position. Given more time, better training and port facilities at San Francisco, and Merritt's own abilities, the VIII Corps suffered far fewer problems in organization, embarkation, and deployment to the Philippines than had Shafter's V Corps. Made up largely of National Guard volunteers from western states, the corps moved to the islands in three contingents. The first group left on May 25. During its passage to the Philippines, it stopped at the Spanish-held island of Guam. Marines and sailors from the escort cruiser USS *Charleston* went ashore on June 20, captured the small garrison, and seized the island, the first Spanish possession to fall to the United States. Two other major contingents left on June 15, and June 25–27, respectively, giving Merritt nearly 11,000 troops.

By the end of July, most of Merritt's force was in Manila Bay. It operated from a base, dubbed Camp Dewey, some three miles south of the city. Camp Dewey allowed VIII Corps sufficient room to train, organize, and prepare for battle. Merritt had his force ready to attack Manila by August 1, and tactically he held all the advantages. Dewey's ships could shell the city at will. Gen. Fermin Juadenes and his 13,000 men faced not only Dewey and VIII Corps but at least 10,000 Filipino insurgents encircling the city. With no hope of relief, Juadenes faced inevitable defeat.

Merritt's real problem was not military but political, for he had to deal with the Filipinos even though U.S. policy was to ignore Aguinaldo and his army. The policy complicated planning an attack, for insurgent forces occupied trenches that lay between VIII Corps and the city. Furthermore, Merritt did not want insurgents involved in any assault. Through informal diplomacy and veiled threats, the corps came to occupy a portion of insurgent trenches running from the bay inland for about three-quarters of a mile.

Early in August, Merritt and Dewey began negotiations with Juadenes to secure his surrender. The parties reached an understanding after nearly two weeks of talks. Dewey agreed not to fire on Manila, and Merritt consented to keep insurgents out of the attack and the city. In return, Juadenes agreed to surrender after a brief skirmish sufficient to satisfy Spanish honor. The opponents established procedures for surrender and set August 13 as the day of battle. Merritt sent a letter to Aguinaldo on August 12 requesting him to remain out of the fight. On the morning of August 13,

Transportation for troops and their equipment during the Spanish-American War campaigns in the Philippine Islands was primitive at best. (National Archives)

Spanish and American troops carried out the sham battle, which lasted two hours and had few casualties. As agreed, VIII Corps units moved into Manila rapidly to keep out insurgents and quickly occupied the Spanish trenches. When night fell, U.S. troops looked outward toward insurgent lines. The last battle of the Spanish-American War occurred where the first battle had taken place, in Manila, a day after the United States and Spain had agreed to an armistice.

ARMISTICE AND PEACE TREATY

In March–April 1898, William McKinley publicly set as his war aims an end to conflict in Cuba and elimination of Spanish sovereignty over the island. As the war progressed, however, new and greater opportunities beckoned. Strategy became intertwined with objectives, each reinforcing the other. Dewey's descent on Manila formed part of the larger naval war plan to attack and hold Spain's vulnerable overseas possessions as hostages to peace talks. Success at Manila opened new vistas not originally part of McKinley's objectives. Visions of an expanded U.S. presence in the Pacific and greater commercial involvement in Asia had been offered for years. Captain Mahan's writings on sea power and command of the sea reinforced this interest in the Pacific. Dewey's presence at Manila, seizure of Guam, and congressional approval to annex Hawaii in late July led President McKinley to reconsider U.S. objectives within the context of these ideas.

Similarly, operations in the Caribbean stimulated broader thinking. Along with Cuba, Puerto Rico became a strategic target in war council discussions by mid-April. Events during the war, especially the *Oregon*'s lengthy journey from the Pacific coast to the Caribbean, brought to mind navalist arguments for an isthmian canal. The coaling difficulties that hindered Admiral Sampson's Caribbean operations emphasized the nation's need for coaling stations in the region. The longer Spain refused to sue for peace, the more determined McKinley became to acquire Spanish cessions, not only to compensate for war costs but to bring stability to the Caribbean and an extended U.S. presence there.

McKinley made specific demands on Spain in early June. Through Ambassador Hay in London, he informally let the Spanish know that the United States expected them to leave Cuba and surrender sovereignty over the island. Cession of Puerto Rico and at least one island in the Marianas was on the list. McKinley's note was vague on the Philippines,

U.S. occupation troops marched into Havana after it was evacuated by the Spanish at the close of the Spanish-American War in 1898. (Library of Congress)

suggesting the United States would want at least temporary possession of a port city there, almost surely Manila. More than a month passed before Spain sued for peace on July 18, but U.S. demands remained unchanged. When the two powers agreed to an August 12 armistice, Spain accepted all terms except the one bearing on the Philippines. Formal treaty discussions began in Paris in October and lasted until December. All the talks dealt with settling the Philippine question. Spain at last gave in. The Treaty of Paris freed Cuba and gave Puerto Rico, Guam, and all of the Philippines to the United States. In return, the United States paid Spain $20,000,000, largely to speed its acceptance of the treaty.

American victory proved a disappointment for Cuban and Filipino insurgents. Once the V Corps captured Santiago, Cuban rebels found that their U.S. allies had lost interest in their cause. Washington maintained an occupation force in the island, as for nearly four years, the U.S. Army governed Cuba. A section of the Apr. 19, 1898, congressional resolution authorizing President McKinley to intervene in the insurgency, the Teller Amendment, disavowed any U.S. desire to annex Cuba. McKinley, and his successor, Roosevelt, however, had no intention of leaving the island until the United States would install a stable, fiscally responsible government. In the interim, U.S. occupation forces improved public health and education and gave instruction in self-government. What the former insurgents wanted most was the right to govern themselves, which did not come until May 1902. However, Congress attached the Platt Amendment to legislation granting self-government. Incorporated into the Cuban constitution at U.S. insistence, the amendment restricted Cuba's freedom to make treaties and incur international debts and granted the United States the right to intervene to insure the island's independence and political stability.

In the Philippines, Spain's cession of the archipelago to the United States created deep disappointment among Aguinaldo's followers, who at first had seen the Americans as liberators. Long after the Cuban and Puerto Rican expeditionary forces returned home, Merritt's Western National Guard volunteers served in watchful waiting in the trenches defending Manila. American-Filipino relations grew tense through the autumn of 1898, with occasional individual conflicts arising, but both sides waited uneasily for the final treaty provisions. In early January 1899, Aguinaldo learned that his country had become a U.S. protectorate. Within a month, American and Filipino soldiers were shooting at each other.

AFTERMATH

The Spanish-American War seemed indeed a "splendid little war" for most Americans—an easy contest against a weak opponent, a relatively brief series of campaigns that brought cheap military victories (on both land and sea) and a ready-made overseas empire. The war heightened U.S. nationalism, represented best by McKinley's appointment of former Confederates such as Joseph Wheeler and Fitzhugh Lee to high military command. Victory also brought the nation new international respect and set patrician New Yorker Theodore Roosevelt on his way to the White House. Amidst the hearty self-congratulations, however, lay unpleasant reminders of war's realities and deep flaws in the U.S. military system. While the country's small towns and big cities welcomed home the volunteers of 1898 and gave heroes' welcomes to Rear Admiral Dewey, Commodore Schley, and Roosevelt and his Rough Riders, soldiers lay dying and the War Department lay wallowing in self-recrimination.

Death and Disease

The great tragedy of the Spanish-American War was that nearly 10 times as many men died of disease as were killed in action or died of wounds. The majority succumbing to disease never left the United States. While 345 officers and men died from combat through the August 12 armistice, nearly 2,500 died from disease. The V Corps suffered the worst among the expeditionary forces, but nearly as many men as the corps lost died at Camp Thomas, Chickamauga Park, Georgia. Threats to the health of volunteer soldiers in the United States did not become evident until late July and early August, just as the war ended. Malaria and typhoid epidemics swept the volunteer camps and overwhelmed the army's ill-equipped, underfunded Medical Department. At Camp Thomas alone, some 4,400 soldiers were in the hospital on August 15.

Ignorance of how malaria, typhoid, and yellow fever were transmitted accounted in part for the disaster. Volunteers displayed a woeful lack of basic camp sanitation, and too many old-time regular officers left health matters to medical officers whom they ignored and often despised. Intent on equipping the overseas forces, the War Department moved slowly to provide proper supplies to the stateside camps. As letters home and inquisitive reporters at last revealed camp conditions, a storm of protest crossed the nation. Once again, Secretary of War Alger and the War Department took the wrath of an outraged press.

Dodge Commission

In order to defend himself, as it was evident President McKinley was not going to, Alger recommended that the president appoint a commission to examine and report on War Department administration and conduct of the war. McKinley agreed and selected prominent Republican railroad executive and former Civil War general Grenville M. Dodge to head the commission. The Dodge Commission met from October through December 1898, taking testimony from bureau chiefs, officers, and enlisted men and visiting several army camps. McKinley used the commission largely to deflect criticism from his administration but got more than he bargained for when General Miles testified early in December. Miles used the Dodge Commission testimony to exact revenge on McKinley and Alger for ignoring him during the war. The arrogant Miles asserted that the administration used his strategy to win but denied him the credit. Further, he charged, it ignored his advice on camp conditions. Most sensational of all, Miles asserted that the War Department issued chemically tainted beef, both frozen and canned, to overseas troops. The so-called embalmed beef scandal implied willful ignorance if not outright dereliction of duty in the War Department. Many of Miles's assertions were clear fabrications. The commission found no evidence of contaminated food, although all admitted the canned beef was extremely unpleasant to eat. Unfortunately, Miles's unsubstantiated charges factionalized the War Department and generated undeserved publicity. Further, the embalmed beef uproar detracted from the War Department's genuine shortcomings so recently revealed. The Dodge Commission found no corruption in the War Department, although it obliquely criticized Secretary Alger for inefficiency.

Although the Spanish no longer ruled the Philippines, peace did not come easily. U.S. soldiers bombard the Spanish church in Mololos in 1899 in an attempt to rout Emilio Aguinaldo's rebels. (U.S. Military Academy Archives)

SUMMARY AND ANALYSIS

The bitter recriminations echoing from the Dodge Commission hearings reinforced strident yellow press coverage of rampant sickness at Montauk Point and the volunteer camps. Early in 1899, the outbreak of the Philippine Insurrection added to postwar disillusionment that national glory and imperial power did not come so cheaply after all. While an antiimperialist movement appeared briefly in response to the insurrection, serious assessment of the conduct and consequences of the Spanish-American War failed to develop. In less than two decades, an American expeditionary army 10 times the size of the force mobilized in 1898 fought in an overseas war of infinitely greater costs and consequences. In the shadow of World War I, the 1898 conflict faded into obscurity or assumed comic-opera overtones.

The Spanish-American War was, however, not an event to be trivialized. The United States entered the war as a North American continental power of potentially great military strength. It emerged from the conflict in August 1898 having demonstrated a remarkable improvisational capacity to extend its power thousands of miles far from its homeland. However inefficiently, whatever the economic and human costs, the United States used its modest navy and undermanned, poorly managed army to defeat a European power and acquire an overseas empire. In the midst of chaotic mobilization, the McKinley administration sent more than 45,000 men overseas to two theaters of war separated by thousands of miles. It improvised these expeditionary forces and the transport fleets that carried them in just over two months, from mid-May to the end of July. By the end of August, the harried War Department had begun to solve its logistical problems, and supplies, too much too late, were flowing to the mobilization camps. In retrospect, the mobilization, organization, and overseas deployment of the U.S. Army in 1898 was the most historically significant aspect of the war. The United States would repeat the performance on a grander scale in two 20th-century world wars.

McKinley proved to be an effective commander in chief. He utilized military force to achieve his war aims while gaining his larger goal of a short, limited war that kept combat casualties low while effective diplomacy prevented Spain from acquiring formal or informal allies. McKinley found it necessary to direct strategic operations and compel the army and navy to work together. Modern cable communications gave the president the ability to oversee operations in the Caribbean and the Philippines simultaneously. McKinley never lost public support for the war. Public opinion strongly favored a war to free Cuba, and although the president altered his war aims in May to seek permanent cessions from Spain, he managed to retain public backing through Senate approval of the Treaty of Paris. It was an adroit performance.

If the larger war effort—mobilization and strategic conduct—appeared impressive, serious problems developed at the organizational, operational, and tactical levels. Organizational difficulties beset the war effort throughout. From the onset, McKinley found it necessary to coordinate joint army-navy operations as there was neither a formal agency nor any inclination within the two services to do the job. While Commodore Dewey and General Merritt worked well together in Manila, interservice rivalry and jealousy dominated Caribbean joint operations. McKinley personally interceded several times to end bickering between General Shafter and Admiral Sampson, and between Sampson and General Miles. The president had to play the same role with the War Department. Divisions there, between Secretary Alger and Miles, and between Miles and the supply bureaus, weakened the army's efforts continually.

More important, the army's antiquated, decentralized organizational system nearly collapsed under the weight of rapid mobilization and overseas deployment. Shafter's V Corps performance suffered from its formation in late April through its return to the United States in August as a consequence of the army's systemic organizational problems. Whatever Shafter's command abilities might have been, they were insufficient to overcome the logistical disorganization he faced when coupled with the administration's demand that he engage the enemy immediately. The campaigns that Generals Miles and Merritt organized and conducted were far smoother, in large part because they had enough time to plan and prepare.

In contrast to the army, the navy's operational performance appeared highly efficient. For both Dewey and the Sampson-Schley team, quick destruction of enemy squadrons in a day won the navy national praise. The navy held advantages not open to the army. It had a general war plan with which all senior officers were familiar. A portion of the force, the North Atlantic Squadron, had trained in peace as a functioning unit. Above all, a point not lost on supporters of Captain Mahan, the navy fought the war with a force in being, that is, peacetime ships and crews. While the navy in part improvised a portion of its wartime fleet—colliers, auxiliary cruisers, and dispatch boats—the squadrons that fought the Spanish existed prior to the war. The navy's performance was not flawless, as exhibited by its stumbling attempts to locate and blockade Admiral Cervera. During the Manila and Santiago battles, naval gunnery was less than impressive, with only 10 percent of the shots fired finding a target. Nonetheless, given the fact that the navy had not fought enemy ships on the high seas since the War of 1812, it deserved the praise it received.

The U.S. approach to war in 1898 resembled that of 1861. A call for volunteers brought forth more than 100,000 men, but at best they were only partially prepared to fight. Political favorites, notably Leonard Wood and Theodore Roosevelt, won military commissions without regard to their qualifications. The army's officers corps was dominated by veterans who held high command based solely on seniority. Of the important generals (Miles, Shafter, Merritt, and Corbin), Corbin, the adjutant general and not in a field command, was the youngest at age 56. President McKinley could not replace Commanding General Miles, except by court-martial, even though he neither liked nor trusted him. Ultimately, victory came at low cost, but none of the field commanders displayed imaginative operational or tactical leadership. Unlike the Civil War, the Spanish-American conflict did not create army heroes, in part because of its brevity but also because of lackluster individual performances. Roosevelt was the only significant figure to make the most of his battlefield notoriety. A new breed of politician, Roosevelt went to war because he had political ambitions, in contrast to numerous predecessors who became politicians because of their military exploits.

In the war to free the Cubans, the United States came to be the colonial rulers of peoples of color. Quickly abandoning the original Cuban revolutionaries and turning its back on the Filipino insurgents, the McKinley administration set out to tutor both Cubans and Filipinos in the essentials of self-rule. The Cubans won semi-independence in 1902, but their brothers in the Philippines would have to wait nearly a half century. A parallel experience awaited black Americans who took part in the war. Unlike the Civil War experience, blacks fought in the Spanish-American War from the start. All four of the army's black regiments, officered by whites, served in Shafter's V Corps and performed effectively. Black National Guardsmen and other blacks ready to volunteer eventually entered service as well. Five all-black National Guard infantry regiments answered McKinley's second call for volunteers in May: 3d Alabama, 6th Virginia, 3d North Carolina, 23d Kansas, and 8th Illinois, the last three of which were led by black officers. Black guardsmen from Ohio, Indiana, and Massachusetts served in smaller units. In the 6th Massachusetts Volunteer Infantry, which campaigned in Puerto Rico, Company L was the only black outfit to serve as part of a white regiment.

In the 10 years following the war, North Carolina, Alabama, and Virginia purged its guard of black soldiers. Within the army, white officers began to question the use of black regulars as combat soldiers, despite their fine performance during the Indian wars and in Cuba. Roosevelt, who had praised black cavalrymen for their role in charging Kettle Hill, joined the effort by later denigrating the troopers as near cowards. By the onset of World War I, the army adopted a policy to deny blacks a combat role in the American Expeditionary Force. Unlike the Civil War, the Spanish-American War was not a war about freedom and rights but one of conquest and assumption of the so-called white man's burden, unfortunately at home as well as abroad.

4

The Emergence of the United States as a Global Power: 1898–1917

While the United States had been an interested, if only a minor, player in international affairs since the American Revolution, the Spanish-American War is generally accepted as the United States' debut on the world stage. From that summer in 1898 until its entry into World War I in 1917, the United States expanded its role as an international player through trade and diplomacy, often backed by military might. Proponents of a new Manifest Destiny, such as John Burgess, John Fiske, and Josiah Strong, laid the groundwork for this foray into world affairs in the 1880s and 1890s. In studying German nationalism, Burgess concluded that Germanic peoples were particularly adept at creating states. It was their assumed mission to direct the political structuring of what is now called the Third World. Fiske and Strong applied Charles Darwin's biological theory of the survival of the fittest to the life of nations. They suggested that the Anglo-Saxon race had a mission to spread its "civilized" ideals of Christianity and justice to the rest of the world, an attitude popularly called the "white man's burden." At the same time, U.S. businessmen and farmers were starting to look abroad, particularly across the Pacific, for outlets for their surplus production.

Such sociological, religious, and economic rationales for expansion, combined with a renewed sense of patriotism, were synthesized by Alfred Thayer Mahan. In his major study *The Influence of Sea Power Upon History, 1660–1783* (1890), he submitted that the British could not have maintained their national security and built their empire without an active merchant marine backed by a strong navy and strategically located coaling stations. Mahan extrapolated from the British example, asserting that the position of any great nation, including the United States, rested on its foreign commerce. Therefore, he supported the development of domestic production, foreign trade, a strong navy, commercial shipping, and colonies that, under American guidance, would develop into civilized nations while providing commercial markets.

EXPANSION IN THE PACIFIC

With its newfound international outlook, the United States began to expand in areas where it had exerted some influence in the past, particularly among the island groups of the Pacific Ocean. Even before the Spanish-American War, journalists, politicians, and naval experts had seen great strategic importance in the harbor of Pago Pago, Samoa. In the Treaty of 1878, the Samoan king had granted the United States a franchise for a coaling station at Pago Pago. Great Britain and Germany were equally interested in the islands. In the course of the next decade, agents of all three nations jockeyed for advantage in Samoa while causing considerable upheaval among the local population. Finally, in 1889, the United States joined Great Britain and Germany in establishing a three-power protectorate over the islands. This theoretically equitable solution proved to be impractical and unworkable, so in 1899, the United States and Germany divided the archipelago. Germany received the two largest islands and the rest, including Pago Pago, went to the United States. Britain received the Solomon Islands (with the exception of Bougainville) and Savage (Savai'i) Island as compensation.

Pres. William McKinley directed Sec. of the Navy John D. Long to govern and protect the islands. In turn, Long made the commandant of the naval station at Tutuila the civil as well as the military commander of American Samoa and later designated him as governor of the islands. In 1903, the first secretary of native affairs was appointed to direct local government. Police activities were undertaken by the Fita-Fita, a native constabulary trained and commanded by a senior marine noncommissioned officer. While this administration grew and developed, the islands remained under control of the U.S. Navy until 1951, when administration was shifted to the U.S. Department of the Interior.

Hawaii

Of greater importance to the United States than Samoa was the acquisition of Hawaii, then known as the Sandwich Islands. From the early 19th century, American missionaries and whalers were based in Hawaii. As early as 1855, Sec. of State John Marcy negotiated a treaty of annexation with the Hawaiian king, but the Senate, in the face of vigorous opposition from American sugar interests, rejected it. A reciprocity treaty was signed with King Kalakaua in 1875; in 1887, the king gave the United States the exclusive right to use Pearl Harbor as a naval base. That same year, white planters and merchants who were now established in Hawaii forced the king to accept a liberal constitution.

Queen Liliuokalani, who came to the throne in 1891, viewed that document as an attempt to subordinate native Hawaiian interests. In January 1893, she tried to impose a new autocratic constitution. Seeing this as a very serious threat, the white elite rose up against the queen, appealing to the U.S. minister, John L. Stevens, for assistance. On January 16, 150 Marines from the USS *Boston* landed in Honolulu, allegedly to protect U.S. lives and property. The following day, Stevens, on his own initiative, recognized the revolutionary government. Thoroughly intimidated by such a show of force, Lilioukalani abdicated, and on February 1, Stevens declared Hawaii a U.S. protectorate. Although the marines were withdrawn quickly, Rear Adm. John Walker stayed in Hawaii until the provisional government under appointee Sanford Dole (former associate justice, Hawaii Supreme Court) became stable.

Representatives of Dole's government rushed to Washington and negotiated an annexation treaty that was submitted to the Senate in the last days of the Benjamin Harrison administration (March 1893). Despite considerable support for the treaty, succeeding U.S. president Grover Cleveland withdrew it from the Senate and appointed a commission under James Blount to investigate the circumstances of the revolt. Blount discovered that the scheme had only succeeded because Stevens had aided the conspirators. However, it was too late to reinstate the monarchy without the use of force. Congress eventually passed two noninterference resolutions. Plans for annexation waxed and waned for the next four years. Finally, on July 7, 1898, undoubtedly inspired by Commodore George Dewey's victory in the Philippines, Congress passed a treaty of annexation.

Guam and Wake Islands

The Spanish-American War brought several other islands under the American wing. On June 4, 1898, the cruiser USS *Charleston,* Capt. Henry Glass commanding, left Honolulu in convoy with the *City of Pekin,* the *City of Sydney,* and the *Australia,* which were transporting troops to the Philippines. Once at sea, Glass opened his sealed orders and found that the convoy was to proceed to the Ladrones Islands and seize Guam. Situated 3,300 miles west of Honolulu, Guam was well suited as a coaling station. At daylight on June 20, the ships arrived at the island. The *Charleston* entered the harbor at Agana alone and opened fire on Fort Santa Cruz. Twelve shots went unanswered. Shortly afterward, the Spanish officer in charge went aboard the *Charleston* to apologize for not returning the American salute, explaining that he lacked the artillery to do so. Glass informed the stunned officer that it had been no salute; their countries were at war, and the shots had been hostile. On June 22, Glass raised the U.S. flag over Fort Santa Cruz and proceeded to Manila with the 56 Spanish marines of Guam's garrison and Governor Marina aboard. They left no official authority in the island.

The early U.S. administration of Guam was a rather slipshod affair. In January 1899, the USS *Bennington* arrived at Guam and Cmdr. Edward D. Taussig formally took possession of the island for the United States as called for in the Treaty of Paris (1899). On February 1, he raised the U.S. flag at Agana, but the *Bennington* departed on February 20, leaving a local U.S. resident as acting governor. On August 7, the USS *Yosemite* arrived at Guam. Capt. Richard P. Leary, captain of the *Yosemite,* was to establish a naval station and to serve as governor of Guam. With Leary was Maj. Allen C. Kelton of the marines, with 123 troops to garrison the naval station. Despite early difficulties with irregular supply and a typhoid epidemic, the marines worked with the native Chamorro population and gradually established a regular station. The island remained under the administration of the U.S. Navy for the next 50 years.

Similarly, Wake Island came under the aegis of the United States on July 4, 1898, when the army's Maj. Gen. Francis V. Greene, on his way to reinforce Dewey in the Philippines, stopped at the deserted island. The *Bennington* visited Wake in the summer of 1899, and Taussig claimed it for the United States. However, unlike the situation at Guam, there was virtually no naval activity on the island until the 1930s.

PHILIPPINE INSURRECTION

Possession of the Philippines came at a much higher price than did that of Guam or Wake. To help rally Filipino support against the Spanish after his stunning initial success at Manila Bay, Dewey allowed the foremost leader of the Philippine independence movement, Emilio Aguinaldo, to return to the islands. While providing no direct support to Aguinaldo, Dewey did give him the impression that the insurgents and the Americans were fighting a common enemy. With the fall of Manila on August 13, 1898, and the armistice between Spain and the United States, the Filipinos expected to receive their independence. Aguinaldo declared a republic with himself as president. He established a provisional capital at Malolos and organized a congress to write a constitution. But in the Treaty of Paris, Spain ceded the Philippines to the United States. The disillusioned insurgents ratified their new constitution, declared an independent Philippine Republic, and shortly thereafter began a bloody war against their new colonial masters.

Fighting erupted in Manila on the evening of Feb. 4, 1899. Maj. Gen. Elwell S. Otis, commanding VIII Corps, quickly committed 12,000 of his 21,000 troops against the 40,000-man Philippine Republican Army. Despite their numerical superiority, the Filipinos were inadequately armed and poorly disciplined. They could not hold out against the mobility and marksmanship of the Americans, who quickly found that the Filipino entrenchments could be breached with flanking attacks. Otis conducted extensive operations around Manila, inflicted more than 3,000 Filipino casualties, and drove the Republican Army from Manila and its environs.

By the end of March, U.S. troops had captured Malolos and Pasig, thus cutting communications between the insurgents in northern and southern Luzon. In April, Otis sent Brig. Gen. Henry W. Lawton south from Manila toward Santa Cruz, and Brig. Gen. Arthur MacArthur moved north from Malolos to San Fernando. During the summer, U.S. troops landed on the islands of Cebu and Negros, but for the most part, Otis's forces consolidated their positions in Luzon and carried out minor operations.

Almost half of the U.S. troops in the Philippines at that time were members of state volunteer units scheduled for demobilization at the end of the war, so Otis was unable to commit the large number of men needed to carry out a sustained campaign against Aguinaldo's forces. The Philippine Insurrection, as it became known, caused Congress to retain the volunteer units until a new army could be raised. The Army Bill of Mar. 2, 1899, provided for a regular army of 65,000 men. It also called for the recruitment of 35,000 volunteers to serve in the Philippines. In general, these units were commanded by professional officers with combat experience. Many of the enlisted men were veterans of the Spanish-American War or the Indian campaigns, so they were well prepared to face both conventional warfare and the guerrilla tactics soon to be employed by the insurgents.

With the arrival of fresh troops in the fall of 1899, Otis launched a three-pronged attack in north-central Luzon. Lawton, on the right, captured San Isidro and moved toward San Fabian on the Lingayen Gulf. MacArthur, in the center, took Tarlac and proceeded to Dagupan, while Brig. Gen. Lloyd Wheaton sailed to San Fabian and moved inland. His men defeated the Filipinos at San Jacinto and linked up with MacArthur at Dagupan. During this campaign, a number of Filipino leaders were killed, vital supplies were destroyed, and Aguinaldo was forced into the hills.

In January 1900, Otis ordered attacks against Aguinaldo's forces in southern Luzon. Wheaton and Brig. Gen. Theodore Schwan moved through Batangas, Laguna, and Tayabas provinces, while Brig. Gen. Walter Kobbe landed his forces in the southeastern provinces of Alby and Sorsogan, driving the defenders into the mountains. A final landing in Ambos Camarines Province by forces under Brig. Gen. James F. Bell effectively eliminated the Republican Army.

With his regular forces dispersed, Aguinaldo attempted to prolong hostilities by engaging in a guerrilla campaign. A clandestine civilian infrastructure supported the irregular forces by paying taxes, hiding weapons, and supplying them with food and shelter. U.S. forces responded with counterinsurgency measures, but President McKinley had directed the army to pacify the islands by winning the respect of the Filipinos, by providing them with individual rights and freedoms, and by pursuing policies of benevolent assimilation. While certainly a humane policy, it seriously restricted the army's actions. General Otis responded by dividing Luzon into departments, with garrisons in a number of towns in each department. Army officers were to establish and guide municipal governments in those towns on the theory that firsthand experience with U.S. principles of justice and equity would lead the Filipinos to abandon the guerrilla cause.

When MacArthur succeeded Otis in May 1900, he continued his predecessor's policies, going so far as to declare a 90-day amnesty period for all guerrillas. But while many officers sympathized with McKinley's principles, they concluded that current conditions demanded military pacification before civil reforms could be implemented. As ambushes and guerrilla attacks continued, MacArthur took a more aggressive approach toward pacification, including the in-

American Possessions in the Pacific, 1860–1910

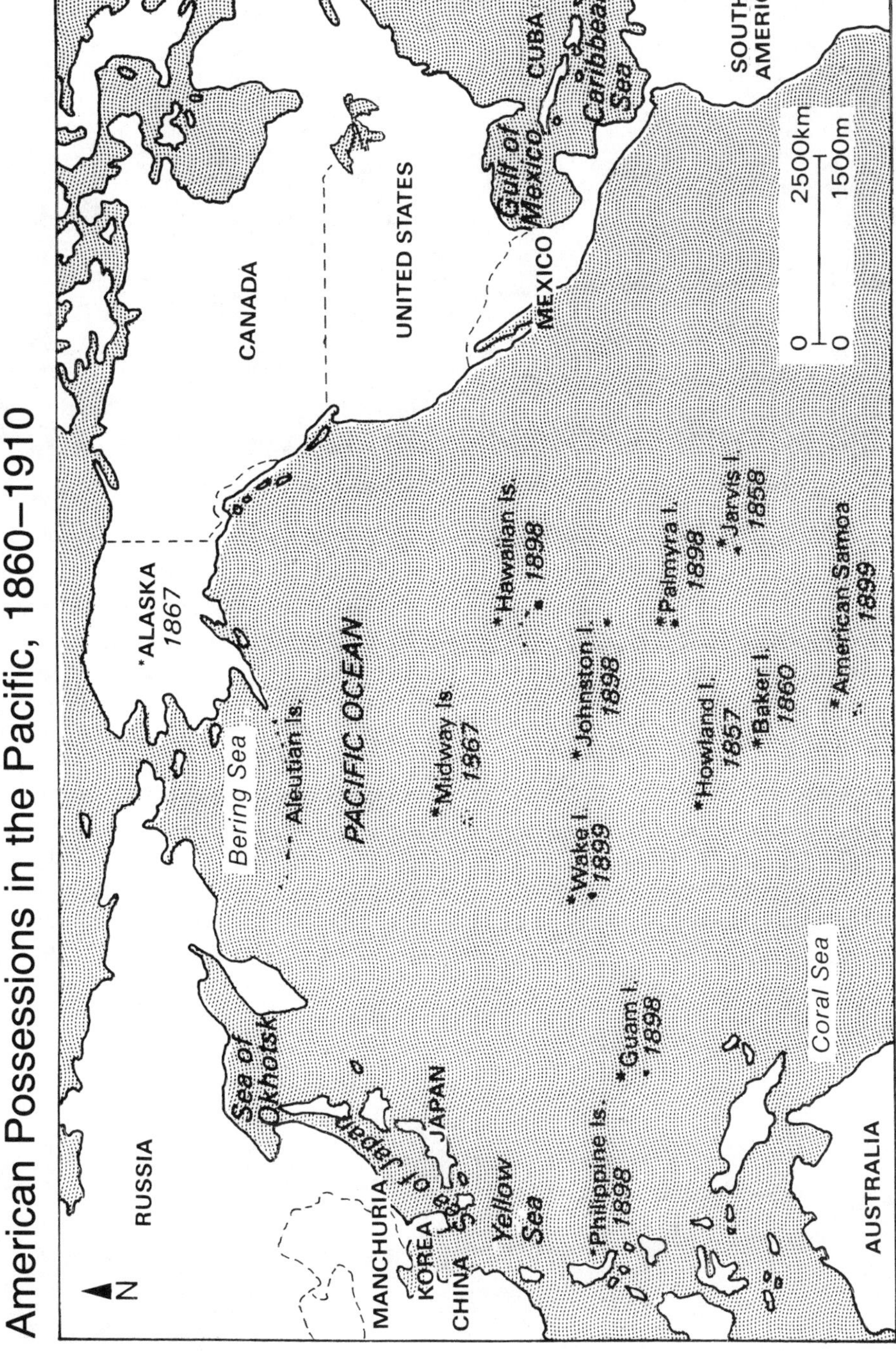

United States possessions are starred and date of aquisition is given.

American troops march through a small town in the Philippines during the insurrection that began in 1899. (U.S. Military Academy Archives)

stitution of martial law, deportations, and a plan to cut off the guerrillas from their urban supporters. The army even took a page from Spanish tactics in Cuba and forced the reconcentration of insurgent towns. In some cases, there was physical abuse of individual Filipinos.

Defeat of the Insurgents

By the end of 1900, the 70,000 U.S. soldiers in the Philippines were placing constant pressure on the insurgents. In March 1901, a party of 84 Filipino scouts and 4 Americans led by Brig. Gen. Frederick Funston captured Aguinaldo at Palanan, thus removing the insurrection's charismatic leader. Aguinaldo's subsequent proclamation, which acknowledged U.S. sovereignty over the islands, made surrender more acceptable to other Filipino commanders such as Juan and Blas Villamor, Mariano Trias, and Juan Cailles. Opposition was now concentrated in Laguna, Tayabas, Batangas, and Samar provinces, and it appeared that pacification would soon be complete.

A major shift toward civil government came in July 1901 when Maj. Gen. Adna R. Chaffee replaced MacArthur and William Howard Taft became civil governor of the Philippines. Troops were ordered to disengage gradually from their civil duties. It became evident, however, that hostil-

U.S. troops repair a low railroad bridge in swampy land in Tarlac, Philippines, in November 1899. (U.S. Military Academy Archives)

Arthur MacArthur (second from the left), *shown here with his staff, served as civil governor of the Philippines in 1900–01.* (U.S. Army Military History Institute)

The U.S. Army Corps of Engineers' bridge-building techniques during the insurrection had to be adapted to the difficult terrain of the Philippines. (U.S. Military Academy)

ities were not over when, on September 28, insurgents massacred Company C, 9th U.S. Infantry, at Balangiga, Samar. Chaffee and his subordinates Brig. Gens. Bell and Jacob H. Smith reacted immediately with draconian campaigns that resulted in many casualties and considerable property damage. Most notorious of these actions was the march of a detachment of marines under Maj. Littleton W. T. Waller across Samar. It was a mission plagued by nearly impassable terrain, swollen rivers, disease, mutiny, and just plain bad luck. Waller had several of the native bearers tried and executed for mutiny. It was an impetuous act (somewhat mitigated by his own serious illness), for which he was court-martialed and acquitted.

Although bloody and unpopular among a vocal segment of the American population, harsh measures seemed to achieve the desired results. By June 1902, the last of the guerrilla leaders had surrendered. Conditions, although not entirely tranquil, were controlled enough for Pres. Theodore Roosevelt to declare that the campaign had come to a successful conclusion.

THE BOXER REBELLION

In the midst of the upheaval in the Philippines, the United States became embroiled in an expedition to China. U.S. merchants had maintained a modest trade with China since the days of the tea clippers, and missionaries of various denominations vied for converts from China's enormous population. European entrepreneurs had been more aggressive than Americans, establishing spheres of influence, setting up concessions, and developing communication and transportation networks. While this expanded trade, it disrupted local commercial patterns, threatened ancient traditions, and resulted in fear and resentment of foreigners by the Chinese. Toward the end of the 19th century, famine and floods throughout China caused tremendous loss of life and further economic dislocation.

Traditionally, the Chinese responded to severe political and economic upheaval by forming secret societies. Sometime in 1897, the I Ho Chuan (the Fists of Righteous Harmony), better known as the Boxers, appeared in Shantung. With their antiforeign, anti-Christian credo and claims of invulnerability, the Boxers quickly spread throughout northern China. Chanting their bloodthirsty slogan "Kill! Burn!," they lashed out at foreigners and Chinese Christians alike, throughout 1898 and 1899. On Jan. 11, 1900, the Dowager Empress Tsu Hsi issued an imperial proclamation supporting the society, and by May 1900, red-sashed Boxers were sabotaging rail and telegraph lines and wandering with impunity through the streets of Peking.

Tientsin Campaign

In a show of support for Americans in China, the USS *Monocacy* sailed to Taku on the Chinese coast in March 1900, and on May 20, the USS *Newark,* commanded by Capt. Bowman H. McCalla, proceeded from Yokohama to Taku. The *Newark* stopped briefly at Nagasaki to coal and take on board Capt. John T. Myers and his 25 men from the marine guard of the USS *Oregon*. The *Newark* joined a number of European warships off the Taku Bar on May 27. In response to a request from James Ragsdale, American consul at Tientsin, McCalla sent Myers and 49 marines ashore at 4:00 A.M. on May 29. Two more landing parties and McCalla himself followed later that day. The 150 Americans marched 4 miles from Taku to the railhead at Tongku. There the authorities would not allow them to make the 30-mile trip to Tientsin by rail, so McCalla chartered a large covered scow to carry his men up the Pei-Ho River to Tientsin. They were the first foreign troops to reach the city. British, French, Russian, Austrian, Japanese, and Italian forces soon joined them.

While troops massed at Tientsin, diplomats in Peking demanded that the Chinese government allow an international force to travel by rail to the capital to reinforce the legations' guards. The Chinese granted permission on May 30, and the next morning, Myers, with 55 men, joined more than 300 European troops for the 90-mile ride to Peking. In a prescient decision, Myers ordered his men to march without baggage, taking instead 20,000 rounds for their rifles and 8,000 rounds for their Colt machine gun.

Looting, burning, and murderous attacks on Chinese Christians increased, and Boxers cut the rail line between Peking and Tientsin on June 6. In a meeting that afternoon, the consuls and senior military officers at Tientsin agreed that Britain's Vice Adm. Sir Edward Seymour would command the combined Western forces. On June 8, after the Boxers cut the telegraph line, the officials met again. When the conference reached an impasse, McCalla reportedly threatened to take unilateral action against the Chinese. Seymour concurred with McCalla, and the others soon decided to join in an expedition to break through to the capital. The first of four trains carrying 2,006 foreign troops in what became known as the Seymour Expedition left Tientsin for Peking at 10:00 A.M. on June 10. The column moved slowly, repairing the line that the Boxers had sabotaged. On the morning of June 18, a large band of Boxers, with units of the Imperial Chinese army, attacked the train near Anting, about 25 miles from Peking. Imperial troops cut the railroad line between the expedition and Tientsin as well. Faced with the overwhelming numerical superiority of the Chinese army, and unable to move ahead or fall back to Tientsin by rail, Seymour reluctantly ordered the expedition to burn the trains and retreat on foot toward Tientsin. They followed the Pei-Ho River, with the wounded, spare stores, and ammunition traveling in a motley assortment of junks and sampans. After a desperate march, the column reached the safety of the Hsi Ku Arsenal, 5 miles from Tientsin, on June 22.

Shortly after the last train pulled out of Tientsin on June 10, the Chinese began to shell the foreign section of the city. The enclave had no real defenses. Only 1,100 soldiers and marines with rifles, side arms, two small cannon, and 12 machine guns remained in the city. Had they been so inclined, the Chinese could have overwhelmed the concession easily. On June 14, Boxers cut both rail and telegraph lines between Tientsin and the coast. The senior naval officers of all the nations represented at Taku met at once and concluded that the first step toward the relief of Tientsin would be to neutralize the forts at Taku and to seize the railroad station at Tongku. The Russian, German, British, Japanese, Italian, and Austrian officers issued an ultimatum to the Chinese commander of the forts at 11:00 A.M. on June 16, demanding that he surrender by 2:00 A.M., June 17. His reply was to open fire on the foreign armada at 12:44 A.M. The polyglot force returned his fire. After four hours of an intense naval barrage, in which the United

States did not participate, the Chinese abandoned the forts, and allied landing parties rapidly occupied them. (Capt. Frederic Wise, captain of *Monocacy,* had orders to protect U.S. interests but to take no offensive action unless first attacked by the Chinese. Wise did not consider the fire from the forts to be directed at his vessel since the United States had not signed the ultimatum, so he moved his ship out of the line of fire.) The Chinese government took the shelling of the Taku forts to be an act of war. It responded by ordering the Imperial army to attack the Seymour Expedition and to lay siege to the international quarter of Teintsin and the legations at Peking.

Immediately after the allied seizure of the Taku forts on June 17, Imperial troops at Tientsin laid down an artillery barrage on the International Settlement. That evening, Herbert Hoover, then a young mining engineer representing a London firm in China, supervised the men of the foreign community and thousands of Chinese Christian refugees as they barricaded the entrances of the settlement with sacks of grain and sugar taken from the godowns (warehouses). Early the next morning, swarms of Boxers assaulted the settlement, which, to their surprise, was now heavily fortified and manned by European troops. The Boxers withdrew, but the Imperial artillery continued to shell the settlement sporadically.

Meanwhile, U.S. Marines from the Philippines, under Colonel Waller, landed at Taku on June 20 and set out by train for Tientsin. After about 15 miles, they found the track demolished and so began to march toward the city. On the road, they linked up with a battalion of Russian soldiers. At 6:30 A.M. on June 21, the combined force ran into 5,000 Imperial troops. After engaging the Chinese for more than an hour, the Americans and Russians retired to a base at Cheng-liang Chang, where they were later joined by a British contingent. Together they advanced about 8 miles on June 22 and forged on the next day through a sandstorm and several serious encounters with Chinese troops to arrive at Tientsin on June 24. Allied troops rested in the settlement until the following morning, when they moved out toward the Hsi-Ku Arsenal to relieve the Seymour Expedition. After evacuating his men, Seymour ordered Japanese and American units to raze the arsenal.

For the next month, Western troops conducted numerous operations against the Chinese in the area, including destroying another arsenal, clearing Boxers from a burned-out section of Tientsin, and patrolling into the countryside. All the while, reinforcements were rushing to China from around the globe. Elements of the 9th Infantry and 325 marines under Col. Robert L. Meade arrived from the Philippines just in time to join the allied assault on the Chinese section of Tientsin on July 13. Later in the month, the 14th Infantry, with Battery B of the 5th Field Artillery, and a regiment of the 6th Cavalry arrived at Tientsin.

U.S. Marines seized control of a section of the Tartar Wall surrounding Peking, smashed the gate with artillery, and effectively ended the Boxer Rebellion in 1900. (U.S. Army Military History Institute)

General Chaffee commanded the combined marine and army forces taking part in the China Relief Expedition.

Relief of Peking

On August 4, the international force of more than 20,000 men began a 10-day trek to relieve the beleaguered legations in Peking. On August 5, Chinese troops attacked the left flank of the Japanese, who led the column. After a fierce six-hour battle, the Japanese, aided by British troops, routed the Chinese from Piet Sang. The following day, U.S. Marines came under small arms and artillery fire and a cavalry charge. A few volleys drove off the Chinese cavalry, and the marines rapidly cleared out small pockets of Boxers from Yangtsun.

Russian troops prematurely forced their way into Peking on August 13. They escaped being cut off only when other allied troops came to their rescue. On August 14, elements of the 14th Infantry and a faction of marines seized a section of the Tartar Wall and provided cover for British troops as they entered the Outer City and relieved the legations. The following day, U.S. marines cleared away barricades from the Chien-men gate, allowing the artillery to take up a position there. A few rounds from their guns smashed the gates to the Forbidden City. For all practical purposes, the Boxer Rebellion was over, and to the many supporters of the U.S. presence in the Philippines, it was vindication of their belief that a military presence in the

Pacific would be important in maintaining and defending the Far Eastern interests of the United States.

MORO WARS

Many of the U.S. troops from the China Relief Expedition returned to the Philippines to find that while pacification efforts were bearing fruit in Luzon, conditions were deteriorating in the southern islands. Early in the Philippine Insurrection, it was decided that the United States would concentrate on suppressing the nationalistic movement in the north. In the south, Brig. Gen. John C. Bates had negotiated a stopgap agreement with the Sultan of Sulu, nominal leader of the Moros, in 1899. According to the Bates Agreement, the sultan recognized U.S. sovereignty. In return, the United States promised to protect the sultan's subjects, pay him an annuity, acknowledge his jurisdiction in criminal cases involving only Moros, respect local religious customs and, by implication, recognize slavery. Despite the agreement, disturbances continued in the south. Unrest centered among the warlike Islamic Moros, a people so ferocious that the Spanish had quietly let them go their own way rather than try to subdue them. The Americans, who were not only foreigners but infidels, provided a new enemy for the Moros, particularly those living around Lake Lanao and north-central Mindanao. In November 1901, Capt. John J. Pershing, with two troops of the 15th Cavalry and three companies of infantry, arrived on Mindanao to win over the Moros. Pershing did gradually gain their trust. With his base at Iligan, he began visiting the sultans in their respective districts and oversaw the construction of roads to connect the many villages. Within a relatively short time, Pershing had won over the Moros along the north shore of the lake. Yet, he could not sway the sultans and *datos* (lesser tribal chiefs) on the southern shore. Ambushes and skirmishes increased. Brig. Gen. George Davis responded by sending 1,200 Americans against the Moros' *cotta,* or fort, at Pandapatan. They took the fort but at a cost of 60 American soldiers dead and many others wounded. Troops then established Camp Vicars on the outskirts of Moro territory.

Pershing was placed in command of the base, and between June 1902 and May 1903, he conducted frequent friendly visits throughout the area, trying to coax and cajole the datos into cooperation. When all else failed, he led his men against the fanatic Moros in their cottas. These were effective expeditions that showed detailed planning as well as Pershing's considerable restraint and marked understanding and respect for the Moros. In a dramatic move, Pershing combined a punitive and an exploratory expedition and made the famous "March Around the Lake." While hostilities did not stop altogether, the march did mark the beginning of a period of greater acceptance of U.S. dominion over the islands.

Members of the Moro constabulary stand at attention on either side of their prisoners, Moro guerrilla fighters, about 1905. (U.S. Army Military History Institute)

Shortly after Pershing returned to the United States in the summer of 1903, the Philippine Commission combined all the areas in which Moros were a majority into a single province and gave the governor broad discretion in dealing with them. Maj. Gen. Leonard Wood became the governor of the Moro province. Wood was completely out of sympathy with the exotic-looking Moros, who were often compared to the American Indian. Wood was particularly determined to eliminate the Moro practice of slavery and end their warrior ways. He was prepared to force them to become a peaceful society. As Wood embarked on his reform program, resistance stiffened and developed into a real guerrilla war. By October 1905, Dato Ali had become such a force that an army expedition of 115 men under Capt. Frank R. McCoy was sent against him. On October 22, they surprised and killed Ali at his cotta near the Malalag River.

Still, the Moros refused to follow Wood's bidding. A large number of them moved to Bud Dajo, the crater of an extinct volcano that provided an excellent defensive position. Early in 1906, rumors to the effect that the U.S. troops were too weak to force them out of Bud Dajo began to spread. The Americans were convinced that this was the beginning of a major insurrection. On March 5, 1906, several battalions of the 6th Infantry under Col. Joseph W. Duncan assaulted the 2,100-foot-high summit. After hacking their way through nearly impassable underbrush and scaling the hill, the Americans stormed the fortified cottas and trenches manned by fanatical defenders. The Americans took Bud Dajo on March 8, at a cost of 18 American and 600 Moro dead.

Pershing's Moro Campaigns

Although only minor disturbances occurred during the next several years, resentment and hostility toward the Americans festered among the Moros. When Pershing returned to the Philippines in 1909, this time as a general in charge of Mindanao, he was distressed by the way that the Moros seemed to have reverted to their barbaric ways. After a year of renewing old acquaintances and rebuilding trust, Pershing concluded that the only way finally to bring peace to the area was to disarm the Moros. He hoped it would stop fanatical assaults against individuals *(juramentado)* and perhaps strengthen the position of weaker tribes who were at the mercy of the more belligerent groups. He carefully worked up to the actual disarmament, issuing the official order on Sept. 8, 1911, although the deadline for turning over weapons was not until Dec. 1, 1911. All the while, he continued to palaver with the datos to coax them into compliance.

Despite his efforts, trouble broke out in October 1911, forcing Pershing to act. On December 3, he sent three parties against the Moros and dispatched five more columns on December 5. The Moros then sent word that they wished to negotiate. The talks dragged on until the Moros began reoccupying Bud Dajo on December 14. Pershing's troops encircled the hill. By December 22, 1,000 Americans were ready to close in on the Moros. Still, Pershing moved slowly, giving the Moros every opportunity to surrender, or at least to send their women and children away. On the morning of December 24, scouts reported to Pershing that Bud Dajo was deserted.

That campaign subdued the Moros for a while, but they still were not completely disarmed or pacified. After two brief skirmishes in January 1913, more than 5,000 Moros, with their wives and children, moved into the fortified positions on Bud Bagsak, another extinct volcano. Tensions mounted throughout the spring. Pershing proceeded with great deliberation, trying to persuade them to return home and to minimize casualties on both sides. Finally, on June 11, a well-coordinated land and amphibious assault by U.S. Army troops and Philippine Scouts began against Bud Bagsak. In hard fighting against well-defended cottas at Languasan, Pujagan, Matunkup, Puyacabao, Bunga, and Bagsak, U.S. troops took Bud Bagsak on June 15, 1913. Moro resistance now gradually petered out.

CARIBBEAN INTERESTS

American actions in the Caribbean, paralleling the thrust of politico-military policy in the Pacific, sought to consolidate the gains that had been made during the Spanish-American War of 1898, which propelled the United States into the world arena. U.S. attention in the Caribbean initially focused on Cuba and Puerto Rico.

Cuba

When the Spanish turned over the island of Cuba to the United States, it was truly in a state of destruction, with no public services and near famine in certain regions. To cope with local conditions, and to prepare the country for self-government as required by the Teller Amendment, the War Department created the Division of Cuba and divided the country into four districts. President McKinley then appointed the army's Maj. Gen. John R. Brooke as the first military governor of Cuba. However, he gave Brooke no specific instructions as to U.S. policy regarding Cuba. Without such guidance, Brooke took a pragmatic approach to his task. His first order of business was to establish a program of food distribution, restore reasonable levels of sanitation, and maintain order. Brooke was quite successful in his relief measures, but he failed to recognize that the military's mandate to prepare the island for self-government was equally important. For the sake of efficiency, he reappointed former Spanish bureaucrats, a politically naive move that angered the Cubans and Americans. McKinley

Dr. Walter Reed, an officer in the Army Medical Corps, determined through research that the Aëdes aegypti *mosquito was the transmitter of yellow fever.* (U.S. Army Military History Institute)

relieved Brooke in December 1899 and replaced him with the dynamic and politically sophisticated Leonard Wood.

A medical doctor by training, Wood pursued the health and educational goals of his predecessor, aggressively supporting public works and hospital construction. After a serious outbreak of yellow fever in Havana in 1900, he created the Yellow Fever Commission and asked Dr. Walter Reed of the Army Medical Corps to head the commission's investigation into the cause of the disease. Together with Drs. Jesse W. Lazear, James Carroll, and Aristides Agremonte, Reed carried out a series of experiments that proved that the *Aëdes aegypti* mosquito transmitted the disease. With the information gained from those experiments, the Medical Corps, under the direction of Maj. William C. Gorgas, destroyed the mosquito breeding grounds and quickly eliminated yellow fever from Cuba.

In addition to his drive to improve living conditions, Wood took an aggressive approach toward preparing Cuba for independence. Unconcerned with offending the old bureaucracy, he replaced more than 90 percent of the government's officials and revamped much of the country's civil procedures. Wood supported the election laws passed in April 1900, and in June of that year, the army supervised the first elections since the war. Another referendum was held in September for a committee to write a new constitution. The document was signed on Feb. 21, 1901. Then on May 28, the Cuban legislature took a major step toward independence when it accepted the Platt Amendment, which granted the United States the right to intervene in Cuba to protect life and property, to preserve liberty and the nation's independence, as well as to aid in the defense of the United States. Once this right of intervention was guaranteed, progress toward independence quickened. Cuba elected its first president, Don Tomás Estrada Palma on December 31, and on May 20, 1902, Wood and the few remaining Americans left Cuba.

Puerto Rico

Puerto Rico was also the scene of fighting during the Spanish-American War, but this 19-day campaign, directed by Nelson A. Miles, Commanding General of the Army, was only a peripheral event of the war. Upon the cessation of hostilities with Spain, the United States established a military government that directed Puerto Rican affairs until Congress passed the Organic Act of 1900 (the Foraker Act). The act established an elected assembly with a council appointed by the president of the United States. This arrangement remained in effect until it was replaced by the Organic Act of 1917 (the Jones Act), which instituted a more responsible government and granted U.S. citizenship to Puerto Ricans.

NAVAL EXPANSION

When Theodore Roosevelt became president in 1901, he brought to the White House his commitment to a "Big Navy" policy. His support of longtime friend and naval advocate Mahan had become a popular sentiment by the turn of the century, as a broad segment of U.S. public opinion began to favor an expanded navy. One of the most vocal and effective promoters of the navy was the Navy League. Made up of financiers, attorneys, exporters, industrialists, retired naval officers, and others interested in fostering U.S. power and prestige, the Navy League brought considerable pressure on Congress when naval matters were debated.

In December 1901, Roosevelt asked Congress for an eight-percent increase in naval appropriations, and in 1903, Congress approved a program that called for laying down two capital ships a year. By 1905, naval expenditures had risen to $117,550,308 from $55,953,078 in 1900 and

Congress had authorized construction of 10 battleships, 4 armored cruisers, and 17 other vessels. Then, in 1905, Roosevelt called for a respite from this frenetic building program, requesting only the replacement of obsolete vessels and the construction of 1 new battleship a year.

But events conspired against this proposed moderation. An exacerbation of anti-Japanese sentiment in California made war with Japan seem like a realistic possibility, so the U.S. presence in the Pacific needed to be maintained and strengthened. More important, in December 1906, the British commissioned the first "all-big-gun" battleship, the HMS *Dreadnought*. Displacing 18,110 tons and carrying 10 12-inch guns in five turrets, its main battery firepower was 2.5 times greater than that of any other battleship. Even the new *Virginia* class battleships of the United States, which displaced 14,948 tons and were armed with 4 12-inch, 8 8-inch, and 12 6-inch guns, had been made obsolete.

This combination of diplomatic and technological challenges reinvigorated Roosevelt, and in December 1907, he proposed construction of 4 all-big-gun battleships, precipitating a bitter debate in Congress. Supporters of the president insisted that the increase was the only way to maintain the United States' naval position among the powers, to deter aggression, and to maintain and protect U.S. foreign commercial interests. Opponents scoffed at the notion that a large navy would deter war. They maintained that it only stimulated arms races, which could lead to economic ruin. They also suggested that the natural security provided by the Atlantic and Pacific oceans made such a major building program unnecessary. Ultimately, Congress authorized construction of two *Delaware* class, all-big-gun battleships and did so again in the 1908–09 session. Yet, construction of other classes such as cruisers and destroyers failed to keep up with the increase in battleships, and the United States arrived at the eve of World War I still lacking those essential elements of an effective navy.

Great White Fleet

One of Roosevelt's most dramatic moves with respect to the navy was his decision to send the battleship fleet on a round-the-world cruise. It was done in part to impress the Japanese, who had recently decimated the Russian fleet at Tsushima, as well as to gain further favorable press that could influence future congressional appropriations. Sixteen battleships, known as the Great White Fleet, sailed from Hampton Roads in December 1907 with Robley D. Evans in command.

The 14-month tour was a technological triumph and a major diplomatic success. The Japanese invited the fleet to call at Yokohama and welcomed the Americans with wild enthusiasm, a reaction that went a long way toward assuaging strained relations between the two nations. In Australia, too, the Americans were the men of the hour, and in the Middle East and Europe, the fleet was greeted as tangible proof of U.S. power and goodwill. By February 1909, when the ships sailed back up the Elizabeth River, the cruise had provided the navy with invaluable experience. It had also persuasively illustrated the need for the construction of U.S. yards and bases overseas.

THE PANAMA CANAL

Since 1898, a major argument for naval expansion was the need for a capability to defend the United States' new Pacific possessions. The difficulty of maintaining a Pacific presence had been graphically illustrated by the heroic dash of the *Oregon* around Cape Horn to Cuba during the Spanish-American War. The trip took 68 days. Clearly, the United States could not defend its insular possessions with a fleet that might require two months to reach them. One possibility, quickly rejected because of economic and political concerns, was the construction of independent battle fleets for the Atlantic and the Pacific. The other alternative was to build a transisthmian canal that would increase the efficiency of the navy. Roosevelt came to office convinced of the necessity of building such a canal.

The idea of a transisthmian canal was not a new one. In 1850, the United States and Great Britain negotiated the Clayton-Bulwer Treaty, which required joint Anglo-American control and the complete neutrality of an unfortified canal. But neither country made a serious attempt at construction. By the turn of the century, conditions had changed drastically, and in February 1900, the United States and Great Britain joined in the Hay-Pauncefote Treaty, which superseded the Clayton-Bulwer agreement. The United States could now build, fortify, own, operate, and defend an isthmian canal. Proponents of both a Nicaraguan and a Panamanian route now began intense lobbying campaigns.

Eventually, the administration concluded that Panama, then a province of Colombia, offered the best route for an transisthmian canal and opened talks with the Bogotá government. However, when the United States refused to increase the payment stipulated in the agreement, the Colombian government rejected the Hay-Herrán Treaty and the project collapsed. But Panamanians—then in Washington, D.C., to lobby for a canal—inferred from their discussions with officials there that, in light of the failure of the treaty, a Panamanian revolt against Colombia might receive U.S. support.

Panamanian Independence

That implication spurred local nationalists to enlist the support of Gen. Victoriano Huerta and the Panama Battalion, a unit of the Colombian army stationed at Panama

City, in a plot against Colombia. When reports of a conspiracy reached Bogotá, the government sent an army regiment to Colón, but railroad authorities there refused to transport the troops to Panama City. Officials did, however, allow the two commanding generals to travel to Panama City, where they intended to take command of the Panama Battalion and arrest Huerta. To their surprise, members of the battalion placed them under arrest immediately upon their arrival at the barracks. The renegade battalion then seized Panama City, and on Nov. 3, 1903, leading rebels proclaimed Panamanian independence.

Although there had been no fighting at Colón, the marine guard from the USS *Nashville* landed early the next morning, ostensibly to protect U.S. lives and property. The USS *Dixie,* having been diverted from fleet maneuvers at Culebra, arrived at Colón on November 5 with a marine battalion under Maj. John A. Lejeune. The marines were under orders, based on the Treaty of 1846, to prevent any troops from approaching within five miles of the rail line or interfering with the transit of the isthmus.

The United States recognized the new Republic of Panama on November 6. There was virtually no local unrest, and Colombia seemed resigned to the loss of the province. Yet, U.S. officials believed the stability of the area to be so important to any future canal project that the marines remained on the isthmus. Lejeune's men went into camp at Emperador, site of an old French Canal Company installation, and marines continued to land in Panama throughout the winter of 1903. On Jan. 3, 1904, Brig. Gen. Commandant George F. Elliott arrived and organized the marines into a provisional brigade of two regiments. There was actually little for them to do, and they devoted most of their energy to topographical surveys and studies for the defense of a canal and Panama City. By February 1904, it was clear that Panamanian independence was secure, so Elliott withdrew most of the marines, leaving Lejeune's battalion to guard U.S. interests.

Immediately after the uprising, the Panamanian government appointed Philippe Bunau-Varilla, one of the financiers of the revolt and Panama's chief lobbyist in Washington, as minister plenipotentiary to the United States. By November 18, he and Sec. of State John Hay had concluded the Hay-Bunau-Varilla Treaty. According to its provisions, the United States permanently leased a 10-mile-wide zone from Panama for $10,000,000, with annual payments of $250,000. The treaty gave the United States extraordinary rights of sovereignty within the Isthmian Canal Zone in return for a guarantee of Panamanian independence.

Col. George W. Goethals, charged with planning and carrying out the construction of the Panama Canal, reviews marine workers stationed at the canal. (U.S. Military Academy Archives)

The upper Gatun locks, shown during construction in 1908–11, are part of a series of locks that lift ships from the Atlantic coast to Gatun Lake, or that lower ships from Gatun Lake to the Atlantic coast. (U.S. Army)

Canal Construction

Sanitary conditions in Panama presented perhaps the greatest challenge to construction of the canal. The isthmus was rife with yellow fever, bubonic plague, and malaria. From 1904 to 1906, Colonel Gorgas, who had eliminated yellow fever from Cuba, directed the draining of swamps, clearing brush and improving sanitary facilities to destroy disease-carrying mosquitoes and rats.

While Gorgas cleaned up the isthmus, Congress concluded that a canal with locks would be cheaper and faster to build than would a sea-level canal. In 1906, Roosevelt sent a civilian commission to Panama to direct construction, but by early 1907, he had become impatient with the rate of construction and the discord among commission members. In an attempt to speed construction, Roosevelt appointed Col. George W. Goethals as chairman of the Isthmian Canal Commission. A 25-year veteran of the Army Corps of Engineers, Goethals was the virtual czar of the Canal Zone, working to solve serious engineering and logistical problems.

Construction included erecting Gatun Dam across the Chagres River, creating Gatun Lake, and building the three locks. The most difficult project was the excavation of the Gaillard Cut, from which 211,000,000 cubic yards of dirt and rock were removed. At the height of the work, more than 43,000 men, mostly from the British West Indies,

Pres. Theodore Roosevelt, on an inspection tour of Panama Canal construction sites, runs a steam shovel at Culebra Cut (later named Gaillard Cut) in 1906. (Library of Congress)

worked on the canal. The gargantuan project was completed in 1914.

CARIBBEAN BASIN

With the Canal Zone now a vital part of U.S. defense planning, the need to protect it meant that the United States would take a more active role in events in the Caribbean. In the aftermath of an intervention by Germany and Great Britain in Venezuela over that country's foreign debt, Roosevelt sought to prevent any further European adventures in the Western Hemisphere. Basing the so-called Roosevelt Corollary on the Monroe Doctrine, and the traditional aim of protecting the United States, Roosevelt acknowledged the right of one nation to intervene in another in the case of flagrant abuses. But he stated that should intervention become necessary in the Western Hemisphere, it would be up to the United States, not a European nation, to act. In effect, he made the United States the policeman of the Caribbean.

Dominican Republic

It was not long before Roosevelt invoked his corollary. During 1903–04, a series of destructive civil wars plagued the Dominican Republic. Ships from the U.S. Atlantic Squadron periodically patrolled the coast during the unrest, and in January 1904, Cmdr. Albert C. Dillingham of the USS *Detroit* landed marines to protect the large foreign populations at Sousa and Puerta Plata. Then on February 1, rebels in Santo Domingo fired on a launch from the USS *Yankee,* killing the launch's engineer. In response to this assault, the cruiser USS *Columbia* arrived at Santo Domingo on February 8. Lt. Cmdr. Marcus L. Miller, captain of the *Columbia,* concluded an agreement with the rebels for the use of docks by foreign vessels. However, when the USS *New York* tried to land on February 11, it came under fire. The Americans responded by landing two battalions of marines and seamen, from the *Columbia* and the *Newark,* under a barrage from the *Newark*'s guns. The troops returned to their ships that night, having made their point. The rebels abided by the agreement.

Besides threatening foreign lives, the anarchy in the Dominican Republic was destroying the economy and causing serious concern among foreign investors. There was some talk of the United States annexing the country, or of establishing a naval base at Samana Bay. Roosevelt, showing admirable restraint, would have none of these suggestions. However, he was determined that there would be no foreign intervention. The solution was to find a way for the Dominican Republic to meet its foreign obligations. At the suggestion of the Dominican president, Carlos Morales, the two governments negotiated a treaty under which the United States would appoint the collector of Dominican customs and the national finance director. Forty-five percent of customs revenues would be applied to current government expenses, with the remainder placed in a trust fund to service the debt and cover the cost of the receivership. Roosevelt submitted the agreement to the U.S. Senate in February 1905.

Anticipating delays in its passage, the two nations implemented the agreement under a modus vivendi based on the terms of the treaty. Under the receivership, the Dominican debt was scaled back from $32,000,000 to $17,000,000. A new issue of $20,000,000 worth of 50-year bonds would fund the adjusted debt. The plan worked well, ushering in a period of unusual stability and prosperity for the country and eliminating the threat of European intervention. The Senate finally ratified the treaty in 1907.

Cuban Intervention

Shortly after the Dominican modus vivendi went into operation, Roosevelt found it necessary to send troops back to Cuba. The December 1905 Cuban election was fraught with corruption and by the summer of 1906, the Liberal party was in revolt against Palma's government. Palma requested that two U.S. warships come to Cuba. Roosevelt reluctantly ordered the USS *Des Moines* and the USS *Tacoma* to Cuban waters because he did not want the habit of revolution to take hold. As the crisis deepened, more ships arrived off Havana. On Sept. 13, 1906, the U.S.

chargé d'affaires, Joseph Sleeper, without instructions from Washington, requested that troops be sent ashore; 130 men from the USS *Denver* then landed. By the following morning, Sleeper had received word that the United States would not intervene militarily unless the commander on the scene deemed it absolutely imperative, so the troops reembarked.

The short landing had a calming effect in Havana, but the situation deteriorated steadily in the western part of the country. On September 14, Capt. William F. Fullam, captain of the USS *Marietta,* sent 33 men ashore at Hormiguero and Soledad to protect U.S. interests, and on September 15, 38 men landed near the Constancia plantation. On September 18, 50 marines landed from the *Dixie* at Cienfuegos and 25 marines reinforced the guard at Soledad. More marines moved into Palmira and Sagua la Grande on September 25, while others provided a special guard for the treasury in Havana.

In the meantime, Roosevelt had sent Secretary of War Taft and Asst. Sec. of State Robert Bacon to help mediate a settlement between the Liberals and Moderates. Taft and Bacon arrived in Havana on September 19 and quickly concluded that the election had indeed been fraudulent. They recommended that new elections be held, but Palma refused to remain as a caretaker while new elections were arranged. He and his cabinet resigned during a session of Congress on September 28, leaving Cuba without a government. After checking with Roosevelt, Taft issued a proclamation taking control of Cuba in the name of the United States as provided in the Platt Amendment. Taft became the provisional governor and ordered the occupation of all trouble spots throughout the island. That same day, a provisional brigade of 2,000 marines commanded by Colonel Waller landed at Havana. In about two weeks, they had disarmed both Liberal forces and the government's Rural Guard. Army units led by General Funston began arriving on October 10, and on October 13, Brigadier General Bell assumed command of the 5,600-man Army of Cuban Pacification.

Also arriving in Cuba was Charles Magoon, named by Roosevelt to be governor of Cuba. Not terribly imaginative, Magoon was in constant communication with Taft. On December 3, he prorogued the Cuban congress and assumed legislative responsibilities. U.S. Army officers quickly took on civil as well as military duties. In fact, by the end of the occupation in 1909, nearly 60 U.S. military officers were guiding Cuba's legal, medical, political, and technical establishments. On Dec. 24, 1906, Magoon appointed an Advisory Law Commission. Headed by Col. Enoch Crowder, the commission wrote laws on elections, the judiciary, and the civil service. Under the direction of the occupying forces, the Cuban congress passed legislation reforming all aspects of government and public service. The commission also set up the Central Election Board, again under Crowder, and supervised new elections in November 1908. José Miguel Gómez became the new president of Cuba, and the last of the occupation forces were withdrawn by Jan. 29, 1909.

U.S. troops returned to Cuba again four years later. The uprising in 1912, the so-called Colored Revolt, was due in large part to the fact that since the 1906 revolt, much of Cuba's black population had felt alienated from the governing process. They organized the Independent Party of Cuba, led by Juan Maso Parra, and took up arms against the government in May 1912. Gómez quickly crushed the rebellion except in Oriente Province. U.S. Sec. of State Philander C. Knox was deeply concerned by the events and warned Gómez that U.S. lives and property must be protected. When Gómez was unable to end the outbreak in Oriente, Knox informed the Cuban government that the United States would land troops, although it should not be considered an intervention. On May 31, a provisional brigade of marines under Col. Lincoln Karmany landed at Daiquiri and moved into the country to protect sugar plantations and mines in the interior. Order was gradually restored, and the marines pulled out late in the summer of 1912.

Nicaraguan Intervention

Cuba was not the only area of U.S. intervention during the early 20th century. On Oct. 10, 1909, a group of prominent Nicaraguans led by Juan J. Estrada, Adolfo Díaz, and Emiliano Chamorro Vargas revolted against Pres. José Santos Zelaya. The rebellion began near Bluefields on the eastern coast of Nicaragua and gradually spread across the Sierra mountains to the western section of the country. Zelaya, a brutal and corrupt dictator, had spent much of his 16-year regime antagonizing or openly fighting with his Central American neighbors. He was also in disfavor with the United States, having flouted the provisions of the 1907 Central American treaties, maintained an offensive attitude toward the U.S. representative in Managua, tampered with official diplomatic communications, and refused to discuss the claims of several U.S. firms against his government.

Relations deteriorated further when his troops captured two Americans, Leonard Croce and Leroy Canon, who were serving as officers in Chamorro's army. Against all advice, Zelaya ordered their execution rather than incarcerating them as prisoners of war. Calling Zelaya a "blot on the history of Nicaragua," Knox severed relations with Nicaragua on Dec. 1, 1909. That same day, the Navy Department organized the Nicaraguan Expeditionary Brigade. The brigade arrived at Cristobal, Canal Zone, on December 12 and proceeded immediately to Balboa, where they embarked aboard the USS *Buffalo,* bound for Corinto.

In mid-December, it became clear to Zelaya that he would not be able to suppress the revolt. He resigned in favor of Dr. José Madriz on December 16 and accepted asylum in Mexico. With Zelaya's departure, the situation improved markedly, and only a few parties of marines and sailors ever went ashore.

The marines aboard the *Buffalo* returned to Panama on Mar. 22, 1910, but the fighting between rebels and forces loyal to the government continued in the area around Bluefields. On May 16, Cmdr. William W. Gilmer, captain of the USS *Paducah* then off Bluefields, issued a proclamation to government and rebel forces alike forbidding any fighting within the city limits. He also requested more troops to enforce his orders. In response, the Navy Department ordered 200 marines from Camp Elliott in the Canal Zone to proceed to Bluefields. The marines, under Maj. Smedley D. Butler, arrived on May 30. Butler issued another proclamation reaffirming Gilmer's policy.

A major issue was control of the Bluefields custom house. In the spring of 1910, Estrada seized it and financed his revolt from its revenues. However, on May 27, Madriz's army reoccupied the bluff and the custom house. Estrada's forces, which still controlled the city, insisted that duties on goods bound for Bluefields be paid to them in the city. Madriz demanded that they be paid at the custom house as usual. The U.S. government was not about to allow a double levy or to decide in favor of Madriz, who appeared to be carrying on in Zelaya's footsteps. Therefore, Washington insisted that since the goods in question were bound for Bluefields, duties should be paid to the Estrada faction, which controlled the city itself.

During their time ashore, the marines kept order in the town, supervised sanitary improvements, and rebuilt the hospital and market. They made virtually no contact with Nicaraguan forces. On August 23, Managua fell to Estrada's troops, and he was inaugurated as president on August 30. The marines pulled out of Bluefields on September 4 and returned to Panama.

Still, all was not serene in Nicaragua. Zelaya's followers were not reconciled to their new status as "outs," and members of Estrada's own party felt that he should distribute the spoils of office more aggressively. Others were displeased with the president's acceptance of new financial agreements with the United States. Street fighting broke out in Managua when Estrada attempted to fire his insubordinate minister of war, Gen. Luis Mena. To keep the peace, Elliott Northcott, U.S. minister in Managua, prevailed upon Estrada to resign in favor of Vice President Díaz.

Estrada's departure proved but a temporary palliative. In the summer of 1912, Mena, supported by Gen. Benjamin Zeledon, withdrew to Masaya in defiance of the government. When revolutionary troops seized the Lake Managua steamships that belonged to the U.S.-owned railroad company, the U.S. government appealed to Díaz for protection. Díaz countered with his own plea for assistance, with which the U.S. government complied. A token force of 100 seamen from the USS *Annapolis* arrived in Managua from Corinto on August 4, while 353 men, again commanded by Butler, rushed to Corinto from Panama. On August 14, three companies of marines and 80 seamen boarded trains for Managua, where they arrived the next day. That afternoon, George F. Weitzel, the new U.S. minister to Nicaragua, composed a note to Mena demanding the immediate return of all U.S. property seized by rebel forces. The reply was negative.

The 1st and 2d marine battalions of the 1st Provisional Regiment under Col. Joseph H. Pendleton joined Butler's troops in Managua on September 6. Pendleton took command of U.S. forces ashore and ordered Butler to open the rail line from Managua to Granada. All went smoothly until the train carrying Butler and three companies of marines approached La Barranca, a hill near Masaya, where Zeledon's forces were besieged by government troops. Butler arranged for a conference between Zeledon and Pendleton, and later with Rear Adm. William H. H. Southerland. After several days of talks, Zeledon agreed to allow the marines to cross his lines, but when they clattered into Masaya on September 19, Liberal troops ambushed them. Their train roared out of the city and finally proceeded on to Granada. At San Blas, just outside the city, Butler told representatives of the ailing General Mena that he would attack Granada if the general did not surrender. Mena acquiesced and was allowed to go into exile in Panama.

Marines now controlled the entire railway with the exception of Zeledon's stronghold in the Barranca-Coyatepe hills, and the cities of Masaya and Leon. On October 2, government troops joined marines in shelling the hills for several hours. At 5:15 the next morning, marines and Nicaraguans stormed the hills and within 40 minutes controlled them both. Government troops then fell on Masaya and engaged in an episode of carnage and looting, while Leon, the last Liberal stronghold, surrendered to U.S. forces, thus ending the revolt. With the uprising over, most of the marines left Nicaragua for Panama in November 1913, although more than 100 remained, ostensibly to guard the U.S. legation but more important to support Díaz's Conservative regime.

Conflict in Mexico

Units of the U.S. Army had begun to move into the Canal Zone in 1911, and by 1914, the last of the marines left Panama aboard the USS *Minnesota* to join elements of the Atlantic Fleet off the east coast of Mexico. Mexico had been torn by civil strife since the 1911 resignation of strongman Porfirio Díaz, president of that country for 30 years. On Feb. 18, 1913, two weeks before Woodrow Wilson's inauguration, the shrewd, hard-bitten Huerta overthrew Francisco Madero, the legitimate president of Mexico, who was shot two days later while allegedly trying to escape. Wilson feared that to recognize Huerta would be to encourage coups d'etat throughout Latin America.

William Jennings Bryan, Pres. Woodrow Wilson's secretary of state (1913–15), urged increased U.S. control in the Caribbean as a safeguard for the Panama Canal. (Library of Congress)

Although the United States traditionally recognized de facto governments, Wilson insisted that he would not recognize a "government of butchers."

He developed a plan whereby the United States would negotiate an armistice between Huerta and his opponents, the Constitutionalists led by Gen. Venustiano Carranza and Álvaro Obregón, pending new elections. To deliver the proposal, Wilson decided to operate outside regular diplomatic channels. He appointed John Lind, former governor of Minnesota and longtime friend of Sec. of State William Jennings Bryan, as his special agent. While Lind was a man of exceptional character, he spoke no Spanish, was anti-Catholic, and had no prior diplomatic experience—circumstances that virtually guaranteed the mission's failure. Indeed, Huerta refused to meet with Lind and rejected the U.S. proposal. In a speech to a joint session of Congress on Aug. 27, 1913, after the Mexican rebuff, the scholarly Wilson declared a complete embargo on all arms shipments from the United States to Mexico. Nevertheless, Huerta continued his struggle against the Constitutionalists. The two presidents had arrived at a real "Mexican standoff."

As part of his policy, Wilson ordered ships from the Atlantic Fleet to the Mexican coast. The vessels shuttled between Veracruz and the port of Tampico, 300 miles to the north. At Tampico, on Apr. 10, 1914, a Huertista officer arrested the paymaster and crew of a whaleboat who had gone ashore to purchase gasoline for one of the *Dolphin*'s motor launches. Gen. Ignacio Moralos Zaragoza, commandant of Tampico, quickly ordered the men released. He then sent a personal apology, along with the information that the offending officer was in custody, to Rear Adm. Henry T. Mayo, commander of U.S. forces at Tampico. However, Mayo found Zaragoza's expression of regret inadequate and demanded a 21-gun salute to the U.S. flag. After much delay, the Mexicans refused to perform the salute without assurances that it would be returned by an American ship.

While diplomats and military men haggled over a point of honor, the *Ypiranga,* a Hamburg-American Line steamship loaded with 200 Remington machine guns and 15,000,000 rounds of ammunition for Huerta's troops, approached Veracruz in direct violation of the embargo. To prevent the landing of those arms, Wilson ordered Rear Adm. Frank F. Fletcher, commander of all U.S. forces in Mexican waters, to seize the custom house at Veracruz. At 11:12 A.M., April 21, the first detachment of marines scrambled into the USS *Prairie*'s whaleboats and headed for shore. Marines and sailors from all the U.S. ships in the harbor soon followed. The Veracruzanos surprised the Americans by taking offense when armed men rushed into their city. Although most of the Mexican regular army had withdrawn from the city, a few remaining individuals, along with civilians and cadets from the Naval Academy, put up a stiff, if disorganized, resistance. Such serious opposition forced Fletcher to order the occupation of the entire city. By nightfall, 1,200 U.S. military men were ashore.

Early on April 21, Fletcher ordered all but one of the vessels at Tampico to proceed at once to Veracruz. More marines landed in the early hours of April 22. In house-to-house fighting, the marines gained control of the city by nightfall, but serious sniper fire continued for several days. Lieutenant Colonel Lejeune took command of forces ashore on April 22. He consolidated his position and established a perimeter as far from the city as the Veracruz-Vegara Road and the pumping stations at Tejar and El Gato. In light of continued sniping, Fletcher declared martial law and instituted a curfew on April 26. By April 28, the firing had stopped, and he lifted the curfew.

That same morning brought the welcome arrival of the army's 5th Reinforced Brigade, Funston commanding. The soldiers landed at once, and Funston took command of all ground forces. They found an orderly, quiet city. The marines began to withdraw on May 1, although Funston's men remained in Veracruz until November 23.

Behind the scenes, there was a flurry of activity to extricate the two countries from their dilemma. The so-called ABC powers—Argentina, Brazil, and Chile—

U.S. troops fire at the enemy at Veracruz, Mexico, in 1914. (U.S. Army Military History Institute, Marvin C. Hepler Collection)

proposed joint mediation of the affair under their offices at Niagara Falls in May 1914. Huerta adamantly rejected most of the proposals. The conference did not result in an evacuation of Veracruz, nor in an end to the internecine struggle within Mexico. Eventually though, Huerta was unable to hold out against Carranza, and in late July, he went into exile. Carranza assumed the presidency on August 20.

Haitian Intervention

While conditions in Mexico seemed to improve, the situation in the island republic of Haiti was approaching anarchy. Cacos, rugged northern hill dwellers who were peasants and part-time mercenaries, were in nearly constant revolt against a series of rapidly changing but uniformly degenerate governments in the capital of Port-au-Prince. In 1914, the Haitian government missed several interest payments on its European debt, and the lenders, particularly Germany, began to use aggressive tactics to collect the delinquent funds. Concerned that internal disorders might lead to full-scale European intervention and prodded by Americans who were concerned about their investments, Secretary Bryan proposed a customs agreement between the United States and Haiti. However, the current Haitian government fell before negotiations were complete.

After a coup in the spring of 1915 placed Jean V. G. Sam in office, President Wilson sent John F. Fort and Charles C. Smith to Haiti to negotiate a plan to stabilize conditions in that country. They, too, failed, and Sam was toppled on July 27, 1915, in one of Haiti's bloodiest coups. Rear Adm. William B. Caperton, commander of the Cruiser Squadron, Atlantic Fleet, proceeded to Port-au-Prince aboard the USS *Washington,* arriving on July 28. A force of 340 marines and sailors landed at Port-au-Prince immediately. The admiral requested reinforcements, and on August 4, Col. Eli K. Cole and the 2d Marines aboard the USS *Connecticut* arrived at Port-au-Prince.

In an attempt to establish some semblance of local civilian rule, Caperton and Capt. Edward L. Beach met with Dr. Rosalvo Bobo, leader of the current revolution, and Philippe S. Dartiguenave, president of the Haitian Senate, on August 8. Dartiguenave appeared to be the more tractable of the two, so on August 12, with the backing of the United States, the National Assembly elected him president of Haiti. Three days later, the 1st Marines and its headquarters staff under Colonel Waller landed in Port-au-Prince.

From the first, Caperton wanted to disarm the Cacos peacefully, and some progress toward that goal was made in and around the capital. But northern Haiti, particularly the Cap Haitien district and the area geographically bounded by Grande Rivière, Fort Liberté, and Ouanaminthe, was in turmoil. On September 20, Cacos ambushed a marine unit patrolling south of Cap Haitien and attacked the detachments that went to their aid. Marines flushed small bands of the peasant/rebels out of Quartier Morin, drove them

U.S. Marine scouts used motorcycles to patrol Haiti in 1915. (U.S. Army Military History Institute, Marvin C. Hepler Collection)

out of Gonaïves, and chased Cacos from Haut-de-Cap, Grande Rivière, and Bahon. On the evening of September 24, about 400 Cacos ambushed a patrol of marines fording Grande Rivière. At daybreak, three squads drove the Cacos from their stronghold at Fort Dipitie and burned it to the ground.

On September 29, Waller concluded an agreement to disarm the Cacos with two of their generals, but the cease-fire lasted only a few weeks. The marines then redoubled their patrolling and pacification efforts. Late in October, a reconnaissance party stumbled across old Fort Rivière, where a large band of Cacos had taken refuge. On November 17, Butler took three companies of marines and the landing party from the *Connecticut* back up Montaigne Noire, and in the Battle of Fort Rivière, they drove out or killed the Caco defenders and razed the citadel.

Violence erupted again in Port-au-Prince in January 1916 with a coup attempt against the Dartiguenave government. A handful of marines and Haitian gendarmes drove off the attackers, and by January 16, all the leaders were in custody. At this time, the Americans began turning over the job of peacekeeping to the Gendarmerie d'Haiti, a national police force that was trained and officered by the U.S. Marines.

The denouement of the Caco rebellion began on Sept. 1, 1916, when Butler took 100 gendarmes and marines on a trek through northern Haiti to the Dominican border. They were searching for a few die-hard Cacos and arms and ammunition supposedly belonging to the Dominican bandit Celidiano Pantilion. On that march, they covered 406 miles through jungles and over mountains. In effect, that marked the end of the rebellion, for, although there were occasional acts of violence against the marines, there was no further organized resistance until 1918. During that interregnum, the marines embarked on impressive public works programs, including the building of schools and markets, the paving of roads, the extension of public utilities, and the improvement of sanitation.

Second Dominican Intervention

Concern over security at the Haitian-Dominican border was prompted by renewed upheaval in the Dominican Republic. The 1911 assassination of Pres. Ramón Cáceres sparked a return to chaos, and with the backing of the republic's army, Eladio Victoria became president. Several dissatisfied factions promptly rebelled against the new leader, an event that interrupted the customs service. President Taft sent Brig. Gens. Frank McIntyre and William T. S. Doyle, backed by the 2d Provisional Regiment of marines aboard the *Prairie,* to set things in order. In accordance with an agreement negotiated with the various parties, Victoria stepped down and Monsignor Nouel, Archbishop of Santo Domingo, became the provisional president. With that, the marines returned to Philadelphia. But even a clergyman was unable to placate the various Dominican factions, and by 1913, Nouel had had enough of public office. He left for Europe in March of that year. After considerable infighting among the various cabals, Gen. José Bordas Valdéz emerged with a one-year term as provisional president.

By December 1913, revenues from customs were not meeting current government obligations. The United States responded to that situation by recommending that U.S. supervision be extended to all areas of Dominican finances. Santo Domingo rejected the proposal; the Americans were insistent; and the Dominicans were equally adamant in their objections. The impasse continued until Bordas's term expired and a new revolt, beginning at Puerta Plata, spread throughout the country. The violence placed U.S. lives and property in jeopardy, so Washington ordered a company of marines under Capt. Arthur E. Harding to the republic. The marines landed at Puerta Plata on May 6, 1914, and withdrew a month later, after the legitimate election of Juan I. Jiménez.

A year later another revolt broke out. The 5th Regiment of marines, under Col. Charles A. Doyen, was dispatched to the island, arriving in Puerta Plata on Aug. 15, 1915. After establishing order there, it sailed around the island to San Pedro de Macoris and moved on to Santo Domingo. It remained in the capital until October 12, by which time Capt. Edward W. Eberle, the senior U.S. naval officer in Dominican waters, had persuaded the rebels to lay down their weapons.

The Wilson administration now decided to support the legitimate government vigorously and to promote efforts to place the country on a sound economic and political footing. But when President Jiménez arrested two supporters of Gen. Desiderio Arias, his secretary of war, the general seized the main fortress in Santo Domingo and his followers took to the streets on April 1916. Jiménez, having little support, withdrew from the city. U.S. minister William W. Russell now feared for American lives. On May 3, he requested that naval vessels be sent to Puerta Plata, Macoris, and Sanchez. Two destroyers were sent to each town, and on May 5, the 6th and 9th companies of marines under Capt. Frederic Wise arrived at Santo Domingo from Port-au-Prince aboard the *Prairie*. The marines occupied the U.S. and Haitian legations and consulates as well as Fort San Geronimo, but they did not actually enter the city. The 4th Company from Port-au-Prince and 150 marines from Guantánamo Bay soon followed, and Admiral Caperton arrived in Santo Domingo on May 12. After consultations with Russell, he issued an ultimatum to Arias ordering him to surrender and disarm by May 15 or the Americans would occupy the city and forcibly disarm the rebels. Arias's troops evacuated on the morning of May 14, and the marines occupied the city without opposition. More American reinforcements arrived on May 23 when Col. Theodore P. Kane, with three infantry companies and the Headquarters Company of the 2d Marine Regiment, landed in Santo Domingo.

Meanwhile, Jiménez had resigned, leaving the cabinet in control. Clearly, the country was on the verge of chaos, so on May 30, Caperton ordered the detachments that had been waiting offshore at Monte Cristi and Puerta Plata to land the next day. The marines at Puerta Plata met determined resistance, and Caperton requested further reinforcement. The 4th Marine Regiment, Colonel Pendleton commanding, landed at Monte Christi on June 18. He immediately began to plan an assault against Arias's base at Santiago. The advance began on June 26, with 840 men moving toward the city. The Americans encountered Arias's troops on June 27 at La Trencheras. In the first example of marines' advancing with support of artillery and machine guns, they drove Arias's men from their fortifications.

The marines met the rebels again at Guyacanas on July 3, but this time there was no good position for the artillery, so the infantry and machine gunners carried the day. On July 4, Pendleton's forces linked up with Maj. Hiram I. Bearss's battalion, which had come from Puerta Plata. The following morning, emissaries from Arias met with Pendleton to report that their leader and Admiral Caperton had come to terms. Pendleton's troops marched unopposed into Santiago on July 6. Organized opposition had come to an end, although the marines still encountered small pockets of resistance. They now set out to rebuild and restore the country, much as their fellow marines were doing in Haiti.

On July 25, the Dominican Congress elected a new president, Dr. Francisco Henríquez y Carvajal. But Henríquez and the U.S. government could not come to an agreement on the direction of the country's finances. Finally, on November 30, Capt. Harry S. Knapp, who had relieved Caperton, declared a military government over the Dominican Republic. This government would direct the country's finances, law enforcement, and the judiciary, although Dominican laws would be enforced. By year's end, the country was reasonably tranquil, and U.S. troops, with the exception of the 2d Brigade, were evacuated. Those troops remained in the Dominican Republic until 1924, during which time the marines actively worked to suppress "banditry" and trained and officered the National Guard, a force similar to the Haitian Gendarmerie.

MEXICAN BORDER CAMPAIGN

Almost simultaneous to the Arias revolt, hostilities between the United States and Mexico erupted once again. In October 1915, the United States recognized the de facto government of Carranza, who had emerged preeminent, if not absolutely victorious, among Obregón, Emiliano Zapata, and Francisco ("Pancho") Villa in their struggles against Huerta. Villa refused to accept defeat and concluded that a war between Mexico and the United States could help him regain his stature by giving him the opportunity to rally support by fighting the Americans.

In January 1916, a group of U.S. engineers who were to reopen the La Cuisi mine in northern Mexico were set upon by Villa's forces at Santa Ysabel. Sixteen of the engineers were killed. Carranza had guaranteed the safety of Americans in Mexico and now promised to catch the assailants, but he did nothing. This episode was followed by a series of border raids. Then, on March 9, Villa and 485 of his men crossed into Columbus, New Mexico, killing 18 Americans, engaging in a brief skirmish with elements of the 13th Cavalry, and disappearing into the Chihuahuan hills. U.S. public opinion demanded immediate action. The government responded promptly by sending General Pershing with the 7th, 10th, 11th, and 13th cavalries, the 6th and 16th infantries, and two batteries of the 6th Field Artillery into Mexico on March 15. Pershing set up camp at Colonia Dublan, just north of Casas Grandes in Chihuahua. From there, he sent out three columns to hunt down the elusive Villa.

Along with infantry and cavalry troops, the 1st Aero Squadron under Capt. Benjamin Foulois was part of the Punitive Expedition. Pershing saw the advantage that aerial observation could have in finding Villa, but the technology of the JN-2s ("Jennies") could not meet the demands of the climate and terrain. All but two of them were lost, and even those played a negligible role in the campaign.

Of greater importance than the planes was the use of truck transport to supply Pershing's troops as they marched

deeper into Mexican territory. Forbidden by the Mexican government from using the railroads, the expedition literally would have starved had not Maj. Gen. Hugh L. Scott, army chief of staff, initially acting on his own authority, purchased a motley assortment of vehicles that managed to keep the men supplied.

As the troops moved further into Chihuahua, Pershing moved his headquarters to the San Geronimo Ranch, 200 miles south of the border. During a tour of inspection, Pershing met with Maj. Frank Tompkins at Bachiniva. When asked where he thought Villa had gone, Tompkins replied that he would expect him to go to Parral. After a brief conversation, Pershing ordered Tompkins to follow his hunch. Tompkins, with two troops of the 13th Cavalry, marched on Parral. On the morning of April 12, he arrived at the outskirts of the town. There, Gen. Ismael Lozano warned him that entry into the town would incense the population. Nonetheless, Tompkins proceeded through Parral where an ugly mob was soon joined by Carranzista troops. The Mexicans attacked and pursued the Americans as they made for Santa Cruz de Villegas, where Tompkins took up a fortified position. Meanwhile, stragglers from Tompkins's column alerted Col. William C. Brown and elements of the 10th Cavalry about Tompkins's plight. Brown and his men raced toward Santa Cruz and relieved Tompkins at 7:30 that evening.

Although Mexico and the United States had agreed to permit mutual border crossings to pursue bandits shortly after the Punitive Expedition began, there was a distinct difference in interpretation of the accord. The Carranza regime held that it applied to all future incursions, while the United States concluded that it was retroactive and applied to the current expedition against Villa. The incident at Parral was a clear manifestation of Mexican opposition to U.S. intervention. But despite Mexican hostility, the Americans continued their pursuit, fighting Villistas at Tomochie, Ozos, Azules, and Agua Caliente. Mexican-American relations were deteriorating to the point of rupture, while Villa remained ever out of reach.

General Scott dashed south and met with Obregón, now Carranza's secretary of war, on May 1 and 2. By May 3, they had hammered out the Scott-Obregón Agreement, which provided for a gradual U.S. withdrawal. But it was not to be. The elusive Villa had doubled back north, crossed the border again, and raided Glen Springs and Boquillas, killing four and kidnapping two Americans. Instead of withdrawing the troops, Wilson activated more than 75,000 National Guardsmen on June 18 and started rushing them toward the Mexican border.

Brig. Gen. John J. Pershing conducted the Punitive Expedition into Mexico, 1916–17, that dispersed the band of Pancho Villa but failed to capture Villa. (National Archives)

A field drill is carried out by the 6th Infantry in 1916, during the Punitive Expedition. (Library of Congress)

On June 17, Pershing ordered Capt. Charles T. Boyd of Troop C, 10th Cavalry, to carry out a reconnaissance of the area around Villa Ahmuda. On June 21, the 75 men of Boyd's party approached Carrizal and were told by Gen. Felix Gómez that they could not pass through the village. Boyd rashly insisted. In the ensuing fight, 14 Americans, including Boyd, were killed and many more were wounded or captured. When Pershing learned of the rout, he sent units of the 11th Cavalry toward Villa Ahmuda to rescue survivors. Officials in Washington believed the Carrizal incident would trigger a full-scale war, but both Carranza and Pershing showed great restraint. The Americans spent the summer patrolling Chihuahua, chasing down rumors, and skirmishing with a few Villistas. As fall turned into winter, a joint Mexican-American Commission arrived at an agreement under which the United States promised to withdraw its troops 40 days after Carranza approved it, so long as Villa carried out no further raids on Americans during that period. On Jan. 27, 1917, the Punitive Expedition began the march north, crossing into Columbus on February 5. National Guard troops were demobilized shortly thereafter, but for the United States, peace was to be short-lived. Not four months later, many of these same troops who had followed Pershing into Mexico would follow him in an even greater undertaking to Europe.

5

The Emergence of a Modern Army and Navy: 1903–1917

The Spanish-American War placed many new responsibilities upon the U.S. military establishment. What kind of armed forces did the United States need to defend U.S. prerogatives against the professional armies and navies of the great imperial powers? What kind of a force could take on the role of territorial constabulary and administrator? What had to be done to correct the many flaws in organization, administration, matériel, and personnel policy that subdued the euphoria of winning the "splendid little war"?

These concerns, buttressed by turn-of-the-century military theories that predicted future wars were likely to be short—possibly decided in one battle—forced many Americans to conclude that the United States had to prepare for war in time of peace. To do this, especially at a time of fiscal conservatism, the U.S. military needed to be reorganized in ways that would promote both efficiency in war and economy in peace.

To lead this new military force, the United States needed a new kind of soldier. Inspired partly by the social and intellectual currents of the Progressive Era, the members of the U.S. officer corps forged a common bond that linked them together as specialists in the conduct of war. To secure their place among "the society of gentlemen," among the learned professions, they especially cultivated the intellectual component of what they called their "military character." The dramatic rise of military professionalism in the pre-World War I years illustrates the armed forces' depth of commitment to efficiency in organization and to proficiency in personnel.

"We separate for service." This was the motto of one West Point class of the post-Civil War years. It effectively acknowledged the sense of isolation—professional as well as physical—that all officers experienced some time in their careers. A new army second lieutenant expected long years of service in small garrisons, his future professional development dependent on the interest of his superiors and the enthusiasm of his peers. Similarly, a new navy ensign expected a predictable rotation of sea duty and shore assignments, spending much more of his time on dry land. A second lieutenant in the very small Marine Corps—there were fewer than 100 officers before 1898—could wait 20 years for promotion to captain. Although many career officers stayed the course from a high sense of personal commitment, their morale flagged.

A compartmentalized, decentralized military organization reinforced the sense of isolation. The services used unwieldy and inefficient bureau systems, each bureau chief tending to treat his office as his personal fiefdom apart from, not a part of, his service. Protection of traditional rights often took precedence over cooperation or efficient administration. Bitter intraservice rivalries separated staff departments from each other and kept troop commanders and bureau chiefs at each other's throats. Even in the combat arms, the lines were so clear that it was unlikely that a cavalry officer would learn the basics of artillery deployment or cooperation with infantry troops; similarly, in the navy, a ship's chief engineer was not likely to learn how to command in battle the ship he so carefully maintained.

This sense of isolation, some historians have argued, fueled increasingly loud calls for reforms to promote new and higher standards of professional conduct. Other scholars, however, have held that this sense of isolation was more illusory than real. Well before 1898, officers served overseas as military attachés, were professors of military science at civilian universities, took temporary assignments in Washington and elsewhere, consulted engineers and scientists at research laboratories, and, after 1898, provided constabulary service overseas. While each opportunity was not equally desirable, each offered chances for professional, intellectual, and even social contacts with a wide assortment of brothers in arms.

U.S. military officers also were not isolated from mainstream society. During the Progressive Era, they learned from civilian professions similarly engaged in forging corporate identities. Military men laid claim to intellectual authority over the art and science of war, the unique body of theory that defined their profession's area of expertise. They demanded strict entry requirements for new officers and pushed for a promotion system based on merit, not seniority alone. They borrowed ideas about postgraduate education, specialized journals, and professional associations to bring together on common ground all members of the officer corps.

Creating a more professional U.S. officer corps did not come without controversy. Military conservatives in and out of uniform did not like the kinds of changes that subverted traditional practices. Still, to build a modern military force, substantial improvement in the quality of its individual elements had to be made first; revitalizing the entire military machine would surely follow in time.

STANDARDS FOR NEW OFFICERS

Nearly everyone interested in promoting the new spirit of military professionalism confronted one basic issue: Who made the best military leaders and what qualifications did they need to enter the profession of arms? In 1900, a regular army second lieutenant could be promoted from the enlisted ranks or he could receive a commission by passing a competitive examination, by graduating from the U.S. Military Academy, or, occasionally, by transferring from a volunteer or National Guard unit.

Few enlisted men rose to officer rank on the basis of their service alone. Usually, like civilian candidates for commissions, they took the competitive examination. Introduced in the 1890s, the testing procedure was itself among the army's first personnel reforms. While the army's Young Turks backed the system of entry examinations, many senior officers, whose own high rank often stemmed from Civil War heroics rather than mastery of the military art, feared that there would be no place for "natural leaders" who did not shine in intellectual pursuits. They saw no benefit to the service in commissioning "a bookworm" if it meant rejecting a hearty man of sterling character. The policy of direct commissions, however, clearly was open to cronyism and political favoritism, and the reformers won. Indeed, before 1898, examinations were also required for promotion through the rank of captain.

Role of West Point

Graduation from the Military Academy was the most professionally respectable avenue to a commission. Throughout its history, critics had attacked West Point for promoting militarians and elitism; more recently, they had argued that the Civil War had proved that the academy could not produce enough officers in a national crisis. As long as congressmen controlled appointments and the War Department handled curricular matters, however, West Point's future was safe.

Between 1865 and 1898, intellectual stagnation plagued the school. In the classroom, daily recitation and rote memorization took precedence over analysis and original thinking. Few of the faculty, mostly West Pointers themselves, held advanced degrees. The French courses were so poor that whenever a prominent visitor from France arrived on post, the instructors would invariably depart on leave. Lessons in military engineering introduced by Dennis Hart Mahan in the 1820s were still dutifully taught without revision in 1885.

West Point's centennial celebration in 1902 brought about a reevaluation of the school's mission and methods. For Sec. of War Elihu Root and other military reformers, West Point had to produce more than soldiers; it had to produce valuable citizens. West Point adopted "Duty, Honor, Country" as its official motto and set about creating a new kind of soldier. Cadets learned that the army officer of the future required both a sound general education as well as a solid grounding in the military arts. Their diplomas proved only that they had mastered the rudiments of their profession.

Certainly, the faculty paid close attention to the military education of cadets. The Department of Tactics taught them to use a wider variety of weapons than ever before and offered extensive hands-on training on many newer weapons including mountain artillery and Gatling guns. Cadets even learned how to do army paperwork, including nearly every form a junior officer was likely to encounter early in his career. Beginning in 1902, the Department of Military Art and Engineering took the first class to Gettysburg to study strategy and tactics, a method so useful that the army's senior schools soon added it to their own curricula.

But it was the cadet's general education that saw a dramatic change. The Board of Visitors demanded that a cadet's education be one "approaching in culture that acquired in the best American colleges." Cadets devoted considerable time to foreign languages, political science, and geography. In 1908, a brand new Department of

After 1902, more attention was paid to the liberal arts in the West Point curriculum; cadets took literature courses along with the traditional grammar courses such as shown above (1903). (U.S. Military Academy)

English and History taught literature courses (not just grammar, once taught by the modern language department) and college-level history, which took the place of a high-school-level civics course. The library also underwent complete reorganization.

On the eve of World War I, West Point believed itself capable of providing the army with junior officers capable of carrying out a lieutenant's duties and perhaps much more. The Class of 1915 was the "class the stars fell on" and included such future luminaries as Dwight D. Eisenhower and Omar Bradley.

Navy and Marine Officers

The route to becoming an ensign in the navy was more restricted. Either a candidate graduated from the Naval Academy or he was appointed directly from civilian life. A few enlisted men with special technical skills, limited to six a year, could rise to officer rank as well.

The navy distinctly preferred Annapolis men. The Naval Academy, according to one secretary of the navy, "produces officers the equal of any in the world. When the best are obtainable, we need not content ourselves with anything less." In 1902, the navy had 1,360 unfilled officer billets in new and scheduled construction and pushed for an expansion of the academy to meet manpower needs. Maintaining high professional standards was critical; the selection process had one central dictum: "It admits none by favor."

To provide officers for the new navy, the academy followed many paths. Addressing the problem directly, several classes between 1903 and 1906 were graduated early to join the fleet; elements of the Class of 1907 left in September 1906, February 1907, and June 1907.

As at West Point, an Annapolis education included both professional and general studies. The Annapolis curriculum, however, had not endured quite so long a period of stagnation. In the 1880s, midshipmen began to take classes in electricity and metallurgy. The Naval Academy of the 1890s experimented in dividing classes into command groups and engineering groups. By 1902, in addition to summer cruises on modern battleships, some midshipmen served on the first navy submarine, the *Holland*. In 1911, the navy's first three pilots flew over the academy from its nearby airfield and made many converts for naval aviation.

West Point and Annapolis, while making great strides in the classroom, had their share of problems and successes outside the halls of instruction as well. On one hand, both suffered through widely publicized hazing scandals that had resulted in the deaths of underclassmen. West Point also endured racial problems stemming from the admission of 13 black cadets before 1898. On a more positive note, however, both schools were at the forefront of intercollegiate athletics. More than recreation and school pride was at stake here; the teamwork required for victory on the playing field taught practical lessons about the cooperation needed in modern war.

Col. Charles Young, Class of 1898, became the third black graduate of West Point and went on to serve honorably on the frontier (1889–94), in the Caribbean (1904–07) and Liberia (1912–15), and in the Punitive Expedition (1917). (U.S. Military Academy Archives)

A candidate for a second lieutenancy in the U.S. Marine Corps might graduate from the Naval Academy or he might be commissioned directly from civilian life. Most new marine officers followed the latter path since Annapolis graduates were far more likely to receive assignments to the fleet. To an unusual degree, however, marine lieutenants were qualified for their commissions and not mere political appointees. Many held college degrees, had served on active duty during the Spanish-American War, or both. Until the great expansion of the Marine Corps for World War I, the service had no trouble attracting qualified officers from civilian life.

CAREER EDUCATION

Military men now knew that a good officer needed more than a good physique and a handsome uniform. Intellectual acumen mattered too. To this end, the services developed systems of postgraduate schools to stimulate career-long study and informed analysis in professional subjects. Graduation from any of these schools offered objective evidence of a man's capacity for greater responsibility and higher rank.

Army Schools

The army's postgraduate school system evolved haphazardly, with no guiding hand. It began in the late 1870s, when Col. Emory Upton breathed new life into the Artillery School at Fortress Monroe. Along with traditional work in ordnance, ballistics, and tactics, Upton discussed the cooperation of artillery with the other arms, especially with the infantry. He used historical examples from Civil War battles to inject immediacy and realism into his theory-based lectures.

Buoyed by Upton's success, in 1881, Gen. William T. Sherman opened the Infantry and Cavalry School at Fort Leavenworth. At first belittled as "the kindergarten" attended only by the greenest officers or perennial troublemakers, the school blossomed in the 1890s with five academic departments: tactics, strategy, law, engineering, and hygiene. Students completed both practical and theory-based work in such diverse fields as hippology, military geography, logistics, staff duties, war-gaming, and international and constitutional law.

Not all officers were chosen to attend these advanced schools, but that did not lessen their obligation to tend to their professional studies. In 1891, by general order, the commander of each garrison manned by at least one company of men had to open a post school, or officers' lyceum, to allow his subordinates time to read and study about topics likely to appear on promotion examinations. A solid performance at the post school often led to selection to the advanced schools.

These schools, chiefly for lieutenants and captains, made up the entire army postgraduate school system until 1898. They were not entirely accepted. Many old soldiers still on active duty believed that "only war teaches war" and sneered at the army's embrace of "educationmania." Others believed the schools were expensive luxuries that taught officers skills they were unlikely ever to need.

The Spanish-American War, however, underscored the need for a first-rate officer education program. Creating "safe leaders" became the goal of all levels of officer education. Introduced at Fort Leavenworth in the 1890s by Capt. Arthur L. Wagner and Eben Swift, "safe leadership" was a concept based on responsibility, reliability, intellectual acuity, and teamwork. To become a safe leader, Wagner and Swift encouraged officers to study military history to learn about the kinds of "perplexities and embarrassments" commanders face. Applying the principles of war to events from past conflicts—called the applicatory method—offered illustrations of problems that came from inattention to security, efficiency, and clarity in written orders.

The spirit of military professionalism did not exclude enlistees. Every garrison opened a school for the military and general education of soldiers in the regular army. Specialty schools such as the Cooks and Bakers School helped remedy glaring shortcomings in the quality and economy of support services. More than one dozen such special schools for enlisted men were started before World War I.

But the education system still catered chiefly to the needs of regular army officers. After 1898, still more schools for officers (and occasionally select enlisted men as well) opened, including the Coast Artillery School, the Engineer School, the Mounted Service School, the Army Signal School, the School of Fire for Field Artillery, the Field Engineer School, the School of Musketry, and the Signal Corps Aviation School.

The Infantry and Cavalry School underwent a most dramatic metamorphosis. No longer only a school for the two combat arms, it now took students from any branch who might qualify for future assignment to the newly formed General Staff. At the newly renamed School of the Line, each officer studied law, tactics, strategy, hygiene, and military engineering. The honor graduates stayed on for a second year at the Staff College, where they learned the duties of staff officers, especially how to write orders. Each man also undertook a substantial research project in U.S. military history.

Army War College

The events of 1898 led directly to the creation of the capstone of the education system, the Army War College. Since the 1870s, various officers had called for a U.S. version of the Prussian Kriegsakademie. In 1901, Secretary Root, citing a need for an institution that could reach "a consensus of matured opinion" on military matters, opened the army's senior school at Washington.

The Army War College initially served as an adjunct to the General Staff, resolving problems assigned to it by the secretary of war or by the chief of staff. Consistent with the school's unofficial motto to "learn things by doing things," in one year, a student completed several extended series of tactical problems—some on maps and some on horseback on local Civil War battlefields—solving them with concise five-paragraph orders. Historical rides to Civil War battlefields in Virginia, Maryland, and Pennsylvania included staff exercises based on actual campaigns, and each student took a turn as commander, chief of staff, or other responsible position. They created map exercises and other instructional material for the rest of the army schools. Finally, they annually reviewed and revised the army's war plan, devoting far more time to issues related to mobilization and organization than to operations and development of doctrine.

With the use of the airplane, aerial photography became another tool for the army; here, at the U.S. Army School of Aerial Photography in Ithaca, New York, an officer in a motorcycle with sidecar watches flying exercises. (U.S. Military Academy Archives)

By World War I, the army's officer education system had taken shape. Graduation and all academic honors were printed in the *Army Register*. Some curricular features won the praise of civilian scholars; the American Historical Association declared the military history seminar at the Staff College a model worthy of emulation. The schools taught army officers "to speak the same language," a key element in safe leadership. It was no small compliment when, after victory in World War I, one U.S. general said, "Thank God for Leavenworth!"

Navy and Marine Education

Advanced education was equally important to the future leaders of the U.S. Navy. The evolution of the navy's education system followed a path quite different from that the army had taken.

Naval officers seldom had felt so much pressure to stay abreast of global diplomatic and navy affairs as they felt now in this age of imperial expansion. Since 1873, the

U.S. Naval Institute had helped keep them informed, but the fleet's future commanders needed more. Like their army counterparts, naval officers looked to a postgraduate school system to bring together men from all parts of the navy—the fleet, the engineers, and the bureaus—to discuss issues of common concern. Also like the army's experience, the navy school system grew haphazardly.

Indeed, the navy's capstone institution for its most senior officers appeared first. On Oct. 6, 1884, the Naval War College opened to offer "an advanced course of professional study for naval officers." Rear Adm. Stephen R. Luce, its driving force and first president, located the school at Newport, Rhode Island, where students could be "lulled to sleep by the Atlantic surf." Luce believed that the school should be "a place where our officers will not only be encouraged, but required, to study their profession proper—war—in a far more thorough manner than had ever heretofore been attempted." The original course of study included classroom work, library research, and fleet tactical problems. By the 1890s, William M. Little brought war-gaming into the classroom. Luce occasionally called upon the North Atlantic Squadron to test the students' solutions.

After 1898, the curriculum evolved to include lectures, a term-long war problem, creation of war charts and defense plans, war games, steam launch exercises, torpedo instruction, and professional reading. Using the army's applicatory system to "enhance the mental process that leads up to a decision," each class also broke down into four committees that created solutions-by-conference, a naval version of safe leadership.

The success of the Naval War College only underscored the problems of naval education. After graduation from Annapolis, an officer had almost no chance for professional study until he had obtained sufficient seniority for an appointment to the Naval War College. A few specialized schools opened—such as the Naval Pay Officers School in 1905—but these did not meet the need for advanced education for most naval officers.

In the technical fields, things were better. On Feb. 1, 1913, the Naval Postgraduate School opened at Annapolis; two years later, its class included 5 officers studying ordnance and 20 more taking engineering. Other officers took courses at civilian universities; in 1915 alone, 20 officers studied engineering at Columbia and 12 more studied naval architecture and ship construction at the Massachusetts Institute of Technology. Eight more served internships with industries that manufactured naval armaments, such as Bethlehem Steel.

The technical nature of many naval skills required the navy—far more than the army—to see to the training of its enlisted men. On the eve of U.S. entry into World War I, a seaman might attend the Torpedo and Seaman Gunners School, the Machinists School, one of two electricians schools, the Artificers School, one of two musicians schools, the Cooks and Bakers School, one of two yeomen schools (or hospital corps training schools), the Fuel Oil School, or the Pensacola Aviation School. Sec. of the Navy Josephus Daniels was proud that the schools "primarily prepare the men for efficiency while serving in the Navy, but they also equip them with an asset which insures them a lifelong means of support if they retire from the service."

The push for professional education did not miss the Marine Corps either. In May 1891, the first School of Application for new second lieutenants and select enlisted men opened at Monroe Barracks. In 10 weeks, the students learned infantry tactics, drill, and naval gunnery and attended the navy's Torpedo School at Newport.

Still, as long as the Marine Corps mission included service as landing parties, light infantry, and ship guards, marksmanship mattered more than intellectual attainment. While the marines' school system expanded slightly with the opening of the Advanced Base School in 1910 at New London, Connecticut (and moved to Philadelphia the next year), marine officers usually attended the navy's (and sometimes the army's) advanced schools. Before World War I, at least, a marine officer's frequent assignments to duty with expeditionary forces all too often kept him out of the classroom and in the field.

Aiding Professional Education

Since only a fraction of the officer corps could attend the postgraduate schools, the services had to find other ways to keep their future leaders current on the most recent military and naval developments. Much of the solution came from a grassroots movement among officers who also became military writers. The blossoming of U.S. military literature included textbooks for the service schools and an attempt at "official history." By far, however, the most popular and accessible form of military reading was the professional journal.

Several short-lived antebellum military journals had failed for lack of money and sustained interest, but the Civil War made a success of William C. Church's *Army and Navy Journal*. Although not officially sponsored by either the War Department or the Navy Department, the journal continued publishing after the war to provide current information on military topics from congressional debates on army and navy appropriations to transfers and retirements of active-duty personnel.

Most journals of this area, however, were sponsored by a professional association that served both as political lobby and sounding board for unresolved military issues. The U.S. Naval Institute, organized in 1873 "for the purpose of discussing matters of professional interest," began publishing its *Proceedings* in 1875. Other Navy Department publications—such as the records of the Washington Naval Observatory—appealed chiefly to the technical specialties.

Others attracted civilian readership as well, most notably the *U.S. Naval Medical Bulletin,* started in 1906.

Army publications were even more numerous. In 1878, with War Department approval, Gen. Winfield S. Hancock founded the Military Service Institution of the United States. Its influential journal started the following year. Successful in publicizing professional issues that cut across the different service branches to bring together all army officers on common ground, the *Journal of the Military Service Institution of the United States* was nearly named the professional journal of the Army General Staff by Chief of Staff Leonard Wood in 1914.

Each of the combat arms also launched its own specialized journal. In 1888, the *Cavalry Journal* began publication. Four years later, the *Journal of the U.S. Artillery* began a long run. The *Infantry Journal* started a few years later, in 1904. Officers were strongly encouraged—and often required—to subscribe to professional journals. The War Department paid attention to subscription figures, using the numbers as one sure measure of a post's intellectual activity.

The *Marine Corps Gazette,* sponsored by the Marine Corps Association organized in 1911, began publication in 1916. From that point on, marine officers turned to the *Gazette* instead of navy journals for the most recent information about their service.

While the journals filled part of the void in U.S. military literature, still more was needed. In addition to the practical studies sponsored by the war and navy departments—engineering reports, for instance—the services wanted to be able to teach and discuss military theory, and they wanted to do so without immediate recourse to European doctrine. They needed a body of military literature that examined the U.S. way of war and the conduct of war in North America. Some of the texts that filled the gap, most notably Capt. Matthew F. Steele's *American Campaigns,* appeared with financial assistance from the War Department. Most authors, however, fended for themselves to find civilian publishers and underwrote publications' costs in hopes that the War Department would later adopt the book for classroom use or for promotion examinations. Except for Capt. Alfred Thayer Mahan, naval authors faced the same kinds of challenges; indeed, sometimes their task was even more difficult since the technological sophistication of naval science was unlikely to attract curious readers outside the navy and engineering communities.

The army also attempted to write an "official history" of the Civil War. Begun by the Army War College in 1912 and designed as a textbook to teach officers about proper and improper applications of the laws of war, the project ultimately failed. Neither the officers who wrote the text nor the General Staff officers assigned to edit the final volume sufficiently understood how to distinguish errors in historical fact from doctrinal disagreements. In concept, however, the "official history" project took a giant step toward advancing the army's professional literature to a level consistent with its desire to cement its intellectual authority over the study of military history, a claim disputed by the academic historical community.

These efforts took U.S. military art and science to a higher intellectual plane than it had ever reached before. There simply were fewer and fewer excuses for not keeping current with the newest military developments.

MILITARY REORGANIZATION

Although the need for reorganization and modernization of the military services was widely recognized by the late 19th century, the need was not universally accepted. Entrenched interests, both military and civilian, often opposed changes that would curtail their power and influence.

Army

Like other bureaucratic institutions of the Progressive Era, the U.S. Army wanted to improve efficiency in administration and effectiveness in organization. The Dodge Commission (1898) explored some of the army's worst institutional problems in the Spanish-American War, and it made many suggestions for improvements in quartermaster and medical services. Military reorganization quickly became a matter for heated institutional, public, and political debate.

The army considered organizational reforms on all levels of command and in all areas of support. Most controversial was the effort to replace the traditional bureau system with a general staff, a centralized office for the planning and coordination of all activities attendant to the conduct of modern war.

Creation of a general staff lay at the heart of many reform agendas. After examining the administration of foreign armed forces in *The Armies of Asia and Europe* (1878), Upton had become an early convert to the campaign. Spenser Wilkinson's widely read *The Brain of An Army* (1891) explained how the German general staff worked, making it the model most often cited by American advocates of institutional reorganization, despite fears that it was not entirely suited to the army of a republic. Still, even in 1900, when the Military Service Institution offered a prize for the best essay in "the organization of a staff best adapted for the United States Army," no entry was deemed worthy of the award. Consensus was impossible.

Nonetheless, Secretary of War Root, desiring organizational reform and willing to face the resistance of his bureau chiefs, organized the Army War College in 1901. This organization, designed to consider "all questions affecting the welfare and efficiency of the army," was—in combination with the Bureau of Military Information—"as near

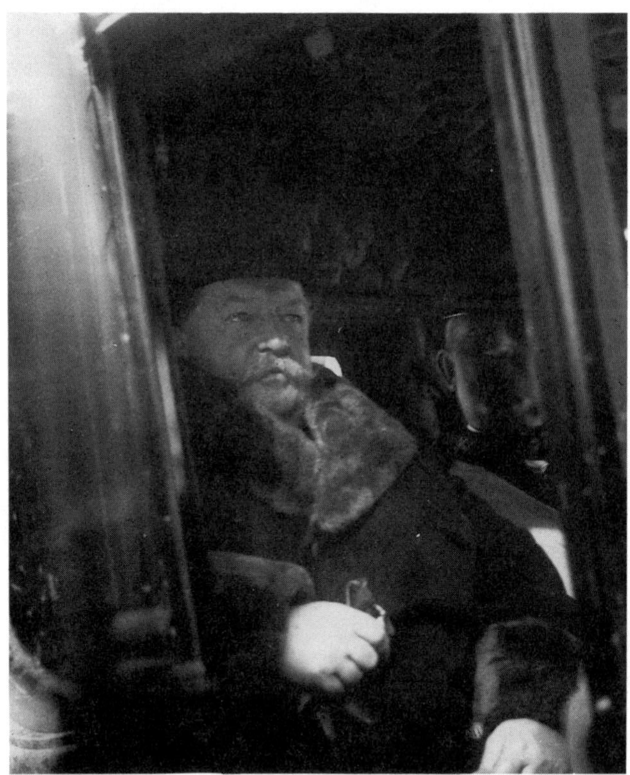

William Howard Taft, secretary of war (1904–09) under Pres. Theodore Roosevelt, oversaw much of the reorganization of the armed forces during his tenure. In the winter of 1908, he made one of his many official visits to West Point. (Library of Congress)

an approach to the establishment of a General Staff as is practicable under existing law.''

Root pushed for congressional approval, but his own subordinates occasionally worked to undercut his efforts. When Root suggested eliminating the position of Commanding General of the Army, former commanding general Nelson A. Miles spoke out against it and against all reforms he deemed more suited ''to the monarchies of the Old World.'' Quick work by another former commanding general, John M. Schofield, helped to save the day.

Finally, on Feb. 14, 1903, Congress passed ''an act to increase the efficiency of the army,'' and created the General Staff. Replacing the commanding general was the new chief of staff. The General Staff Corps included the chief of staff, 2 additional generals, 4 colonels, 6 lieutenant colonels, 12 majors, and 20 captains. Tours on General Staff duty were temporary; after four years, an officer had to return to his own branch. The General Staff was responsible for making mobilization plans and war plans, examining all issues affecting the army's readiness and efficiency, and coordinating military actions of different elements of the army. The chief of staff supervised all troops of the line; all those of the adjutant general's, inspector general's, judge advocate's, quartermaster's, subsistence, medical, pay, and ordnance departments; the Corps of Engineers; and the Signal Corps. The first chief of staff was Lt. Gen. Samuel B. M. Young.

Repeatedly until World War I, the General Staff had to defend itself against attacks by military conservatives in and out of uniform. The strongest challenge came in 1911 when the adjutant general, Frederick C. Ainsworth, refused to carry out Chief of Staff Wood's directives for cutting army paperwork. Ainsworth, a longtime critic of the General Staff plan, was finally court-martialed for insubordination, and his forced retirement was a signal victory for the supporters of the new order.

While the creation of the General Staff was the most ambitious advance in army reorganization, many more were underway as well. To promote economy, the War Department tried to eliminate many ''hitching post'' forts along the long-pacified western frontier. Congressmen interested in protecting the economic investments of constituents—not military necessity—kept many obsolete posts open. As late as 1914, 49 garrisons remained open in 24 states, few with more than 700 troops.

The widely scattered troop dispositions made it difficult for the General Staff to initiate large-unit training exercises. To remedy the problem, Sec. of War Henry Stimson in 1913 organized the garrison troops into divisions, the largest tactical units ever to exist in the U.S. Army in peacetime. Earlier divided into four geographic departments for administrative purposes, the army now had a chain of command and table of organization that simplified the assembly of large numbers of troops; when hostilities threatened on the Texas border with Mexico, Stimson ordered out elements of Brig. Gen. Frederick Funston's 2d Division with a message only five lines long. The army had other needs for larger units, too. By 1914, permanent foreign garrisons, made up of full-strength units—not skeletons as was the usual practice in peacetime—were needed for the Philippines, Hawaii, and the recently completed Panama Canal.

Support services underwent important changes as well. The Medical Corps learned to treat tropical diseases, and in 1913, the U.S. Army became the first army in the world to require inoculations against typhoid. A new Medical Reserve Corps maintained a pool of trained men to fill enlisted slots in a war emergency. In 1901, to correct a problem exposed in 1898, the Army Nurse Corps was founded, opening the first official slot for women in the U.S. military establishment. A Veterinary Corps and a dental detachment also added to the Medical Corps' capabilities before 1917.

Other support departments were overhauled too. The Adjutant General's Department, after scrutiny by the President's Commission on Economy and Efficiency, simplified its muster rolls and payrolls. The Historical Section was added to the General Staff in January 1914, giving an institutional billet to the study of the art and science of war. In another move to promote economy, the Commissary Department and the Paymaster Department were consolidated into the Quartermaster Department in August 1912. Its enlisted men belonged to a new General Service Corps, soon renamed the Quartermaster Corps, which replaced civilian teamsters, clerks, and others with qualified soldiers.

Technological advances suggested still other kinds of organizational refinements. The Quartermaster Corps had to figure out how to fit motorized vehicles into its table of organization. The Signal Corps created an Aviation Section by 1911; by April 1917, the U.S. Army had 55 airplanes of widely varying quality. The army's embryonic Tank Corps experimented with several models but made little progress before World War I. The army gave surprisingly little thought to the use of the machine gun. Each regiment carried only 2–4 machine guns; some National Guard units carried more. Only in November 1916 did the War Department approve the purchase of gas masks. Unfortunately, no part of the army was responsible for chemical warfare, and basic questions about gas-mask design were unceremoniously dumped on the Medical Department.

Army organization had responded both to military needs and to social pressures to improve efficiency and economy. Much of the drive to reform army administration came from the debacle of 1898. World War I would show how far the army had come in a short time. The report card would be mixed.

Navy

The U.S. Navy's organizational revolution began a bit before that of the army. By the mid-1880s, the ships of the technologically sophisticated new navy were on the drawing board. The Naval War College opened in 1884 to teach officers to command the new fleet. But these innovations alone had not prepared the U.S. Navy for war. As Sec. of the Navy John D. Long wrote in late 1898, "Among the most important lessons learned in the war with Spain was that a modern navy cannot be improvised during a war or upon the threshold of a war."

The navy's institutional reorganization began in 1882 with the creation of the Office of Naval Information (ONI) in the Bureau of Navigation. It centralized collection and dissemination of military and technological data from civilian and foreign sources. It also dabbled in questions concerning naval strategy and policy, although this effort ran against the best judgment of some naval leaders. Its studies of centralized administration in the world's major navies buttressed early calls for reforming the inefficient bureau system, in place since the 1840s. The powerful bureau chiefs, at first, were able to block naval Young Turks from accomplishing their goals.

After 1898, however, calls for a general staff organization, much like the one the army wanted, could no longer be ignored. A first step came in 1900 when Secretary Long appointed the General Board, a group of 11 senior officers, headed by Adm. George Dewey. The panel had three jobs: gathering information on the navies of foreign powers, preparing war plans, and training officers for command in war. The General Board also coordinated the efforts of the ONI and the Naval War College and could request their recommendations on everything from officer education to ship design. Since it was only an advisory committee, however, its authority and influence was limited.

Theodore Roosevelt, author of a naval history of the War of 1812 before he became president, agreed with Long and others who wanted a single central office to coordinate all elements of naval operations. But even with the powerful support of the newly formed Navy League, they could not sway Congress. The chairman of the Senate Committee on Naval Affairs, Eugene Hale of Maine, feared that any such reforms would undercut his own authority and consistently restricted his committee to examining defects in ship construction only.

In 1909, working quietly to avoid confrontations, Sec. of the Navy George V. Meyer divided his department into four sections: fleet operations, personnel, matériel, and inspections. Each of the old bureaus fit into one of these new divisions. Each division was headed by a high-ranking line officer—an aide—who, individually, advised the secretary on issues concerning his division; collectively, the aides constituted an advisory council on naval policy. To make the changes permanent, however, Meyer needed the permission of Congress. Legislators refused, apparently fearing that these aides—chosen for their professional expertise, not their political acumen—would be less likely to curry their favor.

Finally, in 1915, over the opposition of Secretary of the Navy Daniels, the Office of Naval Operations formally replaced the aide system. For the first chief of naval operations, Daniels backed Adm. William S. Benson, who was not active in the reform effort, and opposed the ambitious Adm. Bradley Fiske, a major voice in the call for change. The new office centralized naval administration, much as the General Staff had done for the army.

Not all organizational changes occurred on the highest levels of naval administration. Others had a direct link to the combat role of the new fleet that Mahan and his supporters had sought for so long. By 1905, a special committee on naval gunnery outlined a system of firing that set standards until the eve of World War II. By 1907, the Atlantic Fleet had become "the most powerful fleet of battleships under one command in any navy." Its two squadrons were homogeneous; that is, more technologically advanced ships were grouped together rather than mixed in with older ships. Also in 1907, a unified Pacific Fleet was organized for "strategic reasons," all naval forces in Pacific and Asiatic waters working together to illustrate "the idea of perfect mobility." The concentration of ships made possible large-scale tactical exercises, especially in the Atlantic.

The most obvious display of the navy's new prowess was the world tour of the "Great White Fleet" from December 1907 through February 1909. Sixteen battleships, with auxiliary vessels, sailed from Hampton Roads under Rear Adm. Robley D. Evans, covered 46,000 miles, and suffered no major technical problems, effectively silencing the navy's critics.

Even though ambitious junior officers were encouraged to stay in the big ships, technological advances offered still more challenges and promoted still more institutional change. In 1900, the navy commissioned the *Holland,* its first submarine, which stretched for nearly 54 feet and carried a crew of seven. By 1915, a submarine center opened at New London, Connecticut.

Naval aviation was born, by tradition, on May 8, 1910, when Capt. Washington I. Chambers completed contracts for the navy's first two airplanes. The Navy Engineering Experiment Station near Annapolis served as its first home. After civilian pilot Eugene Ely successfully flew his airplane off the deck of the cruiser *Birmingham* in November 1910 and in January 1911 landed it on a special platform on the cruiser *Pennsylvania,* the future of naval aviation seemed promising. In 1913, Secretary Daniels appointed an Aeronautics Board, which recommended the establishment of the navy's first flight center. The Pensacola air station, manned by its first contingent of naval aviators—9 officers and 23 enlisted men—opened in February 1914.

Many naval support services also went through major organizational overhauls. The lack of navy chaplains drew considerable attention. In 1913, the navy carried 24 chaplains on the rolls, the same number as in 1842. The Navy Medical Corps also suffered from a severe shortage of professional personnel; in 1907, the navy's surgeon general reported 67 vacancies with no idea of how to fill them. For surgeons already commissioned into the navy, however, the Navy Medical School offered further opportunities at what was touted as one of "the best postgraduate schools not only of this country, but the world." The surgeon general, arguing that women nurses were "by natural endowment and special aptitude" superior to male nurses and citing the good service of female Japanese nurses in the Russo-Japanese War, obtained authorization to start the Navy Nurse Corps in 1908.

Several other organizational innovations also showed promise for the future. In 1903, a joint board of army and naval officers was named to coordinate interservice planning for mobilization and combined operations. In 1915, 11 scientific associations were invited to name two members each to a Naval Consulting Board that would filter through recent technological advances to find those with practical applications in the naval service. Thomas A.

In January 1911, for the first time, an airplane landed on a platformed deck of the battleship Pennsylvania; *here, the* Pennsylvania (right), *accompanied by the transport* George Washington (background) *and a U.S. subchaser* (foreground), *is shown off the coast of France in December 1918.* (U.S. Army Signal Corps)

A U.S. medical mobile unit and its nurses are prepared to accept war casualties in 1918. (U.S. Army Signal Corps)

Edison accepted the chairmanship of this group that forged a common bond between the military and civilian scientific communities.

All of these organizational changes improved the navy's ability to carry out its mission as the nation's first line of defense. In 1917, as the United States entered World War I, Secretary Daniels wrote proudly that the "years of drilling and practice, of close cooperation in planning and thinking, were evidence of the readiness and quickness with which the Navy moved when the command rang out." While the navy still found holes in its preparedness, it nonetheless had created a much sounder, more efficient organization in a very short time.

Marine Corps

The military establishment's drive for institutional reform carried far greater implications for the U.S. Marine Corps than for any other service. Indeed, its very survival was at issue.

After 1898, with constabulary service in the new U.S. empire expanding the role of the marines from its traditional missions as landing parties and shipboard infantry, the Marine Corps needed to double its prewar strength. With Congress's support, the corps steadily grew from a strength of 211 officers and 6,062 enlisted men in 1899 to 332 officers and 9,521 enlisted men in 1908.

As the corps grew larger, its personnel policy required refinements as well. The post of Marine Corps commandant carried the higher rank of major general, beginning in 1903. His staff grew in size and authority, and its members were promoted to ranks appropriate to their responsibilities. A marine officer was assigned to be one of the president's

In 1915, inventor Thomas Alva Edison chaired a group of scientists that advised the navy on technological advances. (Library of Congress)

naval advisers. For enlisted men, the new rank of gunnery sergeant conferred greater status and higher pay to specialists in the handling of naval ordnance.

But the corps' improved posture soon would be challenged. In Executive Order No. 969, President Roosevelt declared in 1908 that the appropriate missions of the Marine Corps included only garrison duty at naval stations at home and abroad, manning the first line of defense at U.S. naval bases overseas, organizing expeditionary forces as needed, and guarding the Panama Canal Zone.

Gone was the marines' traditional service as shipboard infantry. Roosevelt and his allies argued that the higher quality of navy recruits reduced the likelihood that marines would be needed to provide a positive military example or to enforce discipline. They also agreed that the marines had no specific skills as landing parties or gun crews that sailors could not master for themselves. Marine Corps supporters feared that Roosevelt had taken the first step in support of his contention that the marines "should be absorbed into the army and no vestige of their organization should be allowed to remain. They cannot get along with the navy, and as a separate command with the army the conditions would be intolerable."

But the Marine Corps did not die. In 1909, a sympathetic congressional committee concluded that economy and efficiency both required the return of the marine complement to the ships. They took a hard line, linking the continuation of traditional shipboard duties to their support for an important military appropriations bill. The corps' old missions were restored. Secure in its continued existence, the corps embraced new specialties. Like the army and navy, the Marine Corps was interested in aviation. In May 1912, 2d Lt. Alfred A. Cunningham qualified as the first Marine Corps aviator, and by December 1913, the Marine Aviation detachment swelled to two airplanes, two officers, and seven enlisted men.

The Advanced Base Force was the Marine Corps' most innovative organizational change before World War I. The navy, concerned about the defense of its overseas bases, wanted to prepare and man fixed permanent fortifications at those posts. Although this clashed with the traditional mission of the army's Coast Artillery Corps and the Corps of Engineers, the General Board in 1901 suggested that the Marine Corps create "a military organization of sufficient strength in numbers and efficiency, to enable the Navy to meet all demands upon it . . . without dependence on the cooperation of the Army." It took more than 10 years to clarify the new role, marine officers wavering between support for manning fixed defenses and a mobile defense force to secure bases only until permanent fortifications were in place.

Between 1910 and 1914, the advanced base concept evolved from theory to reality. A permanent expeditionary company was stationed at each Marine Corps barracks. The General Board backed the creation of the new Advance Base School at New London in 1910, at which marines of the Advanced Base Force learned to defend fixed positions and to use artillery, mines, torpedoes, and electrical communications. The advanced base concept was declared a rousing success in 1914, when Col. George Barnett's 1st Advanced Base Brigade shone in naval maneuvers around Culebra Island in the Carribean.

Barnett later expanded the Advanced Base Force, adding minelaying, searchlight, and engineer units. While manpower remained a problem—many of its personnel were siphoned off to the mobile defense forces designed for temporary duty at overseas bases—the new mission helped to forge a much stronger relationship with the navy. The Marine Corps now had a mission essential to the success of the fleet. Far from facing the axe, by 1916, the Marine Corps had discovered a role that made it nearly indispensible.

National Guard

The impulse for institutional reform reintroduced a question as old as the republic itself: Should national defense be entrusted to a professional military establishment or to a levy of "citizens in arms" raised in time of war? As in most times of fiscal conservatism, the minuteman tradition—advocated most strongly by John A. Logan in *The Volunteer Soldier in America*—found many supporters, often for very different reasons. Some viewed standing armies as expensive, others saw a potential threat to American liberties, still others endorsed volunteer military service as a duty of all male citizens. Their opponents, who drew inspiration from Emory Upton, put their faith in a professional army and navy. A well-trained national guard was one way to straddle the question to both sides' satisfaction.

From 1877 to 1892, state troops had been called out 112 times to restore order during labor strikes and domestic unrest, and they resented being called "scabs" or "tin soldiers." In 1879, delegates from 19 state militias founded the National Guard Association, a lobby group to promote the guardsmen's interests during Congress's deliberations on military reorganization.

The guardsmen's banner bearer was Cong. Charles Dick of Ohio. As president of the National Guard Association, he pushed the "Act to Promote the Efficiency of the Militia" through Congress. The Dick Act, passed on Jan. 21, 1903, divided all male civilians into two classes, the National Guard (or organized militia) and the reserve militia of all male citizens between 18 and 45 unenrolled in National Guard units, continuing in principle the Militia Act of 1792 that made military service an obligation of citizenship.

Under the Dick Act, National Guard units were to be organized, trained, and disciplined like regular army troops.

Guardsmen received federal pay for summer training and maneuvers with regulars. They drilled at least 24 times annually and were inspected by regular army officers. The Dick Act had weaknesses; the governor still had the power to decide how to respond to a call for troops, and troops were restricted to nine months of domestic federal service.

States responded differently to the Dick Act. Some resented federal intrusion. Others actively upgraded armories and sent guardsmen into riflery competitions and field maneuvers with other state units and the regular army. Some even wanted closer ties. In 1908, the Division of Militia Affairs in the General Staff centralized administration of the National Guard units, and about the same time, the nine-month limit on federal service and the ban on assignments outside the United States were ended.

In 1911, the National Guard Association hotly opposed Secretary of War Stimson's ideas for a "continental army," a 400,000-man force of citizen soldiers who would train for war but serve mainly in an inactive reserve rather than on active duty. It seemed to downgrade the role of the guardsmen in national defense. Stimson listened to their concerns; his final plan called for a regular army with its own trained reserves, a militia system sufficiently under federal control to provide immediate support for the regulars in wartime, and an army of volunteers as a third line of defense. The National Defense Act of 1916 further secured the guardsmen's place.

Navy Militia

The naval militia enjoyed less initial success. It began much later, Massachusetts starting the first naval militia in May 1888. Also, the naval militia had no Dick Act to support it and no vocal political lobby such as the National Guard Association to look out for it. In 1911, however, the Navy Department authorized an Office of Naval Militia to pay special attention to creating a reserve force. Reinforced in February 1914 by the Naval Militia Act, a new Division of Naval Militia Affairs urged governors of states that fronted on oceans, deepwater lakes, or major rivers to create such units. Membership jumped dramatically, gratifying navy officials who praised the new recruits in this "entirely unselfish service" as "the nucleus of the enlargement of the Navy in case of war."

In 1915, Congress formally established the Naval Reserve, one component being the naval militia. It was a sound organizational move; in April 1917, the naval militias of 24 states provided nearly 16,000 of the 49,000 reservists activated early in the war, thus sustaining the navy's obligation to serve as the nation's first line of defense.

MEXICAN TESTING GROUND

The nation's new military establishment faced its first real test in Mexico. From 1911 through 1916, U.S. naval and land forces discovered how far they had come and how far they still had to go to eliminate inefficiency and ineffectiveness.

Gen. William H. Carter, commander of the 1911 maneuvers in Texas, insisted on cleanliness, order, and uniformity. (Fort Sam Houston Museum)

The army was tested first. In March 1911, Pres. William H. Taft ordered 50,000 troops to Texas for "war games." It may also have been a move to strengthen border defenses if Mexico's political instability threatened U.S. security, a prospect perceived by many as a real possibility.

The Texas maneuvers included so many troops that the War Department authorized the temporary formation of the Maneuver Division on March 12. The army's only permanent tactical units—the regiments—were assigned to brigades within it. Gen. William H. Carter commanded the Maneuver Division. An influential reformer, he launched a mandatory program of antityphoid shots, required that all water for drinking and cooking be boiled before use, and demanded that every soldier bathe at least twice a week. He tried to promote uniformity of weapons and attempted to improve march discipline. He tested new technology under field conditions, predicting good things for air power and wireless radio.

The mobilization also revealed a major lack of transportation. Army planners had assumed the cooperation of civilian-run railroads, and the movement of troops to Texas made clear that railroad company officials did not respond well to mere appeals to patriotism. After the threat of war passed and the Maneuver Division was disbanded in August 1911, Carter returned to Washington to try to remedy the most blatant problems.

Veracruz Occupation

The navy faced a far more challenging test. On Apr. 9, 1914, Mexican forces detained nine American sailors who had inadvertantly entered a restricted zone. The men were released a half hour later, but Rear Adm. Henry T. Mayo

U.S. Intervention in Mexico, 1914–17

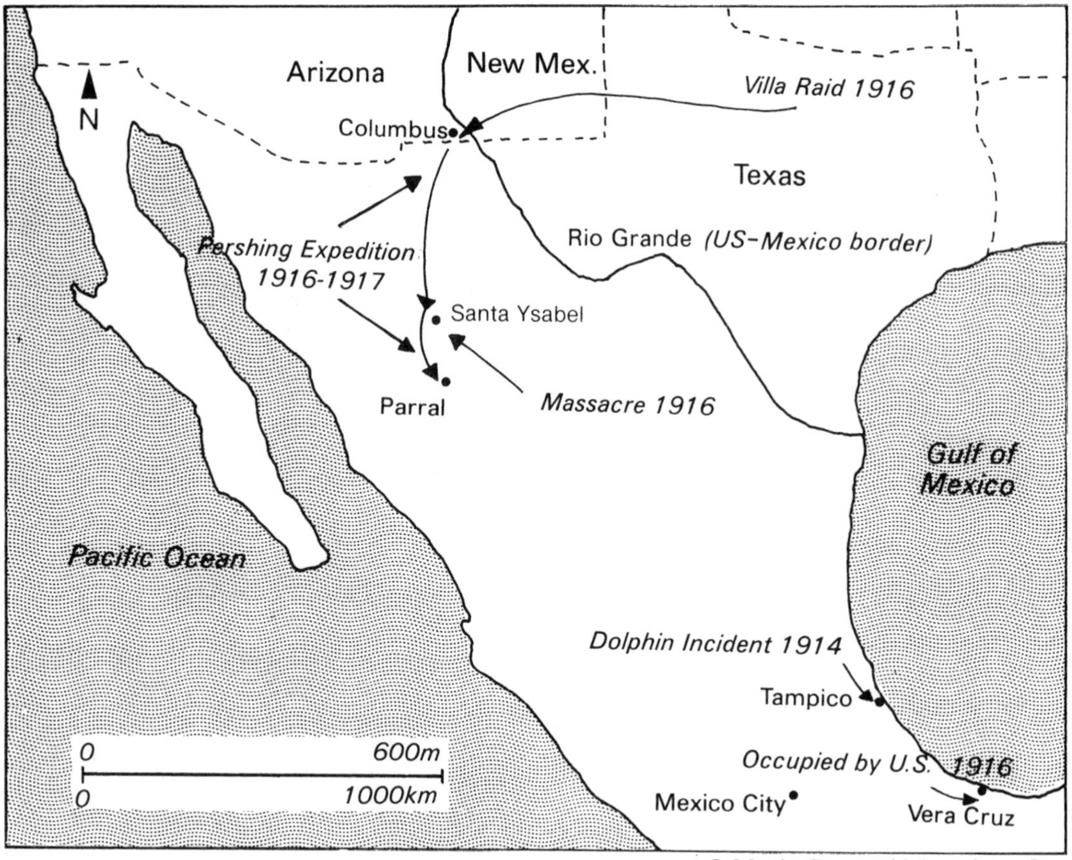

demanded both a formal apology and a 21-gun salute to the U.S. flag. Mexican president Victoriano Huerta offered an apology but would not agree to the salute unless U.S. ships returned it, shot for shot. Pres. Woodrow Wilson refused and ordered the Atlantic Fleet to Mexico's Gulf Coast.

On April 21, a German ship bearing arms for Huerta was due at Veracruz, and Wilson wanted to prevent the delivery. He ordered the town's custom house seized to capture the guns after they were safely out of German hands. Only two hours after receiving the order, a combined force of 787 marines and sailors went ashore at Veracruz. Both sides hoped to avoid bloodshed, but the cadets of Mexico's naval academy and some private citizens resisted the landing. Nonetheless, U.S. troops quickly seized the custom house, completing the occupation of Veracruz by noon on April 22. An army brigade under General Funston replaced the naval and marine contingent shortly thereafter and stayed in Veracruz until November 1914.

The navy learned much in Mexico. First, it discovered that it could mobilize quickly if needed. Within 24 hours of receiving orders, the Atlantic Fleet was headed to the Gulf. The navy met the great logistical challenge as well. As Secretary Daniels bragged, "one giant ship took on 1,000 tons of coal, provisions for 1,000 men for six weeks, huge quantities of various supplies, gathered up officers and men ashore and on leave, and was tugging at her anchor awaiting only the signal to proceed, all in a bare 12 hours."

There were other positive signs, too. Navy lieutenant P. N. L. Bellinger flew the navy's first combat mission to look for mines in the harbor. The Navy Medical Corps prevented epidemics in the military and civilian populations. Perhaps the only sour note was that, despite the Americans' best efforts, the German ship still had been able to deliver its cargo to another port.

Mexican Border Campaign

The army's sternest test began Mar. 9, 1916, when Francisco "Pancho" Villa raided Columbus, New Mexico, killing 18 Americans. The raid prompted Wilson to order Gen. John J. Pershing's Punitive Expedition into Mexico to capture Villa. Pershing decided to advance into Mexico with two complex columns of infantry, cavalry, field artillery, the 1st Aero Squadron of eight airplanes, field hospitals, wagon and ambulance companies, and signal detachments. The first troops did not cross into Mexico until March 16, and the week-long delay proved to one newspaper editor that the army was "not prepared even for a fourth-class skirmish."

Attempts to catch Villa and his men proved futile. Although he was badly wounded and briefly believed to be dead, Villa avoided capture. Between March 29 and June 9, Pershing skirmished with Villa's men at least 10 times,

Gen. John J. Pershing, leader of the Punitive Expedition into Mexico in 1916, stands outside living quarters in Casas Grandes, Mexico. (Library of Congress)

Lt. George S. Patton, later of World War II fame, served as Gen. John J. Pershing's aide-de-camp during the Punitive Expedition. (Fort Sam Houston Museum)

suffering 15 dead and 31 wounded. When Pershing refused to give up the chase after several months of trying to catch Villa, the Huerta government informed him that any future moves in any direction but north could be considered as acts of war. In response, adding to the Texas, Arizona, and New Mexico National Guards already called up, the War Department considered mobilizing at least 65,000 more troops. At Carrizal on June 21, U.S. troops clashed with Mexican government soldiers, withdrawing after taking 44 casualties, the largest loss of the expedition. Even after Villa recovered from his wound and restarted active campaigning in the summer, however, Wilson decided to prevent further hostilities, restricting Pershing to a 150-

U.S. soldiers receive a semaphore message from a hilltop outpost during the 1916 campaign to capture Mexican guerrilla leader Pancho Villa. (Library of Congress)

U.S. soldiers line the trenches in 1916 at an encampment during the Punitive Expedition into Mexico. (Library of Congress)

mile strip of land in northern Mexico. His hands tied, Pershing withdrew to Columbus in February 1917.

The incursion into Mexico offered many good signs, but the problems were far more glaring. Pershing's aircraft suffered from cracked propellers; only two of his eight planes could still fly after one month's active service. Still, the utility of reconnaissance airplanes where terrain did not impede vision was convincing. Experiments continued in aerial photography, gunnery, and bombing.

The quality of the army's machine guns came under scrutiny. Even at Veracruz, the guns had shown a tendency to jam. Additionally, they were sensitive to moisture, even

A grim Gen. John J. Pershing, shown at his encampment at Namiquipa, Mexico, in 1916, was frustrated by the elusive Pancho Villa, who evaded capture. (Library of Congress)

the evening dew. As the *New York Sun* reported, the army's machine gun could "answer the demands made on it between sun-up and sun-down," but it was "not to be depended on after twilight."

Transportation delays, solved only by a quick purchase of 54 trucks, showed how little progress had been made since 1911 concerning logistical demands in rapid mobilizations. While the trucks performed well enough, they probably could have done even more if the drivers and their escorts had not had to build roads as they went. Pershing formed at least 10 truck companies during his campaign, but initially most drivers were civilians. The burden of the supply effort still rested on packtrains and the standard four-mule wagon. Other motorized vehicles, such as the 6 Dodge passenger cars Pershing obtained for his staff, showed promise, but motorcycles with mounted machine guns were not stable enough for the rough terrain. Still, even they showed sufficient promise to merit future trials.

Although the Punitive Expedition gave only a few of his troops genuine combat experience, Pershing made up for it with a massive training program, in which he emphasized mobility and firepower. Instructors paid special attention to marksmanship, fire discipline, and mock battle. Military intelligence services also caught Pershing's attention. Much of what Pershing learned here, he would soon put to good use in Europe on the western front (1917–18).

FACING THE FUTURE

In an amazingly short time, both the new army and the new navy had accomplished many of their goals. With both a centralized and streamlined administration and a more highly trained generation of officers to command these forces in peace and war, the U.S. military establishment had reached new heights of efficiency and professionalism. When the United States entered World War I in 1917, it faced the challenge with armed forces dramatically improved over those that went to Cuba and the Philippines in 1898.

6

World War I—America Prepares for War: 1916–1918

On June 28, 1914, Gavrilo Princip, a Serbian nationalist, assassinated Archduke Francis Ferdinand of Austria-Hungary and his wife in Sarajevo, Bosnia. Although a terrible incident, few in Austria-Hungary, much less the rest of Europe, expected this episode to begin a series of events that would lead to a general European war. Still fewer Americans, protected by the Atlantic Ocean and a tradition of avoiding European disputes, expected that the United States would be drawn into this war.

WAR IN EUROPE: 1914–1917

Europe, just prior to World War I, witnessed an era of unprecedented economic and population growth. A widespread belief in peace, prosperity, and progress was reinforced by a period of cooperation and by the growth of numerous international organizations. Yet, beneath the surface of this peaceful existence lurked forces that would destroy this world. Nationalism—supported by public education, universal military service, and an inflammatory press—heightened natural peacetime rivalries, both economic and political. Economic competition, through the search of raw materials, markets, and colonies, created tensions throughout the world. The need to protect national interests worldwide led to an arms race involving armies and navies of the major powers. To deter potential enemies in Europe, alliance systems were created. On the eve of war, Europe was divided into two armed camps.

Germany, under Kaiser Wilhelm II, played a central role in the instability of Europe. This newly unified country, which had become the major industrial power on the continent, wanted to be a major world power. Acquisition of colonies, a first-class navy, and a powerful army were the tools Wilhelm desired to demonstrate German power. These actions indirectly threatened France, Britain, and other countries. As a result, two separate alliance systems eventually developed: the Central Powers (Germany, Austria-Hungary, and Italy) and the Triple Entente or Allies (France, Britain, and Russia). When war actually came, the smaller nations reconsidered, but the major powers held to the alliances. During most of the war, the Central Powers consisted of Germany, Austria-Hungary, Turkey, and Bulgaria. Italy backed out in 1914. When the war started, the Allies included France, Britain, Russia, Belgium, and Serbia. Later, they were joined by Italy in 1915, Rumania in 1916, and other countries throughout the war. The assassination of the archduke initially seemed a crisis similar to those in Morocco in 1907 and 1911 and in the Balkans in 1912 and 1913. However, this situation was different. Misunderstandings, bungled diplomacy, and rigid military plans would precipitate war.

1914: Failure of the Plans

European military professionals agreed about the nature of the next war. It would be quick, deadly, and decisive. It was expected that the nation that most quickly could concentrate, by conscription, its manpower into a large army and begin movement would have a decisive advantage. Germany, lacking defensible frontiers and faced with a possible war against both France and Russia, developed the Schlieffen Plan to solve its strategic dilemma. To deal with the two-front war, Count Alfred von Schlieffen and the German general staff chose to defeat France first and then to turn to Russia. The plan lacked flexibility to adjust to the possibility of fighting only Russia, without involving France. To obtain a quick victory against the French in order to be able to concentrate against a slower developing but more massive Russian threat, the Schlieffen Plan, modified by Chief of the General Staff Helmuth von Moltke, began with an attack through neutral Belgium on Aug. 4, 1914. In addition to creating an uproar in the international community, the violation of Belgium's neutrality brought a British Expeditionary Force (B.E.F.) to the continent. If the German plan failed to destroy the French army and the B.E.F. by a massive encirclement before the Russians attacked, it made the two-front war inevitable.

French Plan No. 17 called, upon completion of mobilization, for an immediate attack into Alsace and Lorraine, the provinces lost to Germany in 1871. Gen. Joseph Joffre, the French commander in chief, launched his initial attacks on August 14. The result was a disastrous defeat with massive casualties. French eagerness to attack German positions supported by modern weapons became an eagerness to die. As the French attacks toward Germany were in progress, the German movement through Belgium threatened the French army with an envelopment. Once he belatedly recognized the German threat to his rear—using the time provided by the resistance of the small Belgium army, the delay actions of the B.E.F. at Mons and Le Cateau, and the fighting of Gen. Charles Langrezac's French 5th Army—Joffre conducted a masterful repositioning of forces using his superior interior lines and rail net. Coupled with an attack against the exposed German right flank by Gen. Joseph Gallieni (the military governor of Paris who used taxis to move his hastily formed units forward), the German armies paused to reposition units just when the B.E.F. attack at the Marne River on September 6 moved into a gap in the German forces, causing Moltke to order a withdrawal. On September 14, Moltke was replaced by Gen. Erich von Falkenhayn, who served Germany as both chief of the general staff and war minister. The attempts of both sides to turn the exposed flank of the other, known as the "race to the sea," ended when both forces rested their flanks on the North Sea. The bloody repulse of the German attack at Ypres beginning October 20 demonstrated that neither side had sufficient combat power to break the front that winter.

The military professionals had been partially right. The war had been deadly, but it had been neither decisive nor quick. The armies had decimated each other without decisive result. As the armies in France burrowed into the ground, defensive systems (consisting of trenches covered by barbed wire and defended with magazine-fed rifles, machine guns, and quick-fire artillery) stretched 466 miles from the North Sea to the Alps. In France, the tactical problem for the entire war would be how to make a breakthrough of these defenses.

As the plan was failing in France, the Germans, under the team of Field Marshal Paul von Hindenburg and Gen. Erich von Ludendorff, were able to defeat Russian forces at Tannenberg in August and at the Masurian Lakes in September. However, Austria-Hungary suffered severe defeats in Serbia and in Galicia. To regain the initiative on the eastern front, Falkenhayn decided that the German main effort for 1915 would be against the Russians, with defensive operations in France.

By the end of 1914, the war was being fought worldwide. In maritime fighting in the South Atlantic and the Pacific, the British navy swept the German High Seas Fleet and German merchant shipping from the oceans. The British Grand Fleet established a distant blockade from its anchorage at Scapa Flow. A German counterblockade using submarines was instituted. Successful land operations were conducted against German colonies by the Japanese in the Pacific and in China and by primarily British colonial forces in Africa. The exceptional failure was German East Africa where German lieutenant colonel Paul von Lettow-Vorbeck continued operations until after the armistice in 1918. Unsuccessful operations were conducted against the Turks by the Russians in Caucasia. The British Indian army occupied the southern part of Mesopotamia to secure the oil fields. The scope of the war had expanded to well beyond the European continent.

At the end of 1914, the belligerent nations faced a war none had envisioned. The massive losses of the initial campaigns had brought only stalemate and the promise of greater losses in the future. The armies were immobilized, exhausted, and remnants of what they had been only months before. The lack of munitions was general. The home fronts would have to be organized to ensure that the limited resources of their respective nations were efficiently used to sustain the war effort. No nation saw how victory would come, but none saw defeat as inevitable.

1915: Searching for Success

Operations in France in 1915 were a series of uncoordinated and unsuccessful attacks relying more and more on artillery to achieve the breakthrough of the front defenses. Even so, the losses, particularly among the French, were appalling. But it took time to mobilize the munitions industries so that adequate artillery ammunition was available. Both Britain and France faced a "shell shortage scandal" as the governments and the armies sought to create the resources and to develop the techniques needed to achieve the elusive breakthrough. British attempts at Neuve Chapelle in March and at Loos in September were no more successful than those of the French. Ironically, a German limited offensive at Ypres, designed to tie down Allied forces in France while German operations were conducted against Russia, created the gap needed for the breakthrough. On April 22, the Germans released chlorine gas from canisters. Through ghastly deaths and panic, this experiment created a hole in the British line. However, there were inadequate German forces available to exploit this success. The Germans were as surprised as the Allies. The introduction of poisonous gases, expressly forbidden by the Hague Convention, was a serious propaganda setback for the Germans. After this first use of gas, both sides developed defensive chemical warfare equipment, as well as deadlier gases and improved means of delivery through artillery.

International opposition to German actions had increased when Germany decided to conduct unrestricted submarine operations against all shipping on February 4. In response to this violation of the accepted rules of naval warfare, the uproar from neutrals, particularly the United States, was intense. This was reinforced with the sinking of the passenger ship *Lusitania* on May 7. The pressure applied by the United States helped cause the German reconsideration and modification of this policy in September. The submarines were once again placed on a leash, no longer able to sink any ship on sight.

On the eastern front, the Germans and Austro-Hungarians achieved the most successful operation of the war. On May 2, the Gorlice-Tarnow Offensive began with a short artillery preparation supported with gas. Through the gap created, German forces, supported by Austro-Hungarian units, moved 80 miles in less than two weeks. By September, the Central Powers had advanced 300 miles, caused 1,000,000 Russian casualties, taken 1,000,000 Russian prisoners, and liberated Galicia, the Polish salient, and parts of Russia. This contrast with operations on the western front was startling. Following up this success against Russia, a successful fall offensive against Serbia drove the remnants of the Serbian army to the island of Corfu. It was reconstituted there by the French and then moved to Salonika in Greece, where it fought alongside Allied forces landed too late to aid the Serbs earlier.

British leaders such as First Lord of the Admiralty Winston Churchill and Prime Minister David Lloyd George looked for ways to win the war without the slaughter in France. On February 19, in response to an appeal for help from the Russians, the British navy tried unsuccessfully to force a passage through the Dardanelles. On April 25, British and French units under Sir Ian Hamilton landed on the Gallipoli Peninsula, beginning a nine-month campaign known for bungling, lost opportunities, and failure. Landings at Sulva Bay in August were no more successful. The Turkish defense, commanded by German general Liman von Sanders, succeeded after heavy losses on both sides. The only thing that went well at Gallipoli was the exceptionally well-planned and flawlessly executed evacuation. In May, Italy joined the Allies by declaring war against Austria-Hungary. For those who still sought alternatives to operations in France after the fiasco at Gallipoli, Italy and Salonika remained attractive during the war.

In December, Field Marshal Joffre met Allied commanders at Chantilly to coordinate a plan for operations against the Central Powers for 1916. It was agreed to attempt simultaneous attacks in each theater at basically the same time. Although no Allied unified command existed, Joffre was attempting to apply pressure on the Central Powers strategically rather than each theater command attempting to conduct the war in its own manner. The British and the French agreed to attack together along the Somme River valley in the summer.

1916: Stalemate and Attrition

Germany's chief of the general staff Falkenhayn decided that France was to be the main theater in 1916 and ruined the Anglo-French plans by moving earlier. Falkenhayn sought to bring the French to battle where they most easily could be overcome. Verdun was chosen as the place and attrition as the method; the French would be destroyed by firepower. On February 21, the longest and most intense battle of the war began. On December 18, 302 days later, it ended. The tenacious defense made Gen. Henri Pétain a hero and the successor to Joffre. Successful counterattacks in the last months of the battle, directed by Gen. Robert Nivelle, reoccupied much of the lost ground with minimal French casualties. Although Verdun held, 66 French divisions, half of the French army, rotated through Verdun and suffered heavily there.

To reduce pressure on the French at Verdun, Sir Douglas Haig, B.E.F. commander, launched his first offensive at the Somme on July 1. The first day produced 60,000 casualties with limited gains. The battle continued into November. Tanks, developed as a means to break the stalemate, were introduced on September 15. Mechanically unreliable and used in small numbers, the tanks did not perform well. Resistance to the tank at B.E.F. general headquarters did little to ensure a successful initial operation. By the end of the year, the front had moved less than six miles despite the millions of casualties suffered since stalemate in late 1914.

On the eastern front, Gen. Alexi Brusilov launched a successful Russian attack in Galicia on June 12. The Germans sent forces to reinforce the Austro-Hungarians. Hindenburg and Ludendorff, who replaced Falkenhayn in September as Germany's supreme commander, decided to focus the main effort in 1917 against the Russians. The success of the Brusilov Offensive provided Rumania the opportunity to enter the war on August 27. Unfortunately, a masterful winter campaign conducted by Falkenhayn overran the country, and Bucharest was occupied on December 6.

On May 31, 1916, the Battle of Jutland, the only major naval action of the war, was fought. The British Grand Fleet under Adm. Sir John Jellicoe sought battle with the German High Seas Fleet under Adm. Reinhardt von Scheer.

Pres. Woodrow Wilson, determined to maintain U.S. neutrality in the face of the war in Europe, reviews the cadets at West Point in 1916. (U.S. Military Academy Archives)

Scheer's spirited engagement of the British battle cruisers of Adm. David Beatty quickly became a complicated and desperate attempt to break contact and escape under the cover of darkness to his bases in the Baltic when he discovered he faced the entire Grand Fleet. After limited losses by both sides, the battle was a tactical stalemate; but the British, ready for action the next day, retained control of the surface of the seas. If German naval action was to play a part in the war, it would have to rely upon the submarines.

1917: Prospects

Hindenburg and Ludendorff believed Russia could be defeated in 1917. In fact, a revolution occurred in February, but Aleksandr F. Kerenski (Russian revolutionary leader and subsequent war minister) promised the Allies that Russia would continue the war. How long the Russians would be able to continue when the Germans attacked was questionable. The German navy convinced the Kaiser that unrestricted submarine operations would drive Britain out of the war in six months. The risk of neutral intervention, particularly by the Americans, was considered. Even if they did intervene, American military power was potential and could not be delivered immediately. If the submarine campaign worked, then time would not favor U.S. involvement.

For the Allies in 1917, General Nivelle convinced Lloyd George that, with British support, he could conduct a successful offensive based upon the methods used at Verdun. Even when the Germans voluntarily withdrew to more defensible terrain, Nivelle remained confident. When the attack came in April, at the same time that the United States came into the war, it failed with heavy losses. The French soldier lost confidence in his commanders, which led to French mutinies. General Pétain, called upon to rebuild the French army, chose as part of his program the slogan that the French were to "wait for the tanks and the Americans." The Allied situation was becoming bleak as the United States entered the war.

U.S. CONDITIONS

Upon the outbreak of hostilities in Europe in August 1914, Pres. Woodrow Wilson committed the United States to a policy of strict neutrality. He was determined to ensure that U.S. actions would show no favoritism to any belligerent. In the United States—a nation of great ethnic diversity and multicultural ties—this was a politically difficult position, but Wilson received support for his neutrality stance from most Americans, who believed that what happened in Europe was of no concern to the United States.

Actions taken by the Central Powers, particularly Germany, strengthened anti-German sentiment. The unprovoked German declarations of war on France and Russia, the attack on neutral Belgium, along with atrocities committed (magnified by Allied propagandists), shocked and angered many Americans. Germany seemed determined to fight the war in violation of the accepted rules of warfare. This belief was reinforced when the Germans introduced poisonous gas and when they began aerial bombardment of noncombatants in British cities. As heinous as these actions appeared, the most shocking to Americans was submarine warfare.

Demands for money and for war matériel from belligerents increased during the war. As a neutral, the United States was free to trade with all, which it did. Contracts were negotiated with both sides, but more with the Allies than with the Central Powers. Demand, gold, shipping, and geography made business more profitable and reliable with the Allies. Not only had $2 billion of business been concluded with the Allies by 1917, but loans to the Allies approached $2.5 billion, compared to only $45 million to Germany. American banks were betting on eventual Allied success, while American business was depending on freedom of the seas to ship its products to European trading partners.

Freedom of the Seas

Freedom to sail the seas unmolested and to trade with any country it wished was the right of a neutral power. This was a principle in which the United States strongly believed and for which it had fought in the past. International agreements established procedures for blockade, for contraband goods, and for neutral shipping. The United States expected both the Allies and the Central Powers to abide by these rules. Almost from the beginning, British blockade procedures and an ever-lengthening list of contraband goods caused tensions between the United States and Britain. Seizure of cargo by the Royal Navy created unpleasant incidents but no loss of life. Blunt diplomatic notes passed between both countries. Britain chose to modify some of its practices at times, but its blockade remained in force. Tensions decreased as U.S. trade and economic ties shifted toward the Allies. On the other hand, German submarine operations created a major uproar when Germany declared a restricted zone around Britain in an attempt to enforce a blockade of its own. The threat to sink ships on sight, without warning and without following naval prize rules, prompted immediate protest from the United States.

The seizure of cargo by the British was a minor problem compared to the loss of ships, cargo, and lives that the German submarine threat presented. Americans died aboard British ships in the spring of 1915, but the incident that caused the greatest protest was the May 7 sinking of the passenger ship *Lusitania*. Of the 1,198 passengers who drowned, 124 were American. Outrage over the high loss of civilian lives on an unarmed passenger liner was immediate. Sharp diplomatic notes were exchanged between the United States and Germany. Disagreement on these notes to Germany was so strong within the Wilson cabinet that Sec. of State William Jennings Bryan resigned. Bryan feared the United States was being pushed toward war. The U.S. note did not stop German submarine operations. However, after a similar sinking of the passenger ship *Arabic* in August, German submarine commanders were instructed to avoid passenger and neutral shipping vessels. The desire to appease neutrals, particularly the United States, caused the Germans to restrict submarine operations. A wider war was to be avoided if at all possible.

Leonard Wood, U.S. Army chief of staff (1910–14) (seated, left), *with James G. Harbord* (standing) center, *began a voluntary training camp at Plattsburgh, New York, in 1915, in an effort to prepare the nation for war.* (U.S. Army Military History Institute, Washington I. Wallace Collection)

William Jennings Bryan, Pres. Woodrow Wilson's secretary of state (1913–15), remained a neutralist and resigned his office in 1915 when he felt that the United States was edging toward war with Germany over the sinking of the Lusitania. (Library of Congress)

Preparedness Movement

President Wilson's neutrality stance permitted no military preparations that departed from traditional U.S. military policy. He refused to take any actions that would indicate a willingness of the United States to enter the war. Believing unpreparedness to be dangerous, former president Theodore Roosevelt and former U.S. chief of staff Leonard Wood pushed an effort to generate interest among the public to prepare the nation for a war they saw coming.

While chief of staff, Wood had begun a program in which college students received military training at summer camps. This voluntary program was supported by the students who paid for the training. In 1915, Wood opened another voluntary camp at Plattsburgh, New York, for men from the professional and business communities. Expenses were paid by private donations. The success of the Plattsburgh camp led to the creation of other such camps throughout the country.

Nationwide organizations arose, such as the Army League and the National Security League, to lobby for increased military preparedness. Building on the ideas of Roosevelt, Wood, and others, they pushed for a larger army and navy, as well as for conscription. A vocal minority, the preparedness movement kept the poor state of military preparedness in the public view. As with most extreme movements, it generated opposition as well as support. Opponents saw preparedness as a dangerous program that would militarize U.S. society and lead to involvement in a European war where Americans had no business. The nation's lack of preparedness was of little concern to most Americans, who did not see U.S. involvement in a major war as a likelihood.

During this debate over preparedness, a major revision of the U.S. military establishment occurred. The National Defense Act of 1916 addressed the size of the regular army, the designation of a trained reserve force, the need for economic planning, the expansion of the General Staff, and the recognition of conscription in principle. The political debate was heated. Sec. of War Lindley M. Garrison, a partisan of increased preparedness, made a strong appeal for national troops raised by conscription to replace reliance upon soldiers from state organizations, especially the National Guard. Unwilling to compromise, Garrison was replaced by Newton D. Baker. Responding to the demand for an increased readiness and to the political influence of the National Guard, while remaining steadfast to his policy of neutrality, President Wilson signed a compromise bill that totally satisfied few.

The regular army remained the force ready for immediate action. It was to increase to 175,000 over a five-year period. During war, the regular army would expand further to 286,000. The law authorized new units: divisions and brigades. Three brigades were to make up a division; three regiments were to make up a brigade. Although an attempt to put the U.S. Army on a modern basis, it did not provide for corps, armies, nor army groups, larger commands that were common in Europe at the time.

In addition, the problem of an inadequate organized reserve for the U.S. Army was addressed. Federal supervision of the National Guard was increased by the creation of a Militia Bureau of the General Staff. Members of the National Guard swore two oaths, one to the state and a new oath to obey the president and to defend the Constitution of the United States. This solved the problem of calling upon the state militia and not having it available for service outside the continental United States. Once brought into federal service, the National Guard became part of the national army and subject to the same regulations as the regular army. The National Guard was to increase from about 100,000 to almost 400,000 over several years. In addition, several other organizations were created to provide for specialists. A regular army enlisted reserve was established to identify former regular army soldiers for emergency service. An Enlisted Reserve Corps for engineer, ordnance, medical, signal, and quartermaster specialists was created. The summer camps for businessmen and college students were militarized in the Officers' Reserve Corps and the Reserve Officer Training Corps. The National Defense Act made the National Guard, supplemented by these new organizations, the principal trained reserve for the U.S. Army in time of war.

Three additional sections of the act were of importance for the upcoming war in Europe. First, the obligations of every able-bodied male citizen between the ages of 18 and 45 to serve was reaffirmed by designating such a force the Militia of the United States. This laid the basis for conscription if necessary. Second, although economic mobilization for war was seldom addressed, this act permitted the president to place orders for military materials and to regulate (through coercion and compensation) industries involved in military contracts. The secretary of war was to survey the armaments industry. A rider to the August 29 army appropriation bill created the Council of National Defense, an advisory commission to discover the problems associated with economic mobilization. The council, chaired by the secretary of war, consisted of the secretaries of war, navy, commerce, labor, agriculture, and the interior. The third important action was to increase the General Staff to 55 officers, including 3 generals. No more than 26 junior officers were to be assigned duty in or near Washington, D.C., at any one time. This increase in the General Staff was designed to reduce the influence of the bureau chiefs. When war came in 1917, only 19 General Staff officers were on duty in Washington, compared to 232 for Britain and 650 for Germany in 1914. Despite the provisions of the National Defense Act of 1916, the U.S. Army would be largely unprepared when war came. The program embodied in the act was hardly adequate to prepare for modern war, and five years were not available to get ready.

Naval armaments also were an issue in 1916. On February 3, President Wilson supported the recommendations of the navy's General Board calling for a U.S. Navy that in Wilson's words was to become "incomparably the greatest navy in the world." The program called for 10 battleships, 6 battle cruisers, 10 scout cruisers, 50 destroyers, and 67 submarines. Sec. of the Navy Josephus Daniels oversaw this unprecedented buildup of the U.S. Navy. The Naval Act of 1916, which received congressional approval on August 29, called for a three-year building program. This act also authorized a wartime strength of 17,400 for the U.S. Marine Corps. When war began seven months later, the naval building program was just beginning to get underway. A balanced fleet organized around battleships proved unnecessary to meet the unique demands of convoy duty to counter German submarines.

Status of U.S. Army

In April 1916, Sec. of War Newton D. Baker, a former mayor of Cleveland with no military experience, assumed his post after Garrison was removed over the National Defense Act of 1916. Baker's principal advisers were Chief of Staff Maj. Gen. Hugh L. Scott and Asst. Chief of Staff Maj. Gen. Tasker H. Bliss. Both were approaching retirement and had no experience in modern warfare as fought in Europe. Tensions between the bureau chiefs and the General Staff continued despite the Root Reforms. Of the fewer than 20 General Staff officers in Washington, 11 made up the War College Division, which did planning for war.

On the eve of war, no plans existed to send an expeditionary force overseas. In fact, President Wilson chastised the War College for undertaking contingency planning to determine what would be required if forces were to be sent to Europe in the future. To Wilson, this was not neutrality. The U.S. Army had the mission to defend the continental United States and U.S. colonies against attack. The organization of the army into four continental departments and two overseas commands (Hawaii and Philippines) supported this mission. All plans were defensive.

Expansion of the regular army authorized in the five-year program of the National Defense Act of 1916 had not occurred. The regular army numbered about 133,000, a force so small that Peyton C. March (who became chief of artillery for the American Expeditionary Force in 1917) described it as "scarcely enough to form a police force for emergencies within the territorial limits of the United States." Tensions along the Mexican border led Wilson to federalize part of the National Guard. As a result, the 70,000 National Guardsmen on federal service brought the U.S. Army to a total strength of just over 200,000. Only about 130,000 men served as the reserve for this force: 110,000 National Guardsmen, 4,700 regular army reservists, 10,000 enlisted reservists, 4,400 National Guard reservists, and 413 reserve officers. During April 1917, the month that the United States entered the war, the French army *lost* almost as many men in two weeks during the Nivelle Offensive as the U.S. Army *had* on active duty. Compared to the million-man armies in Europe, the U.S. Army had a long way to go to match the numbers. However, numbers alone did not make a modern army, and the U.S. forces were deficient in these areas as well.

Essential equipment was limited in quantity and in quality. Adequate quantities of the Model 1903 Springfield rifle were available for a force of more than 500,000. Beyond that, almost all weapons and equipment required for men in battle were absent or limited in quantity. Fewer than 1,500 machine guns existed. None of the four most common models had interchangeable parts. No light automatic weapon existed. No tanks existed. No gas warfare capability, offensive or defensive, existed. Trench mortars and hand grenades, essential for trench warfare, were nonexistent. Even steel helmets did not exist. The artillery had a few light artillery pieces, but the heavy and medium artillery used by European forces did not exist. Artillery ammunition on hand was described as adequate for a preliminary regimental artillery bombardment of about nine hours. Even aircraft, which Americans invented, were inadequate. Of the 55 planes in the Aviation Section of the Signal Corps, 50 were obsolete and 5 were obsolescent by European standards. Not only was equipment for the regular army inadequate to fight in the modern warfare conditions of Europe, but the ability to expand quickly to a much larger force was virtually nonexistent.

Despite the experience in France where army groups, armies, corps, and divisions fought modern industrialized war, the basic U.S. combat unit remained the regiment. The brigades and divisions authorized in 1916 appeared only on paper. No particular attention had been paid to warfare in Europe, which had been considered irrelevant to immediate U.S. Army needs. Unit training focused on marksmanship and small unit exercises emphasizing fire and movement. Both rifle marksmanship and open warfare methods would be emphasized in France. Ironically, only 40 percent of the regulars qualified better than marksman between 1909 and 1914, and open warfare methods had proven disastrous early in the European war. The U.S. Army was deficient in manpower, equipment, force structure, and doctrine. Except for a determination to make a significant contribution, the U.S. Army would begin the war essentially unprepared for the challenges of modern European war.

Status of U.S. Navy

The first line of U.S. defense traditionally was its navy. Since 1913, Secretary of the Navy Daniels, a former North Carolina newspaperman and politician, ran the Navy Department. His tenure was not without controversy, particularly within the navy, which regarded Daniels as ignorant of naval affairs. Daniels appointed Franklin D. Roosevelt as his assistant secretary. Roosevelt, cousin of the former president, was a strong supporter of the U.S. Navy and a firm believer in the ideas of naval historian Alfred Thayer Mahan. The chief of naval operations (CNO), Rear Adm. William S. Benson, received 15 assistants from the Naval Act of 1916. They helped Benson in issuing instructions in the name of the secretary of the navy. This became the naval equivalent of the army's General Staff. It was also the way that both the navy secretary and the CNO controlled the 8 semi-independent bureau chiefs. The Naval Act of 1916 made the CNO the senior admiral in the navy upon the death of Adm. George Dewey (1837–1917), then president of the navy's General Board.

When war came, the U.S. Navy consisted of approximately 67,000 officers and men, who manned 300 ships and 130 shore stations. It was organized around the battleship, the fleet's primary fighting instrument, in which both Mahan and the navy had long believed. The Marine Corps numbered just over 10,000. The navy was much better prepared for immediate response to war than was the army, but its battleship fleet was ill prepared to be tasked with antisubmarine missions.

DECLARATION OF WAR

In January 1917, the Germans announced the resumption of unrestricted submarine operations effective January 31. Adm. Henning von Holtzendorff, chief of the German admiralty staff, convinced the Kaiser and his principal advisers that Britain could be driven from the war within months. The risk of U.S. involvement was weighed and accepted. The United States was unprepared for war and would take time before it could field a large, modern army. If the submarine campaign worked, the U.S. Army could not cross the Atlantic until too late, and then at great peril.

President Wilson, although just narrowly reelected on the platform that "He kept us out of war," willingly accepted the German challenge. Wilson considered the repeated German threat to American freedom of the seas provocative. Diplomatic relations with Germany were broken on February 3. An inflamed U.S. public was further outraged by what became known as the "Zimmermann Telegram." On February 23, the British provided a copy of a January 16 note from German foreign minister Arthur Zimmermann to his ambassador in Mexico. The note proposed that Mexico join Germany in a war against the United States. In return for its effort in tying down U.S. forces, Mexico was to receive land in Texas, New Mexico, and Arizona. Upon publication of this note, Wilson asked for armed neutrality—that is, the arming of U.S. merchant ships so that they could defend themselves. This note, coupled with sensitivity about activities along the Mexican border, enraged the U.S. public, which pushed Wilson toward war. Wilson resisted, but on March 18, the triple sinking of the ships *Illinois, Vigilancia,* and *City of Memphis,* with heavy loss of life, made a call for war almost inevitable. On March 25, he called additional National Guardsmen to federal service. The United States actually entered World War I over the issue of unrestricted submarine operations.

On April 2, Wilson addressed Congress. The preceding days had been filled with demonstrations both for and against the war. In his address, Wilson asked that Congress "formally accept the status of belligerent which has . . . been thrust upon it" by German actions. He addressed not merely the issue of peace or war but also the means by which he intended the United States to fight the war. He referred specifically to large increases in the armed forces based upon conscription, to economic mobilization, to increased taxation, to suppression of dissent, and to central direction of the war effort by the executive branch of the government. On April 6, by a vote of 82 to 6 in the Senate and 373 to 50 in the House of Representatives, the United States entered the war.

From the beginning, Wilson made clear that the United States had no formal ties to the Allies. The United States would fight as an "associate power" working with the Allies to bring about the defeat of Germany. But Wilson was to fight this war for higher goals. In his address asking for war, Wilson had stated: "The world must be made safe for democracy." Although U.S. entry into the war was triggered by the renewal of unrestricted submarine warfare, Wilson began to espouse broad, ideological goals, which he would codify in his Fourteen Points of January 1918. Although U.S. military forces were desperately sought by the Allies, enthusiasm for Wilson's proclamations by Allied statesmen was subdued.

INITIAL ACTIONS

Intense planning kept the War College Division of the General Staff busy as it grappled with basic, but complex, questions: What size force would be required in France? How would conscription be administered? What would be the role of the regular army? How would the force be equipped and fought? How would industry be organized to support the war effort? The answers to these questions, essential to planning, evolved as requirements were identified, modified, and changed again. The confusion, chaos, and frustration in the War Department was constant throughout the entire war.

Secretary of War Baker relied heavily upon Major Generals Scott and Bliss. When President Wilson sent Scott, the chief of staff, to Russia on a fact-finding mission, the initial War Department efforts were directed by Bliss and his assistant, Brig. Gen. Francis J. Kernan, a member of the General Staff. They were assisted by a limited number of General Staff officers, originally fewer than 20.

Trained General Staff officers were scarce, the demand for them unlimited. Legislation in May increased the number permitted in Washington to a mere 91, of which 47 were assigned to the War Plans Division. Created during the Root Reforms in 1903, the General Staff was modeled after the German army's general staff. As described by Johnson Hagood, a General Staff officer and later a key supply officer in France, the General Staff was composed of "men without war experience, and in imitation of a German system which they did not understand." By September, its number in Washington was down to 24 men.

Determining the requirements, coordinating the War Department bureaus, working with industry, and responding to countless problems placed upon the General Staff the biggest challenges faced by any group of U.S. military planners to that time.

Even if the General Staff positions had been increased, the number of officers trained to fill such positions was limited. Of the 6,000 regular army officers at the beginning of the war, there were about 200 graduates of the Leavenworth Command and Staff College, 343 graduates of the original Leavenworth School of the Line, and fewer than 200 graduates of the Army War College, which produced the General Staff officers. Confusion in the War Department, compounded by the shortage of qualified personnel, prompted Col. Robert L. Bullard to remark, "If we really have a great war, our War Department will quickly break down." By the end of the war in 1918, more than 200,000 officers would be in the U.S. Army, a number greater than its total strength in April 1917.

Immediately after the declaration of war, foreign missions began to arrive in Washington. Britain's mission, headed by foreign secretary Arthur J. Balfour and Lieutenant General Bridges, arrived on April 20. On April 24, the French arrived with Prime Minister René Vivani and Marshal Joffre, the hero of the Marne. Italians, Russians, Rumanians, and Belgians followed. Basically, each mission sought financial assistance, an immediate commitment of forces to France, and a voice in what the U.S. war effort should be. In return, these missions provided the War Department information on the conditions in France. The British and the French both offered to send military missions to assist in the training of U.S. units in the United States. Bridges broached the subject of amalgamation of U.S. soldiers into British units, but the idea was not well received.

After consulting with the French military mission, the War College recommended on May 10 that the regular army not be sent to France immediately. Because of its small size, it was believed best to use the regular army as a training cadre for the massive army that was to be built. Only after 1,500,000 men had been trained would any be sent to France. To establish the foundation for the deployment of this American Expeditionary Force (A.E.F.), the study recommended that the designated commander and a planning staff go to France to determine what was needed in France prior to the arrival of the A.E.F. Although sound militarily, politically this advice was unacceptable. President Wilson decided a force had to be sent immediately.

Maj. Gen. John J. Pershing, who had been commander of the Punitive Expedition in Mexico, was chosen to command the A.E.F. Summoned to Washington, Pershing arrived on May 10, spoke briefly with the president, conferred with the War Department, created his staff, received his instructions, and boarded the USS *Baltic* on May 28 with his staff to make the journey to France. At the same time, the 16th, 18th, 26th, and 28th infantry regiments were formed into the newly created 1st Division, filled to authorized strength with recruits, and sailed on June 14. The U.S. Army was en route to the war.

Rear Adm. William Sims convinced the British that the convoy concept would decrease the number of ships sunk by German submarines during World War I. (U.S. Army Military History Institute)

With war imminent, the Navy Department sent Rear Adm. William S. Sims, president of the Naval War College and former commander of the Destroyer Flotilla of the Atlantic Fleet, to Britain. Sims arrived in London on April 10 and conferred with the First Sea Lord of the Admiralty, Sir John Jellicoe. Sims, known for his pro-British bias, was welcomed. The success of the German submarine campaign was a shock for which he was not prepared. Sims suggested, about the same time that Prime Minister Lloyd George directed, that convoys could be the solution to the problem. Because of its focus on the fleet action, the dull nature of convoy duty, and the difficulties of working with merchant seamen, the Royal Navy had studied and rejected the convoy idea previously. When Sims arrived, one in four ships leaving Britain was sunk. A trial convoy in May was successful, and convoys were permanently established. The loss rate dropped dramatically to one percent. Fighting the submarine threat would become the major function of the navy; destroyers became more important than battleships.

On April 24, the first 6 U.S. Navy destroyers left Boston for the war. On May 4, they took station at Queenstown, Ireland. Within four months, the U.S. Navy presence increased to 37 destroyers, assorted craft to assist in the convoy duty, and 5 battleships. Vice Admiral Sims, promoted in May, remained in London throughout the war as commander of U.S. Naval Forces Operating in European Waters. The U.S. Navy was in action before the A.E.F. sailed and a year before the first major A.E.F. offensive in France.

MOBILIZATION

With the outbreak of war, the War Department found itself taking the lead in the war effort. Secretary Baker, through the General Staff, attempted to coordinate conscription, civilian industry, War Department bureaus, other governmental agencies, and shipping to France. It was a massive undertaking and would take almost 15 months before a semblance of order replaced the chaos described by Colonel Bullard.

Manpower

Secretary of War Baker, upon the advice of Chief of Staff Scott, recommended that President Wilson establish a draft immediately, to which Wilson agreed. Baker called a conference with Scott, his assistant Bliss, Adj. Gen. Henry P. McCain, and Judge Adv. Gen. Enoch H. Crowder, to prepare the legislation. Crowder strongly opposed the draft as not being in harmony with American ideas. He recommended the volunteer system instead. Ironically, it became Crowder's task to draft the bill that he, as provost marshal general, would have to administer. Upon return to his office and particularly with the aid of Hugh S. Johnson, a cavalry captain with a law degree, Crowder drafted the legislation with the express purpose of avoiding the problems that had existed with the Civil War draft. He returned the draft to Baker within 24 hours, a masterful performance that few in the War Department would match.

Although numerous volunteers came forward immediately, the passage of the Selective Service Act of 1917 on May 18 ensured that manpower would not be a problem. This bill authorized a draft of 500,000 for the national army with additional increments of 500,000 men permitted as needed. It also included provisions for increasing the regular army to 286,000, for calling 459,000 National Guardsmen to federal service, and for raising four divisions of volunteers composed of men over the age of 25. The volunteer divisions, championed by Theodore Roosevelt, were not supported by the War Department, and none were raised.

Nothing successful happened by chance in the War Department. The General Staff study conducted by Crowder had carefully reviewed the Civil War draft system. To ensure that the worst mistakes of that experience were not repeated, the draft system was administered by civilians, not the military. Each eligible able-bodied man would register for the draft. Local draft boards, composed of civilian fellow citizens, would receive a draft quota and determine within prescribed regulations which men would serve. Initially, all able-bodied males aged 21–30 were eligible. On August 31, the ages were extended to 18–35. All conscripts were to serve for the duration. This legislation eliminated the worst abuses of the Civil War draft: substitutes, bounties, purchased exemptions, and enforcement by the military. The smooth administration of this system speaks highly for the wisdom and foresight of Crowder.

The General Staff initially considered eliminating volunteers but considered it unwise, given congressional and traditional support for the volunteer system. In fact, the draft acted as an incentive to enlistments in the regular army and the National Guard. Recruitment was curtailed as each reached its authorized strength. In November, it was announced that enlistments by draft-eligible personnel aged 21–30 would be discontinued in December. Army enlistments ceased on Aug. 8, 1918, and navy and marine enlistments in September. Conscription became the only means of recruitment until the end of the war.

Two out of every three men who served were drafted. In 20 months, the strength of the military increased from more than 200,000 to 3,700,000 men, of whom 2,800,000 were draftees. Of the men who served, 10 percent were National Guardsmen, 13 percent were regulars, and 77 percent were draftees of the national army. Most of the conscripts (90 percent) were not married, and 70 percent were farm or manual laborers. The tendency of local draft boards not to conscript married men led to a marriage boom. About 20,000 men sought conscientious objector status, but almost 16,000 changed their minds when faced with an unsympathetic military justice system. To support the war effort, local citizens conducted "slacker raids" to encourage draft-eligible men to register and serve. Some 337,000, about 12 percent of those drafted, failed to show for service. By the end of the war, nearly 4,000,000 men were in the U.S. Armed Forces.

Military Units

After men were raised, it became necessary to house, equip, train, and ship them overseas. The task of housing the influx of recruits fell to the newly created Cantonment Division of the Quartermaster Corps. As commander, Col. I. W. Littell worked with the civilian Committee on Advisory Construction to build 16 cantonments for the National Guard and 16 for the conscripts of the national army. To meet a completion date of Sept. 1, 1917, Littell found it necessary to make adjustments. If most of the camps were located in the South, it would be possible to build 16 tent cantonments for the National Guard units that were expected to ship quickly to France. In addition, 16 wooden barracks cantonments would be established for the national army divisions that would require year-round training fa-

Enlisted men in the army went through training before they were shipped off to the war in Europe; here, "doughboys" (slang for World War I enlisted men) line up for a meal. (U.S. Military Academy Archives)

cilities. With no time for the peacetime competitive bidding process, Littell was one of the first to use the Council of National Defense's controversial cost-plus contract procedures. The contractor received 6–10 percent above cost for completing his project on time. The Cantonment Division, working with civilian builders, met the challenge. It completed the 32 camps almost on schedule and, more important, in time to receive the soldiers.

Clothing the new soldiers stretched the resources of Q.M. Gen. Henry G. Sharpe. Before the war, he had notified the War College that stocks on hand existed for only 75,000 men. Federalizing the National Guard for Mexican border service in 1916 had depleted the reserves' stocks. By August 1917, orders were placed for clothing and equipment for 1,500,000 men. Sharpe requested that the national army draftees not report until October, providing time to finish the cantonments and to acquire the clothing needed from Quartermaster Corps factories and civilian industry. By December, more than 1,600,000 soldiers had been clothed. Despite this Herculean effort, the Quartermaster Corps received criticism in the press and became the subject of a congressional inquiry. In December, Sharpe was replaced by Maj. Gen. George W. Goethals, the builder of the Panama Canal, who was recalled from retirement to become the acting quartermaster general.

Other bureaus and government agencies faced similar difficulties trying to procure various items of personal and unit equipment within a short time span. Although none existed except on paper, divisions had to be created. The exact number of divisions that would be required was unknown, but a system was established for their designation. Regular army divisions were to be numbered from 1 to 25, National Guard divisions from 26 to 75, and national army divisions beginning with 76. No volunteer divisions were raised. Of the 62 divisions organized, 43 saw service in France: 8 regular army, 17 National Guard, and 18 national army. Although they all were composed principally of draftees late in the war, each division had its own personality: the regulars prided themselves on serving as the model, the professionals; the guardsmen prided themselves on their state identities; and the national army draftees saw themselves as the epitome of the citizen soldier who does the difficult task and then goes home. Unit pride and competition got out of hand at times. In August 1918, the War Department found it necessary to declare that henceforth there would be only one army, the Army of the United States.

Training was rudimentary in the beginning. Not only was equipment absent but officers and noncommissioned officers had to be trained. There were not enough experi-

The army uniform of the World War I era reflected the modernization of the armed forces. (U.S. Military Academy)

enced soldiers to go around. An army of 4,000,000 would require more than 200,000 officers. In 1917, there were only 6,000 regular officers and 14,000 National Guard officers. The remainder of those needed were selected, trained, and commissioned from the ranks, from civilian occupations, and from the Officers' Training Corps (OTC). Of the 200,000 officers required during the war, 50 percent were OTC "90-day wonders," 33 percent were commissioned direct from civilian occupations, and 17 percent were direct commissions from the regular army and the National Guard. The noncommissioned officer problem was even more severe. Consequently, military instruction in the United States consisted of the teaching of basic soldier skills and marksmanship, small-unit training, and post schools to train the leaders and specialists needed for modern warfare. Although most divisions trained for almost six months in the United States, the quality and quantity of training was adversely affected by shortages of personnel, leaders, and equipment, as well as by bad weather. Many units would require extensive retraining in France before they would be prepared for the rigors of combat.

Economy

European nations had faced the challenge of adapting their entire society to the demands of total war, but none had anticipated the problems. Each had muddled its way into a centralized, state-controlled economic system. Despite this experience, U.S. prewar preparations were sadly lacking. The National Defense Act of 1916 created the Council of National Defense to provide centralized planning and control of economic mobilization, but little had been accomplished prior to the war other than a survey of 18,000 factories. A February 1917 War College review of each bureau's ability to provide for a 1,000,000-man army identified glaring deficiencies, none of which could be solved quickly nor easily. Attempting to meet the requirements of the U.S. war effort, coupled with Allied contracts for equipment and munitions and a resistance by business

Many troops were trained after arrival in Europe; here, a U.S. soldier at an advance post near Amphersbach, Alsace, Germany, demonstrates the proper method of throwing a grenade from a trench. (U.S. Army Signal Corps)

to centralized control, created immediate chaos in the War Department.

Secretary of War Baker shared with President Wilson the basic belief that civilian leaders should interfere as little as possible in military matters. This had a tremendous impact upon the powers that the War Department would eventually assume in directing the U.S. economy, as well as upon the relationship between General Pershing and the chief of staff. In addition, for political reasons, both the president and Congress were slow to exercise control over the economy. The War Department assumed the lead in the war effort.

In May, Congress authorized the War Department to increase the number of General Staff officers to 100 and authorized the chief of staff to have "rank and precedence over all other officers of the Army." This should have made it possible for a strong chief of staff, if supported by Secretary Baker, to control and direct the actions of the War Department, the General Staff, and bureaus. However, Baker did not push for a strong chief of staff. He used the chief of staff and the General Staff to provide him with advice on the raising, planning, equipping, and shipping of the army, but he chose to let the bureaus continue to exercise full authority in their functional areas. Duplication of effort, waste, inefficiency, and endless red tape resulted.

Allowing Pershing to choose key War Department personnel from both the General Staff and the bureaus for his A.E.F. staff made the problems of the War Department doubly difficult. The War College Division, for example, lost Brig. Gen. Joseph E. Kuhn, its president, and two-thirds of its members. By September, only 24 inexperienced General Staff officers remained. Each bureau suffered similar losses at this critical time. There simply were not enough experienced personnel available for all the important tasks that were happening simultaneously.

Through the General Staff, the chief of staff planned, scheduled, and coordinated the mobilization, training, and transporting overseas of units. A reorganization of the U.S. Army from four to six continental departments—Northeastern, Eastern, Southeastern, Southern, Central, and Western—and from two to three overseas Departments—Hawaii, Philippines, and Panama—was an attempt to simplify the task of the War Department. At the same time, the General Staff was beginning to interact with the A.E.F.'s general headquarters to determine its requirements and to refine plans to meet those needs.

Secretary Baker left each bureau chief responsible for the actual running of his bureau's function in the army. Without central direction, each bureau competed with the others for limited resources. By July, 150 different War Department purchasing committees were running amuck. For example, the adjutant general cornered the market for all typewriters in the United States. No one else could acquire one. The commander of Rock Island Arsenal did the same thing with leather. As he testified before a congressional committee, "It was up to me to look after my particular job, and I proceeded to do so." Nine separate systems existed in the War Department for estimating requirements. None had a system of inventory control to determine what was available. No agency in the War Department was responsible for establishing industrial or transportation priorities. Without central direction, the War Department became its own worst enemy.

The War Industries Board (WIB), a civilian agency established to work with the War Department, was responsible on paper for economic mobilization. Even if the War Department had been able to establish requirements and priorities, the WIB had a difficult task and no authority to enforce its decisions. Frank Scott, its first chairman, quit in October, his health broken. His successor, Daniel Willard, former president of the Baltimore & Ohio Railroad, fared no better and quit in disgust in January 1918. Not only was the War Department in chaos, the WIB was powerless also.

Even if both the War Department and the WIB had worked smoothly, there were still extremely difficult problems that took time for American industry to work through. For example, the French mission requested that more than 10,000 aircraft be built. This was more than existed in all armies in Europe at the time and required a massive expansion of the U.S. aircraft industry. In the process of expansion, the requirements were refined. The industry suffered a series of false, frustrating, and expensive starts. Another problem arose in the manufacture of the French 75-millimeter artillery piece. Because its manufacture specifications were secret and not precise enough for U.S. industry, delays resulted as a gun had to be acquired and each component measured in the United States so that assembly-line procedures could be developed for mass production. Changing requirements, desire to make a profit, and incompatible systems were some of the reasons that industry was resistant to direction of the economy by the government.

Despite these problems and inefficiencies, the War Department, supported by U.S. industry, was able to clothe, feed, and provide basic equipment for units to begin training. But it was clear that this method could not continue long. In December 1917, the supply problems, coupled with massive rail and ocean traffic congestion in New York (45,000 rail cars were backed up as far as Pittsburgh and Buffalo because of a shortage of warehouses, docks, and wharves), created a gridlock that brought public and congressional uproar to a peak and compelled Secretary Baker to take action.

Deployment Overseas

Allied demands for men continued throughout 1917. The U.S. and British navies were successfully dealing with the submarine threat along the 3,000-mile Atlantic route through convoys. However, the shipping available was extremely limited, making the buildup of the A.E.F. slower than the Allies desired. At the beginning of the war, the War Department had four troop ships and three cargo ships. Without other sources, it would be a long time before troops arrived in France.

The Shipping Board was created to obtain tonnage for both personnel and cargo. A decision by President Wilson to cease construction on the large naval ships authorized in the Naval Act of 1916 made it possible to concentrate shipbuilding on merchant shipping and on destroyers and smaller craft needed for escort duty. Industry met the challenge by developing a prefabricated ship that could be quickly constructed. By the end of the war, the United States would be the world's leading shipbuilder. Other sources of shipping were developed by the Shipping Board. Neutral shipping was contracted. Ships were bought from other nations, such as China and Japan. In addition, 444 ships were commandeered, and 91 German ships were seized, including the large passenger ship *Vaterland,* renamed *Leviathan.* Ironically, the *Leviathan,* because of its speed and troop-carrying capacity, carried many members of the A.E.F. to France. With these limited assets, just over a half million Americans arrived in France in the first 13 months of the war. The majority, 1,500,000, were shipped in the last 6 months of the war when the British provided shipping because of the desperate situation in France. Almost 50 percent of all Americans sent to France were shipped in British ships. Efficient use of limited shipping was essential, but lack of central direction and coordination added to the crisis in the winter of 1917–18.

ADJUSTMENTS TO WAR

Difficulties in supply, transportation, and economic mobilization led to a congressional inquiry by the Senate Military Affairs Committee, chaired by Sen. George E. Chamberlain. Members of the inquiry attacked the inefficiency and waste of the War Department. As a solution, it proposed, as Thomas N. Perkins of the WIB had argued, that the British model of a separate, civilian supply organization parallel to the military supply departments be established. This would provide an interface between the military and industry. Since the War Department bureaus were considered bound up by red tape and tradition, it was generally accepted that supply and procurement activities were better suited for businessmen than for soldiers.

War Department Readjustments

Prodded by Congress, the WIB, the General Staff, the business community, and the pressure of events, Secretary Baker began to bring the War Department under better control. The Quartermaster Corps faced the toughest problems and received the harshest criticism. In November, Baker appointed Benedict Crowell, a Cleveland industrialist with a commission in the Quartermaster Corps, as his assistant secretary of war. Crowell was a strong advocate of centralized control of the war effort. In addition, on December 20, Major General Goethals became the acting quartermaster general. A week later, Goethals also became the director of the Storage and Transportation Division, a new General Staff agency created to ensure that the rail and port congestion in New York was resolved and did not recur. Crowell and Goethals were hard-nosed and totally dedicated to bringing the war effort under control. Goethals agreed with the WIB that his Quartermaster Corps was ill prepared for its task. It was a huge purchasing agency, not a military operation. He began to staff it with civilian experts. Edward R. Stettinius became surveyor of supplies. Robert J. Thorne, president of Montgomery Ward and Company, became Goethals's volunteer aide in January 1918. By March, he had become Goethals's principal assistant. A new vigor and firm hand was being applied to a portion of the War Department.

On February 9, a major reorganization of the War Department strengthened centralized control of the war effort. The chief of staff was chartered to supervise and to coordinate the various bureaus, corps, and agencies of the military establishment. The General Staff, his tool for accomplishing this, was responsible now for supervising, not merely coordinating. Five assistant chiefs of staff—executive assistant for administration, control, and

In March 1918, Maj. Gen. Peyton C. March, shown here receiving a decoration from Sec. of War Newton D. Baker, became acting chief of staff and worked to centralize the War Department. (U.S. Army Military History Institute)

intelligence; director of war plans; director of operations; director of storage and transportation; and director of purchase and supplies—were appointed to supervise activities along functional lines. The bureaus and other agencies were to be supervised by these staff sections. The initial structure for centralized control was in place, but it would take a strong chief of staff and further refinements to the organization before the war effort would be a consolidated venture.

On March 4, 1918, over the opposition of Secretary Baker, President Wilson appointed Bernard M. Baruch, a Wall Street financier, as chairman of the WIB. Baruch brought a new firmness to the dealings with industry. With better information from the War Department of what was required and after the Overman Act strengthened the WIB, Baruch orchestrated the economic war effort by allocating scarce commodities to various industries and establishing transportation priorities. The WIB became the key government agency for economic control.

On the same day that Baruch became WIB chairman, Maj. Gen. Peyton C. March became acting chief of staff. March, hardworking and ruthless when it came to bureaucratic inertia, was obsessed with the immediate need to bring the War Department and all of its agencies under the direct control of the chief of staff. Although the February 9 reorganization established the principle, inefficiency and foot-dragging by many agencies continued. March, a harsh taskmaster, made an immediate impact upon the War Department. Those who shared his vision and who met his standards did well; those who did not were replaced. The adjutant general, Maj. Gen. Henry P. McCain, a staunch defender of the rights and privileges of the bureau chiefs, was one of the first to go. He was replaced by Maj. Gen. Peter C. Harris, an infantryman with no respect for red tape nor bureaucratic procedures. Through his persistence, March played a key role in transforming the War Department from a decentralized operation run along bureau lines to a centralized operation organized, and finally run, along functional lines.

Bureau resistance to centralization and rationalization was enormous, particularly by the five supply bureaus. Finally, to create one War Department agency responsible for the majority of logistical issues, the directorate of Purchase, Storage, and Traffic (PS&T) was created on April 16 under Goethals. This new organization combined all the functions and the staff supervision of the bureaus that the directorates of Purchase and Supply and of Storage and Traffic had previously. This new organization made work with the WIB and coordination of logistical effort more efficient, but it still did not bring the logistical functions of the War Department under single control.

Overman Act

Despite the efforts of men such as March, Goethals, and Baruch, without congressional legislation granting them wider powers, they could only plead, suggest, or cajole in many cases when it was imperative to be able to direct. That void was filled with the passage on May 20, 1918, of the Overman Act, which gave the president the authority to reorganize government agencies for greater efficiency for the duration of the war. Using the act's provisions, government tightened its control and its ability to manage the war effort more efficiently. Baruch reorganized the WIB and deepened its control over raw materials, commodities, and transportation assets. The result was a more rational and responsive economic effort that met the needs of the war effort with minimal disruption of the home front.

Final War Department Organization

Adjustments within the War Department continued as problems were confronted, solutions developed, and new organizations created to meet the demands of modern war. The Air Service, Tank Corps, Chemical Warfare Service, and Motor Transport Service were just a few of the new components and demonstrated the variety and complexity of modern armies. The last major reorganization of the War Department during the war occurred on August 26. The General Staff became an active operating agency responsive to the chief of staff, not just the supervising agency it had been. The five General Staff sections became the Executive Assistant Division, the Military Intelligence Division, the War Plans Division, the Operations Division,

The Air Service was one of the new organizations within the War Department created to meet the demands of World War I; above is a Breguet bomber of the 96th Aero Squadron at Amanty, France, in July 1918. (U.S. Army Signal Corps)

and the PS&T Division. The PS&T finally brought all the logistical agencies under one General Staff agency. Many smaller agencies and services were created and merged as the war went on, but an effective War Department organization, responsive to a strong chief of staff and capable of working closely with a strong WIB, finally existed. Despite false starts, seemingly impossible obstacles, and intense bureaucratic resistance, by August, the War Department had undergone a managerial transformation. In less than six months, through the efforts of March, Goethals, and Baruch and the passage of the Overman Act, rational principles of centralized control and decentralized operations overcame the traditional and bureaucratic methods that had dominated the War Department during the first year of the war. This crucial struggle, far from the battlefield, had to be won if support of the A.E.F. was to be possible.

A.E.F.-WAR DEPARTMENT DISAGREEMENTS

Given the unpreparedness for war and the nature of the U.S. war effort, it is not surprising that misunderstandings arose between the War Department in Washington and the A.E.F. general headquarters in France. The magnitude and complexity of the tasks each faced were alien to previous American experience. Neither side developed empathy for the difficulties of the other. Each believed that it was in charge. Transatlantic cables lent themselves to misunderstanding. Fighting overseas, without prior preparation, meant that problems identified rarely had immediate solutions. Confusion and chaos ruled in Washington and in France as insurmountable difficulties were addressed.

Secretary Baker unknowingly made the situation worse. In May 1917, legislation clearly stated that the chief of staff had precedence over all officers. However, in France, Major General Pershing was treated as the commanding general in the sense of the pre-Root Reform commanding general. When March became chief of staff, he pushed for the preeminence of the chief of staff both within and without the War Department. With the creation of the rank of full (four-star) general, March made an issue of date of rank with Pershing. Although Baker sided with March, his dealings with Pershing were unchanged. The A.E.F. staff tended to see all efforts to provide unsolicited assistance as an attempt to undercut its position. It considered the questioning of its requirements by the War Department and the inability of the War Department to meet its timetables as lack of support. It failed to understand the impact of changing requirements from France on the efforts of the War Department. After the war, Pershing had Col. George C. Marshall do a study of the War Department support of the A.E.F. Marshall concluded that the War Department did all that it could under the circumstances to support the A.E.F. The tension that existed during the war broke out into a ''war of the books'' as March and Pershing and their supporters wrote their memoirs after the war.

Several major issues arose between the War Department and the A.E.F. Early on, there was confusion and disagreement on the number of troops required and when they could be available. The War Department accepted the A.E.F. requirements, but as the number of divisions required increased as the war took a turn for the worse, the War Department found the 100-division request not only unwise but undoable. Officer promotions also became an issue as the War Department promoted officers that Pershing had not requested and did not promote some he recommended. A major concern late in the war was the offer made by Secretary Baker to send Goethals to France to assist Pershing with his logistical difficulties. Baker's intention was to assist, but Pershing and his staff took it as an attempt to reduce their authority in France. The offer was refused, and Pershing took Maj. Gen. James G. Harbord, former A.E.F. chief of staff, out of division command and made him the commander of the Services of Supply. Although there was lack of understanding and confidence at times, generally the A.E.F.-War Department relationship was effective.

Col. George C. Marshall (right), *shown here with Brig. Gen. John L. Hines* (seated) *and Col. Campbell King, reported to Gen. John J. Pershing after the war on the support of the War Department during World War I.* (U.S. Army Military History Institute)

Maj. Gen. James G. Harbord (left), *shown with Brig. Gen. Charles G. Dawes, served as commander of the Services of Supply for Gen. John J. Pershing's American Expeditionary Force.* (U.S. Army Military History Institute)

OVERALL HOME FRONT EFFORT

The United States was unprepared for a war of the magnitude and the complexity that it faced during World War I. President Wilson's policy of neutrality, coupled with a tradition of noninvolvement in European wars, made military planning and preparation next to impossible. Compared to its Allied counterparts, the U.S. Army was miniscule. The U.S. Navy was organized for the classic fleet encounter but not prepared for antisubmarine operations. Plans for economic mobilization were nonexistent. The War Department was organized for peacetime and, despite the Root Reforms, still divided between the bureaus and the General Staff. In 20 months, to raise a force of almost 4,000,000, to ship 2,000,000 troops to France, and to get it there faster than scheduled was an amazing feat.

There were many lessons to be learned. President Wilson and Secretary Baker were both slow to support a centralized War Department effort despite recommendations provided from those inside and outside of government. The draft system was a highlight of the U.S. effort. It worked smoothly largely due to the foresight of Maj. Gen. Enoch H. Crowder. In most areas, major deficiencies existed that were resolved through trial and error. The U.S. merchant fleet was inadequate. Without assistance from the British, U.S. forces would not have been shipped to France in 1918. Economic mobilization was poorly executed due to inadequate planning, confusion over requirements, the complexity of the problem, and a general lack of time. The involvement of civilian experts in this process was essential for what success was achieved. Just as the economic war effort was getting under control and poised for a major contribution in 1919, the war ended. Finally, the War Department was not organized to handle the challenges of total war. It took almost 16 months before it developed an effective organization. The experience in World War I affected how the United States would prepare for its next war. Every country that sustained a total war effort in World War I had to grapple with these and similar problems in the midst of war. Most muddled their way through without destroying their war efforts. Given the state of unpreparedness in 1917, the U.S. war effort was amazing. It was not efficient, it was not pretty, but it worked.

7

World War I—America at War: 1917–1919

On May 28, 1917, Maj. Gen. John J. Pershing, commander of the American Expeditionary Force (A.E.F.), departed New York City aboard the *Baltic*. Ten days later, his A.E.F. contingent of 40 regular officers, 2 marine officers, 17 reserve officers, 5 civilian interpreters, and 123 enlisted soldiers and clerks arrived in Britain en route to France. On June 13 in Paris, they began the enormous task of building the A.E.F., an undertaking more demanding and more complex than that faced by any previous U.S. commander. Pershing, a demanding taskmaster, would test all of his organizational, managerial, diplomatic, and military skills time and again in his effort to create an American army 3,000 miles from the United States amidst the demands of war.

CREATION OF THE A.E.F.

Prior to his departure, Pershing, along with Sec. of War Newton D. Baker, visited Pres. Woodrow Wilson. Wilson gave Pershing his complete trust and confidence, but little guidance. Throughout the war, Wilson let Baker run the War Department and Pershing run the A.E.F. with minimal presidential supervision. On May 27, 1917, Pershing received written instructions from Secretary Baker. He was directed to command all U.S. land forces in Europe, to include attached marines. Pershing was to proceed with his staff to France to establish a logistical base to support U.S. participation in the war. Cooperation with the Allies was emphasized, but Pershing was personally empowered to decide when and how the A.E.F. would fight. He was also tasked to ensure that Americans fought as a separate and independent command. Pershing's powers and responsibilities were greater than any other commander in chief in France.

The Challenge

During his initial conferences with the French, Pershing became aware, for the first time, of the mutinies among the French soldiers. The Allied situation was more desperate than he had anticipated, which explained the Allied demands that U.S. soldiers be amalgamated into French and British units as replacements. Pershing would spend more time fighting with the Allies over amalgamation and establishing his logistical base than over any other issues during his first year in France. Other than the hastily thrown together 1st Division on its way to France, there actually was no A.E.F. Pershing and his chief of staff, Maj. James G. Harbord, a fellow cavalryman, oversaw an intense and important period of crucial decision making to make the A.E.F. a reality. Basic questions demanded immediate answers. In what sector of the Western Front would the A.E.F. fight? How would it be supported? How would A.E.F. general headquarters (GHQ) be organized? What size force was required? How would it be organized? How would it be equipped? How would it be trained? Many of these issues had been initially studied aboard the *Baltic,* but specific answers had to be hammered out with the French. An unprecedented organizational and managerial challenge, the answers to these questions were crucial both for the A.E.F. buildup in France and for the War Department mobilization in the United States.

World War I, the Western Front, 1914–18

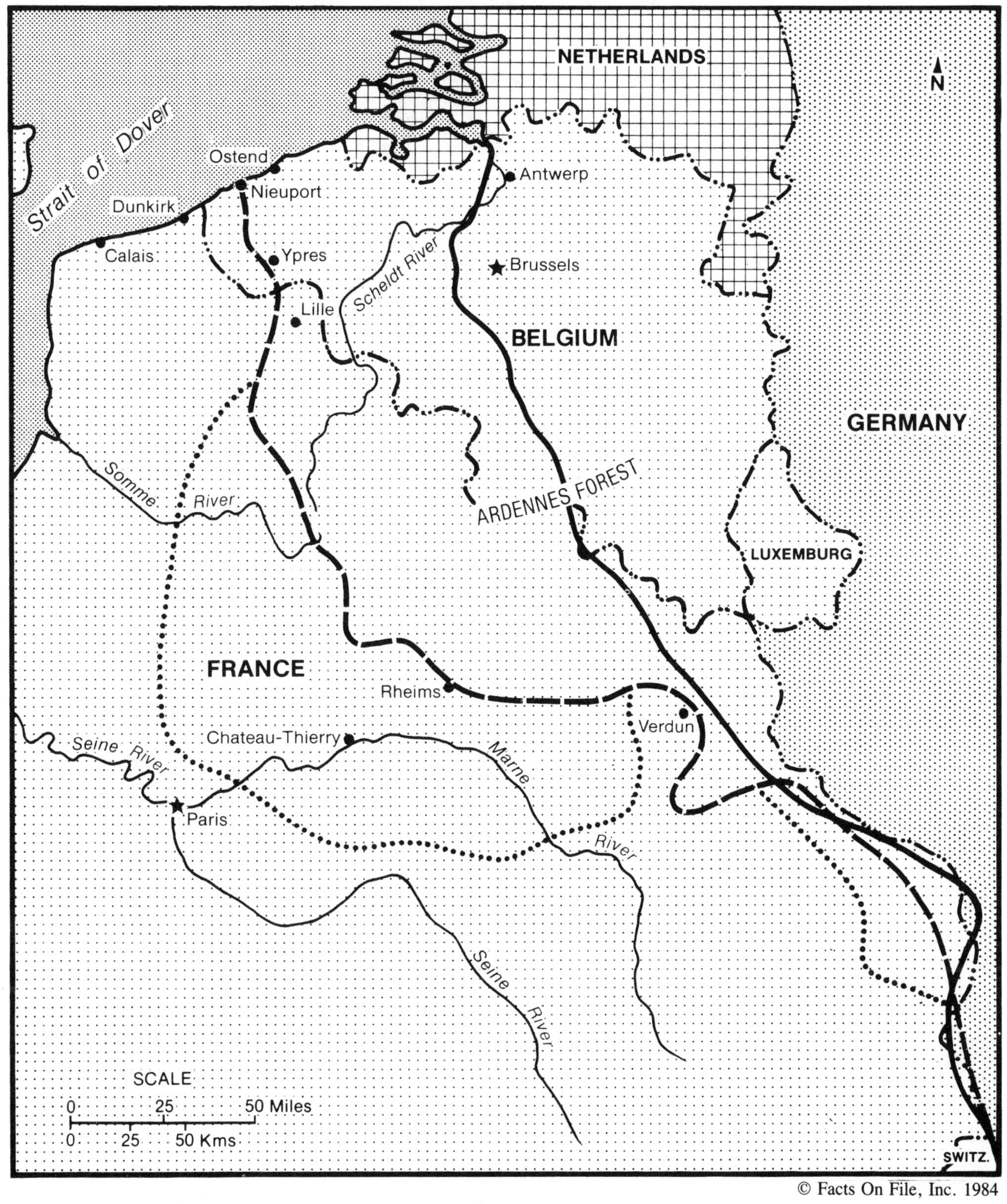

German position, Sept. 1914

Front line, Nov. 1918

Nov. 1914-March 1918 (Siegfried Line)

Gen. John J. Pershing was briefed by France's Marshal Ferdinand Foch on the desperate conditions among the Allied forces; here he escorts Foch from the Leviathan. (Library of Congress)

Initial Decisions

By July 1, Pershing obtained French approval for the A.E.F. to concentrate in Lorraine. This placed the Americans near the fortified German border in the vicinity of Verdun, Nancy, and Épinal. Although difficult to support logistically, this sector offered several strategic opportunities. It threatened a key east-west German railway that ran along the Western Front, as well as Metz, the iron fields around Briey, and the Saar coal fields. German defenses in this sector were well organized and in depth. From the start, GHQ considered the reduction of the St.-Mihiel salient, an operation the French unsuccessfully attempted in 1915, as the first A.E.F. operation.

Logistical, rather than strategic, considerations drove the selection of Lorraine. The ports along the Bay of Biscay were relatively unused compared to the English Channel ports that supported the British Expeditionary Force (B.E.F.). The railroads between the coast and Lorraine were limited. The A.E.F. staff determined that to support a force of 2,000,000 Americans in Lorraine, the railroads needed to handle 50,000 tons of supplies daily. Railroads from Bordeaux and St. Nazaire and from Bourges were considered adequate, with the Marseilles railroad available for an emergency. Despite the average one-way trip of 500 miles, the rail net was adequate to support the large and complex logistical organization required to build up and support a

Strategical Features Influencing Selection of the Lorraine Front for the American Army

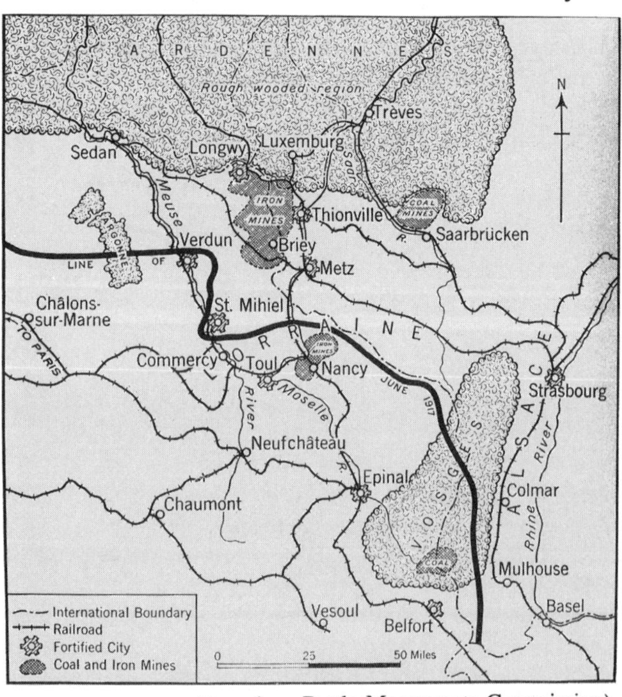

(American Battle Monuments Commission)

separate American army in Lorraine. To oversee A.E.F. logistical problems, the Line of Communications (LOC) was organized on July 5. Brig. Gen. Richard M. Blatchford directed this awesome task. His headquarters were eventually established in Tours, along the crucial railroad in the center of numerous logistical bases.

Initial GHQ organization was established on July 5. The Field Service Regulations of 1914 were modified by the addition of the Air Service. Three general staff sections (operations, administration, and intelligence), three administrative staff sections (adjutant general, inspector general, and judge advocate general), and six technical sections (quartermaster, engineer, ordnance, signal, medical, and air service) reported directly to Pershing. To meet the demands of the war, additional technical staff sections were created. Eventually, the French general staff system was adopted. For most of the war, Avery D. Andrew served as G-1 (administration), Dennis E. Nolan as G-2 (intelligence), Fox Conner as G-3 (operations), George van Horn Moseley as G-4 (supply), and Paul B. Malone as G-5 (training). By September 30, at GHQ in Chaumont, Pershing had 5 general staff sections, 15 administrative and technical staff sections, numerous commanders, and several Allied missions seeking his personal attention. This bulky, centralized staff almost strangled A.E.F. staff work. In March 1918, GHQ would be reorganized as a coordinating staff with 5 general staff and limited administrative sections. The technical section and most administrative sections were placed on the staff of the final A.E.F. logistical organization, the Services of Supply (SOS).

Pershing cabled the War Department on July 6 that at least 1,000,000 men were needed in France by May 1918. He warned that a strong American presence was needed early and suggested that shipping shortages be overcome by an agreement with the Allies. A detailed plan, known as the General Organization Project, followed on July 11. This plan was the product of a joint conference between GHQ and the Baker Board. Secretary Baker had sent a fact-finding team under Col. Chauncey B. Baker, a quartermaster officer, to France to determine what needed to be done. No one notified Pershing, who considered the independent Baker Board as more of a hindrance than a help. This became the first of several incidents that soured relations between the War Department and GHQ. Pershing was adamant that only one recommendation would go to the War Department. It took several days to reach an agreement. The General Organization Project stated that the smallest U.S. force needed in France would be a 1,000,000-man "complete, well-balanced, and independent fighting organization." It needed to arrive by May 1918. Plans for the manufacture of equipment such as artillery, aviation, and tanks were to be based upon an A.E.F. of at least 3,000,000 men. Fortunately, this requirement remained unchanged for almost a year.

This plan called for an independent American army consisting of 5 corps with 30 divisions. Each corps consisted of 6 divisions: 4 combat, 1 replacement, and 1 depot. A division, 28,000 men strong, was composed of 2 brigades of 2 infantry regiments and 1 machine-gun battalion each; 1 field artillery brigade of 3 regiments; 1 engineer regiment; 1 machine-gun battalion; and 1 signal battalion. This division was much different from the 3-brigade division and 3-regiment brigade of prewar force structure. It was designed specifically to have sufficient combat power not only to make a successful initial attack but to sustain it. As a result, the A.E.F. division was as large as two Allied or German divisions in 1918, making the U.S. division almost equivalent to a corps. In August, the War Department began to organize 5 regular divisions, in addition to the 1st and 2d divisions, which were being raised in France, 17 National Guard divisions, and 18 national army divisions. Corps and army units were included in the plan. Only two things were missing from the General Organization Project: engineer and logistical units. Engineer requirements for this force of 1,000,000 were set on July 14 to be 35,000. Determining the logistical requirements took several months.

Most of July and August were spent in organizing the LOC into base, intermediate, and advance sections; in developing the basis for new services such as aviation, tank, and chemical units; and in searching for sources of material to build logistical bases and to equip soldiers. Pershing's decision in September to maintain a 90-day reserve of supplies supported by an automatic supply system, along with the proliferation of new organizations not in the prewar army, created special supply and organizational problems.

On September 10, Pershing approved the Service of the Rear Project, which identified the logistical requirements for the A.E.F. The percentage of support troops increased from an estimated 189,000 in July to 330,000, a number almost 35 percent of A.E.F. combat strength. This increase represented a maturing of GHQ understanding of its logistical challenge. Units and specialists unknown in the prewar army were required to meet unique logistical tasks such as running railroads, establishing forestry operations, supervising ports of debarkation, and building massive supply depots. The Service of the Rear Project established an A.E.F. of 1,300,000 as the minimum required by May 1918. Together, the General Organization Project and the Service of the Rear Project formed the basis of the A.E.F. personnel and force structure.

What was missing from the A.E.F. plan was the Priority of Schedule forwarded to the War Department in early October. This called for shipping units in six increments; the first five each consisted of a corps of six divisions, some corps troops, and limited army troops. The remaining army troops would be in the sixth increment. A progressive, logical buildup of a separate American army was expected. Unfortunately, the inability of the War Department to meet this program, combined with adjustments made to counter the 1918 German offensives, meant that by May 1918, fewer than 400,000 Americans were in France. This was not the 1,300,000-man balanced American army envisioned by the plan. But GHQ had significant obstacles to overcome in France before the A.E.F. would be ready to fight.

Slow Buildup

Rear Adm. Albert Gleaves, responsible for the U.S. convoy system during the war, escorted the transports with the 1st Division into St. Nazaire on June 28. Aboard his flagship *Seattle,* Gleaves explained to Pershing that each of the four 14-transport sections of the convoy was escorted by 1 cruiser and 4 or 5 destroyers. The U.S. Navy had responded quickly to the submarine challenge. The problem was not the submarine but the shortage of shipping. Throughout the war, the shortage of troop and cargo ships hampered the speedy buildup of the A.E.F. more than any other factor.

This convoy, carrying the lead combat elements of the A.E.F., included about 14,500 men. These were the hastily organized units of the 1st Division created from the 16th, 18th, 26th, and 28th infantry regiments, which had been filled to strength with recruits prior to shipping to France. Commanded by Maj. Gen. William L. Sibert, the 1st Division was a division in name only, as the recruits were soldiers in name only; a long period of organization and training would be required before it would become a legitimate combat division. Accompanying the 1st Division was the 5th Regiment of the marines. It would later join the 6th Regiment to become the marines' 4th Brigade under Brig. Gen. Charles A. Doyen. These marine regiments, with the 9th and 23d infantry regiments, formed the 2d Division. The 2d Division, upon activation, was also largely composed of recruits: the marine regiments with 74 percent, and the regulars with 87 percent. Both the 1st and 2d divisions had the distinction of being formed in France. All other divisions were organized in the United States.

Shortage of personnel to work on crucial projects within the LOC caused combat troops to be diverted for use as laborers and stevedores. It became common for combat units to spend time in the ports unloading ships backlogged by port congestion. Port facilities were primitive, labor was difficult to obtain, and shipping too scarce to leave sitting in port waiting to discharge cargo. Throughout the war, the urgency for U.S. combat units to fight Germans remained juxtaposed against the need to build an adequate logistical base.

In the fall, Maj. Gen. Francis J. Kernan assumed command of the LOC, which would evolve in a series of reorganizations to the Services of the Rear, and finally the

Services of Supply of the American Expeditionary Forces

(American Battle Monuments Commission)

Services of Supply. His area of operations stretched 500 miles from the coast to Lorraine. His vast responsibilities and diverse problems rivaled those faced by the War Department's mobilization efforts. His principal Bay of Biscay ports were St. Nazaire, La Pallice, and Bassens. The 23 berths for ships in these ports were inadequate. By the armistice, 89 berths had been built of 160 planned by June 1919. Port operations remained one bottleneck; the railroads were another.

Once men and matériel were disembarked, it became necessary to move them on French railways. French railroads were not in good repair and required special skills that were missing in the A.E.F. Pershing requested a civilian railway expert. William W. Atterbury, vice president of the Pennsylvania Railroad, was commissioned and sent to France to run the A.E.F. railway system. Working with French officials was just one of his challenges. In addition to maintaining the French system and laying 1,000 miles of new track, more than 1,500 locomotives and 18,000 railway cars were shipped in parts from the United States for rebuilding in order to supplement the French railway capacity.

The lack of equipment for the A.E.F. and Pershing's decision to maintain 90 days of supplies in theater generated a tremendous demand for matériel. Equipment and supplies came either from the United States or from purchases in Europe. In September, Pershing appointed Lt. Col. Charles Dawes, a personal friend and Chicago banker, as the general purchasing agent of the A.E.F. His task was to equip and supply the A.E.F. as much as possible from European resources. This was not an easy task. Dawes had to compete with the Allies for scarce resources. He also had to encourage the Allies to sell military equipment for the A.E.F. combat units. The Americans had no helmets, no automatic rifles, no tanks, no aircraft, no medium and heavy artillery. What equipment the A.E.F. did have was inadequate for the 1,000,000-man force envisioned. Through hard work and cooperation with the Allies, Dawes was able to purchase locally 10,000,000 of the 18,000,000 tons of supplies and equipment needed during the war. This reduced the shipping requirements by 55 percent.

Acquisition of supplies and arrival of troops created a huge building program throughout central France. Hospitals, barracks, docks, railheads, bakeries, refrigeration plants, and storage facilities were needed in large numbers. U.S. forestry units provided 200,000,000 feet of lumber and 4,000,000 railway ties. The largest SOS facility was the Gievres Storage Depot, which required 25,000 men to handle 2,300 rail cars daily. It had 4,000,000 square feet of storage, the world's largest refrigeration plant, and 43 miles of railroad inside the facility. The enormity of the logistical effort, along with its unprecedented problems, forced Pershing to spend much of his first six months dealing with logistical issues.

Training Program

Pershing insisted on not sending A.E.F. units into combat until they were trained to his standards. A training section was added to GHQ to oversee unit and school training. A study of French and British training methods criticized their overreliance on trench warfare methods. Although British aggressiveness appealed to Pershing, he became convinced that while trench methods must be taught, they would not be emphasized. If overemphasized, Pershing believed, the soldier would lose confidence in his ability to attack, a condition Pershing observed among French units in particular. The A.E.F. training philosophy stressed offensive action and open warfare methods, despite Allied concern that those ideas had failed in 1914. At the soldier level, Pershing remained convinced that the rifle and the bayonet were the essential infantry weapons. In October, his goal became to enforce upon the A.E.F. the standards he had learned at West Point. American performance upon the battlefield would determine the validity of his ideas.

To instruct officers, noncommissioned officers, and numerous specialists, a school system was established. Courses existed for all units up to division level. Each corps established schools for officers and noncommissioned officers of all arms. Brig. Gen. Robert L. Bullard and Col. James W. McAndrew established the Army Schools Center. GHQ supervised the General Staff College at Langres, the officer training school, the instructor course, and the specialist schools for staff, supply, and other branches. A huge aviation training center was established at Issoudun. Pershing believed that it was essential that the A.E.F. be properly schooled as individuals and trained as units before it was committed to combat.

Divisions arriving from the United States were to have three months to learn the latest tactical and technical techniques of the Western Front and to overcome training deficiencies. This program envisioned a month to work on individual weapons, field craft, and small-unit training. This was followed by a month in the trenches of a quiet sector. Each regiment rotated its battalions to the front line for a 10-day period. The final training period focused on combined arms with all elements of the division conducting offensive operations. Because artillery training was technical and required special facilities, each division lost its artillery brigade during its training. The artillery worked with British or French artillery units and then rejoined the division. During the crisis of 1918, this program was modified. Few units went through each training phase prior to beginning combat operations.

Status at End of 1917

Despite the best efforts of those in the United States and in France, the buildup of the A.E.F. did not go exactly according to plan. Pershing had expected a corps with 32,000 troops by the end of November 1917 and a second corps by February 1918. However, by late December 1917, fewer than 4 divisions and few corps units had arrived, primarily because of shipping shortages. Pershing appealed to the War Department for 4 corps of 24 divisions by the end of June rather than the initial 30 divisions by May. The deployment developed more slowly than expected.

By the end of 1917, only 175,000 Americans were in France. Three National Guard divisions had just arrived or were in the process of arriving: the 26th Division from New England, the 41st Division from the West Coast, and the 42d (or "Rainbow") Division from 26 states and the District of Columbia. These units had yet to begin their training programs. Other than the month spent in the trenches in late October by the 1st Division, no U.S. troops had seen the front line after eight months of war. The Allies were increasingly dissatisfied with the deliberateness of the American buildup.

The year 1917 had been disastrous for the Allies. Other than the success over the submarines and the U.S. involvement in the war, failure dominated Allied operations. After the Nivelle Offensive failed in April, the French mutinies

Brig. Gen. Douglas MacArthur commanded the 84th Brigade, part of the 42d (''Rainbow'') Division; he is shown here in front of his car at St. Juvin Ardennes, France, in 1918. (U.S. Army)

demonstrated the need for a rapid and substantial U.S. buildup. Gen. Henri Pétain did much to restore the discipline of the French army, but it remained primarily a defensive force. The British suffered such casualties from July 31 to November 10 at Passchendaele that Field Marshal Douglas Haig, B.E.F. commander, lost the trust and confidence of David Lloyd George, the British prime minister. Haig's losses would not be replaced. Initial success with tanks at Cambrai on November 20 was prematurely celebrated as an Allied success; by December 3, German counterattacks regained their positions. Failures in other theaters further threatened this weakened Western Front.

By the fall of 1917, Russia was in the throes of revolution. Italy was dealt a near mortal blow at Caporetto. From October 24 to November 12, the Italians lost more than a million men. The Allies rushed limited reinforcements to Italy. At Rapallo, the Supreme War Council was created to deal with this crisis and to coordinate future Allied war efforts. Heads of state or their representatives would meet regularly, but a continuously meeting military committee was to monitor the daily progress of the war. Maj. Gen. Tasker H. Bliss, former army chief of staff, became the U.S. military representative. This bleak strategic situation reinforced the pressure on Pershing to increase the U.S. effort and to amalgamate his forces with the Allies.

AMALGAMATION

Beginning in December 1917, with a German offensive expected, the Allies once again pressed Pershing to provide U.S. companies and battalions for amalgamation into their armies. The Allies argued that the collapse of Russia, coupled with the debacle in Italy, made the immediate future perilous. Extreme measures were required. The British requested 200,000 Americans, and the French requested 100 battalions (approximately 100,000 men). Amalgamation offered several advantages to the Allies. First, it permitted the Americans to make an immediate contribution to the war effort, something the Allies had expected for months. Second, the Allies had divisions, corps, armies, and army groups organized, equipped, and staffed with experienced personnel. By the time the A.E.F. reached this level of experience and organization, the war might be lost. Third, by reducing shipping to only infantry and machine gunners, the shipping needed for units larger than battalions could be eliminated. More fighters could be sent with available shipping. These arguments seemed not only logical but imperative to Pétain and Haig.

Pershing refused to amalgamate. His instructions were to form a separate, independent American army, and he intended to do that. Pershing saw disadvantages with amalgamation. First, the Americans would not receive due credit for helping win the war if they were merely cannon fodder for the Allies. Second, U.S. public opinion demanded an American effort. It would not support using American soldiers only as fillers. Third, language and cultural differences would create difficult problems. And finally, Pershing was unconvinced that the Allies had the correct training philosophy and training program that could defeat the Germans. Pershing did offer, in the event of a crisis, to do whatever was necessary to support the Allied effort.

At Versailles in late January 1918, the British agreed to ship 6 divisions, 150,000 Americans, in British vessels in return for having these U.S. divisions train in the B.E.F. sector. Perhaps Haig thought that once the Americans were there, he would be able to keep them. In all, 10 U.S. divisions (4th, 27th, 28th, 30th, 33d, 35th, 77th, 78th, 80th, and 82d) trained with the B.E.F. The French also remained active in training the U.S. divisions.

In addition, Pershing sped up the training programs of the units in France. On January 20, he organized the I Corps, designating as its commander Maj. Gen. Hunter Liggett, an older and physically larger commander than

U.S. soldiers of Company H, 167th Infantry, have a meal in the trenches near Ancerville, France, in March 1918. (U.S. Army Signal Corps)

most Pershing accepted. In January, the 1st Division entered the French line near Toul. It was followed in February by the 26th Division near Soissons and the 42d Division near Luneville, and in March by the regulars and marines of the 2d Division near Verdun. Divisions arriving in France were sent forward to training areas despite the difficulties that still existed in the logistical base, which was reorganized as the SOS in March.

COMBAT: MARCH–AUGUST 1918

The Allied assessment of German intentions had been correct. During the winter, German general Erich von Ludendorff concentrated 3,500,000 men in 192 divisions on the Western Front. Driven by conditions in Germany and the potential threat of millions of Americans reinforcing the Western Front in the near future, Ludendorff felt compelled to seek a war-winning blow in 1918. He carefully trained his forces to break through the Allied defenses by using a combination of infiltration tactics led by specially trained "shock troops" and by using a complex and sophisticated artillery program mixing high explosive and gas munitions throughout the defensive zone. Allied strongpoints were to be bypassed and cleared by the following forces. These tactics and techniques had been tried in Riga, Latvia, and refined at Caporetto, Slovenia. The Germans developed a tactical and technical solution to the stalemate of the trenches, something the Allies, relying on firepower and tanks, had failed to accomplish despite millions of casualties and the conquest of no more than 10 miles of territory after months of fighting.

German Attack

In the dawn fog of March 21, following a five-hour artillery bombardment, the Germans launched their first attack against the B.E.F. Attacking on a 50-mile front, the Germans quickly overran the British defenses and practically destroyed the British 5th Army. The hole torn in the British line was filled with the last of the British reserves and some French divisions only after the Germans had advanced to a depth of 37 miles in eight days. On March 23, another shock occurred when Paris came under artillery bombardment by specially manufactured guns that fired shells up to 65 miles. Perhaps more devastating than the roughly 900 casualties sustained by the panic-stricken Parisians was the residual psychological impact of the assault. Continuing the attack until April 5, the Germans gained more territory in two weeks than had all the Allied offensives in three years and inflicted about 240,000 Allied casualties. With the B.E.F. barely holding on, with Paris under bombardment, and with French units focusing on the defense of Paris, the Allied situation was bleak.

Unity of Command

Field Marshal Haig requested that the British government offer to place the B.E.F. under the direction of Gen. Ferdinand Foch or some other fighting French general for this emergency. At Doullens, on March 26, the British and the French agreed that Foch would be the coordinator of operations on the Western Front. The next day, Pershing offered Foch, as he had Pétain earlier, the use of whatever U.S. forces he chose to employ. On April 3, at Beauvais, Foch was appointed commander in chief with expanded authority to coordinate the actions of the British, French, and U.S. forces on the Western Front and to conduct the strategic direction of military operations. The temporary expedient of Doullens was replaced with a permanent arrangement at Beauvais.

Lys Offensive

The second German attack, called the Lys Offensive for the river that formed part of the Belgian-French border, again focused on the B.E.F., this time in Flanders. Faced with a desperate situation, Haig issued his "Backs to the Wall" order forbidding any retreat. The tenacious British defense held, and the German attack halted after a 10-mile advance with heavy German losses and about 100,000 British casualties. Ludendorff continued to look for a soft spot that would crumble the front.

During both German attacks, U.S. units continued training with British and French units, both in training areas and in quiet sectors of the front. During the first two offensives, U.S. medical, engineering, and aviation units in the B.E.F. sector had been engaged, without serious losses. The first major U.S. action occurred on April 20 when two companies of the 26th Division were attacked

Tanks were first used in battle during World War I; here a Renault light tank attacks at Seicheprey, France. (U.S. Army Signal Corps)

near Seicheprey along the St.-Mihiel salient. Attacked by 2,800 Germans led by 600 storm troopers supported by an intense box barrage, the Americans suffered from a carefully planned and well-executed German raid. The Germans held the position for 24 hours and then withdrew. When it was over, the 26th Division had lost many as prisoners and suffered 669 casualties. The German losses were not insignificant, but Germany hailed this raid as demonstration that the Americans could be beaten easily. Seicheprey raised again the question of amalgamation and the ability of the A.E.F. to fight large units. The 26th Division discovered, as did other U.S. divisions, that three months in a "quiet sector" still produced casualties, 2,891 to be exact. American units were beginning to inflict and suffer casualties as they made the transition from training to the realities of combat. Yet the balanced, separate, independent 1,000,000-man army planned for May 1918 did not exist. By the end of April, only 430,000 Americans were in France.

Abbeville Conference

A conference of the Supreme War Council was held May 1–2 at Abbeville. Prime ministers, chiefs of staff, and commanders in chief all attended. At this conference, Pershing faced the most severe attacks against a separate American army. The British and French were interested in replacing casualties suffered in the German attacks. Amalgamation was their solution. Joint Note 18, an agreement for shipping more U.S. troops on British boats, was viewed by the French as a British attempt to monopolize U.S. troops. Pershing stood his ground against generals and statesmen alike in a series of heated exchanges. Finally, he stormed out of the meeting. By May 2, it was apparent that Pershing would not budge on the issue of a separate American army. To get U.S. troops to France quicker, the British agreed to increase to 150,000 the number of U.S. troops they would ship in May and in June. The greatest number in any previous month from all shipping sources was 120,000 in April. Beginning in May, 250,000–300,000 Americans would arrive for each of the next five months. A.E.F. plans would be disrupted, this time with 1,000,000 troops arriving in less than six months, compared to 430,000 during the first year. The decision at Abbeville ensured that Americans would arrive in sufficient numbers in 1918 to form a separate American army.

Aisne Offensive

When Ludendorff struck again, this time as a diversion against the French, he was surprised with his success. German units crossed the Aisne River and advanced 20 miles in only 24 hours against slight resistance. This diversion became a major effort. German units reached the Marne River on May 30, within 50 miles of Paris. Reserves, including the U.S. 2d and 3d divisions, were rushed to the front to meet this threat. The rapid movement of the machine-gun battalion of the 3d Division to Château-Thierry on May 31, followed by infantry units, prevented the Germans from crossing the Marne there. The 2d Division arrived June 1 and established a blocking position to the northwest of the 3d Division. French units, reinforced by the Americans, held along the Marne until the German attacks ceased on June 5.

On May 28, the 1st Division, commanded by Major General Bullard, conducted the first U.S. offensive action of the war when it attacked and captured Cantigny. Pershing ensured this operation went well. GHQ was involved in the planning and supervision of the 1st Division preparations. In a carefully planned and well-rehearsed operation, the 28th Infantry, under Col. Hanson Ely and supported by French artillery and 12 tanks, captured the village. The German response was immediate and violent, but Cantigny remained in U.S. hands. At a cost of 1,800 casualties, the 1st Division demonstrated that U.S. troops could attack and hold their objective. The fighting along the Marne, however, overshadowed this attack.

In the weeks of June 6–26, the 2d Division engaged in the heaviest U.S. fighting up to that point. Ordered to capture Belleau Wood, the 4th Brigade of marines, under Pershing's former GHQ chief of staff Harbord, advanced across a wheat field in the prescribed open warfare manner, taking heavy losses. The 5th Marines captured, lost, and recaptured the woods several times during a three-week battle. June 6, 1918, would be the costliest day in Marine Corps history until November 1943 (when the marines took the island of Tarawa from the Japanese during World War II). The village of Bouresches fell to the 6th Marines on June 17. Casualties were high (only 20 marines in the attacking battalion were unwounded), but the objectives were held. The regulars of the 3d Brigade took Vaux on

U.S. soldiers of the 1st Division advance during the Battle of Cantigny, May 28, 1918. (U.S. Army Signal Corps)

July 1. When the 2d Division left the line, it had suffered 7,900 casualties in six weeks of fighting. In honor of the fighting in Belleau Wood, the French renamed it "Bois de la Brigade de Marine."

Counterattacking with the French 10th Colonial Division during June 6-8, the 3d Division, which had raced to Château-Thierry on May 31, also fought well. Maj. Gen. Joseph T. Dickman's division captured Hill 204 overlooking the Marne and held a six-mile front along the river from June 8 to July 14. U.S. losses were just over 400. The eagerness and skill of the U.S. divisions in battle caught the attention of the Allies. Coming at the end of a third German offensive, when U.S. combat ability was still questionable, these successes lifted Allied spirits when they were lowest.

Noyon-Montdidier Offensive

The fourth German offensive from the Noyon-Montdidier sector was anticipated. French counterbattery fire and counterattacks blunted the June 9 attack almost immediately. Within five days, the German attack stopped. Ludendorff was losing forces faster than were the Allies. More than 250,000 Americans were arriving each month. Of the 25 U.S. divisions in France, 7 were in action by June. Pershing was once again assailed with pleas and threats for amalgamation of Americans into British and French divisions. Pershing became convinced that 66 U.S. divisions would be needed by May 1919. He cabled this request to the War Department on June 19. Four days later, Pershing and Foch sent a joint memorandum asking for 80 divisions by April 1919 and 100 divisions by July. The War Department was aghast. These requirements appeared impossible to meet. The stress of repeated German offensives upon Foch and Pershing was showing.

Champagne-Marne Offensive

The city of Reims was situated in the center of the fifth and final German attack, made in the Champagne region on July 15. East of Reims, Gen. Henri Gouraud's French 4th Army halted the German advance in a matter of hours. West of Reims, the Germans advanced to the Marne, which 14 divisions crossed. The fierce fighting along the Marne by Col. Ulysses G. McAlexander's 38th Infantry Regiment blunted the German attack. Fighting in three directions simultaneously, McAlexander held his position. During this battle, the 3d Division earned the nickname "Rock of the Marne." Other U.S. units did not fare so well. Four companies of the 28th Division, which were serving at the front with a French division, were left behind during the retreat. Surrounded, most of the men were killed or captured. The fluid, open warfare battlefield that Pershing had tried to prepare the A.E.F. to fight seemed to exist during these defensive operations against the German attacks.

Aisne-Marne Counteroffensive

Ludendorff had tried to end the war five times and had failed each time. His losses totaled more than 500,000 in less than five months. His expectation of victory in 1918

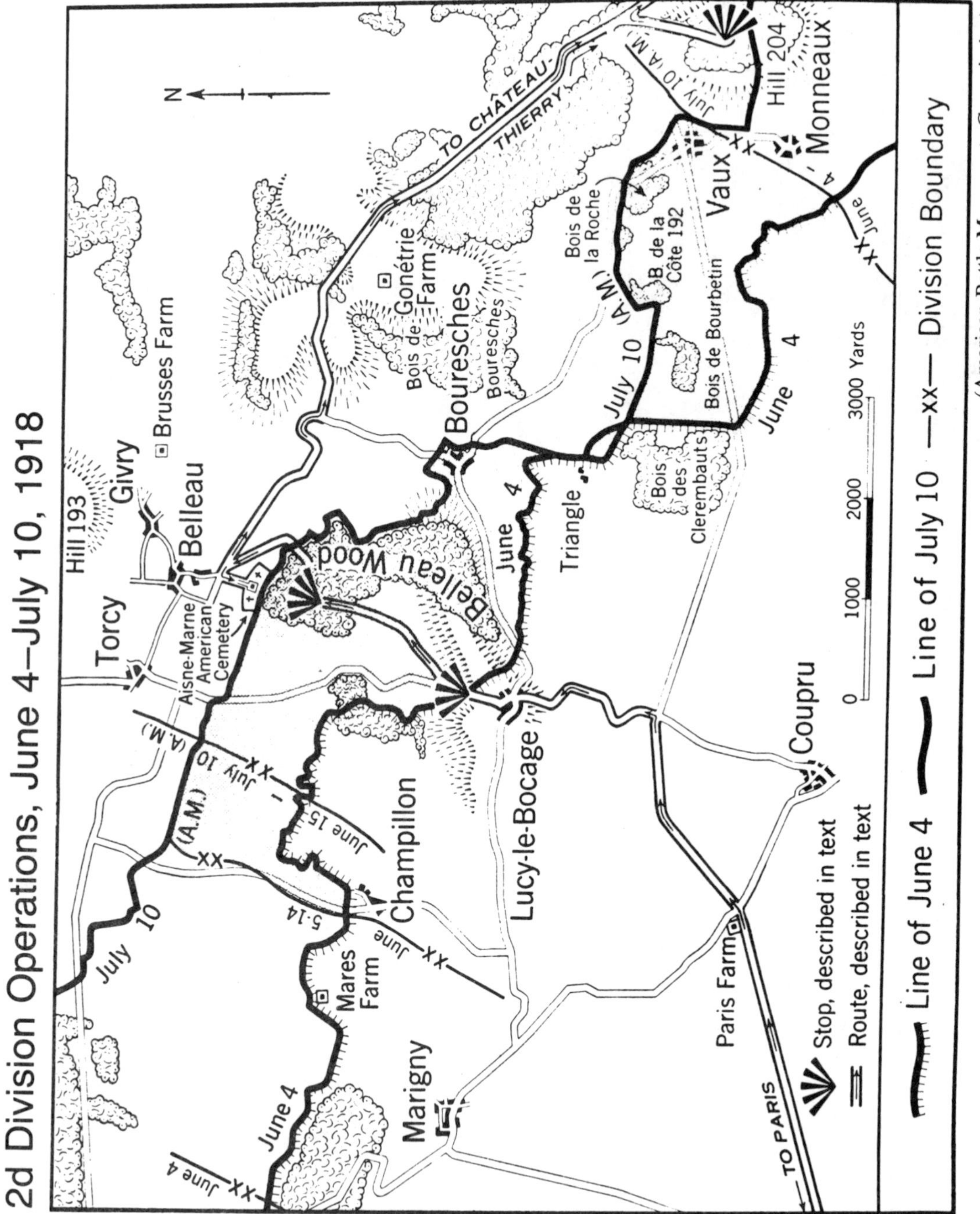

2d Division Operations, June 4–July 10, 1918

(American Battle Monuments Commission)

Location of American Divisions on Western Front August 10, 1918

Line of Aug.10 — 28 Division in Line — (79) Division in Rear Area

International Boundary

(American Battle Monuments Commission)

was gone. The initiative slipped away from the Germans. Whether the Allies had the will and the combat power to counterattack remained to be seen.

Foch, Allied commander in chief, had husbanded units to reduce a series of German salients created during the German advance. The first salient to be struck was the Aisne-Marne. Maj. Gen. Charles Mangin's French 10th Army spearheaded the Aisne-Marne Counteroffensive. The French XX Corps, consisting of the 1st and 2d divisions and the French 10th Colonial Division, made the main attack on July 18 near Soissons. The goal was for XX Corps to drive deep along the base of the salient to cut off the German withdrawal. Both U.S. divisions had new commanders: Maj. Gen. Charles P. Summerall, a hard-driving artilleryman, commanded the 1st Division, and Major General Harbord, the marine brigade commander at Belleau Wood, commanded the 2d Division. The last-minute move of the U.S. divisions to their attack positions precluded any preparations.

Following a rolling barrage, XX Corps advanced with almost 400 French tanks. Within four hours, it advanced more than three miles against surprised German defenders. German resistance stiffened, particularly on July 19, but the advance continued. Both U.S. divisions advanced in a bold and reckless manner, eventually pushing six miles into the German positions. The results were dramatic, but the cost was high: the 2d Division lost 4,300, while the 1st Division suffered 6,900 casualties. It appeared that the Americans, with their willingness to attack regardless of the casualties, were putting a new spirit into the Allied war effort. Other U.S. divisions—the 4th, 26th, and 28th—also took part in the initial attack, fighting alongside French divisions. Before the salient was reduced, four additional U.S. divisions serving in I Corps (Liggett) with the French 6th Army and in III Corps (Bullard) with the French 9th Army joined the pursuit of the Germans to the Vesle River.

Brig. Gen. B. A. Poore (right), *commanding general of the 4th Division's 7th Infantry Brigade, and Maj. A. D. Falconners study plans beside their car in Cherry Chartreuve, France, on Aug. 9, 1918.* (U.S. Military Academy Archives)

U.S. divisions, gaining combat experience and confidence, continued to show an eagerness to fight.

Amiens Counteroffensive

To the north, Haig launched a B.E.F. attack on August 8 against the Amiens salient, following orders from Foch. Led by 400 tanks, British and French armies attacked together. The initial attack was so successful that Ludendorff called August 8 the "Black Day" for the Germans. He finally realized that if the Allies sustained these counteroffensives, his resources were inadequate to hold. He saw no choice but to end the war somehow. The Allied attack continued after a pause on August 11. The Germans were forced to withdraw to the Hindenburg line, their final defensive position. The salient was reduced, and more than 15,000 German prisoners were captured. The morale of the German High Command was beginning to crack.

SEPARATE AMERICAN ARMY

By July 4, more than 1,000,000 Americans were in France. U.S. divisions were fighting in I Corps as well as with French corps. By the end of the month, nine divisions had served at the front either in quiet sectors or during operations against the Germans. Two divisions remained in training; eight new divisions had just arrived. Pershing, anticipating the creation of a separate American army, created additional U.S. corps in June. By early August, I Corps was joined in the B.E.F. sector by II Corps, commanded by Maj. Gen. George W. Read; III Corps, under Major General Bullard, which fought in the Aisne-Marne Offensive; IV Corps, under Major General Dickman; and V Corps, under Maj. Gen. George H. Cameron. Although the groundwork for a separate American army was being laid, the logistical foundation upon which it rested was being weakened.

GHQ faced difficult problems. More Americans had arrived in May and June of 1918 than during the entire first year of U.S. involvement. GHQ had to make constant adjustments to its plans to receive, to transport, to train, and to sustain the 830,000 soldiers who arrived in May, June, and July. Similar numbers were expected in August, September, and October. British shipping, provided initially in May, increased the speed of the A.E.F. buildup, but it also disrupted the carefully developed plans so necessary to field a balanced American army. As in the beginning, chaos again threatened. Corps units were scarce, and army-sized units did not exist, yet several corps and an army were being committed to combat. Training programs were curtailed; in fact, soldiers would go straight from the port to the front before the war was over. Even

Black soldiers of the 369th Infantry, 93d Division, defend a trench in the French sector, May 4, 1918. (U.S. Army Signal Corps)

worse, the SOS was barely able to meet the unprecedented and unplanned demands placed upon it.

Secretary of War Baker, in a July 6 cable to Pershing, offered the services of Maj. Gen. George W. Goethals to run the SOS. Goethals, the builder of the Panama Canal, had been recalled from retirement in December 1917 to fix the War Department logistical system. Baker believed that if Pershing had Goethals run the SOS and used Major General Bliss as his diplomatic intermediary to the Supreme War Council, Pershing could focus on fighting. Baker's intention appears to have been to assist Pershing with his numerous duties. Pershing immediately fired back a cable agreeing to work more closely with Bliss but refusing the offer of Goethals as a coordinate, rather than a subordinate. Pershing subsequently made Major General Harbord commander of the SOS. Pershing and Harbord took a whirlwind tour of the SOS in an attempt to gain a better understanding of its problems. Of the 1,200,000 Americans in France on August 1, about 275,000 were working in the SOS, almost 10 percent less than projected by the Service of the Rear Project. The SOS remained undermanned and inadequately staffed to support the forces in France. Pershing counted on Harbord to keep the logistical system working, despite these handicaps.

Creation of the First Army

On July 24, Foch approved Pershing's request to create the 1st American Army. Its initial attack was to be the reduction of the St.-Mihiel salient, an operation initially envisioned by GHQ planners a year before. Pershing established the 1st Army headquarters on August 10, designating Lt. Col. Hugh S. Drum as chief of staff. Drum organized a headquarters that grew to 600 officers and 1,600 soldiers. Simultaneously, he began planning the St.-Mihiel operation and the concentration of U.S. units into the designated American sector. The 1st Army would be born in battle, created while it was fighting. By August 1, the U.S. forces available were 16 divisions scattered all over France in various stages of training, 5 corps, and an army artillery headquarters. The 1st Army relied heavily upon the French for transport, artillery, tank, and aviation assets during the St.-Mihiel Offensive. Within four weeks of its inception, the 1st Army assumed control of an American sector and two weeks later launched the St.-Mihiel Offensive. Few Allied armies, in sectors already developed to support large forces and with experienced corps and armies in existence, would undertake such an operation in less than six weeks.

On August 30, the day the 1st Army assumed control of its separate American sector, Foch visited Pershing with a new plan. Instead of continuing to reduce salients, Haig had convinced Foch that the war could be won in 1918. What was needed were two major offensives: one in the north by the B.E.F. and one in the south by a Franco-American army under a French commander. Foch wanted Pershing to reduce the scope of the St.-Mihiel operation and to concentrate U.S. forces for an offensive under a French commander between Verdun and Reims. Pershing was livid. He saw this as another attempt to deny the Americans a separate and independent role in the war. After a series of meetings with Foch and Pétain, Pershing agreed at Bombom on September 2 to reduce the St.-Mihiel attack. He also agreed that 10 days after St.-Mihiel the 1st Army would launch a second major offensive between the Argonne Forest and the Meuse River. Pershing had agreed that within 23 days the 1st Army would conduct two major offensives on battlefields more than 40 miles apart, a feat not attempted by even the most experienced Allied army on the Western Front.

St.-Mihiel Salient

Unlike the other salients reduced during the summer of 1918, the St.-Mihiel salient was a well-organized defensive zone developed during four years of German occupation. The salient, 25 miles across at its base, extended 16 miles into the Allied lines. Its two defensive zones, the "Wilhelm" along the face of the salient and the "Michel" along its base, consisted of massive barbed-wire entanglements covering an elaborate system of trenches, concrete shelters, and machine-gun nests. Considered a fortress, the salient was held by units reduced in strength by combat in more active sectors. The Germans occupied the salient with eight divisions forward and five in reserve. Anticipating an American attack in late September, German army detachment C was ordered on September 11 to begin a gradual withdrawal from the Wilhelm to the Michel position to reduce frontage and also to free up units for use elsewhere on the Western Front. The Germans had not begun to execute this order when the 1st Army attacked.

The 1st Army planned to attack the salient with four corps: I Corps and IV Corps, with seven American divisions in line, were to make the main attack from the south along the base of the salient; French II Colonial Army Corps, positioned along the nose of the salient with four French divisions, was to hold German forces in place; and V Corps, consisting of two American and one French division in line, was to attack along the base of the salient from the northwest toward I and IV Corps. The operation was truly a Franco-American effort with 550,000 American and 110,000 French troops supported by 400 French tanks, of which 144 of the 350 light tanks were manned by Americans. Almost 3,000 artillery pieces supported the attack. Nearly all of the corps and army artillery was provided by the French. Col. William B. Mitchell put together the largest aviation effort of the war, more than 1,480 aircraft flown by the Americans, French, Italians, Portuguese, and British. Although the best and most experienced U.S. units were committed to this operation, two of the three corps and four of the nine divisions had not conducted offensive operations before. On the eve of battle, hopes were high.

After a four-hour artillery bombardment, the attack commenced at 5:00 A.M. on September 12. Despite the fact that the tanks were not forward with the infantry to assist initial movement through the wire, the attack proceeded almost as scheduled. Both I and IV Corps units advanced almost five miles the first day. Coming from the northwest, V Corps moved forward two miles. Pershing, sensing that the base of the salient could be cut quickly, ordered the attack to continue into the night with the village of Vigneulles designated the objective for both IV and V Corps. In a bold move, V Corps' 26th Division captured Vigneulles just after 2:00 A.M. on September 13. The U.S. attack continued with almost all objectives secured by dark on September 13. In two days, the 1st Army had attacked and reduced a strongly held German salient. Probing attacks were made into the Michel defensive zone until the attack stopped on September 16. The Germans rushed reinforcements to the area in anticipation of a continued U.S. advance toward Metz and the Briey iron fields. The Americans had suffered fewer than 9,000 casualties, while more than 15,000 German prisoners and almost 450 cannon were captured. More than 200 square miles of French territory had been restored to France. The morale of the Allies and the confidence of the Americans soared.

Preparations for Meuse-Argonne Offensive

Pershing's decision on September 2 to conduct two major operations within 10 days of one another meant that the newly established 1st Army staff had to plan and to prepare for the Meuse-Argonne operation during the preparation

U.S. soldiers fire at the enemy on the first day of the St.-Mihiel Offensive in 1918. (U.S. Army Signal Corps)

and conduct of the St.-Mihiel Offensive. Colonel Drum, 1st Army chief of staff, designated a part of his staff to focus on the Meuse-Argonne operation. Even though the plans were approved four days before the St.-Mihiel operation commenced, massive amounts of men and matériel had to be moved and concentrated before the attack on September 26. Given an inexperienced army staff and the limited road network into and out of the Meuse-Argonne sector, concentrating the U.S. forces in secrecy was an arduous and intricate job. Col. George C. Marshall, a member of the 1st Army Operations Section, was largely responsible for the success of this task. At night, men and matériel moved over three roads that Marshall supervised. In all, more than 220,000 French and Italian soldiers were moved out and almost 600,000 Americans were moved into the sector, about 400,000 from St.-Mihiel. Despite the problems encountered, by the night of September 25, the U.S. forces were in place for the attack.

Gen. Max von Gallwitz commanded the German army group opposite the U.S. sector. He expected a continuation of the attack from the St.-Mihiel region, never anticipating an attack through the 20-mile-wide area between the Argonne Forest and the Meuse River. The terrain there naturally favored the German defense with three successive ridges (Montfaucon, Cunel and Romagne, and Barricourt) running parallel to the U.S. advance. Forward of each of these ridges were strong zones of German defenses, respectively known as the "Hagen/Etzel," "Kriemhild," and "Freya" positions. Considered strong naturally and reinforced by defenses developed over four years to a depth of 10 miles, Gallwitz held this sector with five understrength divisions. Reinforcements, however, were readily available.

The 1st Army planned to overwhelm the German divisions with nine U.S. divisions attacking abreast under three American corps—I Corps in the west, V Corps in the

Plan of Attack of First Army, September 26, 1918

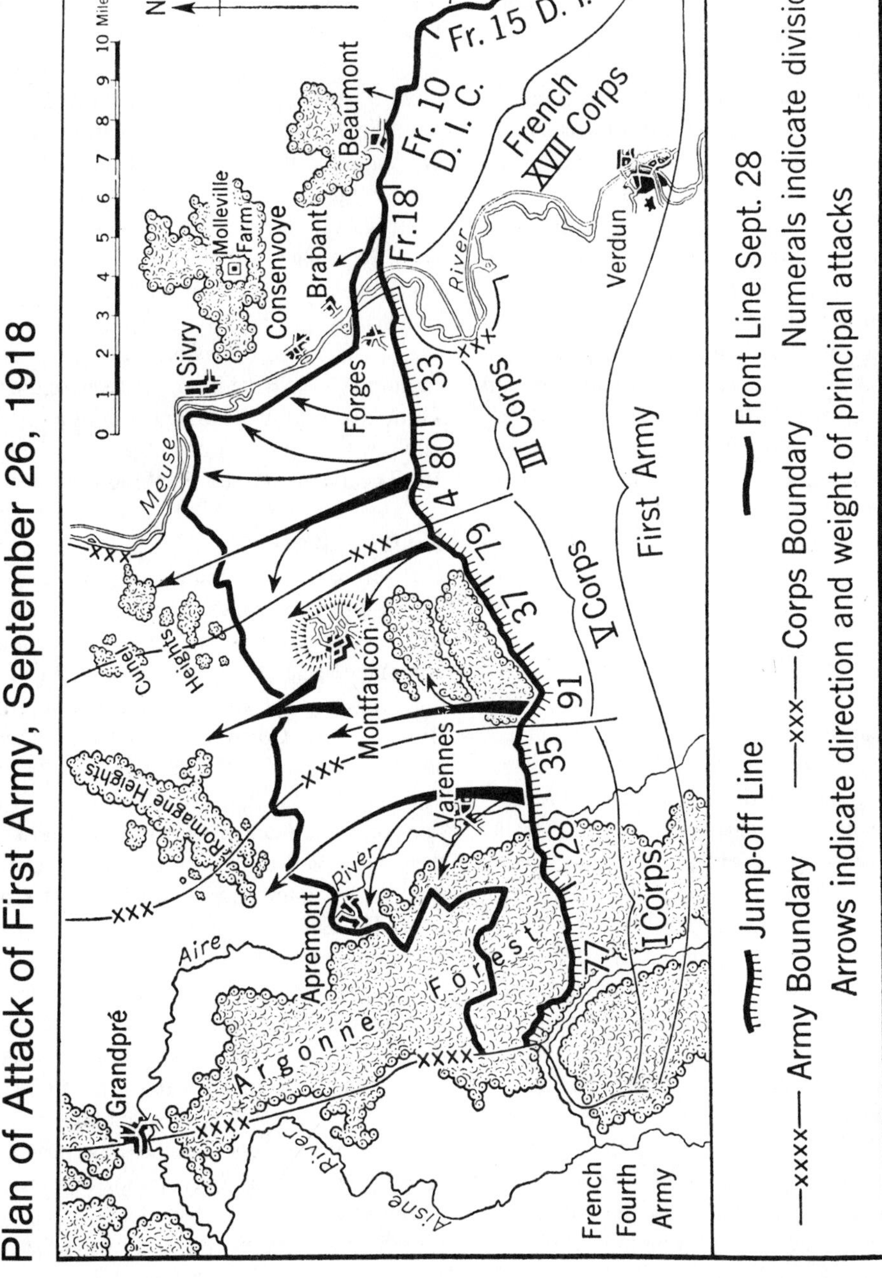

(American Battle Monuments Commission)

center, and III Corps in the east. The plan envisioned an advance of 10 miles the first day through the first two zones, followed by a second 10-mile advance to outflank the Bourgogne Forest to assist the French 4th Army attacking west of the Argonne with the Americans. An initial 1st Army concern was the heights of Montfaucon, which were to be taken in flank. Each corps was provided objective lines to seize. The advance of I and III Corps was to be controlled by the progress of V Corps. The 1st Army would order the advance to successive objective lines.

Because preparations for St.-Mihiel were underway when Foch made the Meuse-Argonne suggestion, the experienced A.E.F. units were not available for the Meuse-Argonne. Of the nine divisions attacking, only five had conducted offensive operations and several were understrength from recent combat along the Vesle. Four of the divisions did not have their own artillery brigades because their training had been incomplete. Tank support was limited, but Lt. Col. George S. Patton commanded 189 light tanks supporting I Corps in the Aire River valley. Col. Billy Mitchell commanded about 850 U.S. and French aircraft. French and U.S. artillery numbering 2,700 supported this attack. This major offensive directed by Foch against strong German defenses in hopes of cutting the railway through Sedan was supported with less matériel and with less experienced units than what was available at St.-Mihiel.

COMBAT: LATE 1918

Following a three-hour artillery preparation, the attack began at 5:30 A.M. on September 26. Despite the hopes and desires of Pershing, the units did not advance 10 miles. In fact, the 79th Division (V Corps) was held up in front of Montfaucon, thus stalling the entire army attack that was tied to its success. The plan was too rigid. Inexperienced units, attacking for the first time through thick morning fog, became lost and disorganized. The German resistance grew stiffer during the day, and reinforcements continued to arrive during the first three days of the battle. Montfaucon and the Hagen/Etzel position fell the second day, but momentum and surprise had been lost. The anticipated rapid breakthrough became a bloody battle of attrition. On September 29, the 1st Army halted the attack to replace worn divisions so that the attack could be renewed. During the lull, a struggle behind the front was fought as engineers and support units tried to get across the desolation of no man's land to provide the fighting units the matériel needed to sustain operations. This struggle, the opening of supply routes across no man's land, was paramount in Pershing's mind. Without supplies, his fighting units would not advance as he demanded. Congestions of the supply routes continued to be a major problem for weeks.

On October 4, V Corps led an attack that continued for several days to break the German Kriemhild position at Romagne. It was supported by III Corps attacks on Cunel. These attacks failed with heavy losses. On October 7, I Corps attacked the eastern edge of the Argonne Forest. After two days of heavy fighting, the Germans were forced to withdraw from the forest to Grandpré, bringing I Corps on line with V Corps. Fighting on the heights east of the Meuse River commenced on October 8 when the 33d Division attacked across the river to join the French XVII Corps in its struggle for the dominating heights. It took more than three weeks of heavy fighting before the heights were finally taken. The 1st Army fought the remainder of the battle with three American and one French corps. Pershing described October 1–11 as the period of "heaviest strain" both on himself and on the 1st Army. Another pause to replace and resupply units was required before the attack was renewed. On October 12, V Corps once again attacked Romagne. III Corps attacked in the vicinity of Cunel. The 32d Division, making a supporting attack, captured Côte Dame Marie, the key to the German position. Through three weeks of heavy fighting, the German Kriemhild position, the first-day objective, finally fell on October 16. The 1st Army and Pershing both needed a break.

Reorganization

On October 12, Pershing reorganized the A.E.F. fighting forces into two armies. Pershing returned to GHQ to command as an army group commander, similar to the other commanders in chief. Hunter Liggett of I Corps was given the 1st Army and the task of continuing the battle. Robert Bullard of III Corps was given the 2d Army and responsibility for much of the inactive U.S. front formerly supervised by the 1st Army. Several division commanders and one corps commander were relieved from command. Others were promoted to replace them. In fact, Liggett had three new corps commanders, Dickman (I Corps), transferred from IV Corps; Summerall (V Corps), raised from 1st Division command; and Maj. Gen. John L. Hines (III Corps), raised from 4th Division command. The A.E.F. now assumed a larger role in the war effort. Each of its divisions were equal in strength to an Allied or German corps, its corps to an army, and its armies to an army group. The Americans were making a major contribution in terms of numbers, but the slow progress of the Meuse-Argonne raised the question of how capable the A.E.F. really was.

Liggett assumed command of the 1st Army on October 16. He immediately began to pull it back together. The 1st Army had been fought to the point of disorganization, and almost to exhaustion. Replacements were in short supply. GHQ had skeletonized seven divisions to send their soldiers forward as replacements for units in combat. In two weeks of hard work, Liggett was able to regain control of many

Operations of First Army, November 1–11, 1918

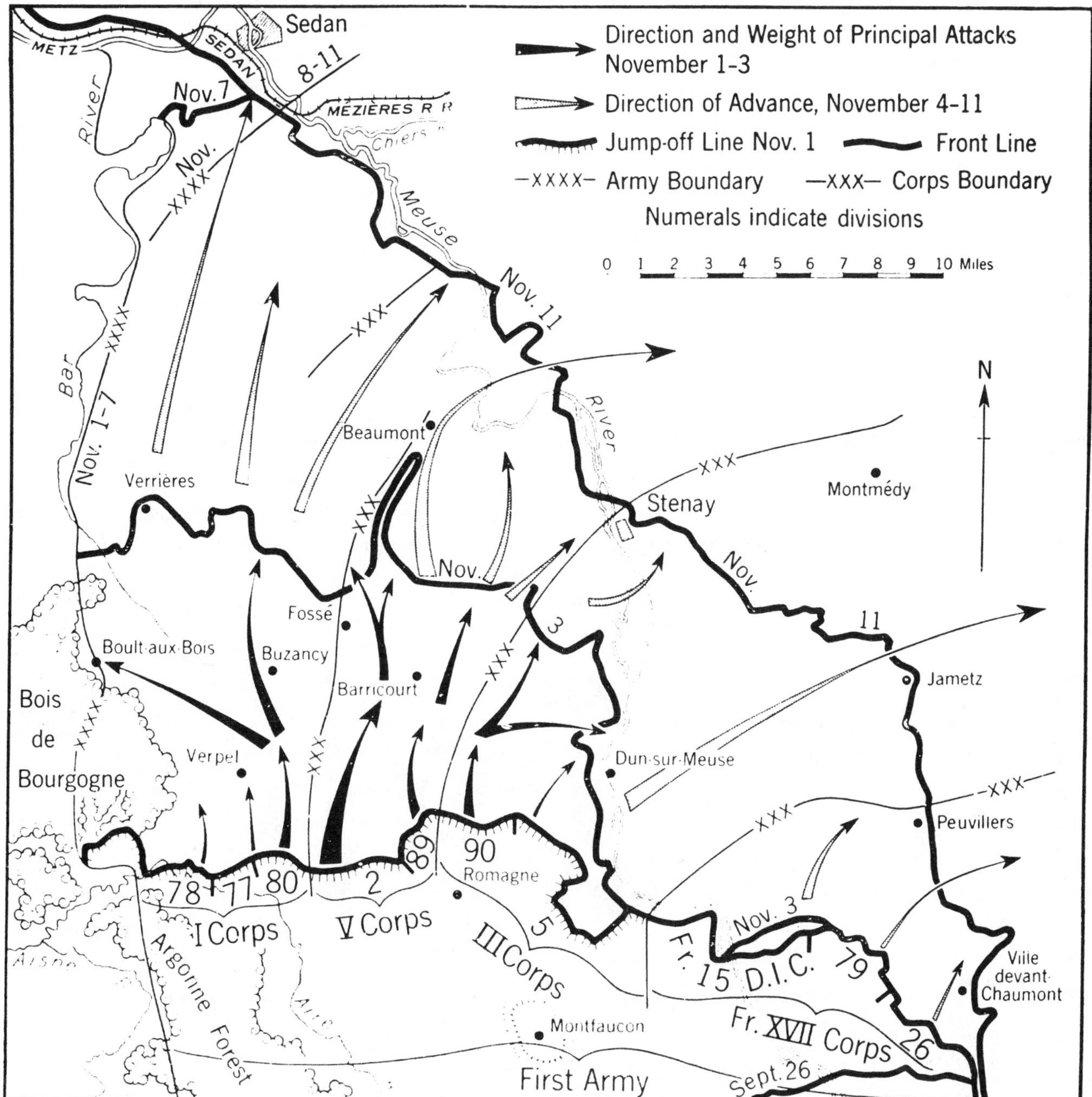

(American Battle Monuments Commission)

soldiers who were lost and straggling, to refocus the army for its next attack, to resupply and replenish the army, and to maintain an aggressiveness toward the Germans. Liggett replaced worn units. He developed a plan not tied to a rigid timetable or to phase lines that hampered the exploitation of the successes of September 26. In the next attack, units would advance regardless of flank protection. To facilitate the breakthrough, he planned to use gas throughout the sector to neutralize enemy strongpoints in a way that the 1st Army had not on September 26. An experienced combat leader, a corps commander since January and in combat almost constantly since July, Liggett brought a unique understanding of operations to the 1st Army.

Final Push

To meet the repeated U.S. attacks threatening their crucial east-west railway, German units had been thrown piecemeal into the battle. Intermixed, understrength, and worn out, their resistance had reached its limit. Reserves were limited. If Liggett could push through the front lines, then open warfare was possible. Massing his artillery to support V Corps as his main effort, Liggett planned that the 2d Division, commanded by the marines' Maj. Gen. John A. Lejeune, and the 89th Division would rupture the German lines. Attacking on November 1, it happened as planned. All along the 1st Army front, by November 2, the Germans were in retreat to the Meuse River. Daring night marches into enemy positions by the Regular Brigade of the 2d Division further disrupted German resistance. By November 7, the 1st Army reached the Meuse near Sedan. The key German east-west railroad was placed under fire from the long-range 14-inch guns mounted on rail. On November 4, elements of III Corps crossed the Meuse and attacked to the east. As peace talks intensified, the A.E.F. repositioned forces for a Franco-American attack planned for November 14. French and U.S. armies were to attack toward Longwy, Metz, and Château-Salins. However, at 11:00 A.M. on November 11, the armistice took effect. The war was over.

For 47 days, the 1st Army—with more than 1,000,000 soldiers, including 135,000 Frenchmen—fought the Germans at a critical point of the Western Front. After a slow start, the final phase of the offensive became a pursuit. At a cost of 117,000 U.S. casualties, the Germans suffered 100,000 casualties, had 26,000 men captured, and lost more than 870 artillery pieces. But the greatest American contribution was enthusiasm and willingness to seek battle. The Germans had to confront an ever-increasing American army, which meant ultimate defeat. This loss of hope in victory led to negotiations and the armistice.

Marine Maj. Gen. John A. Lejeune (center), *commander of the 2d Division, goes over plans with his staff during the last days of World War I.* (U.S. Army Military History Institute)

OTHER AMERICAN OPERATIONS

Although public attention had focused on the gigantic Allied-German clash along the Western Front in 1918, U.S. forces were also engaged in other significant operations. Often, the Americans worked in tandem with forces from other Allied nations.

At Sea

Vice Adm. William S. Sims, commander of U.S. Naval Forces Operating in European Waters, was responsible for 81,000 men who manned more than 370 vessels and operated 47 bases. Sims established his headquarters in London. Five battleships under Rear Adm. Hugh Rodman joined the British Grand Fleet as its 6th Battle Squadron but saw no action, nor did 3 battleships at Bantry Bay, Ireland, under Rear Adm. Thomas S. Rodgers. It was the less glamorous, yet vitally crucial, destroyers and subchasers that did critical work during the war. Vice Adm. Albert Gleaves, commander of the Cruisers and Transport Service, was responsible for convoying U.S. troops to France. At the end of the war, he could claim that no escorted eastbound vessel was sunk, a commendable record. The cruisers and 79 destroyers existing at the beginning of the war performed this duty. A small "splinter fleet" of wooden 110-foot subchasers augmented the antisubmarine force. Stationed in the English Channel and the Strait of Otranto, these vessels were manned primarily by reservists. Their aggressiveness and skill effectively hampered German submarine operations.

Several unusual naval missions were performed during the war. Ten minelayers, commanded by Rear Adm. Joseph Strauss, worked on the North Sea Barrage. To reduce the submarine threat in the North Sea, the U.S. and Royal navies decided to lay a minefield 250 miles wide and 15–35 miles deep consisting of more than 400,000 mines. By the end of the war, the U.S. Navy had laid 56,000 of the 70,000 in the barrage. Upon the end of the war, they commenced to retrieve the mines. During the war, the minefield destroyed four German submarines and possibly four others. The U.S. Navy also provided 112 aircraft to the Northern Bombing Group, which operated from 20 bases in the British Isles. The most unusual naval contribution was the five 14-inch naval guns mounted on special railway cars. Each gun could fire a 1,400-pound shell up to 24 miles. Commanded by Rear Adm. Charles P. Plunkett, these guns fired almost 800 shells between September 6 and the armistice. The principal contribution of the U.S. Navy was the convoying of the A.E.F. to France, but each of its other activities, which included providing marines to the A.E.F., demonstrated a commitment to assisting in any way possible.

In the Air

Beginning the war with 55 obsolete and obsolescent aircraft in the Aviation Section of the Signal Corps, the Air Service in France grew to 740 planes in 44 squadrons by November 1918. Its 767 pilots, 481 observers, and 23 aerial gunners were assigned to 20 pursuit, 18 observation, 1 night-bombing, and 6 day-bombing squadrons. The Air Service performed aerial combat, tactical support of ground forces, day and night bombardment, resupply, photographic, and artillery-fire direction missions. In seven months at the front, 235 U.S. aviators were killed in combat, but they shot down twice as many aircraft as were shot down by the Germans. Eddie Rickenbacker became the unchallenged American ace, with 26 confirmed kills. Brig. Gen. Benjamin Foulois, an aviation pioneer, was instrumental in setting up the Air Service in France. Maj. Gen. Mason M. Patrick, a nonflying engineer, developed the Air Service into the force that assisted the A.E.F. during its battles. Col. Billy Mitchell was the key tactical combat leader. However, despite the numerous obstacles overcome, the Air Service never grew to the 202 squadrons planned nor was it decisive during the war.

With the French

After the creation of the 1st Army, few U.S. units served with the French. As the 1st Army attacked in the Meuse-Argonne, the 2d and 36th divisions were loaned to the French 4th Army, positioned to the west of the 1st Army. On October 3, the 2d Division, led by the Marine Brigade, attacked and captured Blanc Mont, a ridge that had held up the French advance. As a result of this deep attack by the 2d Division, the Germans prepared a hasty withdrawal to the Aisne River. Reinforced by units of the 36th Division, the 2d Division withstood counterattacks while waiting for French divisions to advance to the ridge. Pétain called this action the "greatest single achievement of the 1918 campaign." From October 30 until the end of the war, the 37th and 91st divisions fought under French command in Belgium, an action to which Belgium's King Albert paid tribute after the war.

The most unusual and longest service with French troops was that of four black American regiments that Pershing allowed to be amalgamated into French units. The 15th New York, a National Guard regiment redesignated the 369th Infantry, commanded by Col. William Hayward, served 191 days at the front, more than any other regiment in the A.E.F. Two other former black National Guard regiments, the 370th and 372d, and one national army regiment, the 371st, were incorporated into French divisions. Each of these regiments fought exceptionally well and was commended by the French. After the war, these regiments were designated the 93d Division. Of the 380,000 black soldiers in the A.E.F., only 42,000 were combat troops. The remainder served in service units, primarily as

Eddie Rickenbacker (left) *became America's ace pilot with 26 confirmed kills. He is shown with fellow pilots 1st Lt. Douglas Campbell* (center) *and Capt. Kenneth Marr* (right) *near Toul, France, in June 1918.* (U.S. Army Signal Corps)

stevedores and laborers. The only black combat unit that was organized and fought as a U.S. division, the 92d, performed poorly. This was primarily because of the attitude within the U.S. Army that blacks could not be good combat soldiers. The performance of the black regiments serving with the French disproved this for those that chose to look.

With the British

The U.S. II Corps, commanded by Major General Read, fought with the British. Consisting of the 27th Division, commanded by John F. Ryan (a 44-year-old lawyer and Army War College graduate, also the youngest and the only National Guard division commander), and the 30th Division, II Corps fought in the Somme region during September 24–30 and October 6–21. The fighting was fierce near St. Quentin. On September 27, the 107th Infantry Regiment lost more than 50 percent of its men, the highest loss in a single day by an A.E.F. regiment. During October 6–21, both divisions attacked as part of the British 4th Army general offensive. They advanced almost 12 miles before being relieved.

Other Theaters: Italy and Russia

Except for two detachments, one sent to Italy and one to North Russia, all A.E.F. units fought on the Western Front in France. The 332d Infantry Regiment of the 83d Division was sent to Italy in July 1918 to bolster Italian morale. It trained in Italy and joined the Italian 31st Division during its attack on October 24, beginning the Vittorio-Veneto Offensive. It pursued the Austro-Hungarian forces until the Italian armistice on November 4. The regiment then served on occupation duty in Austria and on the Dalmatian coast until it departed for the United States on Apr. 3, 1919.

On Sept. 4, 1918, the 339th Infantry Regiment, augmented by a battalion of engineers, all from the 85th Division, arrived in North Russia to reinforce British forces already there. Under British command, this regiment soon found itself spread out over a 450-mile front, at times 200

A landing party of U.S. soldiers from the Olympia, *having just returned from patrol, is surrounded by American soldiers of the 339th Infantry Regiment, in Bakharitza, Russia, Sept. 6, 1918.* (U.S. Army Signal Corps)

miles from its main base at Archangel. The soldiers served under extreme climatic conditions and under trying political circumstances. Fighting between Americans and Communist forces occurred. More than 400 casualties were suffered, most after the fighting on the Western Front had ended. By May 1919, the unit was withdrawn to Archangel to prepare to sail to France. U.S. participation ended on August 5.

Although not a part of the A.E.F., another U.S. force, two regiments from the 8th Division in California, under Maj. Gen. William S. Graves, joined Japanese, French, British, and White Russian forces under Adm. Alexander Kolchak in Siberia. President Wilson sent the Americans to counter the Japanese intervention. Graves, strictly following his instructions to assist the withdrawal of the Czech Legion, refused to be drawn into the fighting or into supporting Kolchak. At one time, U.S. forces were stretched along the Trans-Siberian Railroad from Lake Baikal to Vladivostok. Graves, faced with severe difficulties, held until the Czech Legion arrived, and then left by April 1920. Despite the constant potential for fighting, Graves's forces suffered fewer than 90 casualties. The Japanese were eventually forced to withdraw by the Russians in October 1922.

POST-ARMISTICE ACTIVITIES

The armistice was signed on Nov. 11, 1918, and the German army withdrew from France by November 17. On November 23, the newly designated 3d Army, commanded initially by Major General Dickman and later by Lieutenant General Liggett, marched to the German frontier and began its advance to the Rhine River on December 1. By December 9, the 18-mile-deep U.S. bridgehead at Coblenz (Koblenz), Germany, was established. Ten days later, a U.S. force of 240,000 occupied the Rhineland and the bridgehead of Coblenz. Similar bridgeheads were established at Cologne and Mainz by the British and the French. After the Versailles settlement and the rejection of the treaty by the U.S. Senate, U.S. forces were reduced. By July 1919, Americans in the European theater numbered only 16,000 men under Maj. Gen. Henry T. Allen. In January 1923, the last U.S. soldiers left Germany.

Versailles Peace Settlement

Wilson brought the United States into the war to resolve the German submarine menace of 1917. In January 1918, he expanded his vision of a postwar peace when he issued his Fourteen Points, a program of principles upon which he proposed to build a peace without victory, a just peace acceptable to all nations. Viewed by European statesmen as idealistic and unpracticable, Wilson's program faced opposition during the peace conference. The resolution of these opposing views occurred at Versailles, France, where the peace conference convened on Jan. 18, 1919, with 70 representatives from 27 countries attending. It quickly became apparent that the "Big Four"—Prime Minister David Lloyd George of Britain, Prime Minister Georges Clemenceau of France, Prime Minister Vittorio Orlando of Italy, and President Woodrow Wilson of the United States—would determine the peace settlements. Almost immediately, the pursuit of national interests led to disagreement among the victorious Allies. During the months that followed, Wilson was forced to back down on almost each of his Fourteen Points, but he held firm to the need for a League of Nations, an international body to resolve future disagreements that would inevitably arise. On June 28, the Germans were forced to accept a harsh peace treaty and to accept responsibility for the war. With the Versailles Treaty, and those that followed with Austria, Bulgaria, and Turkey, the victorious Allies sowed the seeds for the future conflict Wilson feared. Wilson returned to the United States to seek Senate confirmation of the treaty. During his six-month absence from the United States, Wilson had lost contact with U.S. public opinion. The treaty met immediate resistance from Sen. Henry Cabot Lodge, chairman of the Foreign Relations Committee. On November 19, after a four-month public and congressional debate, the Senate rejected the treaty and, with it, the League of Nations. Wilson's vision of a peaceful order in which the United States and the League of Nations assumed an important role was dead. The United States did not intend to become involved in any more wars in Europe.

Brig. Gen. William ("Billy") Mitchell, World War I ace and champion of the Air Service, inspects planes at Weissenthurm, Germany, in 1922. (U.S. Army Military History)

American Forces in Northern Russia Sept. 4, 1918-Aug. 5, 1919

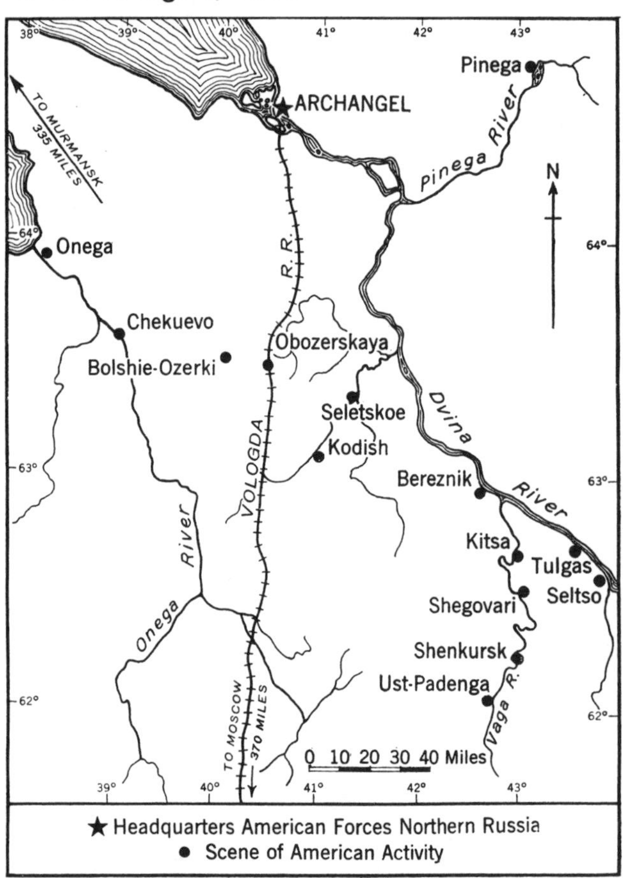

(American Battle Monuments Commission)

Demobilization

Despite War Department preparations, demobilization was as hectic and frantic as mobilization had been. With the war over, everyone wanted to go home immediately. Almost 4,000,000 men had to be demobilized. Those in the United States went home first. In one month, almost 650,000 were processed through 30 hastily organized demobilization centers throughout the country. The goal was established to process each soldier in less than 48 hours. When a man left the demobilization center, he departed with discharge papers, a uniform, a pair of shoes, an overcoat, and $60 cash. Those who served overseas were permitted to keep their helmets and gas masks. Pershing decided when and which units returned from France. In eight months, more than 1,600,000 A.E.F. members left France. The major

Gen. John J. Pershing, leader of the American Expeditionary Force, boards the Leviathan *as he leaves France in 1919.* (Library of Congress)

remnant of the A.E.F. in Europe was the 3d Army at Coblenz. Within nine months, 3,250,000 million Americans had been demobilized.

Industrial demobilization was just as chaotic, yet more disastrous. With the end of the war, $6 billion of contracts were cancelled. Industries had to retool and reorganize for peacetime conditions. How to liquidate supplies on hand was a major problem. Surprisingly, through sale of the material on hand, almost 75 percent of the cost was retrieved. The long-term problem of liquidation of international obligations, which was tied to pay reparations to the victors, took years to resolve, and then not satisfactorily.

CONCLUSION

Credit for the A.E.F. performance in France rests squarely with Gen. John J. Pershing. He planned it, organized it, disciplined it, trained it, sustained it, and fought it. Despite unprecedented challenges and the enormity of the task, in 18 months, the A.E.F. grew from a 187-man advance party to an army group of almost 2,000,000. Of the 43 large U.S. divisions in France, 29 saw combat. Although A.E.F. casualties totaled about 255,000, in military terms, there were no battlefield disasters. The aggressiveness of the A.E.F., which raised Allied morale at a key time in 1918, was of immense value to the war effort. If the war had continued into 1919, the A.E.F. role in victory would have been much clearer.

Pershing did make some questionable decisions. In May 1918, his resistance to amalgamation could have meant the defeat of the Allies. His slowness to place the SOS upon a solid foundation resulted from the complexity of the task, as well as his reluctance to give up any of his responsibilities. His desire personally to conduct the initial battles of the 1st Army delayed his decision to create the 2d Army and, at a time when the A.E.F. was expanding dramatically, took his attention from major problems confronting GHQ. Nonetheless, Pershing's foresight, flexibility, and constant demand for an independent, separate American army ensured that Americans made a major contribution to victory in 1918.

PART II

Biographies

AGUINALDO, EMILIO (1869–1964)

Filipino nationalist leader and president of the first Philippine republic, Aguinaldo, of mixed Filipino and Chinese parentage, was born in Cavite province. In 1896 he, along with Andres Bonafacio, led a revolt against Spain and announced plans to establish a U.S.-style democracy once independence was achieved. Aguinaldo proved to be an adept guerrilla leader and soon had a number of minor military victories. However, a rift developed between his faction and Bonafacio's. After some intrigue, Bonafacio was killed by the Aguinaldo faction. This left Aguinaldo as supreme commander of a now strife-weakened revolution. With the guerrilla force diminished, he and his rebels fled to the mountains of Bulacan, some 60 miles northwest of Manila. In his mountain stronghold, Aguinaldo gained new recruits and was able to hold out against a number of Spanish attempts to destroy them.

Finally, Spain, already weary of another colonial revolt, in Cuba, reached an agreement with Aguinaldo. In return for financial compensation of 800,000 pesos, Aguinaldo agreed to forsake the revolution and go into exile. This pledge was short-lived, for soon he was buying weapons with the money Spain had paid them. Even before the United States was officially at war with Spain, Aguinaldo was in Hong Kong discussing how the United States could help him gain Philippine independence. During those talks, Aguinaldo received assurance that the United States had no designs on the islands as a colony.

This stand by the U.S. government changed in 1898 after George Dewey's naval victory at Manila Bay. Aguinaldo found that the new revolutionary army he had formed would have to take on a new colonial master—the United States. With an army of more than 50,000 poorly armed Filipinos backing him, Aguinaldo proclaimed the first Philippine republic in January 1899 and attempted to fight the U.S. Army in a conventional war. As a result, his army was soon crushed and the remnants took to the hills to fight guerrilla fashion. For the next several years, the United States fought a bloody guerrilla war with the Filipinos. The major resistance ended in 1901 with the capture of Aguinaldo and his pledge of allegiance to U.S. rule. Thereafter, he failed to developed significant power in Filipino politics.

Ted Alexander

AINSWORTH, FRED CRAYTON (1852–1934)

U.S. adjutant general noted for his army personnel recordkeeping, Ainsworth was born in Woodstock, Vermont. He became a physician upon graduating from the University of the City of New York in 1874 and then entered the U.S. Army as a first lieutenant and assistant surgeon.

Early Career. In 1886, after 12 years' service with troops in Alaska and the American West, Ainsworth was assigned to Washington, D.C., to help organize the medical records of the army. At that time, the large number of aging Civil War veterans were pressuring Congress for rapid authentication of their claims for pensions. Unfortunately, medical and personnel records had been produced and stored with virtually no system, necessitating long searches of chronological entries to prove the claims of each separate veteran. As chief of the Records and Pension Division, Captain Ainsworth protected and organized the records and established an elaborate system of indexes to resolve this problem. By 1889, he was so successful that Sec. of War Redfield Proctor placed him in charge of the consolidated medical and personnel records of all Civil War volunteers. In 1892 and 1894, Congress passed laws adding records from previous wars to Ainsworth's office. Finally, in 1898, Ainsworth received control over the publication of the massive *Official Records of the War of the Rebellion*.

Ainsworth, the consummate military administrator and bureaucrat, acquired tremendous political influence because of his ability to satisfy congressional inquiries and veterans' claims in days or even hours. In 1892, he was promoted from captain to colonel under a law specifically designed for his advancement. Promoted to brigadier general in 1899 and major general in 1904, Ainsworth found himself in charge of all army administration as military secretary of the War Department. He was named adjutant general when that title was revived in 1907.

Conflict with Leonard Wood. At the height of his power, Ainsworth came into conflict with Gen. Leonard Wood, chief of staff of the army 1910–14. Wood, like Ainsworth, was a surgeon turned administrator, but he had even more political influence as the friend and wartime commander of Pres. Theodore Roosevelt.

Created in 1903, the General Staff, and especially its chief, seriously threatened the traditional autonomy of the War Department bureau chiefs. The 1903 General Staff Act had specifically exempted Ainsworth's Records and Pension Office from General Staff control, but later changes negated this exemption. In December 1910, Wood directed that all War Department orders be issued through the chief of staff rather than the adjutant general. More important, Wood pressured Ainsworth to merge unit muster rolls with command return and payroll records. This administrative change would have simplified administration in the field, but it was a direct challenge to a man who had built his career on the use of such records.

Forced Resignation. On Feb. 3, 1912, Ainsworth allowed his feud with Wood to affect his judgment. In a written critique of the muster roll proposal, Ainsworth criticized the General Staff (and by implication General Wood) as "incompetent amateurs" who were ignorant of army administration. This flagrant case of insubordination forced Sec. of War Henry Stimson to relieve Ainsworth, whose friends in Congress advised him to resign rather than face a court-martial. Although only a partial victory, the defeat of the powerful adjutant general helped establish the influence of the General Staff.

Bibliography: Deutrich, Mabel E., *The Struggle for Supremacy: The Career of General Fred C. Ainsworth* (Public Affairs Press, 1962); Lane, Jack C., *Armed Progressive: General Leonard Wood* (Presidio, 1978).

Maj. Jonathan M. House

ALGER, RUSSELL ALEXANDER (1836–1907)

U.S political figure and secretary of war, Alger was born in Lafayette, Ohio. He was admitted to the bar in 1859 and moved to Michigan a year later. Despite a questionable war record, he rose to brevet major general of volunteers during the Civil War. He then made a fortune in the lumber industry and served as president of the Grand Army of the Republic. Although Alger was in poor health, in 1897, Pres. William McKinley named him secretary of war, then considered the least demanding post in the cabinet. The war with Spain soon followed and overwhelmed the administrative capabilities of the War Department. The hapless and ineffective secretary, who played little part in the war's direction, became the popular scapegoat for the government's inability to mobilize effectively. He was forced to resign in 1899. Alger was serving as U.S. senator from Michigan when he died.

Richard B. Meixsel

ALLEN, HENRY TUREMAN (1859–1930)

U.S. army officer, Allen was born in Sharpsburg, Kentucky. He graduated from West Point in 1882. Service with the 2d Cavalry was interrupted by a noteworthy exploring expedition through Alaska in 1885. From 1890 to 1895, he was one of the army's first military attachés, assigned to St. Petersburg, Russia. He returned to attaché duty in Berlin, Germany, in 1897.

Allen participated in the expedition to Santiago, Cuba, in 1898, and anxious not to miss the fighting in the Philippines, he obtained command of a battalion of the 43d Volunteer Infantry and arrived in Manila in January 1899. A year later, he was military governor of Samar Island, and when the 43d returned home in May 1901, Captain Allen became military governor of Leyte. His able performance and his familiarity with native troops led William Howard Taft, the first governor general of the Philippines, to appoint Allen commander of the newly formed Philippine Constabulary in July 1901. The position gave the regular army captain the status, but not the rank, of an army brigadier general. Allen held the post until 1907, during which time the constabulary rose in number to more than 6,000 men and bore the brunt of pacifying the islands.

Allen joined the General Staff in Washington, D.C., in 1910. At the outbreak of world war in 1914, Allen helped to repatriate Americans home from Europe. He later served with the Punitive Expedition into Mexico. Allen took the 90th Division to France in June 1918, where it took part in the St.-Mihiel and Meuse-Argonne offensives. He then served as commanding general of the U.S. forces in Germany until 1923. Allen retired the same year.

Bibliography: Twichell, Heath, Jr., *Allen: The Biography of an Army Officer, 1859–1930* (Rutgers Univ. Press, 1974).

Richard B. Meixsel

ALVORD, BENJAMIN (1860–1927)

U.S. military leader, Alvord was born in Rutland, Vermont, and graduated from West Point in 1882. He served in various posts on the frontier and as an instructor at the Military Academy until 1898. Alvord then rotated between command and adjutant general assignments. In 1903, he became the first secretary of the newly formed General Staff. In 1914, he was the chief of staff of the expeditionary force at Veracruz and continued working with Gen. John J. Pershing as the first adjutant general of the American Expeditionary Force (A.E.F.). Promoted to brigadier general in 1917, Alvord returned to the United States in May 1918 due to ill health. He was chief of the Army Personnel Bureau from 1922 until his retirement in 1924.

Capt. George B. Eaton

ATTERBURY, WILLIAM WALLACE (1866–1935)

U.S. railroad executive and military railroad director, Atterbury was born in New Albany, Indiana. He received technical training at Yale University and joined the Pennsylvania Railroad as an apprentice at the huge Altoona shops. He rose quickly and steadily through the ranks of the mechanical and operating departments. By 1911, he was the vice president in charge of operations, the key official in the daily running of the railroad. Atterbury was elected president of the American Railway Association in 1916, and he attracted the notice of Pres. Woodrow Wilson for his coordination of U.S. railroads in the movement of troops and supplies during the mobilization for the Punitive Expedition into Mexico in 1916.

When the transportation mission of the American Expeditionary Forces (A.E.F.) in France grew so large that the French government turned over operation of many rail lines to the A.E.F., Atterbury was the logical choice to become director general of transportation, with an appointment as a brigadier general. After the war, he returned to the Pennsylvania Railroad, becoming its president in 1925. He was responsible for the last major electrification project of a mainline U.S. railroad, accomplished in the depths of the Depression. Ill health forced his retirement in 1935.

Col. Thomas W. Sweeney

BAKER, NEWTON DIEHL (1871–1937)

U.S. secretary of war, Baker was born in Martinsburg, West Virginia. He was a successful lawyer known for his moderate, progressive views. As secretary of war 1916–21, Baker provided Pres. Woodrow Wilson with an even-handed administrator during the highly partisan and divisive preparedness debates prior to the U.S. entry into World War I and a competent, pragmatic official during the war. Controversies surrounding his stewardship of the War Department included his views on the age-old dispute of National Guard versus regular army, civil rights and civilian-military relations, the rift between the War Department's General Staff and bureaus, and the 1918 struggle between the chief of staff of the army and Gen. John J. Pershing. Baker was not an energetic reformer, but he was held in high regard during his public service.

Baker accepted Wilson's call to head the War Department during a bitter 1916 struggle over the nation's attempt to prepare for war. His predecessor, Lindley M. Garrison, had resigned at the first part of the year, signifying his disagreement with the president's lack of support for a scheme to create a 400,000-man reserve force, a proposal known as the "Continental Army Plan." The plan was largely opposed by National Guard supporters who saw it as an attempt to strengthen the regular army at the expense of state military forces. The hot dispute was threatening to split the Democratic party, jeopardizing Wilson's chances for reelection in 1916. Baker supported legislation that reaffirmed the National Guard as the nation's premier reserve force, expanded the regular army, and cut the General Staff. The National Defense Act of 1916 gave something to every contender enmeshed in the preparedness dispute. Wilson won his second term of office.

War Policies. Baker was a recognized progressive. One might expect socially enlightened War Department policies in the administration of a great wartime citizen army, and the massive conscription program that began upon U.S. entry into World War I was effectively and honestly executed. But there were many instances of racial bigotry and callous treatment of conscientious objectors. Baker did little to further the cause of human rights in either case, mainly siding with the view of his officers.

The secretary took a middle course between his two disputing senior generals and, initially, a similar tack in the arguments between the General Staff and the antiquated bureaus. He did try to protect the authority of his office from the encroachments of wartime civilian agencies. Baker waged a rearguard action against Bernard Baruch's War Industries Board, attempting to assert military authority over the country's war production. Baruch did gain on the army bureaucrats, but the secretary of war retained some control over procurement and contracting. At first, Baker resisted siding with either the General Staff or the bureaus, steering a middle course during most of 1917. However, he eventually sided with the chief of staff and began advocating increasing subordination of the bureaus to the General Staff.

Perhaps the greatest wartime trial for Baker was the growing dispute between Chief of Staff Peyton March and Pershing, the commander of the American Expeditionary Force (A.E.F.). This argument became serious in 1918 and was probably inevitable since there was only one significant theater of operations. Pershing naturally insisted that he, as combat commander, should dictate all the parameters for training, organization, matériel, and doctrine. March rightfully insisted that Pershing could not know of the difficulties the army was encountering in the United States and refused to simply distribute A.E.F. requirements to his staff. Baker placed himself squarely between the two generals on some issues and avoided involvement in others.

There were two important wartime national policy issues that Baker did not dodge. He was a strong advocate of a separate front, separate army, and separate place at the peace table for the United States. He backed Pershing's hand in the matter of resisting "amalgamation" of U.S. soldiers into the battle-depleted ranks of French and British forces. Baker was outspoken, at least in official channels, about the involvement of the United States in the ill-fated North Russia Campaign, advising Wilson against sending U.S. troops to Russia. When the president made the decision to do so, however, Baker loyally supported his commander in chief.

Postwar Career. Baker left office in 1921 amid a general air of national appreciation and with little acrimony. He was called to service once again to head a board in 1934 to make recommendations about the thorny issue of independence for the U.S. Army Air Corps. His decision might have been predictable: he advocated retention of the corps within the army as a semiseparate organization with operational freedom. It was a choice that had a degree of satisfaction for everyone.

Baker failed to settle the issues between the National Guard and the regulars or the dispute between the bureaus and the General Staff. He failed to resolve the army's racial problems and did not achieve a lasting solution to the independent air force controversy. However, both the president and the generals could count on his honest, largely apolitical administration of difficult policies. When Wilson needed a pragmatist, he found one in Baker.

Bibliography: Beaver, Daniel R., *Newton D. Baker and the American War Effort, 1917–1919* (Univ. of Nebraska Press, 1966); Cramer, Clarence H., *Newton D. Baker: A Biography* (World, 1961).

Col. (Ret.) Rod Paschall

BATES, JOHN COALTER (1842–1919)

U.S. army officer, Bates was born in St. Charles County, Missouri. He spent the years preceding the Spanish-American War serving in the West and along the Mexican border. With the outbreak of war in 1898, Bates commanded a brigade in Cuba, most notably in engagements at Siboney and El Caney.

In 1899, Bates transferred to the Philippines, where he urged the adoption of a harsh and punitive policy in dealing with the Filipino population. He compiled a distinguished record against the insurgents in actions at Cavité and on the island of Mindanao. In 1906, Bates was promoted to lieutenant general and posted as chief of staff six months before his retirement.

Vernon L. Williams

BELKNAP, WILLIAM WORTH (1829–1890)

U.S. army officer, Belknap was born in Newburgh, New York. After attending Princeton and Georgetown universities, he practiced law from 1851 until the outbreak of the Civil War. Belknap entered the army in 1861 as a major and was promoted to lieutenant colonel in 1862, after the Battle of Shiloh. He was subsequently promoted to brigadier general and then to major general, U.S. Volunteers, at the end of the war.

Although a bluff, unimaginative, and hypocritical man, Belknap served as Pres. Ulysses S. Grant's secretary of war 1869–76. He was impeached for accepting bribes but resigned before the trial began. The charges were then dropped for lack of jurisdiction. When he died in October 1890, it was suspected that he had committed suicide.

Brig. Gen. (Ret.) Uzal W. Ent

BELL, JAMES FRANKLIN (1856–1919)

U.S. army officer, Bell was born near Shelbyville, Kentucky. He graduated from West Point in 1878 and went by the name "J. Franklin" to distinguish himself from other officers named Bell. Subsequent assignments included duty with the 7th Cavalry in Dakota Territory, instructor in military science at Southern Illinois Normal University (1886–89), and staff member at the Cavalry and Light Artillery School at Fort Riley, Kansas (1891–94).

Bell won the Medal of Honor in September 1899 while commanding the 36th Volunteer Infantry in the Philippines. He then directed a harsh but successful pacification campaign in Batangas Province. Promoted from captain to brigadier general in the regular army in 1901, he then became head of the Army Service Schools at Fort Leavenworth, Kansas (1902–06).

Bell is usually considered the first effective army chief of staff, a position created in 1903 and filled by Bell from 1906 to 1910. His reorganization of the staff freed war planners from routine administration while reining in the autonomy of the bureau chiefs. Bell's little-known tenure as commanding general of the Philippines Division (1911–14) was the longest any officer held that post. He implemented the unpopular colonial army system, which replaced the policy of rotating regiments through the islands for two-year periods with the selection of specific regiments to remain permanently on Philippine service.

Bell finished out his army career as commander of the 2d Division in Texas (1914–15) and of the Western Department (1915–17). Poor health kept him from duty with the American Expeditionary Force (A.E.F.), and he died in New York City while in command of the Eastern Department.

Richard B. Meixsel

BENSON, WILLIAM SHEPHERD (1855–1932)

The first U.S. chief of naval operations (CNO), Benson was born in Macon, Georgia. He was one of the first Southerners to enter the Naval Academy after the Civil War. His early career consisted of a variety of ship and shore assignments as he rose slowly through the ranks to become a captain in 1909. After commanding the battleship *Utah,* Benson became commandant of the Philadelphia navy yard in 1913.

In 1915, he was appointed CNO with the rank of rear admiral (full admiral in 1916). He has been criticized unfairly as having been unqualified to be CNO and grossly Anglophobic, but in reality, Benson shaped the office into an effective instrument for centralizing much of the navy's administration. He helped prepare the navy for World War I, capably administered the service through the conflict, and served as the principal U.S. naval adviser at the Paris Peace Conference. Benson retired from the navy in 1919 but continued serving on the U.S. Shipping Board 1919–28.

Bibliography: Klachko, Mary, *Admiral William Shepherd Benson: First Chief of Naval Operations* (Naval Inst. Press, 1987).

Donald A. Yerxa

BENTEEN, FREDERICK WILLIAM (1834–1898)

U.S. cavalry officer, Benteen was born in Petersburg, Virginia. He was commissioned a first lieutenant of the Union's 10th Missouri Cavalry in September 1861 and was promoted to captain the following month. He was at the Civil War's Siege of Vicksburg and thereafter served in the South. After the war, he was commissioned captain of the 7th U.S. Cavalry. He was with Lt. Col. George A. Custer at the Battle of the Washita (Nov. 27, 1868) and at the Battle of the Little Bighorn eight years later, where Custer and his immediate command were annihilated. Benteen came to personify the anti-Custer element of the 7th Cavalry. Consequently, he, along with Maj. Marcus Reno, is often faulted for Custer's defeat. Benteen was competent and respected, however, and his troop was "one of the consistently best'' of the regiment. Benteen later figured prominently in the Nez Percé Campaign.

M. Guy Bishop

BILLINGS, JOHN SHAW (1838–1913)

A pioneer in medical administration and education, Billings was born in Indiana. He graduated from Miami (Ohio) University at age 19 and from the Medical College of Ohio at age 24. His graduation coincided with the outbreak of the Civil War, and he received a Union commission as a regular army medical officer in 1862. During the war, he served as hospital administrator, with the medical director of the Army of the Potomac, and with the Office of the Surgeon General, where he remained until his retirement. In this assignment Billings made his most important contributions to the army by cataloging, indexing, and expanding the surgeon general's library.

Before his death, Billings served on the faculty of the University of Pennsylvania, assisted in the development of the New York Public Library System, and managed the Carnegie Institution for encouraging research. His professional activities elevated the status and credibility of the medical profession in general and the military practitioner in particular.

Bibliography: Garrison, Fielding H., *John Shaw Billings: A Memoir* (Putnam, 1915).

Louise Arnold-Friend

BLACK KETTLE (c. 1801–1868)

Cheyenne leader known for his peace efforts in the face of increased U.S. encroachment combined with increased militancy among many of the young men of his tribe. He and his fellow Indian pacifists did not usually represent a majority of the Cheyenne or other Plains tribes. Thus, they were often criticized for negotiating with the United States and giving away Indian lands.

When war broke out between Indians and U.S. forces in Colorado Territory in the summer of 1864, Black Kettle surrendered his band and was told to camp along Sand Creek. There, at daybreak on Nov. 29, 1864, his village was attacked by Colorado volunteers under Col. John M. Chivington. The resultant ''Sand Creek Massacre'' cost the Cheyenne the loss of nearly half their village. Two-thirds of the dead were women and children. Black Kettle took the survivors of his band south of the Arkansas River and, undaunted by U.S. treachery, still sought peace, taking part in the Treaty Council on the Little Arkansas in October 1865. In 1868, he and his band were in the Washita Valley (in present-day Oklahoma) still trying to deal with U.S. negotiators and military personnel. On November 27, a U.S. force led by George A. Custer traced a Cheyenne raiding party back to Black Kettle's village. In a scene reminiscent of Sand Creek, the soldiers attacked, killing Indians of all ages and both sexes, including Black Kettle and his wife.

Ted Alexander

BLANCO Y ERENAS, RAMÓN (1831–1906)

Spanish military officer and statesman, Blanco y Erenas was born in San Sebastián, Spain. He served in Cuba during that island's 1868–77 war for independence and supported Spain's annexation of Santo Domingo. He later became captain general of Catalonia, Spain.

Blanco was appointed governor general of Cuba 1879–81 and again in late 1897, when the controversial Valeriano Weyler was recalled from that position. Blanco implemented numerous reforms in an attempt to end the rebellion there. His hopes to reach an agreement with Cuban rebels were dashed when war with the United States broke out in April 1898. Blanco tried to get the rebels to join Spain against the United States but was rebuffed. He called for a fleet to defend Cuba, and, when it came, attempted to resist the more powerful U.S. Navy.

Mark Pitcavage

BLISS, TASKER HOWARD (1853–1930)

U.S. army officer, diplomat, educator, and army chief of staff, Bliss was born in Lewiston, Pennsylvania. He graduated from West Point in 1875 and was commissioned in the artillery. He spent little time with his regiment, returning to the Military Academy the next year as an instructor in foreign languages. During his early career, he graduated from the Artillery School at Fortress Monroe, lectured in military science at the new U.S. Naval War College, and studied military education systems in Great Britain, France, and Germany. Bliss was chosen as the aide to Maj. Gen. John M. Schofield, General of the Army, in 1888 and then had assignments with the Coast Artillery and the Commissary Bureau.

When the Spanish-American War broke out in 1898, Bliss returned to serve as a staff officer with the I Corps, commanded by Maj. Gen. James H. Wilson. Bliss accompanied Wilson and one division of the corps on the expedition to Puerto Rico. Although military operations there were brief, he distinguished himself in an attempt to persuade Spanish troops to surrender. The year 1899 found Bliss serving as the customs collector for Cuba, a position he held for the next three and a half years. Bliss worked hard at this job and, with an eye to the future, trained Cubans to replace the U.S. personnel in the customs service. He made his mark, and the War Department respected his opinions in regard to revising U.S. tariffs on Cuban products. After the U.S. withdrawal, Bliss returned to Cuba to negotiate a treaty of reciprocity with the Cuban government.

The wide and varied military career of Tasker Bliss included administration, instruction, foreign relations, and military tactics—an ideal preparation for his appointment to the General Staff in 1915. (U.S. Military Academy)

Outstanding service in Cuba earned Bliss his promotion to brigadier general in 1902. His next assignment was as president of the War College Board. Sec. of War Elihu Root had established the board in 1899 and used it as a de facto War Department general staff until 1903, when the General Staff Corps was formally established. The Army War College was established at the same time, with Bliss as its first president. He spent the first year preparing the curriculum and the faculty. The students were organized into committees, and each committee was tasked to study possible military operations in a certain geographical area. The student committees performed their work under the supervision of General Staff officers. The end product of this process was a plan of operations, including forces required, operational scenario, and a detailed analysis of the proposed area of operations and the likely enemy. In 1906, the employment of the Army of Cuba Pacification was the first use of such a plan.

Bliss's War College, therefore, functioned as the plans agency of the General Staff. This was necessary due to the limited number of personnel authorized by the General Staff Act. The college's first three years saw the beginning of efforts to create long-range thinking and policies in such areas as mobilization and contingency planning, military education, and staff training. Bliss also represented the army on the Joint Army-Navy Board, the forerunner of the current Joint Chiefs of Staff.

Bliss left Washington in 1905 to serve as a member of Sec. of War William H. Taft's diplomatic mission to Japan. Late in the same year, Bliss arrived in the Philippines, where he assumed command of the island of Luzon. Subsequently, he was appointed military governor of Moro Province (1906) and commander of the Division of the Philippines (1908). He returned to Washington in 1909 and served as president of the Army War College for four months. In August 1910, he assumed command of the Department of California. In the period March–June 1911, he commanded a provisional brigade on the Mexican border, following the outbreak of revolutionary activity in Mexico. Much of his time there was spent resolving confrontations and problems resulting from activities on both sides of the border. It was as much a diplomatic assignment as it was a military command.

After two years as commander of the Department of the East, Bliss returned in 1913 to the border area as commander of the Southern Department and Cavalry Division. During this assignment, he became involved in how best to protect the United States's border area from various cross-border illegal activities and revolutionary violence. Opinions within the army on this problem varied. Some advocated a military invasion of Mexico, such as outlined in War Plan Green. Bliss, however, was an advocate of a more limited response: an advance into Mexico to the gulf-to-gulf line between Guaymas and Tampico, thereby establishing the area north of this line as a *cordon sanitaire*. This zone would be occupied by U.S. troops until internal affairs within Mexico were resolved and a stable government established. Neither option was implemented, however, and Gen. John J. Pershing's Punitive Expedition in 1916, a limited response, was the only significant military operation undertaken along the border.

On Feb. 15, 1915, Bliss was appointed assistant chief of staff of the army and promoted to major general. In this position, he was responsible for the General Staff's Mobile Army Division and again had a hand in war planning. Still in this position when the United States entered World War I, Bliss did not handle the army's mobilization very successfully. He was hampered because the war plans considered by the War College did not cover a situation similar to that faced by the United States in the spring of 1917 and because Pres. Woodrow Wilson placed restrictions on the planners that contributed to the lack of preparation for mobilization.

When Gen. Hugh Scott, the army chief of staff, departed on a mission to Russia in May 1917, Bliss became the acting chief. He was formally appointed to the position on Sept. 23, 1917. Although he held this appointment until

May 18, 1918, he did not figure significantly in strategic matters and was absent from the country most of the time. Appointed as the U.S. representative on the Allied Supreme War Council, Bliss arrived in France to assume his new duties in January 1918. His job was to assist in the difficult objective of aligning U.S. efforts with the other Allies to achieve a concentrated effort against the Germans. Chosen as one of the U.S. commissioners to the Paris Peace Conference in 1919, Bliss did have some influence on the technical military portions of the treaty with Germany and perhaps on the conference's attitude toward intervention in Soviet Russia. Bliss returned to the United States to retirement, during which he helped found the Council on Foreign Relations, was an advocate of U.S. membership in the League of Nations, and supported international disarmament.

Bibliography: Challener, Richard D., *Generals and American Foreign Policy, 1898–1914* (Princeton Univ. Press, 1973); Coffman, Edward M., *The War to End All Wars: The American Military Experience in World War I* (Oxford Univ. Press, 1968); Palmer, Frederick, *Bliss: Peacemaker; The Life and Letters of General Tasker Howard Bliss* (Dodd, Mead, 1934).

John A. Hixson

BOLLING, RAYNAL CAWTHORNE (1877–1918)

U.S. aeronautics pioneer who helped lay the foundation of the U.S. Air Service of World War I, Bolling was born in Hot Springs, Arkansas. He was a Harvard-educated lawyer who advocated national defense. He established the First Motorized Machine Gun Company in 1915 and the First Aero Company, New York National Guard, in 1916.

As head of a World War I commission bearing his name, Colonel Bolling led a team of military and civilian experts that determined the course of U.S. military aviation during the conflict. While serving as a liaison officer to the Allies for air matters and as assistant chief of the Air Service, Bolling was killed in action.

Carol E. Stokes

BOURKE, JOHN GREGORY (1846–1896)

U.S. army officer and ethnologist, Bourke was born in Philadelphia. He entered West Point with the Class of 1869 after serving as an enlisted man during the Civil War. In 1871, he joined Gen. George Crook's staff and traveled with the general through the campaigns against the Apache and the Sioux. Throughout these years, Bourke cultivated his interest in American Indian society and culture. By 1886, his ethnographic work, which centered on the southwestern Indians, had become so well known that the U.S. Army granted him a five-year sabbatical to pursue his studies further. Bourke's championing of the Apache irritated some of his superiors, and he never rose above the rank of captain.

Bibliography: Porter, John, *Paper Medicine Man: John Gregory Bourke and His American West* (Univ. of Oklahoma Press, 1986).

Richard F. Kehrberg

BRENT, CHARLES HENRY (1862–1929)

Episcopal bishop and chief of chaplains for the Allied Expeditionary Force during World War I, Brent was born in Newcastle, Ontario, Canada. He received his appointment to head the chaplains on May 1, 1918, and immediately labored to increase the number of chaplains servicing each regiment from one to three. With only one cleric for every 3,600 men, many soldiers went into battle without the spiritual ministrations of a chaplain, a condition Brent called "cruel beyond words." In spite of War Department apathy, he finally succeeded in bringing more religious influence to the front. Brent, a captain, recruited excellent clergymen by dispatching veteran chaplains home to visit local churches. In recognition for his efforts, Brent received the Distinguished Service Medal after the war.

Bibliography: Piper, John F., Jr., *The American Churches in World War I* (Ohio Univ. Press, 1985).

Capt. Karen S. Wilhelm

BROOKE, JOHN RUTTER (1838–1926)

U.S. army officer, Brooke was born in Montgomery County, Pennsylvania. He began his military career in 1861 as a captain of Union volunteers. He earned a reputation as a hard fighter and competent commander in the Peninsular Campaign and in the battles of Antietam, Fredericksburg, Chancellorsville, and Gettysburg. Promoted to brigadier general in 1864, Brooke commanded a division in the final year of the war.

In 1866, he became a lieutenant colonel of the U.S. 37th Infantry. A major general in the Spanish-American War, he assumed command of the 1st Corps and the Chickamauga Camp. In July 1898, he commanded part of the Puerto Rican expedition, landing at Arroyo. Subsequently, he served as head of the military commission and governor for the island and later for Cuba. Brooke returned to the United States and took command of the Department of the East in 1900. He retired in 1902.

Bibliography: Cosmas, Graham A., *An Army for Empire: The United States Army in the Spanish-American War* (Univ. of Missouri Press, 1971); Johnson, Allen, ed., *Dictionary of American Biography* (Scribner's, 1943).

John A. Hixson

BROWN, PRESTON (1872–1948)

U.S. army officer, Brown was born in Lexington, Kentucky. He was graduated from Yale University in 1892. In 1894, he joined the U.S. Army and served as a private and corporal until he was commissioned a second lieutenant of infantry in 1897. Brown advanced through the ranks and was a major by 1916. He accepted a temporary promotion to lieutenant colonel in 1917 and became commander of the 3d Infantry Division for the last month of World War I, during the Meuse-Argonne Campaign. He was awarded the Distinguished Service Medal for his action in that campaign.

After the war, Brown returned to his permanent rank of major. After receiving his Master of Arts from Yale in 1920 and being promoted to major general in 1925, he served in numerous positions of high responsibility, including deputy chief of staff of the army, commander of both the 1st and 6th corps areas, and commander of the Panama Department. He retired in 1934.

Capt. George B. Eaton

BROWNING, JOHN MOSES (1855–1926)

U.S. firearms designer, Browning was born in Ogden, Utah. He ran a firearms factory and designed guns for other manufacturers as well. His rugged but elegant designs were an immediate success. Winchester alone purchased more than 44 designs, and Colt, Remington, Savage, and Belgium's Fabrique Nationale also produced his weapons. The U.S. military adopted Browning designs for pistols, machine guns, and even aircraft cannon in the first half of the 20th century. His machine guns saw service in every U.S. war from the Spanish-American War through Vietnam, and his semiautomatic pistol was standard army-issue for more than 70 years. A plaque at Fabrique Nationale summed up Browning simply as "the greatest firearms inventor the world has ever known."

Bibliography: Browning, John, and Curtis Gentry, *John M. Browning: American Gunmaker* (Doubleday, 1964).

Richard F. Kehrberg

BULLARD, ROBERT LEE (1861–1947)

U.S. army officer, Bullard was born in Youngsboro, Alabama. He graduated from West Point in 1885 and served extensively in the Southwest. During the Spanish-American War, he became a colonel of volunteers and led the 3d Alabama Volunteers, a black regiment that saw service in Cuba. In 1900, Bullard took command of the 39th Volunteer Infantry and fought in the Philippine Insurrection. He returned to the regular army in May 1901 as a major but remained in the Philippines as a district governor until 1904. Advanced to lieutenant colonel in 1906, he served several years in the military government in Cuba. In 1911, Bullard was made colonel of the 26th Infantry. He graduated from the Army War College in 1912 and served on the Mexican border 1915–17.

When the 1st Division sailed for France in June 1917, Bullard received a promotion to brigadier general and went along as a brigade commander. By August, he was a temporary major general and commandant of the infantry school in France. He returned to the 1st Division in December as its commanding officer. After leading it into combat at Cantigny on May 28, 1918, Bullard took command of the III Corps in July. Later that month, the III Corps participated in the Aisne-Marne Offensive. In the midst of the Meuse-Argonne Offensive in September, Bullard was promoted to the rank of temporary lieutenant general and took charge of the newly created U.S. 2d Army. Bullard had proved to be a first-rate field commander and returned home in May 1919 as a permanent major general in the regular army. He retired in 1925.

Bibliography: Coffman, Edward M., *The War to End All Wars: The American Military Experience in World War I* (Univ. of Wisconsin Press, 1986); Millett, Allan R., *The General: Robert L. Bullard and Officership in the U.S. Army, 1881–1925* (Greenwood, 1975).

Daniel T. Bailey

BUNDY, OMAR (1861–1940)

U.S. army officer, Bundy was born in Indiana. He graduated from West Point in 1883 and served as an infantryman on the frontier in Indian campaigns. He was cited for gallantry (and brevetted major) at El Caney, Cuba, during the Spanish-American War and subsequently served three years in the Philippines. Returning to the Philippines in 1905 after three years at the General Service and Staff College at Fort Leavenworth, Bundy achieved distinction while fighting the Moros on Jolo Island in 1906. He sailed to France in 1917 as commander of the 1st Brigade, 1st Division, and commanded the 2d Division in battle in June 1918. Failing to impress Gen. John J. Pershing, Bundy was made commander of a phantom (decoy) corps as part of a U.S. deception plan to support the St.-Mihiel Offensive. He returned to the United States in November 1918 and took command of Fort Lee, Virginia. He was promoted to major general in 1921 and retired in 1925.

Stephen J. Lofgren

BUTLER, SMEDLEY DARLINGTON (1881–1940)

U.S. marine officer, Butler was born in West Chester, Pennsylvania. He joined the Marine Corps in 1898 as a second lieutenant. He served briefly in Cuba during the Spanish-American War and later in the Philippines. In June 1900, he was among the first U.S. troops to land in China in response to the Boxer Rebellion. Twice wounded, Butler participated in the assault on Tientsin and the relief of the Seymour Expedition in July 1900; in August, he marched with the China Relief Expedition to lift the siege of the beleaguered legations in Peking.

Between November 1902 and March 1904, Butler served in various assignments in the Caribbean and Central America. During the years 1905–08 he commanded troops in

Smedley D. Butler, twice winner of the Medal of Honor, commanded marines in the Philippines, Nicaragua, Mexico, and Haiti, as well as in France during World War I. (U.S. Army Military History Institute)

the Philippines, returning to Panama with the Expeditionary Brigade stationed at Camp Elliott in 1909. Late that year, a revolution against strongman Adolfo Díaz sparked a period of turmoil in Nicaragua. The United States responded by sending in the marines. Butler led an expeditionary force to Corinto in December and commanded a landing force at Bluefields May–September 1910. In August 1912, he served with the 1st Provisional Brigade sent to support Nicaragua's U.S.-backed government. The marines defeated rebels at the Battle of Coyatepe, and in a stroke of "shirt-sleeve diplomacy," Butler managed to persuade rebel leader Luis Ména to go into exile.

Butler returned to command Camp Elliott from November 1912 until January 1914, when his marines joined elements of the Atlantic Fleet off the coast of Mexico. As part of an ongoing confrontation between Pres. Woodrow Wilson and Mexican dictator Victoriano Huerta, U.S. Marines, with Butler commanding the 1st Battalion, 2d Regiment, landed at Veracruz on Apr. 22, 1914. He received the Medal of Honor for his part in this action.

In response to another Caribbean coup, this time in Haiti, the 1st Provisional Brigade, with Butler leading the 1st Battalion, landed in Port-au-Prince in August 1915. After suppressing the Caco revolt, he was appointed head of the Gendarmerie d'Haiti, a post he held for three years. Butler received another Medal of Honor for his action at the Battle of Fort Rivière in Haiti.

In October 1918, he took command of Camp Pontanezan, France. After the war, he served as chief of staff and later commander of the marine base at Quantico. Detached from the corps, Butler spent 1924–25 as superintendent of public safety in Philadelphia. During 1926–27, he commanded the marine base at San Diego. Later he led the 3d Brigade in China. In 1929, Major General Butler assumed command of the Quantico base, a post he held until he retired in September 1931.

Bibliography: Schmidt, Hans, *Maverick Marine: General Smedley D. Butler and the Contradictions of American History* (Univ. Press of Kentucky, 1987).

Anne Cipriano Venzon

CAMERON, JAMES DONALD (1833–1918)

U.S. congressman and secretary of war, Cameron was born in Middletown, Pennsylvania. He graduated from Princeton University and served as president of the North Central Railway Company 1863–74. His father, Simon Cameron, was Pres. Abraham Lincoln's first secretary of war and left that post under a cloud of criticism.

In May 1876, Pres. Ulysses S. Grant appointed J. Donald Cameron to head the War Department. Cameron was an unimpressive secretary of war. He failed to protect the army from growing political attacks and left most details to commanding general William T. Sherman. To his credit, Cameron displayed considerable foresight in requesting funds from Congress to preserve the Mathew Brady photo collection. Elected to the U.S. Senate in March 1877, Cameron served in Congress for 20 years.

Bibliography: Bell, William Garner, *Secretaries of War and Secretaries of the Army: Portraits and Biographical Sketches* (Center for Military History, 1982).

Daniel T. Bailey

CANBY, EDWARD RICHARD SPRIGG (1817–1873)

U.S. army commander, Canby was born in Kentucky. He graduated from West Point in 1839 and fought in the Seminole and Mexican wars. During the Civil War, he commanded the Department of New Mexico and successfully opposed the Confederate invasion of that territory in 1862. Later, Canby saw service in other theaters of the war; in May 1865, he accepted the surrender of the last organized Confederate army, commanded by Gen. E. Kirby Smith.

In 1866, Canby was promoted to brigadier general and served in a number of posts until 1873, when he was placed in command of the Division of the Pacific. During the

Modoc uprising that year, Canby headed a peace commission to negotiate with the hostile Indians. He was attacked during the proceedings by Modoc leader Captain Jack and several Confederates, who stabbed and shot him to death. Canby was the only regular army general killed in the history of the U.S.-Indian wars.

Ted Alexander

CAPTAIN JACK (KINTPUASH) (c. 1837–1873)

Modoc leader and key figure in the Modoc War of 1872–73, Captain Jack was born in the vicinity of Lost River near the California border. In 1864, the Modoc signed a treaty that ceded territory and retired the Indians to the Klamath Reservation in Oregon. In 1865, disputes between the Klamath and Modoc led Jack to leave the reservation with a group of followers. After an army attempt on Nov. 29, 1872, to force the Indians back to the reservation, the Modoc fled to the Lava Beds. Negotiations were initiated by Gen. Edward Canby; however, during the second parley with the Modoc on Apr. 11, 1872, the peace commissioners were attacked and Canby was killed. Col. Jefferson C. Davis assumed command of more than 1,000 men and launched an attack. The Modoc surrendered on June 1, 1873. Jack and three warriors were executed on Oct. 3, 1873, and two other Modoc were imprisoned for life.

Bibliography: Payne, Doris Palmer, *Captain Jack, Modoc Renegade* (Binford & Mort, 1958); Riddle, Jeff, *The Indian History of the Modoc War* (Orion Press, 1974).

Deborah L. Mesplay

CARR, EUGENE ASA (1830–1910)

U.S. cavalry officer, Carr was born in Concord, New York. Upon graduation from West Point in 1850, he was appointed a brevet lieutenant, mounted rifles, with duty station at Carlisle Barracks, Pennsylvania. In June 1851, Carr was commissioned a second lieutenant, mounted rifles, and reassigned to Jefferson Barracks. Following participation in several expeditions, he was in Missouri when the Civil War began.

As a colonel with the 3d Illinois Cavalry, Carr participated in the Missouri operations early in the war. His most important military service occurred in Arkansas during the Battle of Pea Ridge (Mar. 7–8, 1862). In command of the 4th Division, he was wounded three times but remained on the battlefield. In addition to promotion to brigadier general of volunteers on Mar. 7, 1862, Carr was awarded the Congressional Medal of Honor for ''distinguished gallantry'' at Pea Ridge.

After the war, Carr reverted to the rank of major of cavalry and joined the 5th Cavalry just in time to participate in the winter campaign of 1868–69 against the Sioux and Cheyenne. Carr stayed on the frontier for the majority of his remaining service. Eventually commanding the 6th Cavalry, he saw continuous service against the Indians, concluding with the Pine Ridge Campaign of 1890–91. Carr retired from active duty as a brigadier general in February 1893.

Lt. Col. Martin W. Andresen

CARRANZA, VENUSTIANO (1859–1920)

Mexican revolutionary and political figure, Carranza was born in Cuatro Ciénegas, Coahuila. From a landholding family, he became governor of the state of Coahuila in 1910. In 1913, he became the nominal head of the struggle against Victoriano Huerta in 1913 as leader of the Constitutionalist party. After victory over Huerta, Carranza broke with his revolutionary allies Pancho Villa and Emiliano Zapata and waged war against them.

The successful Constitutionalist campaigns against Villa gained for Carranza U.S. support and led Villa in 1916 to raid Columbus, New Mexico, touching off large-scale military intervention by the United States. Carranza, capitalizing on a nationalist fervor, aggressively protested the intervention, which did not end until 1917. Carranza, who was elected president in 1917, was assassinated on May 21, 1920, by supporters of a political rival.

Mark Pitcavage

CARTER, WILLIAM HARDING (1851–1925)

U.S. military administrator and reformer, Carter was born in Nashville, Tennessee. During the Civil War, at age 12, he was employed by the Union Quartermaster Department as a mounted messenger (1864–65). Following the war, he moved to New York and later received an appointment to West Point by Pres. Andrew Johnson. Upon graduation in 1873, Carter was commissioned a second lieutenant of infantry and saw extensive service against the Indians for the next 20 years. While a captain, Carter was awarded a Congressional Medal of Honor for rescuing two wounded soldiers despite being wounded himself after encountering hostile Apache at Cibicu Creek, Arizona in 1881.

Carter was assigned to Fort Leavenworth in 1893, where he became an assistant cavalry instructor. Appointed an assistant adjutant general with the rank of major, he reported to Washington, D.C., in 1897. Following the Spanish-American War (1898), Sec. of War Elihu Root selected Carter as his principal adviser. Working tirelessly on Root's behalf, Carter seemed to possess a missionary zeal to reform the army and to introduce modern military management techniques. Among Carter's more significant achievements during this period was the establishment of the General Staff in 1903. He is also credited with encouraging Root to reform the army military school system and to establish the Army War College.

After several command assignments including another tour in Washington as the assistant chief of staff (1909–

11), Carter retired from active service in November 1915. He was soon recalled to active duty with the Senate Military Committee and assisted in the preparation of the National Defense Act of 1916. When the United States entered World War I in 1917, Carter was again recalled and was placed in command of the Central Department. More than 150,000 soldiers were trained and deployed overseas under Carter's direction. In addition to being a capable line and staff officer, Carter wrote several books on military affairs.

Lt. Col. Martin W. Andresen

CERVERA Y TOPETE, PASCUAL (1839–1909)

Spanish admiral whose squadron was destroyed in the Spanish-American War, Cervera y Topete was born in Medina-Sidonia, Spain. When war broke out with the United States in April 1898, Cervera was ordered to sortie to the Caribbean with his squadron of four armored cruisers and three destroyers. He tried unsuccessfully to dissuade the Spanish government from pursuing a strategy that would sacrifice his squadron in a hopeless effort to defeat the vastly superior U.S. naval forces. His squadron slipped into the harbor of Santiago on Cuba's south coast in mid-May. Cervera was soon blockaded by the combined squadrons of Commodore Winfield S. Schley and Adm. William T. Sampson. When U.S. troops in a supporting operation gained the high ground over Santiago, Cervera attempted to escape. On July 3, his force was annihilated by the U.S. fleet, and Cervera was taken prisoner.

Cervera was taken to Portsmouth, New Hampshire, for the remainder of the war, after which he returned to Spain and was honorably acquitted by a naval court of inquiry. In 1902, he was appointed chief of staff of the Spanish navy.

Bibliography: Trask, David F., *The War with Spain* (Macmillan Co., 1981).

Donald A. Yerxa

CHADWICK, FRENCH ENSOR (1844–1919)

U.S. naval officer whose writings contributed to the golden age of U.S. naval philosophy, Chadwick was born in Morgantown, Virginia (now West Virginia). He served in a variety of primarily sea assignments as he rose fairly rapidly in rank in the post-Civil War navy. Throughout the 1880s, he studied and wrote on naval doctrine while carrying out mostly shore assignments. He was naval attaché in London 1882–89, during which time he was promoted to commander. In 1892, he became head of the Office of Naval Intelligence.

In 1897, Chadwick was promoted to captain and given command of the armored cruiser *New York.* While still commanding the *New York,* he assisted in the investigation of the sinking in Cuba of the battleship *Maine,* after which he became Adm. William T. Sampson's chief of staff. During the Spanish-American War, he participated in the Battle of Santiago in July 1898.

Chadwick became president of the Naval War College in 1900 and commander in chief of the South Atlantic Squadron in 1903 with the rank of rear admiral. After his retirement from the navy in 1906, Chadwick authored a three-volume work on the Spanish-American conflict.

Bibliography: Coletta, Paola E., *French Ensor Chadwick: Scholarly Warrior* (Univ. Press of America, 1980).

Donald A. Yerxa

CHAFFEE, ADNA ROMANZA (1842–1914)

U.S. army officer, Chaffee was born in Orwell, Ohio. He rose through the ranks of the 6th U.S. Cavalry from private in 1861 to first lieutenant by the end of the Civil War. He suffered a serious wound at Fairfield, Pennsylvania, on July 3, 1863, but recovered and by 1867 held the rank of captain. Chaffee was cited for bravery a number of times both during the war and afterward in the West fighting Indians. During the Indian wars, he was an officer with a number of different cavalry regiments.

During the Spanish-American War, Chaffee commanded a brigade in the Santiago Campaign and was chief of staff to the military governor of Cuba. In 1900, as a major general, he commanded the multinational relief force that lifted the Siege of Peking during the Boxer Rebellion. In 1902, Chaffee relieved Gen. Arthur MacArthur as commander of U.S. forces in the Philippines. In this capacity, he supervised the final operations against the Philippine guerrillas.

Promoted to lieutenant general in 1904, Chaffee served as chief of staff of the U.S. Army 1904–06. During this period, he introduced a number of reforms to the military. He retired in 1906 and served as president of the Board of Public Works for the City of Los Angeles.

Ted Alexander

CHIVINGTON, JOHN MILTON (1821–1884)

U.S. clergyman whose military career as a commander of cavalry volunteers was characterized by brutality against Indians, Chivington was born in Warren County, Ohio. In 1844, he was ordained a Methodist minister; in May 1860, he arrived in Denver, Colorado, as leader of the First Methodist Episcopal Church. Although Chivington lacked military experience, he was offered a commission as regimental chaplain following the outbreak of the Civil War. Wanting a "fighting" not a "praying" commission, Chivington declined the offer. He later was commissioned a major in the 1st Colorado Regiment. Successful in blunting a Confederate advance at Glorietta Pass (New Mexico) on Mar. 26, 1862, he was appointed commander of the military district of Colorado a year later.

Concerned about an Indian threat, Colorado's Gov. John Evans formed the 3d Colorado Volunteers under Chivington's command in early 1864. Touting a policy of extermination, Chivington led about 1,000 volunteers against a peaceful Cheyenne and Arapaho encampment at Sand Creek, Colorado, on Nov. 29, 1864. The Indians had camped there while negotiating a peace with the commander of nearby Fort Lyon. The Sand Creek Massacre resulted in the death of more than 400 men, women, and children.

Colorado settlers praised Chivington, but the nation was horrified. A report issued by the Joint Committee on the Conduct of the War expressed the hope that the "government will never again be disgraced by acts such as [Chivington's] and those acting with him have been guilty of committing." The massacre was a contributing factor to the Arapaho-Cheyenne War and other Plains Indian hostilities that lasted more than two decades. Chivington resigned his commission in early 1865.

Martin W. Andresen

CONGER, ARTHUR LATHAM (1872–1951)

U.S. soldier and military historian, Conger was born in Akron, Ohio. He graduated from Harvard in 1894 and entered the army in 1898. He saw infantry service in the Philippines and taught in the army schools at Fort Leavenworth (1908–10, 1913–16). During World War I, Conger served as an intelligence officer in France and briefly commanded the 56th Infantry Brigade, 28th Division. He undertook special political and intelligence missions in Germany (1918–19) and later served as military attaché in Berlin (1923–27). He retired in 1928 and eventually became the international leader of the Theosophical Society.

Lt. Col. (Ret.) Charles R. Shrader

CONNER, FOX (1874–1951)

U.S. army officer, Conner was born in Slate Springs, Mississippi. He entered the artillery upon his graduation from West Point in 1898. From then until 1917, Conner alternated among command of various artillery batteries, a teaching assignment at the Army War College, and staff duty in Washington, D.C. Conner, a lieutenant colonel, was one of the staff of fewer than 200 men who accompanied Gen. John J. Pershing to France in May 1917 to begin preparations for the organization and buildup of the American Expeditionary Force (A.E.F.). As assistant chief of staff and then chief of staff for operations, G-3, Conner brought clarity of thought and consistency of purpose to the task of preparing plans for the artillery needs of the A.E.F., for the organization of the standard infantry division, and, as 1918 advanced, for the increasingly large operations of the A.E.F. His efforts were rewarded with promotions to colonel and then brigadier general.

After the war, Conner, who retired as a major general in 1938, held many of the peacetime army's top positions: commander of U.S. troops in the Panama Canal Zone, assistant chief of staff for supply, deputy chief of staff, commander of the Hawaiian Department (1928–30), and commander of the I Corps Area (1930–38). Had he not made known his dislike of service in Washington, he might have become chief of staff when that position fell vacant in 1934. Gen. Dwight D. Eisenhower, who regarded Conner as a model of military professionalism, believed that had Conner been 10 years older, he would have held a top command in World War I; had he been 10 years younger, he would have earned distinction in World War II.

Bibliography: Brown, Charles H., with John Ray Skates, ed., "Fox Conner: A General's General," *Journal of Mississippi History* (Aug. 1987).

Lloyd J. Graybar

CONNOR, PATRICK EDWARD (1820–1891)

U.S. army officer, Connor was born in County Kerry, Ireland, and moved to New York City as a child. He enlisted in the U.S. Army in 1839 and served in the Seminole Wars and in the Mexican War. In 1847, Connor was honorably discharged at Monterrey, Mexico, whereafter he went to the gold fields of California. Because of his strong Union sympathy at the outbreak of the Civil War, Connor was named colonel of California's 3d infantry in 1861. In the fall of 1862, he took his unit to Utah, providing garrison duty to the region through most of the war.

In 1865, Connor, by this time a general, was named commander of the District of the Plains. In this capacity he led the unsuccessful Powder River Expedition against the Sioux, Cheyenne, and Arapaho. Because of this abortive action, he was removed from command. On Apr. 30, 1866, he was mustered out of active service. He returned to Utah and was involved in various business and political activities until his death.

Bibliography: Madsen, Brigham D., *Glory Hunter: A Biography of Patrick Edward Connor* (Univ. of Utah Press, 1990).

Roger D. Launius

CONNOR, WILLIAM DURWARD (1874–1960)

U.S. army officer, Connor was born in Wisconsin. He graduated from West Point in 1897, and his subsequent military career earned him the command of both combat and support units during World War I. He served as chief of coordination on Gen. John J. Pershing's staff until May 1918. He then transferred to the 32d Infantry Division, where he served as chief of staff and later commanded a brigade. When Maj. Gen. James Harbord assumed command of the Services of Supply (SOS), he asked for Connor. Connor was transferred to the SOS to command Base Section No. 2, headquartered in Bordeaux, France.

After the armistice, Connor replaced Maj. Gen. Johnson Hagood as the chief of staff, SOS. In May 1919, he assumed command of the SOS. Following the war, Connor served as assistant chief of staff and commander of U.S. forces in China (1922–26), before being named commander of the Army War College in 1927. He was also superintendent of West Point (1932–38).

Steve R. Waddell

CORBIN, HENRY CLARK (1842–1909)

U.S. army officer, Corbin was born in Batavia, Ohio. His military career began during the Civil War, in 1862, with the 79th Ohio Volunteer Infantry. His wartime service was mostly in the Armies of the Cumberland and Ohio. He advanced in rank through self-study and diligent service, rising to colonel in 1865.

Corbin joined the regular army in September 1866 as a second lieutenant in the 17th Infantry. He spent the next 10 years as an infantry officer, in a variety of assignments in the Southwest. Testifying in 1876 before Congress, regarding the Mexican border situation, gave Corbin his introduction to national politics. Thereafter, politics and the military were solidly intermixed in Corbin's career. He became acquainted with several rising Republican politicians, such as Rutherford B. Hayes, James A. Garfield, and William McKinley. He served as President Hayes's aide for the greater part of the next three years.

In June 1880, Corbin was assigned to the office of the adjutant general. This office, which handled army administration, was the real nerve center of the War Department. Its influence was not lost on Corbin, who also remained a member of the president's inner circle in both the Hayes and Garfield administrations.

He left Washington in 1882 to serve in a series of assistant adjutant general staff positions in various commands. Corbin was promoted to lieutenant colonel in June 1889 and returned to the War Department in 1892. He became the principal assistant the following year and was promoted to colonel in May 1896. On Feb. 25, 1898, he was appointed adjutant general of the army, with the rank of brigadier general.

Corbin served as adjutant general until 1903. His office accomplished many of the functions now commonly associated with a general staff: it was the army's office of record, issued all orders from the secretary of war and the General of the Army, planned for mobilization in time of war, and had charge of the embryonic military intelligence service. Corbin enhanced the influence of this office through his energy, decisiveness, political skills, and good relations with the army's line officers. His tenure as adjutant general spanned a period of great transition in the history of the U.S. Army.

In August 1899, Elihu Root became secretary of war. He found Corbin to be an able assistant and secured his influence and help in promoting his army reforms. Promoted to major general in 1900, Corbin supported Root's efforts to reorganize the army, reform the National Guard, and create a general staff. Root's principal advisers on these matters were mainly members of Corbin's office staff.

Corbin assumed command of the Department of the East in 1904 and conducted the first Army-National Guard maneuvers the same year. He became commanding general of the Division of the Philippines in 1904. Corbin returned to the United States to command the Northern Division and was promoted to lieutenant general in March 1906. He retired six months later.

Bibliography: Cosmas, Graham A., *An Army for Empire* (Univ. of Missouri Press, 1971); Leech, Margaret, *In the Days of McKinley* (Harper & Brothers, 1959).

John A. Hixson

CRAZY HORSE (TASHUNCA-UITCO) (1849?-1877)

Chief of the Ogala Sioux, Crazy Horse was instrumental in resisting the U.S. occupation of the Northern Plains. He was present at the Grattan Massacre (Aug. 19, 1854) near Fort Laramie, Wyoming, which was the occasion of the first military clash between the U.S. Army and the Sioux. Although not present at the destruction of the Ash Hollow Village, Nebraska, on Sept. 3, 1855, Crazy Horse was further provoked by this act of retaliation.

In 1864, a new era of conflict was initiated in the Sand Creek Massacre. The next year, Crazy Horse led the armed Sioux opposition to U.S. plans to construct a new road to the gold fields of Montana. This was followed in 1866 by the massacre of Capt. William J. Fetterman and 80 of his troops, an attack Crazy Horse probably initiated. He was also present at the Wagon Box Fight of Aug. 2, 1867, in Wyoming.

Refusing to honor the reservation provisions of the Second Treaty of Fort Laramie (1868), Crazy Horse led his people into unceded bison territory where they hunted and made war on migrants. During the 1870s he continued his resistance by leading attacks on groups surveying for the North Pacific Railroad. In 1873, he was involved in two minor clashes with Col. George A. Custer on the Yellowstone River.

The discovery of gold in the Black Hills of Dakota Territory in 1874 and the subsequent invasion of Sioux reservation lands by prospectors precipitated another round of confrontation. Brig. Gen. George Crook's attempts to force Crazy Horse from his winter camp were resisted. Joining Cheyenne forces, he attacked Crook at the Rosebud River on June 17, 1876, and forced him to withdraw. He then moved north to unite with the Sioux under Sitting Bull at the Little Bighorn River, where Custer made his last stand on June 25.

Subsequent to this, however, most Sioux surrendered or fled. Crazy Horse fled to the hills, pursued by Gen. Nelson A. Miles in an attempt to force the Indians to deal with government agencies. The cold and hunger finally induced him to surrender to Crook at the Red Cloud Agency, Nebraska, May 6, 1877. Crazy Horse's request to resume his nomadic lifestyle was refused, probably due to the efforts of a treacherous interpreter. On September 5, Crazy Horse was fatally wounded during an effort to escape.

Bibliography: Brown, Vinson, *Great Upon the Mountain* (Macmillan Co., 1975).

Russell Hart

CROOK, GEORGE (1828–1890)

U.S. army officer, Crook was born near Taylorsville, Ohio. He was closely tied to the frontier army during much of his long career in the military, commanding some of the most significant military operations against Indians after the Civil War.

Early Career. Having obtained a congressional appointment to West Point in 1848, Crook graduated in 1853, near the bottom of his class, and was assigned to the 4th Infantry in the Pacific Northwest. While there, he began to develop his ideas on Indian culture and warfare. A hardliner on U.S.-Indian relations, he nonetheless developed a strong respect for the military abilities of Indians. He became an advocate of dealing fairly but strongly with Indian tribes. Most important, he adopted the position that peace would be possible only with the destruction of the Indians' nomadic way of life. Once the Indians had accepted this fact, Crook was committed to treating them fairly.

With the secession of the South and the beginning of the Civil War in 1861, Crook returned to the East and by September had been appointed commander of the 36th Ohio Infantry. He served in West Virginia during the winter of 1861–62, distinguishing himself as an able if unflamboyant commander. Later, Crook commanded the 9th Corps at Antietam. In 1863, he commanded the 2d Cavalry Division at Chickamauga and thereafter served under Gen. Philip H. Sheridan (a West Point classmate) during the 1864 Shenandoah Campaign.

Frontier Career. After the Civil War, Crook was retained in the army and in late 1866 became a lieutenant colonel in command of the 23d Infantry in Idaho Territory. Within a week of taking command, Crook was leading a company of cavalry in the field against renegade Paiute. His winter campaign pursued the Indians as had no other army effort, hunting down encampments, killing men, capturing families, and especially destroying provisions. For nearly two years, Crook pursued the Indians in all weather and over all manner of terrain. The final offensive took place in March 1868 when Crook's men tracked the enemy deep into the mountains and dealt it a decisive defeat, forcing the Indians to sue for peace.

In the early 1870s, Crook was sent to the Southwest to handle the Apache rebellion. Although he disagreed with the efforts of such reformers as Gen. Oliver O. Howard, who wanted to establish a "peace policy" with the Apache, he was respectful of their efforts. When they failed, however, Crook wasted no time in engaging the hostiles. In November 1872, he launched what became an 18-month Tonto Basin Campaign to defeat them. His force, traveling with pack mules and the bare necessities and making use of Indian scouts, pursued the Apache mercilessly in good and bad weather and fought a war of attrition. In April 1873, the beleaguered Apache surrendered to U.S. terms for peace. In part on the strength of this effort, Crook was promoted to brigadier general.

In 1875, Crook was reassigned from Arizona to command the Department of the Platte, under whose jurisdiction the Sioux were restless. The next year, Crook participated in one of the largest operations of the Indians wars. More than 2,000 troops were involved in this campaign. A combination of bad luck and poor judgment, from Crook and from other commanders, led to several setbacks in the campaign, the most serious being Col. George A. Custer's defeat at the Little Bighorn. Accordingly, it was not until May 1877 that the Sioux were brought back onto the reservations.

Crook spent the rest of his career quelling several other Indian rebellions. He was involved with efforts to end the raiding of renegade Apache in Arizona in the 1880s, most notably in fighting Geronimo. In some of these actions Crook sided with the Indians, believing that they were being increasingly ill-treated by the federal government. This eventually led to a breach between Crook and Sheridan that never healed.

Bibliography: Greene, Jerome A., "George Crook," *Soldier's West: Biographies from the Military Frontier,* ed. by Paul Andrew Hutton (Univ. of Nebraska Press, 1987); Schmitt, Martin F., ed., *General George Crook: His Autobiography* (Univ. of Oklahoma Press, 1960).

Roger D. Launius

CROWDER, ENOCH HERBERT (1859–1932)

U.S. army officer, Crowder was born in Edinburg, Missouri. He graduated from West Point in 1881. After frontier service with the 8th U.S. Cavalry, he was twice detailed as professor of military science and tactics at the University of Missouri. During these assignments, he earned a law degree. On Jan. 11, 1895, he was appointed major in the judge advocate general's department, and he remained in that corps for the remainder of his career.

During the Spanish-American War, Crowder served in the Philippines as Gen. Wesley Merritt's judge advocate and after the war as an adviser to Gens. Elwell S. Otis and

Arthur MacArthur. He helped to modify Spanish law to fit U.S. jurisprudence in both the Philippines and Cuba.

In 1911, Crowder was appointed judge advocate general of the army. After World War I, he oversaw the revision of the Articles of War. He retired in 1923, after which he served as ambassador to Cuba until 1927.

David O. Friend

CROWELL, BENEDICT (1869–1952)

Assistant U.S. secretary of war, Crowell was born in Cleveland, Ohio. He was a successful industrialist before World War I. When the United States entered the war, he volunteered his services and was assigned to the General Munitions Board.

Crowell became assistant secretary of war in November 1917 and was given responsibility for the War Department's industrial activities. In 1918, he took on the additional title of director of munitions. He firmly believed in civilian control of War Department procurement activities. Although he supported Maj. Gen. George W. Goethals's attempts to centralize the army's supply services, Crowell retained ultimate control of procurement. The National Defense Act of 1920 reflected his beliefs by officially assigning these matters to the assistant secretary of war.

Bibliography: Huston, James A., *The Sinews of War: Army Logistics, 1775–1953* (Office of the Chief of Military History, U.S. Army, 1966).

Daniel T. Bailey

CROZIER, WILLIAM (1855–1942)

U.S. army officer and firearms inventor, Crozier was born in Carrollton, Ohio. He graduated from West Point in 1876 and, after having served as an artillery officer, he transferred to the Ordnance Corps in 1881. He served in various staff positions until promoted to chief of ordnance in 1901. As chief, Crozier followed a controversial policy of having his ordnance technicians dictate what weapons combat troops would use.

The army's duties before 1917 did not test this practice, but the demands of World War I amply highlighted its faults. Crozier's attitude, along with his difficult personality and penchant for complicated designs, cost him his post at the end of 1917.

Crozier subsequently served on the War Council, a general supervisory agency, and as the head of the Northeastern Department in the United States before his retirement in December 1918. The inventions for which Crozier is best remembered are his wire-wound gun and the Buffington-Crozier disappearing gun carriage (co-invented with Gen. Adelbert R. Buffington).

Bibliography: Crozier, William, *Ordnance and the World War: A Contribution to the History of American Preparedness* (Scribner's, 1920).

Richard F. Kehrberg

CUSTER, GEORGE ARMSTRONG (1839–1876)

U.S. cavalry officer, Custer was born in New Rumley, Ohio. His early education in Ohio included Stebbins Academy in Monroe and McNeely Normal School in Hopedale. In 1856, he qualified to teach grammar school. Believing that he could become rich in the army, Custer obtained an appointment to West Point. He was an undisciplined cadet, who was excellent with horse and saber but poor academically. In 1861, he graduated last in his class of 34.

Civil War. Custer was commissioned a second lieutenant of cavalry and was appointed as an aide to Brig. Gen. Philip Kearny. He then joined the staff of Brig. Gen. William F. ''Baldy'' Smith. Gen. George B. McClellan was impressed enough with Custer to appoint him to his staff as a captain. In April 1863, when McClellan's staff was disbanded, Custer reverted to lieutenant and was assigned to the 5th Cavalry. He was then detailed to the newly promoted Brig. Gen. Alfred Pleasonton's cavalry division staff. In June, Pleasonton became a major general and Custer was again advanced to captain. On June 28, he was promoted to brigadier general, U.S. Volunteers. At the age of 23, Custer was the youngest general in the Union army. Given command of the Michigan Cavalry Brigade, he distinguished himself at Gettysburg, in pursuit of Gen. Robert E. Lee after the battle, and later in the maneuvers of the two armies in Virginia.

Custer designed a flashy uniform that included a blue sailor's shirt and a black velveteen jacket that was ornamented with two rows of brass buttons and a mass of gold braid from cuff to elbow; velveteen trousers adorned with twin gold stripes on each leg were thrust into knee-length spurred boots. He wore a broad-brimmed hat and scarlet necktie and carried a heavy straight sword.

His ''Wolverine'' Michigan Brigade emulated Custer by adopting red ties for themselves. Their commander was dashing, fearless, and reckless, but successful. He was, and remained to the end of his life, a true warrior. Custer was exhilarated by combat, seeming to thrive on and live for battle. His only wound in the Civil War was a slight injury to his leg after a grazing shot ripped one of his boots.

In November 1862, George met Elizabeth Bacon, daughter of Judge Daniel S. Bacon, of Monroe, Michigan. Although the judge did not at first approve of his daughter socializing with a soldier, Elizabeth, known as ''Libbie,'' and George were married on Feb. 9, 1864. Thus began an almost fictional romance. Whenever she could, throughout their marriage, Libbie accompanied Custer; when apart, they exchanged long letters every day.

Western Frontier. By war's end, Custer had won a brevet promotion to major general and command of a cavalry division. After the war, he reverted to captain, 5th U.S. Cavalry. In July 1866, he accepted the lieutenant

Civil War veteran George A. Custer (standing center) *socializes during life on the frontier.* (National Archives)

colonelcy of the 7th Cavalry Regiment. This followed a brevet promotion to major general in the regular army, which had been bestowed on him that May. The 7th, stationed at Fort Riley, Kansas, was typical of those of the day: it consisted of 12 companies, each with 100 enlisted men, a captain, a first lieutenant, and a second lieutenant. Regimental headquarters was authorized a colonel, a lieutenant colonel, and 3 majors.

The 7th, like other regiments employed in the American West, was scattered in small forts and posts. However, Custer led eight companies of the regiment in Gen. Winfield S. Hancock's 1867 expedition against the Indians. Later that year, he was convicted by a court-martial of unauthorized absence from his command (to escort Libbie to Fort Wallace), mistreating captured deserters, and other offenses "to the prejudice of good order and military discipline." He was sentenced to be suspended from rank and pay for a year. However, 10 months later, he was restored to duty and took part in a winter campaign against the Indians. In a dawn attack on Nov. 27, 1868, Custer's 7th Cavalry destroyed Chief Black Kettle's Cheyenne camp on the Washita River in what became known as the Battle of the Washita.

Between 1872 and 1874, Custer wrote a series of articles about his adventures on the frontier. In 1874, these articles were published as a book, *My Life on the Plains*. In the meantime, in 1873, he and his regiment escorted a Northern Pacific Railroad survey party in the Dakota Territory. The following year, he led an expedition into Dakota's Black Hills looking for gold. The presence of gold was ultimately verified, touching off a flood of prospectors and settlers and leading to more Indian warfare.

Sioux Campaign. Custer was slated to have a major command in the 1876 campaign against Sitting Bull and other Sioux. However, before it began, he became involved in an investigation of the sale of post traderships at western military posts. In his testimony in Washington, he gave hearsay evidence implicating Pres. Ulysses S. Grant's relatives in the affair. Grant ordered Custer's removal from command of the Dakota element of the expedition. Intercession by friends allowed him to command the 7th Cavalry in the campaign.

The regiment started from a base camp on the Yellowstone River on June 22, 1876. The 7th numbered 31 officers, 566 enlisted men, 35 Indian scouts, and about a dozen packers and other civilians. Custer had declined the addition of four companies of the 2d Cavalry and a battery of Gatling guns. The Gatlings would slow his column, and the presence of elements from another command would detract from the glory of Custer and the 7th. Custer's orders were to take his command south along the Rosebud Creek in southeastern Montana and cross the Little Bighorn River, where the hostile Indians were believed to be located. As the 7th moved south, Gen. Alfred Terry would continue west along the Yellowstone, then south along the Bighorn and the Little Bighorn. Meantime, Gen. George Crook was heading north from Wyoming to the Rosebud, to trap the Indians in a three-pronged attack.

Early on June 25, Custer found a large Indian village on the Little Bighorn. Fearing discovery, Custer decided to attack. Dividing his command into four detachments, with separate missions, he attacked the village with his detachment of five companies. He and his men were driven off, and all 225 were killed in the Battle of the Little Bighorn. The rest of the regiment held out on nearby bluffs until relieved on June 27.

Custer is faulted by many for recklessness by not waiting until Terry's column joined him before attacking. As a result, "Custer's Last Stand" is famous. He stands forever on the dusty slope overlooking the Little Bighorn, victim of his own confidence and rashness.

Bibliography: Connell, Evan S., *Son of the Morning Star* (Harper & Row, 1984); Kinsley, D. A., *Favor the Bold,* 2 vols. (Holt, Rinehart & Winston, 1967–68); Utley, Robert M., *Cavalier in Buckskin* (Univ. of Oklahoma Press, 1988).

Brig. Gen., PNG (Ret.) Uzal W. Ent

DANIELS, JOSEPHUS (1862–1948)

Editor, reformer, U.S. secretary of the navy and diplomat, Daniels was born in Washington, North Carolina. Influenced by his widowed mother, he became a dedicated Methodist and prohibitionist.

He acquired with borrowed money several newspapers, culminating with the purchase of the influential *Raleigh News and Observer* in 1894. Reflective of his impoverished youth, he championed the poor's cause by promoting federal aid to education, establishment of agricultural experiment stations, and prohibition. Daniels gradually emerged as an important figure in the Democratic party and became an early advocate of Woodrow Wilson. For this he was rewarded with the office of secretary of the navy (1913–21).

As a cabinet officer, he quickly instituted reforms repugnant to the navy's patrician establishment. He required sea service for promotion, provided schools for illiterate common sailors, opened the Naval Academy to enlisted men, and insisted on competitive bidding for navy contracts. In 1914, he banned liquor from naval vessels.

Ranking officials claimed Daniels left the navy inadequately prepared for World War I, a charge repeated before postwar Senate hearings by Adm. William S. Sims, commander of the U.S. fleet in Europe. Daniels defended himself by pointing to the navy's successful performance during the conflict. In his later career, Daniels served as ambassador to Mexico (1933–41).

Bibliography: Cronon, E. David, ed., *The Cabinet Diaries of Josephus Daniels, 1913–1921* (Univ. of Nebraska Press, 1963); Daniels, Josephus, *The Wilson Era: Years of Peace* (Univ. of North Carolina Press, 1941);———, *The Wilson Era: Years of War and After* (Univ. of North Carolina Press, 1946).

Fred Arthur Bailey

DAWES, CHARLES GATES (1865–1951)

U.S. vice president (1925–29) and financier, Dawes was born in Marietta, Ohio. Prior to World War I, he held several prestigious offices, including that of U.S. comptroller of the currency (1897–1901) and president of a major Chicago bank (1902–21).

With the wartime rank of brigadier general, Dawes served the American Expeditionary Force (A.E.F.) in France 1917–19 as its purchasing agent. In 1921, he became the first director of the U.S. Bureau of the Budget. Two years later, he chaired the postwar committee investigating German finances.

The committee's recommendations were released in 1924 as the Dawes Plan, for which he received the Nobel Peace Prize in 1925. The plan proposed stabilizing the German currency through a reorganization of the Reichbank under Allied supervision and called for German reparation payments to offset the costs of the war. (The impoverished Germans could not pay the $33 million indemnity, however, and the resulting financial hardship contributed to Adolph Hitler's rise to power).

In 1924, Dawes was elected vice president as the running mate of Republican Calvin Coolidge. In 1929, Pres. Herbert Hoover appointed Dawes as ambassador to Great Britain. In 1932, Hoover named him to head the Reconstruction Finance Corporation. Under his guidance, the RFC made loans of well over $1.5 billion to U.S. banks, mortgage loan companies, railroads, and other major corporations in hope of turning around the Great Depression.

M. Guy Bishop

DEWEY, GEORGE (1837–1917)

U.S. naval officer, Dewey was born in Montpelier, Vermont. He wanted to go to West Point, but a lack of available appointments forced Dewey to take whatever opening his father's political influence could obtain. In 1854, Dewey secured an appointment to the Naval Academy, where he compiled a record marked by solid academic achievement but tarnished with numerous demerits and discipline violations.

Dewey entered fleet service in 1858 and spent the pre-Civil War years on the Mediterranean, first on board the flagship *Wabash* and later on the *Powhatan* and the *Pawnee*. During his tenure overseas, Dewey observed firsthand naval diplomacy at work in the capitals of Europe and gained valuable experience on board ship as well as ashore. In 1861, he was ordered to the Naval Academy to stand

George Dewey, the first to hold the rank of Admiral of the Navy, was one of the principal agents of change during the navy's modernization. (U.S. Navy)

examination for lieutenant, where he placed third on the list.

Civil War. With the coming of domestic hostilities, Dewey received orders while on leave at home to report for duty aboard the steam frigate *Mississippi*. Dewey spent the beginning months of the war on station along the Atlantic coast performing blockading duties. It was not until the next spring that Dewey would find himself in the thick of battle at New Orleans, a part of the naval flotilla of Adm. David G. Farragut.

The campaign up the Mississippi at New Orleans faced a significant obstacle at the mouth of the river where shallow water, sandbars, and two Confederate forts stood in Farragut's way. The rebels added a boom of cypress logs to further block the Union forces. On Mar. 18, 1862, Farragut began towing his ships across the sandbars at the mouth of the river. It took eight arduous hours of work to drag the *Mississippi* across the bar.

In April, as the Union fleet began to sail past the Confederate guns, Dewey took the helm of the *Mississippi*. His skill in guiding the ship past the Confederate forts while under fire and his success in maneuvering the *Mississippi* in an engagement with the Confederate ironclad *Manassas* were praised in his captain's official report to Farragut. The river fights were but a beginning to Dewey's Civil War service that saw him in action in the western theater and later once again in blockade duty along the southern Atlantic region. Dewey ended the war in the rank of lieutenant commander.

Interwar Years. In the decades that followed the war, Dewey succeeded in slowly advancing in the ranks and improving his position for command. By the time the Spanish-American War arrived, Dewey had taken advantage of political connections in and out of the navy and had served a number of years in Washington, holding posts at the Naval Academy and the Lighthouse Board, as well as several sea assignments with the European Squadron.

In 1889, he was appointed head of the Bureau of Equipment. There, Dewey oversaw the modernization of the fleet. He remained in Washington until 1897, eventually serving as president of the Board of Inspection and Survey and winning promotion to commodore. With the support of Asst. Sec. of the Navy Theodore Roosevelt, Dewey won a behind-the-scenes battle for command of the Asiatic Squadron, setting the stage for his service in the Spanish-American War.

Spanish American War. Arriving in Japan in January 1898, Dewey quickly prepared his small command for the possibility of war. He moved the fleet to Hong Kong, where he received word from Roosevelt that war was imminent and to prepare for offensive operations against the Spanish in the Philippines. When war was declared, Dewey sailed to the Philippines, arriving there on Apr. 30, 1898. In the early morning hours the next day, he found the Spanish fleet at anchor off Cavite, in Manila Bay. In the battle that followed, the American fleet hammered the beleaguered enemy until no Spanish ship remained afloat.

Postwar Honors and Achievements. News of the victory reached the U.S. press and produced such a public outpouring for Dewey that many historians called the phenomenon "Deweymania." It was a year before Dewey arrived back in the United States, but his popularity had not diminished. For the most part, Dewey appeared bewildered by the attention and unable to take advantage of the opportunities that being a national hero afforded. His national status was validated by the creation of a new rank for him: Admiral of the Navy. In addition to grand gift presentations, parades, and untold demands for his appearances, there was talk of his running for president. As Dewey rejected invitations to speak and made himself appear ungrateful, the public turned against him and made him the subject of ridicule and scorn. Dewey never fully understood what had happened to him and spent the rest of his career defending himself.

Perhaps Dewey's greatest contribution to the U.S. Navy came after Manila Bay, during his tenure as president of the navy's General Board 1900–17. During the 17 years he served as the navy's highest ranking officer, Dewey acted as a moderator and facilitator of change as the navy sought to modernize and reform its institutions. For those reformers who sought rapid and radical change, Dewey often appeared conservative and an impediment to progress. He became a mediator between the radical reformers and the traditionists within the navy. Often in sympathy with the reforming elements, Dewey allowed the modernization process to occur slowly, using his prestige and influence to thwart aggressive and impetuous plans.

Bibliography: Dewey, George, *Autobiography of George Dewey, Admiral of the Navy* (Scribner's, 1913); Spector, Ronald, *Admiral of the New Empire* (Louisiana State Univ. Press, 1974); Williams, Vernon L., "George Dewey: Admiral of the Navy," *Admirals of the New Steel Navy,* ed. by James Bradford (Naval Inst. Press, 1900).

Vernon L. Williams

DÍAZ, (JOSÉ DE LA CRUZ) PORFIRIO (1830–1915)

Mexican military leader and dictator, Díaz was born in Oaxaca. After many years of plotting the overthrow of the Mexican government, he succeeded in assuming control in 1876. Between 1877 and 1911, he served eight presidential terms (1877–80, 1884–1911). Díaz brought peace to Mexico for the first time since the colonial period and also effected significant economic developments, including railroad construction, petroleum production, and the encouragement of industry. He solicited foreign investment, especially from the United States. During his regime, 22 percent of Mexico's land surface was U.S.-owned.

Eventually, Díaz's rule caused great hardships. His policies alienated both the peasantry and the political elite. By the early 1900s, there was widespread discontent, which manifested itself in the revolution of 1910. In May 1911, Díaz was deposed by the revolutionary forces of Francisco Madero. Díaz died an exile in Paris.

Mark Pitcavage

DICKMAN, JOSEPH THEODORE (1857–1927)

U.S. army officer, Dickman was born in Dayton, Ohio. He graduated from West Point in 1881 and became a respected cavalryman and a talented tactician. His early military career included active duty against Indians, Spaniards, and Filipinos.

During World War I, in late 1917, Dickman took command in France of the 3d Division, which in March 1918 played a critical role in stopping the German drive on Château-Thierry. This action so impressed American Expeditionary Force commander John J. Pershing that he gave Dickman command of IV Corps in August. His corps did well in the St.-Mihiel Offensive, and, in October, Pershing moved Dickman to I Corps, which had become bogged down in the Meuse-Argonne Campaign. Dickman reorganized the corps' position and on November 1 launched an attack that shattered the German line.

Following the war, Dickman briefly commanded the Army of Occupation in Germany. He retired in 1921.

Joseph T. Dickman was known for his success in organizing troops during World War I. (U.S. Army Military History Institute)

Bibliography: Dickman, Joseph T., *The Great Crusade: A Narrative of the World War* (Appleton, 1927).

Richard F. Kehrberg

DOYEN, CHARLES (1859–1918)

U.S. marine officer, Doyen was born in Concord, New Hampshire. He graduated from the U.S. Naval Academy and was commissioned a second lieutenant in the Marine Corps in 1883. After serving briefly at the marine barracks in the New York navy yard, Doyen transferred to command the marine detachment aboard the USS *Galena* and saw action in strife-torn Panama. Doyen, now a first lieutenant, was then ordered to command the marine detachment at the marine barracks on Mare Island, California. In 1898, he was transferred to the USS *St. Paul,* where he spent the Spanish-American War. He was subsequently fleet marine officer of the North Atlantic Fleet. After being detached as commanding officer of both the 1st and 2d brigades of marines in the Philippines (1904–06), Doyen, a lieutenant colonel from 1905, was assigned to marine headquarters. After serving in various billets as commanding officer,

Doyen, in July 1914, was assigned to command the first marines (5th Regiment) to land on the island of Santo Domingo, where a revolution threatened U.S. lives and interests.

In June 1917, Doyen was reunited with the 5th Marines and sailed for France as the regiment's commanding officer. He was promoted to brigadier general on Oct. 3, 1917, and assumed command of the 4th Brigade on October 24. This brigade consisted of both the 5th and 6th marine regiments, as well as the attached 6th Machine-Gun Battalion. Doyen's skillful leadership soon transferred the inexperienced marines into a combat force in readiness. Due, however, to ill health, Doyen was relieved of command of the 4th Brigade and was assigned to marine barracks command at Quantico, Virginia. In October 1918, Doyen died of influenza.

Leo J. Daugherty III

DRUM, HUGH ALOYSIUS (1879–1951)

U.S. army officer, Drum was born in Fort Brady, Michigan. He received a direct commission as the son of an officer killed in action during the Spanish-American War. Drum served with the 25th Infantry Regiment in the Philippines 1898–1901, where he earned the Silver Star fighting against the Moros. He graduated from the School of the Line in 1911 and from the General Staff College in 1912. He then served as assistant chief of staff for Gen. Frederick Funston at Veracruz in 1914.

When the American Expeditionary Force (A.E.F.) was formed for World War I duty in France in May 1917, Drum was promoted to lieutenant colonel and appointed to Gen. John J. Pershing's A.E.F. staff. With the creation of the 1st Army in July 1918, Drum was promoted to brigadier general and appointed chief of staff; he thus played a major role in the planning of the St.-Mihiel and Meuse-Argonne operations.

Following the war, Drum served in nearly every possible capacity. He held brigade, division, and corps commands. As a general staff officer he became involved in the debate over the creation of a separate air force. He testified against Gen. William (''Billy'') Mitchell at Mitchell's court-martial. He headed the Drum Board and later served on the Baker Board, both of which studied the future of an independent air force.

From 1933 to 1935, he served as deputy chief of staff to Gen. Douglas MacArthur. Passed over for chief of staff in 1935, Drum let anyone who would listen know that he wanted the job. When passed over again in 1939, Drum believed that he was being unfairly treated. Despite Drum's being the most experienced general officer in the army, his plans to be the ''Pershing of World War II'' never materialized. He played no major role in World War II and was forced to retire in 1943.

Steve R. Waddell

EDWARDS, CLARENCE RANSOM (1860–1931)

U.S. army officer, Edwards was born in Cleveland, Ohio. After graduating from West Point in 1883, Edwards fought in western campaigns against Indians, saw duty in the Spanish-American War, and four times earned citations for gallantry against Philippine guerrillas. In the years 1915–17, he commanded U.S. troops in the Panama Canal Zone.

At the onset of U.S. involvement in World War I in 1917, Edwards organized the 26th Division, a group of New England National Guardsmen, which he commanded with the rank of major general (national army). In September 1917, he brought the division to France, where it participated in numerous clashes. Edwards commanded in the Chemin des Dames sector, at the Marne salient, and at St.-Mihiel, and he successfully tied up German opposition near Metz while the Meuse-Argonne Offensive got underway.

Edwards commanded a division on the front lines longer than any other American, yet because of criticism that he lacked aggressiveness, he was relieved on Oct. 24, 1918, and sent home to train new divisions. He was given the rank of major general, U.S. Army, in 1921 and retired the following year.

Bibliography: Sibley, Frank P., *With the Yankee Division in France* (Little, Brown, 1919); Taylor, Emerson Gifford, *New England in France, 1917–1918* (Houghton Mifflin, 1920).

John F. Wukovits

FISKE, BRADLEY ALLEN (1854–1942)

U.S. naval officer and inventor, Fiske was born in Lyons, New York. He graduated from Annapolis in 1874 and for the next quarter century was assigned to a variety of ship and shore billets, most of which he found ''tiresome'' and ''profitless,'' save for the opportunities they afforded him to tinker with electric inventions. He busied himself with problems related to communications, gunnery, and steering, inventing such things as an electric range finder, a naval telescope sight, an electrically powered ammunition hoist, and an electric steering mechanism. Opposition to innovation from conservative senior officers led Fiske to align with other ''Young Turk'' reformist officers who pushed for technological, administrative, and educational reforms they believed were necessary to modernize the U.S. Navy.

As the navy expanded, Fiske advanced through the ranks: lieutenant commander in 1899, commander in 1903, captain in 1907. His first ship commands came in the years 1906–10 aboard the vessels *Minneapolis, Arkansas,* and *Tennessee*. By 1911, Fiske had become a significant figure in the modern navy; he was serving on the navy's General Board, was promoted to rear admiral, and was made president of the Naval Institute, a position he would hold until 1923 (the longest tenure in the institute's history).

From 1913 to 1915, Fiske served as aide for operations, the highest post in the navy at that time. Navy secretary Josephus Daniels sharply opposed Fiske's notions of reorganizing the navy along the lines of the German General Staff as well as Fiske's suggestions on fleet preparedness for war. The conflict between the two became so acute that Fiske resigned, but not before he was able to use his influence on Capitol Hill to create the new post of chief of naval operations.

Fiske spent his last year of active service at the Naval War College, removed from Washington's political maneuverings. He retired in 1916, although he was recalled four times to temporary active duty. In retirement, he wrote five books and continued to warn the nation about the dire risk of naval unpreparedness.

Donald A. Yerxa

FLETCHER, FRANK JACK (1885–1973)

U.S. naval officer, Fletcher was born in Marshalltown, Iowa. He graduated from Annapolis in 1906 and began many years of service in battleships and destroyers. In 1914, Fletcher was serving on the battleship *Florida* while that ship was stationed off Veracruz during Mexico's civil war. A lieutenant, Fletcher was given command of the steamer *Esperanza,* chartered by the United States to serve as a haven for U.S. and other refugees. Snipers fired upon the ship, but Fletcher, who earned the Medal of Honor for his gallant service, kept calm among the hundreds of civilians under his protection. All were brought to safety.

After tours on the staff of Rear Adm. Frank Friday Fletcher (his uncle and the Atlantic Fleet commander) and at the Naval Academy, Fletcher served in European waters during World War I. He received the Navy Cross while commanding the destroyer *Benham* on antisubmarine patrol in 1918.

In World War II, he commanded naval forces in the North Pacific and was a leader in the force that drove back the Japanese from Midway in 1943. He also commanded the carrier task force that supported operations on Guadalcanal.

Bibliography: Butcher, M. E., "Admiral Frank Jack Fletcher, Pioneer Warrior or Gross Sinner?" *Naval War College Review* (winter 1987).

Lloyd J. Graybar

FLIPPER, HENRY OSSIAN (1856–1940)

First black graduate of the U.S. Military Academy at West Point, Flipper was born into slavery in Thomasville, Georgia. Despite his unfavorable beginnings, his early life was characterized by an emphasis on education. After the Civil War, Flipper attended schools run by the American Missionary Association and Atlanta University. While a student at the university, he applied for admission to the Military Academy.

Henry Flipper, the first black graduate of West Point, encountered racial prejudice throughout his four years at the academy and during his five years of duty on the frontier. (University of Texas Institute of Texan Cultures, San Antonio, Texas)

Flipper's controversial appointment, made by Republican Rep. James C. Freeman, was no precedent. A few other blacks had received appointments, equally as controversial. The others, however, succumbed to racial prejudice and the intense rigors of the academy's academic and disciplinary code. Flipper endured both, graduating in 1877. Public reviews of his accomplishment were mixed. The Northern press was largely laudatory while Southern papers reflected their readerships' ugly mood toward Reconstruction.

Upon graduation, Flipper was commissioned a lieutenant in the 10th U.S. Cavalry and served at several frontier posts. While the post commissary at Fort Davis, Texas, he was charged with embezzling more than $3,000 and falsifying his reports to the post commander, Col. William R. Shafter. The ensuing court-martial proceedings and review process found Flipper guilty; on June 30, 1882, he was dismissed from the army.

Flipper spent his remaining years as a civil engineer in the Southwest and in Mexico. His offer to return to military service during the Spanish-American War was rejected. He died of a heart attack on May 3, 1940, in Atlanta, Georgia, having steadfastly maintained his innocence of the charges that had ended his army career 58 years earlier. Recent scholarship indicates he may have been the victim of a plot to oust him from the service, perhaps generated by a romantic entanglement.

Bibliography: Flipper, Henry O., *The Colored Cadet at West Point* (Lee, 1878).

Louise Arnold-Friend

FORSYTH, GEORGE ALEXANDER (1837–1915)

U.S. cavalry officer, Forsyth was born in Muncy, Pennsylvania. Following the outbreak of the Civil War in April 1861, he enlisted as a Union private in the Chicago Dragoons and was soon commissioned a first lieutenant in the 8th Illinois Cavalry. Moving through the ranks quickly, Forsyth was brevetted a colonel of volunteers in October 1864 and a brigadier general in March 1865.

Mustered out in February 1866, Forsyth was commissioned a major of cavalry in July and was assigned to the 9th Cavalry. He spent most of his remaining career in the West fighting Indians. Gen. Philip H. Sheridan chose him as his military secretary (1869–73) and later his aide-de-camp (1878–81). Forsyth also traveled to Europe (1875–76) as a member of a board of officers to inspect the armies of Europe and Asia. Forsyth is best remembered for the battle at Aricharee Fork on the Republican River, where his command of 50 men withstood an attack by some 700 Cheyenne for nine days and where he himself sustained three wounds. Following retirement from active service in 1890, Forsyth wrote two books about military life.

Lt. Col. Martin W. Andresen

FUNSTON, FREDERICK (1865–1917)

U.S. army officer, Funston was born in New Carlisle, Ohio, and grew up in Iola, Kansas. He left the University of Kansas after two and a half years and supported himself as a journalist and railroad ticket taker. In 1890, he obtained a position with the U.S. Department of Agriculture and soon gained recognition as a botanist and explorer. Transferred to Alaska in 1892, he undertook several hazardous solo expeditions to record the territory's flora.

In the summer of 1896, Funston enlisted on impulse in the guerrilla liberation army led by Cuban patriots Máximo Gomez and Calixto García. Despite a decided lack of military experience, he served for 18 months as an artillery commander before returning to the United States in January 1898. After the United States declared war on Spain in April 1898, the governor of Kansas offered Funston command of the 20th Kansas Volunteer Infantry. He accepted and led the regiment to the Philippines in November 1898, too late for operations against the Spaniards but just in time for the 1899 Malolos campaign against the Filipino *insurrectos*. An aggressive but circumspect troop commander, Funston gained a reputation for bravery and efficiency. On Apr. 27, 1899, Funston and 45 men of the 20th Kansas successfully crossed the Rio Grande de Pampanga at Calumpit under fire and drove off 2,500 *insurrectos*. For his part in the action, Funston was promoted to brigadier general of Volunteers and was awarded the Medal of Honor.

After a brief visit to the United States in the fall of 1899, he returned to the Philippines to command the 4th District of the Department of Northern Luzon and carried out a vigorous and successful antiguerrilla campaign. Early in 1901, he learned the location of the secret headquarters of Emilio Aguinaldo, the leader of the *insurrectos,* and devised a hazardous plan to effect Aguinaldo's capture. Leaving Manila on March 14, Funston and four other officers posing as captives, escorted by a party of loyal Macabebe tribesmen posing as their *insurrecto* guards, succeeded in penetrating Aguinaldo's headquarters, captured the rebel leader, and returned him to Manila on March 28. The daring feat led directly to the end of the Philippine Insurrection, and Funston was rewarded by Pres. William McKinley with appointment as brigadier general in the regular army on April 1.

The 36-year-old Funston returned to routine duties in the United States in late 1901. In April 1906, he found himself in temporary command of the Pacific Division in San Francisco and was responsible for the deployment of federal troops to assist in rescue and firefighting efforts during the great earthquake and fire of April 18. His aggressive response was credited with saving lives and property, but he was widely criticized for his decision to dynamite firebreaks in the burning city.

Following brief assignments in Cuba, Kansas, the Philippines, and Hawaii, Funston was assigned in January 1914 to command the 2d Division at Texas City, Texas. He subsequently commanded army troops in the expedition to Veracruz in April and served as military governor of the city until November, when U.S. forces were withdrawn. In early 1916, he was placed in command of all U.S. troops along the Mexican border. After Pancho Villa's raid on Columbus, New Mexico, on March 9, Funston recommended immediate pursuit and oversaw the movements of the Punitive Expedition in Mexico led by Brig. Gen. John J. Pershing.

On Feb. 19, 1917, Funston died suddenly in the lobby of the St. Anthony Hotel in San Antonio, Texas, apparently from a heart attack. His untimely death deprived the U.S. Army of perhaps its most capable and vigorous general officer on the eve of its entry into World War I. It is quite probable that, had he lived, Funston would have been selected to lead the American Expeditionary Forces to France.

Throughout his life, Funston displayed an unusual ability to change and grow professionally with the times. Only a few of his contemporaries were as successful as he in making the transition from the small-scale military forays of the 19th century, in which leaders were expected to display personal courage and individual initiative, to the more complex military operations of the early 20th century, in which leaders were required to be team players and effective managers of resources.

Bibliography: Crouch, Thomas W., *A Yankee Guerrillero: Frederick Funston and the Cuban Insurrection: 1896–97* (Memphis State Univ. Press, 1975); Funston, Frederick, *Memories of Two Wars: Cuban and Philippine Experiences* (Scribner's, 1911); Shrader, Charles R., "Frederick Funston," *Dictionary of American Military Biography*, vol. 1, ed. by Roger J. Spiller (Greenwood Press, 1984).

Lt. Col. (Ret.) Charles R. Shrader

GALL (1840?–1894)

Hunkpapa Sioux chief, Gall was born in South Dakota. Having refused to endorse the Fort Laramie Treaty of 1868, Gall, along with Sitting Bull, Hump, Crazy Horse, and other nontreaty Sioux leaders, embarked on a collision course with the U.S. Army. Gall emerged historically as a leading figure at the Battle of the Little Bighorn in 1876. His men repulsed Maj. Marcus A. Reno's initial assault and overran the positions of Lt. James Calhoun's Company L and Capt. Miles Keough's I Company. Legend long held that it was Gall who killed Lt. Col. George A. Custer.

Gall and Sitting Bull led their bands to Canada after the Custer fight. In 1881, Gall surrendered to the army and settled as a farmer at the Standing Rock Agency in Dakota Territory. In his later years, Gall peaceably worked for the betterment of his people.

M. Guy Bishop

GARCÍA ÍÑIGUEZ, CALIXTO (1836?–1898)

A Cuban soldier and revolutionary, García was born in Holguín, Santiago. He fought against Spanish rule in the Ten Years' War (1868–78) and the Little War (1879–80) before waging a successful campaign in the War for Independence (1895–98). He commanded the rebel forces in eastern Cuba. A careful strategist, he utilized artillery and conventional tactics. In 1898, García helped plan the U.S. landing at Daiquiri Beach aimed at taking Santiago. García supported the landing and the subsequent campaign.

García did not get along with U.S. general William Shafter and later argued with U.S. occupation authorities. He died in Washington, D.C., while in a delegation discussing payment to the Cuban army.

Mark Pitcavage

GARFIELD, JAMES ABRAM (1831–1881)

Twentieth president of the United States (1881), Garfield was born in Orange, Ohio. He was educated at Western

Pres. James A. Garfield's hopes for the improvement of relations with Latin America were never realized, as he was assassinated seven and a half months into his administration. (Library of Congress)

Reserve Eclectic Institute (now Hiram College) and Williams College. He taught at Western Reserve, later was admitted to the bar, and served in the Ohio Senate. During the Civil War, he rose from lieutenant colonel to major general.

From 1863 to 1880, Garfield served in the U.S. House of Representatives; he chaired the appropriations committee 1871–75. He advocated a high protective tariff and a firm Reconstruction policy. Garfield helped establish the U.S. Department of Education and the U.S. Geological Survey and was a regent of the Smithsonian Institute.

Having been nominated on the 36th Republican ballot, Garfield was elected president of the United States in 1880. He was shot on July 2, 1881, in a Washington railroad station by Charles J. Guiteau, a mentally unbalanced office-seeker. Garfield died on September 19.

Bibliography: Bundy, J. M., *The Life of General James A. Garfield* (A. S. Barnes, 1880); Hoyt, Edwin P., *James A. Garfield* (Reilly & Lee, 1964); Smith, Theodore Clarke, *The Life and Letters of James Abram Garfield*, 2 vols. (Yale Univ. Press, 1925).

Brig. Gen., PNG (Ret.) Uzal W. Ent

GATEWOOD, CHARLES BAEHR (1853–1896)

U.S. army officer, Gatewood was born in Woodstock, Virginia. After graduating from West Point in 1877, Gatewood joined the 6th Cavalry in the Southwest and for the next nine years campaigned against the Apache. During this time, he gained a reputation as an outstanding leader of Indian scouts and as an expert on the Apache. The scouts played important roles in Gen. George Crook's 1883 and 1885 expeditions into Mexico. In 1886, Gen. Nelson A. Miles sent Gatewood with two Apache scouts into Mexico to negotiate the surrender of Geronimo. After Geronimo's surrender, Gatewood served as Miles's aide before returning to his regiment to participate in the Pine Ridge Campaign 1890–91. Badly injured while fighting a fire at Fort McKinney, Wyoming, in 1892, Gatewood was forced to retire.

Bibliography: Dunlay, Thomas W., *Wolves for the Blue Soldiers: Indian Scouts and Auxiliaries with the United States Army, 1860–90* (Univ. of Nebraska Press, 1982); Thrapp, Dan L., *The Conquest of Apacheria* (Univ. of Oklahoma Press, 1967).

Richard F. Kehrberg

GERONIMO (1829–1909)

Apache chieftain and medicine man whose name means "one who yawns," Geronimo was born in No-doyohn Canyon on the Gila River, New Mexico. He was a member of a southern band known as the Chiricahua tribe. His early life was marked by the massacre of his entire family at the hands of Mexican troops on the Janos River in Chihuahua State. This event motivated much of his succeeding actions against Mexican troops and civilians.

The 1848 Treaty of Guadalupe Hidalgo, which conveyed the Spanish Southwest to the United States, and therefore the Southwest tribes with it, thus appeared favorable to the Apache. However, included in the agreement was a promise by the U.S. government to restrain Indian raiding in northern Mexico. Displeased with this provision, Geronimo led several raiding parties into Mexico during the 1850s. The arrival of prospectors and other settlers in the region around the Santa Rita copper mines provoked further Apache antagonism, and between 1860 and 1875, Geronimo was constantly involved in raids on northern Mexico and New Mexico.

In 1871, in response to the continuing Indian hostility, Congress appropriated money to finance a forcible collection of the Apache of Arizona and New Mexico onto reservations. Under Gen. George Crook, who arrived to take over the Arizona Department in the same year, the Chiricahua and Geronimo were removed from the Apache pass to the San Carlos reservation in Arizona. In 1875, it appeared as though U.S.-Apache relationships were stable with those Apache tribes receiving guaranteed titles to refuges that almost invariably included their former homelands. However, later in 1875, the Indian Office changed its disposition and began the forcible uprooting of the Indians into concentrated resettlement areas. This obvious breach of promise signaled the beginnings of a new and more bloody round in the Apache wars in which Geronimo was to become a prominent figure.

Chiricahua Apache Geronimo's refusal to be contained on a reservation constantly frustrated the U.S. military. (Library of Congress)

From 1876 to 1878, Geronimo lived as a renegade outside of the agencies, frequently raiding them for provisions. Eventually he was captured, but after a brief internment in 1878, he escaped and fled to the Sierra Madre, where he actively encouraged the breakout of other bands that had been forcibly interned. In May 1878, however, a force under Crook, led by Apache scouts, traced Geronimo's sanctuary to Ojo Caliente, arrested him, and forcibly returned him to the reservation at San Carlos.

In 1881, Geronimo led 70 warriors into the Sierra Madre, an area in which they raided for several months. They finally returned to San Carlos to free those Apache who wished to escape military supervision. Their success was bitter as a Mexican regiment succeeded in ambushing and killing the majority of the women and children in the party as they retreated across the Mexican border.

Until 1883, the Apache subsisted in hostile Mexican territory without more than spasmodic interruption. However, in 1883, the government campaign resumed in earnest when Crook crossed the border and captured Geronimo's base camp. The chief, who was absent on a raid at the time, was forced to meet Crook on his own terms and thus subsequently returned to San Carlos. Geronimo and his band were resettled around Turkey Creek, some miles from the main reservation, and from 1883 continued to uphold the peace treaty. Americanization of Indian habits and Geronimo's suspicion of U.S. promises, however, prompted him to break out again in 1885.

Geronimo returned to his raids and in May 1885 led yet another series of attacks on U.S. settlers. Crook was again sent in pursuit into the Sierra Madre with threats of exile to Florida for Geronimo and his followers. Within a month, the band lost one-third of its women and children and Geronimo lost all family members except his warrior son. Geronimo's base camp was soon captured, and Geronimo again surrendered to Crook, this time hoping for resettlement upon a reservation. It became clear that U.S. patience had run out and accommodation was no longer possible. Crook demanded nothing less than unconditional surrender.

One night after the formal surrender, Geronimo took his band into exile. When Geronimo led his band back over the border into Mexico, public hysteria prompted the escalation of attempts to bring Geronimo to order. Gen. Nelson A. Miles and his regiment of 5,000 soldiers and Indian scouts, together with the aid of the Mexican army, finally induced Geronimo to surrender on Sept. 4, 1887. Geronimo and his followers were deported to Florida, Alabama, and finally Fort Sill, Oklahoma, in 1893, where the Apache adopted a successful farm life.

In his "retirement," Geronimo became a popular public figure but was abused as a commercial property. He converted to Christianity, appeared at two national expositions (Omaha 1898 and St. Louis 1904), and participated in Theodore Roosevelt's inaugural parade. At the same time, Geronimo never ceased appealing for a return to his homeland. He died Feb. 17, 1909, and was buried in the Apache cemetery at Fort Sill.

Bibliography: Debo, Angie, *Geronimo: The Man, His Time, His Place* (Univ. of Oklahoma Press, 1976).

Russell A. Hart

GIBBON, JOHN (1827–1896)

U.S. army officer, Gibbon was born in Philadelphia and graduated from West Point in 1847. He distinguished himself during the Civil War and rose to the rank of major general of volunteers. He returned to the regular army in 1866 as a colonel.

As commander of the 7th Infantry, Gibbon played a key role in the Sioux War of 1876. He led one of three separate columns ordered to converge on the Sioux in southwestern Montana. Although he saw little action in the campaign, his command rescued the survivors of the Battle of the Little Bighorn. The next year, he unsuccessfully intercepted the Nez Percé at the Battle of the Big Hole. Promoted to brigadier general in 1885, Gibbon held various departmental commands until he retired in 1891.

Bibliography: Utley, Robert M., *Frontier Regulars: The United States Army and the Indian, 1866–1891* (Macmillan Co., 1973).

Daniel T. Bailey

GOETHALS, GEORGE WASHINGTON (1858–1928)

U.S. army officer and engineer, Goethals was born in Brooklyn, New York. After graduating from West Point in 1880, he rose in rank to lieutenant colonel in the Corps of Engineers, serving in various capacities including stints as instructor and assistant professor of civil and military engineering at the Military Academy. His practical engineering duties between 1884 and 1894 included construction and improvement projects on the Ohio, Cumberland, and Tennessee rivers; Muscle Shoals Canal; and Colbert Shoals Locks. He served as chief engineer, I Corps, in Puerto Rico during the Spanish American War (1898) and then on various assignments in Block Island, Nantucket, Narragansett Bay, and New Bedford (1900–05). Goethals retired from the army's General Staff in 1907.

Goethals's early assignments were preludes to the challenges he faced between 1907 and 1914, when he controlled the organization responsible for the construction of the Panama Canal. The French earlier had failed to construct a sea-level canal across the isthmus. Engineering and logistical problems were equally daunting for their successor, the U.S. Isthmian Canal Commission. After the unsuccessful attempts of its first two civilian engineers, John Wallace and John Stevens, Pres. Theodore Roosevelt abolished the commission and gave Goethals control over every facet of the canal project.

Goethals succeeded in providing for the well-being of a multinational work force of more than 30,000 men. Under his direction, the Canal Zone became a self-contained machine comprising, for example, its own transportation and law enforcement systems and commissary and sanitation department. Credited for completing the project some six months ahead of schedule, Goethals was promoted to major general by a special act of Congress on Mar. 4, 1915.

George W. Goethals was not only a brilliant engineer, overseeing the construction of the Panama Canal where others had failed, he was also an excellent organizer and administrator who reorganized the Quartermaster Corps during World War I. (Library of Congress)

After the Panama Canal opened, in 1914, Goethals was director of the Purchase, Storage, and Traffic Division and commanding general in the field of army supply during World War I. In spite of his success in supplying and transporting U.S. troops, as well as his receipt of the Distinguished Service Medal for reorganizing the Quartermaster Corps, his reforms barely lasted for the duration of the conflict. Goethals retired in 1919.

Carol E. Stokes

GÓMEZ Y BÁEZ, MÁXIMO (1836–1905)

Cuban patriot and military leader, Gómez y Báez served as an officer in the Spanish army in Santo Domingo. He moved to Cuba to become a farmer and rebelled against Spanish rule there. During the unsuccessful Ten Years' War (1868–78), he rose to command all rebel forces.

In the 1890s, Gómez was recruited by Cuban revolutionary José Martí to fight once more against the Spanish, and he again became commander in chief. In Cuba's War for Independence (1895–98), Gómez was quite successful, avoiding conventional conflict and applying a scorched-earth strategy aimed against plantations. He supported U.S. intervention and sided with the United States in its war against Spain. After the war, Gómez refused to run for office but continued as military chief.

Mark Pitcavage

GORGAS, WILLIAM CRAWFORD (1854–1920)

U.S. army surgeon and sanitarian, Gorgas was born in Toulminville, Alabama. He graduated from the University of the South in 1875 and from Bellevue Hospital Medical College in 1879. Entering the U.S. Army Medical Corps the following year, he observed numerous cases of yellow fever at frontier posts in Texas, North Dakota, and Florida.

During the Spanish-American War of 1898, Gorgas eradicated yellow fever from Havana by destroying mosquito breeding grounds. Appointed chief sanitary officer in Panama in 1904, he eliminated yellow fever from the Canal Zone in less than one year. After serving as surgeon general of the U.S. Army during World War I, Gorgas retired to work with the International Health Board. In England, he was knighted by King George V. Gorgas died in London after suffering an apoplectic stroke.

Bibliography: Gibson, John M., *Physician to the World: The Life of General William C. Gorgas* (Duke Univ. Press, 1950); Gorgas, Marie D., and Burton J. Hendrick, *William Crawford Gorgas: His Life and Work* (Doubleday, 1924).

Capt. James Sanders Day

GRANT, FREDERICK DENT (1850–1912)

U.S. army officer, Grant was born in St. Louis, Missouri, the first child of Ulysses S. and Julia Dent Grant. As a boy he was with his father in a number of Civil War campaigns.

Dr. William C. Gorgas, following Dr. Walter Reed's discovery that mosquitoes transmit yellow fever to humans, developed ways to control mosquito breeding grounds and thus minimize the incidence of yellow fever in the tropics. (Library of Congress)

An 1871 graduate of West Point, he served as an aide to Lt. Gen. Philip Sheridan during several Indian campaigns.

Grant resigned from the army in 1881. He later became U.S. minister to Austria-Hungary and police commissioner of New York City. He was a colonel of volunteers during the Spanish-American War and later served in the Philippines. Grant rose to the rank of major general, regular army, by 1906.

Bibliography: Grant, Julia D., *Personal Memoirs of Julia Dent Grant,* ed. by John Y. Simon (Putnam's, 1975); McFeely, William S., *Grant: A Biography* (Norton, 1981).

Brig. Gen., PNG (Ret.) Uzal W. Ent

GRANT, ULYSSES SIMPSON (1822–1885)

Eighteenth president of the United States (1869–77) and commander in chief of the Union army during the Civil War, Grant was born Hiram Ulysses Grant in Point Pleasant, Ohio. Although not eager to attend, Grant entered West Point in 1839, having been appointed by Cong.

Thomas L. Hamer. Due to Hamer's clerical error, Grant was registered as Ulysses Simpson Grant ("Simpson" was his mother's maiden name), and the misnomer became his official name from then on. Grant graduated in June 1843, 21st in a class of 39. He was brevetted a second lieutenant of infantry.

Grant served with the 4th U.S. Infantry at Jefferson Barracks, Missouri, and New Orleans. In 1846, he served with Zachary Taylor at Corpus Christi. Although detailed most of the time as regimental quartermaster and commissary during the Mexican War, Grant took part in five major battles. He distinguished himself at Monterrey and Mexico City, ending the war as a brevet captain.

Grant married Julia Dent, sister of his West Point roommate, in 1848. He was stationed at a number of Great Lakes posts between 1848 and 1852, when his regiment was sent to Oregon, where he was regimental quartermaster. In July 1853, he was promoted to captain.

He and other officers tried to make extra money at various enterprises. All of Grant's efforts failed. He ran afoul of his commander and was forced to resign or be court-martialed. He resigned in the spring of 1854 and returned, broke, to his wife and children in St. Louis. He was a wood hauler for two years, then tried farming. The Panic of 1857 wiped him out financially. Then cold weather destroyed his crop, and he was invalided by sickness for six months. A series of financial failures ensued. By 1860, Grant was destitute, and he accepted a position in his father's leather store in Galena, Illinois.

During the presidency (1869–77) of Civil War leader Ulysses S. Grant, he advocated the acquisition of Santo Domingo in the Caribbean for the United States as a place where freed slaves could be resettled. (U.S. Army Military History Institute)

Grant had lived in a slave state and hated abolitionists. Yet, in 1859, although desperate for money, he freed his one slave. Grant believed in the principles of federal government and was enraged when Virginia left the Union.

The Civil War. Grant was appointed by the governor of Ohio to command the unruly 7th District Regiment, a unit of undisciplined 90-day enlistees that he whipped into shape in three weeks. Grant was promoted to brigadier general on Aug. 7, 1861, and given command of southern Illinois and southeastern Missouri. On September 6, he occupied the strategic town of Paducah, Kentucky, at the mouth of the Tennessee River. However, his attack on Belmont, Missouri, was repulsed.

At this time, contractors and speculators were rigging government contracts and overcharging the army for grain and forage. Learning of this, Grant canceled all contracts and defied a powerful and influential politician, expelling him from his military district.

His 1862 campaigns brought Grant national attention. Forts Henry and Donelson fell to his forces in February; it was at Donelson that he first demanded unconditional surrender. Grant then proceeded to Shiloh, where he was almost defeated on April 2 by the sudden and unforeseen attack of Gen. Albert Sidney Johnston's army. The arrival of Union reinforcements the next day forced Johnston to withdraw.

In late 1862, Grant's initial attempts to capture Vicksburg, a key Southern fortress on the Mississippi, were repulsed. But in the spring of 1863, he led a swift and brilliant campaign; on July 4, he took the city-fort. Vicksburg cost the Confederacy irreplaceable losses in manpower and opened an avenue for Union troops to strike deep into the Southern heartland.

In late November 1863, Grant won again at Chattanooga, Tennessee. On Mar. 9, 1864, he was promoted to lieutenant general and given supreme command of all Union troops, enabling him to employ his strategy of applying pressure across all Confederate borders.

In the east, where Grant traveled with the Army of the Potomac, that army executed a tenacious, slashing pursuit of Gen. Robert E. Lee, culminating in Lee's surrender at Appomattox in April 1865. Grant provided terms of surrender that saved many men, including Lee, from vengeful postwar persecution.

After the war, Grant was raised to the new rank of four-star general and took command of the army. In mid-1867, he was also made secretary of war, a post he left at the end of the year.

The Presidency. Grant was elected president of the United States on the Republican ticket in 1868 and served two terms. He believed the role of the president to be that of an administrative officer who should obey and enforce the laws of the land. He also believed that the will of the people was expressed in Congress. These lack-of-policy theories doomed his administration to failure in dealing with Reconstruction, a corrupt federal civil-service system, and the numerous scandals that marred his tenure.

Jay Gould and Jim Fisk, two wealthy, unscrupulous businessmen, began the scandals by attempting in 1869 to corner the nation's gold supply and by wining and dining the president in an attempt to have him permit gold prices to rise at will. Grant soon detected something amiss and ordered government gold to be sold, driving the price down. Many honest businessmen were ruined as a result, and Grant's reputation was sullied by rumors of his connection with Fisk and Gould.

Then there was the aborted attempt during his first term to obtain a treaty to take over the small republic of Santo Domingo, which occupied two thirds of a potentially rich island in the Caribbean. Santo Domingo, bankrupt and in revolution, approached the United States with the idea of buying the tiny country. Grant endorsed the idea because he believed that the island nation could easily support 10,000,000 people and thus would be the perfect place to resettle the recently freed slaves. There they could establish several all-black states as part of the United States. To the end of his life, Grant believed this to be one of the finest ideas he ever had. The treaty died in the Senate in 1870, however. Again, Grant was considered by some to have been involved in an unsavory deal.

The heavily subsidized Union Pacific Railroad organized a construction company called the Crédit Mobilier. It built the railroad, but insiders controlled the charges it levied. The company was incredibly profitable, and some members of Congress were paid off in company stock to ignore the situation. The scandal was exposed at the end of Grant's first term, further tainting his administration.

The president waged an unsuccessful battle to reform the corrupt federal civil service. It was undermined by a widespread spoils system. He appointed a commission that recommended rules that would have established a true merit system. Enemies of the plan in Congress torpedoed reform, and Grant failed to pursue the matter further. Reform Republicans and the Democrats, determined to deny Grant a second term, ran liberal journalist Horace Greeley, a poor choice. He was eccentric and disliked by many, and Grant won easily.

The Reconstruction era in the South presented the Grant administration with additional problems. Blacks were authorized to vote but were kept from polling places by fraud and force. Northern-backed local Southern governments were kept in office by military might. Southerners, outraged by these events and by exploitive carpetbaggers, struck out, sometimes violently. The unprecedented social wounds of the recent war created the need for solutions that were beyond the preparedness of Grant and his administration.

Following the financial panic of 1873, Grant vetoed a greenback bill, further eroding his popularity. Other financial scandals, including the corruptions of Sec. of the Interior Columbus Delano, Sec. of War William W. Belknap, and a member of Grant's personal staff, finished the president's political credibility.

Later Years. Upon leaving the White House in 1877, Grant went on a world tour, returning to the United States in 1879. An attempt to nominate him for president in 1880 was unsuccessful. Grant's investments were wiped out in the spring of 1884, leaving him bankrupt. That summer, he learned he had throat cancer. Enduring intense agony, he began writing his memoirs in the fall of 1884 and completed them on July 19, 1885, four days before he died. The book, which restored his wife to financial independence, is considered one of the most objective works of its genre ever written.

Bibliography: Catton, Bruce, *U. S. Grant and the American Military Tradition* (Little, Brown, 1954); Grant, Ulysses S., *The Personal Memoirs of U. S. Grant,* 2 vols. (Webster, 1885–86); Lewis, Lloyd, *Captain Sam Grant* (Little, Brown, 1950); McFeely, William S., *Grant: A Biography* (Norton, 1981); Williams, Kenneth P., *Lincoln Finds a General; Vol. 3: Grant's First Year in the West* (Macmillan Co., 1952).

Brig. Gen., PNG (Ret.) Uzal W. Ent

GRAVES, WILLIAM SIDNEY (1865–1940)

U.S. army officer, Graves was born in Texas. He graduated from West Point in 1889 and spent the next decade with the 7th Infantry in various Western locations. After service in the Philippine Insurrection, he returned to garrison duty in the West. In 1909, he had the first of several tours on the General Staff.

During World War I, Graves was promoted to major general (1918) and was informed that he would lead a division on the western front. Instead, he was placed in command of a U.S. expedition of some 9,000 infantry and support troops ordered to Siberia, where civil war seemed likely in the aftermath of the Bolshevik Revolution. Graves had orders to prevent Allied supplies stockpiled along the Trans-Siberian Railroad from falling into the hands of the Central Powers but not to interfere in Russia's internal affairs. Graves's written account relates the tangled circumstances he faced in Siberia until U.S. personnel were withdrawn in 1920. He later commanded the Panama Canal Department from 1927 until his retirement in 1928.

Bibliography: Graves, William S., *America's Siberian Adventure* (Cape and Smith, 1931).

Lloyd J. Graybar

GREELY, ADOLPHUS WASHINGTON (1844–1935)

U.S. army officer and arctic explorer, Greely was born in Newburyport, Massachusetts. In the summer of 1861 he enlisted in Company B, 19th Massachusetts Volunteer Infantry, and served with his regiment on the Peninsula and in the battles of Antietam and Fredericksburg, advancing to the rank of sergeant and being three times wounded. In February 1863, Greely accepted a commission as second lieutenant in the 81st U.S. Colored Troops and subsequently fought at Port Hudson and in other battles along the Mississippi River. At the end of the Civil War, Greely served with the provost guard in New Orleans and helped to organize the 39th U.S. Infantry and 9th U.S. Cavalry, two renowned black units.

In 1867, Greely was commissioned as a second lieutenant of infantry in the regular army and served in Wyoming and Utah until late 1867, when he was unexpectedly detailed to the Signal Corps. He served as signal officer with Gen. Eugene C. Carr's 1869 campaign against the Cheyenne in Nebraska. In 1870, Greely was assigned to assist Gen. Albert Myer, the Signal Corps chief, in organizing the U.S. Weather Bureau. From 1870 to 1875, Greely gathered data and formulated methods for the River and Flood Service and was soon recognized as an expert meteorologist. From 1875 to 1880, he undertook the important and often hazardous work of constructing telegraph lines in Texas and the Southwest, along the eastern seaboard, and from the Dakotas to Washington State.

Lady Franklin Bay Expedition. In 1881, the U.S. government organized an expedition to Lady Franklin Bay opposite the western coast of Greenland for the purpose of studying arctic weather and climate. Greely was chosen to command the 25-man expedition, which arrived at its station on Aug. 11, 1881. Under Greely's direction, the expedition gathered an important collection of data on arctic weather and tidal conditions, studied the region's flora and fauna, and undertook a number of successful explorations. Greely's leadership was severely tested when the relief vessels scheduled for 1882 and 1883 failed to arrive. On Aug. 9, 1883, Greely and his party abandoned their post and made a long and difficult passage over the ice to Cape Sabine on Bedford Pym Island. Another planned relief expedition under the U.S. Army's Lieutenant Garlington was aborted. Without food or proper shelter, 18 of the 25 Greely expeditioners perished during the winter of 1883–84. Literally within hours of death from malnutrition and exposure, Greely and his remaining 6 companions were rescued on June 22, 1884, by a relief expedition under the command of the U.S. Navy's Capt. Winfield Scott Schley.

As the U.S. Army's chief signal officer, Brig. Gen. Adolphus Greely was responsible for the Signal Corps becoming a permanent branch of the army. (U.S. Army Military History Institute)

The scientific accomplishments of the Lady Franklin Bay Expedition were eclipsed by sensational charges of cannibalism and criticism of Greely's harsh disciplinary methods, but such incriminating talk soon subsided, and Greely received international acclaim for the scientific work carried out in the arctic under his direction.

Signal Corps. Passed over for promotion to the rank of captain while abandoned in the arctic, Greely was finally advanced to that rank in June 1866, and in March 1887, he was appointed by Pres. Grover Cleveland to be chief signal officer of the army with the rank of brigadier general.

During his long tenure as chief signal officer, Greely was instrumental in establishing the Signal Corps as a permanent branch of the army. Under his able direction, the Signal Corps reformed the Weather Bureau and transferred it to the Department of Agriculture in 1891, played the leading role in the construction of telegraph lines and undersea cables, and pioneered the army's use of photography, the telephone, radio, the automobile, and many other modern devices. In 1898, Greely obtained funds to support the attempts of Samuel P. Langley to construct a flying machine for war purposes. Langley's experiments failed but encouraged the Wright brothers to build and fly the first successful airplane in 1903. The Signal Corps subsequently took the lead in military aviation in the United States.

Having refused promotion in order to direct Signal Corps operations in the Spanish-American War in 1898, Greely was finally promoted to major general in February 1906 and left the Signal Corps to command the Pacific Division, with headquarters at San Francisco. Although he was absent at the time of the destructive earthquake and fire in April 1906, Greely quickly returned to coordinate relief and recovery measures. He was retired for age in March 1908.

Legacy. Following a world tour, Greely dedicated himself to writing and to various public service endeavors. A founder of the National Geographic Society in 1888, he remained one of its trustees until his death. On Mar. 27, 1935, he was presented with a special Congressional Medal of Honor. Greely was only the second American so honored for peacetime service, Charles Lindbergh having been the first.

Throughout his career, Greely demonstrated at every opportunity his personal bravery, scientific acumen, and leadership skills, particularly the ability to manage the difficult problem of emerging technology. He was one of a handful of military and naval officers who led the armed services and the nation into the modern world of the 20th century.

Lt. Col. (Ret.) Charles R. Shrader

GREENE, FRANCIS VINTON (1850–1921)

U.S. army officer, Greene was born in Providence, Rhode Island. He entered West Point at age 16 and graduated first in the Class of 1870. He was commissioned in the artillery but transferred to the Corps of Engineers two years later. Greene served as an observer with the Russian army and published an authoritative report entitled *The Russian Army and Its Campaigns in Turkey in 1877–78.*

Promoted to brigadier general of volunteers in 1898, Greene commanded the second expedition to the Philippines. He resigned in 1899 and became police commissioner of New York City in 1903. Returning to New York City after 10 years of construction work in Buffalo, Greene served as a consulting engineer while writing critiques of military policy.

Capt. James Sanders Day

GRIERSON, BENJAMIN HENRY (1826–1911)

U.S. army officer, Grierson was born in Pittsburgh and was living in Illinois at the outbreak of the Civil War. He had been a musician and then a merchant but failed to achieve financial success in either occupation. In 1861, he entered Union service as a lieutenant in an Illinois regiment. He quickly rose to a colonelcy and won national recognition in 1863 by leading his cavalry brigade in a two-week-long raid across the heart of Mississippi. Thereafter, Grierson held various commands in the districts of West Tennessee and West Mississippi.

After the war, he obtained a commission in the regular army, seeing duty in the South and then in various western posts while organizing and then commanding the 10th Cavalry, a regiment manned by white officers and black enlisted personnel. In 1888, Grierson moved up to command the Department of Arizona. He retired in 1890, a few months after promotion to brigadier general.

Bibliography: Leckie, William H., and Shirley A. Leckie, *Unlikely Warrior: General Benjamin Grierson and His Family* (Univ. of Oklahoma Press, 1984).

Lloyd J. Graybar

HAGOOD, JOHNSON (1873–1948)

U.S. army officer, Hagood was born in Barnwell County, South Carolina, the nephew of Brig. Gen. Johnson Hagood, Confederate army officer and governor of South Carolina. He graduated from West Point in 1896, and some of his many postings prior to the U.S. entry into World War I included teaching philosophy at West Point and service with the General Staff Corps.

Following his arrival in France with the American Expeditionary Force (A.E.F.), Hagood commanded the Advance Section of the Line of Communications (LOC) and then became its chief of staff. In February 1918, he presided over the Hagood Board, which led to a reorganization of the A.E.F. staff system and created the Services of Supply (SOS). The reorganization consolidated all supply functions under one command. Promoted to brigadier general, Hagood served as SOS chief of staff for the remainder of the war. He retired in 1936.

Steve R. Waddell

HARBORD, JAMES GUTHRIE (1866–1947)

U.S. army officer, Harbord was born in Bloomington, Illinois. He learned telegraphy and typewriting at Kansas State Agricultural College (now Kansas State University) and in 1889 enlisted in the army as a private, advancing to quartermaster sergeant before becoming a second lieutenant in the 5th Cavalry in 1891. He graduated from the Infantry and Cavalry School at Fort Leavenworth in 1895.

During the Spanish-American War, Harbord held the temporary rank of major in the 2d U.S. Volunteer Cavalry. Promoted to first lieutenant in 1898, he was transferred to the 10th Cavalry and became close friend to another first lieutenant, John J. Pershing. Following promotion to captain in 1901, Harbord was posted to the Philippines, where he served from 1902 to 1914. From 1903, he was assistant commander of the Philippine constabulary, with the equivalent rank of colonel. Promoted to major in December 1914, Harbord went on to attend the Army War College, from which he graduated shortly after the U.S. entry into World War I.

World War I. When General Pershing took the American Expeditionary Force (A.E.F.) to France in April 1917, Harbord, by then lieutenant colonel, went along as chief of staff. He was promoted brigadier general, national army, in August. Harbord played a vital role in organizing the A.E.F. staff during its important formative period in France. On May 6, 1918, he took command of the 4th Marine Brigade of the 2d Infantry Division and led the brigade in the Battle of Belleau Wood in June. Promoted to major general, national army, Harbord took command of the 2d Infantry Division in July and participated in the counterattack at Soissons.

Although a competent combat commander, Harbord made his greatest military contribution in the areas of administration and supply. In late July, Pershing was in need of someone to command the newly created Services of Supply (SOS). Moreover, army chief of staff Peyton March was contemplating the formation of a support command in France beyond Pershing's command. To bring some semblance of order to the chaotic logistical system and to counter March's moves, Pershing selected Harbord to command the SOS.

Promoted to brigadier general, regular army, in November 1918, Harbord commanded the SOS until May 1919, when he once again became chief of staff, A.E.F. In September, Harbord was promoted to major general, regular army, and took command of the 2d Infantry Division once more. When Pershing was appointed chief of staff in 1921, Harbord became his deputy. As such, he oversaw a reorganization of the War Department General Staff along the lines of the former A.E.F. staff. Harbord retired in December 1922, at which time he became president of the Radio Corporation of America (RCA), a position he held until 1930, when he became chairman of the board. In 1942, Harbord was promoted to lieutenant general on the retired list.

Bibliography: Hagood, Johnson, *The Services of Supply: A Memoir of the Great War* (Houghton Mifflin, 1927); Harbord, James G., *The American Army in France, 1917–1919* (Little, Brown, 1936).

Steve R. Waddell

HAY, JOHN MILTON (1838–1905)

U.S. secretary of state, Hay was born in Salem, Indiana, and spent most of his childhood in Warsaw, Illinois. After practicing law briefly in Springfield, he accompanied Pres. Abraham Lincoln to Washington in 1861 as his assistant private secretary. After Lincoln's assassination, Hay served as a field diplomat in three different European capitals. Financial pressures forced him to return to the United States in 1870 to become an editorial writer for the New York *Tribune*. He also enjoyed a successful literary career.

Hay returned to Washington as assistant secretary of state 1878–81. He did not return to public office until 1897 when he became Pres. William McKinley's ambassador to Britain, a position he held during most of the Spanish-American War. He became McKinley's secretary of state in August 1898 and continued to serve Pres. Theodore Roosevelt in that position until his death in 1905. As secretary of state, Hay's most notable accomplishments were his advocacy of the Open Door Policy in China, which became the cornerstone of U.S. Far Eastern policy, and his role in the Hay-Pauncefote Treaty of 1901, which cleared the way for the construction of the Panama Canal.

Bibliography: Dulles, Foster Rhea, "John Hay," *An Uncertain Tradition: American Secretaries of State in the Twentieth Century*, ed. by Norman A. Graebner (McGraw-Hill, 1961).

Donald A. Yerxa

HAYES, RUTHERFORD BIRCHARD (1822–1893)

Nineteenth president of the United States (1877–81), Hayes was born in Delaware, Ohio. He attended Kenyon College and Harvard Law School and was admitted to the bar in 1845. During the Civil War, he was wounded five times and rose to the rank of major general. Having helped found the Ohio Republican party, Hayes served his state in the U.S. House of Representatives (1865–67) and as governor (1868–76).

After a controversially close election (the returns were contested in four states, and a special commission was appointed to tally the votes), Hayes became U.S. president in 1877. As president, he ended the Reconstruction era and made financial appropriations for the South. Congress restored the silver dollar as legal tender over his veto. Hayes obtained the treaty that permitted the United States to control Chinese immigration. In retirement, Hayes devoted himself primarily to Southern public education, prison reform, and aid to blacks.

Bibliography: Davison, Kenneth E., *The Presidency of Rutherford B. Hayes* (Greenwood Press, 1972); Hoogenboom, Ari, *The Presidency of Rutherford B. Hayes* (Univ. Press of Kansas, 1988).

Brig. Gen., PNG (Ret.) Uzal W. Ent

HAZEN, WILLIAM BABCOCK (1830–1887)

U.S. army officer and chief of the Signal Corps, Hazen was born in Vermont. He graduated from West Point in 1855 and served the Union throughout the Civil War, becoming a major general in 1864. Later, he was an arbitrator of Indian and railroad claims during the development of the western frontier and served as a U.S. military observer during the Franco-Prussian (1870) and Russo-Turkish (1877) wars.

In 1880, Hazen became a brigadier general and was put in charge of the U.S. Army Signal Corps. His principal accomplishment was as director of the nation's first weather service. Under his leadership, two Signal Corps research teams explored arctic regions, collecting data that greatly increased the scientific knowledge about an unknown part of the world. Hazen was court-martialed in 1885 for openly criticizing a superior officer.

Carol E. Stokes

HENRY, GUY VERNOR (1839–1899)

U.S. military officer, Henry was born in Fort Smith, Indian Territory. After graduating from West Point in 1861, he served in the 1st Regular Artillery Regiment until November 1863, when he was appointed colonel of the 40th Massachusetts Volunteer Infantry. Following the Civil War, then Brevet Major Henry returned to duty with the regular artillery. In 1870, he transferred to the 3d Cavalry and joined his unit on the frontier, where he remained until 1892. During those 22 years while engaged in several campaigns of the trans-Mississippi Indian wars, "Fighting Guy" Henry earned his reputation as a brilliant and fearless campaigner. During the Spanish-American War, he was promoted to the rank of brigadier general. Initially commanding a brigade under Gen. Nelson Miles in Puerto Rico, Henry later served as the military governor of Puerto Rico.

Lt. Col. Martin W. Andresen

HERRON, CHARLES DOUGLAS (1877–1977)

U.S. army officer and administrator, "Fox" Herron was born in Crawfordsville, Indiana, and graduated from West Point in 1899. He served in the Philippines during the Spanish-American War, followed by stateside service with the 18th Infantry Regiment. Herron entered World War I as commander of the 313th Field Artillery Regiment. He also served on Gen. John J. Pershing's staff and as chief of staff of the 78th Infantry Division, for which service he received the Distinguished Service Medal. He was promoted to brigadier general in 1934, major general in 1937, and lieutenant general in 1940.

Although Herron retired in 1941, he remained active during World War II, testifying before Congress against the relocation of Japanese-Americans. He was soon recalled to active duty to serve on the secretary of war's Personnel Board, making recommendations on general officer retention and promotion for the wartime expansion of the army, and to serve during the postwar demobilization.

David O. Friend

HEYWOOD, CHARLES (1839–1915)

U.S. Marine Corps commander, Heywood was born in Waterville, Maine. He was appointed a second lieutenant in the marines in 1858. His first sea assignment involved seeking out the so-called filibusters who were threatening Nicaragua and other Central American nations. After the Civil War broke out in 1861, Heywood participated in the amphibious raid on Hatteras Island and assisted in the capture of Fort Clark. In November, he was promoted to captain, serving aboard the navy's James River flotilla. During the famous naval battle between the *Merrimac* and the *Monitor,* the *Cumberland,* Heywood's ship, was severely damaged by the *Merrimac*. During the remainder of the war, Heywood served with distinction both ashore and afloat commanding marines and gun batteries in the West Gulf Squadron.

After the Civil War, Heywood continued the normal pattern of sea and land duties as a Marine Corps officer. During the labor riots of 1877, he personally led a full marine battalion in the quelling of the uprisings in Baltimore, Philadelphia, and Reading, Pennsylvania. He then commanded a regiment of marines dispatched to the Isthmus of Panama, where a local rebellion threatened U.S. interests as well as plans for an isthmian canal. Landing with both marines and sailors, Heywood quickly brought the city of Colon under U.S. control.

Soon afterward, Heywood received the command of the marine barracks in Washington, where he was promoted to lieutenant colonel (1888) and later to colonel (1891). Upon the retirement of Commandant Charles McCawley in 1891, Heywood was appointed his successor. He almost immediately implemented measures to increase the professionalism of both officers and enlisted men. He established the School of Application in 1891 for new second lieutenants and selected enlisted men, required officers to take competency examinations, and attempted to remove the older officers and replace them with the new lieutenants coming out of Annapolis. In short, he sought a role for the Marine Corps in the new navy that was now coming on line. The progress made during the first few years of Heywood's commandancy enhanced the readiness of the Marine Corps early in the Spanish-American War in 1898. During this time, the concept evolved of using the marines in amphibious warfare. Heywood retired in 1903 as a brigadier general.

Bibliography: Millett, Allan R., *Semper Fidelis: The History of the United States Marine Corps* (Macmillan Co., 1980).

Leo J. Daugherty III

HINES, FRANK THOMAS (1879–1960)

U.S. army officer and veterans' affairs administrator, Hines was born in Salt Lake City, Utah. The son of a mine superintendent, he studied civil engineering. During the Spanish-American War, Hines served with Utah National Guard units in the Philippines. He joined the regular army in 1901 and served in Coast Artillery units for more than 10 years, during which time he authored *The Service of the Coast Artillery*.

With the U.S. entry into World War I, Hines became the chief of the Embarkation Service. He orchestrated the flow of men and matériel to Europe and represented U.S. interests in Allied transportation allocations. Immediately after the war, Hines headed the Army Transport Service.

After a brief stint in private life, he was called by Pres. Warren G. Harding to reform the Veterans Bureau. For more than 20 years, he devoted his austere and dedicated managerial style to veterans' affairs. Pres. Harry S Truman made him ambassador to Panama in 1945, and he retired in 1948.

Col. Thomas W. Sweeney

HINES, JOHN LEONARD (1868–1968)

U.S. army officer, Hines was born in White Sulphur Springs, West Virginia. Following his graduation from West Point in 1891 and his commission as an infantry officer, he was ordered out West. He was promoted to first lieutenant with the outbreak of the Spanish-American War. He served in Cuba and participated in the Battle of San Juan Hill, where he won the Silver Star for gallantry. Promoted to captain in 1900, Hines helped put down the Philippine Insurrection, including action against the Moro on Mindanao. He served in various administrative capacities, achieving the rank of major in 1912.

When the Punitive Expedition advanced into Mexico in 1916, Hines served as adjutant to Gen. John J. Pershing. In May 1917, Pershing remembered Hines, newly promoted to lieutenant colonel, and appointed him assistant adjutant general for the American Expeditionary Force. World War I brought Hines rapid advancement. Promoted to colonel, he took command of the 16th Infantry Regiment in November 1917. The following May, Hines, as brigadier general, assumed command of the 1st Brigade of the 1st Infantry Division, which he then led in the Battle of Soissons and the Second Battle of the Marne. Promoted to major general, he assumed command of the 4th Infantry Division in August and led it in the St.-Mihiel and Meuse-Argonne operations.

Following the war, Hines commanded the III Corps during the occupation of the Rhineland. He had the distinction of being the only officer to command a regiment, a brigade, a division, and a corps in combat during World War I. From 1924 to 1926, Hines served as army chief of staff. He retired from the military in 1932.

Steve R. Waddell

HOUSE, EDWARD HANDELL (1858–1938)

U.S. foreign policy adviser to Pres. Woodrow Wilson, House was born into a patrician family in Houston, Texas. As a friend of the politically powerful, he influenced several Texas governors. Taking advantage of his acquaintance with British foreign secretary Edward Grey, House secured the English withdrawal of support from Mexico during the Veracruz crisis of 1914.

When the United States entered World War I, House established "The Inquiry," a committee of academics, to advise President Wilson on peace proposals. As the president's personal representative, he coordinated activities with the Allies and later served Wilson at the Versailles Peace Conference in 1919. Their association ended when House counseled compromise with the U.S. Senate on the Versailles Treaty.

Bibliography: Seymour, Charles, *The Intimate Papers of Colonel House,* 4 vols. (Houghton Mifflin, 1926–28).

Fred Arthur Bailey

HOWARD, OLIVER OTIS (1830–1909)

U.S. army officer, Howard was born in Leeds, Maine. After working his way through Bowdoin College, he entered West Point and graduated fourth in the Class of 1854. Like many of his contemporaries, Howard became well known during the Civil War, often for his failures on the battlefield. However, no one questioned his bravery. He lost an arm at Seven Pines but was soon back in the field leading troops.

A war's end, Pres. Andrew Johnson appointed Howard the first commissioner of the Freedmen's Bureau. During this period, Howard was instrumental in establishing and serving as president (1869–73) of the university for blacks in Washington, D.C., that bears his name. He was also active in other endeavors on behalf of the postwar black. However, like his former commander Ulysses S. Grant, Howard was very naive in the political arena. When the Freedmen's Bureau became enmeshed in scandal and corruption, the idealistic Howard refused to believe the evidence brought before him. Because of this attitude, he, too, was soon accused of corruption but was later exonerated.

Howard resumed his military career in the West of the 1870s and 1880s. In 1872, he brought an end to the Cochise War in Arizona by riding into the camp of that Apache chief and negotiating an agreement with him. In 1877, he led troops in pursuit of Chief Joseph and his band of Nez Percé, which helped to force the surrender of Joseph to Gen. Nelson A. Miles. Howard retired from the army with the rank of major general in 1894. He spent the remainder of his life in Burlington, Vermont, where he was active in religious and educational activities.

Ted Alexander

HUERTA, VICTORIANO (1854–1916)

Mexican general and political figure, Huerta was born in Colotlán, Jalisco. Although he had fought to ensure Porfirio Díaz his dictatorship, Huerta transferred his allegiance to the regime of Francisco Madero when Díaz fell in 1911. The right-wing Huerta led campaigns against revolutionaries more radical than Madero, including Emiliano Zapata and Pascual Orozco, while maneuvering to take power himself. In February 1913, Huerta killed Madero and assumed the presidency. Huerta's reign was spent trying to maintain power against growing opposition. Rebels Zapata and Pancho Villa led successful campaigns against him, and U.S. president Woodrow Wilson ordered the occupation of Veracruz in 1914 to weaken him. Huerta fled in July 1914. He died in Texas in 1916, still plotting his return to power.

Mark Pitcavage

JOHNSON, HUGH SAMUEL (1882–1942)

U.S. army officer and legal administrator, Johnson was born in Fort Scott, Kansas. He graduated from West Point in 1903. Serving at cavalry posts from the Mexican border to the Philippines, he became a frontier intellectual, publishing more than 30 stories on frontier life and attending the University of California Law School.

Brought to Washington, D.C., in 1916 for his legal expertise, Johnson assisted the Woodrow Wilson administration in the drafting and implementation of the Selective Service Act. He served on the General Staff and the War Industries Board during World War I and helped to energize the nation's industrial mobilization. Promoted to brigadier general in April 1918, he resigned in February 1919 rather than accept a reduced rank in the postwar army.

Daniel T. Bailey

JOSEPH (HINMATON-YALAKTIT) (c. 1840–1904)

Nez Percé leader, Chief Joseph was probably born in the Wallowa Valley of Oregon. Like most tribes, the Nez Percé was a fragmented, loose association of factions and settlements, with no one chief able to control all elements. The tribe had befriended Meriwether Lewis and William Clark in the early 19th century, and Chief Joseph's father, a leader of one band, was converted to Christianity in 1839. The old chief had his son baptized Joseph, and the tribe lived in peace for many years. However, with the Jakima War of 1856–58, Oregon statehood, and the gold rush of 1861, the Northwest became increasingly populated with U.S. settlers, thus inhibiting the nomadic tribes. When his father died in 1871, Joseph tried to contain his band in the Wallowa Valley, but the U.S. government chose a reservation for the tribe elsewhere. Joseph not only refused to move from the valley, he further refused to have his chosen area declared a reservation.

Serious difficulties between the Nez Percé and the U.S. government arose at a meeting of tribal leaders with Gen. Oliver O. Howard at Fort Lapwai in May 1877. Fighting almost broke out at the meeting itself. Chief Joseph took the lead in keeping calm. Understanding the odds, he agreed to vacate the Wallowa Valley and returned there to collect his people. But when three braves from another band killed some U.S. settlers, hatred grew, reason disappeared, and all of the Nez Percé became fugitives. During the summer of 1877, Chief Joseph and his people joined four other Nez Percé bands and drew 10 columns of U.S. Army troops into a well-publicized 1,700-mile running battle from Oregon, through Idaho, and into Montana. The exhausted Indians finally surrendered to the ever-persistent Col. Nelson A. Miles, and Chief Joseph made his much recorded vow of peace: "From where the sun now stands, I will fight no more forever."

The Nez Percé used impressive tactics, and Joseph was inaccurately described in some accounts as being responsible for their military successes. They used advance and rearguard fighting detachments, skirmish lines, and field fortifications. Their flight was so well conducted that they almost escaped to Canada. Rather than leading in battle, Chief Joseph often remained as the protector for the women, the old, and the infirm.

The U.S. government broke the promise made at the surrender of the Nez Percé; the tribe was not permitted to return to Oregon. Chief Joseph died in Nespelem, Washington, on Sept. 21, 1904.

Bibliography: Howard, Helen Addison, *Saga of Chief Joseph* (Univ. of Nebraska Press, 1965).

Col. (Ret.) Rod Paschall

KELLY, LUTHER SAGE (YELLOWSTONE) (1849–1928)

U.S. army scout in the West, Kelly was born near Geneva, New York. He was eager to serve the Union in the Civil War but, being underage, was rejected by the volunteer unit he tried to join. Early in 1865, he succeeded in joining the 10th U.S. Infantry. The war ended before he saw any action, and Kelly found himself stationed at Fort Ripley, Minnesota. He later was transferred to the Dakota Territory, where he eventually received his discharge.

Kelly spent time among the Sioux in the late 1860s. The intimate knowledge he gained of the tribe won him a job as a army scout in 1873. Vital information provided by him to Gen. Philip Sheridan regarding the Yellowstone River earned Kelly his nickname. After leaving military service, Kelly spent several years as an occasional hunting guide in Colorado and Montana. He came out of retirement in 1877 to join Gen. Nelson Miles's staff in the Nez Percé campaign.

M. Guy Bishop

KENT, JACOB FORD (1835–1918)

U.S. military officer, Kent was born in Philadelphia. He graduated from West Point in 1861 and served with distinction during the Civil War. Following the conflict, he spent almost 30 years in garrison duty in the South and on the frontier and was still a colonel by 1898.

When the Spanish-American War broke out, Kent was commissioned a brigadier general of volunteers and took command of the 1st Infantry Division. This division saw action in the Santiago Campaign and helped take San Juan and Kettle hills in a confused battle in July 1898. Despite clumsiness in handling his division, Kent proved himself a competent commander under fire. He retired in 1898 and was promoted to major general on the retired list in 1915.

Mark Pitcavage

KING, CHARLES (1844–1933)

U.S. soldier and author, King was born in Albany, New York, great-grandson of early American statesman Rufus King. He graduated from West Point in 1866. Joining the 5th Cavalry in 1871, King participated in several Indian campaigns before a troublesome elbow wound forced him to retire in 1878. Nevertheless, he remained active in military matters, especially with the Wisconsin National Guard. His most notable accomplishments, however, were literary. Over the next few decades, King poured out 53 novels, 4 major historical works, and more than 250 short stories.

His fictional works were a great success and served to popularize the frontier army. Moreover, critics noted both his fiction and nonfiction pieces for their realism and accuracy. King's novels made him one of the most popular authors of his day and helped shape the U.S. image of the "Old Army."

Bibliography: King, Charles, *Memories of a Busy Life* (State Hist. Soc. of Wisconsin, 1922).

Richard F. Kehrberg

LAWTON, HENRY WARE (1843–1899)

U.S. military leader, Lawton was born in Manhattan, Ohio, and grew up in Indiana, where he enlisted in a Union regiment in 1861. He won the Medal of Honor during the Civil War and the brevet rank of colonel. Lawton tried his hand at law but reentered the army in 1866 and, as a cavalry officer, won fame when he forced Apache chief Geronimo to surrender after a lengthy chase in 1886.

As a brigadier general of volunteers during the Spanish-American War, Lawton commanded the 2d Division of V Corps in Cuba and led the attack on El Caney in July 1898. He remained in Cuba after the war as governor of Santiago, but a drinking problem soon led to his recall.

Lawton arrived in the Philippines in February 1899, where he assumed command of a division of the VIII Corps. While leading an expedition near Manila, Lawton needlessly exposed himself to enemy fire and was shot dead at San Mateo on Dec. 19, 1899.

Richard B. Meixsel

LEE, FITZHUGH (1835–1905)

U.S. army officer, Lee was born in Fairfax County, Virginia, grandson of Revolutionary War hero Gen. Henry "Light-Horse Harry" Lee and nephew of Confederate commander Gen. Robert E. Lee. He graduated from West Point in 1856, 45th in a class of 49. He was assigned to the 2d U.S. Cavalry in Texas and in 1859 was wounded in a fight with hostile Comanche.

Lee gained prominence during the Civil War as one of Gen. Jeb Stuart's Confederate cavalry commanders. He succeeded to the command of the cavalry corps of the Army of Northern Virginia in 1865, after Wade Hampton, who had succeeded the dead Stuart, was transferred to the Carolinas.

Lee was active in politics after the war, serving a term as governor of Virginia (1886–90). After his defeat for the U.S. Senate in 1893, he was appointed consul general to Havana by Pres. Grover Cleveland, as a reward for his loyalty to the Democratic party. Lee was very controversial during his tenure in Cuba and upset the Spanish with his overt sympathy for the Cuban revolutionary cause.

Pres. William McKinley, a Republican, kept Lee as consul general, and in 1898, he advised the president to send the battleship *Maine* to Havana to protect U.S. interests. When war broke out between the United States and Spain, McKinley authorized the appointments of Lee and former Confederate general Joseph Wheeler as major generals in the U.S. Army. This was done in part to gain the support of the Democratic South. Lee retired from the army with the rank of brigadier general in 1901.

Ted Alexander

LEJEUNE, JOHN ARCHER (1867–1942)

U.S. Marine Corps officer, Lejeune was born in Pointe Coupée Parish, Louisiana, and graduated from the Naval Academy in 1888. In 1890, Lejeune was appointed as a second lieutenant in the Marine Corps. In the Spanish-American War, he participated in the campaign to take Puerto Rico. In 1903, he was promoted to major and given command of a battalion of marines then assembling for use on the Isthmus of Panama. While in Panama he helped to maintain peace among the various political factions there. After a round of assignments at sea and ashore, as well as another deployment to Panama, Lejeune assumed command in June 1908 of the marine brigade in the Philippines and was promoted to lieutenant colonel. He then attended the Army War College before taking command of the Brooklyn-based marine barracks.

When the navy began preparations for the 1914 fleet maneuvers off Puerto Rico, where a marine "advance base force'' was ordered to seize and defend the small island of Culebra, Lejeune saw an opportunity to prove that the corps could act as an advanced base force. He was given command of the 2d Marines and during the maneuvers showed the marines' effectiveness as an advanced base force. In 1915, Lejeune became assistant commandant of the marines.

When the United States entered World War I in April 1917, Lejeune, now a brigadier general, fought to get marines assigned to the first contingent to France and succeeded in getting the 5th and 6th regiments assigned for service with the army. After arriving in France, Lejeune set about to involve marines in combat. Failing to get Gen. John J. Pershing's approval for the formation of a marine division, Lejeune was given command of the marine brigade on July 25, 1917. Three days later, he was named commanding general of the army's 2d Division and was appointed a major general. In late October 1918, Lejeune's 2d Division broke the Hindenburg line, forcing a general German retreat, and on November 10, the first elements of the 5th Marines crossed the Meuse River into Germany.

Returning to the United States in September 1919, Lejeune became commanding general of the base at Quantico, Virginia. On July 1, 1920, he was appointed commandant of the Marine Corps. In 1922, Lejeune established the Marine Corps Institute, an attempt through correspondence courses to raise the educational standards of enlisted men, as well as to establish a system of schools at Quantico for officers and staff noncommissioned officers.

In 1929, after having served nearly three terms as commandant, Lejeune turned down a request to remain and retired. A short time later, he became the superintendent of the Virginia Military Institute, where he remained until 1937, finally retiring from all activities. In August 1942, Congress promoted Lejeune to the rank of lieutenant general (retired). Camp Lejeune, North Carolina, is named for him.

Bibliography: Heinl, Robert D., *Soldiers of the Sea: The U.S. Marine Corps 1775–1962* (Naval Inst. Press, 1962); Lejeune, John A., *The Reminiscences of a Marine* (Dorrance, 1930); Metcalf, Clyde, *A History of the United States Marine Corps* (Putnam's, 1939).

Leo J. Daugherty III

LIGGETT, HUNTER (1857–1935)

U.S. army officer, Liggett was born in Reading, Pennsylvania. He graduated from West Point in 1879 and served in the 5th Infantry Regiment for the next 19 years, primarily along the frontiers in Dakota and Montana. During this period, he commanded troops and served as the regimental adjutant. He was promoted to captain in 1897.

During the Spanish-American War, Liggett served only briefly in Cuba. He was transferred to the Philippines in 1901, where he commanded and held staff positions until his promotion to major in 1902. He returned to the United States and served in staff positions until he commanded a battalion at Fort Leavenworth, Kansas.

Hunter Liggett, noted for his reorganization of the Army War College, was also known for his aggressiveness and strategic planning in combat. (U.S. Army Military History Institute)

Liggett was promoted to lieutenant colonel in 1897, to colonel in 1912, and to brigadier general in 1913. He attended the Army War College 1909–10 and then became its director (1910–13) and president (1913–14). It was during this period that Liggett made his most lasting contributions to the army. He refined the War College curriculum, adding courses in military history, operational planning, and staff responsibilities. He also made the curriculum more difficult and raised the admission standards. These changes enhanced the professionalism of the officer corps by adding a common basis of higher education and by bridging the gap between the older officers accustomed to frontier war and the younger officers who were thinking in terms of 20th-century conflicts.

After subsequent command positions, Liggett was promoted in March 1917 to major general, one of only seven in the army, and took command of the 41st Division. Upon his arrival in France, Allied commanders were reluctant to accept him because of his age (60) and his great girth.

Liggett soon changed their minds. His planning and leadership capabilities were apparent as he honed U.S. units for battle. In January 1918, he was made commander of the U.S. I Corps and took over the first U.S. section of the front. His corps defended at Château-Thierry, participated in the Aisne-Marne Counteroffensive, and was active in the Meuse-Argonne Campaign. The summit of his career occurred when he was made commander of the 1st Army in October. Liggett displayed aggressiveness, good planning, and a calming patience in all aspects of combat operations. Liggett returned to the United States in 1919 and retired in 1921.

Bibliography: Liggett, Hunter, *Commanding an American Army* (Houghton Mifflin, 1925); Spiller, Roger J., ed., *Dictionary of American Military Biography* (Greenwood Press, 1984).

Capt. George B. Eaton

LINCOLN, ROBERT TODD (1843–1926)

U.S. attorney and statesman, Lincoln was born in Springfield, Illinois, the eldest child of Pres. Abraham Lincoln, and the only of the president's four children to survive to adulthood. After graduating from Harvard in 1864, he entered Harvard Law School but departed after four months to accept an appointment to the staff of Gen. Ulysses S. Grant.

Lincoln pursued a legal career after the Civil War. Living in Chicago, he became active in Illinois politics, which led to two appointments at the federal level: as Pres. James A. Garfield's (and subsequently Pres. Chester A. Arthur's) secretary of war (1881–85) and as Pres. Benjamin Harrison's minister to Great Britain (1889–93).

For the next 20 years, Lincoln served as legal counsel for numerous businesses, most notably the Pullman Company, of which he was president 1897–1911. Ill health forced his partial retirement the next year.

Bibliography: Painter, Ruth R., *Lincoln's Sons* (Little, Brown, 1955).

Louise Arnold-Friend

LOOKING GLASS (1823?–1877)

War chief of the Nez Percé tribe during its epic 1,600-mile flight toward Canada in 1877. Looking Glass was one of several Nez Percé chieftains who had refused to sign the 1863 treaty with the United States that would force the tribe onto a small reservation at Lapwal, Idaho. Subsequent U.S. Army attempts to enforce the treaty culminated in the war of 1877. Looking Glass's influence was eclipsed during the conflict, as his counsel for a slower pace on the trek north twice allowed the U.S. Army to intercept the tribe, forcing its subsequent capitulation. Looking Glass, however, never lived to witness the tragic consequence of his counsel. He became the last fatality of the war.

Bibliography: Dockstader, Frederick J., *Great North American Indians: Profiles in Literature and Leadership* (Norbock Books, 1977).

Russell A. Hart

LUCE, STEPHEN BLEECKER (1827–1917)

U.S. naval officer and founder of the Naval War College, Luce was born in Albany, New York. He entered the navy in 1841. He had sailed around the world before joining the second class at the new U.S. Naval Academy in 1848. After service in the Atlantic, Pacific, and Caribbean, Luce reported to the academy as an instructor in 1860.

Transferred to the South Atlantic Blockading Squadron during the Civil War, Luce took part in attacks on Hatteras Inlet, Port Royal, and Charleston. It was during the war that his idea for an institution to study naval warfare took root. Luce devoted much of the next two decades to reforming training for both sailors and merchant seamen. He served as commandant of midshipmen 1865–68 at Annapolis, where he later played a leading part in the founding of the U.S. Naval Institute (1873), which he served as president 1887–98. Instrumental in establishing the Naval War College in Newport, Rhode Island, the first institution of its kind in the world, he served as its first president (1884–86) and appointed Capt. Alfred T. Mahan to its faculty.

Luce commanded the North Atlantic Squadron 1886–89 and retired shortly thereafter. From 1901 to 1910, he was recalled to special duty at the War College. During this time, and until his death, Luce wrote articles in both professional and popular journals championing the cause of expanding and modernizing the U.S. Navy.

Bibliography: Gleaves, Albert, *Life and Letters of Stephen B. Luce: Rear Admiral, U.S.N., Founder of the Naval War College* (Putnam's, 1925).

James C. Bradford

LUKE, FRANK, JR. (1897–1918)

U.S. army officer noted for his aviation feats during World War I, Luke was born in Phoenix, Arizona. Ordered to France in March 1918, 2d Lieutenant Luke joined the 27th Aero Pursuit Squadron, where his daring piloting and scorn of military discipline soon brought both acclaim and approbation. His total of 18 downed German aircraft (4 airplanes, 14 balloons) placed him second behind famed World War I ace Eddie Rickenbacker.

On September 29 after destroying three German balloons, dangerous targets because of their low altitudes and protection by enemy fighters, Luke was attacked by six German Fokkers. Before setting down his damaged plane, the seriously wounded Luke shot down two of his attackers and strafed German troops marching along a road. He then died on the ground, fighting off German soldiers with his

.45 automatic rather than surrendering. For this day's remarkable actions, Luke received the Medal of Honor.

Bibliography: Jackson, Robert, *Fighter Pilots of World War I* (St. Martin's Press, 1977); Whitehouse, Arch, *Decisive Air Battles of the First World War* (Duell, Sloan and Pearce, 1963).

John F. Wukovits

McANDREW, JAMES WILLIAM (1862–1922)

U.S. army officer and administrator, McAndrew was born in Hawley, Pennsylvania. He fought against the Sioux two years after graduating from West Point in 1888 and later participated in the Spanish-American War. After traveling to France in 1917 with the 1st Division, the initial U.S. combat unit to reach Europe in World War I, McAndrew was given command of the General Staff College and army schools at Langres, France, where, under his careful vigilance, inexperienced officers received training in various aspects of trench warfare. In May 1918, he became Gen. John J. Pershing's chief of staff. McAndrew later received the Distinguished Service Medal for his war duty.

Bibliography: Pershing, John J., *My Experiences in the World War* (Frederick A. Stokes Co., 1931).

John F. Wukovits

MACARTHUR, ARTHUR (1845–1912)

U.S. army officer, MacArthur was born in Chicopee Falls, Massachusetts. His distinguished Civil War service landed him a commission in the regular army in 1866. Promotions came slowly, but by the outbreak of the Spanish-American War, he was a lieutenant colonel.

In May 1898, MacArthur was appointed a brigadier general of volunteers and given command of a brigade in the Philippines. He successfully subdued the Filipino rebellion on Luzon by late 1899. Promoted to a brigadier general in the regular army, MacArthur became military governor of the Philippines in January 1900. He returned home the following year after a promotion to major general. In September 1906, MacArthur advanced to lieutenant general and became the ranking officer in the army, but he was denied the opportunity to be chief of staff, a goal attained by his son Douglas. He retired in 1909.

Bibliography: James, D. Clayton, *Years of MacArthur; Vol. 1: 1880–1941* (Houghton Mifflin, 1970).

Daniel T. Bailey

MACARTHUR, DOUGLAS (1880–1964)

U.S. Army officer, MacArthur was born on an army post near Little Rock, Arkansas, the son of Arthur MacArthur. He spent his youth in New Mexico Territory, where his father was serving in the wars against the Apache. MacArthur graduated first in his class from West Point in 1903. His first assignment was with the engineers in the Philippines. In World War I, MacArthur helped organize the ''Rainbow Division'' and at war's end served as its commander. In the 1920s, MacArthur was superintendent of West Point and commander of U.S. forces in the Philippines. From 1930 to 1935, he served as chief of staff of the U.S. Army. During this period, he commanded the troops that dispersed the ''Bonus Army'' (12,000 World War I veterans who marched on Washington, demanding payment of bonuses promised in 1924). His efforts were criticized by some as being heavy-handed.

In 1935, MacArthur was sent to the Philippines as military adviser. In 1937, he retired from the U.S. Army but continued to command the Philippine army as a field marshall. He stayed in the Philippines four years and in 1942 was named Supreme Commander of Allied Forces in the South Pacific. Having a key role in the war effort, he was appointed General of the Army and in August 1945 accepted the Japanese surrender to end World War II. As commander of the United Nations armed forces in the Korean War, he clashed with Pres. Harry S Truman in 1951 over how the campaign should be waged. He was relieved of his command and returned to the United States to a hero's welcome.

Ted Alexander

McCAWLEY, CHARLES (1827–1891)

McCawley was born in Philadelphia, the son of a marine captain. He was commissioned a marine second lieutenant in 1847 and fought in both the Mexican War and the Civil War. After the Civil War, McCawley was assigned to various marine barracks along the eastern seaboard and oversaw the recruiting service. He was appointed lieutenant colonel in 1867 and assumed the post of colonel commandant of the Marine Corps in 1876. While he was commandant, marines helped to quell bloody labor riots in New York, Chicago, and seven other major cities. Marines were likewise dispatched to protect American lives and property in Panama and Chile.

McCawley's major accomplishments while serving as commandant included improving the training of enlisted men and commissioning and promoting officers based on merit. The most important reform introduced by McCawley was the stipulation that all new officers would be drawn from the Naval Academy, a policy that greatly increased professionalism among marine officers. McCawley retired in January 1891 and died later that year after suffering a stroke.

Leo J. Daugherty III

MACKENZIE, RANALD SLIDELL (1840–1889)

U.S. army officer, Mackenzie was born in New York City, the son of naval officer Alexander Slidell Mackenzie. He graduated from West Point in 1862 and commanded a cavalry division in the Civil War as a brevet major general. In 1871, Mackenzie became colonel of the 4th Cavalry, which, for the next six years, he led in a series of Indian campaigns in Texas. He particularly distinguished himself in two such events: an 1873 raid into Mexico to halt Kickapoo attacks across the border and the victorious battle at Palo Duro Canyon that climaxed the Red River War. After further service on the Northern Plains, Mackenzie was promoted to brigadier general in 1881 and in 1883 was assigned to head the Department of Texas. Once back in Texas, however, Mackenzie's physical and mental health collapsed, and he was sent to a New York City asylum. Mackenzie was formally retired from the army in early 1884.

Bibliography: Wallace, Ernest, *Ranald S. Mackenzie on the Texas Frontier* (West Texas Museum Assoc., 1964).

Richard F. Kehrberg

McKINLEY, WILLIAM (1843–1901)

Twenty-fifth president of the United States (1897–1901), McKinley was born in Niles, Ohio. He became a Republican party stalwart after service in the Civil War. He served in the House of Representatives (1877–83, 1885–91) and as governor of Ohio (1892–96). Elected president in 1896, McKinley was immediately concerned with reconciling U.S. and Spanish views over the fate of Cuba, where a revolution was in progress. He reluctantly asked for a declaration of war against Spain on Apr. 25, 1898. Long seen as an ineffective commander in chief who followed the nation into war instead of leading it, McKinley is now considered to have been an able war leader and molder of public opinion. McKinley was a partisan of U.S. expansion in Asia; his decision to retain the Philippines after Spain's defeat led to a protracted campaign against Filipino insurgents. Reelected in 1900, McKinley was shot in Buffalo, New York, by anarchist Leon Czolgosz on Sept. 6, 1901. He died eight days later.

Richard B. Meixsel

William McKinley, president (1897–1901) during the Spanish-American War (1898), took his role of commander in chief seriously and was involved in the formulation of war strategy and decisions. (Library of Congress)

MADERO, FRANCISCO INDALECIO (1873–1913)

Mexican revolutionary and political figure, Madero was born in Parras, Coahuila. In 1910, he campaigned against Mexican dictator Porfirio Díaz for the presidency. When his political intentions were met with repression, Madero began an uprising that started the Mexican Revolution. His rebellion succeeded in early 1911 when rebel general Pascual Orozco captured Ciudad Juárez. Díaz was forced to resign in May, and Madero became president (1911–13).

As leader of Mexico, Madero found himself increasingly cornered by both radical and conservative opponents. Eventually, such radicals as Orozco and Emiliano Zapata revolted, and Madero had to depend on right-wing Gen. Victoriano Huerta to put them down. Given increased power, however, Huerta himself engineered a coup and assassinated Madero in February 1913, proclaiming himself president.

Mark Pitcavage

MAHAN, ALFRED THAYER (1840–1914)

U.S. naval officer and historian, Mahan was born at West Point, New York, the eldest son of Dennis Hart Mahan, a professor of civil and military engineering and dean of faculty at the U.S. Military Academy. Mahan entered the Naval Academy at age 16 and was given a year's advanced standing, something never awarded another student. This concession, combined with his reserved manner, which many ascribed to arrogance and vanity, set him apart from most of his classmates. When Mahan's sense of military honor and religious morality led him to report a fellow midshipman for talking in ranks, many of his peers ostracized him during his final year at Annapolis.

Graduated second in the Class of 1859, Mahan served a tour on the Brazil Station (1859–61) and spent most of the Civil War assigned to blockade duty, first in the *Pocahontas* (1861–62) at Port Royal, South Carolina, then in the screw sloop *Seminole* (1863–64) off Sabine Pass, Texas, and finally in three ships of the South Atlantic Squadron off Charleston, South Carolina. Such service was boring to Mahan who disliked—perhaps feared—the sea and was generally contemptuous of his fellow officers whom he thought his inferiors. Following the war, Mahan served both at sea and ashore. He rose to the rank of captain in 1885.

Career as Naval Scholar. In 1883, Mahan had written *The Gulf and Inland Waters,* a descriptive rather than analytical work that had little literary merit. Yet it apparently impressed Stephen B. Luce, under whom Mahan had served in 1863 when Luce commanded the sloop *Macedonian* on a cruise taking midshipmen to Europe. Luce, who in 1884 founded and became the first president of the Naval War College at Newport, Rhode Island, believed his college's mission to be "the systematic study of military operations, by land or sea, applying the experiences of history to contemporary conditions" and set about finding those who could best contribute to that end. Meeting Luce's criteria, Mahan was selected to join the faculty. He reported to the War College in October 1885 and was given a year to prepare his lectures on naval history and tactics, the first of which he delivered in the fall of 1886. Mahan then succeeded Luce as president of the college (1886–89).

In 1890, Mahan's lectures were published with only slight revision as *The Influence of Sea Power upon History, 1660–1783.* In its first chapter, Mahan discussed the "General conditions affecting Sea Power" (geographical position, physical conformation, extent of territory, number of population, national character, and character and policy of governments), and in the next 12, he examined the effect of sea power on the nations of Western Europe, especially Great Britain, the world's preeminent sea power.

After being sent to the West Coast for a year, he returned to Newport to complete *The Influence of Sea Power upon the French Revolution and Empire, 1793–1812,* published in 1892. The book continued the analysis of its predecessor, showing how England's position off the coast of Western Europe had allowed it to become a worldwide power. As an island, it did not need to support a large army, as did continental nations, and instead devoted the money other nations spent on their armies to build a great navy. England then used its sea power to cut off its rivals from overseas trade and to build for itself a great empire. Geographical position alone was not enough to ensure England's rise. Equally important was a government that understood the value of sea power and its correct usage. To Mahan, this meant the building of a battle fleet that could destroy enemy navies, denying them the use of the sea.

When Mahan visited England as captain of the cruiser *Chicago,* flagship of the European Squadron, 1893–95, he was given receptions by Queen Victoria, the Admiralty, and the Royal Navy Club and received honorary degrees from Oxford and Cambridge. After returning to the United States, Mahan again served briefly as president of the War College (1892–93), then retired voluntarily in November 1896 in order to write full-time.

The next year, he published *The Interest of America in Sea Power, Present and Future,* in which he argued that the same factors that made England the world's leading sea power in the past could make the United States the greatest sea power in the future. Strategically speaking, the United States was basically an island and its position astride the trade route from Europe to Asia could bring it victory in the inevitable competition among nations. What the nation needed was a government willing to (1) build a fleet of capital ships capable of meeting any potential enemy on favorable terms, (2) construct a Central American canal to link its east and west coasts by sea, and (3) establish a series of coaling stations to support its fleet in overseas operations.

Such reasoning reflected a revolution in thinking for Mahan. For many years, he had accepted the U.S. strategy based on commerce raiding and coastal defense and opposed the acquisition of overseas territories because he feared that the acquisition of an empire would bring with it a military aristocracy that could threaten American democracy. Mahan's shift in views can be traced to his growing sense of Christian mission and to his 1885 experience in Panama when, as commander of the *Wachusett,* he had to order marines and bluejackets ashore to protect U.S. lives and property during a rebellion.

Later Years. Mahan was recalled to active duty to serve on the Board of Naval Strategy established at the beginning of the Spanish-American War and served as U.S. delegate to the first Hague Peace Conference in 1899. At that conference, he opposed the granting of immunity from seizure to private property captured at sea and the signing of any arbitration treaties that might limit U.S. freedom of action to enforce the Monroe Doctrine. In 1902, Mahan was elected president of the American Historical Association. Four years later, he was promoted to rear admiral on the retired list.

Mahan continued to write, most notably *Sea Power and Its Relations to the War of 1812* (1905); his autobiography, *From Sail to Steam: Recollections of a Naval Life* (1907); *The Major Operations of the Navies in the War of American Independence* (1913); and hundreds of magazine articles and letters to newspapers. Mahan's influence was even greater abroad than it was at home, and his unsolicited advice to Great Britain that it should attack Germany in a preemptive strike prior to the outbreak of World War I led to protests by those who felt that such statements by so prominent an American violated all rules of neutrality. Mahan did not live to witness much of that war, dying on Dec. 1, 1914.

Legacy. Mahan's fame rests primarily on his writings. Political leaders rarely consulted him on foreign policy or naval matters, and he was strongly disliked by his fellow naval officers. Through his many books and articles, he articulated a theory of sea power that dominated 20th-century naval theory. Even those who reject Mahan's ideas have rarely escaped his shadow, as they argue questions of naval strategy within the framework he devised. His ideas were not original; they were synthetic and reflected the optimism, imperialism, racism, and Christian missionary zeal of his time. An Anglophile, Mahan, through such works as his biography of Horatio Nelson (1897) and *Types of Naval Officers* (1901), helped cement the Anglo-American diplomatic and naval rapprochement of the early 20th century.

Bibliography: Livezey, William E., *Mahan on Sea Power* (Oklahoma Univ. Press, 1981); Puleston, W. D., *The Life and Work of Captain Alfred Thayer Mahan, U.S.N.* (Yale Univ. Press, 1939); Seager, Robert, *Alfred Thayer Mahan: The Man and His Letters* (Naval Inst. Press, 1977); Seager, Robert, II, and Doris D. Maguire, eds., *Letters and Papers of Alfred Thayer Mahan,* 3 vols. (Naval Inst. Press, 1975); West, Richard S., *Admirals of American Empire* (Bobbs-Merrill, 1948).

James C. Bradford

MALONE, PAUL BERNARD (1872–1960)

U.S. army officer and administrator, Malone was born in New York. He graduated from West Point in 1894, and following stateside service with the 13th Infantry Regiment, he served in the Spanish-American War, the Philippine Insurrection, and the Army of Cuban Pacification (as judge advocate and provost marshal general while only a captain). Malone graduated with honors from the Army School of the Line and was sent briefly overseas as an official observer of foreign maneuvers before World War I.

At the beginning of the war, Gen. John J. Pershing appointed Malone the plans and training officer of the American Expeditionary Force. He later sought and received combat assignments, during which he personally led troops in the Meuse River crossing. After the war, Malone, who reached the rank of major general, worked on the War Department General Staff and served as assistant commandant of the Infantry School, where he designed the school crest and motto, "Follow Me." He commanded the 2d and Philippine divisions; the 3d, 6th, and 9th corps areas; and the 4th Army (1935–36) before his retirement.

Louise Arnold-Friend

MARCH, PEYTON CONWAY (1864–1955)

U.S. army officer and chief of staff, March was born in Easton, Pennsylvania. He graduated from West Point in 1888 and saw his first tour of duty with the 3d Artillery Regiment in Washington, D.C.

Early Career. Promoted to first lieutenant in 1894, March served with the 5th Artillery in San Francisco and then studied at the Artillery School. With the outbreak of the Spanish-American War in 1898, he was named to command a battery of light artillery financed by John Jacob Astor. March's duties included recruiting and training the personnel and purchasing uniforms and weapons, three-inch Hotchkiss mountain guns he ordered from Paris. After a brief period of training in New York City, the Astor Battery was ordered to the Philippines. There, under the command of Gen. Arthur MacArthur, it was engaged in one sharp skirmish with the Spanish prior to cessation of hostilities.

The outfit remained in Manila for several months of occupation duty before returning to New York City to be mustered out; at MacArthur's request, March was ordered back to the Philippines to serve as the general's aide. As a major of volunteers assigned to the 33d Volunteer Infantry Regiment, March also saw combat in the Philippine Insurrection, leading his battalion ashore in an amphibious operation along Lingayen Gulf and taking part in other actions against insurgent forces on Luzon. After insurgent leader Emilio Aguinaldo had disbanded his regular forces in order to use guerrilla tactics, March led his men on several hazardous forays into difficult terrain.

March, now a lieutenant colonel of volunteers, concluded his service in the Philippines as commissary general of prisoners. As such, he was responsible for overseeing the care of some 5,000 insurgent prisoners and the compilation of records on each. On July 1, 1901, March yielded his rank in the volunteers to return to the United States and become a captain in the regular army. His service in the Philippines was one of the key events of his career; as a leader of troops, he was outstanding.

March's next duty was with artillery at Fort Riley and then as a member of the newly established General Staff in Washington, D.C. During the Russo-Japanese War (1904–05), March was assigned as an observer to the Japanese 1st Army. He thought the Russian artillery had superior equipment but that Japanese troops excelled in training and morale. The general staff system that the Japanese had learned from the German army also impressed March. He returned to Washington and became one of several officers who formulated plans to divide the Artillery Corps into its two logical components of Coast Artillery and Field Artillery. Promoted to major in 1907, March then saw service with the 6th Field Artillery at Fort Riley.

Between 1911 and 1916, March served primarily with the adjutant general's department, first in departmental and divisional offices in Omaha, Nebraska; Chicago; and Texas City, Texas, where he supervised the handling of correspondence and the maintenance of records. From 1913 on, he was in the adjutant general's office in Washington, where his work involved recruiting and preparing plans for calling up militia units in the event of trouble with Mexico.

March's promotion to colonel in 1916 was soon followed by an assignment to command the 8th Field Artillery Regiment, a newly formed outfit stationed at Fort Bliss, Texas. March, however, was already marked for bigger things. Sec. of War Newton Baker had been particularly impressed by the efficiency with which March handled the task of coordinating all telegraphic communications between the War Department and National Guard units mobilized for active duty along the Mexican border.

World War I. In June 1917, March was ordered to Washington. Slated for promotion to brigadier general, he would be going to France to command the first active artillery brigade of the American Expeditionary Force (A.E.F.). March arrived in France in July and spent most of a month studying British and French artillery equipment and organization. Arrangements were made for March's brigade to undergo training at a camp in France to prepare it for service on the Western Front. Even before his brigade had completed its eight-week training program, March was moved up to become chief of A.E.F. artillery.

In January 1918, Secretary of War Baker notified A.E.F. commander John J. Pershing that he intended to recall March to Washington where March would serve as acting chief of staff. March was the fourth man to have the duties of chief of staff within a year. The General Staff had been overwhelmed with Pershing's demands for personnel, supplies, and equipment. March had much to recommend himself. He was familiar with both the War Department and conditions in France. Furthermore, Baker remembered that March had the qualities the chief of staff would need in wartime circumstances: the ability to see to the heart of complicated matters, the knack of simplifying organizational details, and the strength of character to act promptly and decisively.

Both as acting chief, March's title for his first two months in Washington, and as chief of staff, which carried with it the rank of full general, March acted with typical energy to reorganize supply, transport, and other services; he shifted personnel in the interests of efficiency and established such new agencies as the Chemical Warfare Service, the Air Service, and the Bureau of Aircraft Production. Outraged at seeing War Department offices close down at 5:00 P.M. each day, March soon took pride in seeing the lights in departmental offices on around the clock and seeing officers hard at work, no matter what the time of day, accomplishing the many things that needed to be done during a state of war.

Friction inevitably developed between March and Pershing, for during World War I, Pershing, as chief of the expeditionary forces, reported directly to the secretary of war and to the president, assuming that the chief of staff's primary, if not only, function was to fulfill Pershing's requests. Both March and Pershing were strong-minded and differed over many matters. To neither man's credit, some of their disputes were petty. For instance, March insisted that A.E.F. officers returning to the United States remove the Sam Browne belts worn overseas. Pershing was equally adamant that, when under A.E.F. jurisdiction, his officers wear the belt even though March considered the belt's right shoulder strap a waste of leather.

Ordinarily, matters of substance, such as supply, production, and the optimum size of the A.E.F., were at issue. Pershing, for example, wanted a force of 100 divisions while March believed 80 divisions were all that could be organized and effectively maintained overseas. Pershing requested 194-millimeter artillery for his long-range batteries, but March felt that since no facilities for the production of such a weapon yet existed, Pershing should utilize the large-caliber naval guns that were already available. Authority over promotion of officers to general's rank also created friction between the two men. In one case, March advised Pershing that, while he valued Pershing's recommendations for promotion on officers currently serving with the A.E.F., he (March) commanded the entire U.S. Army, of which the A.E.F. was but one component. He would consider that when finalizing the promotion list. Had the two generals been able to confer in person, perhaps many of their differences could have been avoided or resolved more readily.

Postwar Years. For more than two years after the armistice of 1918, March remained in office trying to shape the organization and size of the postwar army but meeting disappointment in several areas. Congress was in no mood to fund the 500,000-man force March wanted. March, always brusque with congressmen, was simply not the man to extract higher appropriations from Congress when demobilization and retrenchment were the watchwords. Still, March was a superb military manager, one often regarded among the greatest chiefs of staff in the history of the General Staff.

Bibliography: Beaver, Daniel, *Newton D. Baker and the American War Effort: 1917–1919* (Univ. of Nebraska Press, 1966); Coffman, Edward M., *The Hilt of the Sword: The Career of Peyton C. March* (Univ. of Wisconsin Press, 1966);———, *The War to End All Wars: The American Military Experience in World War I* (Oxford Univ. Press, 1968); Hewes, James E., Jr., *From Root to McNamara: Army Organization and Administration, 1900–1963* (U.S. Govt. Printing Office, 1975); March, Peyton C., *The Nation at War* (Doubleday, 1932).

Lloyd J. Graybar

MARSHALL, GEORGE CATLETT
(1880–1959)

U.S. army officer, Marshall was born in Uniontown, Pennsylvania. He graduated from Virginia Military Institute in 1901 and served in the Philippines. He attended the Infantry and Cavalry School (1907) and the Staff College (1908) at

Fort Leavenworth, teaching at the latter until 1910. He served again in the Philippines 1913–16.

During World War I, Marshall sailed to France in 1917 as a 1st Division staff officer with the American Expeditionary Force (A.E.F.). As the division's operations officer in May 1918, he helped plan the first U.S. offensive of the war (Cantigny). Briefly assigned to A.E.F. general headquarters at Chaumont, he helped plan the St.-Mihiel Offensive. "Loaned" to the 1st Army staff where he became assistant chief of staff, Marshall organized the intricate movement of hundreds of thousands of troops and supplies for the Meuse-Argonne Offensive. After a short stint as VIII Corps chief of staff, Marshall served as aide to Gen. John J. Pershing 1919–24.

As army chief of staff (1939–45) and as President Franklin D. Roosevelt's strategic adviser, Marshall played a major role in the Allied victory in World War II. It was as secretary of state from 1947 to 1949 that Marshall formulated the European Recovery Program—to become universally known as the Marshall Plan—to provide economic support in the postwar period. His efforts brought a Nobel Peace Prize in 1951.

Stephen J. Lofgren

MAXIM, HIRAM STEVENS (1840–1916)

U.S. and British inventor, Maxim was born in Sangerville, Maine. He obtained his first patient in 1866 for a hair-curling iron. While much of his early work was in illumination, Maxim's interest in automatic firearms led him to move to London, where, in 1884, he produced the first fully automatic machine gun. The gun enjoyed great commercial success in Europe and in 1903 was adopted by the U.S. Army. The Maxim gun and its derivatives served in European armies through World War I. After the success of his machine gun, Maxim continued to experiment in a wide variety of fields, and in the 1890s, his interests focused on powered flight. In 1900, he became a British citizen and in 1901 was knighted by Queen Victoria.

Richard F. Kerhberg

MAYO, HENRY THOMAS (1856–1937)

U.S. naval officer, Mayo was born in Burlington, Vermont. He graduated from Annapolis in 1876. He served in the Asiatic Squadron (1876–78), with the Coast Survey charting Puget Sound (1879–82, 1886–89, 1892–95), with the Greeley Relief Expedition (1883), and in various ships stationed on the West Coast, including the cruisers *Albany,* his first major command (1907–08), and *California* (1909–10). While commanding the Mare Island navy yard (1911–13), he came to the attention of Sec. of the Navy Josephus Daniels, who selected Mayo to serve as his aide for personnel in 1913. This position paved the way for Mayo's promotion to rear admiral and command of 4th Division, Atlantic Fleet, which patrolled the coast of Mexico during its civil war. Mayo's bellicose behavior during the Tampico Incident (April 1914) pleased Pres. Woodrow Wilson and led to Mayo's further promotion.

Mayo became an admiral and commander in chief of the Atlantic Fleet during World War I. Much of his time was devoted to training the fleet in U.S. waters. On two trips to Europe, he met with Allied leaders and inspected U.S. installations, ships, and personnel. At war's end, Mayo reverted to the rank of rear admiral and served on the General Board. He retired from active duty in December 1920.

Bibliography: Bradford, James C., "Henry T. Mayo: Last of the Independent Naval Diplomats," *Admirals of the New Steel Navy,* ed. by James C. Bradford (Naval Inst. Press, 1990).

James C. Bradford

MENOHER, CHARLES THOMAS (1862–1930)

U.S. army officer and air force pioneer, Menoher was born in Johnstown, Pennsylvania. His graduation from West Point in 1886 was followed by service in the artillery. He graduated from the Artillery School in 1894 and the Army War College in 1907 and was a member of the army's newly founded General Staff.

A colonel when World War I broke out, Menoher advanced to major general by the conflict's end. During the war, he commanded the School of Instruction for Field Artillery at Samur, France; the 42d Infantry Division; and the VI Corps. He was highly decorated by both France and the United States.

In 1919, he was appointed chief of the U.S. Army Air Service and the next year was promoted to major general. Constant friction over policy with his chief subordinate, Col. William Mitchell, led Menoher to seek a troop assignment. Thereafter, he successively commanded the Hawaiian Division (1922–24), the Hawaiian Department (1925), and the IX Corps at San Francisco (1925–26), after which he retired.

Louise Arnold-Friend

MERRITT, WESLEY (1834–1910)

U.S. army officer, Merritt was born in New York City. He graduated from West Point in 1860. During the Civil War, he proved to be a superb combat leader, rising to the rank of major general of volunteers and taking command of a cavalry division. Merritt returned to the regular army in 1866 as lieutenant colonel of the 9th Cavalry. Promoted to colonel in 1876, he took charge of the 5th Cavalry. He participated in several western campaigns and developed a reputation as a skilled Indian fighter.

In 1882, Merritt became superintendent of West Point. He advanced to brigadier general in 1887 and to major general in 1895. He held several important departmental commands and was commanding the Department of the East when the Spanish-American War broke out.

Ordered to seize the Philippines, Merritt hastily organized the VIII Corps and set sail with 15,000 troops. He arrived in late June and immediately laid siege to Manila. Merritt found himself in a difficult situation between Filipino revolutionaries seeking independence and the Spanish forces holding the city. With considerable skill, he succeeded in securing Filipino assistance without committing the United States to Philippine independence and in defeating the Spanish after a brief fight. He remained military governor of the islands for less than two weeks before being called to the peace conference in Paris. In June 1900, Merritt retired from the army, but three years later actively assisted the passage of the General Staff Act.

Bibliography: Cosmos, Graham A., *An Army for Empire: The United States Army in the Spanish-American War* (Univ. of Missouri Press, 1971); Utley, Robert M., *Frontier Regulars: The United States Army and the Indian, 1866–1891* (Macmillan Co., 1973).

Daniel T. Bailey

MILES, NELSON APPLETON (1839–1925)

U.S. army commander, Miles was born near Westminster, Massachusetts. He never went beyond high school but achieved meteoric success as a Union officer in the Civil War. Commissioned a lieutenant, he became an aide to Gen. Oliver O. Howard and later a lieutenant colonel in a New York regiment, winning a Medal of Honor. By the fall of 1864, Miles had become a brevet major general and a divisional commander.

At the end of the war, Miles was named commandant of Fortress Monroe and oversaw the incarceration of Confederate president Jefferson Davis. He was a strict jailer and received a great deal of negative publicity for briefly placing chains on the Confederate president. In January 1866, Miles departed from Fortress Monroe and became a colonel in the regular army. He served a brief tour of duty as a regimental commander in North Carolina, during which he married the niece of Gen. William T. Sherman.

Indian Wars. In March 1869, Miles found himself assigned to Fort Hoyd, Kansas. However, it was not until 1874 that he saw any action. When war with the Cheyenne, Kiowa, and Comanche broke out in Indian Territory and the Texas panhandle (the Red River War), Miles led a column of troops sent from the Department of the Missouri. On August 30, he engaged 600 warriors and drove them off but could not pursue them because his supplies were exhausted. Miles stayed in the field until February 1875, when most of the Indians returned to their reservations.

Miles next saw action the following year, after Lt. Col. George A. Custer's startling defeat by Sioux chiefs Sitting Bull and Crazy Horse at the Battle of the Little Bighorn in late June 1876. Sherman, Commanding General of the Army, sent reinforcements north to the Dakotas, including the 5th Infantry Regiment under Miles, who had pressed Sherman for the assignment. Miles was given the task of holding the main fording places of the Yellowstone River in order to block the Sioux's escape route to Canada. In October, he learned of Sioux movements in his vicinity and caught up with Sitting Bull at Cedar Creek, Montana, on October 20. Miles attempted to persuade the chief to return to the reservation, but when negotiations failed, he fought a two-day running battle with the Sioux.

On October 27, 2,000 Sioux surrendered, but the rest, including Sitting Bull, escaped northward. Miles decided to keep his regiment in the field during the winter to chase the Sioux across Montana. On Jan. 8, 1877, he was attacked by 500 warriors led by Crazy Horse and skillfully repulsed their attacks until a blizzard interrupted the battle. Most of Crazy Horse's band surrendered a few months later to Gen. George Crook. In the spring and summer of 1877, Miles himself defeated the last remnants of the Sioux uprising. His energetic prosecution of the campaign against the Sioux in harsh conditions was chiefly responsible for their surrender.

In September, Miles was sent to help intercept Chief Joseph and his Nez Percé, who were waging a successful mobile campaign in an attempt to link up with Sitting Bull in Canada. Miles raced the Nez Percé to the Canadian border and met them on September 30 in Snake Creek Valley, fighting a sharp engagement in which he lost 24 killed and almost twice as many wounded. Miles suspended the assault and placed the Nez Percé camp under siege. On October 5, Chief Joseph surrendered to Miles and his superior, General Hoard, who had just arrived. The two officers promised Joseph his people could return to Oregon, but they were overruled, and the Nez Percé were sent to Indian Territory, where many died. Not until 1884, with the aid of Miles and others, were the Nez Percé able to go back to the Northwest (although still not to their native Idaho).

After his victory over the Nez Percé, Miles became increasingly aggressive in seeking reward, in 1879 repeatedly requesting a military department for Montana, with himself as its brigadier general. He also wanted permission to pursue Sitting Bull into Canada. When in the summer of 1879 Sitting Bull and his remaining followers reentered the United States to hunt, Miles drove them out of their camp and back into Canada. Miles's impulsiveness angered Sherman, and it was over Sherman's protests that Miles received his brigadier general's star in 1880.

Miles served as commander of the Departments of the Columbia and the Missouri. In April 1886, Gen. Philip H. Sheridan, who replaced Sherman as commanding general, ordered Miles to take command of the Department of

Arizona from General Crook. Crook had been trying for several years to suppress an uprising by the Apache led by Geronimo. Miles had actively campaigned for the assignment, especially since Miles and Crook were among the competitors for a major general's slot.

To capture the elusive Geronimo, Miles organized mobile striking forces and set up heliographs for quick communications. He organized a column specifically to pursue Geronimo and ordered the deportation of many Apache from Arizona to Florida. By September, Geronimo, out of supplies and separated from his tribe, surrendered, ending the Apache uprisings.

In 1890, Miles received a promotion to major general. He commanded the Military Division of the Missouri during the Ghost Dance movement and suspended Col. James Forsyth, who commanded at the Wounded Knee Massacre, but was overruled. In 1894, Miles was ordered to intervene in the Pullman Strike organized by the American Railway union; he helped the railroads quash the strike by ordering federal troops to escort mail trains. The following year, Miles, as senior major general, was appointed Commanding General of the Army.

For Miles, the next several years passed uneventfully, until the conflict with Spain erupted into open warfare after the explosion on the USS *Maine* in 1898. Miles informed Sec. of War Russell Alger and Pres. William McKinley that the army was not able to attack Havana and advised against any Cuban offensive in the summer because of the harsh climate. He argued that the United States should take Puerto Rico first and wait until the fall to attack Cuba, while in the meantime providing assistance to the rebels.

Miles's enthusiasm for attacking Puerto Rico left him out of the subsequent Cuban campaign. Only after the campaign to take Santiago stalled in July was Miles sent to the front. Miles landed with reinforcements on July 11, after negotiations for surrender had begun. Already, yellow fever and dysentery had begun to reach crisis proportions. This led Miles and Gen. William Shafter to agree to Spanish demands for repatriation of prisoners to Spain.

After the surrender of Santiago, Miles left with 3,400 men to take Puerto Rico, where he encountered only token resistance by the Spanish garrison. The Spaniards surrendered on August 12, before he could capture San Juan. After the war ended, Miles found himself mired in controversy over his remarks about the "embalmed beef" sent to the troops in Cuba. This issue caused the resignation of Alger in 1899.

Later Years. The following year, Miles was promoted to lieutenant general, but shortly thereafter was officially censured by Sec. of War Elihu Root for publicly expressing his views on the debate between naval commanders William T. Sampson and Winfield Scott Schley over the Battle of Santiago Bay. Miles also fought with Pres. Theodore Roosevelt over both the conduct of the war against the Filipinos and Roosevelt's Army Reorganization Bill, which would abolish the position of commanding general (after Miles's retirement) and institute a general staff system.

Roosevelt and Root were no doubt relieved when Miles reached mandatory retirement age in 1903. Even after his retirement, however, Miles did not avoid controversy; in 1923, at age 85, he supported Col. William ("Billy") Mitchell's criticism of army leadership.

Bibliography: Amchan, Arthur J., *The Most Famous Soldier in America: A Biography of Lt. Gen. Nelson A. Miles* (Amchan, 1989); Johnson, Virginia Weisel, *The Unregimented General: A Biography of Nelson A. Miles* (Houghton Mifflin, 1962); Trask, David A., *The War With Spain in 1898* (Macmillan Co., 1981); Utley, Robert M., *Frontier Regulars: The United States Army and the Indian, 1866–91* (Macmillan Co., 1973).

Mark Pitcavage

MITCHELL, WILLIAM (BILLY) LENDRUM (1879–1936)

U.S. army officer, Mitchell was born in Nice, France, the scion of a financially and politically prominent Wisconsin family. Up through World War I, he developed a vision of independent air power that eventually transformed U.S. Army air doctrine during the interwar years.

Early Career. With the advent of the Spanish-American War in April 1898, Mitchell left college to enlist in the 1st Wisconsin Volunteer Regiment. He arrived in Cuba with a volunteer signal company the following December, four months after the end of fighting. After supervising the installation of 136 miles of telegraph wire in the province of Santiago, 2d Lieutenant "Billy" Mitchell grew tired of his duties and volunteered for action in the Philippines.

His transfer in October 1898 coincided with the start of a two-year guerrilla war, and Mitchell served as a communications officer with distinction. He might have remained a reserve officer if not for the Army Act of 1901, which authorized a fourfold increase in the regular army to support U.S. commitments overseas. As a result, 1st Lieutenant Mitchell received a permanent commission in the Signal Corps on Apr. 26, 1901. He worked in Alaska, supervising construction of a 1,700-mile telegraph system, and his efforts resulted in another promotion.

As the youngest captain in the U.S. Army, Mitchell next taught at the newly established Signal School (1905) and commanded the communications detachment at Fort Leavenworth, Kansas. He then attended the School of the Line (previously known as the Infantry and Cavalry School) in 1907 and the Army Staff College in 1908–09. After another tour in the Philippines, he joined the army's General Staff in March 1912.

Gen. Billy Mitchell's vision of military aviation in wartime was little used during World War I, but it became the basis for strategy in the air during World War II. (U.S. Army)

World War I. As the only Signal Corps officer on the General Staff, Mitchell first collected information on the Balkan Wars and the subsequent world war in Europe. In 1916, Sec. of War Newton Baker appointed Col. George Squier, Mitchell's former commander at the Army Signal School, to head the aviation section of the Signal Corps. Mitchell became Squire's deputy in June 1916. He was promoted to major a month later and took private flight training, although he did not become a junior military aviator until September 1917.

The War Department then sent Mitchell to Europe as a wartime observer. By the time he arrived in Paris (Apr. 10, 1917), the United States was at war. As a result, the newly promoted Lieutenant Colonel Mitchell enjoyed complete freedom during the two months prior to the arrival of Gen. John J. Pershing and the American Expeditionary Force (A.E.F.). Mitchell consulted with Allied airmen on military tactics and technology, inspected the French and British sectors of the Western Front, and with his own funds established an unofficial U.S. aviation office in Paris.

When Pershing arrived on June 13, he appointed Mitchell aviation officer of the A.E.F. As the senior U.S. airman in France, Mitchell tried vainly to establish an air force with tactical and strategic capabilities. However, although ground commanders only wanted tactical observation and fighter aircraft, even this narrow request was not possible. The U.S. military aviation industry was in its infancy, and the earliest the A.E.F. could expect its consignment of aircraft was the spring of 1918.

Mitchell became a full colonel in September 1917. Pershing, in turn, appointed him commander of the Air Service in the Zone of Advance (the top A.E.F. aviation training position) and then chief of Air Service, 1st Army. Mitchell held the latter position until Pershing demoted Brig. Gen. Benjamin Foulois, the largely ineffectual chief of the Air Service, A.E.F. Mitchell grudgingly vacated his position to succeed Foulois, who generously but unenthusiastically relinquished his post to his more qualified rival.

Mitchell fielded his first combat squadron in April 1918 but never had more than 650 A.E.F. aircraft at the front. He did, however, command a substantial number of Allied aircraft in the only two major battles the A.E.F. fought: St.-Mihiel (Sept. 12–16, 1918) and the Meuse-Argonne (Sept. 26–Nov. 11, 1918). At St.-Mihiel, Mitchell nominally commanded the largest air armada (1,481 aircraft) of World War I, but inclement weather and an organized German retreat minimized the impact of Allied air forces in combat. (The restriction of aircraft to an infantry support role, operating within a 35-mile radius of ground troops, further delimited the role of air power in the battle.) Nevertheless, Mitchell quickly established air superiority over a comparatively small force of 243 German aircraft, and Pershing promoted him to brigadier general.

During the Meuse-Argonne Offensive, Mitchell assumed command of the Air Service, Army Group. Once again, infantry support took precedence in U.S. air operations, although an October 9 raid by 200 French and U.S. bombers against enemy troops suggested the future potential of strategic operations. With the end of hostilities on November 11, Mitchell returned to the United States and began to champion the primacy of air power in national defense.

Intellectual Development. Mitchell's interest in aviation developed slowly. Prior to 1916, he expressed little interest in air power and had little contact with the minuscule Aeronautical Division of the Signal Corps. Allied airmen revolutionized Mitchell's thinking about air power. The French, for example, first convinced him that fighters and bombers achieved maximum results when assigned to army groups rather than to smaller units such as divisions and regiments. Such an arrangement not only enabled airmen to operate over wide areas of the Western Front, it also prevented local commanders from hoarding aircraft. Mitchell concluded that autonomy in the air improved the effectiveness of air attacks against front-line troops.

Mitchell acquired a faith in the air offensive from Britain's Maj. Gen. Hugh Trenchard, commander of the Royal

Flying Corps (RFC) in France. According to Trenchard, only relentless and incessant air attacks could achieve command of the air, a breakthrough on the Western Front, and an erosion of enemy morale. Trenchard also hoped to destroy the infrastructure that supported the German army, although the RFC never reached the size to isolate front-line troops.

That Mitchell accepted French and British thinking soon became apparent. On May 17, 1917, he cabled Washington and recommended that fighters and bombers should receive a higher production priority than reconnaissance aircraft. When Pershing arrived in Europe, Mitchell sought to divide future A.E.F. inventories into tactical and strategical units. The tactical units would have provided reconnaissance and infantry support for each division, corps, and army, while strategical units would have employed Trenchard's offensive tactics against enemy matériel and aircraft located to the rear of the battlefield area. Mitchell believed his strategical units (the "new cavalry of the air") were critical for the success of ground operations, but both the General Staff and Pershing ignored Mitchell for several months.

With the arrival of the Bolling Mission in June, Mitchell added another aspect to his philosophy of air power. Because of their contacts with Count Gianni Caproni, Bolling Mission members popularized the teachings of Col. Giulio Douhet, an Italian who advocated the large-scale use of strategic bombers to destroy an enemy nation's "vital centers"—industrial capacity and morale. As a result, Mitchell corresponded with Caproni and collected data on potential German industrial targets in the Ruhr. However, continued opposition from Pershing's staff and insurmountable equipment shortages prevented Mitchell from testing the ideas he had adopted. His continuous campaign on behalf of increased U.S. air power eventually led to his public criticism of the War and the Navy departments and Mitchell's court-martial, five-year suspension, and resignation in 1926.

Bibliography: Davis, Burke, *The Billy Mitchell Affair* (Random House, 1967); Devine, Isaac Don, *Mitchell, Pioneer of Air Power* (Duell, Sloan and Pearce, 1958); Hurley, Alfred, *Billy Mitchell: Crusader for Air Power* (Indiana Univ. Press, 1975); Mitchell, William, *Memoirs of World War I* (Random House, 1960);———, *Our Air Force* (Dutton, 1921).

Maj. Peter R. Faber

MORRISON, JOHN FRANK (1857–1932)

U.S. army officer and educator, Morrison was born in Charlotteville, New York. He graduated from West Point in 1881, was commissioned a second lieutenant of infantry, and spent much of the next 17 years with the 20th Infantry in the Southwest. During the Spanish-American War, Morrison was in the battle of El Caney and earned a Silver Star for gallantry. Less than a year later, he was in the Philippines, where he remained for three years.

In 1906, he graduated from the Army War College and subsequently joined the faculty of Fort Leavenworth's Army Staff College and Army School of the Line (1908–12). His publications on organization, strategy, and tactics were regarded as authoritative works, and his courses of instruction came to form the basis for today's system of military education. His classroom introduction of new doctrinal ideas and methods of training played a critical role in the U.S. Army's successes during World War I. He was promoted to major general in 1917 and commanded the Western Department in 1918–19. He retired in 1921.

Lt. Col. Martin W. Andresen

MOSELEY, GEORGE VAN HORN (1874–1960)

U.S. army officer, Moseley was born in Illinois. He held a number of junior field commands after graduating from West Point in 1899 but distinguished himself through the quality of his staff work. When the United States entered World War I in 1917, Moseley was chief of staff for the 7th Division. In August, he took command of the 5th Field Artillery Regiment in France.

In April 1918, Gen. John J. Pershing appointed him to head the 4th Section of the General Staff of the American Expeditionary Force (A.E.F.). As "G-4," Moseley oversaw the A.E.F.'s supply organization and later supervised the return of the army to the United States. Following the war, he held a number of senior positions, including commander of the 1st Cavalry Division (1927–29), major general, deputy chief of staff of the army (1930–33), and commanding general of the 3d Army (1936–38). Moseley retired in 1938.

Richard F. Kehrberg

MONTOJO, PATRICIO (1839–1917)

Spanish admiral, Montojo commanded the Spanish naval forces in the Philippines until his defeat at the Battle of Manila on May 1, 1898. With the threat of imminent U.S. attack from Commodore George Dewey's Asiatic Fleet stationed in Hong Kong, Montojo first selected Subig (Subic) Bay to meet the Americans but found defensive positions inadequate for his fleet, forcing him to move his small squadron to Manila Bay adjacent the naval base at Cavite. In the battle that ensued, the U.S. squadron destroyed Montojo's fleet. Montojo returned to Spain in disgrace to face a court-martial for his failure to coordinate with the Spanish army commander ashore.

Vernon L. Williams

MYER, ALBERT JAMES (1828–1880)

U.S. Army officer and founder of the Signal Corps and the U.S. Weather Bureau, Myer was born in Newburgh, New

York. He entered the army in 1854 as an assistant surgeon, but his enthusiasm for the techniques of visual signaling led him to spend much of the next six years lobbying on behalf of the concept. In 1860, he was named the army's first signal officer, with the rank of major, and in June 1861 he was ordered to organize and command the Signal Corps. His Civil War innovations included experiments with balloons for observation, a mobile field telegraph train, and attempts at automating communications. He supervised work on about 5,000 miles of telegraph line to various frontier posts and ran afoul of the U.S. Military Telegraph for what was seen as an attempt to control all telegraphy. He was relieved as chief signal officer in November 1863 until July 1866, when an act of Congress reorganized the corps and made him colonel and chief signal officer. After the war, Myer resumed his interest in weather prediction, and when Congress authorized formation of the U.S. Weather Bureau in 1870, he went on to organize, equip, and direct the new agency for the next 10 years. He died while on active service, two months after being promoted to brigadier general. Fort Myer, Virginia, is named after him.

Carol Stokes

NOLAN, DENNIS EDWARD (1872–1956)

Chief of intelligence for the Allied Expeditionary Force during World War I, Nolan was born in Akron, New York. He graduated from West Point in 1896 and two years later participated in the Spanish-American War, where he saw action in Cuba during the Battle of El Caney and the siege of Santiago. In 1915, he joined the U.S. Army General Staff and headed its intelligence section when the United States entered World War I.

In May 1918, Nolan earned the admiration of his French allies by accurately predicting a massive German attack along the Chemin des Dames. He also briefly commanded a force of Americans in the field during the Meuse-Argonne Offensive. After the war, Nolan, a major general, served in various posts until his retirement in 1936. He received the Distinguished Service Medal and the Distinguished Service Cross for his actions in World War I.

Bibliography: Department of the Army, *The United States Army in the World War, 1917–19* (U.S. Govt. Printing Office, 1948).

John F. Wukovits

OBREGÓN, ÁLVARO (1880–1928)

Mexican soldier and president, Obregón was born near Álamos, Sonora. He was a Sonoran planter who became involved in the Mexican Revolution during the Constitutionalist struggle against Victoriano Huerta in 1913–14. Obregón displayed considerable military skill and became revolutionary leader Venustiano Carranza's favorite general.

Following Huerta's defeat, Carranza split with radical Pancho Villa in late 1914. Obregón waged a brilliant campaign against Villa, defeating him repeatedly and proving himself to be the best military leader of the revolution. During Carranza's presidency (1915–20), the president came to distrust Obregón, and their subsequent rivalry led to Carranza's ouster and death in 1920. Obregón served as president 1920–24. He was assassinated in 1928, after being reelected.

Mark Pitcavage

O'RYAN, JOHN FRANCIS (1874–1961)

U.S. army officer, O'Ryan was born in New York City. He practiced law in New York City and commanded the New York National Guard's 27th ("Bulldog") Division. A major general, O'Ryan constantly trained his troops to prepare them for action rather than allowing them to become "weekend warriors." As a result, they served with high distinction during the Mexican border dispute of 1916.

During World War I, O'Ryan and the 27th were sent to France in May 1918, and they proceeded to break down German opposition at Mont Kemmel in late August. The next month, the division advanced against the heavily fortified St. Quentin Canal, a key sector along the Hindenburg line. In vicious fighting, the 27th dislodged the Germans from their subterranean refuge and punched a damaging hole in the vaunted Hindenburg line. O'Ryan, beloved by his troops, received the Distinguished Service Medal for his duty.

Bibliography: Bullard, Robert Lee, *Fighting Generals* (J. W. Edwards, 1944); O'Ryan, John F., *The Story of the 27th Division,* 2 vols. (Wynkoop Hallenbeck Crawford, 1921).

John F. Wukovits

OTIS, ELWELL STEPHEN (1838–1909)

U.S. army officer, Otis was born in Frederick, Maryland. He served through the Civil War and then during the Indian campaigns in the 1870s, including the Battle of the Little Bighorn. In 1880, Otis began a decade of service in Kansas, establishing a school of instruction at Fort Leavenworth, the first of a long line of military educational institutions at that location.

Appointed major general a few days after the Battle of Manila Bay (Aug. 13, 1898), Otis arrived in the Philippines in late August to relieve Gen. Wesley Merritt as commander of the Department of the Pacific and governor of the Philippines. Otis assuaged Spanish officials during treaty negotiations and maintained a delicate peace with Filipino nationalists as the United States sought to establish control over the islands.

In February 1899, armed conflict began between the United States and the Filipino insurrectionists. Otis quickly secured Manila, but despite a successful campaign against the main insurgent body later that year, Otis failed to grasp that the war was shifting to guerrilla operations.

Otis was relieved by Arthur MacArthur in May 1900 and returned to the United States, where he commanded the Department of the Lakes until his retirement in 1902.

Bibliography: Gates, John M., *Schoolbooks and Krags* (Greenwood Press, 1973); Millett, Allan R., and Peter Maslowski, *For the Common Defense* (Free Press, 1984).

Vernon L. Williams

PALMER, JOHN McAULEY (1870–1955)

U.S. army officer best known for his advocacy of U.S. citizen soldiers and reserve components, Palmer was born in Scott County, Kentucky. He graduated from West Point in 1892 and was commissioned in the infantry.

Early Career. After serving in the Philippine Insurrection, Palmer became one of the first trained General Staff officers in the U.S. Army. He graduated from the General Staff School in 1910 and then served as brigade adjutant in the experimental Maneuver Division of 1911. The same year, he was assigned to the infantry General Staff in Washington.

Palmer's belief in the value of citizen soldiers was conspicuous in an era when most professional officers thought such soldiers could be used only as wartime fillers under regular army command. He acquired this belief gradually but was heavily influenced by his grandfather of the same name, who had excelled as a Civil War corps commander and as U.S. senator and governor of Illinois.

Initially, Palmer shared the general attitude that the National Guard was unusable in that the Constitution severely limited the role of militia forces; instead, he advocated a federal reserve force to replace the Guard. However, he did come to accept the political reality of the National Guard as the primary reserve force of the nation.

World War I. When the United States entered World War I, its National Guard units were organized into divisions based on a General Staff plan that Palmer helped develop. Palmer himself went to France almost immediately, serving as the operations officer of the American Expeditionary Force (A.E.F.) until the pressures of fielding an army caused his mental and physical collapse in August 1917. Before he had recovered completely, Palmer was pressed into service in the A.E.F. school system, organizing the three-month wartime General Staff course. Again exhausted, he returned to duty only in October 1918, commanding a brigade of the 19th National Guard Infantry Division at the end of the war.

National Defense Act of 1920. Palmer's real contribution to defense began in October 1919, when as chief of war plans for the War Department, he was called to testify before James Wadsworth's Senate subcommittee on a postwar military establishment. Palmer's vast technical knowledge and opposition to the large standing army advocated by Chief of Staff Peyton C. March caused Wadsworth to ask for Palmer as an adviser. Palmer and his friend Col. John W. Gulick helped Wadsworth develop a plan that differed markedly from the official War Department position.

On the way to passage of this bill, Palmer had to compromise first by accepting the National Guard and then by sacrificing his plans for universal military training. The resulting National Defense Act of 1920, however, embodied many of his basic ideas. The United States was divided into nine corps areas, each containing a number of regular army, National Guard, and organized reserve divisions, with regular instructors and inspectors to assist the reserve components.

Later Efforts. Unfortunately, the lack of funds and personnel in the interwar period caused this structure to atrophy rapidly during the 1920s. Palmer himself, his promising career stunted by his outspokenness, retired as a brigadier general in 1925. In retirement, he produced a steady stream of works on reserve components.

In November 1941, Palmer's longtime friend, Chief of Staff George C. Marshall, brought him back on active duty to advise on the postwar military establishment. Palmer tried again to create a large, ready reserve and National Guard system manned by universal military training, but politics again blocked this plan. Despite such failures, the reserve components throughout the Cold War continued to parallel Palmer's views with great accuracy.

Bibliography: Holley, Irving B., *General John M. Palmer, Citizen Soldiers, and the Army of a Democracy* (Greenwood Press, 1982); House, Jonathan M., "John McAuley Palmer and the Reserve Components," *Parameters* (Sept. 1982); Palmer, John M., *Washington, Lincoln, Wilson: Three War Statesmen* (Doubleday, 1930).

Jonathan M. House

PARKER, JAMES (1854–1934)

Decorated U.S. army officer, Parker was born in Newark, New Jersey. He graduated from West Point in 1876 before heading to the frontier to battle Indians and earn fame as a cavalry officer. During the chase for Geronimo, Parker (nicknamed "Galloping Jim") received his first Silver Star for action at Devil's Creek on May 22, 1885. After duty in the Spanish-American War, his bravery in the Philippines brought him two more Silver Stars, plus a Medal of Honor for the "most distinguished gallantry" at Vigan on Nov. 4, 1899. He was promoted to brigadier general in 1913 and to major general in 1917. During World War I, Parker commanded the 32d and 85th divisions and participated in the Armentières and St.-Quentin campaigns, for which he was awarded the Distinguished Service Medal. He retired in 1918.

Capt. Ralph P. Millsap, Jr.

PARKER, JOHN HENRY (1866–1942)

U.S. army officer, Parker was born in Tipton, Missouri. He graduated from West Point in 1892 and in 1898 commanded a Gatling-gun detachment in Cuba during the Spanish-American War. The unit gained recognition for its service at the Battle of San Juan Hill, and Parker emerged as the U.S. Army's leading expert on machine guns. After the war, he advocated the increased use of machine guns within the army, wrote a tactical manual for the guns that did exist, and unsuccessfully pushed for the creation of a separate machine-gun corps, with himself at its head. His zealous efforts earned him the nickname "Machine Gun" Parker, but also the ire of his superiors. During World War I, Parker led an infantry regiment and added to his reputation for bravery by earning three Distinguished Service Crosses. He retired as a colonel in 1924.

Bibliography: Armstrong, David A., *Bullets and Bureaucrats: The Machine Gun and United States Army, 1861–1916* (Greenwood Press, 1982).

Richard F. Kehrberg

PATRICK, MASON MATHEWS (1863–1942)

U.S. army engineer, Patrick was born in Lewisburg, West Virginia. He graduated from West Point in 1886, a classmate and friend of John J. Pershing. After being commissioned in the Corps of Engineers, Patrick successfully completed a number of routine assignments, including providing assistance to the survivors of the 1889 Johnstown Flood. In 1916, he commanded the 1st Engineer Regiment in Texas while Pershing was conducting the Mexican Punitive Expedition.

Upon U.S. entry in World War I, Patrick brought his engineers to France and assumed the task of managing American Expeditionary Force (A.E.F.) lines of communication. When a petty dispute between the leaders of the A.E.F. air service erupted, Pershing decided to turn the air service over to the trustworthy, but nonpilot, Patrick, under whom the A.E.F's air arm performed well in the St.-Mihiel and Meuse-Argonne campaigns. In 1918, he was promoted to major general. Following the war, Patrick again became chief of the army's air service (1921–27). He retired in 1927.

Col. (Ret.) Rod Paschall

PERSHING, JOHN JOSEPH (1860–1948)

U.S. army commander during World War I, Pershing was born in Laclede, Missouri. In 1882, he entered West Point, where he was elected president of his class and attained the highest cadet rank, first captain. Upon graduation in 1886, he was assigned to duty with black soldiers on the western frontier and served in both New Mexico and South Dakota, participating in campaigns against both the Apache and Sioux. After a tour as professor of military science at the University of Nebraska 1891–95, Pershing returned to West Point, this time as a tactical officer. It was in this assignment that he earned the nickname "Black Jack," evidently a derisive reference to his command of black troops, a name given by cadets who suffered under his stern tutelage and strict supervision.

Gen. John J. Pershing, leader of the American Expeditionary Force in Europe during World War I, was noted for his efficiency and his organizational skills and emerged from the war a national hero. (U.S. Army)

Philippine Campaigns. Pershing saw considerable action in the Philippines (1899–1903, 1907–08, 1909–13), often fighting the tough and wily Moros of Mindanao. Despite numerous military disadvantages in the Philippines (such as the energy-sapping jungle environs and the enemy's superior knowledge of the terrain), Pershing performed well and earned a reputation for success in battle and coolness in times of danger.

Between his first and second Philippine tours, in 1905, he married Helen Francis Warren, daughter of Sen. Francis E. Warren, chairman of the Senate Military Affairs Committee. In 1906, Pershing found himself advanced from the modest rank of captain to the exalted level of brigadier general in one bound. His promotion was made over 862 officers with more seniority and caused discontent.

Mexican Punitive Expedition. Pershing experienced disappointment and tragedy during 1914–16. Sent to the Mexican border, the general left his wife and three daughters in San Francisco and began dealing with cross-border raids by elusive Mexican bandits. There, in 1916, Pershing received news that his wife and daughters had died in a fire. His depression was heightened by the fact that there had been little success in curtailing border violence. When Pancho Villa made a bloody raid on Columbus, New Mexico, in March 1916, Pres. Woodrow Wilson finally authorized the Punitive Expedition, a U.S. military foray into Mexico with the aim of bringing Villa and his band to justice. All told, Villa and other bandits got the best of the U.S. Army and its leader, who was promoted to major general while in Mexico. There was simply too much desert and too few U.S. soldiers, but Villa's force had been scattered before the U.S. withdrawal in early 1917.

World War I. The announcement of U.S. entry into World War I in April 1917 was followed by Pershing's appointment as commander of the newly created American Expeditionary Force (A.E.F.). He and an advance force were soon in France, where he immediately faced several great problems. The U.S. contingent had no doctrine or experience in European-style fighting nor was there any organizational scheme that minimized the problems brought on by the lack of a large cadre of seasoned officers for a greatly expanded army. Political factors and the delicate state of the French and British armies in France and Belgium during early 1917 made it imperative to send many U.S. soldiers to Europe as soon as possible, regardless of their lack of training. The European Allies wanted to use the Americans as replacements in their own battle-depleted units, a policy called "amalgamation." Amalgamation was resisted by the Americans who wanted their own army, their own sector of the front, and their own place at the peace table.

Pershing's solution to the first problem, the lack of doctrine, was simple, straightforward, and wholly inadequate. The general had an unfounded, possibly bizarre notion that Americans were somehow superior beings. He was convinced the great migration from Europe to the United States had worked to create stronger breeds out of those who severed their cultural roots and survived in a hostile environment. This questionable idea had the weaker species of mankind staying in Europe. Additionally, Pershing believed the U.S. experience produced a skillful individual fighter, a man familiar with rifles, a hunter possessing native field craft, and a soldier with a highly developed characteristic of personal initiative.

Putting it all together, the general chose a doctrine of "open warfare," a vague concept of shunning trenches in favor of offensive tactical maneuver. German machine guns were to be overcome by "concentrated rifle fire." As it turned out, Americans, like the soldier of other armies, did use trenches. By 1917, the United States had become a rather urban country, and, exceptions such as Sgt. Alvin York aside, there appeared to be no particular advantage in U.S. marksmanship. In fact, Pershing complained throughout the war about his troops' lack of skill and facility with rifles. On the whole, practiced U.S. doctrine differed little from European norms on the Western Front.

Pershing's solution for the organizational problem was a good one. He chose an enormous, 28,000-man, "square" divisional structure, two (and in some cases three) times the size of European divisions. The large structure meant that fewer division, regimental, and battalion commanders were needed for the whole army than if a smaller type of division type had been chosen. Therefore, the problem of having only a handful of experienced officers to cadre the growing U.S. force was minimized. An idea that the larger organization would be able to absorb more casualties and continue fighting proved less promising. The big U.S. "square" division was simply given more front-line space to occupy, had more exposure to enemy fire, and thus had more need for replacements to remain functional. Despite a number of valid criticisms about the U.S. combat organization of 1917–18, it was probably the best solution given the circumstances.

The amalgamation problem and lack of training for U.S. forces were largely solved by Pershing. He insisted on an extensive schooling and training system behind the front lines. The general stubbornly refused to commit Americans to battle before they were qualified to fight. In October 1917, Pershing was promoted to the rank of full general. His high rank and his strong support by Sec. of War Newton Baker helped Pershing to maintain his strategy in the face of Allied opposition. Although there were some compromises, particularly during the German spring offensive of 1918, Pershing was finally able to secure his own sector for a large U.S. army. In the main, amalgamation was rejected. The outstanding combat performance of A.E.F. troops, particularly in reducing the St.-Mihiel salient and then immediately shifting fronts to the Meuse-Argonne offensive in 1918, vindicated Pershing's stance.

Later Career. Pershing returned to the United States in 1919 as an unabashed American hero. Congress gave him the title "General of the Armies of the United States," a position previously accorded only to George Washington. Although many military preparedness recommendations during his tenure as chief of staff (1921–24) were rejected, possibly no one could have done much better in the nation's great haste to dismantle the World War I U.S. Army. After his retirement in 1924, Pershing wrote his memoirs of the war, winning a Pulitzer Prize. However, the depression-era publication had been serialized in a newspaper chain and did not sell well. He also served as chairman of the American Battle Monuments Commission.

Pershing's style of command and public image is in the character of a George Washington, Winfield Scott, and Robert E. Lee. He seemed to be aloof, impeccably dressed, and deadly serious. This persona is the antithesis of a Zachary Taylor or Ulysses S. Grant, a more homespun, common-man projection. However, the A.E.F. commander's stoic image is probably overdrawn, as he was also known for his sense of humor and romantic interests. Overall, however, Pershing was a sound American military leader at a time when his country needed such a figure. His flaws are relatively minor when considered in the light of his many accomplishments.

Bibliography: Pershing, John J., *My Experiences in the World War,* 2 vols. (Stokes, 1931); Smythe, Donald, *Guerrilla Warrior: The Early Life of John J. Pershing* (Scribner's, 1973);———, *Pershing: General of the Armies* (Univ. of Indiana Press, 1986); Vandiver, Frank E., *Black Jack: The Life and Times of John J. Pershing,* 2 vols. (Texas A&M Press, 1977).

Col. (Ret.) Rod Paschall

PRATT, RICHARD HENRY (1840–1924)

U.S. army officer and educator of American Indians, Pratt was born in Rushford, New York. After service in the Civil War and a brief period of civilian life, Pratt returned to the army in 1867, receiving a commission as a second lieutenant in the 10th Cavalry Regiment, a newly formed black unit with which he fought against Indians through the early 1870s.

In 1875, while escorting Indian prisoners to St. Augustine, Florida, Pratt cultivated an interest in the formal education of native Americans. In 1879, he requested and received from the army the use of Carlisle Barracks, Pennsylvania, to create a nonreservation Indian school, of which he became superintendent. Believing that Indian students would benefit from ''Americanization'' and consequently tribal separation, Pratt developed a multidisciplinary curriculum at the Carlisle Indian School that stressed vocational training. His opposition to official Indian policy ultimately led to his removal from the school and his retirement in 1904. Pratt spent the rest of his life as an advocate for the rights of native Americans.

Bibliography: Utley, Robert M., ed., *Battlefield and Classroom: Four Decades with the American Indian, 1867–1904* (Yale, 1964).

Louise Arnold-Friend

READ, GEORGE WINDLE (1860–1934)

U.S. military leader, Read was born in Indianola, Iowa. After graduating from West Point in 1883, he served with various units on the frontier, in Cuba, and in the Philippines, as well as on the War Department General Staff. He briefly led an infantry brigade and then the 15th Cavalry Division.

For World War I duty, Read, a major general, was given command of the 30th Division in April 1918. When he arrived in France, however, he was chosen by Gen. John J. Pershing to head the II Corps in the British sector. After a period of tutelage under the British, Read's corps entered combat on its own. It performed well in the 1918 Somme Offensive and earned the praise of its British superiors for its spirit and bravery. After the war, Read held a number of important commands until his retirement in 1924.

Richard F. Kehrberg

RED CLOUD (MAKHPÍYA-LÚTA) (1822–1909)

Eminent Oglala Sioux war leader and statesman, Red Cloud was born in Nebraska near the forks of the Platte River. He first emerged as a war leader against the Pawnee, Crow, Ute, and Shoshone. In 1866–68, he led the Oglala in opposing encroachment by U.S. settlers along the Bozeman Trail. Following the massacre of Capt. William J. Fetterman's command in 1866 and the Wagon Box Fight in 1867, Red Cloud's demands were met by federal officials in the Fort Laramie treaties of 1868. These promised the abandonment of U.S. Army forts in Oglala territory, the closing of the Bozeman Trail, and the creation of a Sioux reserve of some 60,000,000 acres surrounding the Black Hills.

Federal efforts to enforce the treaties proved futile in view of the increased non-Indian settlement spurred by the advance of the Union Pacific Railroad up the Platte River and by the discovery of gold in the Black Hills. Nevertheless, Red Cloud did not again take the warpath but sought to preserve the Fort Laramie treaties by negotiation, while more aggressive leaders such as Sitting Bull chose to lead the Sioux in armed resistance.

Red Cloud's people accepted reservation life but insisted on an agency in their traditional territory near Fort Laramie rather than on the Missouri River. Their demands were met, and they were settled on the Red Cloud Agency in northwestern Nebraska in 1873. In the mid-1870s, Red Cloud visited Washington several times as federal officials sought his agreement to giving up the Black Hills reserve. Following disturbances in 1873–74, the army established Fort Robinson near the Red Cloud Agency, and in October 1876, following Custer's massacre at the Little Bighorn, the Oglala were disarmed. Red Cloud, previously honored by federal officials with the status of ''chief of all the Sioux,'' was replaced by his rival Spotted Tail, and the Sioux were forced to cede the Black Hills and other rights granted by the 1868 treaties. In 1878, Red Cloud's people were forcibly removed to the new Pine Ridge Agency on the White River in South Dakota.

Red Cloud continued to oppose the loss of tribal lands and treaty rights but was eclipsed by younger leaders who advocated armed resistance. Although he supported the spread of the Ghost Dance quasi-religion among the Sioux in 1890, Red Cloud decried the agitation for armed conflict that resulted in the Battle of Wounded Knee in December 1890.

Bibliography: Hyde, George E., *Red Cloud's Folk: A History of the Oglala Sioux Indians* (Univ. of Oklahoma Press, 1976); Olson, James C., *Red Cloud and the Sioux Problem* (Univ. of Nebraska Press, 1965); Utley, Robert M., *Frontier Regulars: The United States Army and the Indian, 1866–1890* (Macmillan Co., 1973).

Lt. Col. (Ret.) Charles R. Shrader

REED, WALTER (1851–1902)

U.S. army surgeon, Reed was born in Belroi, Virginia. He entered the University of Virginia at age 16 and two years later received his M.D. The following year, he earned a second M.D. from Bellevue Hospital Medical College in New York. During the next five years, Reed served as an intern at Kings County Hospital in Brooklyn, as an inspector for the boards of health in both Brooklyn and New York City, and as a physician in Charity Hospital at Randall's Island, New York.

Gaining admission to the U.S. Army as an assistant surgeon, Reed was commissioned a 1st lieutenant in the Medical Corps in 1875. He spent the next 15 years at various frontier posts. In 1890, he received a transfer to Baltimore as an examiner of recruits. During this assignment, Reed continued his graduate studies in bacteriology and pathology at nearby Johns Hopkins Hospital. Reassigned to Washington, D.C., in 1893 as curator for the U.S. Army Medical Museum, he also served as professor of bacteriology and clinical microscopy at the newly organized Army Medical School. In addition, Reed chaired the Department of Bacteriology and Pathology at Columbian (now George Washington) University Medical School. In 1898, he chaired a committee investigating the cause and transmission of typhoid fever, a study resulting from the fever's prevalence among overseas U.S. volunteers. The findings, published in 1904 as *Report on the Origin and Spread of Typhoid Fever in U.S. Military Camps during the Spanish War of 1898,* purported typhoid transmission by flies, dust, and personal contact.

Reed's emphasis changed in 1897 in response to Italian scientist Giuseppi Sanarelli's theory that the *Bacillus icteriodes* caused yellow fever. Sanctioned by the army's surgeon general, Reed and Dr. James Carroll conducted laboratory experiments that refuted the Sanarelli theory. Based on this experience, Reed headed a commission of U.S. Army medical officers investigating the outbreak of yellow fever among army personnel in Havana, Cuba. Intrigued by a theory espousing transmission by the *Stegomyia* mosquito, Reed established a field station near Havana. After seven months' experimentation (June 1900–February 1901), Reed's research team compiled conclusive evidence to support that theory. Army medical personnel and sanitary engineers took immediate steps to reduce the population of the *Stegomyia fasciata* (later reclassified as the *Aëdes aegypti*) mosquito. In stark contrast to the 1,400 reported cases of yellow fever in Havana alone in 1900, the disease was eradicated from all of Cuba by 1902.

While his experimental team conducted its work in Cuba, Reed returned to Washington in February 1901 to resume his work at the Army Medical School and at the Columbian University Medical School. The following year, he received honorary degrees from Harvard University and the University of Michigan. Soon after, Reed died of appendicitis. The U.S. Army's Walter Reed Hospital in Washington is named in his honor.

Bibliography: Bean, William B., *Walter Reed: A Biography* (Univ. Press of Virginia, 1982); Truby, Albert E., *Memoir of Walter Reed: The Yellow Fever Episode* (Hoeber, 1943).

Capt. James Sanders Day

RENO, MARCUS ALBERT (1834–1889)

U.S. cavalry officer, Reno was born in Illinois. He graduated from West Point in 1857 and was assigned to the 1st Dragoons. He served on the frontier at Forts Walla Walla, Washington, and The Dalles, Oregon. During the Civil War, Reno served with the Army of the Potomac 1861–65.

Following a tour of duty at Fort Vancouver, Washington, Reno became a major with the 7th Cavalry on Dec. 26, 1868. He was stationed at Fort Hays, Kansas, 1869–71. Following a tour in the East, Reno commanded the escort for the Northern Boundary Survey June–October 1873. In October 1875, he was assigned to Fort Abraham Lincoln in the Dakota Territory. In June 1876, Reno marched with Lt. Col. George Armstrong Custer toward the Little Bighorn River. Reno's role in the Battle of the Little Bighorn is, perhaps, more controversial than that of any other participant. Failing in his attack on the Sioux village, Reno and his men were besieged on what is now known as Reno Hill while Custer's forces were destroyed just a few miles away. Ever since, Reno has been derided for failing to come to Custer's aid. Reno retired from the army in 1880.

M. Guy Bishop

RHODES, CHARLES DUDLEY (1865–1948)

U.S. army officer, Rhodes was born in Delaware, Ohio. After graduating from West Point in 1889, he was commissioned in the cavalry and served on the frontier. His early combat experiences include the Sioux War of 1890–91, the Santiago de Cuba Campaign, the China Relief Expedition, the Philippine Insurrection, and the Moro Expedition.

During World War I, Rhodes commanded at brigade and division levels—as a brigadier and major general, respectively—through the Aisne-Marne, St.-Mihiel, and Meuse-Argonne offensives. His noteworthy postwar assignments include three tours with the General Staff and brigade commands at El Paso, Texas, and in Panama. Rhodes retired from active duty in 1929.

Capt. James Sanders Day

RICKENBACKER, EDWARD (EDDIE) VERNON (1890–1973)

U.S. army aviator, who in World War I shot down more enemy planes than any other American, Rickenbacker was born in Columbus, Ohio. His early fascination with machinery evolved into an auto-racing career that lasted until May 1917, when he enlisted to fight in the war. He went to France as a driver on Gen. John J. Pershing's staff, but with Col. William (''Billy'') Mitchell's aid, he soon transferred to flight school.

Rickenbacker joined the 94th Aero Pursuit Squadron as a captain and assumed command of the unit when its leader was killed in May 1918. After scoring his initial kill on April 29, Rickenbacker earned ace status within one month. He then tallied a rapidly increasing number of enemy planes and observation balloons. Rickenbacker earned the Congressional Medal of Honor for his exploits on Sept. 25, 1918, when he single-handedly attacked seven German planes and downed two of them. In six months of action, Rickenbacker shot down 22 enemy aircraft and 4 observation balloons.

After the war, he was first an automobile industry executive and, from 1935, was associated with Eastern Airlines, of which he became president. In World War II, he performed special assignments for the army air forces, during one of which he crashed and then endured three weeks on a raft in the Pacific Ocean.

Bibliography: Rickenbacker, Edward V., *Rickenbacker: An Autobiography* (Prentice-Hall, 1967).

John F. Wukovits

ROCKENBACH, SAMUEL DICKERSON (1869–1952)

U.S. military leader, Rockenbach was born in Lynchburg, Virginia. After he entered the U.S. Army in 1891, he demonstrated a flair for administration; his early duties were often as regimental adjutant or quartermaster. In early 1917, upon the entry of the United States into World War I, Gen. John J. Pershing chose Rockenbach to organize the initial supply service of the American Expeditionary Force. Later that year, Pershing chose Rockenbach as the commander of the infant Tank Corps.

Rockenbach's duties were largely administrative, but in August 1918, he took command of the American 1st Army's tankers and led them through the St.-Mihiel and Meuse-Argonne offensives. After the war, he headed the army's tank program until promoted to brigadier general in 1924. Thereafter, Rockenbach held a series of field commands until his retirement in 1933.

Bibliography: Wilson, Dale E., *Treat 'Em Rough: The Birth of American Armor, 1917–20* (Presidio Press, 1989).

Richard F. Kehrberg

ROMAN NOSE (1830?–1868)

Cheyenne warrior, nicknamed ''Wokinh'' (literally, ''hook nose'') by U.S. soldiers. Until the Sand Creek Massacre of 1864, he maintained peaceful relations with U.S. settlers. From 1864, frequent skirmishes between Indians and settlers occurred. Plans to build a stretch of the Union Pacific Railroad across Cheyenne hunting grounds in 1866 led to attacks on wagon trains and track-laying gangs. Col. George A. Forsyth was dispatched with a force to police Indian activity in the area. During Sept. 16–25, 1868, Forsyth and 52 men held off an attack by Roman Nose and several hundred Cheyenne warriors at Beecher's Island, Colorado. Roman Nose was killed on September 17.

Russell A. Hart

ROOSEVELT, THEODORE (1858–1919)

Twenty-sixth president of the United States (1901–09), Roosevelt was born in New York City. He graduated from Harvard and at the age of 23 was elected, on the Republican ticket, to the New York State Assembly. Within two years, he was named assembly speaker. Roosevelt's youth, energy, and crusading zeal provided him with national recognition. His fame was increased by his skill and popularity as a writer, whose works included *The Naval War of 1812,* for many years the definitive work on the subject, and a book that influenced Alfred Thayer Mahan.

Early Career. Roosevelt lost the New York City mayoral election in 1886, coming in third, but in 1889 was appointed to the U.S. Civil Service Commission by Pres. Benjamin Harrison. In 1895, he became president of the New York City Board of Police Commissioners. To every job, he brought his plans for progressive reform and his considerable personal energy to bear. In 1897, newly elected Pres. William McKinley chose Roosevelt to be the assistant secretary of the navy. Roosevelt proved to be more energetic than the secretary, John D. Long, and established himself as one of the administration's most ardent expansionists. As relations with Spain worsened, Roosevelt repeatedly urged war. While acting secretary in Long's absence, Roosevelt helped naval officer and friend George Dewey receive command of the important Asiatic Station. While again acting secretary in February 1898, Roosevelt essentially placed the entire U.S. Navy in a state of alert and ordered Dewey to take offensive actions in case of war. As assistant secretary, Roosevelt was competent but impulsive and headstrong.

Spanish-American War. After war with Spain had been declared, Roosevelt sought to take a more direct part in the conflict. Offered command of a regiment of volunteer cavalry by Sec. of War Russell Alger, Roosevelt declined in favor of his friend Leonard Wood and became second in command as a lieutenant colonel. This unit, the 1st U.S Volunteer Cavalry, was better known as the "Rough Riders."

Roosevelt accompanied his Rough Riders, a mixed group of Westerners and Ivy Leaguers, to Tampa, Florida, where he and Wood worked assiduously, eventually commandeering a transport, to insure they would be included on the imminent expedition to Cuba. The Rough Riders accompanied the U.S. V Corps on its campaign to capture Santiago de Cuba, where the Spanish fleet was bottled up. When Wood received a promotion in Cuba, due to the illness of superiors, Roosevelt assumed command of the regiment and distinguished himself in the battles for the Spanish defensive line east of the city of Santiago, leading a charge to capture the Spanish outpost on Kettle Hill and taking part in the capture of San Juan Hill. Roosevelt was the senior officer on the crest line of the latter hill when it was captured. His "charge up San Juan Hill" won him the status of national hero.

Although a capable officer, Roosevelt was little inclined to respect established authority and was not hesitant about using his fame and influence to his own ends. After the capture of Santiago, he urged that the troops be removed from the area because of rising sickness, and he publicly criticized the War Department for mismanagement of supplies, medical care, and food. Nevertheless, his status influenced McKinley to choose him to be the Republican vice-presidential candidate in the election of 1900.

Presidency. Upon McKinley's assassination in 1901, Roosevelt, at age 42, became the youngest U.S. president. As president, Roosevelt did not hesitate to use military force or the threat of force to further the ends of the United States, as his deployment of naval squadrons to block Columbian military intervention in Panama demonstrated.

Roosevelt's desire to have the United States recognized as a world power led him to sponsor a large increase in the size and ability of the military establishment. His close friend and secretary of war, Elihu Root, lobbied successfully for several army reforms, including the creation of a general staff. Roosevelt and Root also spurred reform of the National Guard, which resulted in the Dick Act of 1903, legislation that increased federal control of state militias. The Militia Act of 1908 further strengthened the National Guard.

For the navy, Roosevelt launched a huge expansion program of battleships, calling for a fleet second only to Britain's. His administration added 16 battleships to the "Great White Fleet," which he sent in 1907 on a triumphant world-circling cruise, announcing the arrival of the United States as a major power. However, despite the large construction program, Roosevelt remained indifferent to organizational reforms of the navy, which would have to wait for subsequent administrations.

Later Years. After leaving office in 1909, Roosevelt still remained active and in the public eye, running for president in 1912 on the Progressive "Bull Moose" ticket and arguing for U.S. involvement in World War I. When war for the United States was declared in 1917, he sought but was denied a military command.

Bibliography: Beale, Howard K., *Theodore Roosevelt and the Rise of America to World Power* (Johns Hopkins Press, 1956); Morris, Edmund, *The Rise of Theodore Roosevelt* (Coward, McCann, & Geoghegan, 1979); Oyos, Matthew M., *The Naval Reform Movement, 1900–16* (unpubl. thesis, Univ. of Nebraska, 1986); Trask, David F., *The War With Spain in 1898* (Macmillan Co., 1981).

Mark Pitcavage

ROOT, ELIHU (1845–1937)

U.S. secretary of war, Root was born in Clinton, New York, at Hamilton College, where his father and older brother taught for many years. After graduating from Hamilton in 1864, he joined a militia company and volunteered for federal service in the Civil War but was rejected because of his frail physique.

Early Career. In lieu of a military career, Root attended New York University Law School (1865–67) and established a New York City law practice that brought him wealth as an attorney for railroads and other major businesses. Pres. Chester A. Arthur appointed him U.S. attorney for southern New York (1883–85), where Root became known for meticulousness in solving and proving complex business frauds. After successfully defending Theodore Roosevelt in an embarrassing 1898 tax case, Root won the gratitude of the rising politician.

Appointed Secretary of War. In July 1899, Root was surprised when Pres. William McKinley nominated him as secretary of war. He accepted only when told that McKinley wanted a legal, rather than a military, expert to direct the military governments of the Philippines, Cuba, and Puerto Rico. Root did well but soon realized that the U.S. Army required major changes. The Spanish-American War of 1898 had shown that existing specialized War Department bureaus were inadequate to plan and conduct modern warfare.

Root introduced a number of major reforms to prepare the army for the future. The concepts behind these changes often came from professional soldiers, most notably the scholarly assistant adjutant general, Maj. William H. Carter.

Carter introduced Root to the philosophy of Emory Upton, who had opposed any reliance on militia or reservists except as individual replacements under regular army command. Root realized that such notions stood no chance with the powerful National Guard lobby in Congress, then led by Rep. Charles W. Dick, who was both head of the National Guard Association and an influential House committee chairman. Working with Dick, Root achieved the

Militia Act of 1903—better known as the Dick Act—the first overhaul of the militia since 1792. This act recognized the National Guard as separate from the general pool of public manpower and provided for the federal standards of organization, training, and equipment. This included federal outlays for instructors/inspectors as well as modern weapons, and it set the stage for the creation of the dual (state-federal) National Guard in 1916.

Root lobbied for a true general staff to give the country the central planning body it had lacked in 1898. Overcoming resistance to the idea, he achieved a modest general staff in 1903. In the process, the position of commanding general was abolished, in favor of a chief of staff subordinate to the secretary of war. Although this General Staff did not have clear authority over the older bureaus within the War Department, it became the nucleus for the planning for both world wars.

To support the General Staff, the National Guard, and the expanded standing army, Root began a hierarchy of military schools that today survives in its outlines. In the late 1800s, a disjointed series of officer-training facilities had existed, but these schools had virtually closed during the Spanish-American War of 1898. When Carter offered Root a revival plan, the secretary likened Fort Leavenworth to Hamilton College as a means to provide a liberal military education for selected junior officers.

As eventually established, Root's system included a network of schools, many of them at Leavenworth, Kansas, for medicine, coast artillery, and engineering, as well as the School of the Line for combat arms officers. Only honor graduates of these schools, equivalent to modern officer advanced courses, would be accepted for a second year of instruction in the Staff School (later the Command and General Staff College). In turn, only honor graduates of the Staff School were theoretically eligible to attend the War College that Root established at what is now Fort McNair in Washington. In early practice, of course, the immediate need to fill General Staff positions meant that many officers were appointed with few formal educational qualifications. Eventually, however, Root's schools produced educated commanders and General Staff officers.

Later Career. Root resigned as secretary of war in 1904 but returned to Washington in 1905 to accept President Roosevelt's appointment as secretary of state (1905–09). He also served as U.S. senator from New York (1909–15) and contributed to the National Defense Act of 1916 that fully implemented many of his previous ideas. In 1912, he received the Nobel Peace Prize for his dedication to the ideals of peaceful arbitration.

Root opposed the prospect of U.S. involvement in World War I and became a key Republican advocate of the League of Nations. He stayed committed to international justice throughout and after the war, and in 1921 was a U.S. delegate to the International Conference on the Limitations of Armaments (Washington, 1921–22).

Bibliography: Hill, Jim Dan, *The Minute Man in Peace and War: A History of the National Guard* (Stackpole Books, 1964); Jessup, Philip C., *Elihu Root,* 2 vols. (Dodd, Mead, 1938); Leopold, Richard W., *Elihu Root and the Conservative Tradition* (Little, Brown, 1954).

Jonathan M. House

SAMPSON, WILLIAM THOMAS (1840–1902)

U.S. naval officer, Sampson was born in Palmyra, New York. He graduated from Annapolis, first in his class, in 1861. After brief tours in the Washington navy yard and on board the *Pocahontas* and *Potomac,* he spent almost two years teaching at the Naval Academy before becoming executive officer on the Union monitor *Patapsco* during the Civil War. His calm leadership when the *Patapsco* was sunk by a Confederate mine helped bring his promotion to lieutenant commander in 1866 even though the navy was retrenching after the war.

Between 1867 and 1878, Sampson served two tours as an academic department head at the Naval Academy and one in the European Squadron. The next 20 years were spent at sea commanding ships and at the Naval Observatory, the Naval Torpedo Station (during which time he helped establish the Naval War College), the Naval Gun Foundry, the Naval Academy (superintendent, 1886–90), and the Bureau of Ordnance (chief, 1893–97).

The Spanish-American War. Sampson's technical expertise led to his appointment as head of the Board of Inquiry that investigated the sinking of the *Maine* in February–March 1898. Transferred to command of the North Atlantic Squadron at the outbreak of the Spanish-American War, Sampson was given direction of all naval forces in the Caribbean. Winfield Scott Schley, although two numbers higher than Sampson on the navy's seniority list, was ordered to serve under him. After cruising to Puerto Rico in an attempt to intercept the Spanish fleet commanded by Adm. Pascual Cervera, Sampson returned to Key West to refuel and then established a blockade of Cuba's northern coast. Learning that Cervera's fleet was at Santiago, he ordered Schley to blockade the port and returned to Key West to convoy army transports to the area.

When Sampson arrived on Cuba's south coast on June 1, he took personal command of the blockade that Schley had been slow to implement. By placing his ships in a semicircle with bows aimed at the harbor and by training searchlights on its mouth at night, Sampson kept his ships ready. On June 21, his squadron was renamed the North Atlantic Fleet and Schley's Flying Squadron was incorporated into it.

Disagreement soon arose between Sampson and Maj. Gen. William Shafter, commander of U.S. land forces around Santiago. Sampson was reluctant to expose his ships to the mines and batteries guarding the entrance to Santiago harbor and wanted the army to destroy the batteries by attacking them from the land. Shafter rejected this plan, proposing instead that Sampson sail into the harbor and destroy the Spanish squadron to prevent it from firing on his troops. Since neither Shafter nor Sampson was in overall command, a deadlock ensued, although the two did cooperate in laying siege to the Spanish. U.S. Marines seized Guantanamo to serve as a coaling station for the navy, which established embarkation and supply bases for the army at Daiquiri and Siboney.

By late June, the Spanish were cut off from contact with the outside. On July 2, Shafter and Sampson agreed to meet and try to coordinate the final attack on Santiago. Just before 9:00 A.M. the next day, Sampson's flagship, the *New York,* headed east toward Shafter's headquarters. A half hour later, the Spanish fleet sortied. Sampson immediately ordered the *New York* to retrace its route at top speed. From its bridge, he watched his captains execute the plan of battle that he had developed the previous month. As the ships moved to "close in towards [the] harbor entrance," as he had ordered, Schley's ship, the *Brooklyn,* nearly rammed the *Texas* as the two attempted to prevent the escape of the Spanish. Quickly recovering, the U.S. ships set off in pursuit of the Spanish as they fled westward along the coast. A running fight ensued in which all six Spanish ships were either sunk or forced to run aground. In contrast to U.S. losses of one sailor killed and one wounded, the Spanish suffered 474 killed or wounded and 1,750 taken prisoner.

For Sampson the victory was bittersweet because the *New York* had not been able to reach the battle in time to contribute to the victory. Many observers believed that Schley, the commander in the midst of the action, earned the credit of victory. Others considered Sampson more deserving of the credit, pointing out that he authored the plans for blockading the Spanish and countering their breakout; they argued that the captains of the U.S. ships executed Sampson's plans without further instructions from Schley. The controversy would hang like a cloud over Sampson for the rest of his life and divide the navy for a quarter of a century.

The U.S. Navy's defeat of the Spanish did not resolve its deadlock with the U.S. Army, whose leaders continued to insist that Sampson attack the land fortifications around Santiago. Even pressure from Washington failed to break the impasse before the Spanish capitulated on July 17, bringing operations in Cuba to an end. Sampson continued in command of the North Atlantic Station until October 1899, when the deterioration of his health led the navy to transfer him to the largely ceremonial command of Boston's navy yard and naval station.

Bibliography: Dawson, Joseph G., "William T. Sampson: Progressive Technologist as Naval Commander," *Admirals of the New Steel Navy,* ed. by James C. Bradford (Naval Inst. Press, 1990); Goode, A. M., *With Sampson through the War* (Doubleday, 1899); Trask, David F., *The War With Spain in 1898* (Macmillan Co., 1981); West, Richard S., *Admirals of the American Empire* (Bobbs-Merrill, 1948).

James C. Bradford

SCHLEY, WINFIELD SCOTT (1839–1911)

U.S. naval officer, Schley was born in Frederick County, Maryland. He graduated from Annapolis in 1860 and during the Civil War served the Union navy in blockade operations off Charleston, South Carolina, and then in the Gulf of Mexico under David Farragut. As acting commander of the *Monongahela,* his aggressive leadership in attacking Confederate shore batteries at Port Hudson during the Vicksburg Campaign earned him Farragut's off-the-record praise. Schley later saw combat while serving on the sloop *Richmond* and in 1863 was named executive officer of the *Wateree,* an experimental ship not assigned to combat.

Promoted to lieutenant commander in 1866, Schley taught at the Naval Academy for several years and then saw duty in the Asiatic Squadron, participating in an 1871 landing operation to punish Korea for a supposed insult to the American flag. After more service at sea and another tour at the Naval Academy, Schley was appointed to the Lighthouse Board. His responsibility was to ascertain that all lighthouses, ships' lights, and buoys along the coasts of Massachusetts and Rhode Island were in proper working order. In 1884, Schley, a superb leader of men, gained national attention when he commanded a three-ship expedition that rescued survivors of a polar exploration party marooned in a remote northern area of Greenland. He subsequently became chief of the Bureau of Equipment and Recruiting with subsequent additional duty as chief of the Bureau of Provisions and Clothing. In this capacity, he gave special attention to securing better clothing and rations for enlisted personnel.

As a captain, Schley received command of the new cruiser *Baltimore* in 1889. Two years later, while in Chilean waters during a time of tension in that nation, Schley authorized a liberty party to go ashore in Valparaiso and found himself again in the news when members of the shore party were attacked. An inquiry supported Schley's account of the incident, and Chile made suitable apologies and paid an indemnity.

After several years of shore duty, Schley received command of the cruiser *New York* in 1895. With the outbreak of war with Spain in 1898, Schley, just promoted to commodore, was named to command the Flying Squadron, a force formed to reassure business and political leaders in the Northeast that their cities were being safeguarded from Spanish naval bombardment. Once it was ascertained that the Spanish fleet was heading toward Cuba, Schley, assigned to the *Brooklyn,* took his force south to establish a blockade of Santiago. There he came under the command of Rear Adm. William Sampson of the North Atlantic Squadron.

While Sampson's flagship was nearly out of sight taking him to a conference with U.S. Army leaders, the Spanish force sortied and met overwhelming defeat in the ensuing engagement. The press hailed Schley as the victor, but ill feelings resulted between Schley and Sampson. Partisans of the two officers engaged in public debate over credit for the victory and whether Schley had acted properly during and prior to the battle. In 1901, a court of inquiry (convened at Schley's request) criticized as inappropriate some of the decisions Schley had made. Schley also failed to gain the unequivocal recognition he sought for the victory at Santiago. The president of the navy's General Board, George Dewey, filed a minority report supporting Schley. Younger naval officers long remembered the dispute as unfortunate. Schley, retired in 1901, prepared to continue the debate over Santiago.

Bibliography: Goldberg, Joyce, *The Baltimore Affair* (Univ. of Nebraska Press, 1986); Langley, Harold D., "Winfield Scott Schley: The Confident Commander," *Admirals of the New Steel Navy,* ed. by James C. Bradford (Naval Inst. Press, 1990); Schley, Winfield Scott, *Forty-five Years Under the Flag* (Appleton, 1904); Schley, Winfield Scott, and J. R. Soley, *The Rescue of Greely* (Scribner's, 1885); West, Richard S., Jr., *Admirals of the American Empire* (Bobbs-Merrill, 1948).

Lloyd J. Graybar

SCHOFIELD, JOHN MCALLISTER (1831–1906)

U.S. army officer, Schofield was born in Gerry, New York. He graduated from West Point in 1853 and gained prominence in the Civil War as the commander of several military departments and armies in both the trans-Mississippi and western theaters. He was promoted to brigadier general in the regular army for his successes at the battles of Franklin and Nashville. At the end of the war, he was sent to France to negotiate for the withdrawal of the French from Mexico.

Schofield held a number of important postwar commands, including a nine-month sojourn (1868–69) as secretary of war under Pres. Andrew Johnson. In 1872, he served on a special mission to the Hawaiian Islands to judge their suitability for U.S. military strategy. At this time, he recommended that Pearl Harbor be acquired as a navy base.

From 1876 to 1881, Schofield served as superintendent of West Point, where he headed the board that exonerated Fitz-John Porter, the Civil War commander who had been dismissed for alleged disloyalty and misconduct at the Second Battle of Bull Run. In 1888, Schofield became commanding general of the U.S. Army, from which he retired in September 1895 with the rank of lieutenant general.

Ted Alexander

SCHWAN, THEODORE (1841–1926)

U.S. army officer, born in Germany. He enlisted in the 10th U.S. Infantry in June 1857 and was commissioned a second lieutenant in the regiment in October 1863. Schwan was cited for bravery and brevetted captain for his role in the Civil War action at Poplar Springs Church, Virginia, Sept. 30–Oct. 2, 1864. He was promoted to major in the Adjutant General's Department in July 1886.

During the Spanish-American War, in May 1898, Schwan was appointed brigadier general of volunteers and commanded the combined force of infantry, cavalry, and artillery that landed at Ponce, Puerto Rico, on July 31. With this column, he advanced 92 miles, fought two skirmishes, and captured nine towns, the most significant advance in this brief campaign. After the war, he returned to the Adjutant General's Department, where he was instrumental in helping to establish the army's General Staff. He served there until his retirement in 1901.

Bibliography: Cosmas, Graham A., *An Army for Empire: The United States Army in the Spanish-American War* (Univ. of Missouri Press, 1971).

John A. Hixson

SCOTT, HUGH LENOX (1853–1934)

U.S. army officer, Scott was born in Danville, Kentucky. He graduated from West Point in 1876 and, while serving on the frontier 1876–98, became an authority on Indian life and on the sign language of the Plains tribes. His expertise assisted in quelling the Ghost Dance disturbances in Oklahoma and in helping the Apache following their relocation to Fort Sill.

Scott spent the Spanish-American War in a southern training camp but served in the military occupation of Cuba. Following this, he was appointed military governor of the Sulu Archipelago in the Philippines. Here, he again demonstrated administrative and leadership ability by helping to pacify the hostile Sulu Moros through a policy of moral suasion backed by military force.

A tour as superintendent of West Point and other normal military postings followed his colonial assignments. During this time, Scott became interested in the problem of modernizing the U.S. Army, which essentially had become an Indian-fighting and colonial police force.

Gen. Hugh L. Scott, an able administrator who served as a military governor in the Philippines and as superintendent of West Point, acquired an expert knowledge of Indian sign language while serving on frontier duty. (U.S. Military Academy)

In 1912, Scott served as a troop commander and diplomatic envoy in the Mexican border area. In 1914, he became chief of staff of the army. During 1915–16, he assisted in resolving border crises, in organizing Gen. John J. Pershing's Punitive Expedition into Mexico, and in mobilizing and moving the National Guard to the border. As a result of this border experience, Scott worked diligently to modernize the army.

Mandatorily retired in 1917, Scott remained active. He served on the Root Mission to Russia in 1917 and commanded training units in the United States. He also retained his interest and activity in Indian affairs.

Bibliography: Clendenen, Clarence C., *Blood on the Border* (Cornell Univ. Press, 1969); Scott, Hugh L., *Some Memories of a Soldier* (Appleton-Century, 1928); Vandiver, Frank E., *Black Jack: The Life and Times of John J. Pershing* (Texas A&M Press, 1977).

John A. Hixson

SEWARD, WILLIAM HENRY (1801–1872)

U.S. statesman, Seward was born in Florida, New York. He graduated from Union College in 1820 and was admitted to the state bar two years later. An ardent Whig, he soon became active in state politics, serving as state legislator and governor. After he served in the U.S. Senate 1849–61, Abraham Lincoln appointed him secretary of state (1861–69).

Seward, an outspoken abolitionist, adroitly oversaw the Civil War State Department, occasionally stepping outside diplomacy to "meddle" in military affairs. His greatest wartime success was preventing the European powers from entering the conflict.

Seward is best remembered for negotiating the 1867 purchase of Alaska from Russia, an action so unpopular at the time as to evoke the label "Seward's Folly." He also sought, with mixed results, annexation of other territories, including various Caribbean islands.

Seward's political career was stunted by his postwar conciliatory attitude toward the South. His health had been seriously handicapped by an 1865 carriage accident and the brutal attack he suffered at the hands of the Lincoln assassination ring.

Bibliography: Paolino, Ernest M., *The Foundations of American Empire: William Henry Seward and U.S. Foreign Policy* (Cornell Univ. Press, 1973).

Louise Arnold-Friend

William Henry Seward, secretary of state under Presidents Abraham Lincoln and Andrew Johnson, is most noted for the purchase of Alaska from Russia in 1867; most of his contemporaries considered the purchase a foolish move. (Library of Congress)

SHAFTER, WILLIAM RUFUS (1835–1906)

U.S. army officer, Shafter was born in Kalamazoo County, Michigan. A decorated officer during the Civil War, he spent the next 30 years fighting Indians, breaking strikes, and commanding garrisons, reaching the rank of brigadier general in 1897. He achieved fame and notoriety in the Spanish-American War (1898), when he was given command of a expeditionary force to Cuba. Shafter proceeded to Tampa, Florida, to organize the recruits there into an army. He was ordered to capture Santiago when the Spanish fleet was discovered there. His command landed at Daiquiri and captured the city quickly. Because of his ill health, immense weight, and loose control, however, Shafter's role was questionable. He was criticized at the time for the toll taken on his troops by poor logistics and disease. He retired in 1899.

Mark Pitcavage

SHANKS, DAVID CARY (1861–1940)

U.S. army officer, Shanks was born in Salem, Virginia. After graduating from West Point in 1884, he served in infantry units in the West and as an instructor at Virginia Polytechnic Institute. He saw duty in the Philippines in four separate tours between 1899 and 1917, serving in two infantry regiments, as civil governor of Cavite Province, and as inspector for the army in the Philippines.

Shanks, promoted to brigadier general in 1917, assumed command of the Port of Embarkation, Hoboken, New Jersey, during World War I. There, he oversaw the movement of 1,600,000 U.S. soldiers to Europe. Shanks's service culminated with duty as the commander of the 4th Corps Area in Atlanta. He retired as a major general from that position in 1925.

Col. Thomas W. Sweeney

SHARPE, HENRY GRANVILLE (1858–1947)

U.S. army officer and quartermaster general, Sharpe was born in Kingston, New York. He graduated from West Point in 1880. In 1905, he was appointed commissary general of subsistence and worked actively to improve army rations. Appointed quartermaster general in September 1916, Sharpe struggled against political indifference and the fledgling General Staff to prepare the army's supply service, but the massive World War I mobilization of 1917–18 soon outstripped his best efforts to provide adequate support. He was replaced as quartermaster general and retired in 1920.

An innovative thinker, Sharpe wrote several important works on the supply of modern armies. He is representative of both the powerful old bureau chiefs and the progressive young officers of the early 20th century.

Lt. Col. (Ret.) Charles R. Shrader

Philip H. Sheridan, a Union Civil War hero, later contributed greatly to the defeat of the Indians in the West and their removal to reservations. (U.S. Army Military History Institute)

SHERIDAN, PHILIP HENRY (1831–1888)

U.S. army commander, Sheridan was born in Albany, New York. He graduated from West Point in 1853 and went on to become one of the Civil War's most illustrious generals, noted for his grasp of cavalry tactics and strategy. At the conclusion of the Civil War, Major General Sheridan was in command of the 5th Military District (Texas and Louisiana). On Feb. 29, 1868, he took over the Department of the Missouri, headquartered at Fort Leavenworth, Kansas. This command placed Sheridan at the forefront of the Plains Indians wars. Indian hostility and turbulence mounted as the U.S. population pressed the frontier ever westward. Conflict between the two was inevitable, and it became Sheridan's duty to oversee the clash of the two cultures.

In August 1868, Sheridan ordered Col. George A. Forsyth into the field to locate and fight any belligerent Indians. Forsyth found the Indians and engaged them with disastrous results at Beecher Island. After this defeat, Sheridan organized and launched an Indian campaign on the Southern Plains. The major result of the Southern Plains War (1868–69) was Col. George A. Custer's attack on Black Kettle's peaceful Cheyenne camp on the Washita River (November 1868). Sheridan was delighted by Custer's preliminary success and assured Gen. William T. Sherman, commanding the Division of the Missouri, that there soon would be "no more Indian troubles" in his department.

In March 1869, Sheridan was ordered to report to Fort Hays, Kansas, where he learned that newly elected Pres. Ulysses S. Grant had named him lieutenant general and

After the Civil War, Gen. William Tecumseh Sherman served as Commanding General of the U.S. Army (1869–83), during which time he worked to expand educational opportunities for officers and to advance military professionalism. (U.S. Army)

that he was now to command the Division of Missouri succeeding Sherman, who was to become commander in chief of the army (Grant's former position). Sheridan's promotion came as a surprise to many. Grant had said nothing concerning his intentions until the day of his inauguration. In many people's minds, both Gens. Henry Halleck and George G. Meade were considered more likely candidates.

Sheridan's new command covered more than 1,000,000 square miles and was considered home by most of the still-hostile Indian population in the United States. His new headquarters were in Chicago, and from there Sheridan administered his military domain until 1883. While this location gave a much wider scope to his operations, it severely limited Sheridan's opportunity to take the field in person. Yet, in this new office, as in his former, he had a profound influence on military, Indian, and civil developments over a vast western frontier.

Sheridan took an active role in formulating Indian policy; made decisions regarding the establishment, construction, and maintenance of forts within the division; and promoted railroad construction in the West. He also took an interest in fostering reform and in putting an end to wasteful, pork-barrel spending by the military and at Indian agencies.

Militarily, Sheridan directed the Red River War (1874–75) against recalcitrant Commanche, Kiowa, and Cheyenne in the Indian Territory (Oklahoma) and east Texas. In this instance, he left his Chicago headquarters to take up residence at Fort Sill in order to supervise operations more closely. His success here finally brought relative peace to the Southern Plains.

Sheridan also did much of the planning for the Sioux War of 1876. The most significant single action of this campaign was the Custer fight on Montana's Little Bighorn River. Sheridan also oversaw the closing phases of the attempt to block the Nez Percé flight toward Canada. The importance of his role in bringing eventual peace to the Plains is problematical; any dedicated military officer might have done as well. But he was the one with overall direction during a major part of the Indian wars, and his contribution was great.

Bibliography: Hutton, Paul Andrew, *Phil Sheridan and His Army* (Univ. of Nebraska Press, 1985); Rister, Carl Coke, *Border Command: General Phil Sheridan in the West* (Univ. of Oklahoma Press, 1944); Utley, Robert M., *Frontier Regulars: The United States Army and the Indian, 1866–1891* (Univ. of Nebraska Press, 1973).

M. Guy Bishop

SHERMAN, WILLIAM TECUMSEH (1820–1891)

U.S. army commander, Sherman was born in Lancaster, Ohio. He graduated from West Point in 1840 and became one of the most celebrated Union generals of the Civil War. His 1864 "March through Georgia," which included the burning of Atlanta, made him a hero in the North and a reviled figure in the South. His postwar achievements (from 1865 until his death) reveal accomplishments that easily rival his brilliant war record. Immediately after the collapse of the Confederacy, Sherman devoted considerable effort in furthering the fortunes of his wartime superior and comrade, Ulysses S. Grant. As the commander of one of the five territorial divisions, Sherman became involved in keeping order, managing Indian affairs, and furthering the growing U.S. transportation system. After Grant's inauguration as president in 1869, Sherman became the Commanding General of the Army, having to endure a succession of secretaries of war, suffering through unending bureaucratic battles and struggling with the unwieldy U.S. military command system. Although the legal power and authority of his office was limited, Sherman quietly worked behind the scenes, laying the foundations for a competent, apolitical professional officer corps. In an era known for greed and avarice, he set a badly needed example for selfless service and established standards that U.S. military leaders would need for the coming century.

Postwar Service. After the Civil War's close, Sherman, a lieutenant general, found himself alternating his attention between keeping order in a large part of the American West and tending to distasteful political chores involving rivalries among Washington's bickering politicians. With his headquarters and family in St. Louis, Missouri, the general put his rapidly diminishing troop units to work dealing with the troublesome Sioux, Arapaho, Kiowa, and Cheyenne tribes as well as marauders and bandits who were robbing and committing outrages on the newly freed blacks in and around Missouri. Sherman became interested in the transcontinental rail network then in construction and used his forces to assist its completion. At his suggestion, military district boundaries were redrawn so as to secure better the rapidly extending rail link. Called back to Washington at Pres. Andrew Johnson's request in late 1866, the general discovered the commander in chief wanted him to take over command of the U.S. Army while General Grant was dispatched to Mexico. However, Sherman saw through the announced purpose and came to believe Johnson just wanted the popular Grant out of Washington for an extended period. More important, Sherman found his longtime friend was intent on disobeying a lawful order of the president of the United States.

Sherman solved the problem, albeit with considerable sacrifice. The ostensible purpose of the mission to Mexico was to accompany a U.S. envoy and demonstrate U.S. support for a supposedly indigenous republican government standing in opposition to the bogus regime of Emperor Maximilian. In a typically straightforward way, Sherman told the president that Grant would not go, but that he, Sherman, was ready, willing, and able to take on the task. Seeing his plot foiled and evidently unwilling to risk public censure by chastising Grant, Johnson sent Sherman, diplomat in tow, toward Mexico. Grant's dilemma was solved. Despite extended travels, Sherman never did locate the "legitimate" Mexican government. He then returned home, but once again found himself embedded in Washington's political storms.

In early 1868, one of the great American political crises began to unfold and Grant was once more in the middle of the dispute. Congress had passed a law denying the president the right to dismiss a congressionally confirmed official. Johnson met this challenge to his office head-on, fired his secretary of war, Edwin M. Stanton, and appointed Grant to take over the vacated position. Grant balked. He pointed out to the president the law imposed a fine of $10,000 and five years' imprisonment for the transgressor. Sherman rushed to the aid of his friend, trying to find a substitute secretary of war, one the U.S. Senate might approve. Grant was taken off the hook, largely because Johnson's act constituted one of the articles of impeachment preferred against him by Congress. The American people, wearied of the destructive behavior of their politicians, elected Grant—still more a military hero than a political figure—to the presidency in November 1868.

Commanding General. That Grant would appoint Sherman as his successor came as no surprise, but Grant's attitude toward his old position, Commanding General of the Army, greatly disappointed Sherman. As soldiers, both had agreed that the army's high-level structure had to be reorganized. Their view had been that while the secretary of war should handle the army's legal and budgetary matters, the commanding general should have full authority over the officers, bureaus, and territorial divisions. However, as president, Grant was persuaded by a deputation of politicians that various laws precluded much of a change in the top structure of the army. There was too much political patronage at stake to turn over so much power to a soldier, particularly one like Sherman, an officer with a well-deserved reputation for honesty and efficiency. Sherman, therefore, grudgingly submitted to the authority of a number of secretaries of war until his retirement in 1883.

Eventually moving his office from Washington to St. Louis, Sherman, now a full general, began to transform the officer corps into a more professional cadre. Starting with the artillery school at Fortress Monroe, he nurtured the institution, ensuring that it was adequately staffed and supported. He then turned his attention to the Essayons Club in New York, a fledgling association of army engineer officers devoted to furthering their profession. Sherman brought the club into the army's official structure, creating the Engineering School of Application. Next, in 1881, came the School of Application for Infantry and Cavalry at Fort Leavenworth, Kansas. Thus, in 10 years, Sherman had created a rather complete system of postgraduate education for the U.S. Army officer corps.

At the same time, Sherman looked abroad to learn from the mistakes of others and studied the experiences of the Civil War to advance military professionalism in the United States. Sending one of his protégés, Emory Upton, on a worldwide trip, the commanding general launched a systematic study of several foreign armies, a study that resulted in the publication of Upton's *The Armies of Asia and Europe* (1878). Sherman traveled abroad also, visiting old battlefields and broadening his own knowledge of the profession of arms. During his tenure, the U.S. Army began a decided shift from French to German military practices, a shift mainly influenced by the quick and decisive outcome of the Franco-Prussian War. When he wrote his memoirs of the Civil War, Sherman devoted a thoughtful section to lessons of the war, a section aimed clearly at future practices and coming wars.

Despite a number of opportunities, Sherman steadfastly resisted efforts by others to get him into politics. However, upon his retirement from the army in 1884, Sherman was again approached by campaign strategists. A faction of the Republican party made a strong effort to draft Sherman as its presidential candidate. The general turned several appeals away, and finally, on June 5, 1884, when another urgent request to submit his name in nomination came, Sherman sat down and wrote out his now famous reply: "I will not accept if nominated, and will not serve if elected." One of his sons later stated his father had been tempted somewhat to run for the presidency, explaining that his father was perhaps most enticed by the prospect of being empowered to appoint members of the U.S. Supreme Court. Sherman was evidently concerned that the costly fruits of the Civil War might be lost in the courts unless the right choices were made by the country's highest-ranking justices.

The great legacy of Sherman was the exemplary standard he set for his successors. After the 1880s, a successful army officer had to be professionally competent, apolitical, and the soul of integrity. Although Sherman accepted a house in Washington, D.C., as a postwar gift, he constantly complained he could not afford to heat or maintain it. Eventually, he had to remodel the house, dividing it so that he could take in a tenant. Even though he aided the cause of railroad companies involved in the transcontinental link, there is no proof he ever profited from efforts on their behalf. In an age of rapaciousness, Sherman was widely respected as a man of honesty.

Bibliography: Liddell Hart, B. H., *Sherman: Soldier, Realist, American* (Dodd, Mead, 1929); Merrill, James M., *William Tecumseh Sherman* (Rand McNally, 1971); Sherman, William T., *Memoirs of Gen. W. T. Sherman,* 2 vols. (Charles Webster & Co., 1891).

Col. (Ret.) Rod Paschall

SIBERT, WILLIAM LUTHER (1860–1935)

U.S. army engineering officer, Sibert was born in Gadsden, Alabama. He joined the engineering corps after graduating from West Point in 1884 and first gained recognition by improving navigation in the Ohio, Allegheny, and Monongahela rivers. In 1908, he was given command of excavating and constructing the Panama Canal north of Gatun Lake, a task he admirably completed.

During World War I, Major General Sibert was sent to France in 1917 as commander of the 1st Infantry Division. The next year, he returned to the United States to organize the Chemical Warfare Service. His successful work in this area led to effective contributions by chemical weapons units along the Western Front and earned Sibert a Distinguished Service Medal. He retired from the army in 1920.

Bibliography: McCullough, David G., *Path Between the Seas* (Simon & Schuster, 1977); Society of the First Division, *History of the First Division During the War, 1917–1919* (John C. Winston, 1922).

Capt. Ralph P. Millsap, Jr.

SIEBER, ALBERT (1844–1907)

U.S. military scout, Sieber was born in Germany and emigrated to the United States as a boy. In 1862, he enlisted in the 1st Minnesota Infantry. He saw Civil War action at Antietam, Fredericksburg, and Gettysburg, where he was badly wounded. After the war, he went to California and, later, Nevada.

In 1872, Sieber signed on with Gen. George Crook as a scout for the impending campaign against hostile Apache and Yavapai Indians. Sieber played an important role in the September 25 Muchas Cañones fight on the Santa Maria River. He led more than 80 Hualapais scouts and was commended by Crook. On July 17, 1882, near Arizona's Fort Apache, Sieber played a crucial role in saving Capt. Adna R. Chaffee and his troops from an Apache ambush. When Crook organized his great Sierra Madre Expedition of 1883 against the Apache, he selected Sieber as his chief of scouts, Sieber's last significant military action. Sieber was killed in a construction accident at Roosevelt Dam, Arizona.

M. Guy Bishop

SIGSBEE, CHARLES DWIGHT (1845–1923)

U.S. naval officer, Sigsbee was born in Albany, New York. He served on the Union blockade during the Civil War, taking part in attacks on Mobile and Fort Fisher. In command of the U.S. Coast Survey steamer *Blake* (1875–78), he mapped the bed of the Gulf of Mexico and invented several devices for taking soundings and collecting animal and water specimens. He was promoted to captain in 1897 and commanded the *Maine* at the time of its destruction in Havana harbor (Feb. 15, 1898). Transferred to command of the *St. Paul* in the subsequent Spanish-American War, he captured a British collier carrying fuel to the Spanish fleet in May 1898 and defeated two Spanish warships off Puerto Rico in June. In 1903, he was promoted to rear admiral, and in 1905, he commanded the flotilla of ships sent to France to return the body of John Paul Jones to the United States. Sigsbee retired in 1907.

James C. Bradford

SIMONDS, GEORGE SHERWIN (1874–1938)

U.S. army officer, Simonds was born in Iowa. He graduated from West Point in 1899 and served in China in 1901 in the aftermath of the Boxer Rebellion before seeing action in the Philippines (1901–02). He occupied a series of positions prior to World War I, including that of instructor at Fort Leavenworth's General Staff College and at West Point. After the United States entered World War I in 1917, the War Department appointed Simonds to a board of officers whose job was to determine how best to use the vast numbers of soldiers soon to follow. As a brigadier general and II Corps chief of staff, Simonds handled the administration and command of U.S. divisions stationed behind British sectors. After his war service, for which he received the Distinguished Service Medal, Simonds taught at the Army War College, was a brigade commander in the Panama Canal Zone (1925–27), and as a major general was deputy chief of staff of the army (1935–36).

Bibliography: Department of the Army, *The United States Army in the World War, 1917–19* (U.S. Govt. Printing Office, 1948).

John F. Wukovits

SIMS, WILLIAM SOWDEN (1858–1936)

U.S. naval officer, Sims was born in Port Hope, Ontario, Canada (of U.S. parents), and grew up in Pennsylvania. He graduated from Annapolis in 1880 and served in the Atlantic and Caribbean as a junior officer. While on leave, he studied French in Paris (1888–89) and, after service on the Pacific and Asiatic stations, returned to Paris as naval attaché to France and Russia (1897–1900). In this capacity, he organized a network for gathering intelligence during the Spanish-American War. After the war, he returned to the Far East, where he learned the "continuous aim" method of gunfire control from Royal Navy captain Percy Scott, who had developed it. As inspector of target practice (1902–09), Sims introduced the method into the U.S. Navy. His concurrent appointment as naval aide to Pres. Theodore Roosevelt (1907–09) placed him in a position to further the reforms in naval administration, officer promotion, and ship design advocated by fellow junior officers. Frustrated when they could get only the aid system, and not the establishment of a chief of naval operations, Sims may have been pleased to spend much of the next eight years at sea or the Naval War College.

In March 1917, when war loomed with Germany, Sims was sent to London to discuss possible joint operations against Germany. A month later, war was declared, and Sims became U.S. naval attaché to Great Britain and was appointed commander of U.S. naval forces operating in European waters. From London, Sims bombarded Washington with requests for additional aid to Britain, suggestions for closer cooperation with the Allies, and recommendations for operations. His virtual demands that more ships be sent to Europe and his discounting of the U-boat threat in U.S. waters differed with the priorities set by Chief of Naval Operations William S. Benson. Also, Sims's opposition to the offensive operations against U-boat bases advocated by Pres. Woodrow Wilson and Admiral Benson weakened support for him in the United States but increased his stature in British eyes. Many U.S. naval leaders resented what they considered Sims's meddling in their affairs and virtually charged him with putting the interests of Britain ahead of those of the United States.

At the end of the war, Sims returned to the states to take command of the Naval War College. His criticism of the navy's administration during the war embittered relations with other officers and led to a 1920 congressional investigation, which failed to reach any conclusions. His book *The Victory at Sea* (1920) won a Pulitzer Prize and kept alive controversy about the navy's role in the war. Sims retired from the navy in 1922 but continued writing articles for the popular press, championing naval reform—in particular air power, which he believed rendered battleships obsolete.

Bibliography: Morison, Elting E., *Admiral Sims and the Modern American Navy* (Houghton Mifflin, 1942).

James C. Bradford

SITTING BULL (TATANKA YOTANKA) (c. 1830–1890)

Hunkpapa Sioux medicine man and chief, Sitting Bull was born along South Dakota's Grand River. As a boy, he was known as "Jumping Badger." Later, he bore the name of "Four Horn." By the time he was 14 years old, he had accompanied his father on many bison hunts as well as on raids against the Crow—natural enemies of the Sioux. By 1857, his bravery and skill as a hunter led to the changing of his name to "Sitting Bull" (his father's name). By the time he reached maturity, he was looked upon by the Hunkpapa as their principal chief and was held in the highest regard by his people. Whether he was also the head chief of the Teton Sioux is debatable, but it is clear that Sitting Bull played a much more important role among the Sioux than simply that of medicine man. His intractability in dealing with U.S. factions led early historians to emphasize the importance of more malleable Sioux leaders such as Gall in an attempt to minimize Sitting Bull's importance, especially in regard to the Indian wars.

Sitting Bull took an active part in the Plains wars of the 1860s, leading a raid against Fort Buford, North Dakota, in December 1866. He was on the warpath with his band from 1869 to 1876, especially against the Crow but also against the Shoshone and occasionally against U.S. adversaries. In 1876, he either refused to obey or did not know of the U.S. government requirement that he bring his people to a reservation. This led to extensive military operations against the Sioux, culminating in the Battle of the Little Bighorn (June 25), in which the Indian forces decimated Lt. Col. George A. Custer's 7th Cavalry. Sitting Bull was in the hills "making medicine" throughout the fight and took no actual part in the Custer engagement. But the fact that he has remained the looming Indian presence ever since is clear evidence of the representative place he held in both Indian and non-Indian minds.

After the Reno-Benteen siege at the Little Bighorn ended, the great Indian encampment broke up. Sitting Bull, with

Sitting Bull, medicine man and chieftain of the Hunkpapa Sioux tribe, became the symbol of Indian resistance to subjugation and removal to reservations during the 1860s and 1870s. (Library of Congress)

his band and others, ravaged the Northern Plains. In October, Sitting Bull had an inconclusive conference with Gen. Nelson Miles, with the Indian insisting he wanted to live free and the general insisting that Sitting Bull surrender and come into the reservation. A resulting fight at Clear Creek, Montana, brought the death of 5 Indians and the wounding of 2 U.S. soldiers. About 2,000 Sioux surrendered in the aftermath. Sitting Bull and other recalcitrants fled northward, eventually finding refuge in Canada. In 1881, under a pledge of amnesty, he returned to Fort Buford and was later held at Fort Randall, South Dakota, until 1883. He remained largely unreconciled and refused to meet U.S. demands.

Sitting Bull, however, acknowledged his transcultural fame and on June 6, 1885, signed a personal-appearance contract with Buffalo Bill's Wild West Show. He appeared in the show for four months, receiving $50 a week along with the right to charge for his photograph. While touring the United States with the show, Sitting Bull was frequently reviled as a villain, but he was treated royally in Canada.

It was at Sitting Bull's Standing Rock Agency that Kicking Bird organized the first Sioux Ghost Dance. It is unclear whether Sitting Bull influenced this movement or was actually more influenced by it. But the Ghost Dance was the pretext for his attempted arrest in 1890. His biographer Stanley Vestal contends that the Ghost Dance had nothing to do with the arrest, but that it was because Sitting Bull had come to be regarded as an obstacle to the management of the Sioux. Due largely to his opposition, for instance, the Sioux had rejected an offer to sell their land in 1888. Regardless of the real reason, Sitting Bull was shot and killed in a scuffle resulting from the arrest attempt. Agent James McLaughlin of Standing Rock later wrote, "The shot that killed Sitting Bull put a stop forever to the domination of the ancient regime among the Sioux of the Standing Rock Reservation." Some claim that was the true objective of his slaying.

Bibliography: Utley, Robert M., *Frontier Regulars: The United States Army and the Indian, 1866–1891* (Univ. of Nebraska Press, 1973); Vestal, Stanley, *Sitting Bull: Champion of the Sioux* (Univ. of Oklahoma Press, 1969).

M. Guy Bishop

SOUSA, JOHN PHILIP (1854–1932)

U.S. composer and Marine Corps bandmaster (1880–92), Sousa was born in Washington, D.C. As leader of the Marine Corps Band, he built a prestigious organization by improving its instrumentation, repertory, and performance level. During World War I, he enlisted in the navy, orga-

John Philip Sousa's marches, especially Stars and Stripes Forever *(1897), inspired patriotism both on the battlefield and at home.* (Library of Congress)

nizing band units at the Great Lakes Naval Training Center and assisting in Liberty Loans and Red Cross drives. He held the rank of lieutenant commander in the U.S. Naval Reserve upon his discharge in 1918.

Known as the "March King," Sousa inspired patriotism and internationally popularized band music, standardizing the march form. Among his 136 march compositions are *Semper Fidelis* (1888), *Liberty Bell* (1893), and *Stars and Stripes Forever* (1897).

Bibliography: Bierley, Paul E., *John Philip Sousa: A Descriptive Catalog of His Works* (Univ. of Illinois Press, 1973).

Lois Kriner Millsap

SQUIER, GEORGE OWEN (1865–1934)

U.S. military engineer, chief signal officer of the army, scientist and inventor, Squier was born in Dryden, Michigan. He graduated from West Point in 1887 and from Johns Hopkins University in 1892. In a career that spanned the Spanish-American War and World War I, Squier helped science and scientific research to gain acceptance in the military; saw the opening of two army laboratories, one at Fort Monmouth, New Jersey, for radio work, and the other at Langley Field, Virginia, for aviation research; made numerous contributions in the fields of magnetization, telegraphy, and broadcasting; and held a number of patents for his discoveries in telegraphy and telephony. During the Spanish-American War, he served as a signal officer and was made a first lieutenant upon returning to the regular army's Signal Corps. He served with the corps at various locations from 1900 until 1911, when he briefly became chief signal officer in Washington before being named military attaché at the U.S. Embassy in London. In February 1917, he was appointed chief signal officer, with the rank of brigadier general, remaining in the post until his retirement in 1932. During World War I, he studied the technical work in radio and aviation being done by the British. As the chief signal officer, he directed the cable and radio links between the United States and the American forces in Europe. For his service during the war, he was awarded the Distinguished Service Medal and also received commendations from Britain, Italy, and France.

Carol Stokes

STERNBERG, GEORGE MILLER (1838–1915)

U.S. physician and army surgeon general, Sternberg was born at Hartwick Seminary, of which his father was principal, in Otsego County, New York. He briefly attended, then taught at the seminary before pursuing a career in medicine. Receiving his medical degree in 1860 from the College of Physicians and Surgeons in New York (later part of Columbia University), he practiced briefly in Elizabeth, New Jersey, and joined the Union army at the outbreak of the Civil War. He was captured at the First Battle of Bull Run; after his release and recovery from typhoid, Sternberg served in general hospitals in Rhode Island and Ohio.

Remaining in the postwar army, Sternberg was assigned to widely scattered posts. While at Fort Barrancas, Florida, 1872–75, he began to study yellow fever, a study that continued through the next two decades during various assignments. In 1893, he was appointed surgeon general of the army, a post to which he brought numerous innovations, including his establishment of the Army Medical School, the Dental Corps, the Nurse Corps, and the Army Tuberculosis Hospital. Most notable was his 1900 creation of the Yellow Fever Commission headed by Maj. Walter Reed, who ultimately identified the transmitter of the disease. Sternberg retired in 1902 and spent the rest of his life working in the field of public health, specializing in bacteriology and preventive medicine.

Bibliography: Sternberg, Martha L., *George Miller Sternberg: A Biography* (Amer. Med. Assn., 1920).

Louise Arnold-Friend

STIMSON, HENRY LEWIS (1867–1950)

U.S. statesman, Stimson was born in New York City. He earned degrees from Yale University and Harvard Law School. His background of affluence and education made him well suited to join a powerful, Northeast-based political and social movement that was just beginning in the 1890s. Progressivism sought to sweep away the era of greed and avarice that characterized the 1870s and 1880s. The movement prized public service over personal wealth and was aimed at banishing poverty, disease, and ignorance. Theodore Roosevelt and Elihu Root were at the forefront of this movement, and Stimson grew close to both men.

Joining Root's New York law firm, Stimson found himself in Republican Party politics and public service. Appointed by President Roosevelt as a U.S. attorney for the Southern District of New York in 1906, Stimson began waging a successful battle against abusive, arrogant corporations. He ran for governor of New York state in 1910 but lost. The next year, President Taft appointed Simpson secretary of war (1911–13). In that role, he furthered the reforms that his predecessor and mentor, Root, had initiated at the turn of the century. Stimson pressed for a better trained U.S. Army, siding with Chief of Staff Leonard Wood and the General Staff Corps in arguments against undue political influence in War Department matters. He also fought the power of entrenched army bureaucracies.

Although Stimson returned to private life when the Democrats took power in 1913, he soon joined the preparedness bandwagon, vigorously advocating a strong American armed force as Europe was caught up in the stalemated tragedy of World War I. On the U.S. entry into the war in 1917, Stimson was given an army commission and went to France.

There he served in the artillery, seeing combat in the Lorraine sector. During the war, he reached the rank of lieutenant colonel.

In the years following the war, Stimson remained an influential public figure. Pres. Calvin Coolidge appointed him governor general of the Philippines (1927–29) and Pres. Herbert Hoover chose him as secretary of state (1929–33). During World War II, Stimson regained national prominence as Pres. Franklin Roosevelt's secretary of war (1940–45).

Bibliography: Stimson, Henry L., and McGeorge Bundy, *On Active Service in Peace and War* (Harper & Brothers, 1947).

Col. (Ret.) Rod Paschall

SULLY, ALFRED (1821–1879)

U.S. army officer, Sully was born in Philadelphia. He graduated from West Point in 1841 and fought in the Mexican War and several Indian campaigns before the Civil War. As colonel of the 1st Minnesota, he served with distinction in the Peninsular Campaign and at Antietam. Promoted to brigadier general in 1862, he participated in the battles of Fredericksburg and Chancellorsville before being ordered west in 1863 after the Sioux uprising in Minnesota. Over the next three years, Sully led several expeditions against the Sioux in the Dakotas. While these operations kept the Indians away from white settlements, they failed to bring the conflict to a decisive conclusion. In 1868, he campaigned against the Southern Cheyenne before becoming superintendent for Indian affairs for Montana (1869–70). He also campaigned against the Nez Percé in 1877.

Bibliography: Jones, Robert H., *The Civil War in the Northwest: Nebraska, Wisconsin, Iowa, Minnesota, and the Dakotas* (Univ. of Oklahoma Press, 1960).

Richard F. Kehrberg

SUMMERALL, CHARLES PELOT (1867–1955)

U.S. army officer, Summerall was born in Lake City, Florida. He graduated from West Point in 1892 as first captain of the Corps of Cadets. Assigned to the infantry, he transferred to the artillery at the first opportunity. He first saw combat during the Philippine Insurrection, during which he won two Silver Star medals while serving with Reilly's Artillery Battery. The unit was also assigned to the China Relief Expedition, during which he earned another two Silver Stars. Summerall braved Chinese fire to mark targets on the gates of Peking with chalk so that his platoon would have clear aiming points. For most of the decade after 1905, he held assignments as an instructor of tactics at West Point and as a lecturer at the Army War College and at the War Department.

In early 1918, Summerall, then a colonel, went to France with a mission headed by Col. Chauncey Baker to evaluate, independent of Gen. John J. Pershing, the needs of the American Expeditionary Force (A.E.F.). Members of the Baker Mission and A.E.F. officers agreed on many points, but a strong disagreement took place between Summerall and Fox Conner, representing Pershing's Operations Division. Summerall believed that Conner had not planned for sufficient artillery. Conner, also an artillery expert, won the day, but Pershing was impressed with Summerall's forceful presentation and requested the War Department to assign Summerall to duty with the A.E.F.

Summerall soon returned to France in command of an artillery brigade in the Rainbow Division. He was shortly transferred to the 1st Division. Pershing, who considered Summerall one of his ablest field commanders, promoted him to command the division during the Soissons Offensive in July 1918. Assigned to the French 10th Army along with another American division, the 1st was ordered to attack for several days in a row before relief became available. Summerall, now a major general, personally went among men and officers to explain what was being asked of them.

In mid-October, as preparations for the final phases of the Meuse-Argonne Campaign were going forward, Summerall was given command of V Corps in the American 1st Army. Expected to provide more energetic leadership than the previous commander of V Corps had supplied, he received key assignments and handled them well. In the war's last days, however, Summerall, anxious to win for himself and for the A.E.F. the glory of capturing Sedan, pushed his corps into a sector assigned to another U.S. corps. Confusion resulted, angering both French and U.S. officers. Some wished to see court-martial charges brought against Summerall. His army commander, Lt. Gen. Hunter Liggett, was angry with Summerall's behavior but decided not to take disciplinary action. Pershing dismissed the incident as "a misconception of orders."

As much as any officer in the A.E.F., Summerall emerged from the war with an enhanced reputation. Although histrionic and considered by some to be a glory seeker, he was admired both for his aggressive leadership and for his tactical innovations, especially in the employment of artillery. "Artillery exists only to protect and support infantry," he said, and his actions underscored his remark. He often deployed 75-millimeter guns at the front lines, used a modified rolling barrage with great effect, and demanded quick and reliable communications between his infantry and artillery commanders in order to register German machine-gun and artillery positions with the greatest possible precision.

After the war, he served as army chief of staff (1926–30) and was promoted to full general in 1929. He retired in 1931 and became president (1931–53) of The Citadel.

Bibliography: Liggett, Hunter, *Commanding an American Army: Recollections of the World War* (Houghton Mifflin, 1925); MacCloskey, Monro, *Reilly's Battery: A Story of the Boxer Rebellion* (R. Rosen Press, 1969); Miller, Henry Russell, *The First Division* (Crescent Press, 1924); ———, *History of the First Division During the World War: 1917–1918* (Crescent Press, 1922); Pratt, Fletcher, *Eleven Generals: Studies in American Command* (William Sloane, 1949).

Lloyd J. Graybar

SWIFT, EBEN, JR. (1854–1938)

U.S. army officer, Swift was born in Fort Cadbourne, Texas. After graduating from West Point in 1876, he served in a number of Indian campaigns (1876–93), in the Spanish-American War (1898), and in the Philippines (1899–1901, 1912–13). His important contributions to the army, however, came through his association with the emerging military education system, especially the schools at Fort Leavenworth. Along with Arthur L. Wagner, Swift pioneered the curriculum and methods of instruction used there. Chief among his contributions was the development of a standardized system for writing field orders. He held a variety of field and staff commands but always continued to write on topics such as military history, weapons, tactics, and training. After service in World War I, Swift retired in 1918 as a brigadier general.

Bibliography: Nenninger, Timothy K., *The Leavenworth Schools and the Old Army: Education, Professionalism, and the Officer Corps of the United States Army, 1881–1918* (Greenwood Press, 1978).

Richard F. Kehrberg

TAFT, WILLIAM HOWARD (1857–1930)

Twenty-seventh president of the United States (1909–13) and chief justice of the United States (1921–30), Taft was born in Cincinnati, Ohio. After earning degrees from Yale University and Cincinnati Law School, he augmented a law career by becoming involved in Republican politics, first in Ohio and then nationally.

His national prominence began in 1890 when he was appointed U.S. Solicitor General. In 1900, he became head of the commission to the Philippines that was to organize the civil government there. Subsequently, he was named the islands' first civil governor (1901–04). Taft became Pres. Theodore Roosevelt's secretary of war in 1904 and a close adviser to the president in Latin American affairs.

Elected to the presidency in 1908, Taft essentially continued Roosevelt's policies. Deterioration of the Taft-Roosevelt relationship split the Republican vote in 1912 and resulted in the election of Woodrow Wilson. Taft retired from public life in 1913 and taught law. He was appointed chief justice in 1921.

William Howard Taft, secretary of war before succeeding Theodore Roosevelt to the presidency in 1909, oversaw the construction of the Panama Canal. (Library of Congress)

Bibliography: Butt, Archibald W., *Taft and Roosevelt* (Doubleday, 1930); Minger, Ralph E., *William Howard Taft and United States Foreign Policy: 1900–1908* (Univ. of Illinois Press, 1975); Pringle, Henry F., *The Life and Times of William Howard Taft* (Farrar & Rinehart, 1939).

John A. Hixson

TERRY, ALFRED HOWE (1827–1890)

U.S. army officer, Terry was born in Hartford, Connecticut. He studied law at Yale University and, during the Civil War, was commissioned colonel of the 2d Connecticut Infantry in 1861. By the end of the war, he was a major general of volunteers. Following the war, he commanded the Department of Dakota (1866–68, 1873–86). Although inexperienced in Indian fighting, Terry was in overall command of the main theater of operations during the Sioux wars of 1865–68 and 1876. In October 1877, he headed a commission to Canada to try to persuade Sitting Bull to return to a reservation in the United States. However, the angry Sioux chieftan would barely speak to Terry, advising him to "go home." In 1886, Terry was promoted to major general and given command of the Division of the Missouri.

M. Guy Bishop

TITUS, CALVIN PEARL (1879–1966)

U.S. soldier, Titus was born in Vinton, Iowa. He volunteered for service in the Spanish-American War, enlisting with the 1st Vermont Volunteers, but he saw no overseas service before the war ended. After the war, he remained in the army to participate in the Philippine Insurrection, serving as a bugler with the 14th U.S. Infantry Regiment. His unit was sent to China in the summer of 1900 to participate in the Boxer Rebellion. During heavy fighting at Peking, Titus overhead his commander speaking of the need to scale the Tartar Wall and answered with the now-famous "I'll try, Sir." With no equipment, he climbed the 30-foot obstacle, followed by two companies of his regiment whose covering fire allowed British troops to breach the Boxer stronghold.

The next year, Titus received an appointment to West Point. For his China heroics, Titus was awarded the Congressional Medal of Honor, which was presented him by Pres. Theodore Roosevelt during his plebe year at the academy.

Following his 1905 graduation, Titus was commissioned in the infantry. He served with Pershing's Punitive Expedition to Mexico with the 15th Infantry Division in the United States during World War I, and overseas for three years with the Army of Occupation after the war. From 1927 to 1930, he taught leadership at the Infantry School at Fort Benning, then retired as a lieutenant colonel.

Louise Arnold-Friend

TORAL, JOSÉ (1832–1904)

Spanish army general, Toral spent much of his military career in the Spanish colonies. During the Spanish-American War, he commanded Spanish forces in Cuba. Toral's army suffered heavy casualties in the battles around Santiago, and food as well as other supplies ran low. When the Spanish fleet was destroyed at the Battle of Santiago Bay (July 3, 1898), Toral, realizing that his position was untenable, entered into negotiations with U.S. commander Gen. William Shafter. Toral asked for a number of concessions, including the right for his men to keep their arms. Instead, a compromise was reached, and Toral and his 22,000 troops in Cuba gave up their arms to the U.S. victors and were transported back to Spain at the expense of the United States.

Ted Alexander

TRACY, BENJAMIN FRANKLIN (1830–1915)

U.S. attorney and secretary of the navy, Tracy was born near Owego, New York. As Pres. Benjamin Harrison's navy secretary (1889–93), he advocated a strong, battleship navy. Tracy supported the Naval War College by providing it with resources to develop strategy and war plans and ordered the formation of a squadron of evolution to test tactics and strategy. He also imposed a merit rather than a patronage system on navy yards, convinced Congress to build four battleships and three cruisers (all larger and more powerful than previous U.S. ships), established the naval militia, and streamlined the Navy Department administratively. One of Harrison's closest advisers, Tracy strongly influenced the president's expansionist foreign policy and the firm positions taken by the United States in the Valparaiso Incident, the controversy over fur sealing in the Bering Sea, and the conflict over the right of asylum in the Barrundia case.

Bibliography: Cooling, B. Franklin, *Benjamin Franklin Tracy: Father of the Modern American Fighting Navy* (Archon, 1973).

James C. Bradford

UPTON, EMORY (1839–1881)

U.S. army officer and military tactician, Upton was born near Batavia, New York. He graduated from West Point in 1861 and went on to serve in the Civil War with distinction, attaining the rank of brevet major general. Immediately following the war, he reverted to the rank of captain and was posted west but soon returned east. Reaching the grade of lieutenant colonel in mid-1886, he labored on a proposed change in tactics and asked to present his ideas to a board of general officers. Assigned to West Point, he began simultaneously teaching cadets and making his arguments before the first two boards. His superiors agreed with the young officer, and the army adopted his concepts in August 1867. Upton's wife, Emily, died in 1870, and for the next five years, Upton was a humorless, strict commandant of cadets at West Point.

The Commanding General of the Army, William T. Sherman, chose Upton to tour foreign armies with a view toward reforming American military institutions. Upton's 1875–76 travels resulted in his publication of *The Armies of Asia and Europe* (1878). He preferred German military practices, not least because they had been successful on Franco-Prussian War battlefields. Upton advocated changes in the U.S. Army's organization, but his most controversial proposal dealt with the makeup of a wartime U.S. fighting force. His ideas were little different from John C. Calhoun's notions of an expansible army: citizen soldiers led by professionally trained officers.

Upton's ideas were seized upon by politicians as unhealthy European concepts that threatened to transform the United States into an autocracy, and these detractors won out. Until World War I, the United States was destined to depend on a small professional army in peace and on a larger, ill-trained, volunteer force led by a few professionals and politically well-connected amateurs in war. In truth, there was not much "democratic" about the inefficient U.S. militia system and not much autocratic about either Calhoun's or Upton's proposals. Upton began work on a new book, a study of U.S. military policy when he was given command of the 4th Artillery in San Francisco in 1880. (The manuscript was incomplete at the time of his death but was published by Sec. of War Elihu Root in 1904). On Mar. 15, 1881, Upton used a pistol to commit suicide. Probably the victim of a brain tumor, Upton had been in physical pain, but he also had suffered unreconciled grief over his wife's death and had bitterly concluded that the army would never adopt some of his more "controversial" recommendations.

Bibliography: Ambrose, Stephen E., *Upton and the Army* (Louisiana State Univ. Press, 1964); Michie, Peter Smith, *Life and Letters of General Emory Upton* (Appleton, 1885).

Col. (Ret.) Rod Paschall

VICTORIO (c. 1825–1880)

Mimbres Apache chief in the southwestern part of present-day New Mexico. He first came to public attention in 1853 when he put his "X" to a "provisional compact" with the United States. He subsequently became known as "Lucero" to Americans in the Southwest. Following a gold strike near Pinos Altos, New Mexico, he reportedly became involved with warlike activities. He was known to be present with Cochise and Mangas at the Battle of Apache Pass (July 1862), when hostile Apache fought the U.S. Army's California Column. Finally subdued, Victorio and his people were moved in 1872 to a reservation at Tularosa, in what is now New Mexico. Later, they were removed to San Carlos, Arizona. Unaccustomed to this region, the Mimbres became restive. Victorio and some followers broke out of the reservation in September 1877. Following years of skirmishes with U.S. troops, Victorio was killed in a fight near New Mexico's Palomas River in 1880.

M. Guy Bishop

VILLA, FRANCISCO (PANCHO) (1878–1923)

Mexican bandit and revolutionary leader, Pancho Villa was born Doroteo Arango in Rio Grande, Durango, Mexico. He was an outlaw in northern Mexico until drawn into the Mexican Revolution by his patron Abraham Gonzalez, who supported Francisco Madero's uprising against dictator Porfirio Díaz. Villa joined the revolution and in 1911 played a role in the decisive capture of the border city of Juarez. Villa supported the subsequent Madero regime but found himself a revolutionary again in 1913 when Gen. Victoriano Huerta assassinated Madero and proclaimed himself president. Villa took up arms against Huerta and became the leading revolutionary in north-central Mexico. Nominally under Venustiano Carranza, the head of the revolutionary Constitutionalists, Villa was in reality an independent commander with his own army, the Division of the North. Depending on supplies from the United States, he waged a successful campaign against the federal forces in Chihuahua. In late 1913, he captured the city of Torreon and established himself as the most powerful rebel leader. He recaptured Juarez and the city of Chihuahua before the year was out, and by summer, Huerta had resigned.

In the absence of a common foe, a rift opened between Carranza and Villa, which led to all-out war by November 1914. The war against Carranza saw Villa pitted against Álvaro Obregón, the military leader of the Constitutionalists and the most talented military figure of the revolution. Obregón, using modern tactics and weapons, repeatedly decimated the Villistas' frontal attacks over the next nine months. Villa's defeats led the United States to recognize and support Carranza in hopes of ending the revolution. Such U.S. support manifested itself in Villa's defeat at Agua Prieta on Nov. 1, 1915, when Constitutionalist forces, transported across U.S. territory by rail to reinforce the town, defeated a night attack by Villa, whose troops were blinded by searchlights powered from the United States.

Growing hostility toward the United States and a desire to regain popularity led Villa to kill 15 Americans at Santa Isabel in Mexico in January 1916 and then to raid Columbus, New Mexico, on March 9. This cross-border attack resulted in the death of 17 more Americans and formed anti-Mexican feelings in the United States. In retaliation, the United States organized a Punitive Expedition, under Gen. John J. Pershing, which chased Villa across northern Mexico for months and inflicted serious casualties on his forces but which failed to catch him. Instead, Villa's forces grew stronger throughout 1916 and briefly recaptured Chihuahua and Torreon. Villa himself became a popular hero for his resistance against the U.S. troops. For the next two years, Villa waged a skillful guerrilla war against the Carranzistas. In June 1919, he launched a surprise attack on Juarez, eliciting a counterattack by U.S. troops, who chased Villa from the city. This defeat led Villa to make peace with Carranza's successor, Obregón, and to retire in 1920. Villa was assassinated in retirement in 1923.

Bibliography: Clendenen, Clarence C., *The United States and Pancho Villa: A Study in Unconventional Diplomacy* (Cornell Univ. Press, 1961); Knight, Alan, *The Mexican Revolution,* 2 vols. (Univ. of Nebraska Press, 1986).

Mark Pitcavage

WAGNER, ARTHUR LOCKWOOD (1853–1905)

U.S. military educator, Wagner was born in Ottawa, Illinois. He graduated from West Point in 1875 and brought six years of frontier regimental duty and four years' experience as an instructor in military science at East Florida Seminary (now the University of Florida) to the faculty of the Infantry and Cavalry School, which he joined in 1886. Established at Fort Leavenworth, Kansas, in 1881, the school at first stressed drill, ceremony, and memorizing outdated texts. Wagner was determined to make the school a true war academy in the fashion of the German *Kriegsakademie*. During his 10 years at the school, he authored standard texts on army organization, tactics, and military history and helped professionalize the school's curriculum. Wagner served in staff positions in Cuba and the Philippines and helped found the Army War College. His promotion to brigadier general coincided with the time of his death.

Richard B. Meixsel

WALLER, LITTLETON WALLER TAZEWELL (1856–1926)

U.S. marine officer, Waller was born in York County, Virginia. He served in the Cuban theater during the war with Spain (1898) and took part in operations at San Juan de Puerto Rico and at Santiago de Cuba and was present at the destruction of Adm. Pascual Cervera's fleet at Santiago on July 3.

Beginning in 1899, Waller served on the Asiatic Station in operations against Filipino insurgents and in suppression of the Boxers in China. He was acquitted on charges of murder resulting from his orders to execute native guides on Samar in 1902. From 1903 to 1917, Waller commanded marines in campaigns in Panama; Cuba; Veracruz, Mexico; and Haiti. In 1917, he returned to the United States for his last assignment, commanding the Advance Base Force in Philadelphia.

Vernon L. Williams

WEYLER Y NICOLAU, VALERIANO (1838–1930)

Spanish statesman and military figure. He served as a military attaché during the American Civil War and prized his association with Gen. William T. Sherman. In 1896, Weyler became governor general of Cuba, appointed to end the insurrection there by any means. He used forts to partition the island into three regions in order to isolate and contain the rebels at both ends. To further deprive them of food and assistance, he ordered farmers and their families to move into reconcentration camps. These camps caused great suffering and tens of thousands of deaths. Despite such brutal measures, Weyler failed to contain the rebellion. Amid public U.S. outcries against his activities, he resigned in late 1897, when a new Spanish government favoring Cuban autonomy took power.

Mark Pitcavage

WHEATON, LOYD (1838–1918)

U.S. army officer, Wheaton was born in Pennfield, Michigan. In the Civil War he enlisted in the 8th Illinois Infantry and was commissioned as a first lieutenant in July 1861. He rose to lieutenant colonel by the end of the war and later in 1865 received a regular army commission as a captain. He spent the post-Civil War period in assignments with the 34th and 20th infantry divisions. Wheaton was a senior commander throughout operations in the Philippines during the Spanish-American War (1898) and sought to undermine the emerging policy of benevolent pacification initiated during the U.S.-Philippine conflict with Filipino insurgents. He actively asserted his antipacification policy in the campaign and strongly advocated a strategy of repression to meet the terror and treachery employed by the rebels. Wheaton commanded the Departments of Northern Luzon and Northern Philippines from 1900 until 1902, when he retired with the rank of major general.

Vernon L. Williams

WHEELER, JOSEPH (1836–1906)

U.S. army officer and political figure, Wheeler was born near Augusta, Georgia. He graduated from West Point in 1859 and became a renowned Confederate cavalry commander during the Civil War.

After the war, he became a successful Alabama cotton planter. He served in the U.S. House of Representatives (1881–82, 1883, 1885–1900), where as a member of the Military Affairs and Ways and Means committees, he advocated traditional white rule in the South, opposed civil rights legislation, promoted industrialization, and espoused reconciliation between the South and the North.

As a major general of U.S. Volunteers, Wheeler commanded cavalry forces in Cuba during the Spanish-American War. He also served as a brigadier general of volunteers during the Philippine Insurrection until his retirement in 1900.

Bibliography: Dyer, John P., *"Fightin' Joe" Wheeler* (Louisiana State Univ. Press, 1941).

Capt. James Sanders Day

WILLIAMS, CLARENCE CHARLES (1869–1958)

U.S. ordnance chief, Williams was born in Georgia. He graduated from West Point fourth in the Class of 1894. Commissioned in the artillery, he soon transferred to ordnance and was appointed assistant chief of ordnance in February 1917, on the eve of U.S. involvement in World War I. Williams went to France nine weeks later as chief ordnance officer of the American Expeditionary Force, where he gained the rank of brigadier general.

As a major general and chief of ordnance (1918–30), Williams reorganized the Ordnance Department, increased efficiency, and decentralized the procurement process. He fostered a partnership between ordnance arsenals and industry by planning for industrial mobilization. Involving the combat arms in weapon development, he produced the 75-millimeter antitank gun and the semiautomatic rifle, important weapons during World War II. He retired in 1930 but returned to active duty in 1942–43.

Bibliography: Sterling, Keir B., *Serving the Line with Excellence, 1775–1987* (U.S. Army Ordnance Center and School, 1987).

Maj. James Sanders Day

WILSON, JAMES HARRISON (1837–1925)

U.S. army officer and administrator, Wilson was born in Shawneetown, Illinois. He graduated from West Point in 1860 and briefly served in the Corps of Topographical Engineers. During the Civil War, he distinguished himself as a combat commander of cavalry in both the eastern and western theaters of operations. He also displayed extraordinary administrative talents when he commanded the Cavalry Bureau for several months in early 1864.

During the postwar army reorganization, Wilson became lieutenant colonel of the 35th Infantry Regiment but was quickly reassigned to the engineers. Until his 1870 resignation, he oversaw internal navigational improvements, primarily along the Mississippi River.

Wilson spent the remainder of his life engaged in private business pursuits and public service. He reentered military service in the Spanish-American War (1898), serving as a major general of volunteers in Cuba and Puerto Rico, and soon after participated in the Boxer Rebellion. In 1901, he was placed on the retired list. Wilson was a prolific author of numerous professional journal contributions, biographies of his stellar contemporaries, and a two-volume autobiography, *Under the Old Flag*.

Bibliography: Longacre, Edward G., *Union Stars to Top Hat: A Biography of the Extraordinary General James Harrison Wilson* (Stackpole Books, 1972).

Louise Arnold-Friend

WILSON, (THOMAS) WOODROW (1856–1924)

Twentieth-eighth president of the United States (1913–21), Wilson was born in Staunton, Virginia. He graduated from Princeton University in 1879, briefly practiced law, and then entered Johns Hopkins University, earning a doctorate in history in 1886. He joined the faculty of Princeton in 1890 and later served as the university's president (1902–10). After serving as Democratic governor of New Jersey (1911–12), Wilson's reputation for reform led to his nomination and election as president in 1912. Although committed to the democratic ideal, his intellectual hauteur and moral indignation led him into complicated and unwelcome foreign involvements. Events in Latin America and Europe compelled him to use the U.S. military more than any president since Abraham Lincoln.

Despite Wilson's anti-imperial inclinations, protection of the Panama Canal necessitated his involvement in the Caribbean Basin. He retained the Marine Corps presence in Nicaragua and sent the marines to quell unrest in Haiti (1915) and in the Dominican Republic (1916–22).

In 1913, Wilson refused on principle to grant diplomatic recognition to Mexican dictator Victoriano Huerta. The arrest of U.S. sailors at Tampico (April 1914) afforded Wilson the excuse to seize the Mexican port of Veracruz, an action that, rather than toppling Huerta, inflamed the Mexican people and created a diplomatically embarrassing withdrawal. Huerta soon fell, but other difficulties ensued. Provoked by Francisco ''Pancho'' Villa's cross-border raids into New Mexico, in 1916, Wilson ordered Gen. John J. Pershing and 12,000 cavalrymen into Mexico. Failing to capture Villa, they were withdrawn in 1917, leaving behind a bitter Mexico sympathetic with Germany in the mounting world war.

Although Pres. Woodrow Wilson consistently advocated a policy of isolationism, circumstances drew the United States into war during his administrations. (Library of Congress)

In 1914, Wilson proclaimed U.S. neutrality in the European war. He soon discovered that U.S. trade was threatened by both the Allies' contraband policies and Germany's submarine warfare. While he protested the former, the latter moved him toward conflict with the Central Powers. Designating the submarine a ''terror'' weapon inflicted upon innocent non-combatants, Wilson forced Germany to suspend its use in May 1916. Nine months later, a desperate Germany resumed unrestricted submarine warfare; on Apr. 2, 1917, Wilson urged Congress to declare war on Germany.

Seeing the war as a moral crusade, Wilson suppressed dissent at home, and on Jan. 8, 1918, he presented his ''Fourteen Points'' address in which he stressed his idealistic goals. His peace would be built upon the foundations of open diplomacy, freedom of the seas, free trade, disarmament, and a league of nations.

Following Germany's surrender in 1918, he personally traveled to Versailles. Confounded by pragmatic European ministers opposed to his values, Wilson compromised his goals and returned to the United States with a treaty that at least salvaged his quest for the League of Nations. Given

Wilson's refusal to compromise further with the U.S. Senate, the treaty failed. During the last months of his second presidential term, he languished, paralyzed by a stroke.

Bibliography: Bailey, Thomas A., *Woodrow Wilson and the Great Betrayal* (Macmillan, 1945); Blum, John Morton, *Woodrow Wilson and the Politics of Morality* (Little, Brown, 1956); Garraty, John A., *Woodrow Wilson: A Great Life in Brief* (Knopf, 1956); Link, Arthur S., *Wilson the Diplomatist* (Johns Hopkins Press, 1957); ———, *Woodrow Wilson and the Progressive Era, 1910–1917* (Harper & Row, 1954).

Fred Arthur Bailey

WINSLOW, JOHN ANCRUM (1811–1873)

U.S. naval officer, Winslow was born in Wilmington, North Carolina. During the Civil War, his screw sloop *Kearsarge* sank the feared Confederate raider *Alabama* off Cherbourg, France, in June 1864, in what proved to be the last one-on-one encounter in history between major wooden warships. Winslow's victory, and his continued cruising for Confederate raiders in European and Caribbean waters, made him a popular naval hero in the North throughout the remainder of the war.

After the war, Winslow commanded the Gulf Squadron (1866–67) and the Portsmouth navy yard (1869–70) before he was promoted in 1870 to the rank of rear admiral and given command of the Pacific Squadron. When poor health forced him to end his naval career in 1872, a grateful U.S. Congress refused to place him on the retired list.

Bibliography: Fowler, William M., Jr., *Under Two Flags: The American Navy in the Civil War* (Norton, 1990); Reynolds, Clark G., *Famous American Admirals* (Van Nostrand-Reinhold, 1978).

Donald A. Yerxa

WOOD, LEONARD (1860–1927)

U.S. army physician, officer, and administrator, Wood was born in Winchester, New Hampshire. He graduated from Harvard Medical School in 1884 and entered the army in 1885 as a contract surgeon. Joining the 4th Cavalry Regiment at Fort Huachuca in Arizona Territory, Wood seized the opportunity a year later to participate in an expedition to capture the Apache leader Geronimo, who had led a small band of disgruntled warriors off of the San Marcos reservation. Officially the expedition's medical officer, Wood voluntarily assumed a more active role, traveling with the Indian scouts and briefly commanding the infantry company assigned to the expedition. In 1898, he received the Congressional Medal of Honor for his conduct during the chase, which had forced the Apache surrender in September 1886. Also in 1886, he had received a commission as an assistant surgeon in the army's medical department.

An advocate of military preparedness, Gen. Leonard Wood urged vigorous training programs. (U.S. Army Military History Institute)

Promoted to captain in the Medical Corps in 1891, Wood was serving in Washington, D.C., four years later when he became the personal physician to Pres. Grover Cleveland. When William McKinley became president in 1897, Wood became the physician to his invalid wife. It was at this time that Wood began his lifelong friendship with Theodore Roosevelt (then assistant secretary of the navy), and the two men shared an enthusiasm for physical fitness and a belief that the United States should play a more active and competitive role in world affairs. Roosevelt's patronage would contribute greatly to Wood's rapid rise in the army.

Spanish-American War. Roosevelt and Wood used their political connections to obtain commissions in one of the federal volunteer regiments authorized by Congress at the start of the Spanish-American War (1898). Roosevelt turned down the offer to command in favor of the more experienced Wood, and the two began recruiting for the 1st U.S. Volunteer Cavalry Regiment, popularly known as the ''Rough Riders.'' Colonel Wood's direction of the regiment in combat at Las Guasimas as the V Corps approached Santiago, Cuba, showed more enthusiasm than competence, but he soon moved up to command the 2d Brigade, which he led at the battle of San Juan Hill. After the fighting, Wood remained in Cuba, first as governor of Santiago (July–October 1898) and then as commanding general of the Department of Santiago and governor of the province (October 1898–December 1899). Wood, now a major general of volunteers, replaced Maj. Gen. John Brooke as commanding general of the Division of Cuba in December 1899. In addition, by February 1901, Wood had parlayed political contacts and exemplary service as a colonial administrator into a brigadier general's commission in the regular army, leapfrogging over the 509 more senior officers.

Philippines. The U.S. military occupation of Cuba ended in May 1902, and after temporary assignments in Europe and the United States, Wood was ordered to the Philippines. As commanding general of the Department of Mindanao and first governor of the coterminous Moro Province, Wood forced a grudging acceptance of U.S. rule upon the area's truculent Muslim inhabitants. Wood was promoted to major general in August 1903 and in February 1906 took command of the Philippines Division.

Wood's authority in Cuba and Mindanao had encompassed both military and civil duties, but his new assignment was restricted to control of the U.S. Army garrison in the archipelago. Of necessity, he turned his energy to military reform during his two years at division headquarters in Manila. Remote from the constraints of congressional and public oversight, the Philippines was ideal for trying out the tenets of the military reform movement, and Wood implemented a vigorous training program that emphasized preparation for war. Returning to the United States in 1908, Wood commanded the Department of the East for two years and then, in April 1910, became army chief of staff.

Chief of Staff. Established in 1903, the General Staff was still in its formative period. Many officers were unclear as to the nature of their duties, and the army's powerful bureau chiefs were determined to retain their independence from the General Staff. The old commanding generals of the army had been unable to subdue them, and the new chiefs of staff initially fared little better. Wood's primary goal was to assert his authority as the bureaus' superior and as the army's sole link with the secretary of war. The newness of that concept and the unorthodox manner in which Wood had become the army's senior general inevitably led to conflict.

After becoming chief of staff, Wood began encroaching on the adjutant general's domain in such areas as officer assignments and recruiting. Only by control of such everyday affairs could Wood initiate reforms leading to military preparedness for war. Ironically, Adj. Gen. Frederick Ainsworth had also entered the army as a contract surgeon. Wood forced Ainsworth to resign but was only partially successful in subordinating the bureaus to his direction. Subsequent congressional legislation reduced both the size of the General Staff and the length of time officers could serve on it without returning to their regiments. The National Defense Act of 1916 also allowed bureaus once again to report directly to the secretary of war.

The defects of an army perceived as an aggregate of regiments also drew Wood's attention. He brought units together to provide training with brigade- and division-size organizations. In contrast to other reform-minded officers who had little faith in the citizen-soldier concept, Wood believed that short-term training would produce competent soldiers. In 1913, he supported a summer camp program to provide military instruction to select college students. Wood believed that officers could then be obtained from among the students in time of emergency.

World War I. Following completion of his tour of duty as chief of staff in April 1914, Wood again took command of the Eastern Department. From its headquarters at Governor's Island, New York, he continued to argue for a federal reserve force. His advocacy of increased military preparedness led to the highly successful ''Plattsburgh'' camps (after a training camp held at Plattsburgh Barracks, New York, in August 1915), which provided the models for the officer training camps of World War I. However, Pres. Woodrow Wilson's distrust of the military and the close association between the Preparedness Movement and the Republican Party brought Wood into increasing conflict with the administration.

As the leading proponent of military preparedness and the army's highest-ranking officer when the United States entered World War I, Wood seemed well placed to lead U.S. troops abroad. And indeed, the administration did want to send the general overseas—but to Hawaii or the Philippines. Wood's insubordinate conduct during the preparedness campaign and his public contempt for Wilson's prewar policies had cost him the government's confidence. The more experienced and slightly older Gen. John J. Pershing commanded the American Expeditionary Force (A.E.F.) instead. Along with other generals excluded from field command, Wood made a short tour of the A.E.F. in France, but he spent most of the war in Kansas training divisions for combat. Under fire for denying a battlefield command to Wood, the administration considered giving him a division in Italy, but Pershing suspected that Wood would make a fractious subordinate and was adamant in refusing him any position in Europe.

Postwar Activities. Campaigning in uniform on a law-and-order platform that emphasized the threat posed to the United States by radical elements, Wood was a leading contender for the Republican Party's presidential nomination in 1920. He lost to Warren G. Harding, and his hope of being named secretary of war in Harding's cabinet came to naught. Instead, Harding offered Wood the governor-generalship of the Philippines. At first angered by what seemed to be yet another attempt to exile him from public life in the United States, Wood then agreed to lead a mission of inquiry to the islands.

He had maintained a genuine interest in Philippine affairs. After the inquiry conducted by former governor general W. Cameron Forbes and himself criticized the conduct of the islands' administration, Wood accepted the offer to become the new governor in August 1921 and retired from the army in October. Although often showing little sympathy for the sensibilities of local politicians, for the next six years, Wood strove to implement the same standards of honesty, economy, and efficiency in government that had characterized his rule in Cuba a quarter of a century earlier.

Wood led a vigorous and active life, but he had in fact suffered from increasingly poor health since sustaining a head injury in Cuba in 1898. He had also been seriously injured by an accidental mortar explosion in France in 1917, and he had undergone two brain operations. In May 1927, he returned home on an official visit and arranged to have yet another operation. He died unexpectedly on August 7 and was buried alongside other Rough Riders in Arlington National Cemetery.

Bibliography: Gleeck, Lewis, E., Jr., *The American Governors-General and High Commissioners in the Philippines* (New Day, 1986); Hagedorn, Hermann, *Leonard Wood: A Biography* (Harper & Brothers, 1931); Lane, Jack C., *Armed Progressive: General Leonard Wood* (Presidio, 1978).

Richard B. Meixsel

WOOD, ROBERT ELKINGTON (1879–1969)

U.S. army officer and business executive, Wood was born in Kansas City, Missouri. He graduated from West Point in 1900 and served in the Philippine Insurrection. He was transferred to the Panama Canal Zone in 1905 and soon became chief quartermaster of the Canal Zone and director of the Panama Railroad and Steamship Line. Instrumental in the building of the canal, he retired in 1915.

When the United States entered World War I in 1917, Wood volunteered and was commissioned a colonel. He went to France but returned to the United States early in 1918 to became quartermaster general. He worked closely with his former Panama Canal superior, Maj. Gen. George W. Goethals, to create a centralized supply system for the army. Wood retired from the army once again in 1919 and became a successful businessman, holding executive positions in the Montgomery Ward (1919–24) and Sears Roebuck (1924–39) companies.

Daniel T. Bailey

WOTHERSPOON, WILLIAM (1850–1921)

U.S. military administrator and army chief of staff, Wotherspoon was born in Washington, D.C. At age 20, he began his military career in the U.S. Navy. The highlight of his three years of naval service came in the harbor at Marseilles, France, where he boarded a burning oil ship, attached it to a tug, and had it pulled into open waters.

He sought and, in October 1873, received from Pres. Ulysses S. Grant a commission as second lieutenant in the U.S. Army. After service with several infantry regiments, including a stint in the Philippines during the insurrection there, he was appointed to the General Staff College at Fort Leavenworth.

In November 1904, Lieutenant Colonel Wotherspoon was appointed director of the newly created Army War College, a post he held for the next seven years (and from which he was interrupted for several temporary assignments). His administrative abilities came to the attention of Pres. Theodore Roosevelt, who in 1909 promoted him to brigadier general. That same year, Wotherspoon's title changed to president of the Army War College, where he remained until promoted to major general in 1912. Several other assignments preceded his April 1914 appointment as army chief of staff, a post he held only until November, when he reached mandatory retirement age.

His assignments and capabilities made Wotherspoon one of the primary architects of the professional U.S. Army. The army's efficient conduct of World War I was due in large part to the training its officer corps received at the War College. Following his retirement, Wotherspoon served as New York State Commissioner of Public Works and oversaw the completion of the state canal system.

Louise Arnold-Friend

Aviation pioneers Orville (left) *and Wilbur Wright pose in 1909, the year that the U.S. Army accepted the first army plane after months of extensive analysis and testing.* (Library of Congress)

WRIGHT, WILBUR (1867–1912) AND ORVILLE (1871–1948)

U.S. aviation pioneers, the brothers Wilbur and Orville Wright were born in Millville, Indiana, and Dayton, Ohio, respectively. Each experienced only brief periods of formal education and neither completed high school. In 1892, the Wright brothers established a bicycle shop in Dayton, and three years later, they began manufacturing bicycles.

By 1898, they had developed a strong interest in aviation, reading articles and books on the emerging field of aeronautics. They soon built a biplane kite (1899) and started conducting man-carrying glider experiments at Kitty Hawk, North Carolina (1900). Unable to find much scientific information on aircraft design and construction, the two men built a wind tunnel (1901) and tested the operation of some 200 wing and bi-wing surfaces of their own design. They painstakingly worked out major innovations in aircraft control.

In October 1902, they began building a powered aircraft. When completed, their machine weighed 750 pounds and carried a 170-pound, 12-horsepower gasoline engine. On Dec. 17, 1903, at Kitty Hawk, Orville Wright made the first piloted flight in a powered aircraft, remaining aloft for 12 seconds and soaring a distance of 120 feet. Of the four flights completed that day, Wilbur flew the longest one: 59 seconds for a distance of 852 feet. Upon returning to Dayton, the Wright brothers steadily improved their airplane. By the end of 1905, they were able to keep the craft aloft for 38 minutes and travel 24 miles. They eventually obtained a patent for the aircraft (1906). In 1909, following extensive testing and evaluation, their machine was accepted by the U.S. Army. Commercial aviation and manufacture of the Wright airplane also began that year.

M. Guy Bishop

YORK, ALVIN CULLUM (1887–1964)

Celebrated World War I hero, York was born in Pall Mall, Tennessee. He at first refused induction into the armed services on religious grounds, writing on his draft notice, "I don't want to fight." When his request for conscientious objector status was denied, York joined the 328th Regiment, 82d Division, and took part in the battles of St.-Mihiel and Argonne Forest. On Oct. 8, 1918, during the Argonne Offensive, Corporal York, an incredibly skilled marksman, singlehandedly eliminated a German machine-gun position. When a German major offered to surrender, 132 enemy soldiers eventually gave themselves up to the surprised York. York was promoted to sergeant and received more than 50 decorations, including the U.S. Congressional Medal of Honor and the French Croix de Guerre. He returned to Tennessee after the war, acclaimed as one of the war's greatest heroes. In 1941, he was immortalized in the Academy Award-winning motion picture *Sergeant York*.

Bibliography: Brandt, Nat, "Sergeant York," *American Heritage*, vol. 32; Toland, John, *No Man's Land* (Doubleday, 1980).

John F. Wukovits

Sgt. Alvin York, originally a conscientious objector, went on to win more than 50 decorations for bravery in World War I. (U.S. Army Military History Institute)

YOUNG, SAMUEL BALDWIN MARKS (1840–1924)

U.S. army officer, Young was born in Pittsburgh, Pennsylvania. He first saw service in the Civil War, enlisting in 1861. He served in Cuba during the war with Spain (1898) and in 1899 went to the Philippines, where he was promoted to brigadier general (1900) and major general (1901). There he was perhaps the most extreme of a group of officers promoting a harsh policy for the treatment of Filipinos. Young, a commander under Gen. Loyd Wheaton in the Department of Northern Luzon, was impatient with benevolent trends in the islands. Among the changes he sought included supreme powers of life and death over all natives, press censorship, use of assassination and murder in retaliation for acts in kind by rebels, and movement of all civilian populations into U.S. controlled zones. Wheaton supported these measures but did not recommend them for fear of U.S. public opinion. As a lieutenant general, he briefly commanded the army in 1903 before his retirement.

Vernon L. Williams

ZEILIN, JACOB (1806–80)

U.S. military officer, Zeilin was born in Philadelphia. He became a Marine Corps second lieutenant in 1831 and received a variety of sea and shore assignments before the Mexican War, during which he saw action in California and served as the military commandant of San Diego. After the Mexican War, Zeilin accompanied Commodore Perry during the historic trip to Japan and saw extensive action early in the Civil War before being promoted to colonel commandant in 1864.

Inheriting a Marine Corps torn by sectional differences, low morale, and an extremely high desertion rate, Zeilin sought to reestablish the Marine Corps and restore its traditional sea-going character, tasks made more difficult after the war as military budgets shrank. In 1867, he approved the adoption of the army's new drill and tactical manuals. Before his retirement in 1876, Zeilin laid the foundation for the revitalization of the Marine Corps under Col. Commandant Charles C. Heywood in 1893.

Leo J. Daugherty III

PART III

Battles and Events

ADOBE WALLS, BATTLE OF
(June 27, 1874)

Battle fought at Adobe Walls, a supply post for buffalo hunters on the Main Canadian River in the Texas Panhandle, between the post's 29 residents and a mixed group of 700 Indians, mainly Comanche and Cheyenne. The Indians, upset that the post had opened deep in Indian territory without a government license and further angered when U.S. soldiers did nothing to break it up, attacked at dawn on June 27, 1874. Two hunters were quickly killed and scalped, but the remainder reached the relative safety of the post's few buildings. From those positions poured a steady stream of accurate fire from seasoned hunters using telescopic rifles, which succeeded in repelling initial mounted attacks. By midafternoon, low on ammunition, the Indians retreated with 15 dead and a large number wounded.

Bibliography: Brown, Dee, *Bury My Heart at Wounded Knee* (Bantam Books, 1972); Leckie, William H., *The Military Conquest of the Southern Plains* (Univ. of Oklahoma Press, 1963).

John F. Wukovits

AISNE-MARNE OFFENSIVE
(July 15–August 4, 1918)

World War I operation in which French and U.S. forces defeated the Germans in northern France. The 1918 German counteroffensive drove a salient into Allied lines on the Marne River. On July 15, Gen. Erich F. W. Ludendorff launched the 1st, 3d, and 7th German armies (Gens. Bruno von Mudra, Karl von Einem, and Max von Boehn) toward Châlons-sur-Marne and Épernay in a renewed effort to expand the salient. The attack, launched without the element of surprise, merely drove the Germans deeper into a trap; on July 18, French general Ferdinand Foch (the Allies' supreme commander) launched a long-prepared offensive to nip out the salient. The French 10th Army (General Magin) attacked eastward from the Villers-Cotterêts forest against German positions on the Aisne-Ourcq rivers line. Simultaneously, Gen. Jean Marie J. Degoutte's 6th Army, on Magin's right flank, attacked the westernmost German positions between the Ourcq and the Marne.

Gen. Henri R. Pétain, directing operations, employed massed light tanks in a surprise attack on the lines of Cambrai. Subsequently, the French 5th and 9th armies (Gens. Marie Antoine H. de Mitry and Henri M. Berthelot), to the right of the 6th, assaulted the Germans south of the Marne and southwest of Rheims. The Germans stemmed the French advance sufficiently to withdraw and straighten their line, by August 2, along the Vesle River from Reims westward to the Aisne confluence and then parallel to the Aisne to a point west of Soissons, which was abandoned to the enemy.

Russell A. Hart

AMERICAN EXPEDITIONARY FORCE (A.E.F.) (1917–1919)

U.S. Army troops, under the command of Maj. Gen. John J. Pershing, sent to Europe during World War I. In April 1917, after the entry of the United States into the War, the A.E.F. was raised and sent to France. Since not technically one of the Allies, Pershing was directed to maintain the A.E.F. as "a separate and distinctive component of the combined forces, the identity of which must be preserved." A total of 2,084,000 men and 42 divisions were eventually shipped to southwestern French ports (without the loss of a single troopship) to take over the Lorraine sector of the front from east of Verdun to the Swiss border. A total of 29 divisions and 1,390,000 men saw combat in 13 major operations before the armistice on Nov. 11, 1918. Pershing first stepped foot in France on June 14, 1917. The vanguard of the 1st U.S. Division followed 12 days later.

The first U.S. offensive of the war occurred at Cantigny on May 28, 1918, as U.S. forces rushed to halt the May 27 German offensive (Third Battle of the Aisne). Although essentially a local operation, its success against Hutier's veteran 18th Army was a much needed boost to Allied morale after recent reverses.

On May 30, 1918, the U.S. 2d and 3d divisions counterattacked the German offensive on the Marne River in what has become known as the Battle of Château-Thierry, driving the Germans back across the Marne. In the days of June 5–7, the 2d Division counterattacked once again and recaptured Vaux, Bouresches, and Compiègne.

June 1918 saw the establishment of the first three U.S. corps, and on July 4, U.S. troop strength in France passed the 1,000,000 mark. On July 18, the 1st and 2d divisions spearheaded the French assault on the Marne and played a role in the subsequent elimination of the Marne salient. U.S. troops conducted the St.-Mihiel operation on September 12, but this proved a sideshow for the largest U.S. offensive of the war. On September 26, the newly formed 1st U.S. Army launched the 47-day Meuse-Argonne Campaign during which 22 divisions were committed to combat. By the armistice, Pershing's troops were at the gates of Sedan. Total A.E.F. casualties during the war amounted to 50,280 killed and 205,690 wounded.

Bibliography: Braim, Paul, F., *The Test of Battle: the A.E.F. in the Meuse-Argonne Campaign* (Univ. of Delaware Press, 1987); Smythe, Donald, *Pershing: General of the Armies* (Univ. of Indiana Press, 1986).

Russell A. Hart

APACHE CAMPAIGN (1871–1873)

Efforts by the U.S. government to enact a peace proposal based on the forced resettlement of the Southwest's Apache Indians. The Apache situation in Arizona had become so unstable by the end of the 1860s that local civilians, disgruntled by the military's failure, sought retribution.

The Camp Grant massacre of friendly Apache by the Tuscon Committee of Safety shocked the nation and highlighted the failure of the treaty system to solve the Indian problem.

Pres. Ulysses S. Grant, therefore, inaugurated a new peace policy that entailed the resettling of the Apache on four reservations: Fort Apache, Camp Verde, Tularosa Valley, and Camp Grant. The peace policy's strongest proponent was Indian Commissioner Vincent Colyer. Colyer's efforts were frustrated on two counts in 1871. Incensed Arizona settlers planned to exterminate the Apache who had gathered at the Southern Apache Agency at Canada Almosa to await Colyer's arrival. Thus, most of the Apache had fled by the time of Colyer's arrival. Nonetheless, he went on to establish the Fort Apache Reservation on Sept. 7, 1871, and subsequent reservations at Camps Grant and Verde. The second obstacle to Colyer's plans was the resurgence of advocates of a military solution. This led to the dispatch, in June 1871, of Gen. George Crook to Arizona with orders to compel the Apache onto reservations.

Crook's Campaign. On July 11, 1871, Crook moved, with little success, against Cochise's Chiracahua. Protests by peace policy proponents temporarily forced Crook to abandon hostilities. Convinced that it was only a matter of time before the peace policy was discredited, Crook made extensive preparations to force the Apache into submission. Notably, he allied with Reservation Apache, taking them on as scouts, thereby turning Apache against Apache.

Colyer's departure from Indian Territory only strengthened Crook's hand, and when violent outbreaks occurred during the summer and fall of 1871, the government endorsed a military solution. In December 1871, Crook ordered all Apache to be on their reservations by Feb. 16, 1872, or be hunted down as renegades.

The specter of war, however, caused a resurgence of the peace party, and so Gen. Oliver O. Howard was sent to work alongside Crook. The two successfully resettled the Apache on a new reservation at San Carlos. Howard's peace efforts and Crook's incessant campaigning induced Cochise to make peace on Oct. 13, 1872. With this obstacle removed, Crook was able to implement fully the hunting down of renegades and the imposition of a daily muster on the reservations, actions he had planned for since his arrival.

On Apr. 1, 1873, the beaten Apache signed the Peace of Camp Verde, and all but the most diehard renegades were rounded up by the summer. Although the Apache problem was not completely solved, Crook's campaigning had broken the back of Apache resistance.

Bibliography: Cole, D. C., *The Chiracahua Apache 1846–1876: From War to Reservation* (Univ. of New Mexico Press, 1988); Ogle, Ralph, *Federal Control of the Western Apache* (Univ. of New Mexico Press, 1970).

Russell A. Hart

APACHE CAMPAIGN (1876–1886)

U.S. military action against those Apache who resisted U.S.-imposed resettlement. In 1875, the Apache wars seemed to be at a hiatus. The death of Cochise in 1874 fragmented the Apache into quarreling factions. Many tribes accepted protected refuge. But in 1876, the Indian Bureau began a policy of concentration. All Apache were to be resettled at the San Carlos reservation on the Gila River. Half of the tribe heeded the order to go to San Carlos. The remainder, led by Geronimo, fled to Mexico and to the Sierra Madre, from where they conducted sweeping raids across Arizona and northern Mexico.

In 1877, the Warm Springs Apache of Ojo Caliente reservation were also ordered to San Carlos. On Sept. 2, 1877, Victorio led his men from the reservation only to surrender at Fort Wingate, New Mexico, in October. They were allowed to return to Ojo Caliente while the governor decided how best to deal with the Apache problem. Upon hearing that they would be forced to return to San Carlos, Victorio and 90 men took to the mountains. They then terrorized settlements while managing to evade the army by fleeing into Mexico whenever U.S. troops approached. Their freedom was curtailed, however, by lack of food and bad weather, and in 1879, Victorio talked to an agent at the Mescanero Apache reservation east of the Rio Grande about resettling there.

The request was rejected. Victorio and 60 men counterattacked by completing a sweep on Troop E of the 9th Cavalry near Ojo Caliente, killing 8 black soldiers on guard there and stealing 46 horses. Joined by some 150 new warriors, he began a series of raids on cross-country travelers. In November, Victorio ambushed and killed 18 Mexicans and a search party of 15 in the Candelaria Mountains of Chichuahua. He continued raiding, until 1880, from Chichuahua into west Texas, New Mexico, and Arizona.

In 1880, Col. Edward Hatch and the 9th Cavalry pursued the band into New Mexico and at Hembrillo Canyon and at Black Range almost succeeded in capturing the renegades. In July, Victorio attempted to reenter the United States via Texas but was driven back by a well-coordinated attack under Col. Benjamin H. Grierson and the 10th Cavalry out of Forts Davis and Stockton. By fall, the raiders began to tire and moved farther east. In September, Col. George P. Buell led a force of 350 Mexican militia across the Mexican border. At the same time, Col. Joaquin Terrazos, an experienced Apache fighter, went east to deal with the beleagured Apache. These initiatives were doomed, however, as Terrazos refused to cooperate with the U.S. forces and consequently ordered them out of Mexico. However, by October, Terrazos's Mexican troops had surrounded the Apache at Tres Castillos, Chichuahua. Large quantities of Indian stock were captured, and the Apache were driven into the hills. In the subsequent Indian advance, 78 Apache were killed and 68 taken prisoner. Victorio was

During the Apache Campaign, Indian police stand in front of the guardhouse on the San Carlos Reservation in 1880. (U.S. Army Military History Institute)

found dead. His death ended one era of the Apache campaign, but it did not end the war. The survivors of Tres Castillos moved north under Nane, ultimately to ally with Geronimo.

Until summer 1881, the Apache were concerned mainly with regrouping and the army with keeping the peace on the San Carlos reservation. However, the attempted arrest of Nakaidoklini, a medicine man who was preaching a subversive new religion on reservation land, led to the mutiny of the White Mountain Scouts and the Battle of Cibicue Creek on Aug. 30, 1881. On September 1, the Apache also attacked Fort Apache but were driven back. The newspapers portrayed the whole affair as a massacre, which provoked further garrisoning of the San Carlos reservation. On September 30, Geronimo, Nacho, and 76 Indians broke out of the San Carlos reservation and united with the remainder of Victorio's band in Mexico.

Campaign Against Geronimo. In April 1882, a war party under Geronimo attacked San Carlos and left with hundreds of Warm Springs Apache. At Horseshoe Canyon, they fought off Col. George A. Forsyth and continued into Mexico. In July, Natiosh led another raid by the White Mountain Apache on stockmen in the Tonto basin, only to be wiped out at the Battle of Big Dry Wash on July 17.

Later that year, Gen. Orlando Willcox was replaced at the Arizona Agency by Gen. George Crook, who organized five companies of White Mountain Apache to seek out the raiders in the Sierra Madre. His cross-border campaign proved successful and resulted in the return of Geronimo and others to San Carlos.

In May 1885, the Apache broke out again and were pursued by Crook into Mexico. After a campaign lasting many months, Crook persuaded the Chiricihua to talk. At the conference at the Canyon de los Embudos Mar. 25, 1886, Geronimo finally surrendered, but almost immediately bolted to the mountains. Crook was replaced by Gen. Nelson A. Miles. From Fort Huachuca, Miles combed the Sierra Madre. Captured Apaches were sent to detention camps in Florida and San Carlos. Lt. Charles B. Gatewood opened formal talks with Geronimo, who formally surrendered at Skeleton Canyon in Arizona, September 1886.

Bibliography: Worcester, Donald, *The Apaches: Eagles of the Southwest* (Univ. of Oklahoma Press, 1979).

Russell A. Hart

ARMISTICE (November 11, 1918)

The end of the combat of World War I, as effected at 11:00 A.M., Nov. 11, 1918, six hours after Germany signed a treaty of peace. Negotiations for an armistice began on Oct. 6, 1918, with a request from the German army. The original basis of armistice negotiations was Pres. Woodrow Wilson's Fourteen Points. During the course of negotiations, the Weimar Republic was proclaimed, and on November 10, the Kaiser abdicated. The final terms of the armistice bore little resemblance to Wilson's Fourteen Points and were, in effect, an unconditional German surrender. The German army had to evacuate all occupied territories and leave behind all heavy military equipment. Additionally, Germany evacuated territory west of the Rhine, surrendered all submarines, and interned all other warships. The Allied blockade of Germany remained in effect.

Capt. George B. Eaton

ARMY-NAVY BOARD (1898)

The U.S. military board that validated the usefulness of a joint agency to coordinate the strategic planning of the U.S. Army and Navy. To facilitate joint planning for the expected war against Spain, a two-man Army-Navy Board was established in late March 1898. Army lieutenant colonel Arthur L. Wagner and navy captain A. S. Barker outlined a plan for a joint assault on Cuba. Submitted to the service secretaries on Apr. 4, 1898, their plan, although subsequently modified, provided the basic outline for the joint campaign in the Caribbean. Deemed a workable agency, this board led to the creation of the more permanent Joint Army-Navy Board in 1903.

Lt. Col. (Ret.) Charles R. Shrader

ARMY WAR COLLEGE (1901)

The U.S. Army's institution of higher learning. The Spanish-American War of 1898 revealed a number of inadequacies in the U.S. Army's ability to plan, coordinate, and manage large-scale military operations. As part of his overall reform program, Sec. of War Elihu Root sought to create an agency with dual academic and planning/coordination responsibilities that would "study and confer on the great problems of national defense, of military science, and of responsible command." Congress appropriated funds for the project in May 1900, and the Army War College was formally established by War Department General Order No. 155 on Nov. 27, 1901. The first officers were assigned to the new college in July 1902, and in February 1903, Root laid the cornerstone for its permanent home in Washington, D.C.

From 1901 to 1917, the War College operated as the third division of the newly formed War Department General Staff. Its primary tasks were war planning, the supervision of the army school system, and the preparation of strategic and tactical problems for the instruction of army officers. The first resident class of nine officers began its course in November 1904. Subsequent courses have included officers of the other services, civilian agencies, and allied nations.

The Army War College shared the growing pains of the new General Staff and was not particularly successful in preparing officers for the challenges of World War I, but a beginning had been made. Courses were suspended in 1917. When they were resumed in the fall of 1919, the college had shed its staff planning and coordination responsibilities and had been refocused on a broader, more clearly educational mission. Between 1919 and 1941, the college became the capstone of the army officer education system and successfully prepared a generation of officers for the great challenges of World War II. Courses were again suspended in 1941 on the eve of war, but the college reopened in February 1950 at Fort Leavenworth, Kansas. It was moved to its present home, Carlisle Barracks, Pennsylvania, in July 1951.

The establishment of the Army War College was a landmark in the process of creating a progressive system of professional education for army officers begun in the 1880s. Today the college stands at the apex of an international respected system of officer education. Most general officers of the army are graduates of the college, which also plays an important role in the formulation of army organization and doctrine.

Lt. Col. (Ret.) Charles R. Shrader

BANNOCK WAR OF 1878

One of several minor campaigns in which the U.S. Army sealed the fate of the smaller Indian tribes of the Northwest. The war was caused by U.S. incursions by white settlers on the Camas Prairie southeast of Boise, Idaho. The camas root was a principal foodstuff of the Bannock and Paiute, and the livestock, particularly hogs, of the U.S. settlers destroyed the roots of the plants. Compelled by hunger, the Bannock and Paiute began a last futile protest of their fate in the spring of 1878 with raids, led by the Bannock chief Buffalo Horn, on U.S. settlements. Leadership of the group of about 450 warriors soon fell to the Paiute chief Egan and the shaman Oytes.

After chasing the rebellious Bannock and Paiute over very rugged terrain and fighting several sharp engagements, the 1,000 troops commanded by Capt. Reuben F. Bernard forced the surrender of Oytes on August 12 and ended the war in a final engagement in Wyoming one month later. During the brief campaign, 31 U.S. civilians were killed; the loss of U.S. soldiers was 9 dead, 15 wounded. An estimated 78 Indians were killed; the survivors fled to refuge with the Sheepeaters in the Salmon River Mountains.

Bibliography: Robert M. Utley, *Frontier Regulars: The United States Army and the Indian, 1866–1890* (New York: Macmillan, 1973).

Lt. Col. (Ret.) Charles R. Shrader

BEECHER'S ISLAND, BATTLE OF (September 17–25, 1868)

U.S. military engagement against hostile Indians in Kansas. In the summer of 1868, Gen. Philip Sheridan ordered Maj. George A. Forsyth to raise a company of 50 frontiersmen and to protect the railroad around Fort Wallace, Kansas. In mid-September, Forsyth's men pursued a warm trail up the Arikara Fork of the Republican River. At dawn on September 17, 600–700 Sioux and Cheyenne warriors attacked the army camp. Forsyth moved his men onto a small island, where they held off three Indian charges. Rebuffed, the Indians besieged the small force. Several scouts managed to slip past the besiegers, however, and retrieve help from Fort Wallace. On September 25, a column of the 10th Cavalry lifted the siege. Militarily the battle was of little significance, but it became part of army lore.

Richard F. Kehrberg

BELFORT RUSE (August–September, 1918)

A U.S.-conducted operation designed to deceive the Germans as to the actual point of a U.S. attack, the Belfort Ruse was only partially successful. The ruse was suggested to Gen. John J. Pershing when the French general Henri P. Pétain discovered widespread and embarrassingly accurate stories in Paris about a forthcoming U.S. offensive. Col. Arthur L. Conger of Pershing's staff, along with a number of unwitting unit representatives, were dispatched to the French city of Belfort near the German and Swiss borders to create enough communications and reconnaissance activity to appear convincing. The Germans were taken in, sending three divisions to Mulhausen, directly opposite Belfort. However, these units were not taken from the St.-Mihiel region, the object of the planned U.S. offensive. The Americans, however, did achieve surprise in their first major offensive in World War I, a success that could partially be attributed to Conger's work.

Col. (Ret.) Rod Paschall

BELLEAU WOOD, BATTLE OF
(June 6–26, 1918)

World War I battle that represented the final attempt by the German army to advance on Paris and the first major engagement of U.S. troops, particularly the 4th Marine Brigade, in the war. Prior to the battle, U.S. troops had been either engaged in training or occupying the quiet sectors of the front lines, while British and French troops were rushed to block the massive German onslaught that threatened to break through the Allied line that spring.

German advances during Gen. Erich F. W. Ludendorff's Chemin des Dames offensive against the Aisne Heights (May 27, 1918) threatened to cut the Allies' northern front into two, thus allowing the Germans unhindered access into Paris. Conferring with his staff and the U.S. commander-in-chief, Gen. John J. Pershing, French marshall Ferdinand Foch ordered the U.S. 2d Division eastward toward the front lines with the mission of saving Paris.

On June 1, 1918, the 6th Marine Regiment, commanded by Col. Albertus Catlin, relieved the French forces northwest of Château-Thierry, while to their right, the 5th Regiment was positioned to guard the 6th's flank. Maj. Gen. James G. Harbord, commanding officer of the 2d Division, of which the 4th Marine Brigade was attached, began a general advance on June 6, in order to correct the bulge that had developed after the initial German advances in the Château-Thierry sector. This mission involved the marine brigade in some of the heaviest fighting thus far on the Western Front. The marines were to lay the groundwork for the Allies' general counteroffensive that would eventually drive the German army back beyond the Hindenburg line. The Belleau Wood operation thus became part of the larger offensive in the Château-Thierry sector, with the marines leading the assault. The first part of that offensive commenced on the morning of June 5, when part of the 1st Battalion, 5th Marines, was ordered to seize a formidable German machine-gun emplacement on Hill 142 in Belleau Wood.

The terrain of this former hunting preserve made the operation complex. Belleau Wood was the largest of a number of small forests visible from the dominating heights surrounding the woods. The woods themselves were approximately 1.2 miles from north to south, a little more than 0.5 mile from east to west. The terrain was rough, high ground, strewn with boulders and rock formations interspersed with deep ravines and gullies. The thick underbrush severely restricted visibility. The woods themselves were broken up by large wheat fields bordered by another line of dense woods. This was where the 5th and 6th Marines placed their reserves and utilized the site as a jumping-off point for the attack. Thus, Belleau Wood was a natural fortress, offering the German defenders an excellent field of fire. It became the task of Gen. John A. Lejeune's 4th Marine Brigade to dislodge the Germans from the woods and prevent the Germans from advancing on Paris.

Early Combat Operations. Broken up into two phases, the early morning assault on June 6 secured the first in a series of German strong points on Hill 142. By noon, Turill's battalion, after incurring heavy casualties in an attack that covered only a half a mile, had seized a critical point in the German defenses in Belleau Wood. The second phase of the attack involved the 3d Battalion, 5th Marines, commanded by Maj. B. S. Berry, and the 2d and 3d battalions, 6th Marines. Despite the fierce German resistance, the marines advanced in fighting that at times was hand-to-hand and were able to achieve a toehold along the edge of the woods and the neighboring village of Bouresches.

The main objective of the 2d Division was not only to secure Belleau Wood but also to take the towns of Torcy, Bussaires, and Bouresches. Defended by some of the best troops in the German army (the 461st Infantry Regiment and the 237th Division), Harbord had hoped that the attack would catch the enemy off guard, but the advancing marines came under intense artillery and machine-gun fire.

By late evening of that first day, the marines were able to secure the edge of the forest but had suffered heavy casualties. By the end of the day, the marines had suffered 1,087 casualties in killed, wounded, and missing—a greater loss than the Marine Corps had ever suffered in any previous battle.

After their initial setback, the Germans rushed in reinforcements and further strengthened their defenses in the woods. As the marines, assisted by artillery, readied to resume the offensive, German artillery and machine-gun fire pounded them at the end of the forest. Only on June 9 was the 1st Battalion, 6th Marines, able to advance to where Sibley's marines had ended up before being halted.

On the morning of June 11, the 2d Battalion, 5th Marines, attempted to link up with the 1st Battalion, 6th Marines, and to launch a major offensive designed to clear the Germans from Belleau Wood. This assault not only netted the marines a break in the main German line, but it also cracked all German resistance in Belleau Wood as a whole. By 8:40 P.M., the marines controlled nearly 90 percent of Belleau Wood. As the marines dug in that night, the Germans prepared a counterattack.

The marines' position in Belleau Wood was still precarious, being exposed to German artillery fire and an expected infantry attack, which came at 4:00 A.M., June 13. After nearly five hours, the Germans were beaten back, due largely to the fact that their commanders had expended their reserves.

Last Phases. As the Germans sought to replace and reinforce their depleted units for one last counterstroke, front-line American marine units were withdrawn temporarily until they could be reinforced and brought up to strength before being committed in Belleau Wood. The U.S. Army's 23d Infantry Division and 7th Infantry Regiment were dispatched to relieve the marines at Bouresches. The Germans likewise reinforced their depleted units with that of the 87th Infantry Division, which replaced the battered 28th Division.

On June 23, the last major attack was launched to drive the Germans from Belleau Wood. Having had sufficient time to dig in deeper, the Germans were preparing for the final stand against the anticipated major U.S. onslaught, which came that evening. By 9:30 P.M., June 25, the last pockets of German resistance had been crushed. The U.S. troops had not only saved Paris from the German offensive, but they had proven beyond any doubt that, militarily, the United States was prepared for war. The French, who had disputed the abilities of the American soldier, were so grateful that they renamed the Belleau Wood sector "Bois de la Brigade Marine."

Bibliography: Heinl, Robert D., Jr., *Soldiers of the Sea: The United States Marines, 1775–1962* (Naval Inst. Press, 1965); McClellan, Edwin N., *The United States Marine Corps in the World War* (U.S. Govt. Printing Office, 1920); Millett, Allan R., *Semper Fidelis: The History of the United States Marine Corps* (Macmillan Co., 1980).

Leo J. Daugherty III

BLACK HILLS EXPEDITION (1874)

A U.S. military mission of exploration that violated a Sioux treaty and invoked a gold rush. The Sioux treasured the Black Hills of present-day South Dakota for the richness of the game, the sheltered valleys, and the abundant firewood. Sprawling over the western portion of the Great Sioux Reservation, the tribe believed the area safe from white intrusion. Then, in the fall of 1873, Gen. William T. Sherman determined to conduct a reconnaissance of the Black Hills. Lt. Col. George A. Custer was assigned to explore the Black Hills. Officially, the purpose of the expedition was to find a site for a military post. An unstated goal was to scout for mineral wealth, particularly gold. In the contemporary U.S. imagination, the Black Hills offered the last great mining frontier of the West. The Treaty of 1868 guaranteeing the Black Hills to the Sioux infuriated Dakotans. The Black Hills Expedition marched out of Fort Lincoln in July 1874. When his men found traces of gold, Custer quickly made the information public, thus starting the Black Hills gold rush.

M. Guy Bishop

BOXER REBELLION (1898–1900)

Unsuccessful uprising by a Chinese secret society, primarily against foreigners. Sparked by hatred of foreign "spheres of influence" in their country, members of the covert I Ho Chuan (Society of Righteous and Harmonious Fists) fomented rebellion against Westerners near the end of the 1800s. Labeled the "Boxers" because of their practice of Chinese martial arts, they blamed all of China's problems, including serious famine and devastating floods, on foreigners and found a ready following among the country's illiterate peasants and former soldiers.

The Boxers spread rapidly through much of northern China when the Dowager Empress Tzu-Hsi, who also hoped to counter European influence, adopted a lenient approach to the Boxers' violent actions. Inflammatory signs urged people to "Protect our country, drive out foreigners, and kill Christians." Christian missionaries in outlying regions bore the movement's initial fury. On Dec. 31, 1899, a British missionary was killed, followed by further such incidents in the next five months.

As the Boxers neared Peking (Beijing), the foreign legations situated inside dispatched pleas for aid from troops stationed near the coast. On May 31, 1900, 340 soldiers of various nationalities, including 50 U.S. Marines led by Capt. John T. Myers, entered the Legation Quarter, a 1.5-square-mile stretch of embassies and foreign businesses in Peking, and started constructing barricades for its defense. While 24 foreign warships gathered off the Chinese coastal forts at Taku, Boxers rapidly moved in on Peking to threaten the legations. As conditions deteriorated, the Chinese foreign office informed each legation that relations had been broken and they must depart within 24 hours, a situation made worse when the German minister was shot to death while on his way to the Chinese foreign office. War erupted when foreign ships fired on the Taku forts.

Foreign diplomats, their families and staffs, and Chinese Christians gathered in the Legation Quarter. A force of 409 soldiers from eight nations, supported by only 4 field weapons and 125 civilian volunteers, quickly established a defense perimeter keyed by a section of Peking's huge Tartar Wall held by Myers's marines. British minister Claude MacDonald assumed command while a Methodist missionary, Dr. Frank Gamewell, directed construction of defenses. Food for the besieged 3,000 foreigners, including 1,000 cases of imported champagne from the Peking Hotel, appeared sufficient for the time being.

Chinese regular troops and Boxers relied mainly on continuous artillery and rifle fire to pin down legation defenders while other troops gradually moved closer. Twice, buildings lying adjacent to legation positions were torched, but neither resulted in any significant Boxer gains. Surrounded by howling mobs, foreigners tied their hopes to relief from Western forces gathering near the coast.

Those forces experienced problems of their own, however. British admiral Sir Edward H. Seymour led more than 1,800 troops out of Tientsin on June 10. The Chinese government, upset that a large conglomeration of foreign troops was heading toward Peking, ordered its own military to join angry Boxers in stopping Seymour. A June 15 attack was followed by a stronger assault on June 18 that forced Seymour, low on supplies and burdened by wounded soldiers, to fall back to Hsiku Arsenal, where he held out until relieved on June 24 by a contingent of U.S. Marines. The combined force rushed back to Tientsin's foreign settlements, now practically surrounded by Boxers. On July 13, a large multinational assault led by Japanese troops succeeded in driving out 24,000 Chinese regular and Boxer troops from Tientsin.

Meanwhile, in Peking the Chinese centered on Myers's crucial section of the legation defense by constructing a high wall that enabled them to fire down on the U.S. position. When the Chinese advanced this wall to within 25 feet of the Americans, Myers led a desperate charge against the numerically superior Chinese that succeeded in driving them back. U.S. minister Edwin H. Conger later tabbed this charge the "bravest and the most successful event of the whole siege."

The Chinese reverted to their strategy of constant artillery and rifle fire while probing for a weak sector. The nerves of those inside the Legation Quarter became frayed from unrelenting heat, endless duty shifts at the wall, and continuous worry about their fate.

Partly as a result of successful allied action at Tientsin, a 12-day cease-fire commenced in Peking in mid-July. During that time, the first word that a relief expedition was being organized reached the besieged legations, which now were concerned with rapidly dwindling food supplies. In early August, everyone went on half-rations.

Relief of Peking. Knowing an allied relief expedition was being planned, Chinese forces around Peking ended the cease-fire with heavy pushes against legation defenses, now manned by every available fighter, even the wounded. An August 13 thrust led by officers shouting "Don't be afraid—we can get through!" almost succeeded, but at a critical moment a Chinese barricade collapsed, permitting British forces to gun down the attackers behind. In the middle of the assault, defenders heard the sounds of fighting to the Chinese rear, indicating that the relief expedition had finally arrived.

The expedition almost arrived too late, partly because allied commanders wasted an entire month debating strategy. Finally, a 16,000-strong eight-nation force, led by large contingents from the United States, Russia, Japan, and England, departed for Peking on August 4. Maj. Gen. Adna R. Chaffee commanded 2,000 U.S. troops, including marines, the 6th U.S. Cavalry, and the 14th U.S. Infantry.

In the next two days, Chinese forces battled the expedition at Peitsang and Yangsun but inflicted little damage. After a third clash at Tungchow, only 14 miles from Peking, allied commanders plotted their strategy for breaking through to the legations. After advancing in parallel columns to a jump-off point, Russian, Japanese, American, and British forces would each charge one of Peking's four gates situated along its eastern wall. As each nation was eager to be first into Peking, all were to advance simultaneously on the morning of August 13.

However, when Russian troops jumped off ahead of schedule, the other foreign contingents followed hastily behind. In the confusion, troops attacked the wrong objectives and threw the assault into disarray. Chaffee quickly led his men through an open gate and battled the Chinese in severe street fighting. Supported by Capt. Henry J. Reilly's Light Battery F of the 5th U.S. Artillery, Chaffee's troops slowly advanced from building to building until they neared the American Legation. At 4:00 P.M., they sighted a U.S. Marine happily waving a U.S. flag from the Tartar Wall. Unknown to Chaffee's men, a British detachment had already arrived at the legation.

While U.S., Japanese, and Russian forces encountered stiff opposition, British troops piled through their gate against minimal resistance and rushed toward the Legation Quarter. After being told by an American defender of an entry point through a sluice gate, British soldiers poured through to relieve the weary defenders.

Chaffee led the 14th Infantry against Forbidden City, a walled section of Peking, on August 14, while Russian, Japanese, and British forces consolidated control over the rest of Peking. With Reilly's artillery in support, the infantry fought through two of Forbidden City's three successive gates, at which time a cease-fire order halted the Americans before they broke into the inner confines of Forbidden City. Two days later, a column of soldiers relieved the last group of Westerners under siege when it advanced against the French Pei-tang Cathedral two miles from the Legation Quarter.

The ordeal had cost the defenders 49 percent casualties, caused the deaths of as many as 50,000 Chinese Christians, and brought 60 Medals of Honor to U.S. troops. It ended in a debauchery of Western looting throughout Peking while the Dowager Empress fled in disguise to the old capital of Sian. The severe Boxer Protocol, implemented on Sept. 7,

1901, ensured continued Chinese hatred for foreign domination with its insistence on the destruction of Chinese coastal defenses, the execution of high officials, formal apologies, a prohibition of arms imports, and a huge indemnity to Western nations.

Bibliography: Dupuy, R. Ernest, and William H. Baumer, *The Little Wars of the United States* (Hawthorn Books, 1968); Heinl, Robert Debs, Jr., *Soldiers of the Sea* (Naval Inst. Press, 1962); O'Connor, Richard, *The Spirit Soldiers* (Putnam's, 1973); Purcell, Victor, *The Boxer Uprising* (Cambridge Univ. Press, 1963); Tan, Chester C., *The Boxer Catastrophe* (Columbia Univ. Press, 1955).

John F. Wukovits

BROWNSVILLE INCIDENT
(August 13–14, 1906)

An alleged racial confrontation of dubious origin, in which black army enlistees were implicated. When shots were fired in Brownsville, Texas, on the night of Aug. 13–14, 1906, the mayor and other inhabitants of the town blamed black soldiers from nearby Fort Brown for the resulting death of one white man and the wounding of another. An army investigation resulted in the discharge of 167 enlisted men of the 1st Battalion, 25th Infantry, on the orders of Pres. Theodore Roosevelt, although the men were never convicted of any crime. (The rest of the regiment, along with the army's other black troops, was soon sent to the Philippines.) A U.S. Senate inquiry in 1907–08 upheld the order, but a minority report lent credence to claims that the soldiers were not involved in the affair. The army reinstated 14 of the soldiers in 1909, but not until 1972 did it reopen the case and reverse all of the dismissals. Only one soldier remained alive to collect a pension authorized by Congress.

Richard B. Meixsel

BUFFALO SOLDIERS

Name given by Indians to black Indian-fighting U.S. cavalrymen in the late 1860s. The use of black soldiers was initially viewed as experimental by the army. In August 1866, Gen. Ulysses S. Grant directed that a regiment of black cavalry be organized for service on the frontier. This new regiment, designated as the 9th and 10th U.S. cavalries, was placed under the command of Cols. Edward Hatch and Benjamin Grierson, respectively. Despite the possibilities for greater rank and rapid advancement, many white officers refused to command black troops. Still, some excellent officers were eventually procured for these units, including Lt. Col. Wesley Merritt and Maj. Albert P. Morrow.

By early 1867, the 9th Cavalry was stationed in west Texas at Fort Davis and the 10th at Fort Leavenworth, Kansas. The westward movement of these regiments marked the beginning of more than two decades of continuous service on the Southern Plains and in the mountains and deserts of New Mexico and Arizona by black cavalrymen.

Grierson and the 10th Cavalry fought on the Southern Plains in 1868–69. The 10th was assigned to provide safety in the Indian Territory and along the Smoky Hill and Santa Fe overland routes. Before long, Indian antagonists were referring to these hard-fighting foes as "buffalo soldiers"—a name referring to their hair, which the Indians likened to bison fur. The men of the 10th, and later the 9th, Cavalry wore this name with pride.

The 9th Cavalry, operating out of Forts Davis and Stockton, had the mission, from 1867, of protecting the mail and stage route between San Antonio and El Paso, campaigning against marauding Indians, and maintaining law and order along the troubled Rio Grande. Patrolling the vast, sparsely settled region was a difficult task. In late October 1867, a hostile Indian band killed two buffalo soldiers near Fort Stockton. The next month, another soldier was killed. To counter these raids, Merritt set in motion plans to drive the marauding Apache south into Mexico. However, the 9th was spread too thin over the Texas plains and their enemies were too numerous. Military control was not established until summer 1869.

Sgt. Christian A. Fleetwood fought with the Buffalo Soldiers, the name given to black troops by the Indians, who thought the soldiers' hair resembled bison fur. (U.S. Army Military History Institute)

In May 1918, soldiers of the U.S. 28th Infantry go over the top of the ridge on which Cantigny is located and fight their way toward the town. (U.S. Signal Corps)

While considerable success with the Mescalero Apache could now be claimed, the Kiowa, the Commanche, and the Lipan Apache remained a sore spot for the 9th Cavalry. The lack of decisive victories over their elusive foes frustrated the commanders of the 9th. By the end of 1871, the 9th Cavalry had seen nearly five years of the hardest kind of service with no respite. Grierson's 10th Cavalry fared better, playing an instrumental role in the 1879–80 Victorio War. Overall, the buffalo soldiers of both the 9th and 10th U.S. cavalries were first-rate soldiers, equal to the challenges of the western frontier.

M. Guy Bishop

CAMP GRANT MASSACRE
(April 30, 1871)

Brutal attack and slaying of Apache villagers by a civilian faction from Tucson, Arizona. In 1869, Pres. Ulysses S. Grant adopted a peace policy designed to curb hostilities between Indians and U.S. settlers. Bvt. Maj. Gen. George Stoneman was assigned to implement this policy in the Department of Arizona. Trying to impose peace "through the medium of their bellies," Stoneman established a "feeding station" near Camp Grant (located on the lower San Pedro River) for Arivaipa and Pinal Apache. Arizonans, particularly the "Tucson Ring," adamantly opposed the policy since it would hurt their livelihood of supplying military expeditions. In Tucson, a Committee of Safety was formed, dedicated to active resistance to Grant's policy.

Just after daylight on Apr. 30, 1871, a group from Tucson (6 Anglos, 48 indigent Mexicans, and 94 Papago Indians who had long suffered at the hands of the Apache) raided an Apache rancheria near Camp Grant. Led by William S. Oury and Jesus M. Elias, the group slaughtered and mutilated an estimated 125 Apache, nearly all of whom were women and children. Another 29 children were carried off and sold into bondage in Sonora, Mexico. While Arizonans applauded the massacre, President Grant and the rest of the nation were appalled. After Grant threatened to impose martial law, more than 100 alleged participants were brought to trial. It took a Tucson jury just 19 minutes to render a "not guilty" verdict. Unfortunately, the bitter legacy of the Camp Grant Massacre would affect the Arizona Territory for another two decades.

Lt. Col. Martin W. Andresen

CANTIGNY, BATTLE OF
(May 28–31, 1918)

World War I battle in northern France, in which the United States executed its first offensive action of the war. In May 1918, the 1st Division (under Maj. Gen. Robert L. Bullard) of the American Expeditionary Force (A.E.F.) was directed to seize the town of Cantigny, then held by German general Oskar von Hutier's 18th Army. Located approximately three miles northwest of Montdidier, at the tip of the

Amiens salient, Cantigny sat on a low, but tactically significant, ridge that overlooked the U.S. front lines.

The Allies knew that the coming battle would be a critical test of the inexperienced U.S. soldiers, commanders, and staffs. Gen. John J. Pershing reportedly declared that once the town was taken, "no inch was to be given up."

The division staff prepared what became a one-regiment attack. The principal planners were operations officer Lt. Col. George C. Marshall and artillery brigade commander Brig. Gen. Charles P. Summerall. They thoroughly orchestrated the attack, leaving little to chance. Aerial photographs, terrain models, and intelligence from German prisoners were used in planning, and, behind division lines, a model of Cantigny was laid out. The regiment scheduled to make the attack, the 28th Infantry under Col. Hanson E. Ely, was pulled out of line and put through two full rehearsals of the planned attack.

The attack began on the morning of May 28. A two-hour artillery bombardment was so successful that the first wave of attacking troops essentially walked in and claimed Cantigny. Infantrymen used flamethrowers to root out surviving Germans who were hiding in cellars. Suffering few casualties, they took 100 prisoners by 8:00 A.M. Some Germans avoided capture and inflicted casualties on reserve troops moving forward to support the assault force.

The regiment failed to establish a secure perimeter defense and faced repeated German counterattacks for the next two days. But German infantry assaults were ill-coordinated with their artillery, and Ely's men defeated the multiple attacks. Nevertheless, heavy German artillery fire over the next two days caused many U.S. casualties and impeded communications. The division could not counter the German artillery because French heavy artillery and air support had been rushed south to meet a new German offensive. The 1st Division's own guns could break up German infantry assaults but lacked the range for counter-battery fire. After 48 hours, the regiment, reinforced with almost a full battalion, had lost almost one-third of its original strength. Exhausted, the regiment was replaced on the night of May 30–31 by Col. John L. Hines's 16th Infantry. The Germans, however, who had suffered approximately 1,800 casualties, then decided to make no further efforts to retake Cantigny.

While not significant operationally, Cantigny was a tactical and psychological success. In rendering two German infantry regiments largely combat-ineffective, the 1st Division won an important psychological victory for the A.E.F. Marshall wrote later that the "price paid was a heavy one [approximately 1,000 casualties] but it demonstrated conclusively the fighting qualities and fortitude of the American soldier." Pershing was elated. The Germans correctly interpreted the battle as evidence of the A.E.F.'s rapid maturation.

Stephen J. Lofgren

CARRIZAL AFFAIR (June 21, 1916)

Military skirmish in a northern Mexican village, in which U.S. forces, under the command of Gen. John J. Pershing, were defeated by the Mexicans. During the 1916 Punitive Expedition into Mexico, U.S. troops scoured the countryside in search of Pancho Villa and members of his band. As the expedition penetrated deeper into Mexico, the Carranza government, which had permitted the entry of U.S. troops into the country, became increasingly belligerent. On June 21, 1916, a patrol of the 10th Cavalry attempted to enter the town of Carrizal without the permission of the local Carranzista commander. A sharp gunfight followed in which the U.S. contingent lost 12 men killed, 11 wounded, and several others captured. The fight awoke both sides to the real possibility of a major war between them and served to dampen the hot tempers that had preceded it.

Bibliography: Clendenen, Clarence C., *Blood on the Border: The United States Army and the Mexican Irregulars* (Macmillian Co., 1969).

Richard F. Kehrberg

CHÂTEAU-THIERRY, BATTLE OF (May 30–June 26, 1918)

World War I battle between U.S. and German troops in northern France. On May 27, 1918, Gen. Erich F. W. Ludendorff launched a diversionary German assault along a 25-mile section of the French front on the Chemin des Dames, better known as the Third Battle of the Aisne. This rapid breakthrough across the Aisne River to the Marne River forced Gen. John J. Pershing to rush U.S. troops to the defense of the Marne. On May 30, the 2d and 3d U.S. divisions (under Maj. Gens. Omar Bundy and Joseph Dickman, respectively) moved against the nose of the German penetration across the Marne. The 3d Division denied the Marne bridges at Château-Thierry to the enemy, then subsequently counterattacked and, with the assistance of rallying French troops, threw the Germans back across the Marne. Meanwhile, the 2d Division halted all German efforts to advance west of Château-Thierry.

The timely intervention of U.S. troops stemmed the rout of the French forces and contributed directly to Ludendorff's decision to halt his offensive on June 4. The following day, the 2d Division went on the offensive. The advance was spearheaded by Brig. Gen. James Harbord's 4th Marine Brigade, composed of the 5th and 6th marine regiments and the 6th Marine Machine-Gun Battalion. The attack was supported by elements of the 9th and 23d infantry regiments of Brig. Gen. Edward Lewis's 3d Infantry Brigade. Additionally, on the division's flanks, troops of the French 10th Colonial and 167th Infantry divisions pursued diversionary attacks aimed at tying down German reserves.

The initial assault proved successful, with the early capture of Bouresches on June 6. On that same day, elements of the 23d Infantry Regiment, due to confusion over orders, advanced well beyond their designated objectives, leaving their flanks exposed and the unit unsupported. German counterattacks during the night of June 6–7 drove the Americans back to the original halt line with heavy casualties. By June 7–8, the advance into Belleau Wood had also stalled in the face of entrenched machine-gun positions and German infiltration tactics. The thick undergrowth provided excellent defensive cover, and consequently the woods proved murderously difficult to clear.

U.S. troops withdrew somewhat on June 9, preparatory to a major artillery barrage by U.S. and French artillery. This facilitated further advances, and on June 11, U.S. troops occupied Hill 169 deep inside the wood. A renewed German push on Compiègne, begun on June 9, was stopped by French and U.S. troops by June 12. Casualties were heavy due to stiff German resistance and employment of gas attacks. By June 15, losses amounted to 4,400 personnel, of which only 2,740 could be replaced immediately. By this stage, the 4th Marine Brigade had exhausted itself after two weeks of nonstop, heavy combat. Relief, though, proved impossible. Nevertheless, steps were made to shorten the marines' front, thereby allowing the withdrawal of several battalions to the rear for rest.

Renewed efforts were made to eliminate the continuing enemy resistance along the northern edge of the wood. The U.S. troops experienced difficulty gaining ground because of German infiltration back into sectors of the woods previously cleared. Such groups disrupted communications and launched spoiling attacks aimed at throwing the Americans off stride. On June 16, the 7th and 23d infantry regiments (3d Brigade) joined the attack in order to regain the offensive's lost momentum. Finally, by June 25, the last Germans were driven from their positions on the northern tip of the woods and at Vaux and Compiègne.

Although a relatively small engagement with limited strategic value, the fact that this was the first significant clash of U.S. and German forces gave the battle a special psychological importance on both sides. The defending Germans were determined to bloody the inexperienced U.S. troops. To this end, German commanders led their troops to believe that the Americans would not take prisoners. Consequently, the fighting proved bitter and bloody. Between June 5 and June 26, the 2d Division drove the Germans from their positions at Vaux, Bouresches, Compiègne, and also at Belleau Wood, whose name this battle often bears. However, the cost of these successes was high. The 4th Marine Brigade incurred 5,000 casualties, more than 50 percent of its strength.

In retrospect, however, the Battle of Château-Thierry proved one of the highlights of the combat performance of the American Expeditionary Force (A.E.F.) in the last year of the war. The dogged and energetic push of the 2d U.S. Division, and especially its marine brigade, transmitted an important message to the Germans—that the A.E.F.'s presence in France was firmly established and that it represented a force with which to be reckoned.

Bibliography: Department of the Army, *The U.S. Army in the World War, 1917–1919: Military Operations of the American Ground Forces* (U.S. Govt. Printing Office, 1948); Lawrence, Joseph D., *Fighting Soldier: The A.E.F. in 1918* (Colorado Assoc. Univ. Press, 1985); Smythe, Donald, *Pershing: General of the Armies* (Univ. of Indiana Press, 1986).

Russell A. Hart

CHEYENNE CAMPAIGN (1878)

U.S. military action against those Cheyenne who fled the poor conditions of their reservation to return to Montana. In 1876, the U.S. government decided to consolidate all Cheyenne peoples on reservations in the area of the Arkansas River. In 1878, the northern Cheyenne signed a treaty agreeing to accept the same position as the southern Cheyenne on the Cheyenne-Arapaho reservation. After their surrender, 1,000 Cheyenne were moved under military escort south to Darlington Reservation in what is now Oklahoma.

The conditions on the southern reservation were much different from those the Cheyenne had experienced in the north. Montana, their homeland, was high, dry, and plentifully supplied with bison. Southern Indian territory was hot and humid, and food there was scanty. Consequently, during the winter of 1878, many Cheyenne starved and 41 were killed by disease. After requests to be allowed to hunt bison to supplement their diet were turned down, one-third of the band, under Dull Knife (also known as Morning Star) and Little Wolf, fled the reservation on Sept. 10, 1878.

Gen. Philip H. Sheriden, fearful that the escape proved army incompetence and undermined the viability of the reservation system, ordered Gen. George Crook to spare nothing in order to kill or capture the escapees. Major Mizner was dispatched from Fort Reno with U.S. cavalry and Indian scouts to track the renegade band. Mizner's troops pursued the Cheyenne band and finally overtook it on September 13, near the Cinammon River. Mizner called on Dull Knife to surrender and peacefully return to Darlington Reservation. On his refusal, Mizner ordered the cavalry to charge the Indians from the north, but they were driven back in the direction of Dodge City. Two days later, the cavalry returned and was again repulsed.

Only minor skirmishes accompanied the Cheyenne on their way to Montana. North of the Platte River, the band divided into two groups. Lt. W. P. Clark and his force cut off Little Wolf, who surrendered and eventually enlisted in the U.S. Army as a scout against the Sioux. Dull knife moved farther west and subsequently gave up at Fort Robinson, West Nebraska. On the trek north, 64 Cheyenne were killed, but many made it to their Montana homeland, where they finally persuaded the government to grant them a reservation on the Tongue River. Dull Knife was eventually allowed to rejoin his people at their new reservation.

Bibliography: Grinell, George, *The Fighting Cheyennes* (Scribner's, 1915).

Russell A. Hart

COLUMBUS RAID (March 9, 1916)

Attack by Mexican revolutionary leader Pancho Villa on a U.S. Army post at Columbus, New Mexico. On Mar. 9, 1916, the remains of Villa's once-large revolutionary army, only 300 strong, responded in anger to recent U.S. intervention in Mexican affairs. Villa hoped to create an incident that would draw support to his cause. His raid was costly in the short term. Against 17 U.S. deaths (including 9 civilians), the Villistas lost approximately 170 to U.S. resistance and pursuit. The raid also prompted Pres. Woodrow Wilson to organize the so-called Punitive Expedition, which chased Villa for months. However, the raid did renew Villa's popularity, and he continued his campaigns for several years.

Mark Pitcavage

CUBAN PACIFICATION, ARMY OF (1906–1909)

Expeditionary force assembled by the United States for its second intervention into Cuban affairs. Growing out of electoral frauds, the Cuban civil war of 1906 drew Pres. Theodore Roosevelt into intervention under the terms of the Platt Amendment. Planning for an expeditionary force to Cuba began with a general staff study of the problem in 1905. This study became the plan for the organization, movement, and logistic support of the force to be sent to Cuba should the need arise.

On Sept. 29, 1906, the plan went into effect, and the Army of Cuban Pacification, a force of some 5,600 U.S. personnel, was assembled and moved to Cuba. The occupation dragged on, with little military action or fundamental change in Cuban society, for three years. In the winter of 1909, the Army of Cuban Pacification began to withdraw from the island.

This was the first real test of the new army general staff. Intended as a planning agency, the general staff and its individual members played a much larger role in the expeditionary force itself. In both preparing plans and controlling their execution, the new general staff functioned in a manner very similar to the great German General Staff, the model upon which it was based.

Bibliography: Langley, Lester D., *The Banana Wars: United States Intervention in the Caribbean, 1898–1934* (Dorsey Press, 1985); Millet, Allan R., *The General: Robert L. Bullard and the Officership in the United States Army 1881–1925* (Greenwood Press, 1975); ———, ''The General Staff and the Cuban Intervention of 1906,'' *Military Affairs* (fall 1967).

John A. Hixson

DICK ACT (1903)

Officially entitled the Militia Act of Jan. 21, 1903, the Dick Act laid the basis for the U.S. Army's modern reserve system. The Spanish-American War of 1898 made it clear that the army required some sort of organized reserve other than the traditional state militias. Sec. of War Elihu Root was determined to address the problem, and his military advisers, ignoring the popular and partially trained state National Guard units, urged the formation of a federal volunteer reserve. Recognizing the political liabilities of such a plan, Root sought a compromise solution that would satisfy such National Guard supporters as Cong. Charles W. Dick of Ohio. The two came to respect each other and framed a bill acceptable to all parties involved.

The Dick Act was the first fundamental revision of the Militia Act of 1792. The law established two different reserve formations. Retaining the principle of universal military obligation embodied in the Militia Act, all able-bodied men in the states constituted the ''Reserve Militia''—an unorganized manpower pool to be tapped in a national emergency. The ''Organized Militia'' consisted of the National Guard units organized by the states. To enhance their usefulness, the law required the federal government to provide them with arms, financial assistance, and military instructors. In return, the National Guard agreed to hold at least 24 drills and a five-day summer camp each year. The regular army also opened its school system to National Guard officers and agreed to participate in joint maneuvers with the National Guard.

Bibliography: Millett, Alan R., and Peter Maslowski, *For the Common Defense: A Military History of the United States of America* (Free Press, 1984); Weigley, Russell F., *History of the United States Army* (Indiana Univ. Press, 1984).

Daniel T. Bailey

DODGE COMMISSION (September 1898–February 1899)

Post-Spanish-American War commission created to examine questionable wartime activities of the U.S. War Department. Despite military successes, the War Department was criticized severely for its management of the Spanish-American War effort. While much of the criticism was the result of distortion, falsification, and exaggeration, there were problems with the administration of the war. The scapegoat became Sec. of War Russell Alexander Alger. Indeed, by mid-1898, ''Algerism'' came to symbolize corruption and incompetence. Angered by calls for his resignation and the realization that he was losing Pres. William McKinley's confidence, Alger asked for a commission to investigate his department's wartime administration. McKinley quickly approved the request and appointed Grenville Mellon Dodge—an experienced Civil War commander, successful railroad executive, and prominent Republican—to head the commission. Other commission members included Gen. Alexander M. McCook, Gen. James M. Wilson (chief of engineers), Gen. James A. Beaver, Col. James A. Sexton, Col. Charles Denby, Capt. Evan P. Howell, former Vermont governor Urban A. Woodbury, and Dr. Phineas T. Connor of Ohio.

The Dodge Commission was tasked with probing every bureau and agency of the War Department. McKinley's written instructions to the commission stated, "If there have been wrongs committed, the wrongdoers must not escape conviction and punishment." After months of testimony, no spectacular instances of stupidity, malfeasance, or corruption were uncovered. Then, on Dec. 21, 1898, Maj. Gen. Nelson A. Miles, Commanding General of the Army, appeared before the commission and charged that tainted and "embalmed" beef containing poisonous chemicals had been provided the troops, many of whom subsequently became ill. Possessing political aspirations, Miles focused on the beef controversy through the media.

Unaffected by the controversy, the Dodge Commission issued its report on Feb. 9, 1899. Based on volumes of testimony and documents, the commission concluded that the War Department was innocent of deliberate negligence or widespread corruption but that it "had been poorly managed." Overall, the report portrayed hardworking, conscientious officials struggling to deal with a very difficult situation. Feeling vindicated by the report, Secretary Alger vowed to remain in office. However, following a confrontation with McKinley, Alger submitted his resignation on July 19, effective Aug. 1, 1899.

Lt. Col. Martin W. Andresen

DOLPHIN

U.S. dispatch boat in service 1885–1921, the first of the "new navy" warships to be commissioned. During its early years, the USS *Dolphin* (PG-24) cruised extensively with the North Atlantic Squadron, the Pacific Squadron, and the Squadron of Evolution. It was assigned to the blockade of Havana and Santiago during the Spanish-American War (1898). After the war, the *Dolphin* was assigned to the secretary of the navy as a special dispatch vessel, often transporting the president and serving in ceremonial functions.

From 1908 to 1921, the *Dolphin* was assigned to the Caribbean as flagship of the Third Squadron, Atlantic Fleet (1908–17); the American Patrol Detachment (1917–20); and the Special Service Squadron (1920–21). With the Third and Special Service squadrons, its primary duties were to assist in missions of gunboat diplomacy and to show the flag. Its World War I service with the American Patrol Detachment revolved around protecting maritime traffic from an expected U-boat threat that never materialized.

Bibliography: *Dictionary of American Naval Fighting Ships,* vol. 2 (Historical Div., U.S. Navy).

Donald A. Yerxa

ENDICOTT BOARD (1885–1886)

Following release of the "Gun Foundry Board" report in 1884, Congress directed in the Fortification Appropriations Act of Mar. 3, 1885, that a special board be appointed to examine all facets of the nation's coastal defenses. Known as the Endicott Board, it was chaired by Pres. Grover Cleveland's newly appointed secretary of war, William Crowninshield Endicott. Other board members included Brig. Gens. Stephen V. Benet (chief of ordnance) and John Newton (chief of engineers), Lt. Col. Henry L. Abbot, Capt. Charles S. Smith, Commanders W. T. Sampson and Caspar F. Goodrich, and civilians James Morgan, Jr., and Erastus Corning. After eight months of investigation, the board submitted its report to Speaker of the House John G. Carlisle on Jan. 23, 1886. Citing numerous deficiencies, the board concluded that U.S. coastal defenses were "unable to cope with modern iron- or steel-clad ships of war."

Although the Endicott Board's report was well received and often cited as a model for future boards, neither Congress nor the War Department took any action on the board's recommendations. Indeed, alarmed at the board's estimated costs associated with upgrading coastal defenses (more than $126 million), Congress even failed to appropriate funds for maintaining existing coastal defense works in both 1886 and 1887. In 1898, as relations with Spain deteriorated, Congress took a renewed interest in the Endicott Board's report and appropriated limited funds to improve the overall conditions of U.S. coastal defenses.

Lt. Col. Martin W. Andresen

FENIAN RAIDS (1866, 1870)

Raids into Canada by anti-British Irish veterans from the Civil War who believed the best way to hurt Britain was to attack Canada. Named after the Fianna, soldiers of a legendary leader in Irish mythology, the Fenians first poured across the border on June 1, 1866, when John O'Neill led 1,000 men in the capture of Fort Erie near Niagara. The next day, he bested a force of Canadian militia at nearby Ridgeway, but withdrew on June 4 when he learned that 1,700 British regulars were approaching. Three days later, a separate Fenian force crossed Missisquoi Bay in Quebec but retreated within 48 hours. Little more occurred until May 25, 1870, when Fenian groups from Vermont and New York advanced separately into Canada and were easily repulsed. The Fenian raids increased popular support in Canada for confederations.

Bibliography: Callwood, June, *Portrait of Canada* (Doubleday, 1981).

John F. Wukovits

FETTERMAN MASSACRE (December 21, 1866)

Battle near Fort Kearny, Wyoming, where 2,000 Sioux warriors led by Red Cloud annihilated 80 U.S. soldiers commanded by Capt. William J. Fetterman. Red Cloud hoped to destroy the fort, which protected entrances into western gold fields, and decided to lure soldiers out of their encampment by attacking a detail sent out to gather wood. When initial gunshots were heard, Col. Henry Carrington ordered Fetterman to lead his detachment of 80 men to rescue the detail. Carrington specifically stated that Fetterman was only to bring back the detail and was in no case to pursue the Indians beyond nearby Lodge Trail Ridge. Fetterman, who had earlier boasted he could conquer the Sioux with only 80 men, chose not to follow orders.

A decoy of 10 Sioux, reportedly including Crazy Horse, continually taunted Fetterman's force from a distance in hopes of drawing it farther from the fort. Once Fetterman's men advanced beyond Lodge Trail Ridge, the 10 decoys split into two parties and rode across each other's path, the prearranged signal for the 2,000 hidden Sioux to charge from two sides. Fetterman's hopelessly outnumbered squad fought hand-to-hand with the enemy but was wiped out. The Sioux lost almost 200 dead and wounded in the encounter they call the Battle of the Hundred Slain. However, they failed to seize Fort Kearny when a blizzard prevented them from attacking the fort before army reinforcements arrived from Laramie.

Bibliography: Brown, Dee, *Bury My Heart at Wounded Knee* (Holt, Rinehart, 1971); Connell, Evan S., *Son of the Morning Star* (North Point Press, 1984); Tebbel, John, *The Compact History of the Indian Wars* (Hawthorn Books, 1966).

John F. Wukovits

FORT LARAMIE TREATIES (April–November 1871)

A series of peace agreements between the U.S. government and approximately 200 Indian leaders. The treaties promised that the Sioux would control the Black Hills of South Dakota in perpetuity, that the Powder River area of northern Wyoming and southern Montana would remain independent Indian territory, and that the Bozeman Trail, along with the U.S. Army forts that defended it, would shut down. In the last case, the closures freed an army regiment to protect newly constructed portions of the Union Pacific Railroad. The intrusion of the railroad, along with the Black Hills gold strike of 1874 and continued military expeditions through sacred hunting grounds, perpetuated Indian violence and doomed the treaties.

Bibliography: Brown, Dee, *Bury My Heart at Wounded Knee* (Holt, Rinehart, 1971).

Maj. Peter Faber

FREEDMEN'S BUREAU

Post-Civil War agency directed by the War Department. Established by an act of Congress in March 1865, the Bureau for the Relief of Freedmen and Refugees (commonly known as the Freedmen's Bureau) was mandated to assist with the socioeconomic concerns of newly freed slaves and homeless white rufugees in the South. The bureau was headed by Maj. Gen. Oliver O. Howard. Despite Howard's honesty and idealism, charges of inefficiency and corruptness soon were being lodged against the agency. However, it still accomplished a considerable amount, particularly in the area of black education.

Radical Republicans hoped to pass new legislation to strengthen the bureau and continue its work, but Pres. Andrew Johnson vetoed the bill, on the grounds that it represented the harsh military reconstruction policies of the Radicals. Although his 1866 veto was overridden, the bureau's powers were gradually diminished, and it went out of existence in 1872.

Ted Alexander

GERMAN OFFENSIVES (March–July 1918)

World War I operations against British forces by the Germans. In the spring of 1918, Germany made a final effort on the Western Front to win the war before U.S. troops could intervene. Utilizing new tactics and specially trained infantry, Gen. Erich F. W. Ludendorff directed a series of five offensives intended to drive Great Britain from the war. The first occurred in March, with the others following monthly. Except for the final offensive, each was tactically successful and resulted in notable gains in territory (and in Allied panic). Ludendorff, however, lacked a well-formulated plan, and the German army had not overcome the fundamental problems that constrained World War I offensives. Germany's finest infantry was squandered in achieving tactical successes that ultimately left a weaker Germany, with Germany's enemies on the strategic offensive.

Stephen Lofgren

GHOST DANCE MOVEMENT (1889–90)

One of several native American quasi-religions that attempted to offset cultural disaster with messianic religious frenzy. Preceded by similar spiritual outbreaks among the Columbia River tribes in the 1870s, the White Mountain Apache in 1881, and the Crow in Montana in 1887, the Ghost Dance can be traced to the Paiute shaman Wovoka.

Wovoka preached a peaceful blend of Christian and native beliefs that promised a bliss-filled eternal life in which believers would be reunited with dead friends and relatives, game (particularly the bison) would be plentiful,

French soldiers and U.S. troops of the 168th Infantry, 42d Division, advance during a raid on the German's Mecklenburg Trench at Badonvillier, France, in March 1918. (U.S. Army Signal Corps)

and, above all, the "white man" would be absent. Believers could glimpse the world to come through praying, singing, and performing the Ghost Dance from which the movement takes its name.

Although Wovoka enjoined on his followers a strict moral code and complete pacifism, in the hands of his Sioux apostles Short Bull and Kicking Bear, the movements took on an aggressive tone. The Sioux Ghost Dancers perverted Wovoka's doctrines and claimed the millennium might be hastened by wearing bullet-proof "ghost shirts" and destroying the white intruders. The popularity of the movement among the militant Sioux led directly to the Battle of Wounded Knee in December 1890, which marked the end of the Indian Wars.

Lt. Col. (Ret.) Charles R. Shrader

GRAND ARMY OF THE REPUBLIC (G.A.R.)

Organization of Union veterans of the Civil War. Founded in 1866 in Illinois, the G.A.R. soon grew nationally. Its political power also expanded, as was evidenced by the key role the organization played in the presidential election of Ulysses S. Grant in 1868. This clout was instrumental in electing Republican presidents, most of them former Union officers, through the end of the century (Democrat Grover Cleveland was the only candidate able to defeat the Republicans during this period).

With a membership of nearly half a million by the 1890s, the G.A.R. was able to lobby for and get passed important legislation that favored Union veterans. Pension bills were passed with G.A.R. support, and Memorial Day became a national holiday. By the early decades of the 20th century, the G.A.R.'s influence on national politics diminished along with its size. In 1949, the organization held its last national encampment, with only a handful of veterans in attendance. Its last member died in 1956.

Ted Alexander

GRANT'S PEACE POLICY (1869–1874)

Policy of Indian affairs developed by the administration of Pres. Ulysses S. Grant, based on the untried premise "of endeavoring to conquer by kindness." It was a compromise between those factions within the government espousing military control of Indians and those espousing civilian control. Its main points were as follow:

1. Civilian supremacy in conducting Indian affairs would exist.

2. Indian agents and superintendents would be selected by church groups, primarily Quakers.

3. A Board of Indian Commissioners (all philanthropists), serving without pay, would oversee disbursement of Indian appropriations.

4. An end to treating Indian tribes as "domestic dependent nations" would be effected.

5. Concentration of Indian tribes on reservations, where they would be educated, Christianized, and assisted to become agriculturally self-supporting, would be realized.

6. The Indian Bureau would be given "exclusive control and jurisdiction" of all Indians on reservations.

7. The U.S. Army would be given jurisdiction of all Indians off reservations. These Indians were to be treated as hostile.

8. The U.S. Army would not interfere with reservation Indians unless invited by the agent or his superiors.

The policy failed. The agents failed to keep Indians on reservations, and the army failed to punish those who left. Arrest of individual Indians on the reservation also failed. In 1874, the army was permitted unrestricted entrance to reservations, ending their use by Indians as refuges between forays against U.S. adversaries.

Bibliography: Utley, Robert M., *Frontier Regulars: The United States Army and the Indian* (Macmillan Co., 1973).

Brig. Gen., PNG (Ret.) Uzal W. Ent

GREAT SIOUX UPRISING (1862–1864)

The militant actions of the Sioux in Minnesota for what they regarded as the unjust consequences of U.S. expansion; part of the Sioux Wars of 1854–90. After the Sioux ceded land east of the Red and Big Sioux rivers to the United States, they expected a period of peace. However, they were left with poor hunting areas, and settlers encroached upon their lands. In August 1862, Chief Little Crow led an attack against an army detachment on the upper Minnesota River. After defeating that contingent, the Sioux besieged Fort Ridgely. On August 24, New Ulm, Minnesota, residents were attacked and massacred by Sioux raiders.

Because regular troops were involved in the Civil War, the defense of Minnesota rested on volunteers units. Minnesota governor Henry Sibley raised a unit and defeated Little Crow at Wood Lake on September 23. Little Crow escaped but was shot and killed by a farmer the next year. Campaigns against the Sioux continued through the summer of 1864.

Capt. George B. Eaton

GREAT WHITE FLEET

Force of 16 front-line battleships assembled by Pres. Theodore Roosevelt in 1907 to circumnavigate the world. In light of growing Japanese Far East ambitions, Roosevelt wanted to remind Japan that the United States would protect its interests in the region. He also hoped a grand tour of the world by a U.S. fleet, bedecked with white paint, would gain domestic support for the construction of a larger navy. The fleet began its 14-month voyage on Dec. 16, 1907, from Hampton Roads, Virginia, and anchored in Tokyo Bay on Oct. 18, 1908. After a warm welcome in Japan, the fleet returned by way of the Atlantic Ocean, finally arriving home on Feb. 22, 1909. The successful 14,000-mile cruise offered superb training conditions for the crews, gained worldwide respect for the U.S. Navy, and reasserted U.S. power in the Far East.

The U.S. Marine encampment at Camp M'Calla, Guantánamo, Cuba, served as a logistics support base during the Spanish-American War in 1898. (Library of Congress)

Bibliography: Alden, John D., *The American Steel Navy* (Naval Inst. Press, 1972); Costello, John, *The Pacific War* (Quill Books, 1982); Hart, Robert A., *The Great White Fleet* (Little, Brown, 1965).

John F. Wukovits

GUANTÁNAMO BAY

Site of the oldest U.S. overseas naval base, situated at the southeastern tip of Cuba. Guantánamo Bay's strategic location athwart the Windward Passage and its spacious harbor made it a site of increasing interest to the U.S. Navy as U.S. power and influence in the Caribbean grew in the late 19th century. The navy used Guantánamo during the Spanish-American War as a logistics support base. In 1903, after delicate negotiations with newly independent Cuba, the United States received a perpetual lease of Guantánamo in order to develop a naval station.

Prior to World War II, Guantánamo was never developed as a major naval installation. The navy used it primarily for fleet training and emergency repairs, although war planners viewed it as a first line of hemisphere defense. It was also a staging area for interventions in Cuba during periods of unrest prior to the abrogation of the Platt Amendment in 1934.

During World War II, Guantánamo became increasingly important for antisubmarine efforts and as a focal point for several vital convoy routes. In the postwar years, the base continued its fleet training functions and served symbolically as an "outpost of freedom" in Fidel Castro's Cuba.

Bibliography: Coletta, Paolo E., and K. Jack Bauer, eds., *U.S. Navy and Marine Corps Bases, Overseas* (Greenwood Press, 1985).

Donald A. Yerxa

GULFLIGHT INCIDENT (May 1, 1915)

The attack on a U.S. tanker by a German submarine off the Scilly Isles near the southwest tip of England. The incident occurred during World War I but two years prior to U.S. entry into the conflict.

In February 1915, the German government declared a war zone around Great Britain and Ireland and warned that all merchant ships found "within this zone will be destroyed." On May 1, the German commander of submarine U-30 sighted a large vessel being escorted by two British patrol boats. Assuming that the vessel was transporting munitions, the commander fired a torpedo, which damaged the *Gulflight* and caused three U.S. deaths.

The vessel was towed safely into port by British patrol boats, but the U.S. government swiftly condemned this attack on a neutral ship. The German government apologized and offered to pay damages, but the whole affair was overshadowed within one week by the sinking of the British luxury liner *Lusitania*.

Bibliography: Bailey, Thomas A., and Paul B. Ryan, *The Lusitania Disaster* (Free Press, 1975); Hoehling, Adolph A., *The Great War at Sea* (T. Y. Crowell, 1965).

John F. Wukovits

HAITI: 1915–1919

Situated on the western half of the island of Hispaniola, Haiti had been torn by coups d'etat and internal political upheavals. Haiti had also been the scene of an intense struggle among the United States and France and Germany for control of the strategic Windward and Mona passages as well as the vital naval base at Môle St. Nicholas. It was these two factors that prompted a full-scale intervention by the United States, starting in 1915.

Fearing both an internal revolution and possible foreign intervention, the U.S. State and Navy departments had been prepared to act, with Rear Adm. William B. Caperton ordered off the Haiti coast with a marine force. On July 28, 1915, Caperton and a marine company landed at Port-au-Prince, beginning what would be a 19-year occupation. In the meantime, another marine company had been sent from Guantánamo Bay, Cuba, to join Caperton's forces to restore order and to protect the lives and property of U.S. personnel.

These forces were soon augmented by the 1st Brigade, commanded by Col. Littleton "Tony" W. Waller, an experienced counterinsurgency expert. Two other marine units, the 1st Regiment and the Artillery Battalion, were sent in as well. The marines were charged with restoring the legitimate Haitian government and enforcing the strict martial law that the U.S. State Department had ordered.

Meanwhile, a new Haitian president had been elected, and the Haitian Assembly had enacted a new constitution, which recognized the legitimacy of the U.S. occupation as a means of restoring order. While the political reorganization continued under Caperton, the marines set out to crush the Cacos (bands of Haitian political thugs) that controlled the northern part of the country, which took several months.

While much of the brigade was involved in heavy fighting, the marines also assisted in the establishment of the Gendarmerie d'Haiti, a native constabularly force composed of Haitians and led by U.S. personnel. Basically ignored during World War I, Haiti received close attention from 1918 as anti-U.S. guerrilla activity accelerated. Hard fighting finally subdued the rebels, whose leaders had been killed.

For the Marine Corps, the Haitian intervention brought into use, for the first time anywhere, aircraft in a close air-support role. Marine infantrymen later found the Haitian service useful in Nicaragua. Marines would later incorporate all of the lessons learned in Haiti and Nicaragua into the famed *Small Wars Manual,* which has been the conceptual groundwork for Marine Corps counterinsurgency doctrine.

Marine and navy personnel gained vital training in civil affairs programs during the intervention years in the Caribbean, particularly in Haiti, experiences later drawn upon in Vietnam. The establishment of the Gendarmerie became not only the foundation of the Haitian army but the primary springboard for Haitian politicians (particularly the Duvaliers). First viewed with suspicion by the Haitian elite, it soon became an important stepping stone to political advancement.

The lasting legacies, however, of the first years were mixed. On one hand, the United States attempted to restore political and economic stability to Haiti. But this was accomplished through what was often viewed as an extension of dollar diplomacy. Haiti has never fully recovered from the political violence that shook it in 1915.

Bibliography: Heinl, Robert D., Jr., *Soldiers of the Sea: The United States Marine Corps, 1775–1962* (Naval Inst. Press, 1962); Millett, Allan R., *Semper Fidelis: The History of the United States Marine Corps* (Macmillan, 1980).

Leo J. Daugherty III

HAY-BUNAU-VARILLA TREATY (1903)

Agreement signed on Nov. 18, 1903, granting the United States in perpetuity the use and control of a 10-mile strip of land across the Isthmus of Panama. At the start of the Spanish-American War in 1898, the 66 days required by the battleship *Oregon* to sail around the tip of South America had demonstrated the importance of a canal to U.S. military interests. The United States had been attempting a canal project as early as 1846, but the agreements reached failed to gain ratification by all parties. The failure of Colombia to sign such a treaty in 1903 led to a revolt in which Panama declared its independence of Colombia. On Nov. 18, 1903, U.S. Sec. of State John Hay and Philippe J. Bunau-Varilla, Panama's first minister to the United States, signed a document agreeing to independence for Panama and the leasing of a 10-mile-wide corridor—the Panama Canal Zone. Panama was to be paid $10,000,000 outright and an annual fee of $250,000 starting nine years after ratification. The U.S. Senate approved the agreement on Feb. 23, 1904.

In the 1930s, talks began on modifying the arrangement, and a new accord was signed on Mar. 2, 1936. Because of strong opposition from the U.S. military, the treaty was not approved by the Senate until July 25, 1939. Along with a larger annuity, the new agreement gave the United States expansion rights as well as the promise of joint action in the event of any aggression seen as endangering "the security of the Republic or the neutrality or the security of the Panama Canal." This was taken to mean that the United States had strengthened its military control as well as its commercial interests in the region.

Edward T. Jasek

HAYFIELD FIGHT (August 1, 1867)

A brief battle in which 12 U.S. civilians (engaged in mowing hay) and 20 soldiers of the 27th Infantry held off an assault of mostly Cheyenne warriors. The attack followed an agreement made by Sioux, Cheyenne, and some Arapaho to wipe out two U.S. military installations, Forts Phil Kearny (Nebraska) and C. F. Smith (Montana). The fight took place at a hayfield 2.5 miles from Fort Smith. Since the soldiers were armed with the new breechloading Springfield rifles using metallic cartridges and had had the foresight to erect a log enclosure in case of an attack, they held the upper hand. The Indians mostly used bows and arrows, making several assaults, one of them on foot. The commander of the troops, Lt. Sigismund Sternberg, was killed by a bullet early in the fight. The besieged hay-mowing party and its escort suffered three killed and two wounded. Estimates of Indian casualties varied widely.

Col. (Ret.) Rod Paschall

HAY-HERRÁN TREATY (January 22, 1903)

Proposed agreement between the United States and Colombia for lease of a canal zone across the Isthmus of Panama (then part of Colombia). With the passage of the Hay-Pauncefote Treaty in November 1901, the Theodore Roosevelt administration entered into negotiations with Colombia for a canal agreement. After much haggling, Sec. of State John Hay and Colombian envoy Thomas Herrán signed the Hay-Herrán Treaty on Jan. 22, 1903. Under this agreement, the United States would lease at a bargain rate a six-mile-wide strip through Panama for 99 years, with renewal options. Although Colombia would retain nominal sovereignty, the United States would gain the right to intervene militarily without Colombian consent during times of crisis.

The U.S. Senate approved the treaty in March, but the Colombian legislature, suspicious of U.S. imperialism and offended by U.S. niggardliness, defeated it in August. The treaty's defeat encouraged Panamanian secessionists to revolt in November 1903.

Bibliography: McCullough, David, *The Path Between the Seas: The Creation of the Panama Canal, 1870–1914* (Simon & Schuster, 1977).

Donald A. Yerxa

HAY-PAUNCEFOTE TREATY (November 18, 1901)

Agreement between the United States and Great Britain that abrogated the Clayton-Bulwer Treaty of 1850 and permitted the United States to construct, control, and defend a canal across the isthmus between the Caribbean Sea and the Pacific Ocean. U.S. interest in a Central American canal accelerated after the Spanish-American War, and in 1899, Sec. of State John Hay entered into discussions with British ambassador Sir Julian Pauncefote on a new canal convention. In February 1900, the first Hay-Pauncefote Treaty was signed, allowing the United States the right to build a canal unilaterally, but the treaty foundered in the U.S. Senate over provisions stipulating the waterway's neutrality and nonmilitarization. Britain, strategically overstretched and diplomatically isolated, compromised to generate American goodwill. The second Hay-Pauncefote Treaty was signed on Nov. 18, 1901, and was ratified promptly.

The Hay-Pauncefote Treaty was one of the great diplomatic accords of the 20th century. It not only acknowledged U.S. supremacy in the Caribbean, but also signaled a profound improvement in Anglo-American relations that would be a fundamental feature of 20th-century diplomatic history.

Donald A. Yerxa

INTERVENTION, NORTH RUSSIAN (1918–1919)

Aspect of both World War I and Russia's civil war in which U.S. troops served in and near the North Russian port cities of Murmansk and Archangel. Following the Bolshevik Revolution and the formal termination of hostilities between the Central Powers and Russia, the Allies sought ways to minimize the advantages derived by their enemies' victory in the East. An Allied presence in North Russia might accomplish several things: forestall the possibility of the Germans occupying the ice-free port of Murmansk for use as a submarine base, keep Allied military stores at Murmansk and Archangel from falling into German hands (any supplies there had already been, or would soon be, removed by the Bolsheviks), lead possibly to a

The bleakness of the U.S. blockhouse at Toulga on the Dvina River in Russia affected the morale of the soldiers stationed there during the North Russian Intervention of 1918–19. (U.S. Army Signal Corps)

reopening of an Eastern Front, and aid the formation of anti-Bolshevik Russian forces, whose personnel the British would train.

Preparations. Allied representatives had begun discussing sending forces to North Russia as early as March 1918. A mixed group of Allied troops began to assemble in Murmansk between March and June; included among them were several dozen U.S. marines from the old cruiser *Olympia,* which docked at Murmansk in May, also bringing with it Maj. Gen. Frederick Poole, the British officer who would command Allied personnel in North Russia. However, it was early August before Allied troops disembarked at Archangel, a city near the mouth of the Northern Dvina River several hundred miles closer to the Russian heartland than Murmansk. White Russians in the area overthrew local Bolshevik leadership just as the Allies arrived.

Reluctant to send U.S. Army troops to Russia, Pres. Woodrow Wilson agreed to do so in June 1918 after numerous discussions between U.S. and Allied representatives. Although Wilson subsequently advised the Allies that he had no intention of allowing U.S. troops to participate in "organized intervention" in Russian affairs, in practice, U.S. personnel did as their British superiors ordered. Assisting the Whites ranked much higher among British and French goals than Wilson seemed to realize.

The U.S. units selected for duty in North Russia consisted of three battalions of infantry from the 339th Regiment (sometimes called "Detroit's Own"), a battalion of engineers, a field hospital, and an ambulance company. Lt Col. George E. Stewart, who had won the Medal of Honor as an enlisted man in the Philippine Insurrection, commanded the force of some 4,500 men. Already ravaged by an attack of Spanish influenza on the ships bringing them from England where they had been billeted, the Americans landed at Archangel in early September, diverted there from Murmansk on General Poole's orders. In November, Poole was officially replaced by Maj. Gen. Edmund Ironside, who had already been acting commander for some weeks.

Operations. By the time the various Allied units had arrived in Archangel, events on the Western Front had made it unlikely the Germans would take any initiative in North Russia. But by the signing of the Armistice in November, Allied forces, including the bulk of the U.S. infantry, had moved into forward positions along the one railroad into Archangel and along the Northern Dvina River, which linked Archangel and the interior of Russia. The most advanced units were some 200 miles from Archangel. The combined forces in the Archangel area then totaled about 18,000 men and included British, French, U.S., and Canadian personnel, as well as White Russians being trained by British instructors.

Six feet of snow was on the ground by December, and in January 1919, Red forces launched an attack to drive the Allies from Archangel. The Red attack was halted far short of its objective but did force Russian and U.S. troops to pull back from the important city of Shenkursk. By this time, the 339th had been dispersed among a dozen positions, rarely in as much as company strength in any single location. If Allied positions were overextended, as Ironside believed they were, it was to provide the Whites with a wider recruiting area and perhaps to facilitate an eventual linkup with another White force that was attempting (unsuccessfully) to push northwest from Siberia.

In February, a Yorkshire infantry regiment refused to go from Murmansk to the front. Similar problems were experienced in a French colonial battalion and then in a U.S. company that balked at returning to the front after some time in a rear area. Accounts about the degree of discontent differ. In any case, the problems were resolved, and the purpose of operations in the Archangel area, the only scene of significant combat in North Russia, was at last clarified: holding out until the return of warmer weather opened the ice-bound port of Archangel and made evacuation feasible. The organization and training of White personnel would continue until then.

Withdrawal. President Wilson had decided by February 1919 to withdraw U.S. personnel but was reluctant to act separately from the Allies. Political pressures, however, caused Wilson to direct Sec. of War Newton Baker to announce that two companies of railway troops would be shipped to Murmansk to improve the supply situation of troops in the field until evacuation was possible. Baker assured Congress and the press that Brig. Gen. Wilds P. Richardson, who had extensive service in Alaska, would go to North Russia to organize and command the U.S. departure, which would commence at the earliest feasible time. The Allies made similar decisions, the British sending to North Russia several thousand fresh troops, many of whom were volunteers, to cover the evacuation.

By the end of May, U.S. personnel had been withdrawn to barracks near Archangel. Five separate contingents sailed from Archangel in June and July. The caskets of those 139 Americans who had died while in the Archangel area were shipped home for reburial in August. In addition to the dead, nearly 300 had been wounded. Ironside was the last ranking Allied army officer to depart. The Whites vainly attempted to hold out, their leader Gen. Eugene Miller and many of his officers going into exile in February 1920. The White cause elsewhere in Russia was faring almost as poorly.

Americans served in Siberia as well as in North Russia, and other Allied forces appeared elsewhere along the periphery of the Russia state. Their presence failed to contribute to the defeat of the Central Powers, whose fate was sealed on the Western Front. Rather, their primary use in most areas of Russia was to equip and train the Whites and, on some occasions, as in North Russia, to fight alongside them, but to no avail. Allied personnel were always limited in number, and, especially after the end of the war, morale decreased; enlisted men, at least, now wondered why they were serving in Russia. Perhaps the surprising thing, therefore, is not that U.S. personnel in North Russia apparently displayed some discontent but that morale problems were not more pervasive.

Bibliography: Cudahy, John, *Archangel, the American War with Russia* (A. C. McClurg, 1924); Ironside, Sir Edmund, *Archangel, 1918–1919* (Constable, 1953); Kennan, George F., *Soviet-American Relations, 1917–1920; Vol. 2: The Decision to Intervene* (Princeton Univ. Press, 1958); Rhodes, Benjamin D., *The Anglo-American Winter War with Russia, 1918–1919* (Greenwood Press, 1988); Strakhovsky, Leonid I., *Intervention at Archangel* (Princeton Univ. Press, 1944); ———, *The Origins of American Intervention in North Russia* (Princeton Univ. Press, 1937); Unterberger, Betty Miller, *The United States, Revolutionary Russia, and the Rise of Czechoslovakia* (Univ. of North Carolina Press, 1989).

Lloyd J. Graybar

INTERVENTION, SIBERIAN (1918–1920)

Aspect of both World War I and Russia's civil war in which U.S. troops landed in Siberia. One of the most bewildering aspects of the last stages of the war and the first two years thereafter was the sending of Allied military personnel to Russia, then in the midst of chaos following the Bolshevik seizure of power in Petrograd (Saint Petersburg) in October 1917. At first opposed to the idea of stationing U.S. troops in Russia, Pres. Woodrow Wilson yielded to Allied requests and authorized the dispatch of small contingents of U.S. troops to Archangel in European Russia and to Vladivostok. A grandiose and logistically impossible proposal to reestablish an eastern front (Russia had surrendered to the Central Powers in early 1918) by first sending 100,000 or more Allied troops to Siberia had already been rejected.

Preparations. Maj. Gen. William S. Graves, an officer Chief of Staff Peyton March regarded as "loyal, levelheaded, and firm," was assigned command of the Siberian expedition. Graves's orders (written in Wilson's own hand) were to prevent large amounts of Allied supplies—nearly $1,000,000,000 worth in and near the city of Vladivostok alone—stockpiled along the Trans-Siberian Railway from falling into the hands of the Central Powers. He was to assist some 50,000 Czech military personnel, formerly held captive by the Imperial Russian Army but now willing to fight for the Allied cause under French direction, in moving safely out of Russia.

Graves's instructions also said not to interfere in Russia's internal affairs, namely the struggle for power between the Bolsheviks and a variety of anti-Bolshevik, or White, forces, then shaping up. However, he was authorized to help the Russian people determine their own future, raising the question, Graves came to realize, of which Russian people—Red or White—he was to assist. U.S. Sec. of War Newton Baker handed Graves the envelope containing the president's instructions and advised Graves that his assignment in Siberia would require a careful step. It would be akin to "walking on eggs loaded with dynamite."

Arrival. Two understrength infantry regiments then in the Philippines would proceed to Vladivostok, the initial elements arriving there in August 1918. Graves would bring reinforcements from the United States, raising the total U.S. force to 296 officers and 9,056 men. Initially, Graves disappointed his superiors by requesting more troops and authorization to send U.S. personnel as far west as Omsk, nearly 4,000 miles west of Vladivostok. The firm response from the War Department, determined not to become more deeply committed in Siberia, was to send no troops west of Lake Baikal. As Graves became more familiar with the situation in Siberia, he came to realize the extraordinary circumstances prevailing there: The resident White government under Adm. Alexander V. Kolchak in distant Omsk did not have the support of ordinary Russians; groups of Cossacks under the command of two different leaders acted with a cruelty that brought the White cause into increasing contempt; the French who were represented by a handful of colonial troops and the British who had a considerable number of officers but only a battalion of men in Siberia hoped to aid Kolchak in overthrowing Bolshevism throughout Russia; not to be left out of the Allied intervention, Italy also had military personnel in Siberia. The Japanese military, by far the largest Allied contingent, with about 70,000 instead of the 7,000 President Wilson had anticipated, hoped that if confusion reigned long enough in Siberia, they might be able to detach the eastern or maritime areas to become a client state under a Russian body acting as a Japanese puppet.

Withdrawal. Graves assiduously followed Wilson's orders, and when his force remained on after the Armistice in Europe, it was clear that the continued U.S. presence in Siberia was meant primarily to act as a restraint upon the Japanese, something that was not in his original instructions but was from the beginning an underlying reason for sending Graves's expedition. Wilson had not been forthright in regard to this aspect of the Siberian intervention since Japan was a nation with which the United States was at peace. Furthermore, any mention of anti-Japanese sentiments easily could have been construed as pro-Bolshevik given the frenzied hatred of Bolshevism then developing in the United States. Despite pressure to aid Kolchak from various State Department officials, especially consular personnel assigned to posts in Siberia or other locations in Asia, Graves remained steadfast in his refusal to interfere in Russian affairs. Graves's orders were in fact amended to guard a section of the Trans-Siberian Railway. Once this commitment was made, his personnel, as Graves recognized, were in effect aiding Kolchak since weapons and ammunition were being shipped to White forces. On another occasion, some of his men helped rescue civilians caught in a cross fire between Reds and Whites in Vladivostok. But such a situation was the exception, and the U.S. presence remained limited in both size and commitments.

With Wilson preoccupied with the Versailles Treaty and then taken gravely ill, policymaking in Washington was uncertain for much of the time the U.S. expedition was in Siberia. Once the war was over, however, U.S. congressional leaders and important elements of the U.S. press became more outspoken about the little-understood U.S. presence in Siberia. By the fall of 1919, the Kolchak government had collapsed, and the Czechs would at last be departing. Finally, the State Department and the War Department, often at odds in the previous year, agreed that nothing was to be gained by keeping the U.S. force in Siberia. Graves received orders to withdraw. The first U.S. troops began embarking in January 1920, and the remainder embarked at intervals; Graves and the last personnel sailed on Apr. 1, 1920. Fewer than one percent of his men had suffered combat deaths or wounds, testimony to Graves's success in complying with his original instructions.

Assessing the U.S. intervention of Siberia is difficult. Graves was in a position at least as risky and perplexing as Gen. John T. Pershing had faced in Mexico in 1916. Whereas arguments can be made that the Punitive Expedition to Mexico drove Pancho Villa's forces far enough from the border so that he could no longer carry out raids on U.S. soil, no U.S. territory was jeopardized by events in Siberia. Furthermore, the U.S. expedition provided the Communists with just one more reason to feel they were encircled by hostile capitalist forces. If anything at all positive was accomplished by the U.S. presence in Siberia, it was in the restraint the international nature of the intervention placed upon the Japanese, who withdrew their own forces in 1922.

Bibliography: Graves, William S., *America's Siberian Adventure, 1918–1920* (Cape and Smith, 1931); Kennan, George F., *Soviet-American Relations, 1917–1920; Vol. 2: The Decision to Intervene* (Princeton Univ. Press, 1958); Morley, James William, *The Japanese Thrust into Siberia, 1918* (Columbia Univ. Press, 1957); Unterberger, Betty Miller, *America's Siberian Expedition, 1918–1920: A Study of National Policy* (Duke Univ. Press, 1956); White, John Albert, *The Siberian Intervention* (Princeton Univ. Press, 1950).

Lloyd J. Graybar

JACKSBORO AFFAIR
(May 18–June 8, 1871)

A violent incident during the implementation of the Indian peace policy begun by the U.S. government in 1867. It started with the Salt Creek Prairie massacre in northwest Texas, where the Kiowa leader Satanta and his followers killed 8 teamsters, burned 10 wagons, and stole 41 mules. Nine days later, Satanta boasted of the attack to an Indian agent at Fort Sill, Oklahoma, who ensured the warrior leader's arrest by Gen. William T. Sherman. While en route to trial at Fort Richardson, Texas, Satanta was killed after he attacked one of his guards. His fellow conspirators, Big Tree and Satank, received life sentences. Despite the affair, neither army strategy nor the U.S. government's Indian peace policy underwent a change.

Bibliography: Utley, Robert M., *Frontier Regulars* (Macmillan Co., 1973).

Maj. Peter Faber

KIOWA CAMPAIGN (1874–1875)

Last rising of the southern prairie Indians (Arapaho, Commanche, Cheyenne, Kiowa, and Kiowa Apache) from the reservation around Fort Sill, Oklahoma. Reservation life and the disappearance of the bison were the chief causes for the rising. During the summer of 1874, under the leadership of Quanah Parker (chief of the Quahada Commanche from the staked plains of Texas), 700 warriors initially attacked the Wichita Agency at Anadarko. After further unsuccessful attacks against Adobe Walls in the Texas Panhandle (July) and Buffalo Wallow (September), the band fled deeper into Texas pursued by Gen. Ranald Mackenzie. Quanah's Quahada Commanche were the last to be forced into surrender at Fort Sill on June 24, 1875.

Russell A. Hart

KRAG-JÖRGENSEN RIFLE

Adopted for use in 1892, the Krag-Jörgensen (or simply, Krag) rifle was the U.S. Army's standard issue shoulder weapon for 14 years. In 1878, the search had begun for a smaller caliber replacement for the Springfield models, which had a tendency to foul with heavy use.

An ordnance board convened in 1890 and, after testing 53 models, selected the Krag-Jörgensen system two years later. The field tests with troops included firing 500 consecutive rounds without cleaning and rusting the rifles before they were fired. While various U.S. models, including the "trapdoor" Springfield, were tested, none qualified as highly as the Krag, which was of Norwegian design.

Outrage of U.S. designers was translated into congressional legislation that required the army to test further U.S. magazine weapons. These models again failed to match the Krag's performance, and the Krag was officially adopted on May 16, 1893.

Bibliography: Shockley, Philip M., *The Krag-Jörgensen Rifle in the Service* (World-Wide Gun Report, 1960).

Louise Arnold-Friend

LADY FRANKLIN BAY EXPEDITION (1881–1884)

Twenty-five-man scientific expedition to study arctic conditions, commanded by 1st Lt. Adolphus W. Greely, U.S. Army Signal Corps. Greely's team established a station at Fort Conger on Lady Franklin Bay opposite the western coast of Greenland on Aug. 11, 1881. During the next two years, expedition members collected an impressive mass of data on arctic climate and tides and on the region's flora and fauna. Their program of exploration and discovery included the attainment of the "Farthest North" (83° 24′N) by 2d Lt. James B. Lockwood and Sgt. David L. Brainard on May 13, 1882.

It was from Fort Sill in Oklahoma that soldiers pursued the renegade Indians who fled the nearby reservations in the 1870s during the Kiowa Campaign. Shown here is an infantry inspection at Fort Sill in 1897. (Library of Congress)

When the relief vessels scheduled for 1882 and 1883 failed to appear, Greely and his men withdrew south on Aug. 9, 1883, according to prearranged plans. After a perilous 51-day passage over water and ice, they arrived at Cape Sabine on Bedford Pym Island. There they established Camp Clay to await relief. The subsequent winter of 1883–84 became a nightmare of despair as starvation, disease, and accident ravaged the party. With the assistance of a few dedicated subordinates, notably Sergeant Brainard, Greely struggled to maintain control through harsh discipline. Just hours away from death by malnutrition and disease, the survivors were finally rescued by a relief expedition led by Capt. Winfield Scott Schley, U.S. Navy, on June 22, 1884. Only 6 of the expedition's 25 members survived.

The scientific achievements, hardships, and stirring rescue were overshadowed for a time by lurid accusations of murder and cannibalism at Camp Clay. Today, the expedition is reckoned a success in that the scientific data collected proved of enormous value to our knowledge of the earth's climate and tidal patterns.

Bibliography: Greely, Adolphus W., *Reminiscences of Adventure and Service: A Record of Sixty-Five Years* (Scribner's, 1927); ———, *Three Years of Arctic Service: An Account of the Lady Franklin Bay Expedition of 1881–1884 and the Attainment of the Farthest North,* 2d ed. (Scribner's, 1894); James, Bessie Rowland, ed., *Six Came Back: The Arctic Adventure of David L. Brainard* (Bobbs-Merrill, 1940); Schley, Winfield S., and J. R. Soley, *The Rescue of Greely* (Scribner's, 1885); Shrader, Charles R., "Greely," *Army Communicator* (winter 1982; spring 1982); Todd, A. L., *Abandoned: The Story of the Greely Arctic Expedition, 1881–1884* (McGraw-Hill, 1961).

Lt. Col. (Ret.) Charles R. Shrader

LAFAYETTE ESCADRILLE (1916–1918)

Contingent of U.S. airmen originally in volunteer service to the French air force in World War I. On Mar. 21, 1916, the Escadrille Américaine was activated as a U.S. unit attached to the French army. Officially designated Escadrille No. 124, the unit's commander, Capt. Georges Thenault, and his chief assistant were French, but the pilots were Americans. The most notable of them was Raoul G. V. Lufbery, who had 17 confirmed kills before his own death in 1918.

The first enemy aircraft shot down by an Escadrille member was credited to Kiffin Y. Rockwell on May 18, 1916, but there would be many more victories. Because of the unit's popularity, it soon became part of the larger Lafayette Flying Corps, whose other units also included U.S. flyers. In all, a total of 267 Americans enlisted in the unit, and its members are credited with destroying 199 enemy aircraft. On Christmas Day, 1917, 93 members of the unit transferred to the American Air Service while another 26 joined the air arm of the U.S. Navy. The Escadrille became the American 103d Aero Squadron on Feb. 13, 1918, and remained active through the rest of the war.

Bibliography: Hudson, James J., *Hostile Skies: A Combat History of the American Air Service in World War I* (Syracuse Univ. Press, 1968).

Roger D. Launius

The difficult terrain in the lava beds made fighting the Modoc demoralizing for U.S. troops. (U.S. Army Military History Institute)

LAVA BEDS, BATTLE OF THE (January 17, 1872)

Principal military engagement of the Modoc War of 1872–73. On the night of Jan. 16, 1872, elements of the 1st U.S. Cavalry and 21st U.S. Infantry, augmented by three companies of Oregon and California militia, surrounded fewer than 60 Modoc warriors under Captain Jack (Kintpuash) in the jagged lava beds south of Tule Lake in northern California. The almost impenetrable area was well known to the Modoc and later came to be called "Captain Jack's Stronghold."

The 335-man force commanded by Lt. Col. Frank Wheaton, Maj. John Green, and Capt. Reuben F. Bernard advanced at dawn on January 17, supported by artillery that soon was masked by the troops advancing in the broken terrain. Held up by the early morning fog, the tumbled and sharp lava rocks, and very determined Modoc resistance, the troopers attempted to consolidate their lines but found themselves directly under the Modoc rifles when the fog lifted in the afternoon. They were quickly demoralized, and, having lost 11 men killed and 26 wounded, withdrew under cover of darkness without having actually seen a single Modoc, all of whom escaped to continue the war for another five months.

Bibliography: Utley, Robert M., *Frontier Regulars: The United States Army and the Indian, 1866–1890* (Macmillan, 1973).

Lt. Col. (Ret.) Charles R. Shrader

LITTLE BIGHORN, BATTLE OF THE (June 25, 1876)

The ill-fated culmination of the U.S. Army's attempts to subdue the Sioux and Northern Cheyenne in the Dakotas and Montana who refused to comply with the U.S.-imposed reservation system; known colloquially as "Custer's Last Stand." Gen. Philip H. Sheridan hoped to catch the Indians in their winter camps and force them to the reservations. However, military planners did not anticipate the difficulties of campaigning in the severe winter that blanketed the northern Great Plains that year. Consequently, progress was slow, and what started as a winter advance began to look more and more like a spring or summer campaign.

Sheridan's plan called for Gen. George Crook to move against the western flank of the Sioux while Gen. Alfred H. Terry's forces advanced from the Dakota Territory to the east. But, much to Sheridan's dismay, early scouting reports placed the Indians to be encamped much farther west than expected.

On June 17, the Sioux engaged Crook's forces along Rosebud Creek in southern Montana. Completely ignorant of Crook's battle or of the current hostile tendencies of the Sioux, Terry pressed westward toward the valleys of the Tongue and Powder rivers. He and Gen. John Gibbon now expected to find the Sioux well to the west of the Rosebud, while in fact they were camped just northwest of the creek in the Little Bighorn Valley.

With orders to ascend the Rosebud from the east, Lt. Col. George A. Custer and the 7th Cavalry marched southwest from Montana's Yellowstone River, scouting for the hostile band of Sioux. They left Terry's command on the morning of June 22. By June 24, Custer had reached a point where the trail of the Sioux diverged to the west. Terry's plan called for Custer to unite with his forces on June 26 at the mouth of the Little Bighorn River. Instead, Custer turned west, following the trail to the divide between the Rosebud and the Little Bighorn.

The 7th Cavalry rested while scouts fanned out to reconnoiter the hilly country. Custer now planned to attack on June 26, the day appointed for Terry to arrive at the Little Bighorn. At dawn on June 25, Custer's scouts spied the Sioux village about 15 miles distant. Unable to see the village, Custer relied on his scouting reports and prepared to attack. Convinced that the Sioux knew of the soldiers' presence, Custer refused to allow them the opportunity to slip away. Although his regiment was exhausted from a forced march, Custer pushed ahead with his plan, unaware of the strength of his foe.

Topping the summit of the divide at noon on June 25, Custer sent three troops, 125 men, under the command of Capt. Frederick W. Benteen, to scout the left, or south, flank. Since the exact position of the Sioux village was still unknown, this move may have reflected Custer's continuing apprehension that the Indians might get away. Unknown to Custer, however, the Sioux were prepared and eager to fight.

Custer then assigned three more troops to Maj. Marcus A. Reno, retained five troops under his personal command, and left one in the rear to escort the pack animals. Custer and Reno then continued to follow the Indian trail down the valley toward the Little Bighorn. Ahead, a line of bluffs hid the river, as well as the Sioux village, from their view. Immediately in front of the column, a party of about 40 Indian warriors, the rear guard of a small camp moving to join the larger village, came into view. To Custer, this clearly indicated that the Indians knew of the soldiers and were attempting to escape. He ordered Reno to attack the village, promising to support him. Custer then advanced up the ridge toward the expected village.

The Sioux village, still unseen by Custer, extended for three miles along the Little Bighorn. It included not only Sioux but Cheyenne visitors as well. If the Indians had any warning of the approaching troops, as Custer believed, it was not much. The exact number of fighting men in the village is unknown, but estimates place the figure at between 1,500 and 3,000 warriors. Many were armed with rifles, some even having the efficient Winchester repeater. The firepower in the village certainly equaled that carried by the 7th Cavalry.

After fording the river and advancing two miles down the Little Bighorn Valley, Reno attacked the upper end of the village. When Sioux swarmed out to confront him, Reno stopped the charge and dismounted his men to fight in a skirmish line. Flanked on his left, Reno ordered a retreat into a cottonwood grove on his right. Warriors soon infiltrated this position, so Reno remounted his men and led them in a mad dash back across the river to a better position on the nearby bluffs. Reno's advance, battle, and retreat lasted about 40 minutes. He had lost, in killed and wounded, almost half of his command.

Reno had expected Custer's support from the rear, but instead, Custer had veered to the north, attacking the village farther up river. Upon seeing the size of the village, Custer sent his trumpeter, Giovanni Martini, back with a note to Benteen to come quickly with the ammunition packs.

As Custer attacked the center of the village, Indians poured out to repulse the onslaught. The Hunkpapa chief Gall, counterattacking from the south, is reputed to have led the defense. Then more warriors led by Crazy Horse struck the 7th from the north. Trapped in broken terrain more suitable to the Indians' style of fighting, the command quickly fragmented. Custer and a small remnant of his men gathered at the northern end of the battle ridge. The fight was sharp and short—within an hour it was over. No U.S. cavalryman survived.

Benteen's scout to the left had proved fruitless. He soon joined Reno's bedraggled forces on the bluffs. They could hear firing from Custer's direction, and some officers wanted to go to his support. Reno wisely refused their requests. Sioux and Cheyenne, returning from the Custer fight, laid siege to the soldiers on the bluffs. During the night, the Indians retreated to the south. The reason for their exodus became clear on the morning of June 26 when the forces of Terry and Crook marched up the Little Bighorn Valley, right on schedule. Terry's scouts found the bodies of Custer and his men where they had fallen. Reno had lost an additional 47 killed and 53 wounded.

Controversy has surrounded the Battle of the Little Bighorn ever since. What if Custer had followed Terry's plan? What if Reno had stormed the village as ordered? What if Custer had attacked with his entire regiment? Yet, as history concludes, the ultimate responsibility for the catastrophe lies with Custer. He departed from Terry's plan. He precipitated the battle a day early with tired men and horses. He went into battle without complete knowledge of his enemy's strength or location.

Bibliography: Connell, Evan S., *Son of the Morning Star: Custer and the Little Big Horn* (Harper & Row, 1984); Utley, Robert M., *Cavalier in Buckskin: George Armstrong Custer and the Western Frontier* (Univ. of Oklahoma Press, 1988); ———, *Frontier Regulars: The United States Army and the Indian, 1866–1891* (Univ. of Nebraska Press, 1973).

M. Guy Bishop

LOST BATTALION (October 1918)

Name given to a 600-man force of U.S. soldiers that became virtually trapped by the Germans after being separated from the main U.S. contingent during World War I. The American Expeditionary Force's 77th Division manned the 1st U.S. Army's left flank as it moved northward through the Argonne Forest during the Meuse-Argonne Offensive. On Oct. 2, 1918, six companies of the 308th Infantry Regiment and two companies of the 306th Machine-Gun Battalion penetrated enemy lines by advancing through a half-mile gap in the German front. Later, Company K of the 307th Infantry Regiment joined the detachment on the north slope of a ravine east of Charlevaux Mill, approximately one-half mile north of friendly lines. These units, separated from the main body when German units reoccupied the line, became known as the "Lost Battalion."

Realizing its plight, the detachment attempted a breakout toward friendly forces on October 3, but German troops repulsed the attack. Consequently, this small U.S. force settled into a perimeter measuring 350 by 75 yards. The steep terrain rendered artillery fire ineffective, but German small arms, trench mortars, and flamethrowers kept the Americans under constant fire. Food, ammunition, and medical supplies were scarce, and continual attempts to reinforce and resupply by ground and air proved futile.

Refusing a German offer to surrender on October 7, the depleted detachment, now at one-third its original strength, fought off the fiercest of the German attacks. Later that day, after five days of repeated assaults, a flanking attack by I Corps and a general advance by the 77th Division drove German forces back and relieved the Lost Battalion.

Bibliography: American Battle Monuments Commission, *American Armies and Battlefields in Europe* (U.S. Govt. Printing Office, 1938); ———, *77th Division: Summary of Operations in the World War* (U.S. Govt. Printing Office, 1944).

Capt. James Sanders Day

LUSITANIA, SINKING OF THE (May 7, 1915)

Sinking of the British Cunard Line transatlantic passenger ship by the German submarine U-20 off the coast of Ireland. Bound for Liverpool from New York on May 7, 1915, the luxury liner *Lusitania* had almost completed its run when, at 2:15 P.M., a single torpedo struck amidship. The *Lusitania* sank within 20 minutes, taking with it 1,198 passengers and crew, including 128 Americans. Anger toward Germany built in the neutral United States, and Pres. Woodrow Wilson condemned the attack. The German government countered that the *Lusitania* illegally carried munitions, thereby making it a justifiable target, and that U.S. citizens had been warned that British ships were subject to attack. In September, Germany called off its unrestricted submarine warfare, but resentment toward Germany continued to grow in the United States.

Bibliography: Bailey, Thomas A., and Paul B. Ryan, *The Lusitania Disaster* (Free Press, 1975); Hough, Richard, *The Great War at Sea, 1914–1918* (Oxford Univ. Pres, 1983).

John F. Wukovits

LYS OFFENSIVE (April 1918)

World War I action, part of German general Erich F. W. Ludendorff's Peace Offensive of 1918, that began in Flanders on April 9 with a breakthrough of British lines along the Lys River. German forces, attacking south of Ypres, penetrated 10 miles along a 12-mile front. With only 8 American Expeditionary Force (A.E.F.) divisions in France, the U.S. commitment in this area was minimal. The 16th Engineers Regiment, the 28th (Aero) Pursuit Squadron, and elements of the 30th Engineers occupied positions within the British sector. While these units rebuilt railways to support Allied counterattacks, the A.E.F. deployed an additional 10 combat divisions to France. Of these, the

27th and 30th divisions reinforced British attacks throughout the summer months. Relieved in early September, both divisions joined the final Allied assault on the Hindenburg line.

Bibliography: American Battle Monuments Commission, *American Armies and Battlefields in Europe* (U.S. Govt. Printing Office, 1938); ———, *30th Division: Summary of Operations in the World War* (U.S. Govt. Printing Office, 1944); ———, *27th Division: Summary of Operations in the World War* (U.S. Govt. Printing Office, 1944).

Capt. James Sanders Day

MACKENZIE'S RAID (May 17–19, 1873)

Surprise U.S. cavalry attack led by Col. Ranald S. Mackenzie against hostile Kickapoo Indians whose raids from Mexico into the United States were on the increase following the Civil War. Diplomatic efforts by the United States to have the Mexican government halt the cross-border raids failed in the face of strong opposition from Mexican merchants who handled the stolen plunder. Exasperated over the continued depredations, the U.S. Army moved Mackenzie's 4th Cavalry to Fort Clark, Texas, in the spring of 1873. Sec. of War William Belknap and Gen. Philip H. Sheridan arrived at Fort Clark in early April, and in a closed-door meeting, they ordered Mackenzie to halt the Kickapoo raids in any manner he saw fit. For the next month, Mackenzie drilled his men and collected intelligence on the Indian villages in Mexico.

In the early hours of May 17, a force of 400 cavalrymen and Indian scouts slipped across border. After a hard, fast march, the column struck the Kickapoo village just after sunrise. The attack achieved complete surprise, and the soldiers quickly drove off the inhabitants and burned the village. After a few hours rest, the column gathered its captured horses and 50 prisoners and proceeded back across the border. The weary force arrived at Fort Clark on May 19 after marching a total of 159 miles in 32 hours. Mackenzie's raid had the desired effect: Kickapoo raids across the border stopped, and the other tribes in the region also ended their forays into Texas for fear of meeting a similar fate.

Bibliography: Clendenen, Clarence C., *Blood on the Border: The United States Army and the Mexican Irregulars* (Macmillan Co., 1969).

Richard F. Kehrberg

MAINE, SINKING OF THE (February 15, 1898)

The sinking of a U.S. battleship moored in a Cuban harbor, an event of questionable cause and an incident used to precipitate the Spanish-American War. In January 1898, amid public outcries in the United States over Spanish mistreatment of Cubans, the USS *Maine* was ordered to make a courtesy call in Havana. The voyage was scheduled because a mob led by Spanish officers besieged newspaper offices in Havana protesting the publication of antimilitary articles, and, although U.S. citizens in the city were in no apparent danger and there had been no damage to U.S. property, the American consul, Fitzhugh Lee, informed Washington that he could not guarantee the safety of U.S. lives or property. Pres. William McKinley then dispatched the warship, a rather standard late-19th-century reaction to such reports. The *Maine* entered Havana harbor on January 25.

Under the command of Capt. Charles Sigsbee, the berthed ship and its crew passed a quiet if watchful three weeks. Although the captain was graciously received and extended courtesies by his Spanish hosts, he did not allow his men ashore. He was influenced by a political tract thrust into his hands by a stranger upon the ship's arrival. The pro-Spanish pamphlet ended with an exhortation: "Death to Americans! Death to Autonomy." Sigsbee permitted his officers to go into the town, but only in civilian attire. He dispensed with the normal light anchor watch routine for a friendly port and ordered a quarter watch, about one-fourth the crew up and about during hours of darkness.

On February 15, 9:30 P.M., a muffled explosion was heard. In an instant, another, much louder explosion rent the air. The massive blast raised the battleship up, and the center of the ship erupted in flames. The explosions were located primarily near the enlisted quarters, and about two-thirds of the crew was killed immediately. In all, there were 260 dead or missing out of 328 on board.

Since that fateful night, interest in the *Maine* has focused largely on the cause of the two explosions. The first formal investigation, a few weeks after the blasts, included an underwater examination by divers that determined the keel was pushed up, indicating a mine placed under the ship. However, there were arguments for an internal blast, perhaps from the ship's heavily loaded magazine.

There is no doubt the great tragedy in Havana harbor contributed to U.S. anger at Spain and inflamed the U.S. press, most notably tabloid czars William Randolph Hearst and Joseph Pulitzer, who perpetuated the cries for war and promoted the rallying call to "Remember the *Maine!*" But the incident was likely only one of several reasons for the actual outbreak of war. Most of the McKinley administration's actions immediately following the event were aimed at tamping down war hysteria and determining the reason for the disaster.

After the Spanish-American War, the hulk of the *Maine* was reexamined and then sunk in deep water. The cause of the explosions has never been explained satisfactorily.

Bibliography: Weems, John Edward, *The Fate of the "Maine"* (Henry Holt & Co., 1958).

Col. (Ret.) Rod Paschall

The explosion of the U.S. battleship Maine *in Havana harbor on Feb. 15, 1898, was blamed (although never proven) on the Spanish and was one of the key events that precipitated the Spanish-American War.* (Library of Congress)

MALOLOS CAMPAIGN (1899)

Philippine land campaign, in which U.S. forces began to oppose Filipino nationalists in northern Luzon. In February 1899, fighting erupted between Filipino and U.S. forces in the suburbs of Manila. In the months since the close of the Spanish-American War, tension had increased as the United States sought to acquire the archipelago in opposition to Filipino desires for independence. The skirmish in February began a campaign in which Gen. Elwell Otis, the U.S. commander, sought to establish control over the island of Luzon and crush the insurgent movement.

In the early hours of the battle on February 4, the U.S. response was savage and swift, surprising even Emilio Aguinaldo, leader of the Filipino forces. U.S. units relentlessly pursued the rebels, and U.S. lines grew dangerously long as the pursuit extended deep into the insurgent countryside. Against a more adept adversary, Otis could have lost the war before it really began.

After one day of fighting, more than 3,000 Filipino dead lay scattered over the city. Surprised and shocked at the fierce onslaught, Aguinaldo sent a representative to Otis requesting a truce. Otis refused the truce, replying that the fighting would not be stopped until he had won.

To secure Luzon, Otis ordered a two-prong offensive against the Filipinos, with one force under Gen. Arthur MacArthur driving northward toward Malolos, the insurgent capital, and Gen. Thomas Anderson taking a southeasterly direction in hopes of sealing off the southern territory.

Otis's plan rested upon the premise that MacArthur would take northern Luzon and destroy the insurgent movement as he did so. Because Aguinaldo and other Filipino leaders had established the capital of the republic at Malolos, Otis reasoned that the fall of Malolos, if done swiftly, could end the opposition to U.S. control of the islands.

Heavy artillery and troops are supported by a pontoon bridge during the advance on Malolos, the insurgent capital, in the Philippines in 1899. (U.S. Military Academy)

On February 10, with a division that included a regiment of volunteers from Kansas and another from Montana, MacArthur began his march toward Malolos using Luzon's only railroad for his communications with Manila. His first objective was Caloocan, a small town three miles north of Manila. The Filipinos waited in prepared trenches dug among a grove of trees. Using ships anchored offshore and artillery accompanying his force, MacArthur shelled Filipino positions before deploying his forces. MacArthur sent one regiment attacking along a line with the forest, while the other regiment charged across rice fields using the irrigation earthworks to shield them from rebel fire.

The Filipinos held their ground with heavy fire brought to bear by both sides. Eventually, soldiers from the Montana regiment flanked the rebel positions, forcing them to flee into the woods. As the Americans entered Caloocan, MacArthur sent patrols from house to house in order to clear the town of rebel sharpshooters. Filipino bodies cluttered the landscape as his troops pursued the retreating rebels. MacArthur ordered the town torched to drive out the last rebel snipers. The U.S. flag was hoisted on the church steeple, signaling the fall of Caloocan.

Filipino resistance such as MacArthur encountered at Caloocan convinced him that Aguinaldo intended to make a stand at Malolos. All along the way, U.S. troops encountered stiff opposition, confirming MacArthur's prediction of a decisive battle at the rebel capital. Aguinaldo never planned such an encounter, intending instead to wear down the Americans by using delaying actions as he made his escape to San Isidro, 35 miles north of Malolos. Despite the relative ease in taking rebel positions above Manila, MacArthur and other commanders were handicapped by an overcautious Otis, who ordered his units to return to the capital after each successful foray into rebel-held territory. MacArthur often ignored such instructions, pushing farther north in an effort to force the insurgents into the "final battle" he expected at Malolos.

When at last MacArthur arrived at Malolos, he rushed ahead of his troops into the town, foolishly exposing himself to danger. Fortunately for the general, the town was empty, the rebels having abandoned the city in favor of safer ground to the north. Despite orders from Otis to the contrary, MacArthur pushed his force five miles north of Malolos to a strategic rail crossroads at Calumpit. Catching Aguinaldo's rear guard by surprise, MacArthur prevented Gen. Antonio Luna from destroying the rail bridge. In a fight with Luna, the Americans inflicted such heavy casualties upon the rebel force that the Filipinos retreated in disarray, leaving the victorious MacArthur in control of the bridge.

On the surface, it appeared that the Malolos Campaign was successful in meeting U.S. objectives to hold territory and destroy the rebel movement. In spite of initial U.S. victories, Otis's unrealistic claims in the press, and Aguinaldo's failures in the field, the only real consequence of MacArthur's campaign was to drive the rebels deeper into the north, where they adopted guerrilla tactics against their opponents and forced the U.S. government to increase its commitment to the subjugation of the archipelago.

Bibliography: Karnow, Stanley, *In Our Image: America's Empire in the Philippines* (Ballantine Books, 1989); Miller, Stuart, *Benevolent Assimilation: The American Conquest of the Philippines, 1899–1903* (Yale Univ. Press, 1982).

Vernon L. Williams

MANCHU LAW (1912)

Colloquial name given to a congressional amendment to the Army Appropriation Bill, the passage of which (Aug. 24, 1912) prohibited certain officers from an apparent evasion of regimental duties. Often using political connections, line officers frequently managed to get detached from service with their regiments along the frontier or overseas and assigned to staff duties in Washington, D.C. These "plush" assignments were noticed by Congress following the creation of the General Staff in 1903, especially since promotion-seeking officers often spent most of their time politicking on Capitol Hill.

In an effort to curb such "homesteading," the War Department's General Order No. 68, promulgated on May 26, 1911, announced that "officers will be detailed in the General Staff Corps for a period of four years . . . and except in case of emergency or in time of war will not be eligible to further detail . . . until they have served for two years in the branch . . . to which they belong." To reinforce that general order, Congress tacked onto the Army Appropriation Bill a provision designed to limit the tours of duty in Washington to four years out of every six. Thus ended the enjoyable and often rewarding Washington tours for many officers.

About this same time, China's Ch'ing, or Manchu, dynasty abruptly ended as the result of a revolution, thereby removing the Manchu bureaucrats from office. In the eyes of the officers "exiled" from Washington, the recent War Department order and congressional legislation had the same effect as did the Chinese Revolution. Hence, the legislation became known as the "Manchu Law" and affected officers were dubbed "Manchus."

Martin W. Andresen

Commodore George Dewey led the U.S. Asiatic Fleet that successfully outmaneuvered and completely destroyed the Spanish fleet in Manila Bay, Philippines, on May 1, 1898. (U.S. Navy)

MANILA BAY, BATTLE OF (May 1, 1898)

Spanish-American War naval battle, in which the United States destroyed the Spanish fleet in Philippine waters and led the way for land operations, effectively ending Spanish control of the islands. Commodore George Dewey arrived in Japan on Jan. 3, 1898, and assumed command of the Asiatic Squadron, at that time numbering four ships. It was clear to Dewey that war was imminent, and he proceeded to make preparations. He moved the small fleet to Hong Kong and began an immediate program of repairs and crew training. Dewey reasoned that Hong Kong presented the best location from which to launch an attack on the Philippines. Soon after his arrival on the Chinese coast, he received a telegram from Asst. Sec. of the Navy Theodore Roosevelt, who urged him to make all preparations for action and who stated that, in case of war, Dewey was to make for the Philippines and commence offensive operations against the Spanish fleet there.

Dewey purchased two ships to serve as supply vessels. The protected cruiser *Raleigh* arrived at Hong Kong from Europe on February 18, and three additional ships joined the fleet in April. Leaving an incapacitated old paddlewheeler in China, Dewey's squadron for Philippine service consisted of four protected cruisers, two gunboats, one revenue cutter, and the two supply vessels.

On April 23, British authorities ordered Dewey to move his vessels out of British waters in accordance with neutrality statutes. This was the first indication to Dewey that the United States was indeed at war with Spain. The next day, he sailed from Hong Kong and positioned his fleet at Mirs Bay, waiting for official word from Washington to attack the Philippines. Sec. of the Navy John Long cabled Dewey that war had begun, ordered the Asiatic fleet to proceed to the Philippines, and urged Dewey to capture or destroy the Spanish vessels he found there.

On April 27, Dewey received intelligence on the situation in the islands from the U.S. consul, Oscar F. Williams, who had sailed to Mirs Bay from Manila to confer with Dewey. Williams indicated that the Spanish planned to contest Dewey at Subig Bay. Dewey sailed for the islands on the same day, reaching the west coast of Luzon on April 30. Dewey dispatched two vessels to Subig Bay to locate the Spanish fleet while he waited with the rest of his ships off the entrance to Manila Bay.

Unknown to Dewey or Williams, Adm. Patricio Montojo, commanding the Spanish fleet in the archipelago, had second thoughts about Subig Bay and had moved his fleet back to Manila, where he had shore artillery positions that could support his vessels. With word that the Spanish were not at Subig Bay, Dewey ordered the fleet to move into Manila Bay. At 11:30 P.M., the first ships entered the Boca Grande Passage steaming in column at eight knots. Dewey encountered sporadic fire from Spanish batteries along the southern shoreline but suffered no damage.

Wanting to arrive off Manila at daybreak, Dewey sailed at slow speed across the bay during the night, arriving near the city at dawn. As soon as the U.S. ships came within range, the Spanish fired on the attacking ships from shore positions at Manila and across the bay at the naval base at Cavite. Montojo added his guns, firing from his 10 ships stationed in line across the front of Cavite. Dewey steamed along the front of the city of Manila and turned toward the facing Spanish fleet. At 5:41 A.M., Dewey opened fire on the Spanish ships as his ships passed them along the port side. The U.S. force made five passes, keeping up a continuous fire until 7:35 A.M., when Dewey ordered the ships out of range.

Dewey received an erroneous report that he was low on ammunition and decided to give the men breakfast and a respite while he conferred with his officers. Shore batteries still bombarded the U.S. squadron, forcing Dewey to send word to the Spaniards in Manila that if the firing continued from that area, he would have no alternative than to shell the city. Firing ceased immediately.

Finding the ammunition report to be untrue, at 11:16 A.M., Dewey renewed the fight, which lasted another hour. The Spanish fleet lay sunk or burning, with the survivors swimming to the safety of shore at Cavite. Spanish casualties included all engaged ships lost and at least 370 men killed. No losses in ships or men were suffered by the United States.

Although Dewey could not initiate a landing and take the city of Manila until army reinforcements arrived later in the summer, the stunning defeat in May spelled the beginning of the end of Spanish rule in the Philippines.

Bibliography: Dewey, George, *Autobiography of George Dewey, Admiral of the Navy* (Scribner's, 1913); Spector, Ronald, *Admiral of the New Empire* (Louisiana State Univ. Press, 1974); Williams, Vernon L., "George Dewey: Admiral of the Navy," *Admirals of the New Steel Navy*, ed. by James Bradford (Naval Inst. Press, 1990).

Vernon L. Williams

MANILA, BATTLE OF (August 13, 1898)

Spanish-American War battle, in which the United States took control of the city of Manila and in turn, the Philippines. On May 1, 1898, Adm. George Dewey defeated the Spanish fleet in Manila Bay but did not have the necessary land forces to take and hold the city. By August, sufficient forces had arrived to make operations possible. Gen. Wesley Merritt formulated a plan with Dewey for the siege of Manila, and on August 7, Dewey and Merritt forwarded a joint message to the Spanish commander at Manila, imposing a 48-hour deadline for surrender of all Spanish forces. The U.S. attack on August 13 encountered little resistance from the Spanish. Unknown to the Americans or the Spanish in the islands, an armistice had been agreed upon by the two nations on August 11. Word did not reach the Philippines until August 16.

Merritt and Dewey took control of the city, occupying all former Spanish positions, keeping Filipino nationalists at bay until orders were received from Washington clarifying their status within the U.S. occupation. The War Department cabled that no joint occupation with the insurgents was to be allowed. Washington indicated that "insurgents and all others" were to recognize the authority of U.S. military and naval occupation. This marked the beginning of deteriorating relations between the Filipinos and U.S. forces, eventually leading to open conflict in February 1899.

Bibliography: Spector, Ronald, *Admiral of the New Empire* (Louisiana State Univ. Press, 1974).

Vernon L. Williams

MEDICINE LODGE TREATIES

Unsuccessful U.S.-Indian agreements created in the wake of the U.S. government's Indian concentration policy, which began in 1867 and stressed conquest by kindness. The policy advocated peaceful negotiations rather than violence, and the transformation of nomadic, warrior-huntsmen into "civilized" farmers. In this spirit, Kiowa, Comanche, Kiowa-Apache, Cheyenne, and Arapaho leaders signed treaties at Medicine Lodge Creek, Kansas, on Oct. 21 and 28, 1867. The Indians relinquished all rights to territories outside of two planned reservations, one north of Nebraska and one south of Kansas. Yet railroads would traverse these vast areas, and army military posts would dot them (the posts would prevent Indian depredations and insulate them from the "evils" of U.S. society). The treaties failed within a year due to continued violence between U.S. and Indian factions.

Bibliography: Wooster, Robert, *The Military and U.S. Indian Policy, 1865–1903* (Yale Univ. Press, 1988).

Maj. Peter Faber

MEUSE-ARGONNE OFFENSIVE
(September 26–November 11, 1918)

World War I operation in which U.S. forces severed a crucial German supply line in northeastern France; one of the war's concluding Allied campaigns. In September 1918, Supreme Allied Commander Ferdinand Foch and the Allied commanders in France agreed on a plan for a general offensive in the west, consisting of a series of convergent and near simultaneous assaults. The first two attacks were scheduled for September 26. Gen. John J. Pershing's 1st U.S. Army on the west bank of the Meuse River attacked northwest of Verdun with initially 9, and later 15, divisions toward Buzancy-Stonne. The attack was supported by 2,775 artillery pieces and 189 French light tanks. Concurrently, the French 4th Army, with 22 divisions, assaulted the western side of the Argonne Forest north of Suippes and between the Suippe and Aisne rivers toward Mézières. Its objective was to cut the German supply line of the Sedan-Montmédy railway and the Châlons-Mézières road.

Pershing's army faced difficult terrain of forest, hills, and deep valleys. Moreover, it had only two weeks to relocate and ready itself in preparation for the offensive, and several of Pershing's best divisions remained locked up in the St.-Mihiel operation. In addition, during the preceding three years, the Germans had constructed four defensive positions. Although heavily outnumbered, the defending German troops were generally of superior quality to those faced by U.S. troops in earlier offensives. Among the defenders were two Prussian guard divisions.

Adding surprise to a five-to-one superiority, Pershing kicked off with nine assault divisions in three corps (I, III, and V). The offensive began according to plan with the early capture of Vauquois, on September 26. The dominating heights of Montfaucon in the center held out until the following day, thereby checking the offensive's initial momentum. The terrain, strong resistance, unimaginative tactics, and the inexperience of many U.S. troops resulted in heavy casualties and limited advances.

October Combat. On October 4, Pershing renewed the stalled offensive by attempting to overwhelm the main German defensive positions with sheer weight of numbers. Pershing expanded the attack to the east bank of the Meuse, where the French XVII Corps, reinforced by the 29th and 33d U.S. divisions, was detailed to capture the Meuse Heights that overlooked the main axis of the advance. The XVII Corps stormed onto its lower slopes on October 8, occupying Consenvoye, but were beaten back from Richene Hill by fierce resistance. Meanwhile, on the main axis, Gesnes fell on October 5. At the same time, the 1st Battalion, 308th Infantry Regiment, found itself cut off and encircled. When this "Lost Battalion" (as it became known) finally succeeded in breaking out, it had been reduced to 194 effectives. All along the U.S. 1st Army's sector, the attack had slowed to a crawl by October 10 and came to a complete halt the following day when the assaulting corps temporarily went over to the defensive. This pause allowed the shuffling of formations, including the withdrawal of the 91st Division, which had suffered 9,387 casualties. At this point, total casualties for the offensive had passed the 100,000 mark, less than half of which could be immediately replaced.

At this point, Pershing realized—perhaps belatedly—that the attack had to be expanded even farther eastward where the terrain was more favorable for an assault. On October 12, therefore, Pershing created the U.S. 2d Army, commanded by Maj. Gen. Robert L. Bullard of III Corps, to take over the sector from the Meuse to the Moselle. On October 16, Pershing handed over command of the 1st Army to Gen. Hunter Liggett, formerly commander of I Corps, thereby removing himself from field command.

Under Allied pressure, Pershing again renewed the attack on October 14. The reasoning behind the renewal of the drive and of continuing Allied criticism of U.S. performance was political. The American Expeditionary Force (A.E.F.) had to renew the attack in order to gain for the

United States a position of influence at the upcoming peace conferences—it was clear that the German army was at the end of its tether.

The focal point of the third attack remained the Aisne-Meuse sector. However, the U.S. assault units were spent. The 5th Division pushed forward on October 14, only to reel back when counterattacked the following day. Pershing immediately relieved its divisional commander, soon followed by those of the 3d and 26th divisions. However, the attack managed to occupy Romagne, thereby piercing the main defensive position, the Kriemhilde Stellung. On October 30, Aincreville fell, thereby completing the occupation of the Kriemhilde position, at which point the advance halted. The flanking assault on the Meuse Heights proved unable to advance farther up its lower slopes. Nevertheless, the Metz-Sedan-Mézières Railroad had now been brought within heavy artillery range.

By late October, the U.S. assault divisions were clearly in need of rehabilitation and replenishment. Up to 100,000 "stragglers" roamed the rear areas, and these had to be rounded up and returned to their units. Such was the shortage of manpower that two divisions had to be broken up and smaller authorized ration strengths established.

German Defeat. As it became clear that the Germans were on the verge of collapse, the attack was renewed for the fourth time on November 1. All along the front, the Allies were advancing. By November 4, the 1st Army had advanced 12 miles, and German resistance had begun to crumble. Buzancy had fallen on November 2 and Barricourt on the following day. On the night of November 4, the Germans began a phased, general withdrawal—the Kriegsmarsch—behind the Meuse. As this withdrawal began, the 2d Army to the east joined the attack. That same day, the 1st Army secured a bridgehead over the Meuse along the Meuse Heights and proceeded the following day to draw up to the Meuse on a broad front just 5 miles southeast of Sedan. Pershing's order to the I Corps to seize Sedan caused mortification among the neighboring French 4th Army, in whose avenue of advance Sedan lay. It was only with difficulty that Pershing was able to halt his forces just short of Sedan, where they remained until the armistice on November 11.

A total of 22 divisions and 1,200,000 men, 850,000 of whom were combat troops, fought in the campaign. A total of 44 enemy divisions were engaged, and U.S. casualties totaled 117,000. Although the U.S. Army's performance was creditable, it was by no means outstanding. The unsophisticated frontal attacks and U.S. combat inexperience caused higher casualties than there might otherwise have been. U.S. use of artillery also left something to be desired.

In retrospect, many U.S. troops proved to have been too hastily trained, and, moreover, some of that training proved to have been misdirected. Thus, the U.S. soldier learned the hard way. But, to their credit, those of the U.S. 1st Army learned fast. If there remains an unresolved issue surrounding the Meuse-Argonne Offensive, it is why Pershing refused to shift the emphasis of the later attacks farther to the east. An attack east of the Meuse in the more negotiable terrain of the Woëvre Valley would almost certainly have resulted in greater achievements at lower cost.

Cavalrymen, led by Brig. Gen. John J. Pershing, cross a river in Mexico in 1916 during the search for Pancho Villa in the Punitive Expedition. (Fort Sam Houston Museum)

Bibliography: Braim, Paul F., *The Test of Battle: the A.E.F. in the Meuse-Argonne Campaign* (Univ. of Delaware Press, 1987); Brook-Shepherd, Gordon, *November 1918: The Last Act of the Great War* (Collins, 1981); Gregory, Barry, *Argonne* (Ballantine Books, 1982); Smythe, Donald, *Pershing: General of the Armies* (Univ. of Indiana Press, 1986).

Russell A. Hart

MEXICAN PUNITIVE EXPEDITION (March 15, 1916–February 5, 1917)

Campaign in which a U.S. force under the command of Gen. John J. Pershing invaded Mexico in a military retaliation for the cross-border raiding by Mexican revolutionaries. Following the assassination of Mexican president Francisco Madero in 1913, several powerful candidates plunged the country into revolution as they vied for the presidency. Reactionary Victoriano Huerta was the first to gain the office, much to the dismay of U.S. president Woodrow Wilson. Subsequently, Wilson used the U.S. Navy to block European arms shipments to the new Mexican government, a policy that resulted in the U.S. occupation of Veracruz in 1914. Venustiano Carranza assumed the presidency when Huerta's government collapsed in 1915.

While Wilson supported the Carranza regime, factional fighting continued with Mexico. Northern revolutionary leader Francisco "Pancho" Villa had assiduously cultivated good relations with the United States throughout this period in the hope of gaining U.S. support for his campaign for the Mexican presidency. But Wilson's recognition of Carranza as president, coupled with several military defeats at the hands of Carranza's army, turned Villa against the United States. In late 1915, Villa's supporters began attacking U.S. citizens in Mexico and increasingly joined the cross-border raids that had plagued the U.S.-Mexican frontier since the beginning of the revolution.

Having little success against the Carranza government in Mexico, Villa decided to attack the United States. Villa's exact motives remain unclear. Possibly he hoped to provoke U.S. intervention to make Carranza look weak and bring popular support to his cause. He may have hoped to involve Mexico in a war with the United States in order to unseat the government, or he simply may have sought revenge for what he considered U.S. offenses against him.

Whatever his motives, Villa led more than 400 of his men ("Villistas") across the border and attacked Columbus, New Mexico, in the early hours of Mar. 9, 1916. In a confused hour-long battle, Villistas, U.S. citizens, and soldiers from the 13th U.S. Cavalry fought in the streets of Columbus. As the Mexican raiders retreated toward dawn, Maj. Frank Tompkins mounted a portion of the 13th Cavalry and pursued them across the border for a short distance.

Operations in Mexico. U.S. public opinion following the Columbus raid demanded immediate action against Villa. The U.S. Army's Southern Department commander, Maj. Gen. Frederick Funston, began concentrating troops and supplies at Columbus and fashioning plans to support an expedition into Mexico. Permission from Washington to enter Mexico followed a few days later, and on March 14, Brigadier General Pershing officially took command of the Punitive Expedition with orders to pursue and destroy Villa's band. The expedition, organized as a provisional division with two cavalry brigades and an infantry brigade, moved into Mexico on March 15.

Split into two columns, the expedition moved by forced marches toward the Mexican town of Casa Grandes, 100 miles south of Columbus. Pershing received information, however, that Villa's band was even farther south. While establishing a forward supply base at Colonia Dublan, he dispatched three fast-moving cavalry columns forward to search the countryside. By moving parallel to one another, Pershing hoped that one of these columns would strike Villa's group as it attempted to evade the others.

Col. George H. Dodd's column of the 7th Cavalry moved south on March 18. After following up several false trails, Dodd learned that 500–600 Villistas had occupied the village of Guerrero just west of his own position in Bachineva. On March 29, after a long, cold night approach march over a rough mountain trail, the 7th Cavalry's 370 men attacked the village. The surprised Mexicans quickly retreated, and the "battle" consisted of a series of skirmishes between small groups of soldiers and Villistas. The cavalry lost 5 men wounded while they counted 35 dead Villistas, including Nicolas Hernández, one of Villa's most trusted lieutenants.

As Dodd's men moved toward Guerrero, the expedition's other two columns, both drawn from the 10th Cavalry, moved south as well. The two columns scoured the countryside to the east of Dodd's force but could not find any Villistas. Col. William C. Brown attempted to coordinate his column's movements with the local Carranzista commanders, but these efforts also failed. Knowing the 7th was marching toward Guerrero, Brown decided to move his command in that direction as well. As the regiment neared the village of Aguas Calientas on April 1, a force of 150 Villistas fired on the column. The cavalrymen quickly deployed and scattered the attackers. After searching the surrounding countryside for fugitives, Brown received orders from Pershing on April 10 to march toward Parral, a town nearly 400 miles south of the border.

Behind these first columns, Pershing sent out a series of smaller "flying columns" to block possible escape routes, comb the countryside, and reinforce the large columns if necessary. Four flying columns, drawn from the 13th and 11th cavalry regiments, left Colonia Dublan after March 20. As the expedition moved deeper into Mexico, the cooperative spirit of the Carranza government, never strong to begin with, measurably decreased. On April 12, Tompkins's squadron of the 13th Cavalry entered Parral. After an angry crowd had gathered around the troopers, Tompkins moved his men out of the town. As they left, however, the local Carranzista garrison attacked and forced Tompkins into a fighting withdrawal to Santa Cruz de Villegas. Word of the attack at Parral reached Colonel Brown that evening, and he quickly marched the 10th Cavalry to Tompkins's aid. The following day, two squadrons from the 11th Cavalry arrived to further bolster the U.S. force. Brown assumed command of the combined columns, and for the next few days, the U.S. and Mexican forces anxiously eyed one another.

The Parral affair dramatically altered the political and military situation in Mexico. A war between the United States and Mexico had become a real possibility. Pershing ordered Brown to pull back and then changed his tactics. Henceforth, each of his five cavalry regiments would patrol its own military district. Before the 7th Cavalry could reach its patrol area, however, it met and defeated Candelario Cervantes's band of Villistas near Tomochic on April 22. Pershing's new tactic paid further dividends as Maj. Robert L. Howze's squadron of the 11th Cavalry destroyed Julio Acosta's band at Ojos Azules on May 5. Battles between the Punitive Expedition and Villistas tapered off after Howze's fight with Acosta, although two more of Villa's senior officers, Julio Cárdenas and Cervantes, died in small skirmishes with U.S. patrols in May.

Tensions between the United States and Mexico deepened in early May as Mexican raids, in some cases led by Carranzista officers, increased on the lower Rio Grande. On May 9, President Wilson ordered the National Guard mobilized for service on the border. The mobilization was slow, and many guard units arrived in poor shape and without proper equipment, but by July, more than 112,000 guardsmen were on duty along the border.

Tensions were near the flash point in late June when a patrol of the 10th Cavalry attempted to enter the town of Carrizal without the permission of the local Carranzista commander. In the fight that followed, more than half the U.S. force was killed, wounded, or captured. The fight shocked both governments and moved them to the bargaining table. As talks began, the tempo of operations in the Punitive Expedition decreased, and Pershing concentrated his forces around Colonia Dublan. For the next six months, the expedition's soldiers undertook a program of limited patrolling, intensive training, and marking time. Although the talks with the Carranza government had been inconclusive and Villa had assembled a new army farther south, Wilson decided to withdraw the Punitive Expedition in late January 1917. On February 5, the last U.S. soldier crossed the border into the United States.

Results. The Punitive Expedition ably succeeded in fulfilling its mission. While Villa was not captured, the expedition shattered the Villista army and killed most of its senior commanders. Furthermore, raids on the New Mexico and west Texas borders virtually ceased during the U.S. penetration into Mexico. And, while Villa was able to assemble a new army later, he never again threatened the United States.

However, the importance of the expedition went beyond Villa and his raiders. The U.S. Army's operations in Mexico provided a training ground for officers and men who would subsequently see action on World War I battlefields. The mobilization of the National Guard highlighted problems of mobilization planning, organization, and logistics that had to be solved if the United States was to send a force to fight in France. While the expedition marked the last extensive use of horse cavalry by the U.S. Army, it also provided the military with its first experience in using machine guns, motor trucks, radios, and airplanes in the field. The experience gained by the army during the Punitive Expedition proved to be of inestimable value just three months later, when the United States declared war on Germany.

Bibliography: Clendenen, Clarence C., *Blood on the Border: The United States Army and the Mexican Irregulars* (Macmillan Co., 1969); ———, *The United States and Pancho Villa: A Study in Unconventional Diplomacy* (Amer. Hist. Assoc., 1961); Thomas, Robert S., and Inez V. Allen, *The Mexican Punitive Expedition under Brig. Gen. John J. Pershing, U.S. Army, 1916–1917* (Office of the Chief of Military History, U.S. Army, 1954); Tompkins, Frank, *Chasing Villa: The Story Behind Pershing's Expedition into Mexico* (Mil. Serv. Publ. Co., 1934); Toulmin, H.A., *With Pershing in Mexico* (Mil. Serv. Publ. Co., 1935).

Richard F. Kehrberg

MODOC WAR (1872–1873)

U.S.-Indian conflict in which 1,000 army troops were held at bay by about 70 warriors for six months in the Lava Beds, a natural volcanic fortress in northern California. The Modoc, a northern California tribe, signed a treaty in 1864, which ceded territory and retired the Modoc to the Klamath Reservation in Oregon. Outnumbered by the Klamath Indians, the Modoc were harassed, and repeated disputes induced a group of Modoc, under Captain Jack, to leave the reservation and return to California. In 1872, the U.S. Army was sent to force the Indians back to the reservation. In what became known as the Battle of Lost River, one Indian was killed and one wounded. The army lost two dead and six wounded. Jack and his followers escaped to the Lava Beds.

On Jan. 17, 1873, a second battle, the Battle of the Stronghold, resulted in further losses for the army. To avoid additional bloodshed, Gen. Edward Canby, the military commander for the district, initiated negotiations. Canby, with Indian agent L. S. Dyer and the federal peace commissioners Alfred Meacham and Rev. Eleasar Thomas, met with Jack's band.

Dissensions arose within the Indian group, and Jack was forced to agree to kill Canby the next time they met. During a conference on April 11, the commissioners were attacked. Canby and Thomas were killed, and Meacham was seriously injured. Col. Jefferson C. Davis assumed command and launched an attack with more than 1,000 men. The Modoc all surrendered by June 1873. Captain Jack and three other Modoc were hanged on October 3.

Bibliography: Palmberg, Walter H., *Copper Paladin: A Modoc Tragedy: A Story of the Two Principal Role-players in the Modoc Indian War of 1872–73* (Dorrance, 1982); Riddle, Jeff, *The Indian History of the Modoc War* (Urion Press, 1974).

Deborah L. Mesplay

MORO CAMPAIGNS (1902–1915)

U.S. military and pacification operations conducted against the Moro tribesmen of the southern Philippines after the end of the Filipino Insurrection in 1902. These were difficult operations against a fierce adversary, required four times as long to conclude as did the insurrection, and featured many of the best-known U.S. soldiers of the period. In Moro Province (Mindanao and the Sulu Archipelago), establishment and operation of the government

Capt. John J. Pershing, seated (second from right) *among his fellow officers, was governor of Moro Province, Philippines, and led the assault against the Moros who were fortified atop their sacred mountain, Bud Dajo, in December 1912.* (Library of Congress)

were U.S. Army responsibilities, with a true civilian government to be instituted at some later date.

The Moros were Malays converted to Islam in the spread of that faith from Borneo and Malacca in the 14th and 15th centuries. On Mindanao, as on the smaller islands of the Sulu Archipelago to the southwest, they established a feudal society that successfully defied the Spanish colonial army and terrorized the Christian Filipinos and Chinese living in the small seacoast villages.

There were numerous Moro chieftains, each ruling his band of gaudily dressed and armed fighting men, along the coasts, lakes, and rivers. Some numbered their followers in thousands, others had only a handful. The business of the Moro leadership was war, which provided the Moro warriors with women and slaves and the satisfaction of bloodshed and conquest. Although not well armed as a whole, guns being generally of obsolete pattern and ammunition scarce, every warrior carried a hand weapon. Against these physically tough opponents, the weapon of choice for U.S. soldiers on outpost duty or on patrol point was the 12-gauge pump shotgun.

The Moros lived in fortified villages called "cottas," which were on the shores of lakes or streams, in swamps, or on difficult terrain. Each cotta was protected by rock walls and usually "lantakas," small muzzleloading cannon. The cottas' walls were generally too thick to be easily penetrated by the army's field guns, making them, along with their siting, difficult to attack.

It was a fiction, believed by both the Spanish and U.S. governments, that the Sultan of Sulu actually governed the Moro people. While he was undoubtedly the titular head of the Islamic religion in Mindanao and the Sulu Islands, he was not the temporal leader. No government, as Westerners understood the word, existed; everything depended upon power and custom. The Spanish had been at war with the Moros for more than three centuries, and they informed the Americans that it would require 100,000 regular troops to subdue them. Gen. John C. Bates, as a U.S. representative, signed a convention with the sultan called the "Bates Agreement" in 1899. This agreement, similar to earlier Spanish-Moro agreements, stipulated that the U.S. governor might interfere in Sulu only in the event of a crime against a foreigner.

In spring 1902, the governor's first emissary to the Moro datus (chiefs) around Lake Lanao found them sullen and dangerous. In March, they killed their first U.S. soldiers. It appeared that they had interpreted the U.S. policy of conciliation as a sign of weakness. As a result, it was modified in favor of a more proactive approach. The U.S. Army was thus directed to establish government presence, programs, and patrol posts throughout the province; negotiate for the datus' allegiance; and work slowly for the elimination of slavery. The program reflected army experience in Cuba, Puerto Rico, and the northern Philippines. It was broad based and called for the following: establishment of schools, improvement of sanitation, encouragement of agriculture, construction of roads, institution of law with U.S. judges, disarmament, organization of civil government by districts (along natural lines governed by natural rulers), and enactment of an antislavery law (with gradual abolishment through purchase). Also, the Islamic religion was to be left entirely alone. It was a program intended to show and persuade the Moros that life under such a system was a better way to live. Behind this program was the military, U.S. regulars and Philippine Scouts, ready to force what could not be achieved through moral suasion.

Early Operations. Although the Bates Agreement was not formally abrogated until Mar. 21, 1904, operations to enforce the new policy began in May 1902 with expeditions under Col. Frank Baldwin and Capt. John J. Pershing against the Moros around Lake Lanao. The 1,200-man combined force of infantry and cavalry mauled the Moros in a pitched battle at Bayan and impressed the local datus that the Americans were serious about establishing posts in the interior and ending slavery. It also ended the faint U.S. hope that pacification could be achieved without a much larger commitment of troops and money.

Early in the pacification effort, it became apparent to experienced army officers, such as Pershing, Leonard Wood, Hugh L. Scott, James G. Harbord, Robert L. Bullard, and John White, that few regulars were really fit to manage these type operations. They also later stated that much of the subsequent fighting might have been avoided if those officers who knew the Moros had been encouraged to remain among them. This would have required a program featuring fair promotion opportunities, adequate pay, and retirement. Such a program was never instituted by the War Department. Many mistakes and much costly relearning took place with each rotation of commanders from province level down to the small detachments in the field.

Military operations centered on the three major areas of Moro population: the Rio Grande valley and the Lake Lanao regions of Mindanao and Jolo Island in the Sulu Archipelago. Nonetheless, the manpower requirements to outpost, patrol, provide adequate operational reserves, and administer the civil government required a garrison of approximately 5,000 regular troops, supplemented by Philippine Scout companies. A major burden on the army was the need to provide officers to administer the civil government. This rapidly used up the older and more experienced officers and left the operational units with the younger and less experienced. In 1910, for example, the commander of an infantry regiment noted that all 12 of his companies and 2 battalions were commanded by lieutenants. Additionally, maintaining so many small garrisons took away from the troops available for field operations. By 1905, it was apparent that if a company had 90 personnel present for duty, only 45 were available for field service and training due to garrison duties and sickness.

Most of the operations against the Moros were small in size and conducted in response to some lawless act. During 1906, for example, 16 operations in the Cotabato Valley and 6 in the Lake Lanao area were conducted on Mindanao. On Jolo, during this period, only 4 operations were conducted. All of these, with one exception, were similar, involving 50–300 troops and lasting 7–10 days. Casualties were normally quite light, with sickness accounting for more than combat. Standard organization for these operations featured a fairly mobile, combined-arms team of infantry and cavalry and one or two pieces of artillery.

One major operation was mounted in the Sulu District in 1906. Colonel Scott, the military governor, had negotiated for months with a group of outlaws who had gathered 600 followers and fortified the summit of Bud Dajo, a 2,100-foot extinct volcano. Although the sultan and other leaders publicly disavowed these rebels, they were sympathetic to their defiance of U.S. authority. In March, Scott decided to settle the issue by force of arms. At daylight on March 7, 600 regulars and a constabulary company assaulted the crater fortress. Twenty-four hours were required to complete the operation, during which almost all the Moros were killed. At the time, it was believed that such a severe lesson would not have to be repeated, yet six years later, it recurred on the slopes of Bud Bagsak, not far from Bud Dajo.

In September 1903, a Moro constabulary was established under the command of Colonel Harbord. This force was intended eventually to assume the task of maintaining law and order in the province. Although many army officers had their doubts, the constabulary soon proved its trustworthiness and ability to do the job. In May 1904, General Wood first used the constabulary for scouts in support of an army expedition against Moro outlaws on Mindanao. The constabulary was ideal for such purposes. Its success here resulted in its use as scouts and advance guards in subsequent operations. By 1910, the expansion and success

Members of the Moro constabulary, shown squatting in front of their U.S. officers, were used mainly as scouts from 1904 during the Moro Campaign. (U.S. Army Military History Institute)

of the constabulary and Philippine Scout programs permitted the reconcentration of regular troops into larger garrisons.

Later Campaigns. On Sept. 8, 1911, Pershing, as governor of the province, issued Executive Order No. 24—the formal order for disarmament of the Moros. It was now unlawful for a Moro to possess a firearm or carry a cutting weapon. Although many Moros admitted its wisdom, few felt that it could succeed without a fight, especially in the district of Jolo. It was clear, before the deadline for surrendering firearms on December 1, that many Moros were not going to comply. They attacked a U.S. base camp in Jolo on November 28, and Pershing put punitive columns in the field five days later. He received word on December 15 that 500–800 Moros, armed with an estimated 200 rifles, had again fortified themselves atop Bud Dajo, their sacred mountain. By December 22, Pershing had ringed the mountain with approximately 1,000 troops. The assault was launched on the day before Christmas. There was close fighting for the next two days. Operations concluded on December 27 with a casualty list of 3 U.S. wounded and 12 Moro killed; 300 Moros surrendered.

Although thousands of guns were surrendered, the rebels on Jolo remained defiant, even after the defeat at Bud Dajo. In late January 1913, there were two clashes with the Moros on Jolo, who, numbered at 5,000–10,000, then withdrew to their forts on top of Bud Bagsak. Pershing, through use of deception, cover of darkness, and speed, was able to encircle and trap the Moros atop the mountain before they were aware that the troops were moving against them. The combined force of U.S. cavalry, infantry, and artillery and Philippine Scouts began operations against the Moro positions on June 11 and continued through June 15. Government losses were 15 killed and 25 wounded. Moro losses were at least 500 killed and an unknown number of wounded. Due to the Moro custom of taking their families with them, approximately 5–10 percent of the killed were women and children.

Hand in hand with field operations went the army's development of an efficient intelligence service, mapping, and road building; the improvement of communications among outposts and the islands; and the acquisition of new weapons and equipment. Improved weapons were obtained with receipt of the Model 1903 Springfield rifle and Vickers-Maxim machine gun in 1906 and the adoption of the Model 1911 .45-caliber automatic pistol. In addition to improved weapons, the army adopted new tactics to hamper the Moros' fondness for nighttime infiltration and the sudden rush. By 1912, field bivouacs were routinely enclosed with barbed wire and the troops entrenched.

Although the standard operational pattern continued, no major fighting with the Moros took place after 1913. The constabulary, with a strength of 60 officers and 972 enlisted personnel, assumed responsibility for the maintenance of public order in 1915. This signaled the end of what is commonly termed the Moro Campaigns, although the U.S. government was still not established in the more remote areas of the province; 5 regiments of regulars and 14 companies of Philippine Scouts remained as a garrison, and rebellious outbursts would continue to occur.

Bibliography: Miller, Stuart C., *Benevolent Assimilation: The American Conquest of the Philippines, 1899–1903* (Yale Univ. Press, 1984); Storey, Moorfield, and Marcial P. Lichauco, *The Conquest of the Philippines by the United States, 1898–1925* (1926; reprint, Ayer Co. Pub.).

Lt. Col. (Ret.) John A. Hixson

MORRILL ACT OF 1862

Act of Congress that granted states vast tracts of public land for the creation of colleges and universities. Passed on July 2, 1862, it required such land-grant schools to teach a course in military tactics.

After the Civil War, Congress empowered the president to detail army officers to schools to teach military tactics and to issue surplus small arms and ammunition for training. The army made little attempt to utilize the graduates of this training until the beginning of World War I and the creation of the Reserve Officers Training Corps (R.O.T.C.) in 1916. Following the model of the Morrill Act, the National Defense Act of 1920 firmly rooted the R.O.T.C. in land-grant institutions and other college campuses.

Daniel T. Bailey

NATIONAL DEFENSE ACT OF 1916

An act of Congress that ended 15 years of discussion about the military establishment necessary for the United States and the military utility of the National Guard. Most regular officers not only doubted the ability of guard units but believed that such units were militarily useless because the Constitution in effect forbad deployment of militia outside the United States. By contrast, National Guard supporters argued that their forces were more in accordance with U.S. tradition and stood ready to volunteer for overseas duty.

In late 1915, Sec. of War Lindley Garrison forced the issue by endorsing a General Staff plan for a larger regular army, backed by a purely federal reserve force to be known as the Continental Army. National Guard supporters led by Rep. James Hay opposed Garrison's plan so strongly that Pres. Woodrow Wilson tried to compromise between the two versions, prompting Garrison to resign.

The sudden mobilization to intervene in Mexico against Pancho Villa resulted in a hasty compromise in May 1916. The resulting act authorized the regular army to expand to 175,000 over five years and to 286,000 in the event of war, including an enlisted reserve force. It also authorized organization of this force into tactical brigades and divisions and gave the president authority over arms manufacturing.

More important, the National Defense Act transformed the National Guard into a dual state-federal force. All members were required to swear allegiance to the federal as well as the state government, and the War Department was to establish standards for guard officers, pay for 48 drills per year, and provide instructors and supplies for the Guard. This combination of federal oaths, standards, and pay was intended to circumvent constitutional limitations by making the National Guard into a deployable, federal reserve force. As such, it went to war in Europe a year later.

Bibliography: Hill, Jim D., *The Minuteman in Peace and War: A History of the National Guard* (Stackpole, 1964); Weigley, Russell F., *History of the United States Army* (Macmillan, 1967).

Maj. Jonathan M. House

NAVAL WAR COLLEGE

The U.S. Navy's institution of higher learning. In an address before the Newport branch of the U.S. Naval Institute on Apr. 4, 1883, Commodore Stephen B. Luce proposed the establishment of "a postgraduate course for study of the science of war." The idea received a cold reception from most navy officers, but Luce obtained the support of Sec. of the Navy William E. Chandler, and on Oct. 6, 1884, Navy General Order No. 325 established "a college for an advanced course of professional study for naval officers" at Newport, Rhode Island. The first course, conducted for eight student officers in September 1885, included lectures on military science, the art of naval warfare, and marine international law.

At first, the Naval War College was little appreciated by many naval officers and struggled to maintain its existence. However, opposition gradually subsided as the reputation and usefulness of the college steadily improved under the direction of Admiral Luce, naval strategist Alfred Thayer Mahan, Capt. William M. Little (who introduced war gaming, an important part of the early college curriculum), and Adm. Henry C. Taylor, president of the Naval War College 1893–96. An important function of the college faculty during this early period was the preparation of plans for naval campaigns. Originally under the Bureau of Navigation, the college was placed under the chief of naval operations in 1915 and became a purely educational institution when its planning responsibilities were assumed by that office.

The operations of the Naval War College were suspended during the Spanish-American War and again during World War I. During the interwar years, the college instituted a number of improvements, including a course for junior officers, and worked with the Army War College on joint operations. Its strategic studies on a potential war with

Japan were of particular importance. Courses were again suspended in May 1941 for the duration of World War II but were resumed in 1946. Today, the Naval War College is a central fixture of the navy's system of professional education for officers.

As the first senior service college, the U.S. Naval War College provided a model for creation of the Army War College in 1901 and for similar institutions in other nations. The college early established its role as a center for the formulation and study of strategic problems particularly through the medium of the war game, and it retains that key role today.

Bibliography: *History of the United States Naval War College, 1884–1963* [and Succeeding Annual Command Historical Report Supplements] (U.S. Naval War Coll., 1966); Spector, Ronald, *Professors of War: The Naval War College and the Development of the Naval Profession* (Naval War Coll. Press, 1977).

Lt. Col. (Ret.) Charles R. Shrader

NEZ PERCÉ WAR (1877)

Three-month campaign in which an 800-man group of Nez Percé under Chief Joseph led the U.S. army on an epic chase of some 1,700 miles through some of the most rugged terrain in North America. The conflict began in March 1877 with a request by the Indian Bureau for army assistance in moving the Nez Percé to a reservation in Idaho. En route, three young braves of White Bird's band killed four whites on June 14, and the Nez Percé fled toward their mountainous Idaho homeland pursued by an ever-increasing number of army detachments. The 300 warriors and 500 women and children apparently then decided to cross the Rockies to the bison-filled plains of Montana. Moving fast and in unexpected directions, they avoided being cornered by the pursuing soldiers, although they fought several sharp engagements, notably at White Bird Canyon on June 18, on the Clearwater River on July 12, at Camas Meadows on August 20, and at Canyon Creek on September 13.

Finally, troops under Col. Nelson A. Miles managed to race ahead and surround the Nez Percé at Bear Paw Mountain on September 30. Miles laid siege to the Indian camp with his artillery and forced negotiations. On October 5, Chief Joseph surrendered with 400 of his people and uttered his stirring words: "Hear me, my chiefs! I am tired. My heart is sick and sad. From where the sun now stands I will fight no more forever."

About 300 of the Nez Percé escaped from Bear Paw Mountain and eventually took refuge with Sitting Bull in Canada, but most of the Nez Percé, including Chief Joseph, were detained first at Fort Leavenworth, Kansas, and then in Indian Territory. In 1884, they were at last permitted to return to reservations in the Northwest, but no Nez Percé were allowed to return to their Idaho homeland.

Some 180 U.S. citizens, mostly soldiers, died in the campaign and another 150 were wounded. The Nez Percé lost 120 dead, about half of whom were women and children. Although the outcome was never really in doubt, the high level of strategic and tactical skill displayed by the Nez Percé was unusual and earned them a reputation unmatched by any other native American people. The campaign seriously tarnished the reputation of several well-known Civil War veterans and Indian fighters, including Gen. Oliver O. Howard and Cols. John Gibbon, Samuel D. Sturgis, and Wesley Merritt. Only Miles, who finally cornered the elusive Indians, managed to enhance his own career.

Bibliography: Brown, Mark H., *The Flight of the Nez Percé* (New York: Putnam's, 1967; reprint Univ. of Nebraska Press, 1982); Josephy, Alvin M., Jr., *The Nez Percé Indians and the Opening of the Northwest* (Yale Univ. Press, 1965); Utley, Robert M., *Frontier Regulars: The United States Army and the Indian, 1866–1890* (Macmillan Co., 1973).

Lt. Col. (Ret.) Charles R. Shrader

NICARAGUA, INTERVENTION IN (1909–1933)

Series of intrusions by the United States into Nicaraguan affairs, starting in late 1909 when the United States supported a successful revolt against Nicaragua's government. The temporary landing of U.S. marines in 1909 and again in 1910 set a precedent for future U.S. involvement in Central America and helped to foster a climate of anti-Americanism in the region. Nicaragua was of particular interest in 1909 because of U.S. fears that the alternative route through Nicaragua for the Panama Canal might fall into foreign hands in a revolt. The interventions came about in part because of the "dollar diplomacy" policies of Pres. William Howard Taft's administration. Philander C. Knox, Taft's secretary of state, met with Nicaraguan president Adolfo Díaz, and they came up with the Knox-Castrillo Convention in 1911. The accord provided for U.S. intervention as well as for the refinancing of Nicarargua's national debt. The U.S. Senate never ratified the treaty, and Nicaraguans also were unhappy with the arrangement. A revolt started, and President Taft, saying that American lives and property were threatened, in August 1912 sent in a substantial force, primarily composed of marines. A marine presence was maintained until 1925. When a new disturbance broke out in 1926, Pres. Calvin Coolidge spoke of the "moral responsibility" of the United States as he sent back a force of marines. These troops were removed in 1933.

Leo J. Daugherty III

OVERMAN ACT

Act of Congress, passed on May 20, 1918, that gave Pres. Woodrow Wilson the authority to create, abolish, or reorganize government agencies to meet the demands of the war emergency. It came after months of confusion and disarray in the World War I mobilization effort.

The Overman Act permitted the War Department to address serious flaws in the U.S. Army's supply system. Chief of Staff Peyton C. March was able to consolidate command of supply functions within the General Staff by the creation of the Purchase, Storage, and Traffic (PS&T) Division. Headed by Maj. Gen. George W. Goethals, builder of the Panama Canal, the PS&T Division provided central direction to the army's logistical network and strengthened the power of the General Staff.

Bibliography: Coffman, Edward M., *The War to End All Wars: The American Military Experience in World War I* (Univ. of Wisconsin Press, 1986); Weigley, Russell F., *History of the U.S. Army* (Univ. of Indiana Press, 1984).

Daniel T. Bailey

PAIUTE WAR (1867–1868)

Conflict that resulted from the depredations of the Paiute tribe on U.S. settlers in the Oregon Territory during 1865–66. In 1864, the Paiute had agreed to settle on the Klamath Lake Reservation, but in the next year, they began raiding stagecoaches, freight trains, gold camps, and ranches. With settlers up in arms about the army's seeming inability to deal with the marauders, Lt. Col. George Crook was called in to take command in December 1866.

Directing the 23d Infantry and 1st Cavalry in the use of mule trains instead of wagons, Crook achieved unprecedented logistical mobility. His strategy was simple: relentless pursuit. He studied the habits of his quarry, insisted on personal reconnaissance, and used Indian trackers, mostly Shoshone.

The war came to an end in 1868. There had been 40 separate fights, 14 of them large enough to be called engagements. The infantry and cavalrymen had steadily pursued the Paiute for a year and a half. There were more than 300 Indians killed and 225 captured. In June 1868, Paiute chief Old Weawea realized that his people could stand no more and asked Crook for terms. A settlement was reached during the next month.

Bibliography: Utley, Robert M., *Frontier Regulars: The United States Army and the Indian, 1866–1890* (Macmillan Co., 1973).

Col. (Ret.) Rod Paschall

PALO DURO CANYON, BATTLE OF (September 28, 1874)

U.S. cavalry attack during the Red River War in which several columns converged on the Texas panhandle in order to locate and crush hostile Indians. Col. Ranald Mackenzie's 4th Cavalry formed the southern column, and in mid-September 1874, his scouts brought back reports of a large Indian encampment in Palo Duro Canyon. At daylight on September 28, the 4th Cavalry charged down the steep canyon walls. While most of the Indians successfully fled, the cavalrymen captured the village and its pony herd intact. After cutting out the best animals for his own men, Mackenzie had the lodges, food stores, and remaining horses destroyed. While suffering very few casualties, the battle proved to be a severe defeat for the Indians as most of their horses and winter stores were lost.

Bibliography: Wallace, Ernest, *Ranald S. Mackenzie on the Texas Frontier* (West Texas Museum Assoc., 1964).

Richard F. Kehrberg

PANAMA CANAL

U.S.-engineered waterway, about 40 miles long, crossing the Isthmus of Panama from Colon on the Caribbean Sea to Panama City on the Pacific Ocean. Locks at each end lift ships from sea level into a freshwater channel that passes miles of jungle, the continental divide, and the Gatun Lake with its massive earthen dam. Although talk of a canal started not long after the discovery of America, various attempts and treaties failed to produce results until 1903. By this time, U.S. military interest in the canal was intense, primarily because of the difficult logistics encountered during the Spanish-American War of 1898 in shifting forces from the Atlantic and Pacific oceans. Pres. Theodore Roosevelt intervened on behalf of Panama in its dispute with Colombia by recognizing the newly formed Panamanian government. The Hay-Bunau-Varilla Treaty was quickly drawn and ratified, and the Isthmian Canal Commission took up where France's Ferdinand de Lesseps had failed in 1899.

Work on the canal began in 1904, and it opened for commercial use in 1914, months ahead of schedule. Lt. Col. George W. Goethals, an army engineer, is credited with overcoming the daunting obstacles to construction, while Col. William C. Gorgas oversaw the medical efforts that drastically reduced the ravages of yellow fever and other tropical diseases. Using modern engineering and management techniques, Goethals hired 30,000 multinational workers to defeat hostile climate and geography. Congress recognized his work by promoting him to major general and awarding him the Distinguished Service Medal.

Although the Panama treaty was renegotiated several times over the years, Panamanian cooperation lessened. By 1964, growing nationalism and resentment over U.S. sovereignty in the 10-mile Canal Zone led to violent confrontations in which U.S. lives were lost. U.S. presidents from that time grappled with the issue of Panamanian sovereignty over the Canal Zone. Pres. Jimmy Carter, in the face of intensive national and political opposition, signed the 1977 Panama Canal Treaties with Panama's Pres. Omar Torrijos. The Canal Zone ceased to exist on Oct. 1, 1979. At the same time, a process began to grant Panama full control of the canal at the end of 1999.

Carol E. Stokes

PARIS PEACE CONFERENCE
(January 12–June 28, 1919)

Conclusive World War I peace talks in which the victorious Allies debated and agreed upon the terms of a treaty to be offered to the Central Powers of Germany, Austria-Hungary, Bulgaria, and Turkey. The defeated nations were not allowed to participate until May 7, the beginning of the ''official'' portion of the conference. The major participants of the conference were U.S. president Woodrow Wilson, French statesman Georges Clemenceau, British prime minister David Lloyd George, and Italian prime minister Vittorio E. Orlando. The result was the Versailles Treaty signed by Germany on June 28, 1919, and the collateral treaties of St. Germain (Austria), Sèvres (Turkey), Neuilly (Bulgaria), and Trianon (Hungary).

The Fourteen Points. On Jan. 18, 1918, Wilson announced his Fourteen Points. Intended as a general program for peace, not as a treaty, the Fourteen Points were grouped into four major concerns: the denunciation of secret diplomacy and treaties, the right to national self-determination based on ethnic and cultural groups, freedom of the seas and free trade, and, most important to Wilson, the establishment of some form of world government.

When the Fourteen Points were first announced, there was only a grudging acknowledgment of the points from the Allies, while Germany denounced the program as an Allied propaganda ploy. However, by September 1918, Germany was beginning to crack, and on October 4, Prince Max of Baden, the new German chancellor, sent a note to Wilson requesting peace negotiations based on the Fourteen Points. After some hard inter-Allied negotiations, Wilson notified the Germans that peace negotiations could be based on the points with two minor reservations. First, Great Britain had refused to commit itself on the issue of the freedom of the seas. Second, France refused to set a prior limit on the level of monetary restorations Germany would have to pay. Germany agreed to these modified terms. Meanwhile, Great Britain had unilaterally accepted the surrender of Turkey, and Austria had voluntarily withdrawn from the war and was disintegrating into varied ethnic groupings.

The actual terms of the armistice foreshadowed the myriad problems that would be encountered during the peace conference. Germany, expecting the just peace promised by the Fourteen Points, was embittered after next being forced to accept an armistice that amounted to unconditional surrender. The German army was forced to surrender all heavy weapons and evacuate all Allied territory. The Imperial High Seas Fleet was interned, and the Allies occupied the Rhineland bridgeheads over the Rhine. After these humiliations, the Germans were informed that they would not participate in the peace conference but would be allowed to attend only after all terms had been agreed upon by the Allies.

Preconference Events. More major events occurred before the peace conference could convene. In the United States, the congressional elections of 1918 were a blow to Wilson. The president had campaigned expecting that war enthusiasm would secure a Democratic majority in the Congress. However, his plan backfired when his moves

U.S. forces such as the 2d Division, shown in March 1919 massed behind Gen. John J. Pershing and Maj. Gen. Joseph T. Dickman, occupied Germany while the provisions of the Treaty of Versailles were being ironed out at the Paris Peace Conference. (Library of Congress)

were seen as blatantly political. The Democrats lost the election, and the Republican party had a firm majority in the House and Senate. Wilson exacerbated his already difficult position as a minority president by failing to appoint a single Republican to the peace conference delegation. Even before the first article of the treaty had been agreed upon, Wilson faced opposition in the Senate, which would eventually be asked to ratify the treaties.

In Great Britain, Lloyd George decided to use the peace euphoria to gain an election victory. He held a relatively moderate position on the treatment of defeated Germany, but in the heat of campaigning, he raised expectations of a harsh treaty. Such campaign slogans as ''Hang the Kaiser'' and ''Squeeze Germany until the pips squeak'' later forced the British delegation to take an intransigent stance.

The Conference. As the Paris Peace Conference opened in January 1919, it became immediately apparent that all 32 Allied Powers could not participate in the negotiations. France, Great Britain, Italy, and the United States were soon the only key players. Most of the detail work was done by committees and then decided upon by the leaders of the four primary delegations.

The conference soon became caught up in the personalities of Wilson, Lloyd George, and Clemenceau. Wilson came to the conference with the belief that he alone was acting in the best interests of the peoples of Europe and the world. He had an inherent distrust for diplomacy and diplomats and viewed the other delegates as unprincipled. In addition, Wilson refused to allow his delegation to draw up a proposed treaty. He intended to improvise and convince the others of the correctness of his position. Lloyd George was moderately disposed toward the German people, as opposed to the German military, but his chief concern was British interests and the establishment of reparations to pay the entire cost of the war. Clemenceau was a realist and power politics advocate. He had experienced both the Franco-Prussian War and World War I, and he intended to insure that Germany would never again be able to threaten the existence of the French state. These three principals clashed repeatedly over the terms of the peace treaties, with Clemenceau walking out of sessions and Wilson going so far as to make an appeal to the people of Italy over the head of Italy's legitimate government.

The major accomplishments of the Paris Peace Conference were the establishment of the Covenant of the League of Nations and the acceptance of the concept of collective security. These two related issues were the primary points of intersection of French, British, and U.S. interests. Clemenceau's demands for French security forced the conference to consider the method of imposing the will of the League of Nations on aggressor nations. Being a land power, France demanded some form of League-directed police force. Clemenceau's great concern was the threat from Germany. The United States and Great Britain, as sea powers, were reluctant to get entangled in promises to defend France, yet both eventually agreed to more power for the League and to guarantee France's security.

The greatest failings of the conference were the unjust treatment of Germany as a military power and the failure to establish limits to reparations payments. Without representation at the Peace Conference, Germany regarded the Treaty of Versailles as a dictated peace. This was seen as a contradiction of the spirit of the prearmistice negotiations. Unlimited reparations payments were also seen as a violation of the Fourteen Points; however, most of the treaty did conform with the points—self-determination and the League of Nations were at the heart of Wilson's program.

The military aspects of the Treaty of Versailles, not covered by Wilson's Fourteen Points, were as disgruntling to Germany as were the unlimited reparations. Germany's army was reduced to 100,000 men on long-term enlistments. It's military aircraft and submarines were banned. The German navy was reduced to a force just barely capable of patrolling the German coastline. These restrictions on the German armed forces, which had not given up any German territory at the time of the armistice, coupled with the requirements to accept guilt for the outbreak of the war and to make unlimited reparations, which would hinder the Germany economy, immediately created German national resentment of their treatment at the hands of the Allies.

Ratification Problems. The establishment of the League of Nations doomed the Paris treaties to failure in the United States. The U.S. Senate saw the power of the League of Nations as infringing on national sovereignty and refused to ratify the treaties. With the failure to ratify also came a refusal to guarantee French security. The United States returned to an isolationist foreign policy after negotiating separate peace treaties with Germany and the other Central Powers in 1920. The terms of these treaties were essentially the same as the Paris treaties, with the exception of any reference to the League of Nations. The failure of the Paris Peace Conference to meet the needs of the Allies adequately and the perceived unjust treatment of Germany and the Central Powers planted the seed for disharmony and conflict that would erupt into World War II 20 years later.

Bibliography: Albrecht-Carrie, Rene, *A Diplomatic History of Europe Since the Concert of Vienna* (Harper & Row, 1973); Keynes, John Maynard, *The Economic Consequences of the Peace* (Harcourt, 1920); Ross, Graham, *The Great Powers and the Decline of the European States System, 1914–1945* (Longman Group, 1983); Seymour, Charles, *American Diplomacy During the World War* (Archon, 1964); Smith, Daniel M., *The Great Departure* (Wiley, 1965); Stokesbury, James L., *A Short History of World War I* (Morrow, 1981).

Capt. George B. Eaton

PEACE COMMISSION OF 1867

Negotiations initiated by the U.S. Congress in 1867 to bring about an end to the Indian raids that continued to terrorize U.S. settlers. The legislation established a commission composed of critics of certain U.S. Army officers and the army's actions against the Indians. The commission members were encouraged to find suitable reservations for the Indians, land that would be barred to U.S. settlers. First, the emissaries treated with Kiowa, Comanche, Kiowa-Apache, Cheyenne, and Arapaho, arriving at what would come to be known as the Medicine Lodge Treaties. Later agreements were made with the Crow and Sioux. Essentially, the negotiations resulted in U.S. government promises to supply the Indians with their needs, provide education, and keep encroaching settlers out of Indian reservations. The Indians, in turn, agreed to confine themselves to their designated areas and cease raiding U.S. settlements. Neither side kept its promises.

Col. (Ret.) Rod Paschall

PHILIPPINE CONSTABULARY

U.S.-Filipino military police force created in the Philippines at the onset of civil government in 1901. The U.S. Army's difficulty in fighting guerrilla forces in isolated regions of the islands and the desire to end military occupation of the country as soon as possible after the end of the war in the Philippines led Vice Gov. Luke E. Wright to suggest the creation of a paramilitary force to maintain law and order. The establishment of the Philippine Constabulary in July 1901, with U.S. Army captain Henry T. Allen as its first chief, met his goal. The force numbered 2,500 U.S. officers and Filipino enlisted men by the end of 1901 and assumed both military and police duties throughout the archipelago. In 1917, Gen. Rafael Crame became the constabulary's first Filipino chief. The Philippine Constabulary formed part of the new Philippine army from 1935 to 1938 and contributed its 2d Division to the 1942 campaign against Japan.

Richard B. Meixsel

PHILIPPINE SCOUTS

Filipino military force recruited by the U.S. Army to assist U.S. troops during the Philippine Insurrection. Following a recommendation made by 1st Lt. Matthew Batson in 1899, Filipino soldiers from the village of Macabebe (north of Manila) who had served Spain were consolidated into a U.S.-supporting contingent first known as Native Scouts. By 1901, the army had raised 50 companies of nearly 100 men each from throughout the islands and designated them Philippine Scouts. In 1904, the army regrouped the companies into battalions and, in 1918, into infantry and artillery regiments. A cavalry regiment, the 26th, was formed in 1922. The reduction of U.S. troop strength in the islands had, by 1922, left the Scouts the mainstay of the archipelago's regular garrison. Recruited to their statutory limit of 12,000 men in 1941, the Scouts were among the ablest defenders of the islands against Japan in World War II.

Richard B. Meixsel

PLATT AMENDMENT (1901)

Congressional amendment to the 1901 Army Appropriation Bill, the passage of which (Mar. 2, 1901) resulted in the withdrawal of the U.S. forces that had remained in Cuba after the Spanish-American War to maintain order and deter intervention by a foreign power. The Platt Amendment (named for Sen. Orville H. Platt) stipulated the following: (1) Cuba could not make any diplomatic or financial agreements with any foreign power that might lead to foreign intervention in Cuba or foreign control of any part of the island; (2) the United States would be at liberty to intervene in Cuba to preserve order or Cuban independence; (3) Cuba would have to lease or sell sites to the United States for naval and/or coaling stations.

The amendment was incorporated into Cuba's constitution on June 12, and the U.S. troops were withdrawn in May 1902, much to the surprise of many Latin American and European nations. Invoking the amendment's provisions, the United States intervened in Cuba several times (the longest period was 1906–09) before the Platt Amendment was eliminated by a new U.S.-Cuban treaty signed May 29, 1934.

Bibliography: Pérez, Louis A., *Cuba Under the Platt Amendment, 1902–1934* (Univ. of Pittsburgh Press, 1986).

James C. Bradford

POWDER RIVER, BATTLE OF THE (March 17, 1876)

Skirmish that occurred after Gen. George Crook ordered army forces under Col. Joseph J. Reynolds to pursue Sitting Bull's hostile Sioux warriors in early 1876. Reynolds's command included three squadrons of the 3d U.S. Cavalry and several Indian scouts, altogether about 300 men. On March 16, in unfavorable winter conditions, Reynolds's scouts picked up the trail and subsequently found an encampment of about 200 Cheyenne and Oglala Sioux warriors and their families along the Powder River in Montana.

Reynolds's plan for attacking the camp from two directions miscarried due to inadequate reconnaissance. However, on March 17 one squadron did enter the camp and drive out the inhabitants while another squadron captured the Indian pony herd. The Cheyenne and Sioux warriors then counterattacked and routed Reynolds's command, which hastily withdrew, leaving behind the bodies of two troopers killed in the fight. The victorious Indians also recovered their pony herd the following night.

Reynolds lost four men killed and six wounded but inflicted few casualties on the Indians and failed to achieve his objective. The bedraggled force returned to Fort Fetterman, and Crook subsequently charged Reynolds with mismanagement of the skirmish. The ineffectual foray demonstrated the difficulties of pursuing small bands of hostiles across difficult terrain in severe winter weather without adequate intelligence.

Lt. Col. (Ret.) Charles R. Shrader

PREPAREDNESS MOVEMENT

Campaign to prepare Americans for military service. The military preparedness movement was born at a time when the United States was at peace during the years before World War I erupted in Europe. Public debate over universal military training had raged without resolution throughout the years before U.S. entry into the war. Civil and military advocates of "preparedness" strove to advertise the United States' lack thereof and instill in the citizenry a sense of public stewardship and obligation to the country's service.

Despite proponents' claims to the contrary, the concept of preparedness early on assumed some partisan political aspects. Numerous organizations, such as the American Defense League, the Army League, and the National Security League, were formed to combat Pres. Woodrow Wilson's reliance upon the National Guard as the sole means of increasing the nation's defense capabilities. The National Security League, the most influential of all the advocacy groups, was founded by New York attorney S. Stanwood Menken and was quite politically active during and after the war.

In 1913, Army Chief of Staff Maj. Gen. Leonard Wood, himself an advocate of a strong defense establishment, had started two experimental student military instruction camps for college students during their summer vacations. Students attended for five weeks at their own expense. The success of these camps (located at Gettysburg, Pennsylvania, and the Presidio or Monterey, California) led to the expansion of the program to four camps in 1915.

Plattsburgh Concept. The preparedness concept began to spread to the general population after the May 1915 sinking by the Germans of the passenger ship *Lusitania*. Citizens of New York sought and received government support to establish a camp modeled on those of the students to provide military training for civic leaders and average citizens. The first camp, with 1,200 enrollees, opened at Plattsburgh, New York, on August 8. The idea spread throughout the country during the next two years, and numerous camps were developed with civil-military cooperation.

Along with the growth of the Plattsburgh concept came the development of a professional organization. The Military Training Camps Association (MTCA) was formally organized on Feb. 4, 1916, largely through the efforts of New York attorney Grenville Clark, an early advocate of preparedness who had long worked behind the scenes in developing national consciousness on the issue. The organization not only coordinated many of the camps' administrative aspects but also served as a lobby group pressing Congress for reform in military policies, with a particularly strong advocacy for universal military training.

As war with Germany loomed in 1917, the MTCA played an increasingly active role in supplying officers to train and operate the volunteer forces that would be necessarily raised for the conflict. In April 1917, the MTCA successfully urged the War Department to create officer training camps, at which a commission could be earned after a 90-day course of instruction. Most prewar Plattsburghers attended these camps. The MTCA also assisted the army with wartime recruitment and a variety of clerical duties.

The actual accomplishments of the preparedness movement were miniscule in comparison to the tremendous war effort of 1917–19. The Plattsburghers were, however, instrumental in raising public awareness of defense issues and establishing a dialogue between the civil and military sectors of U.S. society. This heightened awareness translated into some legislative initiatives with lasting implications, most notably the National Defense Act of 1916, which contained provisions for a permanent reserve officers training corps.

The coming of World War II brought a revival of the preparedness movement. Clark and his associates began a second attempt to reform national defense policy. They were, however, never successful in institutionalizing one of the mainstays of their platform, universal military training.

Bibliography: Clifford, John G., *The Citizen Soldiers: The Plattsburg Training Camp Movement, 1913–1920* (Univ. Press of Kentucky, 1972); Perry, Ralph B., *The Plattsburg Movement: A Chapter of America's Participation in the World War* (Dutton, 1921).

Louise Arnold-Friend

PUERTO RICO CAMPAIGN
(July–August 1898)

U.S. military operation against Spanish forces in Puerto Rico during the Spanish-American War. Prior to the outbreak of hostilities, neither the War Department nor the Department of the Navy had established any firm plans regarding operations against Puerto Rico. During the early strategic deliberations, retired general John M. Schofield and retired navy captain Alfred Thayer Mahan recommended that the initial assaults against Spanish territory should be directed at Puerto Rico and the Philippines rather than at Cuba. Gen. Nelson A. Miles, General of the Army, also favored this strategy.

Intelligence on the Spanish garrison and on the internal situation of the island itself was available to U.S. army and naval planners during the period preceding the U.S. landings. Additional intelligence was obtained from a ground

Gen. Theodore Schwan and his officers arrived in Puerto Rico in July 1898 to supplement the troops being gathered under the command of Gen. Nelson A. Miles during the capture of Puerto Rico from the Spanish. (U.S. Military Academy)

reconnaissance of the island conducted by army lieutenant Henry H. Whitney. Posing as a British merchant seaman, Whitney was able to determine accurately Spanish troop dispositions, topography, availability of resources and supplies, and the condition of the harbors. He estimated the size of the Spanish garrison to be approximately 8,200 regulars and 9,100 volunteers.

In late May 1898, Miles proposed a plan for an attack on Puerto Rico. Pres. William McKinley eventually accepted the idea for a operation against Puerto Rico, to follow immediately the capture of Santiago, Cuba. On June 26, orders were issued for a Puerto Rican Expedition to consist of five army divisions, with a total strength of about 27,000 troops. Miles was to assume command of the expedition once operations began.

On July 17, Miles requested authorization from the War Department to proceed to Puerto Rico with a small advance force of 3,400 men and a strong navy escort. His intent was to seize and secure a beachhead, covered by navy guns, that would be used by follow-on forces from the United States. He spent the next few days, however, antagonizing his naval contemporaries with his many requests for support and his ideas concerning the employment of naval forces in the Caribbean. The president, tired of interservice squabbling, directed the navy on July 20 to supply the ships Miles wanted and get on with the operation against Puerto Rico. Miles departed Cuba on July 21 with his small advance force and escorting ships.

Miles planned to land at several points around the periphery of the island and advance toward San Juan. By doing so, he intended to avoid frontal assaults and use maneuver to accomplish the conquest of Puerto Rico. It was also agreed that the advance force of the expedition would land at Cape Fajardo on the north coast of the island. The Spanish commander, Governor General Macías, placed most of his forces in the northern part of the island, where he expected the landing to occur. In an effort at deception, he also deployed a battalion at Ponce and Mayagüez, with small detachments around the island to give the impression of an area defense.

Invasion. While at sea, Miles changed his landing site. His intelligence led him to believe that the original site, near Cape Fajardo, was known to the Spanish and that they had concentrated their forces there. He persuaded the naval commander to land the force at Guánica, an area that he understood to have few Spanish troops, a good harbor, plentiful food and forage, and a receptive civilian population. After feinting toward the original landing site, during the day on July 24, the force then sailed around the island to Guánica. On July 25, a small force of infantry and artillery landed and, after a brief encounter, secured the town and sheltered harbor. The following day, a column under command of General Garretson advanced and opened the road to Ponce. The first reinforcements from the United States arrived off Guánica on July 27. This brigade, under Major General Ernst, was directed to land at Ponce, where it conducted a coordinated attack with the column from Guánica. The Spanish garrison withdrew toward San Juan.

After the capture of Ponce, Miles issued a proclamation stating that U.S. forces had come to liberate Puerto Rico and that personal and property rights would be respected as far as possible. It apparently had the right effect in that the local populace gladly collaborated with the U.S. forces, providing guides, food, forage, and pack animals. While Miles consolidated his position in Ponce, more U.S. troops, under Gen. Theodore Schwan, arrived on July 31. In the days of August 3–5, more than 5,000 men under the command of Maj. Gen. John R. Brooke debarked at Arroyo, 40 miles east of Ponce. Additional small detachments continued to arrive. Altogether, Miles's force totaled approximately 18,000 troops, about equal the strength of the Spanish garrison. Absent were the originally anticipated troops of Gen. William R. Shafter's V Corps, who were otherwise engaged in Cuba.

Unlike in Cuba, the landing in Puerto Rico came off fairly smoothly, and there were adequate local transportation and supply resources available to meet the needs of the U.S. units. While his force assembled and prepared, Miles planned the subsequent advance on San Juan. The Spanish had reconcentrated in the low mountains that form an east-west spine through the middle of the island. Miles planned to use four columns to isolate and envelop the Spanish positions. The western column, under Schwan, was to march north from Guánica and circle the western end of the mountain chain. A second column, commanded by Brig. Gen. Guy V. Henry, was to move on Schwan's right, along a trail discovered by the engineers, and rendezvous with Schwan at Arecibo on the north coast. The third column, under Maj. Gen. James H. Wilson, was directed toward the Spanish concentration at Aibonito. The mission of the fourth column, under Brooke's command, was to move from Arroyo to cut the road behind the Aibonito position.

All four columns commenced their advances on August 9. Spanish resistance was weak, with too few troops trying to defend too many positions. Schwan's column made the most spectacular advance, covering 92 miles and capturing 9 towns and 192 prisoners before the armistice was declared on August 12.

Miles's campaign was soundly planned and aggressively executed. By the end of hostilities, his forces had captured or exposed every Spanish position outside San Juan at the cost of 4 dead and approximately 40 wounded. His operations in Puerto Rico laid the basis for the U.S. claim to the island as part of the peace settlement.

Bibliography: Cosmos, Graham A., *An Army for Empire* (Univ. of Missouri Press, 1971); Trask, David F., *The War with Spain in 1898* (Macmillan Co., 1981).

Lt. Col. (Ret.) John A. Hixson

PULLMAN STRIKE (June 21–July 20, 1894)

Landmark U.S. labor dispute, in which unprecedented federal military intervention was employed. Irritated over failed attempts to bargain with George Pullman over better working conditions and wages for the workers of the Pullman Car Company in Chicago, the local independent union, in June 1894, called upon the American Railway Union, headed by Eugene V. Debs, to boycott cars manufactured by Pullman's company. The ensuing strike tied up rail service throughout the Midwest. By the end of June, U.S. Atty. Gen. Richard Olney (a former railroad lawyer) had 3,400 special deputies sworn in to keep trains running. When violence broke out, Pres. Grover Cleveland, over the protest of Illinois governor John Peter Altgeld, sent federal troops to restore order, safeguard the mail, and protect interstate commerce. A federal judge issued an injunction forbidding the strikers from interfering with the transportation of the U.S. mail. By mid-July, Debs was in jail for contempt, the troops had restored order to the nation's railroads, and the strike was smashed.

Eugene V. Debs organized the strike by employees of George M. Pullman's Pullman Palace Car Company that ultimately involved the railroad workers' union and rioting and led to the use of military guard for all trains. (Library of Congress)

M. Guy Bishop

RED RIVER WAR (1874–1875)

U.S. military campaign against Cheyenne, Kiowa, and Comanche bands in Texas and Oklahoma along the Red River and its tributaries. The conflict involved some of the army's best-known frontier fighters and marked the end of an experiment in dividing responsibilities between military and civilian governments at the reservation border. Prior to this, the reservations were refuges where the military could not pursue hostile Indians. After a series of raids in early 1874, the army received permission to pursue the Indians wherever they moved. Gen. Philip Sheridan devised a plan to strike at the Indians from all directions. After some 14 pitched battles, culminating in the Battle of Palo Duro Canyon, the Indian threat was eliminated. With the

The Red River War

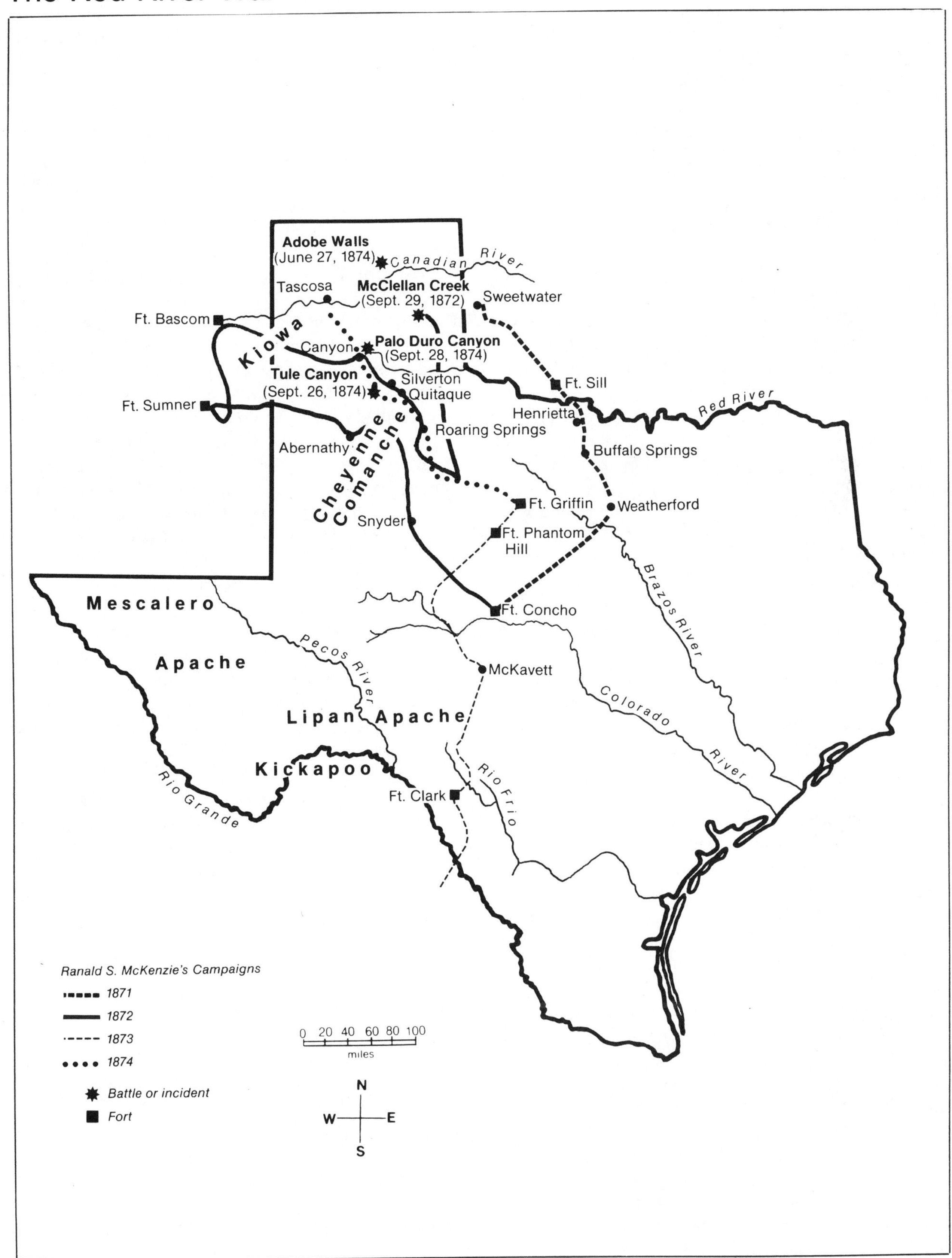

surrender of Chiefs Satanta and Woman's Heart, the Indian Wars on the Southern Plains ended.

Capt. George B. Eaton

REPUBLICAN RIVER EXPEDITION
(June 1869)

U.S. cavalry operation that forever broke the military effectiveness of Cheyenne "dog soldiers" operating in northwest Kansas, bordered by the Republican River to the north and the Smoky Hill River to the south. On June 9, 1869, Maj. Eugene Carr left Fort McPherson, Nebraska, with eight troops from the 5th Cavalry and a three-company battalion of Pawnee scouts. The 500-man force eventually came upon a largely Cheyenne band led by Tall Bull at Summit Springs, Colorado. As the Indians waited to ford the swollen South Platte River and join Sioux bands to the north, they failed to detect the presence of 250 troopers and 50 Pawnee scouts until they were 150 feet away. At the cost of 1 wounded soldier, the attacking cavalry force killed 52 Indians and destroyed 84 of their lodges.

Bibliography: Utley, Robert M., *Frontier Regulars* (Macmillan Co., 1973).

Maj. Peter Faber

ROOT REFORMS

U.S. army reforms instituted in the name of Sec. of War Elihu Root. These amendments contributed to the modernization of the army but were neither wholly new nor wholly successful. The most important of them concerned the reorganization of the army's top leadership strata, the formation of a European-style general staff, the refinement of the officers' progressive education system, and revisions in the nature of the militia (National Guard) and its relationship to the regular army.

Root, a respected New York lawyer, brought few of his own ideas about army reform to office. He was selected for the secretary's position primarily because the U.S. success in the Spanish-American War in 1898 gave the United States colonial possessions that the army would have to administer. Root's abilities included a talent for resolving the coming problems of dealing with the Philippines, Puerto Rico, and Cuba. But Secretary Root soon learned the United States would have to reorganize and streamline its army if it were to succeed in its new colonies. His conclusion merely affirmed what Maj. Gen. Grenville M. Dodge had reported to the president about the army's travails during the war: the high command had to be more centralized, and efficient procedures had to be introduced. The Dodge Report inferred that the U.S. success during the war was as much a function of Spanish incompetence as it was of U.S. military proficiency.

Root listened to several bright officers, did research on his own, and made his way carefully through Washington's bureaucracies and the capital's political pitfalls. The adjutant general, Maj. Gen. Henry C. Corbin, and Lt. Col. William H. Carter became two of his trusted advisers. Root studied the Dodge Report and then read Col. Emory Upton's 20-year-old manuscript titled *The Military Policy of the United States,* and he arranged for its publication in 1904. Root was also influenced by Spenser Wilkinson's *The Brain of an Army* (1895), an argument in favor of the German general-staff system. From Upton's writings and his officer advisers, Root saw a need to reform the nation's militia laws. Through Wilkinson and Upton, he was influenced in the direction of a general staff. All of this, however, was much in keeping with progressive ideas of the day that were reshaping both U.S. government and industry. What Root added was his energy, selflessness, keen political acumen, and knack for choosing the right moment and environment to argue for a new course.

Reform and Resistance. From 1900 until Congress established the General Staff in 1903, Root and his aides worked to eliminate the position of Commanding General of the Army, destroy the powers of the embedded and inefficient War Department bureaus, and install a functional general-staff system. The chief obstacle was Gen. Nelson A. Miles, the army's commanding general since 1895. A second hurdle was the combined resistance of the bureaus and their patronage-linked relationship with Congress. Root first established an ad hoc War College Board, a group of prominent officers who performed some planning for war contingencies. Having a basic planning structure in hand, the reformers demonstrated the need for a full general staff, highlighting the inability of the bureaus to perform modern-day military functions.

Root's plan included a provision for the new General Staff officers to alternate their tours between troop duty and staff positions, eliminating the specter of some officers never getting beyond the confines of Washington. Although the reformers got their staff, they were not fully successful in consolidating the functions of the bureaus within the General Staff.

Perhaps the greatest change came about in the demise of the position of Commanding General of the Army. Ever since the American Revolution, control of the army had been divided between the secretary of the war and the army's senior general. Historically, the two offices were at odds as much as in agreement, a situation that created damaging petty politics in peace and confusion in war. There was some argument for an overall U.S. military commander as long as there was a possibility of war in North America.

In Root's opinion, that prospect, in 1900, was remote. U.S. wars were likely to be waged abroad, and the country's senior military officer would remain in Washington, advising the president. Miles disagreed and argued his point accordingly. Root's solution was to have the ranking general act as a presidential adviser, through the secretary of war. The secretary would be the superior. The senior officer would head the General Staff, would not command, and would have the title "Chief of Staff of the Army." Miles tried to rally a coalition in Congress, targeting Democrats, antiimperialists, and old guard conservatives, in an attempt to kill the General Staff initiative. After a stubborn fight in which Root's opponents raised fears of importing European militarism, Miles finally lost and retired, refusing to serve a day bearing the new title.

The new General Staff was in place, but its members were in need of better professional preparation. During William T. Sherman's tenure as the commanding general, a progressive education system for officers had been established, but the level of instruction rarely got above regimental or divisional tactics.

In 1901, Root directed the schools of instruction for officers, which included West Point, service schools (artillery, engineer, cavalry, etc.), a general staff and service college at Fort Leavenworth, and a war college. His premise was to require attendance at the reorganized Leavenworth school prior to war college attendance. Between 1900 and 1912, a rational, progressive system of professional education was instituted. By World War I, however, fewer than 20 army officers had graduated from both the new course at Fort Leavenworth and the Army War College.

The last of Root's major reforms involved a reorganization of the militia and its redefined relation to the regular army. The reform was captured in the Dick Act of 1903, named for Rep. Charles W. Dick of Ohio. The legislation separated the militia into two classes, the organized militia (National Guard) and the reserve militia. The latter category was to include all able-bodied males in the republic. The reserve militia thus became the new manpower pool for universal conscription in time of national emergency, and the National Guard became the volunteer military organization of the states, a resource that could be called into national service. Under the arrangement, the regular army was to supply advisers to the National Guard, the federal government was to fund certain guard activities and pay for equipment, more training was to be observed, and the guard formations were to reflect regular army organizational patterns.

The Dick Act did not satisfy all of Root's advisers, and the law was revised in 1908 and again in 1914. Constitutional arguments broke out when Congress certified that the Guard could be sent overseas, a murky issue that was still being aired as late as 1988. And, both the states and the federal government failed to live up to their obligations of funds and equipment. The act was, however, a decided improvement over the chaos that existed before, and given the strong, reasonable arguments on both sides of these issues, it was probably the best that could be done prior to World War I.

The Root Reforms are best seen as steps in an evolutionary process, not as dramatic innovations. Furthermore, many of these changes were only partially achieved prior to World War I. The importance of Root's efforts is that they made the duties of his successors considerably easier.

Bibliography: Jessup, Philip C., *Elihu Root,* 2 vols. (Dodd, Mead, 1938); Nelson, Otto L., *National Security and the General Staff* (Infantry Journal Press, 1946); Root, Elihu, *Five Years of the War Department* (U.S. Govt. Printing Office, 1904).

Col. (Ret.) Rod Paschall

ROSEBUD, BATTLE OF THE (June 17, 1876)

Brief but intense conflict between advancing U.S. cavalrymen and alerted Sioux warriors. By mid-June 1876, Sitting Bull's Hunkpapa Sioux were encamped along southeastern Montana's Rosebud Creek to hold a sun dance. On June 16, Sioux hunters brought word of many U.S. soldiers on the upper Rosebud. This column, under the command of Gen. George Crook intended to link up with the forces of Lt. Col. George A. Custer later in June. On the morning of June 17, the Sioux attacked Crook. Fierce fighting, reputedly some of the hardest of the Indian wars, ensued for six hours. The broken terrain along the Rosebud prevented any effective action by Crook's cavalry. Although he had numerical superiority, Crook was never able to gain the initiative. Because he was left in possession of the battlefield at day's end, Crook forever after claimed victory at the Rosebud. Yet he was forced to limp back to his supply base and refused to do battle with the Sioux again until reinforced. Less than 10 days later, Custer would meet these same Sioux a few miles north on the Little Bighorn River.

M. Guy Bishop

ROUGH RIDERS

Nickname of the 1st U.S. Volunteer Cavalry Regiment, one of three such regiments authorized in 1898 in the Spanish-American War. Its commander was Pres. William McKinley's personal physician, Leonard Wood, but the regiment's lieutenant colonel, Theodore Roosevelt, was better known. The Rough Riders, well equipped due to the political and financial connections and energy of their officers, took part in the Santiago Campaign in Cuba. Roosevelt assumed command when Wood was promoted and helped take the San Juan ridge line overlooking Santiago.

The Rough Riders were competent soldiers, but their commanders regularly ignored U.S. Army routine and bordered on insubordination. In the United States, civilian popularity for these men overshadowed military criticisms,

Undersecretary of the Navy Theodore Roosevelt resigned to join the 1st U.S. Volunteer Cavalry Regiment, nicknamed the "Rough Riders," in 1898. Roosevelt led his men in the charges up Kettle and San Juan hills in Cuba during the Spanish-American War. (Library of Congress)

and the regiment's well-publicized performance insured Roosevelt's political career.

Mark Pitcavage

ROUND ROBIN LETTER (1898)

Controversial piece of correspondence sent to the United States from Cuba during the Spanish-American War, on behalf of certain gravely ill U.S. soldiers in Cuba. After the Santiago Campaign, the U.S. Army led by Gen. William Shafter began falling sick to malaria and yellow fever. Shafter and his principal subordinates agreed that most troops should be sent home; to this end, Col. Theodore Roosevelt drafted a letter describing conditions in Cuba, and the subordinates signed it. Shafter forwarded copies of the letter to the War Department and to the Associated Press.

The letter greatly embarrassed Pres. William McKinley and Sec. of War Russell Alger, who considered it a criticism of their leadership. It also risked upsetting the ongoing negotiations with Spain. In its aim, however, it was successful; shortly thereafter, Shafter's army was ordered to Long Island.

Mark Pitcavage

ST.-MIHIEL, BATTLE OF (September 12–16, 1918)

Battle fought in northeastern France to eliminate the Germans' St.-Mihiel salient; the first major U.S. offensive of World War I. Gen. John J. Pershing, commander of the American Expeditionary Force (A.E.F.), had long viewed the relatively exposed and vulnerable salient as the appropriate and logical target for the A.E.F.'s first offensive, but he had lacked the means to conduct such an operation. With the formal assignment of that task to the A.E.F. on July 24, 1918, and the activation of the U.S. 1st Army on August 10, detailed planning commenced with alacrity.

Located southeast of Verdun, France, between the Meuse and Moselle rivers, the salient was approximately 16 miles deep by 25 miles wide, with western and southern sides. St.-Mihiel stood at the apex. The Germans had held the salient since the Western Front stabilized in 1914, and they had developed elaborate defenses. The region had not been the site of heavy combat since 1915, however, and by mid-1918, the Germans no longer manned it heavily or with first-rate troops. The German garrison in the salient resembled an occupation army. The A.E.F. estimated the German strength to be seven divisions in line with two in reserve and with the capability to reinforce with four more divisions within three days.

The operation—the A.E.F.'s trial by fire—would be important for several reasons. Such an operation would bring the A.E.F. much-needed experience in large-unit operations, while simultaneously—assuming it were successful—dealing a heavy blow to German morale. From the Allied strategic perspective, eliminating the salient would both restore the Paris-Nancy railroad and remove a possible threat to the U.S. right flank during future operations. Finally, a successful offensive, and the initiation of large-scale U.S. combat contributions, would increase the status of the United States as a co-belligerent and increase the weight of U.S. opinion in debates concerning the war effort.

At first, A.E.F. operational planning focused on overwhelming the Germans in the salient, breaking through their operational defenses (Hindenberg line), and opening up an avenue for a possible advance on Metz. But unexpected events influenced A.E.F. planning. The Allied high command reacted to the sudden breakdown of the German

U.S. troops advance across a plain during the battle for the St.-Mihiel salient, the first major U.S. offensive of World War I. (National Archives)

army in August 1918, and to the opportunity that that provided, by accelerating the tempo of its war plans. Pressured to involve the A.E.F. in a large strategic offensive, but without the A.E.F. divisions united under American 1st Army control, Pershing agreed on September 2 that the A.E.F. would undertake another offensive 60 miles to the north and west only two weeks after the operation began. Thus, not only would the 1st Army staff have to assemble and deploy disparate A.E.F. units from all over France around the salient, it also would have to redeploy them for the second offensive, later known as the Meuse-Argonne. The redeployment process had to begin even before the first day of fighting at St.-Mihiel was completed.

While a deception plan known as the Belfort Ruse tried to draw German troops away from the salient by dissembling an attack farther south toward Mulhouse, A.E.F. planning continued. One of the greatest planning handicaps was logistical. Not only did the 1st Army need to be built, it also had to be equipped. Tanks, which, like artillery and airplanes, had to be borrowed from the French and British, were available in fewer numbers than had been anticipated or desired.

The final plan was simple. As the A.E.F.'s report stated after the war, "Any study of the St.-Mihiel salient inevitably led to the conclusion that its reduction involved a nutcracker operation involving two attacks—one against the south face and one against the west face—to pinch out the salient." The IV and V Corps would carry out the main and secondary attacks, respectively. If the attack succeeded, the two corps would cut the salient at Vigneulles, trapping the Germans troops within the salient. Meanwhile, the French and I Corps would conduct supporting attacks at the apex and at the salient's right shoulder.

The 1st Army assembled a prodigious force of approximately 550,000 Americans and 110,000 French, along with 1,500 aircraft and 3,000 artillery pieces (almost half operated by French gunners), for the operation. The order of battle for the initial attack (beginning with the eastern end of the southern side and moving right-to-left) was as follows: U.S. I Corps (Lt. Gen. Hunter Liggett), comprising the 82d, 90th, 5th, and 2d divisions; U.S. IV Corps (Maj. Gen. Joseph T. Dickman), with the 89th, 42d, and 1st divisions; the French II Colonial Corps, with three divisions; and the U.S. V Corps (George H. Cameron), with the 26th and 4th divisions and the French 15th Colonial Division. Six divisions remained in reserve.

Knowing the psychological importance that the first U.S. offensive be successful, Pershing invested in the attack his veteran divisions: the 1st, 2d, 26th, and 42d divisions. Balancing the veteran units was the inexperience of the corps and army staffs, as well as the continued rain, which diminished the potential effectiveness of tanks (which were supposed to break paths through the rows of barbed-wire entanglements). Still, one brigadier general told Pershing, "You are going to have a walkover." The Americans did not know that the 23,000 Germans were preparing to abandon the salient.

Combat. The infantry attack began early on September 12 after 4- and 7-hour artillery bombardments on the southern and western faces. Prior to the attack, U.S. opinion had been divided between staff planners who wanted a longer bombardment (18 hours) to ensure that the wire was broken and corps commanders who wanted no preparatory bombardment (unless the ground were too muddy for the tanks to move) in order to ensure tactical surprise. Pershing finally had decided in favor of the shorter bombardments partly for the psychological lift it would provide his troops, and to ensure that the wire was at least damaged.

At 5:00 A.M., along the southern face, infantrymen climbed out of their trenches and attacked through a drizzling rain. They discovered the German wire only partially damaged, but the men found ways to get through the wire, from blowing it apart with Bangalore torpedoes to heaving rolls of chicken wire over entanglements and then walking over it (one French officer reportedly attributed the success in wire-crossing to large American feet). Everywhere in the south, the Americans advanced against varying degrees of German resistance.

The Germans' defense was disorganized because they already had begun to withdraw from the salient. In some cases, the Germans seemed disinclined to fight, as Sgt. Harry J. Adams of the 89th Division discovered when he "captured" 300 Germans while armed with only a pistol. German artillery fire was weak. Much divisional artillery had already been displaced and could not fire. By evening, the units attacking the south face were a day ahead of schedule. On the western face, where the assault jumped off at 8:00 A.M., progress was not as quick, although the 26th Division achieved a deep narrow penetration in the direction of Vigneulles.

Pershing saw the possibility of cutting off the retreating Germans. At 7:00 P.M. on September 12, he ordered the IV and V Corps commanders to press their advances toward Vigneulles "with all possible speed." A regiment of the 26th Division advanced through the night and reached Vigneulles shortly after 2:00 A.M., where they were joined shortly before dawn by men from the 1st Division. Approximately 16,000 Germans, and more than 400 guns, were trapped in the salient. Minor German counterattacks on the night of September 13–14 were repelled. The two-day cost to the A.E.F. had been 7,000 casualties, partly the result of U.S. tactical inexperience. Meanwhile, French units were already replacing U.S. units as the redeployment for the Meuse-Argonne Offensive began.

The easy victory, facilitated by the German withdrawal, cloaked A.E.F. operational problems. The A.E.F. used its overwhelming numerical advantage to crush disorganized German resistance. The campaign did not last long enough for command and control problems, or traffic and supply problems, to affect operations significantly. An omen for the Meuse-Argonne Offensive was the fact that a huge traffic jam had developed by the second day of the St.-Mihiel Offensive. Col. William "Billy" Mitchell, who flew above it, later wrote, "Never have I seen such congestion on a European battlefield." More significant, as a result of the participation of the best U.S. divisions in the St.-Mihiel Campaign, inexperienced divisions were forced to make initial attacks in the upcoming Meuse-Argonne Offensive.

Bibliography: Department of the Army, *The United States Army in the World War, 1917–1919; Vols. 4–5: Military Operations of the American Expeditionary Forces* (1948); Braim, Paul F., *The Test of Battle: The American Expeditionary Forces in the Meuse-Argonne Campaign* (Univ. of Delaware Press, 1987); Coffman, Edward, *The War to End All Wars* (Oxford Univ. Press, 1968); Paschall, Rod, *The Defeat of Imperial Germany, 1917–1918* (Algonquin Books, 1989); Pershing, John J., *My Experiences in the World War,* vol. 2 (Frederick A. Stokes Co., 1931).

Stephen J. Lofgren

SALEE FORTS, BATTLE OF THE (1871)

Engagement between Korean pirates and U.S. naval and marine forces. In June 1871, while U.S. diplomats were negotiating with the kingdom of Korea for a treaty to ensure safety of shipwrecked sailors, the U.S. fleet was fired on by Korean pirates positioned in forts along the Salee River. On June 10, gunboats bombarded the forts, and on June 11, a marine unit was sent into action. After several hours, the marines entered the fort and in hand-to-hand fighting killed or wounded all the defenders. In the assault, 243 pirates were killed; U.S. casualties were 2 killed and 2 wounded.

Leo J. Daugherty III

SAMOA

U.S. archipelago in South Pacific, 2,300 miles southwest of Hawaii, with the Samoan kingdom. The United States had been interested in Samoa as early as 1839 and under a 1878 treaty obtained rights to a naval station in Pago Pago. Germany and Great Britain were also interested in the archipelago, and an 1889 conference in Berlin established a tripartite protectorate over the islands. Differences and tensions continued, however, and on Mar. 16, 1889, the three powers sent warships to Apia Harbor, where a severe, two-day hurricane interrupted an intended confrontation and damaged or sank all but the British vessel. After continued disagreements, the division of Samoa was approved in another tripartite document signed in December 1899. The United States received five islands (American Samoa), Germany received two (Western Samoa), and Britain surrendered its claims in exchange for other Pacific concessions. New Zealand occupied Western Samoa in 1914 as World War I began and received a League of Nations mandate over it in 1920. The islands of American Samoa were ceded to the United States by their chiefs in 1900 and in 1904, the year in which a naval station, staffed by a detachment of marines, was established at Apia Harbor.

Leo J. Daugherty III

Subject to extreme heat and tropical diseases, the 7th Infantry mans the trenches at San Juan Hill during the 1898 Spanish-American War campaign to capture Santiago, Cuba. (U.S. Signal Corps)

SAND CREEK MASSACRE
(November 29, 1864)

Extreme example of how volunteer U.S. militias were often inclined to act toward Indians on the frontier. Led by Col. John Chivington, once a minister in the Methodist Episcopal Church, the 3d Regiment of the Colorado Volunteer Cavalry staged a punitive expedition near the present-day city of Lamar, Colorado. On Nov. 29, 1864, it discovered a Southern Cheyenne village ostensibly under the protection of a U.S. Army detachment at Fort Lyons. Despite the U.S. and white flags raised over Chief Black Kettle's tent, Chivington's men slaughtered and mutilated approximately 200 men, women, and children. The incident was a watershed, since it steeled the resolve of Plains Indians to resist the encroachment of U.S. settlers on their lands.

Bibliography: Hoig, Stan, *The Sand Creek Massacre* (Univ. of Oklahoma Press, 1961).

Maj. Peter R. Faber

SANTIAGO CAMPAIGN (June–July 1898)

U.S. military operation in Cuba, the largest land campaign of the Spanish-American War. It was marked by inefficiency and confusion but nevertheless accomplished its objectives in less than a month.

The U.S. Army had done little to plan for a war with Spain, and even before the declaration of war in April 1898, Sec. of War Russell Alger was forced to admit to Pres. William McKinley that the army could not mount a major expedition for some time. Army planning therefore emphasized providing aid to the insurgents in Cuba. On April 29, Maj. Gen. William R. Shafter was ordered to Tampa, from where he was eventually to lead a landing with 6,000 regulars on the southern coast of Cuba. Shafter was to land, contact insurgent leader Máximo Gómez, and provide him with arms and supplies before returning. However, the departure of the Spanish fleet from the Cape Verde Islands toward the Caribbean caused the expedition to be cancelled. Other plans were discussed, including the capture of Havana, but the news of the arrival of the Spanish fleet at Santiago de Cuba caused their abandonment. McKinley decided on May 26 to attack Santiago with the troops Shafter currently was assembling at Tampa.

Tampa, however, was a scene of confusion and disarray. Troops and supplies had been sent to Tampa with no priorities or higher purpose. The only two rail connections out of the town were overloaded. This disorganization led to repeated delays, until an impatient McKinley ordered Shafter on June 7 to set sail with whatever force he had ready. Even then, a mistaken report of two Spanish warships off Cuba led to a further week's delay.

Shafter left with his V Corps, composed of 17,000 men (only 2,500 volunteers) and a small amount of artillery. His orders were to proceed to Santiago, land east or west of the city, and, with the aid of the U.S. Navy, destroy the Spanish fleet there. This led to differences between Shafter and William T. Sampson, the naval commander. Sampson felt the expedition's purpose to be the capture of the batteries at the entrance to Santiago's harbor. Shafter, however, felt that a major land campaign was needed.

On June 20, the convoy arrived off Santiago. Shafter and Sampson met with Calixto García, the commander of rebel forces in eastern Cuba, and decided to land at Daiquiri, east of Santiago, on June 22, while the Cubans made diversions elsewhere. Daiquiri had only a few Spanish defenders, who withdrew under naval bombardment. Nevertheless, the landing did not go smoothly, since there were few small craft and no one experienced in amphibious landings. Within eight hours, some 6,000 men were on shore, and an equal number landed the next day. This was largely due to help given by the navy. Shafter also decided to land some troops at Siboney, about eight miles closer to Santiago, on June 23. By June 26, all the troops were landed, the only casualties being two soldiers who drowned at Daiquiri.

Once ashore, Shafter ordered his force inland along the road from Siboney to Santiago. The V Corps consisted of two infantry divisions under Brig. Gens. Jacob Kent and Henry Lawton, a cavalry division under ex-Confederate Maj. Gen. Joseph Wheeler, and two brigades. Wheeler headed the advance and on June 24 won a "skirmish" at Las Guásimas against Spaniards already ordered to retreat. This buoyed U.S. morale and opened the way to the Spanish lines around Santiago.

On the instructions of the Spanish commander, Arsenio Linares, these lines extended around the city and were consequently thinly held. Moreover, Santiago's level of supplies was low. However, the Spaniards, numbering slightly more than 10,000, had modern weapons and occupied well-prepared positions. The Spanish and the Americans spent the five days of June 26–30 building up their respective positions. The U.S. forces faced severe difficulties. The troops had no supplies with them initially, nor any way to haul them. They had to use mule trains to supply the entire army, which could only be supplied along one small road. Moreover, growing problems with yellow fever, malaria, and other tropical diseases incapacitated teamsters and packers as well as soldiers.

Spanish Defeat. On June 28, Shafter discovered that Spanish colonel Federico Esario was headed toward Santiago with a reported 8,000 (actually 3,700) reinforcements and decided to attack before the Spaniard's arrival. Shafter wanted to attack the hamlet of El Caney, a strong defensive location northeast of Santiago, to remove a Spanish flanking position and to block the road to Guantánamo. His main attack would be against Kettle and San Juan hills, which flanked the road to Santiago. Lawton was to capture El Caney then move to support Kent and Wheeler against the San Juan Heights.

This plan fell apart quickly, however. Divisions did not begin to move until the afternoon of June 30. Wheeler fell ill and so too did the 300-pound, gout-afflicted Shafter. Shafter made little effort to coordinate movements, and none of the senior officers were experienced in commanding large forces. Lawton attacked El Caney at 7:00 A.M. on July 1 with 5,400 men, expecting to capture it within two hours. However, the 500 well-sheltered defenders held on for the entire day, depriving the attack against the San Juan Heights of Lawton's support.

That attack went no better. Kent's division and the cavalry division, now under Gen. Samuel Sumner, moved into position around El Pozo, within the range of Spanish artillery. A U.S. observation balloon betrayed the troops' line of march, and the U.S. troops were demoralized by the accurate Spanish fire. Finally, at 1:00 P.M., Sumner and Lt. John Miley, an aide to Shafter, authorized an attack. Kent's infantry, with support from Gatling guns, advanced up the southern section of the San Juan Heights, while Sumner's men, including Theodore Roosevelt's ''Rough Riders,'' chased the Spanish off Kettle Hill and continued on to the northern part of San Juan Hill.

Once in possession of the heights, the U.S. soldiers halted. Only 3,000 of their 15,000 troops had gained the heights, and they had suffered almost 1,400 casualties (against 600 Spanish). Moreover, the next line of Spanish defenses was even stronger. The U.S. contingent was considerably demoralized; on July 2, Shafter even debated retreating. To make matters worse, Colonel Escario entered Santiago with his reinforcements that night.

However, the Spaniards were in worse condition, and in desperation the Spanish fleet sortied on July 3, only to be defeated by the U.S. blockading squadron. This victory heartened Shafter, who that day demanded a surrender. Negotiations went on for two weeks, during which time Gen. Nelson Miles arrived with reinforcements. The Spaniards finally capitulated on July 17, surrendering not only the soldiers in Santiago but all of those in eastern Cuba, some 23,000. Spanish resistance in eastern Cuba was finished.

After the capitulation, however, the V Corps experienced its worst days in Cuba. Disease ravaged the U.S. Army starting on July 6, with malaria and dysentery being especially virulent. By July 28, 4,270 men were on the sick roster, and not until mid-August did the army move to a more healthy location.

The final U.S. casualties at Santiago were 243 combat deaths, 1,445 wounded, and 771 deaths due to sickness. The campaign, despite its relative brevity, was ill-managed and haphazard. Victory was due less to U.S. planning or foresight than to the hopelessness of the Spanish position.

Bibliography: Carlson, Paul H., *''Pecos Bill'': A Military Biography of William R. Shafter* (Texas A&M Univ. Press, 1989); O'Toole, G. J. A., *The Spanish War: An American Epic—1898* (Norton, 1984); Trask, David F., *The War With Spain in 1898* (Macmillan Co., 1981).

Mark Pitcavage

SEICHEPREY, BATTLE OF (April 20, 1918)

World War I battle in northeastern France, an action preparatory to the St.-Mihiel Offensive. On Apr. 20, 1918, as the American Expeditionary Force (A.E.F.) moved into the line, German forces launched a 1,200-man raid against the 26th Division in the southern sector of the St.-Mihiel salient. The 26th, the National Guard's ''New England Division,'' occupied sectors near Seicheprey, having replaced the 1st Division earlier in the month. With raiding parties poised for the assault, German artillery bombarded the U.S. defenses with a two-hour barrage. Isolating the trenches with indirect fire, German troops destroyed dugouts, a battalion aid station, and a field kitchen; they then withdrew before a limited counterattack force reoccupied the trenches. The Americans were able to down two German aircraft during the fighting, but the ultimate price of battle was high: A.E.F. losses totaled 634 casualties (80 killed in action) and 130 prisoners of war.

Bibliography: American Battle Monuments Commission, *26th Division: Summary of Operations in the World War* (U.S. Govt. Printing Office, 1944); Van Every, Dale, *The A.E.F. in Battle* (Appleton, 1928).

Capt. James Sanders Day

SELECTIVE SERVICE ACT (1917)

U.S. draft law enacted in anticipation of U.S. entry into World War I. The unfortunate experience with the draft during the Civil War, with its use of bounties, substitutes, and provost marshals to enforce compliance, led army planners under Adj. Gen. Enoch Crowder to propose a more equitable and politically adept draft law for World War I. Under the Selective Service Act of May 18, 1917, all male citizens (and aliens who intended to become citizens) ages 21 to 30 inclusive (in August 1917 extended to ages 18 and 35) registered with local draft boards. Members of the 4,600 boards then selected the registrants for service or exemption. Unmarried farm workers and manual laborers provided the bulk of the draftees. The military preferred conscription and, by September 1918, no longer accepted volunteers. In all, the draft provided about 67 percent of the armed forces' manpower in World War I.

Richard B. Meixsel

SERVICES OF SUPPLY (SOS)

U.S. contingent of logistical support of the American Expeditionary Force (A.E.F.) within France during World War I. At its largest in November 1918, the SOS had almost 25 percent of the total personnel of the A.E.F.

One of the most immediate concerns of the A.E.F. when it deployed in 1917 was logistical sustainment. Matériel had to be purchased and then shipped to Europe, and systems had to be established to handle matériel once it arrived in France. Col. Johnson Hagood, who accompanied Gen. John J. Pershing to France, immediately began to organize all aspects of logistics.

By February 1918, the scope of logistical sustainment was so large that management had to move from A.E.F. headquarters. In March, the Lines of Communications was designated as Services of Supply, and Maj. Gen. Francis Kernan was made commander. Under this arrangement, all logistics activities came under the control of a single commander. In July, Maj. Gen. James G. Harbord was placed in command and was given authority to communicate directly with the War Department.

By war's end, the SOS was involved in all aspects of logistics including procurement, hospital care, railroad transport, building construction, storage, salvage, and food production. Some SOS soldiers grew vegetables in the Garden Service, and others made more than 5,000,000 pounds of chocolate a month. Perhaps the most lasting contribution of the SOS was that a precedent was set giving an overseas commander control of all his logistical support within his theater of operations.

Bibliography: Hagood, Johnson, *The Services of Supply* (Houghton Mifflin, 1927); Huston, James A., *The Sinews of War: Army Logistics, 1775–1953* (U.S. Army, 1966).

Capt. George B. Eaton

SHEEPEATER WAR OF 1879

Essentially unjust pursuit, by the U.S. Army, of the Sheepeaters, a mixed group of "renegade" Bannock and Shoshone who inhabited the rugged Salmon River Mountains of Idaho. In early 1879, the Sheepeaters were wrongly accused of murdering five Chinese prospectors on Loon Creek. Protected by fewer than 30 warriors, the Sheepeaters led the army on a three-month chase in bad weather over some of the most difficult terrain in North America. The group of 51 men, women, and children was finally forced to surrender by Lt. Edward S. Farrow and a group of Umatilla Indian scouts on October 2 and were subsequently settled on the Fort Hall Reservation.

Bibliography: Utley, Robert M., *Frontier Regulars: The United States and the Indian, 1866–1890* (Macmillan Co., 1973).

Lt. Col. (Ret.) Charles R. Shrader

SIOUX WAR (1865–68)

Post-Civil War subjugation by the U.S. Army of hostile Indians in the West. By 1866, Maj. Gen. William T. Sherman commanded the Division of the Missouri, headquartered at St. Louis. Sherman hoped for a year or two of peace on the Great Plains while he rebuilt his army. His strategy through 1866, therefore, was one of defense—if the army could simply hold the line against ever-increasing Indian belligerence, Sherman would be satisfied.

The army was obligated to protect work crews of the Union Pacific Railroad, emigrant wagon trains, freight trains, and stagecoaches. The potential for Indian war loomed on all sides. Major wagon routes to the West spanned Sherman's command in the Departments of the Dakota, the Missouri, and the Platte. Officials of the Bureau of Indian Affairs felt certain that a comprehensive set of treaties negotiated with the warlike tribes of the region would bring lasting peace to the Great Plains. The Indians became increasingly restive, however, as the railroad pushed ever westward and emigrants flooded the Oregon Trail to the West and the Bozeman Trail to Montana.

Col. Henry B. Carrington, commanding at Fort Phil Kearny on the Bozeman Trail in northern Wyoming, expected to overcome any opposition from the Sioux and Cheyenne by "patience, forebearance, and common sense." But Carrington received a more accurate reading of the prospects for peace when he met Chief Standing Elk of the Burlé Sioux at Fort Laramie in June 1866. Standing Elk informed Carrington that the "fighting men" had refused to come to Laramie. By the end of 1866, though, the vicinity around Fort Kearny was alive with Sioux warriors.

On December 21, Capt. William J. Fetterman (who once boasted, "Give me 80 men and I would ride through the whole Sioux nation"), along with 80 men, rode to the rescue of a wood-cutting party near Fort Kearny. A Sioux ambush wiped out Fetterman's entire command.

Western newspapers proclaimed the Powder River country to be in the grip of a full-scale war by 1866–67. The Fetterman massacre shocked and outraged the army. "We must act with vindictive earnestness against the Sioux,"

Sherman informed Gen. Ulysses S. Grant, "even to their extermination, men, women, and children." At western military posts, attitudes toward Indians hardened noticeably.

The major theater of operations against the Sioux continued to be along the Bozeman Trail through 1867–68. The Powder River country of northern Wyoming filled with camps of hostile Sioux and Cheyenne under the umbrella of Red Cloud's leadership. The Oglala Sioux chief and his followers actively sought to drive out the soldiers and shut down the road to Montana.

Between 1867 and 1868, encounters between the army and the Sioux were frequent. During July 1867, Sioux warriors chose to carry their fight with the soldiers to the vicinity of Fort C. F. Smith. Only a 20-mile ride from the Little Bighorn River, the fort was within easy striking range for Red Cloud's warriors.

As with Fort Kearny, whenever the troopers at Fort Smith left the safety of their enclosure, they were threatened by Indians. On the morning of August 1, 12 civilian haycutters and their escort of 19 soldiers were ambushed near the fort and found themselves trapped inside a wooden corral. The Sioux maintained a withering fire, mostly of arrows, until early afternoon. Outnumbered at least 6 to 1, the defenders held their position for more than six hours, sustaining casualties of 3 killed and 2 wounded.

While incidents like the Hayfield Fight (as it became known) had no clear victor, in the aftermath of the Fetterman Massacre, engagements like this bolstered U.S. morale. The Sioux were not invincible. On a strategic level, however, the Sioux War of 1865–68 and the defense of the Bozeman Trail represented a large commitment of manpower and expense to keep the West open to U.S. settlers.

M. Guy Bishop

SIOUX WAR (1876)

Military campaign, sometimes known as "Sitting Bull's War," provoked by U.S. incursions into the Black Hills and by federal policy aimed at denying the Sioux access to that area. The Sioux considered this region of present South Dakota to be sacred. But by 1875–76, some 15,000 gold-hungry miners had invaded the Blacks Hills in violation of a government treaty. At the same time, the Bureau of Indian Affairs decided to launch a move to force the Sioux onto reservations and insisted that the Indians cede much of their land in the Black Hills. All Sioux in unceded territory were ordered to move to reservation land by Jan. 31, 1876.

The government's ultimatum was quickly carried to the Indians' winter camps along the Yellowstone River and its tributaries. Even had they been allowed ample time, and even if the season had been conducive to travel, it is doubtful many Sioux would have made an effort to comply. The stage had thus been deftly set for the anticipated U.S. military campaign against the Sioux. "Sitting Bull's War" had begun.

Gen. Philip H. Sheridan felt that a successful campaign depended upon a quick move while the Indians lay vulnerable in the winter camps. Much to Sheridan's dismay, reports in early February showed the Sioux were not in camp along the Dakota's Little Missouri River but were, in fact, 200 miles farther west.

Army efforts were further hampered by the unanticipated severity of winter on the Northern Plains. Gradually, Sheridan's winter campaign began to look more and more like a spring, or even summer, campaign. Gen. George Crook's expedition, with plans of moving against the Sioux from its western flank, did not leave Wyoming's Fort Fetterman until late February. Gen. Alfred H. Terry's forces marched on the Sioux from the east.

In mid-June, Sitting Bull's Hunkpapa held a sun dance along Montana's Rosebud Creek. At this time, Sitting Bull had a vision of many soldiers "falling right into our camp." Immediately following the sun dance, the camp was moved across the Wolf Mountains to a spot on the Little Bighorn River. There, on June 16, Sioux hunters brought news of many soldiers approaching the Rosebud. Seeing the fulfillment of Sitting Bull's vision on the horizon, eager warriors rode back to Rosebud Creek.

On the morning of June 17, as Crook's troops paused for coffee, the Sioux struck. After the initial moments of confusion, the soldiers held the Indians at bay. Fierce fighting raged along the Rosebud for much of the day. After nearly six hours, the Indians broke off the fight and abandoned the battlefield. Crook's forces, which had numerical superiority, had failed to carry the fight. In fact, during the early stages of the Battle of the Rosebud, it was only the heroic efforts of Crook's Crow and Shoshone auxiliaries that stayed off a disastrous defeat. In Crook's defense, it should be noted that the Sioux and Cheyenne fought with an unanticipated unity and tenacity likely encouraged by Sitting Bull's vision. Eight days later, Lt. Col. George A. Custer and the 7th Cavalry were wiped out by these same inspired warriors a few miles away at the Little Bighorn.

On the morning of June 22, Custer left Terry's camp with orders to trap the Indians along the Little Bighorn and pinch them between his troops and Terry's, who would advance up the Rosebud, the primary object being to keep the hostiles from escaping. By June 24, the 7th Cavalry reached a point where the Indian trail moved off toward the west. Instead of adhering to Terry's containment plan, Custer turned west in pursuit of the Indians. On June 25, Custer attacked the Sioux village and met disaster: he and more than 200 of his men were annihilated at the Battle of the Little Bighorn. The battle all but marked the end of the Sioux War of 1876, and the subsequent scattering of the victorious Indians greatly deterred the U.S. effort to subdue them.

M. Guy Bishop

SOISSONS, BATTLE OF (July 18–21, 1918)

World War I battle in northern France, in which an Allied counteroffensive turned the tide of war in favor of the Allies. Gen. Erich Ludendorff launched Germany's fifth offensive of the year on July 15, 1918, attacking on either side of Reims, France. The Germans established a bridgehead across the Marne River, but their attack was spent after three days. On July 18, Gen. Ferdinand Foch unleashed the Allied counterattack (known as the Aisne-Marne Offensive) with the goal of eliminating the Marne salient.

Foch's initial objective was to cut the Soissons-Château-Thierry highway and the Paris-Soissons railroad, the two main supply lines into the German salient, and thereby compel a German withdrawal. Four French armies attacked all around the salient, with the French 10th Army conducting the primary attack. The French XX Corps, comprising the U.S. 1st and 2d divisions and the French Moroccan 1st Division, spearheaded the attack toward Soissons and the supply lines.

The corps attacked before 5:00 A.M. on July 18. Held behind the front until the last moment in order to maintain operational secrecy, some U.S. units had to double-time in order to reach the line of departure on time. Timing was crucial since, in order to achieve surprise, there would be no preparatory bombardment, only a rolling barrage. Surprise was achieved, and the corps made great gains the first day. Despite advances of three to four miles, however, no unit achieved a breakthrough. By day two, with the advantage of surprise gone and German defenses stiffening, progress was more difficult. By nightfall, the 2d Division, commanded by Maj. Gen. James G. Harbord, had advanced seven miles, captured 3,000 prisoners, and suffered approximately 5,000 casualties. The division was withdrawn. The 1st Division, under Maj. Gen. Charles P. Summerall, forged ahead for two more days. Before it was relieved on July 21, the division had cut the two German supply lines and captured 3,500 prisoners at the cost of 7,000 casualties. His position untenable, Ludendorff evacuated Soissons and the Marne salient and withdrew behind the Vesle River.

Stephen J. Lofgren

SOMME OFFENSIVE (August 1918)

World War I Allied campaign in northern France. British forces launched the offensive in August 1918, with the American Expeditionary Force's 33d Division in reserve of the British III Corps and its 80th Division units assigned to the British IV, V, and VI Corps. In the days of August 9–13, the 131st Infantry Regiment of the 33d Division reinforced the British 58th Division and the Australian 4th Division in attacks on Chipilly Ridge, Gressaire Wood, and Etinehem, thereby capturing 700 prisoners, 30 artillery pieces, 1 airplane, and more than 100 machine guns. One battalion of the 80th Division's 317th Infantry Regiment supported a New Zealander advance, while other elements defended against German raiding parties. In late August, both the 33d and the 80th divisions were reassigned to the American 1st Army in the Verdun and St.-Mihiel sectors, respectively.

Bibliography: American Battle Monuments Commission, *80th Division: Summary of Operations in the World War* (U.S. Govt. Printing Office, 1944); ———, *33d Division: Summary of Operations in the World War* (U.S. Govt. Printing Office, 1944).

Capt. James Sanders Day

SOUTHERN PLAINS WAR (1868–1869)

Series of military campaigns that furthered the U.S. Army's goal of clearing the territory between the Arkansas and the Platte rivers of Indians. In 1866, the War Department established a policy of attempting to confine the Sioux tribes north of the Platte River while relegating the Arapaho, Southern Cheyenne, Kiowa, and Commanche to the Southern Plains. Gen. Philip Sheridan assumed command of the Department of the Missouri in 1868. Sheridan now had the responsibility to safeguard civilians who had poured into the region since passage of the Homestead Act of 1862. The Cheyenne and Arapaho had been guilty of occasional raids against non-Indians since 1867, and Sheridan determined to attack these Indians during the winter of 1868–69. It was felt that if they could surprise the Indians in their winter camps, a decisive victory might be gained. Lt. Col. George A. Custer played a leading role in Sheridan's plan. Marching south from Fort Dodge, Kansas, in November 1868, Custer and his 7th Cavalry aimed for the Cheyenne-Arapaho Reservation in Indian Territory (present-day Oklahoma). Custer located the Indian camps along the Washita River. Sheridan's orders to Custer were to hang all warriors not killed in battle, take the women and children prisoner, destroy the Indian camp, and kill their ponies. At the Battle of the Washita (November 29), Custer reportedly killed 103 Cheyenne warriors and destroyed 51 lodges. Ironically, this was the village of Black Kettle, a peaceful Cheyenne chief. The Cheyenne and Arapaho fled west toward the upper Red River. Sheridan considered the Washita only the opening volley in his campaign to subdue the Indians of the Southern Plains. The next several months witnessed similar attacks against the Kiowa and the Commanche.

M. Guy Bishop

SUMMIT SPRINGS, BATTLE OF (July 11, 1869)

U.S. military attack on belligerent Cheyenne in eastern Colorado. Eight companies of the 5th U.S. Cavalry and

Brig. Gen. Benjamin A. Poore (second from left), *commander of the U.S. 7th Infantry Brigade, and his aide-de-camp, Maj. A. D. Falconners* (center), *review plans on Aug. 9, 1918, during the Somme Offensive in France.* (U.S. Signal Corps)

more than 150 Pawnee scouts under the overall command of Bvt. Maj. Gen. Eugene A. Carr left their encampment on the Republican River in early June 1869. They followed that watercourse and other creeks westward for more than 300 miles. Their destination was Summit Springs, Colorado, where a band of Cheyenne "dog soldiers" held U.S. settlers captured in retaliation for a massacre of Cheyenne, Sioux, and Arapaho by troops under Carr's command in May.

The Indian encampment was located by chief of army scouts, Col. William Cody. The attack began at about 4:00 A.M. on July 11. At Carr's command, the entire mounted force advanced upon the unguarded encampment, and within five minutes, the Cheyenne had suffered their last major defeat before they were settled in Oklahoma in 1870. Carr's force rested for two weeks at Fort Sedgwick before returning to their station.

Bibliography: Weingardt, Richard, *Sound the Charge; The Western Frontier: Spillman Creek to Summit Springs* (Jacqueline Enterprises, 1978).

Louise Arnold-Friend

SUPREME WAR COUNCIL

During World War I, an interallied body for coordinating the war effort and ensuring the best use of Allied resources. Allied reversals in 1917 capped by the Italian defeat at Caporetto in November led British Prime Minister David Lloyd George to suggest the creation of such a council. Lloyd George also hoped to circumvent his senior army commanders, in whom he had little confidence, and to divert the war effort away from the futile offensives along the Western Front. The French ultimately sought unified command under a French supreme commander.

The Supreme War Council, agreed to at a conference at Rapallo, Italy, on Nov. 7, 1917, was a compromise solution. Council members included the prime minister of Britain and the premiers of France and Italy, with subordinate permanent military representatives who were to act as technical advisers to the council. General staffs and field commanders remained responsible to their own governments.

Lloyd George had encouraged U.S. participation in the council from the start. Pres. Woodrow Wilson, who had brought the United States into the war not as an "ally" but as an "associate" of the entente, wanted to preserve U.S. diplomatic independence once the war was won. At the same time, he supported the concept of a coordinated Allied military effort. Thus, he never attended the council meetings nor did he allow anyone to attend in his place as a political representative. He did, however, appoint a permanent military representative with the brevet rank of full general, the very able and respected retiring U.S. Army chief of staff, Tasker H. Bliss. Bliss commanded the dozen officers and 40 enlisted men of the U.S. section of the Supreme War Council until the end of the war.

The political leaders of the council met only 8 times during the war; their military representatives met 51 times at the seat of the Supreme War Council at Versailles. The role of the council was to study and provide joint advice on how to deal with military problems on the Western Front. The members met informally as well to work out differences and ensure that proposals would meet with general approval before being presented to the council.

One of the most contentious issues facing the Supreme War Council was the use of U.S. troops. British and French officials wanted to transport only infantrymen across the Atlantic and incorporate them into existing Allied formations. For purposes of national prestige and to have greater influence in determining postwar peace policy, the United States wanted to form a distinct American army in Europe. Bliss was generally more sympathetic to the Allies on this issue, but he subordinated his view to that of Gen. John J. Pershing, who adamantly opposed the amalgamation of U.S. troops with the armies of Britain and France. The military representative of the council played an instrumental part in working out an acceptable policy on the use of U.S. troops.

Although its promise remained greater than its achievement, the Supreme War Council of 1917–18 was a notable advance toward reconciling the inherent difficulties of waging coalition warfare and provided a model—however limited—for later Allied unity of command.

Bibliography: Trask, David F., *The United States in the Supreme War Council* (Wesleyan Univ. Press, 1961).

Richard B. Meixsel

TAMPICO INCIDENT (April 1914)

Military affair between the United States and Mexico during a period of political strife between the two nations. In 1914, Mexican revolutionaries encircled Tampico, on the Gulf Coast of eastern Mexico, and ships of the U.S. Navy stood offshore to protect U.S. citizens and property. When sailors from the USS *Dolphin* were detained briefly by Mexican officials on April 9, 1914, Rear Adm. Henry T. Mayo demanded a public apology, the raising of the U.S. flag, and a 21-gun salute. After Mexico rejected the demands, Pres. Woodrow Wilson backed Mayo and authorized him to seize Tampico. U.S. troops assembled in Texas, and the rest of the Atlantic Fleet sailed to Mexican waters. When Wilson learned that a ship carrying munitions was due to dock at Veracruz, he ordered U.S. forces to occupy that city (April 21). Thus, attention shifted from Tampico, where Mayo's forces took on board U.S refugees before departing in November.

Bibliography: Quick, Robert E., *An Affair of Honor: Woodrow Wilson and the Occupation of Veracruz* (Norton, 1962).

James C. Bradford

TONTO BASIN CAMPAIGN (1872–1873)

Campaign mounted by Maj. Gen. George Crook against Apache Indians who fled their reservation to live in the Tonto Basin in Arizona Territory. Crook wisely adopted Apache tactics, such as the use of Apache scouts and specially trained men who were able to endure more hardship and move faster than those on previous expeditions. Crook started his campaign in November 1872, believing winter would impede his elusive quarry, and he emphasized to his six separate columns that if they uncovered an Apache trail they were to follow it doggedly until they located their foe. Two major actions punctuated a series of minor clashes—the Battle of the Cave (Dec. 28, 1872), in which 75 Apache died, and the struggle at Turret Peak (Mar. 27, 1873), in which Crook's infantrymen scaled a cliff to surprise their opponents. With this action, Apache resistance virtually ended.

Bibliography: Brown, Dee, *Bury My Heart at Wounded Knee* (Bantam Books, 1972); Tebbel, John, *The Compact History of the Indian Wars* (Hawthorn Books, 1966); Wormser, Richard, *The Yellowlegs* (Doubleday, 1966).

John F. Wukovits

TREATY OF PARIS (December 10, 1898)

Agreement that formally ended the Spanish-American War. Under the terms of the treaty, Spain renounced sovereignty over Cuba and ceded Puerto Rico and Guam to the United States. Spain sold the Philippines to the United States for $20,000,000. More important than the actual terms were the implications for the U.S. armed forces. Transfer from Spain to the United States did not solve any of the domestic problems in the Philippines. The army was soon combating the Philippine Insurrection, which lasted until 1902 and established a lasting U.S. presence in the islands. The navy gained coaling stations in the Caribbean and enhanced the power and ability of the United States to intervene in Central and South America. In addition, the navy gained a global role, as it now had to maintain lines of communication with the Philippines.

Capt. George B. Eaton

UTE WAR (September–October 1879)

U.S. military action against a faction of Ute Indians who resisted U.S. suppression and geographical confinement. In 1868, a U.S. treaty commission worked out an agreement with seven Colorado bands of the Ute tribe, giving them a slice of western Colorado as their reservation. Then, in the early 1870s, mineral strikes in Colorado subjected the Ute to severe stress from encroaching miners. By autumn 1879, the Ute of the White River Agency in northwestern Colorado were incensed and expressed a particular disregard toward their U.S. agent, Nathan C. Meeker, who made constant demands that they abandon their nomadic ways and settle down as farmers. Meeker's call for aid from the U.S. Army in September 1879 heightened the Ute discontent. On September 29, the approaching troops were met by 100 well-armed warriors. After skirmishing with the soldiers, the Ute returned to the agency and slaughtered Meeker and nine others. The Ute War continued until mid-October, when more than 1,500 U.S. troops were sent to quell the uprising. As a consequence of their belligerence, the White River Ute were removed to the Utah Territory.

M. Guy Bishop

VALPARAÍSO INCIDENT (October 1891–January 1892)

Affair in central Chile in which U.S. servicemen were assaulted by angry Chileans. Anti-American feeling was high in Chile after the United States tried to keep arms from reaching rebels who ultimately triumphed in a Chilean civil war. On Oct. 16, 1891, Capt. Winfield S. Schley of the *Baltimore,* one of three ships sent to protect U.S. lives and property during the civil war, unwisely granted leave in Valparaíso to 117 crewmen. After an incident in a bar during which Chileans were accused of spitting in the face of an American, a mob attacked the U.S. sailors with knives, clubs, and stones, killing 2 and injuring 17 others. Pres. Benjamin Harrison and Sec. of the Navy Benjamin F. Tracy considered it a deliberate attack on U.S. honor and demanded an apology and reparations. When Chile rejected the demands, both sides prepared for war. In January 1892, Chile bowed to the inevitable, apologized, and ultimately paid $75,000 in reparations.

Bibliography: Goldberg, Joyce S., *The Baltimore Affair* (Univ. of Nebraska Press, 1986).

James C. Bradford

VERACRUZ (April 1914)

U.S. military occupation of Veracruz, on the Gulf Coast of eastern Mexico, as a result of U.S. political opposition to the newly assumed Mexican government. Following the late-19th-century involvement in the Spanish-American War and other foreign entanglements, the United States became increasingly withdrawn from the world arena. Isolationism became the watchword of U.S. diplomacy, particularly under the direction of Pres. Woodrow Wilson. Wilson's idealistic approach to the conduct of foreign policy came into direct conflict, however, with his desire for nonintervention in the affairs of other nations shortly after his inauguration (Mar. 4, 1913). Less than two weeks earlier, Victoriano Huerta had seized control of the unstable presidency of Mexico.

Wilson was morally offended by Huerta's method of obtaining power, which the U.S. president viewed as symbolic of all the political ills of the Latin American republics. Believing that those nations should be governed by democratically elected governments, Wilson refused to recognize the new Mexican regime. Soon after Huerta established himself in control, opposition groups appeared throughout his country, and Wilson encouraged rebellion there. Wilson lifted the heretofore ineffective ban on shipping U.S. arms to Mexico, and by early 1914, the most potent opposition force became an army led by Francisco "Pancho" Villa. Huerta took no substantive steps to quell Villa in the central part of the country, and other Constitutionalist armies led by Álvaro Obregón and Pablo Gonzalez developed power bases elsewhere throughout Mexico. These three forces were loosely allied to Venustiano Carranza, governor of the state of Coahuila. Huerta used his own troops mainly to garrison railroad junctions and failed to make the opposition forces a military target.

By early April 1914, Villa's army occupied much of northern Mexico and was heading unhindered toward Mexico City. Carranza and Villa developed a difference of opinion, and Carranza began to hinder the Villista advance, hoping the capital would be occupied by Obregón or Gonzalez. At the same time, to strengthen his own relative position, Carranza moved on the oil-rich city of Tampico, loosely defended by a 2,000-man garrison commanded by Gen. Ignacio Zaragoza.

U.S. warships had been stationed at Tampico for several months to protect U.S. lives and property. Vessels under Rear Adm. Henry T. Mayo at Tampico and Rear Adm. Frank F. Fletcher at Veracruz shuttled back and forth between the two cities. Expecting trouble at the approach of Carranza's forces, Mayo requested that Fletcher reinforce Tampico. On April 5, opposition forces attacked, and for the next several days, the city was in a state of confusion. With normal channels of procurement interrupted, U.S. troops needed supplies, particularly gasoline. On April 9, Lt. Comdr. Ralph K. Earle of the gunboat *Dolphin* ordered crewmen to take a whaleboat inland to obtain the needed gasoline from a German civilian. The marines who made the trek were arrested and briefly detained by Zaragoza's forces. Although the men had been quickly released and an apology to Admiral Mayo from General Zaragoza was quickly forthcoming, the U.S. officer considered the apology insufficient. He viewed the detention of his men as an act hostile to the United States and felt that any apology should be made to the country and should include a 21-gun salute, which would be returned.

Wilson received a briefing on the Tampico Incident the next day, concurring with Mayo's course of action and viewing it as an opportunity to force Huerta's hand diplomatically. With the full blessing of the Mexico City government, the demands were not met. In retaliation, Wilson ordered a U.S. fleet to occupy Veracruz. At least in his own mind, he was acting with a diplomatic precedent. On April 14, Wilson ordered the Atlantic Fleet to offshore Mexico to reinforce Mayo at Tampico and Fletcher at Veracruz. This show of force consisted of seven battleships and four transports full of marines, escorted by cruisers and destroyers, all under the command of Vice Adm. Charles T. Badger.

Wilson released a public statement on April 15 in which the incident at Tampico was listed as only one of several affronts to Americans in Mexico. In Veracruz itself, a naval mail orderly had been arrested and imprisoned, and in Mexico City, an official U.S. dispatch had been withheld by Mexican authorities. In Wilson's eyes, the United States was singularly bearing the brunt of unjustified Mexican harassment. Diplomatic and other attempts to get the Mexican government to comply with the Mayo/Wilson ultimatum failed. On April 21, the president ordered the seizure of the Veracruz custom house to prevent the delivery of weapons heading to the port on a German liner.

Occupation. The decision to land at Veracruz rather than Tampico surprised Fletcher, most of whose vessels were at Tampico. Despite an oncoming storm, Fletcher directed the battleship *Utah* to remain outside the harbor to prevent the German ship from landing with its weapons. Personnel on the gunboat *Prairie* were put ashore to occupy the docks, the custom house, and the railroad station. The Mexican commander in the city, Gen. Gustavo Maas, understood that the Americans outnumbered him but said he would return fire if fired upon. About noon, a Mexican soldier fired into U.S. troops advancing on the custom house. The sailors and marines returned fire, and throughout the day, their losses were 4 killed and 20 wounded. Within an hour of the first shot, Fletcher ordered sailors from the *Utah* ashore.

By nightfall, reinforcements from Badger's Atlantic Fleet and vessels from Tampico were arriving, with Fletcher retaining operational control of the force. At daybreak on April 22, he ordered the forces on shore to take control of the city, as he could find no effective government from whom to request a cease-fire. The city was firmly in U.S. control by noon.

On April 30, the U.S. Army 5th Brigade arrived ashore to share occupation duties with the marines. A military government, headed by Gen. Frederick Funston, set about to restore order to the city. While President Huerta never recognized the legitimacy of the U.S. occupiers, neither did he made any serious attempt to resist them. Faced with increasing power of opposition leaders, he resigned on July 15. The power vacuum was filled by Carranza, but the warring factions within the opposition were leading Mexico to civil war.

Wilson's satisfaction at Huerta's departure from power was soon dampened by Carranza's refusal to hold popular elections. The new Mexican leader was primarily interested in U.S. departure from Veracruz. An oral agreement for withdrawal was reached with U.S. diplomats on September 16, but Funston felt he needed a month for an orderly transfer of power to Carranza's appointee and sought guarantees there would be no reprisals against refugees and those who had aided the Americans. Carranza, like Huerta before him, refused to capitulate to U.S. requests. Diplomatic haggling, with Carranza finally superficially yielding to Wilson's demands, held up the U.S. evacuation until November 23.

Bibliography: Quirk, Robert E., *An Affair of Honor: Woodrow Wilson and the Occupation of Veracruz* (Univ. of Kentucky Press, 1962); Sweetman, Jack, *The Landing at Veracruz: 1914* (U.S. Naval Inst. Press, 1968).

Louise Arnold-Friend

WAGON BOX FIGHT (August 2, 1867)

Military incident in which a U.S. frontier fort was attacked by Sioux warriors protesting the existence of such forts along Indian hunting grounds. During the Civil War, John M. Bozeman established the first viable wagon route through the Bighorn country to Montana and northern Wyoming. His route, devised as a shorter passage to and from Colorado and Montana gold fields, became attractive not only to gold seekers but also to the flood of settlers heading west at the end of the war.

The popularity of the Bozeman Trail led to an outcry for protection along its route, for it traversed hunting grounds of hostile Sioux. In 1866, the Indian Bureau opened ultimately unsuccessful negotiations with the Indians, particularly Red Cloud of the Sioux, to assure safe passage along the trail. For the next year, the Sioux battled the U.S. Army and its forts along the Bozeman Trail. Spring 1867 brought renewed hostilities. Close Indian scrutiny forced the army to cease all but the most heavily guarded operations. Resupply for the coming winter had already commenced when the annual Indian sun dance brought together Sioux, Arapaho, and Cheyenne, all vowing to destroy Forts Phil Kearny and C. F. Smith. A force of 800 braves headed for the former installation and on August 1, attacked, only to be beaten near the fort in the "Hayfield Fight."

The next day, a thousand Indians, led by Red Cloud, attacked Fort Kearny, defended by a company of the 27th Infantry under Capt. James W. Powell. Taken by surprise, some of the defenders were caught outside the fort, taking cover in a corral constructed of wooden wagon boxes. The Indians attacked the wagon box corral for four and a half hours before a rescue party from the fort relieved the defenders with howitzer fire.

Neither the Hayfield Fight nor the "Wagon Box Fight" deterred the Indian desire to rid themselves of the Bozeman Trail forts. The battles did, however, strengthen the resolve and morale of its defenders and convinced eastern policymakers that a properly armed and supported force could maintain a cogent defense against an Indian force of superior numbers.

Bibliography: Appleman, Roy E., "The Wagon Box Fight," *Great Western Indian Fights* (Univ. of Nebraska Press, 1960).

Louise Arnold-Friend

As chairman of the War Industries Board, financier Bernard M. Baruch was authorized to set production priorities and control natural resources in order to mobilize U.S. economic resources during World War I. (Library of Congress)

WAR INDUSTRIES BOARD

The primary U.S. agency of economic mobilization during World War I, the War Industries Board (WIB) was created in July 1917. Not the Wilson administration's first attempt to coordinate the economy, the seven-member WIB was only an advisory body and suffered from its lack of authority to dictate the priorities of industrial production.

Finally, on Mar. 4, 1918, Pres. Woodrow Wilson appointed Bernard Baruch chairman of the WIB and, against the wishes of Sec. of War Newton D. Baker, granted Baruch the authority to determine production priorities, build factories, and control natural resources. Under Baruch's strong leadership, the WIB succeeded in mobilizing the economic resources needed for the war effort.

Bibliography: Coffman, Edward M., *War to End All Wars: The American Military Experience in World War I* (Univ. of Wisconsin Press, 1986).

Daniel T. Bailey

WASHITA, BATTLE OF
(November 27, 1868)

Part of Maj. Gen. Philip H. Sheridan's 1868–69 Southern Plains Campaign to force several tribes to treat for peace, the Battle of Washita (Oklahoma) was a brutal attack on a Cheyenne village by the U.S. 7th Cavalry. The action led to criticism of the 7th Cavalry commander, Lt. Col. George A. Custer, and was a harbinger of Custer's reckless tactics at the Little Bighorn eight years later.

Sheridan was under pressure from his superiors as well as from settlers in Kansas and Texas to bring an end to Indian raids in the Southern Plains. One of the more aggressive tribes, the Cheyenne, was particularly worrisome. Black Kettle, a prominent Cheyenne chief, told army authorities that he could not control some of his young braves. The army decided on a winter campaign under the theory that soldiers could endure more hardships than could the Indians, burdened as they were with the caretaking of their families and food reserves. Sheridan ordered two columns to push toward his strong, offensive force, the 7th Cavalry. Custer, with 800 troopers, moved from Fort Sill into Texas and then turned northeast, striking out for the valley of the Washita River in the Oklahoma Territory.

Coming upon about 50 tepees, Custer threw caution aside and ordered a charge without a reconnaissance. A considerable number of fleeing Indians were slaughtered, including the peaceable Black Kettle and his wife. In the camp, the cavalrymen found U.S. captives recently taken in raids. The Indians had killed two prisoners during the assault, but two others survived. Custer discovered he was in an area where there were large numbers of camps, stretching for about 10 miles along the river. He was told of Arapaho, Kiowa, and Comanche groups nearby. During the skirmish, a group of 15 cavalrymen under Maj. Joel H. Elliott pursued a group of Indians, and the small detachment was overwhelmed by Indians. Back at the village, however, the fate of Elliott and his troopers was unknown. Suddenly, Indians began gathering on hilltops overlooking Custer's cavalrymen. The cavalrymen burned the tepees, slaughtered some 800 Indian ponies and gathered up the Indian women and children. Boldly leading a unit down the river valley, Custer feinted a further attack. The ploy was convincing enough to make the surrounding Indian braves move back to protect their own camps. Temporarily alone, Custer withdrew with his captives, making good the regiment's escape.

Immediately after the incident, controversies erupted. Army officers criticized Custer for abandoning Elliott. Indian sources refuted the cavalrymen's claim of killing 103 warriors, citing the deaths of many women and children. A prominent Indian agent resigned in protest, castigating Custer and the army. However, Sheridan regarded the "battle" as vindication of his winter campaign strategy. Unfortunately, the battle did not put an end to Indian raids. It did result in more winter campaigns.

Bibliography: Keim, Randolph, *Sheridan's Troopers on the Border: A Winter Campaign on the Plains* (1891).

Col. (Ret.) Rod Paschall

WESTERN FORTS

U.S. military installations on the western frontier from the 19th century. When Maj. Gen. William T. Sherman assumed his first post-Civil War command in the Division of the Missouri, his new domain swept west from the Mississippi River to the crest of the Rocky Mountains and north from Texas to Canada. What he saw were multitudes of emigrants pouring west on the Oregon-California, Santa Fe, and Smoky Hill trails. They, along with railroad construction crews, freighters, and others, needed military protection.

The establishment of western forts became the focal point of U.S. military power in the West and Southwest. These fortifications housed the troops safeguarding the frontier. Fort Abraham Lincoln (North Dakota), Forts Laramie and Phil Kearny (Wyoming), and Fort Leavenworth (Kansas) were the principal bastions of the Northern Plains. Fort Apache (Arizona); Forts Brown, Clark, and Richardson (Texas); and Fort Sill (Oklahoma) anchored the Southwest and the Southern Plains.

Fort Abraham Lincoln (1872–91) was one of the most significant forts of the West. First known as Fort McKeen when it was established in the spring of 1872, it was renamed in honor of the former U.S. president that fall. Built in the midst of Sioux country, the fort was intended to provide military protection for work crews from the Northern Pacific Railroad and to help maintain peace on the Northern Plains. This was the post from which Lt. Col. George A. Custer left in 1876 on his way to the Little Bighorn River.

Fort Laramie (1849–90) was founded as Fort Williams in 1834 by the Rocky Mountain Fur Trading Company of William Sublette, Robert Campbell, and others. It had a palisade 18 feet high with bastions on two diagonally opposite corners. It was later sold to Milton Sublette and Jim Bridger. The structure became a U.S. military post in 1849, at which time it was renamed Fort Laramie. This former stockaded trading post soon emerged as a key military establishment. Travelers along the California-Oregon Trail welcomed this sign of U.S. presence as they moved west. The Bozeman Trail to Montana's gold fields angled off from Fort Laramie. Over the years, it was the site of several U.S.-Indian peace conferences.

Fort Phil Kearny (1866–68), built by Col. Henry B. Carrington, was intended as the keystone of the Bozeman Trail. For most of its brief existence, however, the fort was virtually kept under seige by hostile Sioux warriors. It was from Fort Phil Kearny that Capt. William J. Fetterman rode to his infamous death in 1866.

Fort Leavenworth (1827–), in eastern Kansas, was called by General Sherman "the most valuable military reservation in the West." The fort was long the headquarters of the U.S. Cavalry in the West. It served for years as headquarters for the Department of the Missouri. In 1874, the U.S. Military Prison was established at Fort Leavenworth.

Fort Apache (1870–1922), in east-central Arizona, was so remote when it was built, and the chance of a direct Indian attack so slight, that there was no stockade. During the 1870s and 1880s, it served as headquarters for Gen. George Crook's Apache expeditions.

Fort Brown (1846–96), located at Brownsville at the southernmost tip of Texas, was initially an earthwork fort constructed as a base of operations against Mexican bandits and marauding Indians. Rehabilitated in 1867, Fort Brown became part of a line of military posts extending from northern Texas to the Rio Grande.

Fort Clark (1852–62, 1866–1949) was a center for military raids against hostile Indians. The post saw heavy use during the 1870s as the U.S. military sought to control border-crossing raids by Apache, Comanche, and Kiowa. An 1871 reorganization of the military system in Texas saw the 4th Cavalry, under the command of Gen. Ranald Mackenzie, become what some considered the best cavalry unit in the army. Mackenzie led his ''Raiders'' from Fort Clark on strikes that even reached into Mexico.

Fort Richardson (1867–78), a cluster of stone buildings located at Jacksboro in northern Texas, was kept particularly busy by post-Civil War Reconstruction duties. It also served as a center in the ongoing military campaigns of the 1870s and 1880s against bandits and Indians.

Fort Sill (1869–), located in south-central Oklahoma, was established on a grassy site at the eastern base of the Wichita Mountains. The spot was chosen by Maj. Gen. Benjamin H. Grierson. His black troops (Buffalo Soldiers) began to erect substantial stone buildings for a post that Gen. Philip H. Sheridan named in honor of a West Point classmate slain in the Civil War. Troops from Fort Sill played an active part in the Southern Plains War of 1869 and the later Red River Campaign.

Bibliography: Andrist, Ralph K., *The Long Death: The Last Days of the Plains Indians* (Macmillan, 1964); Hart, Herbert M., *Tour Guide to Old Western Forts* (Pruett, 1980); Utley, Robert M., *Frontier Regulars: The United States Army and the Indian, 1866–91* (Univ. of Nebraska Press, 1973).

M. Guy Bishop

WOUNDED KNEE, BATTLE OF (December 29, 1890)

Final engagement in the Indian Wars of the Great Plains, occurring at Wounded Knee Creek on the Pine Ridge Indian Reservation in South Dakota. The events at Wounded Knee were an outgrowth of several occurrences. The U.S. Army in the West continued to harbor the hatred of the Sioux that resulted from the Little Bighorn catastrophe in 1876. And the Sioux, like other western tribes, had become impoverished and downtrodden from years of reservation life.

Of great influence to western Indians at that time was the Paiute messiah Wovoka, who in 1889 and 1890 prophesied of a new world in which Indians would be reunited with dead friends, game would be plentiful, and whites would no longer be able to hurt the Indians. In order to bring to pass this millennial experience the Indians had to dance the Ghost Dance and pray to the Great Spirit to come. Wovoka's religion was peaceful, telling of a great flood in which all whites would perish. The religion blended elements of Christianity with old native beliefs. ''You must not fight,'' Wovoka implored his followers.

Soon, most of the western tribes were in the grip of the Ghost Dance, always following Wovoka's directive for nonviolence. Among the Sioux, however, the religion turned militant. Shaken by abuses within the reservation system and broken promises by the United States, the Sioux had no patience for a peaceful solution. In this bitterness and despair, they let their Ghost Dance apostles Short Bull and Kicking Bear persuade them that Wovoka's millennium might be hastened by destroying white people. The Sioux believed they would be protected from harm by wearing ''ghost shirts'' said to repel bullets. The Pine Ridge Sioux eagerly embraced this badly perverted version of the Ghost Dance religion.

By March 1890, Maj. Gen. Nelson A. Miles, commander of the Division of the Missouri, believed a peaceful solution to the Indian problem was no longer possible. By November, enthusiasm caused by the Ghost Dance had brought at least two Sioux agencies—Pine Ridge and Rosebud—to the brink of anarchy. Finally, on November 13, Pres. Benjamin Harrison ordered the army to the reservations to stem any violence. Col. James Forsyth of the 7th Cavalry, a veteran of Little Bighorn, commanded the troops.

As the army approached, the Sioux promptly hoisted a white flag in the middle of their camp as a sign of their good intentions. But the appearance of the army divided the camp into what the army classified as ''friendlies'' and ''hostiles.'' By early December, all ''hostiles'' had taken refuge along Wounded Knee Creek.

Big Foot, a Sioux chief at Pine Ridge, was identified as a supporter of the dancers, and U.S. troops were sent to arrest him. On the morning of December 29, the 340 Indians at Wounded Knee, including about 100 warriors, awoke to find themselves surrounded by 500 soldiers. Forsyth demanded that the Sioux surrender their weapons. The process of disarmament provoked a scuffle resulting in a murderous face-to-face melée between soldiers and Indians. The line of troops replied instantly against the Sioux, firing a volley point blank into the crowd. Possibly as many as half of the warriors were killed instantly. At about the same time, soldiers manning Hotchkiss guns on a nearby hill opened fire, and many fleeing Indians were killed. When the brief, but intense, fight ended, more than 150 Sioux, including Big Foot, were dead. Less than 50 U.S. soldiers died, most apparently victims of their comrades' bullets. Witnesses agreed that the 7th Cavalry failed to act as a well-disciplined unit and rather behaved as men bent only on butchery. With this defeat and the failure of the Ghost Dance, the Plains Indians lost their resolve and further resistance to the advance of U.S. civilization ended.

Bibliography: Brown, Dee, *Bury My Heart at Wounded Knee: An Indian History of the American West* (Holt, Rinehart & Winston, 1971); Utley, Robert M., *Frontier Regulars: The United States Army and the Indian, 1866–1891* (Univ. of Nebraska Press, 1973).

M. Guy Bishop

ZIMMERMANN TELEGRAM (1917)

World War I communication from Germany to Mexico, the disclosure of which helped to further a U.S. commitment to the Allied cause. In February 1917, British intel-

U.S. soldiers who fought at Wounded Knee pose around a Hotchkiss gun after the battle in 1890. (U.S. Army Military History Institute, Washington I. Wallace Collection)

ligence passed to the United States an intercepted January 1917 telegram to the German ambassador in Mexico from the German foreign minister, Arthur Zimmermann. The telegram contained a proposal for an anti-American alliance among Mexico, Japan, and Germany, with Mexico to regain the territory of Arizona, New Mexico, and Texas. The telegram provided impetus to Pres. Woodrow Wilson's movement to extend de jure recognition to the Mexican government of Venustiano Carranza. The telegram's timing, shortly after Germany began unrestricted submarine warfare (which the telegram had announced), reinforced the Wilson administration's belief in German duplicity. Wilson released the telegram to the press on March 1 (incredibly, Zimmermann acknowledged the telegram's veracity), and it contributed significantly to the final deterioration of U.S.-German relations.

Stephen J. Lofgren

Bibliography

1. The Organization of Military Forces: 1865–1919

Brodie, Bernard, and Fawn M. Brodie, *From Crossbow to H-Bomb,* rev. ed. (Indiana Univ. Press, 1973).

Coletta, Paolo Enrico, *The American Naval Heritage in Brief* (Univ. Press of America, 1978).

Department of the Army, *The Army* (1978).

Department of the Army, *Army Heritage,* pamphlet 355-27 (Aug. 7, 1963).

Department of the Navy, *The United States Navy* (Naval Hist. Div., 1969).

Dupuy, R. Ernest, *The Compact History of the United States Army,* rev. ed. (Hawthorn Books, 1961).

Glines, Carroll V., Jr., *The Compact History of the United States Air Force,* rev. ed. (Hawthorn Books, 1973).

Goldich, Robert L., ''Historical Continuity in the U.S. Military Reserve System,'' *Armed Forces and Society* (fall 1980).

Hagan, Kenneth J., ed., *In Peace and War: Interpretations of American Naval History, 1775–1978* (Greenwood Press, 1978).

Hinter, Edna J., ''Combat Casualties Who Remain at Home,'' *Military Review* (Jan. 1980).

Kreidberg, Marvin A., and Merton G. Henry, *History of Military Mobilization in the United States Army, 1775–1945* (Office of the Chief of Military History, U.S. Army, 1955).

Matloff, Maurice, ed., *American Military History* (Office of the Chief of Military History, U.S. Army, 1969).

Maurer, Maurer, *Aviation in the United States Army, 1919–1939* (Office of Air Force History, U.S. Air Force, 1987).

Millett, Allan R., *Semper Fidelis: The History of the United States Marine Corps* (Macmillan, 1980).

Mills, Walter, *Arms and Men: A Study of American Military History* (Mentor Books, 1956).

Parker, William D., *A Concise History of the United States Marine Corps, 1775–1969* (Historical Div., U.S. Marine Corps Hdqrs., 1970).

Paullin, Charles Oscar, *Paullin's History of Naval Administration, 1775–1911* (Naval Inst. Press, 1968).

Rector, Frank, ed., *The Air Force Blue Book 1961; Vol. 2: Air Force Facts* (Bobbs-Merrill, for Military Publ. Inst., 1960).

U.S. Armed Forces Information School, *The Army Almanac* (1950).

U.S. Army Air Forces, *AAF: The Official World War II Guide to the Army Air Forces; A Directory, Almanac and Chronicle of Achievement* (Bonanza, 1988).

Weigley, Russell F., *The American Way of War: A History of United States Military Strategy and Policy* (Macmillan, 1973).

———, *History of the United States Army* (Macmillan, 1967).

Williams, T. Harry, *The History of Americans: From 1745 to 1918* (Knopf, 1981).

2. Reconstruction and the Indian Wars: 1865–1891

Ambrose, Stephen E., *Upton and the Army* (Louisiana State Univ. Press, 1964).
Athearn, Robert G., *William Tecumseh Sherman and the Settlement of the West* (Univ. of Oklahoma Press, 1956).
Bartlett, Richard A., *Great Surveys of the American West* (Univ. of Oklahoma Press, 1962).
Cooling, B. Franklin, *Benjamin Franklin Tracy: Father of the Modern American Fighting Navy* (1973).
Cooper, Jerry M., *The Army and Civil Disorder: Federal Military Intervention in Labor Disputes, 1877–1900* (Greenwood Press, 1980).
Dawson, Joseph G., III, *The Late 19th Century U.S. Army, 1865–1898: A Research Guide* (Greenwood Press, 1990).
Dinges, Bruce, "New Directions in Frontier Military History: A Review Essay," *New Mexico Historical Review* (Jan. 1991).
Ellis, Richard N., *General Pope and U.S. Indian Policy* (Univ. of New Mexico Press, 1970).
Gray, John S., *Centennial Campaign: The Sioux War of 1876* (Old Army, 1976).
Hagan, Kenneth J., *This People's Navy: The Making of American Sea Power* (Free Press, 1991).
Hutton, Paul Andrew, *Phil Sheridan and His Army* (Univ. of Nebraska Press, 1985).
Hutton, Paul A., ed., *Soldiers West: Biographies from the Military Frontier* (Univ. of Nebraska Press, 1987).
Miller, Darlis A., *Soldiers and Settlers: Military Supply in the Southwest, 1861–1885* (Univ. of New Mexico Press, 1989).
Nenninger, Timothy K., *The Leavenworth Schools and the Old Army: Education, Professionalism, and the Officer Corps of the United States Army, 1881–1918* (Greenwood Press, 1978).
Rickey, Don, *Forty Miles a Day on Beans and Hay: The Enlisted Soldier Fighting the Indians Wars* (Univ. of Oklahoma Press, 1963).
Sefton, James E., *The United States Army and Reconstruction, 1865–1877* (Louisiana State Univ. Press, 1967).
Smith, Sherry L., *Sagebrush Soldier: Private William Earl Smith's View of the Sioux War of 1876* (Univ. of Oklahoma Press, 1989).
Spector, Ronald, "The Triumph of Professional Ideology: The U.S. Navy in the 1890s," *In Peace and War: Interpretations of American Naval History, 1775–1984,* ed. by Kenneth J. Hagan (Greenwood Press, 1984).
Tate, James P., ed., "The American Military on the Frontier" (proceedings of 7th Military History Symposium; Office of Air Force History, 1978).
Utley, Robert M., *Cavalier in Buckskin: George Armstrong Custer and the Western Military Frontier* (Univ. of Oklahoma Press, 1988).
———, *Frontier Regulars: The United States Army and the Indian, 1866–1891* (Macmillan, 1973).
Wooster, Robert, *The Military and United States Indian Policy, 1865–1903* (Yale Univ. Press, 1988).

3. The Spanish-American War: 1898

Carlson, Paul H., *"Pecos Bill": A Military Biography of William R. Shafter* (Texas A&M Press, 1989).
Cosmas, Graham A., *An Army for Empire: The United States Army in the Spanish-American War* (Univ. of Missouri Press, 1971).
———, "San Juan Hill and El Caney, 1–2 July 1898," *America's First Battles, 1776–1965,* ed. by Charles E. Heller and William A. Stoft (Univ. Press of Kansas, 1986).
Dierks, Jack Cameron, *A Leap to Arms: The Cuban Campaign of 1898* (Lippincott, 1970).
Foner, Philip S., *The Spanish-Cuban-American War and the Birth of American Imperialism, 1895–1898,* 2 vols. (Monthly Review Press, 1972).
Friedel, Frank B., *The Splendid Little War* (Little, Brown, 1958).
Gatewood, Willard B., Jr., *Black Americans and the White Man's Burden, 1898–1903* (Univ. of Illinois Press, 1975).
Gould, Lewis L., *The Spanish-American War and President McKinley* (Univ. Press of Kansas, 1982).
Hard, Curtis V., *Banners in the Air: The Eighth Ohio Volunteers and the Spanish-American War* (Kent State Univ. Press, 1984).
Jones, Virgil Carrington, *Roosevelt's Rough Riders* (Doubleday, 1974).
Linderman, Gerald F., *The Mirror of War: American Society and the Spanish-American War* (Univ. of Michigan Press, 1974).
Millis, Walter, *The Martial Spirit: A Study of Our War With Spain* (Houghton Mifflin, 1931).

O'Toole, G. J. A., *The Spanish War: An American Epic, 1898* (Norton, 1984).
Risch, Erna, *Quartermaster Support of the Army: A History of the Corps, 1775–1939* (Center of Military History, U.S. Army, 1989).
Spector, Ronald H., *Admiral of the New Empire: The Life and Career of George Dewey* (Louisiana State Univ. Press, 1974).
———, *Professors of War: The Naval War College and the Development of the Naval Profession* (Naval War College Press, 1977).
Steele, Matthew Forney, *American Campaigns,* vol. 1 (U.S. Infantry Assoc., 1922).
Trask, David F., *The War With Spain in 1898* (Macmillan, 1981).
Venzon, Anne Cipriano, *The Spanish-American War: An Annotated Bibliography* (Garland, 1990).

4. The Emergence of the United States as a Global Power: 1898–1917

Bailey, Thomas A., *A Diplomatic History of the American People* (Prentice Hall, 1970).
Beale, Howard K., *Theodore Roosevelt and the Rise of America to World Power* (Collier, 1973).
Bemis, Samuel Flagg, *The Latin American Policy of the United States* (Norton, 1971).
Bombardment of the Taku Forts in China (57th Cong., 1st Sess., House Doc. No. 645).
Chapman, Charles E., *A History of the Cuban Republic* (Macmillan, 1927).
Cline, Howard K., *The United States and Mexico* (Atheneum, 1969).
Coletta, Paolo E., *Bowman Hendry McCalla* (Univ. Press of America, 1979).
Cox, Isaac J., *Nicaragua and the United States, 1909–1927* (World Peace Foundation, 1927).
Fuller, Stephen M., and Graham Cosmas, *Marines in the Dominican Republic 1916–1924* (U.S. Marine Corps, 1974).
Ganoe, William A., *The History of the United States Army* (Appleton-Century, 1943).
Gates, John M., *Schoolbooks and Krags: The United States Army in the Philippines, 1898–1902* (Greenwood Press, 1975).
Healy, David F., *Gunboat Diplomacy in the Wilson Era: The U.S. Navy in Haiti, 1915–1916* (Univ. of Wisconsin Press, 1976).
———, *The United States in Cuba, 1898–1902* (Univ. of Wisconsin Press, 1963).
Langley, Lester D., *The Banana Wars: United States Intervention in the Caribbean, 1898–1943* (Univ. of Kentucky Press, 1985).
Lejeune, John A., *The Reminiscences of a Marine* (Arno Press, 1979).
Link, Arthur S., *Woodrow Wilson: The New Freedom* (Princeton Univ. Press, 1956).
Livezey, William E., *Mahan on Sea Power* (Univ. of Oklahoma Press, 1947).
McCullough, David, *The Path Between the Seas* (Simon & Schuster, 1977).
Metcalf, Clyde H., *A History of the United States Marine Corps* (Putnam's, 1939).
Millett, Allen, *Semper Fidelis* (Macmillan, 1980).
Morison, Elting E., *Admiral Sims and the Modern American Navy* (Boston, 1942).
Nalty, Bernard C., *The United States Marines in Nicaragua* (U.S. Marine Corps, 1968).
Potter, E. B., *The United States and World Sea Power* (Prentice Hall, 1955).
Quirk, Robert E., *An Affair of Honor* (Univ. of Kentucky Press, 1962).
Schott, Joseph L., *The Ordeal of Samar* (Bobbs-Merrill, 1964).
Smythe, Donald, *Guerrilla Warrior: The Early Life of John J. Pershing* (Scribner's, 1973).
Sprout, Harold, *and Margaret Sprout, The Rise of American Naval Power 1776–1918* (Naval Inst. Press, 1966).
Sweetman, Jack, *The Landing at Vera Cruz, 1914* (Naval Inst. Press, 1987).
Taussig, Joseph K., "Experiences During the Boxer Rebellion" (U.S. Naval Inst. proceedings, Apr. 1927).
Tompkins, Frank, *Chasing Villa* (Military Service Publ., 1934).
Welch, Richard E., *Response to Imperialism: The United States and the Philippine-American War 1899–1902* (Univ. of North Carolina Press, 1979).
Welles, Summer, *Naboth's Vineyard,* 2 vols. (Payson & Clarke, 1928).

5. The Emergence of a Modern Army and Navy: 1903–1917

Abrahamson, James L., *American Arms for a New Century* (Free Press, 1981).

Ambrose, Stephen E., *Upton and the Army* (Louisiana State Univ. Press, 1964).

Bacon, Robert, and James B. Scott, *The Military and Colonial Policy of the United States: Addresses and Reports by Elihu Root* (Harvard Univ. Press, 1924).

Ball, Harry P., *Of Responsible Command: A History of the U.S. Army War College* (Alumni Assoc., U.S. Army War College, 1983).

Bledstein, Burton J., *The Culture of Professionalism: The Middle Class and the Development of Higher Education in America* (Norton, 1976).

Braddy, Haldeen, *Pershing's Mission in Mexico* (Texas Western Press, 1966).

Clendenen, Clarence C., *Blood on the Border: The United States Army and the Mexican Irregulars* (Macmillan, 1969).

Dastrop, Boyd L., *The U.S. Army Command and General Staff College: A Centennial History* (Sunflower Press, 1982).

Derthick, Martha, *The National Guard in Politics* (Harvard Univ. Press, 1965).

Dupuy, R. Ernest, *The National Guard: A Compact History* (Hawthorn Books, 1971).

Hagan, Kenneth J., *This People's Navy: The Making of American Sea Power* (Free Press, 1990).

Hammond, Paul Y., *Organizing for Defense: The American Military Establishment in the Twentieth Century* (Princeton Univ. Press, 1961).

Hattendorf, John B., B. Mitchell Shipton III, and John R. Wadleigh, *Sailors and Scholars: The Centennial History of the Naval War College* (Naval War College Press, 1985).

Hewes, James E., Jr., *From Root to McNamara: Army Organization and Administration, 1900–1963* (Center for Military History, U.S. Army, 1975).

Hunt, Elvid, and Walter E. Lorance, *History of Fort Leavenworth, 1827–1937,* 2d ed. (Command and General Staff College Press, 1937).

Huntington, Samuel P., *The Soldier and the State* (Harvard Univ. Press, 1957).

Janowitz, Morris, *The Professional Soldier: A Social and Political Portrait,* 2d ed. (Free Press, 1971).

Karsten, Peter, *The Naval Aristocracy: The Golden Age of Annapolis and the Emergence of Modern American Navalism* (Free Press, 1972).

Millett, Allan R., *Military Professionalism and Officership in America* (Mershon Press, 1977).

———, *Semper Fidelis: The History of the United States Marine Corps* (Free Press, 1980).

Nelson, Otto, Jr., *National Security and the General Staff* (Infantry Journal Press, 1946).

Nenninger, Timothy K., *The Leavenworth Schools and the Old Army: Education, Professionalism, and the Officer Corps of the United States Army, 1881–1918* (Greenwood Press, 1978).

Reardon, Carol, *Soldiers and Scholars: The U.S. Army and the Uses of Military History, 1865–1920* (Univ. Press of Kansas, 1990).

Steele, Captain Matthew Forney, *American Campaigns,* 2 vols. (Byron S. Adams, 1909).

Sprout, Harold, and Margaret Tuttle Sprout, *The Rise of American Naval Power,* rev. ed. (Princeton Univ. Press, 1942).

Sweetman, Jack, *The Landing at Veracruz: 1914, the First Complete Chronicle of a Strange Encounter in April 1914, when the United States Navy Captured and Occupied the City of Veracruz, Mexico* (Naval Inst. Press, 1968).

Weigley, Russell F., *A History of the United States Army,* rev. ed., (Indiana Univ. Press, 1984).

Weibe, Robert H., *The Search for Order, 1877–1920* (Hill & Wang, 1967).

6. & 7. World War I

American Battle Monuments Commission, *American Armies and Battlefields in Europe* (U.S. Govt. Printing Office, 1938).

Coffman, Edward M., *The War to End All Wars: The American Military Experience in World War I* (Oxford Univ. Press, 1968).

DeWeerd, Harvey A., *President Wilson Fights His War: World War I and the American Intervention* (Macmillan, 1968).

Hagan, Kenneth J., *In Peace and War: Interpretations of American Naval History, 1775–1984* (Greenwood Press, 1984).

Hagood, Johnson, *The Services of Supply: A Memoir of the Great War* (Houghton Mifflin, 1927).

Harbord, James, *The American Army in France, 1917–1919* (Little, Brown, 1936).

Hewes, James E., Jr., *From Root to McNamara: Army Organization and Administration, 1900–1963* (Center of Military History, U.S. Army, 1975).
Huston, James A., *The Sinews of War: Army Logistics, 1775–1953* (Center of Military History, U.S. Army, 1970).
Kennedy, David M., *Over Here: The First World War and American Society* (Oxford Univ. Press, 1980).
Liggett, Hunter, *A.E.F.: Ten Years Ago in France* (Dodd, Mead, 1928).
———, *Commanding An American Army: Recollections of the World War* (Houghton Mifflin, 1925).
March, Peyton C., *The Nation at War* (Doubleday, Doran, 1932).
Naulty, Bernard C., *Strength for the Fight: A History of Black Americans in the Military* (Free Press, 1986).
Pershing, John J., *My Experiences in the World War,* 2 vols. (Frederick A. Stokes Co., 1931).
Sparrow, John C., *History of Personnel Demobilization in the United States Army* (Dept. of the Army, 1952).
Stallings, Laurence, *The Doughboys: The Story of the A.E.F., 1917–1918* (Harper & Row, 1963).
Weigley, Russell F., *History of the United States Army* (Macmillan, 1967).

Index

Boldface numbers indicate entries in Parts II and III;
italic numbers indicate illustrations.

Y

Z